M000310601

Applications of Self-Regulated Learning across Diverse Disciplines

A Tribute to Barry J. Zimmerman

Applications of Self-Regulated Learning across Diverse Disciplines

A Tribute to Barry J. Zimmerman

edited by

Héfer Bembenutty
Queens College of The City University of New York

Timothy J. Cleary
Rutgers, The State University of New Jersey

Anastasia Kitsantas
George Mason University

INFORMATION AGE PUBLISHING, INC.
Charlotte, NC • www.infoagepub.com

Library of Congress Cataloging-in-Publication Data

Applications of self-regulated learning across diverse disciplines : a
tribute to Barry J. Zimmerman / edited by Hifer Bembenutty, Queens College
of The City University of New York, Timothy J. Cleary, Rutgers University,
Anastasia Kitsantas, George Mason University.
    p. cm.
 ISBN 978-1-62396-132-9 (pbk.) – ISBN 978-1-62396-133-6 (hardcover) –
ISBN 978-1-62396-134-3 (ebook) 1. Learning. 2. Self-culture. 3. Study
skills. 4. Students–Self-rating of. I. Zimmerman, Barry J. II.
Bembenutty, Hifer, editor of compilation. III. Schunk, Dale H. Barry
Zimmerman's theory of self-regulated learning.
 LB1060.A65 2013
 370.15'23–dc23

                                                              2012042640

Copyright © 2013 Information Age Publishing Inc.

All rights reserved. No part of this publication may be reproduced, stored in a
retrieval system, or transmitted, in any form or by any means, electronic, mechanical,
photocopying, microfilming, recording or otherwise, without written permission
from the publisher.

Printed in the United States of America

CONTENTS

CONTRIBUTORS

Taylor W. Acee
Texas State University–San Marcos
San Marcos, TX

Clare V. Bell
University of Missouri
Kansas City, MO

Héfer Bembenutty
Queens College of the
    City University of New York
New York, NY

Jean-Louis Berger
Swiss Federal Institute
    for Vocational Education
    and Training
Switzerland

Peggy P. Chen
Hunter College of the
    City University of New York
New York, NY

Noreen M. Clark
University of Michigan
Ann Arbor, MI

Timothy J. Cleary
Rutgers, The State University
    of New Jersey
New Brunswick, NJ

Nada Dabbagh
George Mason University
Fairfax, VA

Susan Dass
George Mason University
Fairfax, VA

Irini Dermitzaki
University of Thessaly
Thessaly, Greece

Maria K. DiBenedetto
Baruch College of the
    City University of New York
New York, NY

Marios Goudas
University of Thessaly
Thessaly, Greece

Steve Graham
Arizona State University
Temple, AZ

Applications of Self-Regulated Learning across Diverse Disciplines, pages vii–viii
Copyright © 2013 by Information Age Publishing
All rights of reproduction in any form reserved.

Karen R. Harris
Arizona State University
Temple, AZ

Faye C. Huie
George Mason University
Fairfax, VA

Stuart A. Karabenick
University of Michigan
Ann Arbor, MI

Anastasia Kitsantas
George Mason University
Fairfax, VA

Anthanasios Kolovelonis
University of Thessaly
Thessaly, Greece

Andju S. Labuhn
German Institute for International
    Educational Research
Germany

Gary E. McPherson
University of Melbourne
Melbourne, Australia

Adam R. Moylan
University of California
San Francisco, CA

Siw G. Nielsen
Norwegian Academy of Music
Oslo, Norway

Stephen J. Pape
Johns Hopkins University
Baltimore, MD

James M. Renwick
University of Sydney
Sydney, Australia

Paul D. Rossi
Hunter College of the
    City University of New York
New York, NY

Tanya Santangelo
Arcadia University
Glenside, PA

Dale H. Schunk
University of North Carolina at
    Greensboro
Greensboro, NC

Ellen L. Usher
The University of Kentucky
Lexington, KY

Marcel V. J. Veenman
Leiden University
The Netherlands

Claire Ellen Weinstein
University of Texas at Austin
Austin, TX

Marie C. White
Nyack College
New York, NY

Iffet Elif Yetkin-Ozdemir
Haceteppe University
Ankara, Turkey

FOREWORD

In recent years, there have been substantial developments in theorizing and experimentation on the issue of self-regulation. Among the major topics of interest are the metacognitive processes and motivational beliefs and feelings that underlie self-initiated and self-sustained efforts to acquire competencies in diverse fields. This focus on acquiring mastery of important academic and non-academic skills has been termed self-regulated learning.

I initially became interested in the self-enhancement of learning processes as a youth. My father was an extraordinary teacher who emphasized the roles of studying and practicing as key to success in both academic and non-academic endeavors (e.g., music, sports). He was a firm advocate of setting specific qualitative or quantitative standards for oneself and tracking one's daily progress. As an adult researcher, I drew on these formative experiences to define and assess the impact of these and other self-regulatory processes empirically. This pursuit not only provided convincing answers to many of my questions, it was attractive to students, colleagues, and other researchers. I am deeply honored that many of them have contributed richly to this important volume.

The editors of this text have done an admirable job of assembling major contributors to this burgeoning field. Although there have been a number of previous texts that reviewed research in self-regulated learning, the only exclusive effort to focus on the impact of pedagogical interventions designed to develop or enhance self-regulatory processes and beliefs was published more than a decade ago, when instructional applications were still in a nascent stage. During the ensuing period, extensive applications have been conducted, and this body of research is well described and analyzed regarding its effectiveness in this important text.

Applications of Self-Regulated Learning across Diverse Disciplines, pages ix–x
Copyright © 2013 by Information Age Publishing
All rights of reproduction in any form reserved.

In my efforts to develop an effective theory of self-regulation, I sought to explain individual differences in learning, such as experts versus regular learners, and I also sought to produce increases in competence with novice or challenged learners. The research reported in this book achieves both purposes well. Most especially, the chapters provide educators with detailed descriptions of instructional practices designed to enable students to gain greater control of their learning outcomes. These compelling accounts provide a firm base for optimism regarding future applications of self-regulation research. Becoming a self-regulated learner can be more than a personal wish; it can become a pedagogical reality.

—**Barry J. Zimmerman**

PREFACE

From a social cognitive perspective, self-regulated learning refers to a multidimensional process whereby learners proactively generate, monitor, and adapt thoughts, behaviors, and feelings in pursuit of personal goals. Self-regulated learners are highly proactive individuals who, empowered with a strong sense of competency and skills, actively seek to transform their environments, adapt their thinking or ways of approaching a task, and sustain motivation in order to attain their goals. Despite a relatively robust literature base demonstrating the link between various types of self-regulatory processes, such as goal-setting, self-monitoring, self-evaluation, and performance outcomes, there has been increased interest among researchers, educators, and applied professionals in developing innovative ways to apply self-regulation principles to a diverse array of contexts and situations.

Whether it is a coach teaching athletes how to effectively dribble a basketball, a medical doctor helping his or her patients learn how to manage debilitating health conditions such as diabetes or asthma, or a middle school teacher modeling how to react adaptively to a failing test grade or course grade, a key question for all of these experts involves, "How can one most effectively enhance people's domain-specific skills as well as their capabilities to proactively and efficiently self-manage their learning and execution of adaptive skills?" In recent years, researchers and practitioners have begun to address this emergent question through their development of applied self-regulation intervention programs in both academic and non-academic contexts—an initiative that has been greatly influenced by the theoretical and empirical contributions of Professor Barry J. Zimmerman.

Applications of Self-Regulated Learning across Diverse Disciplines, pages xi–xv
Copyright © 2013 by Information Age Publishing
All rights of reproduction in any form reserved.

PURPOSE OF THE BOOK

We have two primary goals for this edited book. First, we honor the achievements of Professor Zimmerman, an emeritus and distinguished professor of the Graduate School and University Center of the City University of New York. His extraordinary career, which has spanned more than five decades, has involved the study of social cognitive learning with a focus on modeling and self-regulation across several disciplines, including academic, health, and athletic functioning. Overall, he has written more than 200 research articles, book chapters, and professional conference papers, and he has written or edited more than 10 books. Over the past forty years, Zimmerman has conducted ground-breaking research on the effects of various self-regulatory processes, such as goal-setting and self-monitoring, and has underscored the importance and value of modeling and strategy instruction. From our perspective, one of his greatest contributions has been the articulation and refinement of a social-cognitive, cyclical account of self-regulation that emphasizes the proactive and sustained management among cognition, motivation, and behavior.

Zimmerman's seminal work has clearly positioned self-regulation as a hallmark of a learner's ability to remain task-focused and goal-oriented while engaging in learning or clinical tasks. With his passion for teaching and learning and his dedication for rigor in authentic research, Zimmerman's scholastic work has helped promote a belief that while our educational system is experiencing extraordinary social and technological transformations, learners need to be proactive in directing their learning experiences and in guiding their behavior. He also has laid bare the notion that self-regulation of learning is an essential skill linked to attaining long-term and temporarily distant goals, particularly amidst the challenges experienced by millennium learners.

Our second goal was to provide a platform for scholars who are interested in applying self-regulation principles to diverse contexts and who have been influenced, inspired, or motivated by the theoretical and empirical contributions of Zimmerman. In each chapter, the contributors: (a) provide relevant theoretical frameworks underlying their line of research, (b) discuss how their research agenda supports, extends, or is otherwise linked with Zimmerman's theories and research, (c) discuss interventions or theoretical grounds for interventions, and (d) discuss educational implications and future research directions. In addressing these four broad areas, we hope that this research-to-practice book provides a forum for highlighting cutting-edge scholarship in self-regulation intervention research across diverse fields and methodologies and an opportunity to celebrate the broad impact of Zimmerman's scholarly work across both academic and non-academic settings. It is our hope that this book will serve as a useful guide for researchers, graduate students, educators, health practitioners, coaches, and other professionals interested in translating self-regulation theory to intervention development and implementation. Specifically, we believe that this book may be used as a general resource regarding current trends in self-regulated learning and motivation interventions and may prove to be particularly helpful to professionals interested in designing learning activities, tasks, and assignments that foster self-regulated learning of others or perhaps themselves.

ORGANIZATION OF THE BOOK

In the introductory chapter, Schunk and Usher present an overview of Zimmerman's theory of self-regulation while highlighting the unique contribution and role that his scholarly work has played in education and psychology. They describe the historical grounds that gave birth to self-regulation of learning and detail how Zimmerman's theoretical models and research impacted many disciplinary fields, such as education, psychology, health, sport, technology, and music.

The application of self-regulatory principles has been well established within educational circles. In the arena of mathematics, Pape, Bell, and Yetzin-Özdemier describe their vision of mathematics education within a self-regulated learning framework and classroom connectivity technology context. They provide compelling case examples illustrating intervention procedures that can be used during mathematics instruction to help learners become more strategic and self-directed learners. Harris, Graham, and Santangelo describe a self-regulation writing intervention, with an emphasis on its development, implementation, and scaling up over the past twenty years. The authors describe their intervention in detail and offer illustrations that are directly applicable to elementary classroom settings. Along a similar vein, Cleary and Labuhn detail the nature and characteristics of two distinct self-regulation interventions implemented in high school science contexts, underscoring the applicability of Zimmerman's three-phase cyclical model to interventions implemented at a classroom level and a small group or individualized context.

Self-regulation intervention programs have also been successfully applied to college contexts and have included programs that focus on a more a narrow set of self-regulatory processes. In this volume, Moylan examines the implementation and effectiveness of a broad self-regulation intervention with academically at-risk college students. This program, which evolved directly from Zimmerman's theoretical models, focused primarily on creating effective pathways to provide feedback to students and to help them engage in effective self-reflective error analysis. Bembenutty uses Zimmerman's learning academy model of self-regulation as a framework for devising an innovative intervention with pre-service teachers. This intervention has been used to help teachers structure homework activities so that students' self-regulatory skills and subsequent achievement are optimized. At the college level, Weinstein and Acee describe a well-established instructional model whereby college students learn to develop, use, and refine their use of study strategies. In this latter chapter, the authors also highlight interventions and initiatives designed to help foster college students' self-regulated learning. Finally, Karabenick and Berger provide an extensive overview of the empirical support for help-seeking as an intervention. They discuss how educators might facilitate help-seeking in social contexts, such as a classroom.

Two chapters highlight the metacognitive dimension of self-regulation. Chen and Rossi describe the components and essential implementation procedures of a calibration accuracy intervention with at-risk high school students and underscore how calibration intersects with the different phases of Zimmerman's cyclical feedback model. Veenman's chapter addresses the instruction and training of metacognitive skills and discusses the role of motivation for inciting the execution of metacognitive skills.

The importance of self-regulation intervention has also been demonstrated in sports, health domains, and music and has been postulated to have a direct link with technological advancements. With regard to the latter innovation, Kitsantas, Dabbagh, Huie, and Dass provide guidelines for using learning technologies such as Web 2.0 to facilitate self-regulated learning in postsecondary education settings. The direct link between self-regulation theory and music instruction was underscored in great detail by McPherson, Nielsen, and Renwick. In short, these authors describe self-regulation interventions and the development of music expertise based on research they have conducted with beginning, intermediate, and advanced level music learners.

Influenced by Zimmerman's theory and research, Goudas, Kolovelonis, and Dermitzaki describe implementation of self-regulation interventions in physical education and sports contexts. They also offer practical suggestions regarding the use of processes and techniques for enhancing self-regulated learning in sports and physical education and illustrate an instructional approach to help coaches and physical educators comprehend key issues in implementing self-regulation. Clark adds to the impressive array of self-regulation intervention programs included in his volume by discussing a comprehensive self-regulation intervention model for managing chronic heart disease. She describes the intervention procedures in specific detail, helping a reader clearly understand the key components in implementing the intervention program.

The volume concludes with a tribute to Zimmerman as an exemplary mentor. Following a review of classic and contemporary theories on mentoring, DiBenedetto and White argue that Zimmerman's developmental model of self-regulatory competence can be used to understand the psychological mechanisms through which mentees become competent during the mentoring process.

In summary, this research-to-practice book demonstrates that self-regulation theory and principles can be successfully applied to enhance the regulatory skills of individuals across the developmental spectrum and in various contexts. Researchers have also shown the value of using multiple types of methodological designs to examine the implementation and effectiveness of these programs. Of greatest importance, however, is that each of the programs presented in this book are linked in some way to Zimmerman's highly influential and seminal models of self-regulation. We are greatly indebted to Professor Zimmerman for his scholarly innovations as well as for the clarity of his professional vision.

ACKNOWLEDGMENT

We thank all the authors who have contributed chapters to this volume. Their commitment to this project, prompt responses to our inquiries, and eagerness to produce first-class chapters have been highly appreciated and have made this volume one that is expected to have a significant impact on the academic and professional lives of learners, educators, and health practitioners. With much respect and humbleness, we also want to thank Professor Zimmerman for giving each of us the opportunity to work with him during our graduate training and throughout our careers. He has been an exemplary mentor who has graced us with his intellectual and scholarly sophistication as well as his extremely kind and generous spirit. He has enriched our lives and we look forward to continued collaboration with him in the years to come. Finally, as editors of this volume, we contributed equally. Thus, authorship is presented alphabetically.

—**Héfer Bembenutty**
Timothy J. Cleary
Anastasia Kitsanta

Applications of Self-Regulated Learning across Diverse Disciplines, page xvii
Copyright © 2013 by Information Age Publishing
All rights of reproduction in any form reserved.

CHAPTER 1

BARRY J. ZIMMERMAN'S THEORY OF SELF-REGULATED LEARNING

Dale H. Schunk and Ellen L. Usher

The focus of this volume is on explicating Barry Zimmerman's theory of self-regulated learning and its applications to diverse domains involving human learning and performance. Devoting an entire volume to this focus is a fitting and long-overdue tribute, because there is no name more strongly associated with self-regulated learning than his. Over the past 25 years, he has developed a social cognitive theory of self-regulated learning, conducted research to clarify the operation of self-regulatory processes, and offered practitioners multiple ways to apply these ideas to improve student learning and academic performance. Working often with collaborators—many of whom were graduate students with him at the Graduate Center of the City University of New York—Barry Zimmerman has provided the education profession with a coherent theoretical, empirical, and applied picture of self-regulated learning.

As used in this chapter, *self-regulated learning* (or *self-regulation*) refers to the process whereby learners systematically organize and direct their

Applications of Self-Regulated Learning across Diverse Disciplines, pages 1–28
Copyright © 2013 by Information Age Publishing
All rights of reproduction in any form reserved.

thoughts, feelings, and actions to attain their goals. As Zimmerman (1986) stated in his earliest publication on the topic:

> Self-regulated learning theorists view students as metacognitively, motivationally, and behaviorally active participants in their own learning process. Metacognitively, self-regulated learners are persons who plan, organize, self-instruct, self-monitor, and self-evaluate at various stages during the learning process. Motivationally, self-regulated learners perceive themselves as competent, self-efficacious, and autonomous. Behaviorally, self-regulated learners select, structure, and create environments that optimize learning. (p. 308)

In this chapter, we discuss the various components of this conceptualization, which has proven itself worthy to guide the field. Influenced by Zimmerman's early research and writings, professionals have increasingly devoted attention to conducting research on self-regulated learning and applying self-regulatory principles to situations involving teaching and learning. As a consequence, we now have a clearer understanding of the key role played by self-regulatory processes in learning, motivation, and performance.

Our objectives in this chapter are to discuss Zimmerman's theory of self-regulation, to include representative research testing his ideas and models, and to describe applications of these models to settings involving teaching and learning. To help set the context for Zimmerman's theory, we initially discuss a behavioral perspective on self-regulation, which served as the background for a contemporary social cognitive theory of self-regulation. We follow with an explanation of key principles of Bandura's (1977, 1986) social cognitive theory to include his original perspective on self-regulation. Zimmerman's (2000) theory then is discussed under three headings corresponding to its major areas of contribution: dimensions, phases, and levels of self-regulated learning. For each of these we cover theory, representative research, and applications to teaching and learning. The chapter concludes with suggestions for future research to extend the influence of Zimmerman's theory.

BACKGROUND

In 1986, Barry Zimmerman organized and chaired a symposium at the annual meeting of the American Educational Research Association entitled, "Development of self-regulated learning: Which are the key subprocesses?" This symposium was a critical event that stimulated interest among researchers in self-regulated learning. It is instructive to examine the state of self-regulation theory and research at this time to appreciate the radical departure that Zimmerman and others were to bring about. To gain this historical perspective, we examine key ideas from behavior theory.

Behavior Theory

A behavior theory perspective on self-regulation that was prominent for many years derived from the theory of operant conditioning by Skinner (1953). Researchers working within this tradition applied operant principles in diverse settings with children and adults to help reduce dysfunctional behaviors and teach adaptive behaviors (Mace, Belfiore, & Hutchinson, 2001; Mace, Belfiore, & Shea, 1989).

From the perspective of behavior theory, self-regulation involves selecting from different behaviors and deferring immediate reinforcement in favor of delayed (and typically greater) reinforcement (Mace et al., 1989). Individuals self-regulate by deciding which behaviors to regulate, establishing discriminative stimuli for the occurrence of desired behaviors, providing self-instruction as needed, and self-monitoring their performances to determine success. The last phase often includes deliberate self-recording of behavior. People administer self-reinforcement when desired behavior occurs. Three key self-regulatory processes used in this framework are self-monitoring, self-instruction, and self-reinforcement.

Self-Monitoring

Self-monitoring is deliberate attention to one or more aspects of one's behavior, such as quality, quantity, rate, and originality (Mace & Kratochwill, 1988). Self-monitoring is a necessary first step because people cannot self-regulate if they are unaware of what they do. The self-recording that often accompanies self-monitoring may be as simple as recording the frequency and duration of behavior. If Kristen, for example, wants to increase her study time, she might record how many study breaks she takes and the time she spends studying. Self-regulation would address decreasing study break time and increasing study time. To be effective, self-monitoring should occur regularly and proximal to the behavior being monitored. For study time to be improved, Kristen should monitor it daily (rather than once per week) and record the breaks when she takes them (rather than at the end of the night). Non-regular and distal recordings can yield misleading results.

Self-Instruction

Behavior theory emphasizes self-instruction, or the process of establishing discriminative stimuli that set the occasion for self-regulated behaviors leading to reinforcement (Mace et al., 1989). Self-instruction can involve arranging the environment to provide discriminative stimuli; for example, if Kristen needs to review her science notes in the morning, she may write herself a note to that effect and put it where she will easily see it in the morning. Self-instruction also can involve statements (steps, subtasks) to use to complete a task. Kristen may develop a list of steps to follow in reviewing her notes, such as highlight key points, rewrite anything that is unclear, and stop periodically to summarize. These items on her list guide her behavior as she studies her notes.

Self-Reinforcement

Self-reinforcement refers to the process whereby persons reinforce themselves contingent on their performing a desired response, which increases the likelihood of future similar responding (Mace et al., 1989). Kristen may establish a self-reinforcement contingency for her studying. If she studies for five nights and takes no more than two 10-minute breaks per night, she takes the sixth night off. In operant conditioning, a reinforcer is defined by its effects. Whether the opportunity to take a night off reinforces her studying is determined by whether she regularly earns the reinforcement. If she finds herself taking more than two 10-minute breaks per night, then the opportunity to earn a night off is not an effective reinforcer. To increase her studying, she will need to determine what reinforces studying better for her.

Researchers within and outside of the operant tradition have determined that self-monitoring, self-instruction, and self-reinforcement can increase on-task behavior and academic performance. Self-monitoring is a key component of many models of self-regulation and can, by itself, lead to behavioral improvements (Belfiore & Hornyak, 1998). Reid, Trout, and Schartz (2005) reviewed the literature on self-regulation interventions among children with attention deficit disorders and hyperactivity. Self-monitoring alone and in combination with self-reinforcement often was a key component in effective interventions. Self-instruction has been used effectively in many interventions, especially with students with learning disabilities or attention deficit disorders (Kosiewicz, Hallahan, Lloyd, & Graves, 1982).

Critique

Although behavioral methods can promote functional behaviors, a behavior theory approach has some problems. By focusing only on behavior, behavior theory ignores the metacognitive and motivational aspects of self-regulation. Behavior theories tend to define motivation in behavioral terms as an increased rate or duration of behavior, but this neglects the important cognitive and affective components of motivation such as beliefs and emotions. Behavioral methods are effective in the short term for increasing on-task behaviors, but cognitive and affective methods of self-regulation become more important over the longer term, such as when writing a dissertation or obtaining a college degree. A more elaborate perspective on self-regulation is needed for behaviors that extend beyond the immediate.

SOCIAL COGNITIVE THEORY

Social cognitive theory is a contemporary theory of learning emphasizing the idea that much human learning occurs in social environments. By interacting with others, people learn knowledge, skills, strategies, beliefs, rules, and attitudes. Through their observations and interactions with other people, individuals also learn about the appropriateness, usefulness, and consequences of behaviors. People act in accordance with their beliefs about their capabilities and the expected outcomes of actions.

Although there are different social cognitive perspectives, this chapter focuses on Bandura's (1977, 1986, 1997, 2001) social cognitive theory. Bandura's theory emphasizes the importance of vicarious, symbolic, and self-regulatory processes for learning, motivation, and performance. It is the theoretical framework on which Zimmerman's theory and research on self-regulation are based.

Reciprocal Interactions

A central tenet of Bandura's theory is that human behavior operates within a framework of *triadic reciprocality* involving reciprocal interactions among three sets of influences: personal (e.g., cognitions, beliefs, skills, affects), behavioral, and social/environmental factors. How individuals interpret the outcomes of their actions informs and changes their environments and their personal factors, and in turn these interpretations inform and alter subsequent behaviors (Figure 1.1).

These interacting influences can be demonstrated using the personal factor of *self-efficacy*, or one's perceived capabilities for learning or performing actions at designated levels (Bandura, 1997). With respect to the interaction of self-efficacy and behavior, much research shows that self-efficacy influences achievement behaviors such as task choice, effort, persistence, and use of effective learning strategies (Schunk & Pajares, 2009). These behaviors also affect self-efficacy. As students work on tasks and observe their learning progress, their self-efficacy for continued learning is enhanced.

The link between personal and social/environmental factors can be illustrated with students with learning disabilities, many of whom hold low

Person ◄──► Behavior

Person ◄──► Social/Environment

Social/Environment ◄──► Behavior

Figure 1.1   Triadic reciprocality in social cognitive theory.

self-efficacy for performing well (Licht & Kistner, 1986). Individuals in their environments may react to them based on common attributes (e.g., low skills) rather than their actual capabilities. In turn, social/environmental feedback can affect students' self-efficacy. When a teacher tells a student "I know you can do this," the student's self-efficacy may increase.

The link between behaviors and social/environmental factors is seen in many instructional sequences. Social/environmental factors direct behaviors when a teacher points to a display and says, "Look here," which students do without much conscious effort. Students' behaviors can alter their instructional environments. When teachers ask questions and students give incorrect answers, teachers are apt to re-teach the material rather than continue with the lesson.

Social cognitive theory reflects a view of human *agency* in which individuals are proactively engaged in their own success and development (Schunk & Pajares, 2005). They hold beliefs that allow them to exert a large degree of control over their thoughts, feelings, and actions. In turn, people are influenced by the outcomes of their actions and other environmental inputs. But the scope of this reciprocal influence is broader than individuals because they live in social environments. *Collective agency* refers to people's shared beliefs about what they are capable of accomplishing as a group. As is the case with individuals, groups also affect and are influenced by their actions and environments. For example, mathematics teachers in a middle school may collectively decide to use more hands-on activities to deepen students' understanding of mathematical concepts. They develop and implement these activities and continue to refine them based on students' experiences and learning.

Enactive and Vicarious Learning

In social cognitive theory, learning occurs *enactively* through actual doing and *vicariously* through observing modeled performances (e.g., live, filmed, symbolic; Bandura, 1977). Enactive learning involves learning from the consequences of actions. Behaviors that result in success tend to be retained, whereas those that are unsuccessful are discarded or modified. Unlike behavior theories stressing that consequences strengthen responses, social cognitive theory contends that consequences inform and motivate. They inform people of the accuracy or appropriateness of behaviors. People who are rewarded for their actions understand that they are performing well, whereas punishments convey inappropriateness of behaviors. People are motivated to learn and perform behaviors that they believe will have desirable consequences and do not try to learn behaviors that they believe will be punished.

Much human learning occurs vicariously, or without actual performance by learners at the time of learning. Vicarious learning accelerates what people would learn if they had to perform every action and also saves them from undesirable consequences. Observing or reading about safety techniques prevents individuals from acting in potentially dangerous ways. As with enactive learning, observers are more motivated to learn actions leading to successes than those that are unsuccessful. People attend to successful models who demonstrate actions that they believe will benefit them (Bandura, 1986; Schunk, 1987).

Self-Regulatory Processes

From the perspective of social cognitive theory, self-regulation reflects the idea of triadic reciprocality among personal, behavioral, and social/environmental factors (Zimmerman, 2000). While working on tasks, learners may self-regulate personal factors, such as by setting goals, monitoring and evaluating their progress, assessing their self-efficacy for continued learning, and creating a positive emotional climate for themselves. They may exert behavioral self-regulation by employing learning strategies, verbalizing aloud or covertly steps to follow, and self-recording their progress. They exert social/environmental control when they create productive work environments and seek assistance from others when needed. In turn, the results of their personal, behavioral, and social/environmental self-regulation affects their self-efficacy, goals, strategy use, and other self-regulatory behaviors (Pintrich & Zusho, 2002).

An early social cognitive perspective viewed self-regulation as comprising three phases: self-observation, self-judgment, and self-reaction (Bandura, 1986; Kanfer & Gaelick, 1986). These phases bear some similarity to the behavioral phases of self-monitoring, self-instruction, and self-reinforcement, but there are important differences reflecting social cognitive theory's emphasis on cognitions and motivation.

Self-observation refers to deliberate attention to aspects of one's behavior and may involve recording their frequency or intensity. People regulate their behaviors to conform to their internal standards and goals. *Self-judgment* refers to comparing present performances against goals or standards. Prior to embarking on a task, individuals determine their goals and strategies to use. As they work on tasks, they cognitively assess their progress against their goals and decide whether to continue or alter their strategies. *Self-reactions* involve the cognitive and behavioral responses to one's self-judgments. As people reflect on their experiences, they interpret them and determine what their next steps should be. The belief that they have learned and made progress strengthens their self-efficacy and motivates them to continue learning.

ZIMMERMAN'S THEORY

By the 1980s, Barry Zimmerman had conducted and published much research that validated many principles of social cognitive theory (Rosenthal & Zimmerman, 1978). Importantly, this research showed that by observing others, individuals could acquire new skills and strategies that were not copies of behaviors displayed but rather reflected observers' adaptations of what they had observed. These findings fit well with the notion that people self-regulate their behaviors, cognitions, and environments, to attain their goals.

We summarize Zimmerman's theoretical ideas and models of self-regulation under three headings: dimensions, phases, and levels of self-regulated learning. Although there is overlap among these aspects, we believe that discussing them separately will present a clearer picture of their operation and allow for better integration into the larger social cognitive theoretical framework. For each of these three areas, we discuss theory, summarize some representative research, and describe how the ideas have been or could be applied to situations involving learning.

Zimmerman's theory and the various models it includes have clarified and expanded the traditional social cognitive perspective on self-regulation. His investigations of the dimensions of self-regulation explicated the key self-regulatory processes that learners use. His model on the phases of self-regulation expanded the traditional view by addressing self-regulatory processes before and after task engagement, not just those that occur during it. This model also stresses the cyclical nature of self-regulation, in line with Bandura's (1986) framework of reciprocal interactions among personal, behavioral, and social/environmental factors. Lastly, Zimmerman's model of self-regulation development offers a theoretically and empirically based framework to use with students to help them develop skills and strategies.

Dimensions of Self-Regulated Learning

A key contribution of Zimmerman's theory is its showing that self-regulated learning is not a simple phenomenon but rather a complex one that includes multiple dimensions. These dimensions are important theoretically and empirically, as they comprise different types of self-regulatory processes that work in concert and because they indicate ways to help students become better self-regulated learners. These dimensions are shown

TABLE 1.1   Dimensions of Self-Regulated Learning

Dimension	Key Processes
Motive	Goals; self-efficacy
Method	Strategies; routinized performance
Time	Time management
Behavior	Self-observation; self-judgment; self-reaction
Physical environment	Environmental structuring
Social environment	Social networking; selective help seeking

in Table 1.1, along with some key self-regulatory processes (Zimmerman, 1994, 1998, 2000).

Learner choice is a critical element of self-regulated learning. Students can engage in self-regulation to the extent that they have choices in one or more dimensions. If all dimensions are regulated by others (e.g., teacher specifies exactly what students are to do), then students' activities are highly externally regulated. Development of students' self-regulatory skills requires that they be taught these skills and given opportunities to apply them.

Motive

The motive dimension addresses the issue of why one engages in self-regulated learning. Learners are apt to use self-regulatory processes if they believe that these processes will help them learn and perform better on tasks whose outcomes are important to them. This belief can help initiate task engagement and sustain motivation.

Key self-regulatory processes involve goals and self-efficacy (Zimmerman, 2011). Prior to engaging in a task, self-regulated learners set learning goals and divide them into subgoals as needed. They also hold a sense of self-efficacy for goal attainment. As they work at the task, they monitor and assess their goal progress. The belief that they are making progress sustains their motivation and strengthens their self-efficacy. When self-regulated learners perceive their progress as inadequate, they may adjust their strategy, alter their goal, seek assistance, or otherwise attempt to improve their goal progress. Their self-efficacy should not decline if they believe they have ways available to them to foster their learning (e.g., use of a better strategy).

Method

The method dimension addresses how self-regulated learning will occur. Self-regulated learners select learning strategies and procedures to use that they believe will be effective. As learners become more skillful, their choices and implementation of methods can become routinized. The self-regulatory processes involved in this dimension are selection and use of learning strategies and implementation of routinized performance. Self-regulated learners have a repertoire of strategies to use and select those that they believe will be effective for the task and circumstances. Researchers working in the information processing tradition have identified a range of strategies including rehearsal, elaboration, organization, comprehension monitoring, and affective awareness (Weinstein & Mayer, 1986; Winne, 2001, 2011). As learners become more skillful, strategy implementation may occur automatically and reflect a routinized performance. Learners who believe they understand and can apply effective strategies feel self-efficacious and motivated to learn. If their strategies are not leading to acceptable goal progress, they are apt to change their strategies to ones they believe will be more effective.

Time

A third dimension is time. Self-regulated learners choose when they will engage in a task and how long they will do so. The key self-regulatory process is time management. Self-regulated learners plan and monitor their time so that they use it effectively. They understand that certain tasks require more cognitive effort and motivation than others, so they schedule times to work on these when they will be mentally fresher. They also know their limits, so they plan to engage in a task for the amount of time that they believe they can be effective. While working on tasks, they sustain motivation and defer distractions.

Behavior

The behavior dimension refers to the outcome or competence level that learners seek. They spend less time on tasks when their outcome is familiarization than when they strive to attain higher levels of skill. Behavioral outcomes require that learners establish their goals accordingly and monitor and assess their performance to determine whether they have attained the desired outcomes.

Key self-regulatory processes are those discussed earlier: self-observation, self-judgment, and self-reaction. Self-regulated learners observe their performances, judge their progress toward their goals, and react by continuing their approach or changing to a method that they believe will be more effective.

Physical Environment

This dimension refers to where individuals will learn—the physical environment and elements in it. Self-regulated learners are environmentally sensitive and resourceful. They create productive learning environments that minimize distractions and allow them to be successful. Self-regulatory processes involve those associated with environmental structuring, such as selecting the setting and elements in it. Self-regulated learners choose an environment in which they feel comfortable learning. They gather the materials and equipment they will need for the task. They optimize their environment by eliminating distractions (e.g., noise, electronic devices), but if they find that the environment is not conducive to their learning, they may find a new location or attempt to remedy the problems (e.g., use headphones).

Social Environment

The social environment dimension comprises the persons with whom self-regulated learners engage. Self-regulated learners choose effective teachers, coaches, and partners, to learn with and from. They are socially sensitive and resourceful. They seek out models from whom they believe they can learn the skills they need to attain their goals. When working with peers, they choose those who are effective study partners with whom they interact well.

Important self-regulatory processes involved in this dimension are social networking and selective help-seeking. Self-regulated learners form strong social networks composed of like-minded persons. They seek assistance when they believe it will help them learn. They are sensitive to task demands and select models and learning partners consistent with their learning goals. When individuals make poor social environmental choices, their learning and self-efficacy suffer.

Representative Research

Researchers investigating self-regulated learning dimensions typically focus on identifying the self-regulatory processes that students use while learning, how these change with development and learning, and which are most beneficial for various types of content and contexts. Research supports the validity of these dimensions and indicates important developmental and contextual influences.

A representative research study was conducted by Zimmerman and Martinez-Pons (1986), who interviewed high school students to determine their use of self-regulated learning strategies during class and while studying. The researchers presented students with scenarios tapping six different learning contexts: in classrooms, at home, when completing written assignments outside of class, when completing mathematics assignments outside of class, when preparing for and taking tests, and when poorly motivated. For each context, students identified the techniques they used to participate in class, to study, and to complete their assignments.

Students' responses were coded and categorized. The results indicated a variety of techniques that students used, including self-evaluation, organizing, goal setting, seeking information, monitoring, environmental structuring, seeking assistance from others (peers, teachers, other adults), reviewing (tests, texts, notes), and rehearsing. Students' responses reflected several of the dimensions identified by Zimmerman (1994, 1998). This study also compared students from higher and lower achievement tracks. Of the 14 categories of strategies identified, the higher-track group reported greater use of 13 of the strategies compared with the lower-track group. Categories that distinguished best among students involved seeking information, keeping records and monitoring, and organizing and transforming.

Subsequent research (Zimmerman & Martinez-Pons, 1988) validated students' reports of these 14 categories by showing a strong correlation between students' reported self-regulatory skills and teachers' ratings of students' skills ($r = .70$). Factor analyses of teachers' ratings with students' scores on standardized mathematics and English tests revealed the existence of a self-regulated learning factor that accounted for 80% of the explained variance. These results indicate both convergent and discriminative validity for a self-regulated learning construct.

Applications

Theory and research on self-regulation dimensions have implications for teaching and learning. To help students develop self-regulatory skills, teachers can select one or more dimensions, teach students effective strategies, and arrange favorable conditions for students to learn and use these strategies to improve their learning. With respect to time management, for example, teachers could have students keep a written record for a week showing how they spent out-of-class time. Students could bring their records to class and discuss them, receiving suggestions for improving time management. For the method dimension, teachers could teach students various strategies and show how to adapt strategies for use on different tasks. When teachers give assignments, they can ask students to write down what strategies they used to complete the assignments and evaluate how effective those strategies were. To help students structure their physical environments to be productive for studying, teachers might ask students to list the potential distractions and then discuss with them ways to eliminate or minimize these distractions.

It is imperative that students be given opportunities to use self-regulated processes. This requires that teachers not over-regulate assignments; some choices by students are necessary for them to practice self-regulatory skills. Moreover, the self-regulatory strategies that work best for individuals may differ. Thus, teachers will need to exercise flexibility in their assignments. For example, a teacher may assign students to read a book and write a report. There may be certain elements the teacher wants covered in the report (e.g., setting, theme). For students to develop self-regulatory skills, however, they must be given some choices. Thus, they might be allowed to choose their books, when and where they read them and write their reports, and other elements to include in the report. If they have to give oral reports, they might be allowed to choose the formats and visuals they will use.

Summary

In his model, Zimmerman captured the multidimensionality of self-regulated learning and offered practitioners a useful starting point for targeting interventions. Teachers and parents can help by providing learners with a degree of choice that invites them to be agents of their own learning, encouraging learners to try diverse self-regulatory methods and to routinize those that are most effective, helping learners to identify the appropriate behaviors to achieve their goals within a given time frame, and allowing learners to select the optimal physical and social environments in which to carry them out. Changes made in any of these dimensions and the self-regulatory processes they comprise can lead to powerful transformations in learning (and life) outcomes.

Phases of Self-Regulated Learning

The dimensions of self-regulated learning constitute a critical aspect of Zimmerman's theory because they specify what people self-regulate: namely, their motives, methods, time, outcomes, and physical and social environments. The dimensions illustrate the complexity of self-regulation and extend it far beyond the narrow behavior theory focus on overt behaviors. While these dimensions are important, they do not illuminate the process by which self-regulation occurs. Social cognitive theory emphasizes the interaction of personal, behavioral, and social/environmental factors (Bandura, 1986; Zimmerman, 2000, 2001). Zimmerman (2000) built upon this framework by developing a model that cast self-regulation as a cyclical process because these factors typically change during learning and must be monitored. Such monitoring can lead to changes in individuals' cognitions, behaviors, and affects. This dynamic nature is captured well by Zimmerman's theory in its emphasis on phases of self-regulated learning: forethought, performance/volitional control, and self-reflection (Zimmerman, 1998, 2000; see Figure 1.2). This conception also expands the classical social cognitive theoretical view of self-regulation—which addressed

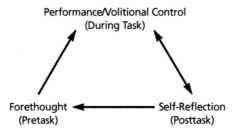

Figure 1.2 Phases of self-regulated learning.

task engagement—because it includes self-regulatory processes performed before, during, and after task engagement.

Forethought

The forethought phase precedes actual performance and includes processes that set the stage for action. Forethought includes task analysis and motivational beliefs (Zimmerman, 2000, 2008a). Prior to beginning tasks, learners set goals for specific learning outcomes. These may be process goals, which focus on the steps and procedures that one will employ, and product goals, or the expected performance outcomes. Learners also engage in strategic planning to decide which strategies and procedures they will use initially to help them learn.

Motivational beliefs also are central. Learners enter tasks with an initial sense of *self-efficacy for learning*, which influences their subsequent effort and persistence during task engagement (Schunk & Pajares, 2009). They hold *outcome expectations*, or beliefs about the expected outcomes of their actions. Learners who believe that their use of procedures and strategies will produce outcomes they desire (e.g., learning, recognition) will be more motivated to engage in the task than those who question whether their task engagement will lead to desirable outcomes. *Values*, or the personal importance learners attach to the learning, also are important. Individuals are more motivated to engage in activities with expected outcomes they value than those whose outcomes are less valued (Wigfield & Eccles, 2002). Finally, *goal orientations*, or one's reasons for learning, are important. Goal orientations have been described in various ways, but a common distinction is between mastery and performance. Students holding a mastery goal orientation engage in learning because they believe it is important and desire to learn the skills. Those with a performance goal orientation are more concerned about the actual outcomes and less interested in the process. Goal orientation researchers have obtained positive relations between mastery goal orientation and various indexes of task motivation (Elliot, 2005; Maehr & Zusho, 2009).

Performance/Volitional Control

This phase of the self-regulatory cycle occurs during task engagement. Two key processes that occur are self-control and self-observation (Zimmerman, 2000). Such self-control processes as self-instruction, focusing attention, and applying task strategies, keep learners engaged in the task and motivated to improve. During self-observation, learners attend to aspects of their performances and outcomes. It is important that such self-observations are accurate, because learners who misperceive or distort their observations will have difficulty improving their performances.

Zimmerman, Bonner, and Kovach (1996) advocated the use of self-recording as a self-observation technique. Self-recording when conducted close in time to the task performance increases the likelihood that observations will be informative and accurate. Students who record the start and stop times of their studying may be surprised to learn that they are studying much less than they think they are. Such records then can show improvements as learners engage better with the task.

Self-Reflection

Periods of self-reflection occur when individuals pause while working on tasks and when work is complete (Zimmerman, 2011). Two important self-reflective processes are self-judgment and self-reaction. *Self-judgment* involves self-evaluating one's performance and making causal *attributions* (perceived causes of outcomes) for the outcomes. Learners compare their present performances against their goals to determine progress. The belief that they are making progress strengthens self-efficacy and motivation (Schunk & Pajares, 2009). The attributions they make for their progress are important. For example, learners who attribute progress to their strategy use and effort are apt to feel self-efficacious about continuing to do well, whereas those who attribute outcomes to factors outside of their control (e.g., luck, teacher help) should not experience the same level of self-efficacy.

Learners may react to the judgments in various ways. If they perceive they are making acceptable progress, they are likely to feel self-satisfied and motivated to continue. The perception of inadequate progress may stimulate feelings of self-dissatisfaction, which can lead learners to alter their strategies or seek assistance to improve. Self-dissatisfaction will not necessarily lower self-efficacy, however, if learners believe they can improve; for example, they attribute lack of acceptable progress to a poor strategy and then shift to one they believe will be more effective. The dynamic nature of Zimmerman's model is evident during self-reflection because depending on their assessments learners may continue with the task or return to the forethought phase to plan a new strategy.

Representative Research

Research on self-regulated learning phases typically examines students' personal, behavioral, and social/environmental factors at the different phases to determine how these change and how they are affected by instructional or experimental factors. Representative research on this facet has been done by Schunk (1996) and Schunk and Ertmer (1999).

Schunk (1996) conducted two projects in which children received modeled explanations and demonstrations of fraction solution strategies and practice opportunities. During the forethought phase, children judged self-efficacy for learning fraction solution strategies. During the performance control phase, they received instruction under process (learning how to solve problems) or product (solving the problems) goal conditions. In the first project, half of the students in each goal condition engaged in daily self-evaluation of their problem-solving capabilities during the self-reflection phase. Compared with students in the product goal without self-evaluation condition, those in the process goal with or without self-evaluation and the product goal with self-evaluation conditions demonstrated higher self-efficacy, self-regulated motivation, achievement, and mastery orientation (desire to independently master academic work) and lower performance goal orientation (desire to perform well to please the teacher and avoid trouble). In the second project, all students self-evaluated their learning progress once during the instructional program. The process goal led to higher self-efficacy, self-regulated motivation, achievement, and mastery orientation, and lower performance goal orientation, than did the product goal. When students self-evaluate less often during periods of self-reflection, self-evaluation may complement process goals better than product goals and exert desirable effects on self-efficacy and self-regulated learning.

Schunk and Ertmer (1999) worked with college students on a computer application (Hypercard). Students were tested on Hypercard self-efficacy and achievement, and on how well and how often they performed various strategies while learning computer skills. These strategies tapped five of Zimmerman's (1994, 1998) dimensions: motives, methods, performance outcomes, and social and environmental resources. Students were assigned to one of four conditions: process goal (with or without self-evaluation), or product goal (with or without self-evaluation). At the start of each of three sessions, process goal students received a goal of learning to perform various Hypercard tasks, which coincided with the unit objectives, whereas product goal students were advised to try their best. At the end of the second session, students assigned to the self-evaluation conditions evaluated their progress in acquiring the skills (self-reflection).

Providing process goals with or without self-evaluation led to higher self-efficacy and strategy competence and frequency than did providing product goals and no self-evaluation. The process goal plus self-evaluation led to higher self-efficacy than did the process goal without self-evaluation and the product goal with self-evaluation. Of the students in the self-evaluation conditions, those who pursued process goals evaluated learning progress greater than those who received product goals. These results corroborate those of Schunk (1996) in showing that engaging in self-evaluation less often during periods of self-reflection is more beneficial for self-efficacy and self-regulation when accompanied by process goals that students pursue during the performance control stage.

Researchers also have obtained evidence for individual differences across the three phases. For example, DiBenedetto and Zimmerman (2010) studied the self-regulation processes of high school students who were high, average, or low achievers in science. Compared with students who were average or low achievers, high achievers employed more self-regulatory processes during each of the three phases, spent more time studying science, and displayed higher achievement.

Applications

The cyclical nature of self-regulated learning suggests that educators should not confine their teaching of self-regulatory skills to only those that students employ during the performance control stage. Rather, educators need to work with students on self-regulatory processes before, during, and after task engagement.

Interventions to improve students' self-regulation can target various combinations of these processes. A useful place to start is with the forethought processes of goal setting and strategy selection. Students can be taught, prior to beginning a task, to set goals for the time they will spend on it and which strategies they will use. While they are engaged in the task they can be taught to self-control their performances by applying the strategies conscientiously and by observing their progress. This stage may be accompanied by self-recording. Having students self-evaluate their self-efficacy and goal progress during periods of self-reflection is especially helpful because students likely are not used to doing this. Teachers also help students decide what to do if their strategies are not producing the level of performance that they desire.

We want to underscore the point that attention be given to all three phases. Some students—especially those with attention problems and learning disabilities—may be inclined to move quickly to the performance phase without giving adequate forethought to processes, such as setting goals and deciding which strategy to use. They also may not be inclined to pause during performance and engage in self-reflection, such as assessing their task progress, deciding whether to continue their approach or change, and judging their self-efficacy for learning. These phases can be built into instructional sequences as teachers can have students engage in forethought planning before they begin and then have them periodically stop to self-reflect.

Summary

As the scholarly work of Zimmerman and his collaborators has shown, self-regulation that occurs during task completion, though important, is insufficient for securing desired outcomes. Zimmerman's phases of self-regulation demonstrate how learning and performance can be optimized when individuals engage in self-regulatory processes before, during, and after learning tasks. Practitioners should design instruction that provides a mechanism for learners to engage in multiple self-regulatory processes at each phase of skill acquisition and performance. Learners would benefit from paying particular attention during the forethought and self-reflection phases, which often are overlooked.

Levels of Self-Regulated Learning

A third major component of Zimmerman's theory addresses the process whereby self-regulatory skills are developed. This aspect, which emphasizes systematic teaching and practice, involves the levels of observation, emulation, self-control, and self-regulation (Zimmerman, 2000). This model predicts that self-regulatory skill development begins with social (external) sources and shifts to self (internal) sources over the course of these four levels (Schunk & Zimmerman, 1997; Zimmerman, 2000; Zimmerman & Schunk, 2004; Table 1.2).

Observation

At the initial observation level, learners acquire basic skills and strategies—although they may not be able to perform them—from social sources such as modeled demonstrations and coaching. This level strongly reflects the social cognitive emphasis on observational learning. By observing live or symbolic (e.g., televised, computer-based) models, learners form cognitive representations of the skills and a basic understanding of them.

Emulation

With practice, feedback, and encouragement that occur during the emulation level, learners' performances begin to approximate the models' general forms. The emulation phase is performance based; observers attempt to practice what they have learned through observation. The major difference between these two levels is that learning transpires vicariously through instruction and observation at the observation level, whereas at the emulation level learners actually can perform the behaviors, albeit in rudi-

TABLE 1.2   Levels of Self-Regulatory Development

Level	Key Processes
Observation	Observation of models; basic cognitive understanding
Emulation	Directed practice; skill refinement based on feedback and encouragement
Self-control	Independent practice; internalization of skills
Self-regulation conditions	Adaptation of skills and strategies to changing self-motivation

mentary ways. Both sources are primarily social because learners require exposure to live or symbolic models. Internalization (discussed later) has begun, but learning is not internalized because learners require external assistance to perform skills and strategies (Schunk, 1999).

Self-Control

At the third level—self-control—learners can employ the skills or strategies on their own when performing similar or related tasks. Learners operating at this level can accomplish behaviors outside of the learning setting, such as at home or with peers. Internalization occurs, although learners still are modeling their actions after their models. They have yet to develop the capability to modify internally their performances based on what adaptations are necessary in given situations.

Self-Regulation

A higher level of functioning is experienced at the self-regulation level, where learners can adapt their skills and strategies based on their understanding of what alterations are needed to succeed under changing personal and contextual conditions. Because learners have internalized skills and strategies at this phase, they can initiate their use, adjust them to fit contexts, and maintain their motivation through their goals, perceptions of goal progress, and self-efficacy (Zimmerman, 2000).

Internalization

Internalization is a critical element in this social-to-self (external-to-internal) progression (Schunk, 1999; Schunk & Zimmerman, 1997; Zimmerman & Schunk, 2004). Knowledge and skills are internalized when they are under the learner's self-regulatory control, unlike non-internalized actions that primarily are under the control of others. Although learning can occur without internalization (e.g., when one is told what to do), internalization is necessary for self-regulated skill improvement over time and beyond the initial learning settings.

Internalization begins with learners at the observation and emulation levels, increases with the shift to the self-control level, and becomes established at the self-regulation level. Because of internalization, learners acquire personal (self) influences that they can employ in self-regulated fashion to sustain motivation and learning. Key self-influences include goal setting, progress self-evaluations, strategies, self-corrective feedback, and self-efficacy.

The role of self-efficacy is noteworthy because research shows that it influences learning, motivation, and achievement (Schunk & Pajares, 2009; Usher & Pajares, 2008). Bandura (1986) postulated that individuals acquire information to gauge their self-efficacy from performance accomplishments, vicarious (non-performance) experiences, social persuasion, and physiological indicators (e.g., heart rate). Performance accomplishments show people what they can do, so they are the most reliable source. To be sustained, gains in self-efficacy brought about by information acquired from the other sources must be substantiated by subsequent personal performance successes. Thus, observing models perform a task at the observation level (vicarious experience) may raise learners' self-efficacy and motivation, but learners subsequently must perform successfully for this increase to be sustained. Internalized skills strengthen self-efficacy because people are able to perform them independently (at the self-control and self-regulated levels) in various contexts (Schunk, 1999).

Representative Research

Research studies on the levels of self-regulated learning typically implement an intervention to help develop students' skills. This intervention consists of instruction, practice, and feedback, and is designed to move learners through the levels. Researchers often determine the key self-regulatory processes at different levels and effective ways to help learners progress.

A study with college undergraduates on writing revision skills operationalized the observation and emulation levels (Zimmerman & Kitsantas, 2002). At the observation level, participants observed an experimenter applying the strategy to several exercises, each of which included six to ten kernel sentences that were to be combined into non-repetitive sentences. The observation level was varied for participants depending on their experimental condition. Some observed a mastery model, where the experimenter skillfully worked all revision exercises. Others observed a coping model, where the experimenter initially made errors but corrected them and gradually improved to the point of the mastery model. Students in a third condition were not exposed to models. The emulation level was defined as participants applying the strategy to revision exercises; depending on their experimental condition, some participants in each of the three modeling conditions received encouragement and feedback while revising, whereas others did not.

Students who are learning skills may benefit more from observing a coping rather than a mastery model because they may perceive the coping model as more similar in competence to themselves, which can raise observers' self-efficacy (Schunk & Pajares, 2009). Encouragement and feedback are postulated to be critical elements in helping learners acquire and refine skills at the emulation level. The results of this study supported predictions. Observing a coping model led to higher gains in self-regulatory development and writing skill compared with observing a mastery model; students in the latter condition outperformed no-model students. Providing feedback assisted learners in all modeling conditions.

The shift from the self-control to the self-regulation level was addressed by Zimmerman and Kitsantas (1997) using dart throwing with high school students. After receiving explanation and modeled demonstration of the task (observation level), participants practiced throwing darts (emulation level). Some participants received a process goal of performing the actions properly, whereas others received a product goal of attaining a given score. The self-control level was defined as the consistent throwing of darts using the prescribed strategy. At that point, some participants were asked to shift from a process to a product goal, which was designed to facilitate self-regulation as participants had to adapt their strategy to attain the desired score. The self-regulation level was operationally defined as a shift away from following a specific strategy to adapting the strategy on one's own.

The results showed that shifting from a process to a product goal led to higher self-regulation, self-efficacy, and achievement compared with pursuing only the process goal. Students in the latter condition outperformed those who pursued only a product goal. This study also employed self-recording (writing down outcome scores), which enhanced skill acquisition and self-efficacy.

Applications

The phases of self-regulatory development closely align with actions in a typical teaching sequence. Teachers generally explain and demonstrate skills (observation level), after which students receive guided practice (emulation level). Independent practice (self-control level)—such as completing homework—helps to further develop skills. In teaching students to subtract from zeros (e.g., $100 - 57$), a teacher might explain and demonstrate problem solving to the whole class, after which students solve problems under the teacher's guidance. Students then could engage in independent seatwork and be given some problems for homework. For students to attain a self-regulation level they must refine and adapt skills to changing requirements. Homework assignments can mix subtraction problems of different formats including those with zeros in different positions (e.g., $6002 - 2379$).

The phases also are useful in one-to-one instruction. For example, a teacher might work with a student to improve clarity and coherence in the student's writing. Initially the teacher might model revision skills by demonstrating them in a paper written by the student (observation), after which the student revises under the teacher's guidance (emulation). Outside of school the student can practice revising papers and bring them to the teacher for feedback (self-control). The self-regulation level can be attained as the student applies revision strategies on different assignments, making adaptations to accommodate differences in content and expectations of teachers.

The levels of self-regulatory skill development emphasize teaching with modeled explanations and demonstrations. It is possible to acquire self-regulatory skills on one's own, such as through self-teaching. As learners begin to experience performance success, their initial self-efficacy is substantiated and their motivation to learn continues. However, this situation fails to capitalize on the power of observational learning (Bandura, 1986; Zimmerman, 2000). It also minimizes the role that vicarious influences play in increasing self-efficacy, which also can raise motivation to engage in the task.

Summary

Individuals become self-regulated learners first by observing others and by slowly internalizing the self-regulatory repertoires they see. Individuals begin to implement those strategies and skills they have acquired through exposure to social models, receiving feedback and assistance along the way. In the next level of the self-regulatory process, learners exercise self-control through independently enacting their newly-learned skills. Over time learners become flexible self-regulators, capable of adapting their strategies to different contexts and in light of new or changing demands. To the extent that learners have internalized the appropriate self-regulatory skills set, they are able and motivated to face the diverse challenges before them without the intervention of others.

FUTURE RESEARCH DIRECTIONS

As indicated in this and the other chapters in this volume, Barry Zimmerman's theory and research have expanded our understanding of self-regulated learning processes: what they are, how they function, how they change, and how teaching can influence them. Drawing on this theory and research base, we suggest three profitable areas for future research: motivation and affect, online learning, and cultures.

Motivation and Affect

A major advance of Zimmerman's theory over the earlier behavior theory view is its emphasis not only on behaviors but also on cognitive, metacognitive, motivational, and affective factors. Most self-regulated learning research has focused on behavioral, cognitive, and metacognitive variables, such as learners' use of self-instruction and learning strategies.

Fortunately this situation is changing. In his own research, Zimmerman (2008a, 2011) has addressed motivational and affective factors by examining students' goals, self-efficacy, attributions, and ways to establish a positive affective climate for learning. But clearly more research is needed.

There are two lines of research on the role of motivation and affect in self-regulated learning. One is determining how these factors affect self-regulated learning and are influenced by achievement outcomes. There is good evidence that motivation and affect can influence self-regulated learning and in turn are influenced by it (Schunk & Zimmerman, 2008). For example, holding an initial sense of self-efficacy for learning promotes task motivation and application of self-regulatory processes. As learners perceive that they are improving their skills, this perception strengthens their self-efficacy and motivation for continued learning (Joo, Bong, & Choi, 2000; Schunk & Pajares, 2009; Usher & Pajares, 2008).

Self-efficacy for self-regulated learning is also related to academic achievement. Students who hold a robust belief in their capabilities to use self-regulatory strategies outperform those who doubt what they can do (Usher & Pajares, 2006, 2008). Future research should be aimed at exploring such relationships among self-regulated learning, motivation, and affect in diverse learning contexts.

A second line of research is directly examining the self-regulation of motivation and affect. Research shows that students can learn to self-regulate motivational and affective factors (Boekaerts, 2011; Wolters, 2003; Zimmerman, 2011). We recommend further research on motivation and affect to determine the complex ways that they integrate with the behavioral, cognitive, and metacognitive aspects of self-regulated learning.

Online Learning

Compared with only a few years ago, the number of online and distance education courses continues to increase at all educational levels. Even traditional face-to-face courses routinely incorporate online learning. These trends surely will accelerate in the future as technological advances make online instruction more accessible and affordable.

Self-regulated learning is important in all circumstances, but it seems critically important when external regulation is low. Compared with face-to-face traditional courses where teachers and peers can exert immediate influence on students' learning, online learning requires high levels of motivation, persistence, and self-regulated behaviors. Research has shown that computer-based learning environments can help develop students' self-regulatory skills and that their use of such skills promotes achievement (Azevedo, Johnson, Chauncey, & Graesser, 2011). Further research is needed to determine what skills students need to succeed in online environments and how they can best acquire those skills and the motivation needed to use them.

Zimmerman and Tsikalas (2005) noted that to develop self-regulated learners, interventions should be clearly linked to the forethought, performance/volitional control, and self-reflection phases so that students learn cognitive, metacognitive, behavioral, motivational, and affective consequences of their actions and develop self-efficacy and motivation for continued learning. Computer-based learning environments that address all three phases of the cycle are more apt to produce enduring benefits. To date, most technological applications have addressed only one or two of Zimmerman's (2000) phases. We recommend future research covering all three phases. Research on self-regulatory processes during online learning can be enhanced by the use of online tracing methods that reveal which learning strategies students employ (Zimmerman, 2008b).

Cultures

Most research on self-regulated learning has been conducted with students in Western societies (Klassen & Usher, 2010; Pajares, 2007). This situation is changing as self-regulated learning research is becoming more global. The increasing presence of technology-rich "classrooms without walls" places learners from diverse contexts side by side, and students' success will depend on their self-regulatory repertoire. Overall the theoretical principles discussed in this chapter have been found to be cross-culturally relevant, despite some cultural differences that have been observed (McInerney, 2008).

Additional investigations are needed to determine whether the dimensions, phases, and levels postulated by Zimmerman's (2000) theory operate consistently across cultures. For example, cultures vary in the extent that they stress individual or collective efforts (McInerney, 2008). For cultures that stress individual responsibility, the social-to-self progression of the development of self-regulatory skills makes sense and should prove highly applicable. For cultures where collective responsibility is more prevalent, however, the social sources may be sufficient to instill self-regulatory competence as students work collaboratively to learn and achieve. This and other cross-cultural issues are in need of further research (Pajares, 2007).

CONCLUSION

Barry Zimmerman has made ground-breaking contributions to the theory, research, and practice of self-regulated learning, as the chapters in this volume show. His clear theoretical formulations of the dimensions, phases, and levels of self-regulated learning have clarified its operation in learning and performance and offer guidance to practitioners for helping students improve their skills. Research by Zimmerman and others has validated his predictions and suggested further avenues for development. We are confident that the next several years will continue to solidify his unique and fitting legacy in self-regulated learning.

REFERENCES

Azevedo, R., Johnson, A., Chauncey, A., & Graesser, A. (2011). Use of hypermedia to assess and convey self-regulated learning. In B. J. Zimmerman & D. H. Schunk (Eds.), *Handbook of self-regulation of learning and performance* (pp. 102–121). New York, NY: Routledge.

Bandura, A. (1977). *Social learning theory.* Englewood Cliffs, NJ: Prentice Hall.

Bandura, A. (1986). *Social foundations of thought and action: A social cognitive theory.* Englewood Cliffs, NJ: Prentice Hall.

Bandura, A. (1997). *Self-efficacy: The exercise of control.* New York, NY: Freeman.

Bandura, A. (2001). Social cognitive theory: An agentic perspective. *Annual Review of Psychology, 52,* 1–26.

Belfiore, P. J. & Hornyak, R. S. (1998). Operant theory and application to self-monitoring in adolescents. In D. H. Schunk & B. J. Zimmerman (Eds.), *Self-regulated learning: From teaching to self-reflective practice* (pp. 184–202). New York, NY: Guilford Press.

Boekaerts, M. (2011). Emotions, emotion regulation, and self-regulation of learning. In B. J. Zimmerman & D. H. Schunk (Eds.), *Handbook of self-regulation of learning and performance* (pp. 408–425). New York, NY: Routledge.

DiBenedetto, M. K. & Zimmerman, B. J. (2010). Differences in self-regulatory processes among students studying science: A microanalytic investigation. *International Journal of Educational and Psychological Assessment, 5*(1), 2–24.

Elliot, A. J. (2005). A conceptual history of the achievement goal construct. In A. J. Elliot & C. S. Dweck (Eds.), *Handbook of competence and motivation* (pp. 52–72). New York, NY: Guilford Press.

Joo, Y. -J., Bong, M., & Choi, H. -J. (2000). Self-efficacy for self-regulated learning, academic self-efficacy, and Internet self-efficacy in Web-based instruction. *Educational Technology Research and Development, 48*(2), 5–17.

Kanfer, F. H. & Gaelick, L. (1986). Self-management methods. In F. H. Kanfer & A. P. Goldstein (Eds.), *Helping people change: A textbook of methods* (pp. 283–345). New York, NY: Pergamon.

Klassen, R. M. & Usher, E. L. (2010). Self-efficacy in educational settings: Recent research and emerging directions. In T. C. Urdan & S. A. Karabenick (Eds.), *Advances in motivation and achievement: Vol. 16A. The decade ahead: Theoretical perspectives on motivation and achievement* (pp. 1–33). Bingley, United Kingdom: Emerald Publishing Group.

Kosiewicz, M. M., Hallahan, D. P., Lloyd, J., & Graves, A. W. (1982). Effects of self-instruction and self-correction procedures on handwriting performance. *Learning Disability Quarterly, 5,* 71–78.

Licht, B. G. & Kistner, J. A. (1986). Motivational problems of learning-disabled children: Individual differences and their implications for treatment. In J. K.

Torgesen & B. W. L. Wong (Eds.), *Psychological and educational perspectives on learning disabilities* (pp. 225–255). Orlando, FL: Academic Press.

Mace, F. C., Belfiore, P. J., & Hutchinson, J. M. (2001). Operant theory and research on self-regulation. In B. J. Zimmerman & D. H. Schunk (Eds.), *Self-regulated learning and academic achievement: Theoretical perspectives* (2nd ed., pp. 39–65). Mahwah, NJ: Erlbaum.

Mace, F. C., Belfiore, P. J., & Shea, M. C. (1989). Operant theory and research on self-regulation. In B. J. Zimmerman & D. H. Schunk (Eds.), *Self-regulated learning and academic achievement: Theory, research, and practice* (pp. 27–50). New York, NY: Springer-Verlag.

Mace, F. D. & Kratochwill, T. R. (1988). Self-monitoring: Applications and issues. In J. Witt, S. Elliott, & F. Gresham (Eds.), *Handbook of behavior theory in education* (pp. 489–502). New York, NY: Pergamon.

Maehr, M. L. & Zusho, A. (2009). Achievement goal theory: The past, present, and future. In K. R. Wentzel & A. Wigfield (Eds.), *Handbook of motivation in school* (pp. 77–104). New York, NY: Routledge.

McInerney, D. M. (2008). The motivational roles of cultural differences and cultural identity in self-regulated learning. In D. H. Schunk & B. J. Zimmerman (Eds.), *Motivation and self-regulated learning: Theory, research, and applications* (pp. 369–400). New York, NY: Taylor & Francis.

Pajares, F. (2007). Culturalizing educational psychology. In F. Salili & R. Hoosain (Eds.), *Culture, motivation, and learning* (pp. 19–42). Charlotte, NC: Information Age.

Pintrich, P. R. & Zusho, A. (2002). The development of academic self-regulation: The role of cognitive and motivational factors. In A. Wigfield & J. S. Eccles (Eds.), *Development of achievement motivation* (pp. 249–284). San Diego, CA: Academic Press.

Reid, R., Trout, A. L., & Schartz, M. (2005). Self-regulation interventions for children with attention deficit/hyperactivity disorder. *Exceptional Children, 71*, 361–377.

Rosenthal, T. L. & Zimmerman, B. J. (1978). *Social learning and cognition.* New York, NY: Academic Press.

Schunk, D. H. (1987). Peer models and children's behavioral change. *Review of Educational Research, 57,* 149–174.

Schunk, D. H. (1996). Goal and self-evaluative influences during children's cognitive skill learning. *American Educational Research Journal, 33,* 359–382.

Schunk, D. H. (1999). Social-self interaction and achievement behavior. *Educational Psychologist, 34,* 219–227.

Schunk, D. H. & Ertmer, P. A. (1999). Self-regulatory processes during computer skill acquisition: Goal and self-evaluative influences. *Journal of Educational Psychology, 91,* 251–260.

Schunk, D. H. & Pajares, F. (2005). Competence perceptions and academic functioning. In J. Elliot & C. S. Dweck (Eds.), *Handbook of competence and motivation* (pp. 85–104). New York, NY: Guilford Press.

Schunk, D. H. & Pajares, F. (2009). Self-efficacy theory. In K. R. Wentzel & A. Wigfield (Eds.), *Handbook of motivation at school* (pp. 35–53). New York, NY: Routledge.

Schunk, D. H. & Zimmerman, B. J. (1997). Social origins of self-regulatory competence. *Educational Psychologist, 32,* 195–208.

Schunk, D. H. & Zimmerman, B. J. (Eds.). (2008). *Motivation and self-regulated learning: Theory, research, and applications.* New York, NY: Taylor & Francis.

Skinner, B. F. (1953). *Science and human behavior.* New York, NY: Free Press.

Usher, E. L. & Pajares, F. (2006). Sources of academic and self-regulatory efficacy beliefs of entering middle school students. *Contemporary Educational Psychology, 31,* 125–141.

Usher, E. L. & Pajares, F. (2008). Sources of self-efficacy in school: Critical review of the literature and future directions. *Review of Educational Research, 78,* 751–796.

Weinstein, C. E. & Mayer, R. E. (1986). The teaching of learning strategies. In M. C. Wittrock (Ed.), *Handbook of research on teaching* (3rd ed., pp. 315–327). New York, NY: Macmillan.

Wigfield, A. & Eccles, J. S. (2002). The development of competence beliefs, expectancies for success, and achievement values from childhood through adolescence. In A. Wigfield & J. S. Eccles (Eds.), *Development of achievement motivation* (pp. 91–120). San Diego, CA: Academic Press.

Winne, P. H. (2001). Self-regulated learning viewed from models of information processing. In B. J. Zimmerman & D. H. Schunk (Eds.), *Self-regulated learning and academic achievement: Theoretical perspectives* (2nd ed., pp. 153–189). Mahwah, NJ: Erlbaum.

Winne, P. H. (2011). A cognitive and metacognitive analysis of self-regulated learning. In B. J. Zimmerman & D. H. Schunk (Eds.), *Handbook of self-regulation of learning and performance* (pp. 15–32). New York, NY: Routledge.

Wolters, C. A. (2003). Regulation of motivation: Evaluating an underemphasized aspect of self-regulated learning. *Educational Psychologist, 38,* 189–205.

Zimmerman, B. J. (1986). Becoming a self-regulated learner: Which are the key subprocesses? *Contemporary Educational Psychology, 11,* 307–313.

Zimmerman, B. J. (1994). Dimensions of academic self-regulation: A conceptual framework for education. In D. H. Schunk & B. J. Zimmerman (Eds.), *Self-regulation of learning and performance: Issues and educational applications* (pp. 3–21). Hillsdale, NJ: Erlbaum.

Zimmerman, B. J. (1998). Developing self-fulfilling cycles of academic regulation: An analysis of exemplary instructional models. In D. H. Schunk & B. J. Zimmerman (Eds.), *Self-regulated learning: From teaching to self-reflective practice* (pp. 1–19). New York, NY: Guilford Press.

Zimmerman, B. J. (2000). Attaining self-regulation: A social cognitive perspective. In M. Boekaerts, P. R. Pintrich, & M. Zeidner (Eds.), *Handbook of self-regulation* (pp. 13–39). San Diego, CA: Academic Press.

Zimmerman, B. J. (2001). Theories of self-regulated learning and academic achievement: An overview and analysis. In B. J. Zimmerman & D. H. Schunk (Eds.), *Self-regulated learning and academic achievement: Theoretical perspectives* (2nd ed., pp. 1–38). Mahwah, NJ: Erlbaum.

Zimmerman, B. J. (2008a). Goal setting: A key proactive source of academic self-regulation. In D. H. Schunk & B. J. Zimmerman (Eds.), *Motivation and self-regulated learning: Theory, research, and applications* (pp. 267–295). New York, NY: Taylor & Francis.

Zimmerman, B. J. (2008b). Investigating self-regulation and motivation: Historical background, methodological developments, and future prospects. *American Educational Research Journal, 45*, 166–183.

Zimmerman, B. J. (2011). Motivational sources and outcomes of self-regulated learning and performance. In B. J. Zimmerman & D. H. Schunk (Eds.), *Handbook of self-regulation of learning and performance* (pp. 49–64). New York, NY: Routledge.

Zimmerman, B. J., Bonner, S., & Kovach, R. (1996). *Developing self-regulated learners: Beyond achievement to self-efficacy.* Washington, DC: American Psychological Association.

Zimmerman, B. J. & Kitsantas, A. (1997). Developmental phases in self-regulation: Shifting From process goals to outcome goals. *Journal of Educational Psychology, 89,* 29–36.

Zimmerman, B. J. & Kitsantas, A. (2002). Acquiring writing revision and self-regulatory skill through observation and emulation. *Journal of Educational Psychology, 94,* 660–668.

Zimmerman, B. J. & Martinez-Pons, M. (1986). Development of a structured interview for assessing student use of self-regulated learning strategies. *American Educational Research Journal, 23,* 614–628.

Zimmerman, B. J. & Martinez-Pons, M. (1988). Construct validation of a strategy model of student self-regulated learning. *Journal of Educational Psychology, 80,* 284–290.

Zimmerman, B. J. & Schunk, D. H. (2004). Self-regulating intellectual processes and outcomes: A social cognitive perspective. In D. Y. Dai & R. J. Sternberg (Eds.), *Motivation, emotion, and cognition: Integrative perspectives on intellectual functioning and development* (pp. 323–349). Mahwah, NJ: Erlbaum.

Zimmerman, B. J. & Tsikalas, K. E. (2005). Can computer-based learning environments (CBLEs) be used as self-regulatory tools to enhance learning? *Educational Psychologist, 40,* 267–271.

CHAPTER 2

SEQUENCING COMPONENTS OF MATHEMATICS LESSONS TO MAXIMIZE DEVELOPMENT OF SELF-REGULATION

Theory, Practice, and Intervention

**Stephen J. Pape, Clare V. Bell,
and Iffet Elif Yetkin-Özdemir**

THE CALL FOR SELF-REGULATED LEARNING IN MATHEMATICS EDUCATION

Several key issues have dominated reform efforts in mathematics education and together make a focus on teaching self-regulated learning (SRL) within the context of K–12 mathematics education imperative. Current conceptions of mathematical competence have been broadened beyond procedural fluency to include conceptual understanding, strategic competence, adaptive reasoning, and productive dispositions (Kilpatrick, Swafford, & Findell, 2001). In addition, situative/sociocultural theoretical perspectives on teaching and learning argue that students develop their understand-

Applications of Self-Regulated Learning across Diverse Disciplines, pages 29–58
Copyright © 2013 by Information Age Publishing
All rights of reproduction in any form reserved.
29

ing of what it means to behave competently in mathematics through interactions within their classroom contexts (Gresalfi, 2009; Gresalfi, Martin, Hand, & Greeno, 2009). As a result of 12 years of mathematics education, graduates should possess skills, behaviors, and positive dispositions toward learning mathematics that will enable them to regulate their behaviors, cognitions, and emotions as they further their education. However, the number of learning-to-learn and no-credit preparatory courses at the college level continues to increase (Porter & Polikoff, 2011; Tuckman & Kennedy, 2009), which might be alleviated by explicitly incorporating SRL instruction within the K–12 classroom.

Additionally, the global economy mandates 21st century skills that depend on a strong mathematics education. Disparities between U.S. and international students as well as between white, middle class students and students of color and or lower SES students within the U.S. translate into differential access to future opportunities in higher education and employment. For example, because algebra functions as a gate-keeping course, individuals who fail to complete algebra courses are filtered out of higher education, often limiting career opportunities (Kelly, 2009; National Research Council, 1989; Schoenfeld, 2002; Thompson & Lewis, 2005). These disparities may be addressed with greater emphasis within K–12 schools not only on mathematics content but ways of learning the content.

Finally, students must possess some level of SRL to engage in classroom instruction focused on learning via problem solving, for example, as outlined by the National Council of Teachers of Mathematics (NCTM, 2000). We argue, however, that instruction aligned with reform as depicted in mathematics education today will also support subsequent SRL development (Pape, 2005; Pape & Smith, 2002; Randi & Corno, 2000). For these reasons, ways of understanding complex material or solving real problems, which are associated with SRL behaviors, as well as deeper and more resilient mathematics understanding must be a focus at the K–12 level.

In this chapter, we present an intervention that integrates mathematics classroom practices sequenced and integrated to recognize "the importance and centrality of self-regulation in the context of the prevailing new conception of school mathematics" (De Corte, Verschaffel, & Eynde, 2000, p. 721). We draw upon both social cognitive (e.g., Zimmerman, 1989, 1990, 2000, 2008) and situative/sociocultural (e.g., Gee, 2008; Gresalfi, 2009; Gresalfi et al., 2009) perspectives for our understanding of SRL and contexts that support its development. This theoretical understanding is further informed by research literature in the area of problem-solving interventions as well as our own observations and analyses of middle and secondary mathematics classrooms (Bell, 2008; Bell & Pape, in press; Yetkin, 2006; Yetkin-Ozdemir & Pape, 2011a, 2011b, 2012). We conceptualize intervention as a multi-treatment package that coordinates components of effective instructional practices emerging from mathematics education and psychological traditions. The proposed intervention sequences instructional practices to highlight Zimmerman's (2000) three phases of SRL (i.e., forethought, performance, and self-reflection) to make the SRL phases and subprocesses explicit for learners. Additionally, the intervention situates these instructional sequences within Zimmerman's (2000, 2002) levels of SRL development (i.e., observation, emulation, self-control, and self-regulation). By situating Zimmerman's (2000, 2002) model of SRL phases within his levels of SRL development, we argue that instruction to support SRL development must attend to the interaction between these two models as students slowly progress toward self-regulation. School administrators are encouraged to implement systematic, building-level programs for developing students' disposition toward learning as an effortful process that requires self-regulation including mathematics-specific strategic behavior.

CYCLICAL PHASES AND DEVELOPMENTAL LEVELS OF SRL

As a foundation for understanding how Zimmerman and colleagues' phases of SRL (Schunk, 2001; Zimmerman, 2000) will frame the lessons within our intervention, we briefly describe individual behaviors, cognitions, and key processes in which self-regulated learners engage within each of the three phases of SRL. During the forethought phase, self-regulated students engage in task analysis to determine the requirements of the task and set performance goals based on this analysis. These goals are used as standards against which students monitor progress and inform their engagement with strategies presently within their repertoire. Throughout this process, they draw on self-motivational beliefs such as beliefs in their ability to accomplish the task (i.e., self-efficacy), expectations for the outcomes of engaging in the task, and orientations toward learning (i.e., mastery vs. performance orientation; Dweck, 2000). Each of these self-beliefs impacts students' subsequent academic behaviors, persistence while performing a task, and future cognitions.

During the second phase, performance, self-regulated learners implement "self-control processes, such as self-instruction, imagery, and attention focusing, and task strategies" (Zimmerman, 2000, p. 18). Throughout the performance phase, they record their accomplishments and make observations to determine their progress toward their goals. This information is used in the self-reflection phase as learners make judgments about their progress and adjust their behaviors if they judge themselves to be falling short of accomplishing their goals. They also make attributions for their successes or failures, which may lead to self-reaction. Information regarding progress toward attaining goals and attributions for success and failure serves as the basis for self-appraisals and future behaviors.

Zimmerman and colleagues (Schunk, 2001; Schunk & Zimmerman, 1997; Zimmerman, 2000, 2002) also identified four developmental levels of regulatory skill: (1) observation, (2) emulation, (3) self-control, and (4) self-regulation (Table 2.1). The development of academic skill begins with co-regulation and social sources for information on how and when to carry out a strategy as the teacher both models the behavior and supports students to engage in the behavior, gradually shifting to self-control and self-regulation. Teachers and students support *observational* learning by modeling (demonstrations) and verbalizing thoughts and reasons for their actions. Teachers may make their thinking explicit for their students and ask students to share their mathematical processes and thinking. When individuals articulate how to solve a problem or justify mathematical steps, their processes and thinking are revealed to the class, becoming objects of discourse for class examination (Cobb, Boufi, McClain, & Whitenack, 1997).

TABLE 2.1   Teacher and Student Classroom Behaviors within Levels of SRL Development

Level	Description of student and teacher classroom behaviors
Observation	Students observe the behaviors of the teacher or others in the class. Teacher or other students in the class model and support students' learning of the behaviors and ways of thinking through the following behaviors: • Thinks aloud • Explains processes • Demonstrates • Verbalizes reasons for actions
Emulation	Student begins to imitate learned behaviors. Teacher provides tasks that allow students to imitate regulatory behaviors, guidance in using these behaviors, and feedback on students' imitative behaviors.
Self-control	Student engages with minimal guidance. • Analyzes tasks • Sets goals • Works on task Teacher provides tasks that allow students' independent work, observes students' actions, provides feedback, and adjusts the task or supports students' understanding of the task when they encounter difficulty.
Self-regulation	Student self-regulates learning behaviors. • Student adapts strategies to varying conditions. Teacher may provide tasks, provides assistance as requested, redirects student work as required, and challenges students to adapt their SRL behaviors for varying conditions.

Students' decisions to take on a model's behaviors and mathematical thinking, which results in *imitation* or *emulation*, is partially determined by whether these behaviors resulted in success or failure or were followed by reward or punishment. This vicarious information helps inexperienced learners formulate outcome expectations. At this level, the learner begins to take on the model's behaviors and is supported by the teacher to enact these behaviors in an imitative way. At the *self-control* level, the learner begins to control the selection and implementation of strategies for specific contexts but is still supported by both teachers and peers in the class when they articulate their behaviors and receive feedback. Such feedback, which is critical to development during earlier levels, is gradually faded out as students become increasingly independent. Further, learners use this feedback to develop standards for performance and give themselves reinforcements for accomplishing desired behaviors at the level of these standards. At the *self-regulation* level, the individual chooses to conduct the behaviors, is able to implement a strategy without assistance, and can adapt these skills to varying conditions. This level is characterized by strong, positive self-efficacy beliefs and consistent use of self-regulatory processes.

As the individual most likely to impact students' SRL development in school, the teacher's responsibility is to make strategic behavior and SRL processes explicit and to provide differential support so that students have equitable opportunity to interact with the mathematics content. Teachers' instructional decisions and practices should be informed by students' level of SRL development. As students move from observation through emulation, self-control, and toward self-regulation, instructional support is slowly withdrawn. Thus, when we consider instruction to support SRL development, we must consider the interaction between the phases of SRL and the levels of development. Table 2.2 provides an overview of teacher-directed activities that support the development of SRL organized in terms of the phases of SRL.

In this chapter, we forward the position that to provide these different levels and types of support, teachers must construct appropriate tasks, establish classroom norms, guide discourse, and use mediational tools that facilitate collective inquiry through the examination of student work. This examination is made possible when students' mathematical thinking and constructions are publicly displayed so that they may be taken up for exploration within whole-class discussion. Such discussion exposes students to a variety of ways of acting and thinking mathematically. Critical examination of multiple strategies must emphasize that no one way of acting or thinking (e.g., teacher's or students') is expected. As stated earlier, a situative/sociocultural perspective posits that classroom interactions influence students' notions of what it means to act competently in mathematics (Gresalfi, 2009; Gresalfi et al., 2009). Students' conceptions of what it means to be self-regulated learners also depend largely on the demands placed on them by the

TABLE 2.2   Selected Teacher Behaviors Across Phases of a Lesson to Support SRL Development

Phase of SRL	Selected teacher behaviors to support development of SRL
Forethought Phase	

Task Analysis and Goal Setting	• Provide worthwhile tasks or problems that require students to use varied strategies and/or multiple representations.
	  – (O; E*) Provide clear discussion of task or expectations for understanding before students implement a plan for solution.
	  – (S-C) Support students' use of strategies for analyzing a task or problem in alternative contexts.
	• Provide advanced organizer or orient students to the class-level goals for the class period.

Activate Prior Knowledge	• (O) Conduct whole-class discussions to elicit students' prior knowledge of concepts, terms, and notations. • (E) Activate students' prior knowledge by asking questions, including questions that make relationships between related concepts explicit. • (S-C) Remind students to search prior knowledge to support their understanding of a new situation.

Activate Strategic Knowledge/Strategic Planning	• Elicit initial conjectures about the task or problem, including ways of thinking about and solving the task or problem.
	  – (O) Model strategy selection.
	  – (E) Activate students' prior knowledge with questions about different strategies.
	  – (S-C) Remind students to think about different strategies and support them to use strategies in broader contexts.

Self-beliefs	• Create norms for classroom behavior that is conducive to learning (e.g., examination of correct and incorrect answers; sociomathematical norms).
Performance control	

Implement Self-control Processes	• Prepare students for self-instruction, imagery, and attention focusing (for example, using Polya-like steps for problem solving).
	  – (O) Model use of an heuristic in a think-aloud while solving a complex problem with the class.
	  – (E) Provide multiple problems and engage students in implementing the heuristic systematically.
	  – (S-C) Continue to provide opportunities to use the heuristic and occasionally remind students about the heuristic.

Implement Strategic Behavior	• Provide opportunities to exercise strategic behavior to solve a problem or accomplish a task individually, in small groups, or as a whole class.

(continued)

TABLE 2.2   Selected Teacher Behaviors Across Phases of a Lesson to Support SRL Development (continued)

Implement Strategic Behavior (*continued*)	• Conduct whole-class discussions of strategy. – (O) Create opportunities for students to observe models solving a problem using a particular strategy (Peer and teacher modeling). – (E) Provide multiple problems and engage students in implementing particular strategies to solve a problem. – (S-C) Continue to provide opportunities to implement the strategy in increasingly different contexts.
Self-monitor	• Conduct whole-class discussions of students' mathematical thinking and mathematical constructions. • Create norms for explanations and justifications within whole-class discussion. • Create expectation for examination of correct and incorrect answers. • (O; E) Provide instruction on and opportunities for collecting data on the relationship between students' strategic effort and outcomes (self-observation, e.g., Pape et al., 2003). • (S-C) Remind students periodically to monitor the efficacy of their academic strategies.
Adjust Strategic Behavior	• (O) Model coping with mistakes, re-examining understanding of a task or problem, and changing strategic direction. • (E; S-C) Remind students about the importance of monitoring progress and making adjustments.
Self-reflection	
Self-judgment	• Provide feedback and make students' mathematical thinking and constructions objects of whole-class exploration. – (O) Model exploration of students' mathematical thinking and constructions. – (E; S-C) Elicit explanations and justifications following individual or small group work to understand a problem and encourage students to request explanations and justifications during small-group work. • Convey expectations regarding personal progress rather than normative evaluations. • Create opportunities for self-evaluation based on goals, prior/current understandings, and self-observations.
Causal Attributions	• Recognize student work and strategic behavior. • Support positive attributions including descriptions of strategy use and recognizing relationships between strategy implementation and academic outcomes (e.g., Pape et al., 2003).
Self-reaction	• Support students to develop adaptive reactions to their own and others' successes and failures, such as self-satisfaction/affect. • Create interactions that provide information about students' reactions to self-reflection.

Note: We delineated different levels and types of teacher behaviors that support students' development of SRL at different levels. (O) indicates the observation level. (E) indicates emulation. (S-C) indicates self-control. The self-regulation level is not included in this table because of the focus on early development of self-regulation. Table adapted from Zimmerman, 2000.

interactional patterns of the classroom as well as the expectations for articulating their thinking and reasoning and the procedures they use. As ways of thinking mathematically are revealed to the class through whole-class discussion, they are also being co-determined through negotiation by and with the class of students. That is, creating a learning environment in which students' and teacher's mathematical thinking and reasoning are objects of classroom discourse requires more than exposing the teacher's expectations or ways of behaving mathematically. Creating a learning environment involves processes of discussion and negotiation of expectations and norms with the students (Hufferd-Ackles, Fuson, & Sherin, 2004; Yackel & Cobb, 1996). The mathematics education intervention research discussed in the following section provides further detail of components of classrooms that support SRL. We review this literature to highlight common characteristics important to classrooms that support SRL.

SRL INTERVENTIONS IN MATHEMATICS

We present Schoenfeld's (1985, 1992) work with college mathematics students because it includes several common features emerging from intervention research that informs our intervention. Schoenfeld's goals were for students to learn and use problem-solving steps similar to Polya's (1945/1957) heuristic (i.e., understand the problem; devise a plan; carry out the plan; and look back to check the solution). His version of these steps included: (1) Analyze the problem, (2) Design a global plan, (3) Explore with the goal of transforming the problem into a routine task, (4) Implement the solution, and (5) Verify the solution. These problem-solving behaviors were taught through four instructional techniques. First, students viewed videotaped episodes of other students modeling problem solving. Second, Schoenfeld explicitly modeled strategies in problematic contexts. Third, he engaged his students in whole-class discussions of problem solutions. Fourth, the students worked in small groups to solve problems while Schoenfeld probed the groups' work with three questions: (1) "What (exactly) are you doing? (Can you describe it precisely?)"; (2) "Why are you doing it? (How does it fit into the solution?)"; and (3) "How does it help you? (What will you do with the outcome when you obtain it?)" (Schoenfeld, 1987, p. 206). The instructor elicited strategies from the students and then helped them expand their repertoire gradually until they were using a variety of strategies on their own.

Reflection on mathematical behaviors, processes, and thinking provides a context in which students may alter their initial thinking and behavior. Schoenfeld's students improved their mathematical problem-solving abilities and achievement, adopted the self-regulated stance toward solving problems that is implicit in more expert problem solvers, and developed more positive dispositions toward problem solving.

More recently, problem-solving intervention research within upper-elementary classrooms (see De Corte et al., 2000 for a summary; Verschaffel & De Corte, 1997; Verschaffel et al., 1999) sought to impact students' SRL behavior as well as their ability to model realistic problems mathematically. An initial requirement for teaching problem-solving skills or mathematics content through problem solving is a "complex, realistic, and challenging" (De Corte et al., 2000, p. 714) task that requires students to use varied strategies and/or multiple representations (Pape, Bell, & Yetkin, 2003). Similar to Schoenfeld's (1985, 1987, 1992) work, students were required to use a series of problem-solving steps:

Step 1: Build a mental representation of the problem.
Step 2: Decide how to solve the problem.
Step 3: Execute the necessary calculations.
Step 4: Interpret the outcome and formulate an answer.
Step 5: Evaluate the solution. (Verschaffel et al., 1999, p. 202)

The lessons followed a sequence that included modeling strategies, small group or individual problem-solving activities, and whole-class discussion. During each of these lesson components, the teacher provided support for problem solving that was gradually reduced or faded over time. Within the intervention, there was careful attention to the development of socio-mathematical norms (see McClain & Cobb, 2001; Yackel & Cobb, 1996). "These norms related to the role of the teacher and the pupils in the classroom...and [are] about what counts as a good mathematical problem, a good solution procedure, or a good response" (De Corte et al., 2000, p. 716). Performance on posttests strongly supported the efficacy of the intervention. Students in the treatment group outperformed the control group in solving non-routine problems, held more positive beliefs about and attitudes toward mathematical problem solving, and showed greater achievement overall.

Some SRL interventions have emphasized the attributions students make for their successes and failures (Borkowski, Weyhing, & Carr, 1988). Students need multiple opportunities to make explicit connections between their behaviors and success or failure. In earlier work, we implemented an intervention to increase seventh-grade students' awareness of their use of strategies (Pape et al., 2003). Students were asked to articulate how they would study prior to a test, estimate their score before seeing their corrected exams, and reflect on the relationship between their strategies and actual test results. Students were then asked to discuss their strategies, which were sorted according to categories developed in prior research (Pape & Wang,

2003; Zimmerman & Martinez-Pons, 1986). Several factors important to the development of self-regulation within a mathematics classroom emerged, such as the importance of rich mathematical tasks that enabled the use of multiple representations and classroom discourse that engaged students in explanations of their strategies and justifications of their mathematical thinking. But more importantly, our findings clearly established that students needed different levels of explicitness and support to incorporate strategic behavior within their repertoires. For example, while we discussed and classified the strategies the students used, we did not specifically model for students who were in the observation phase of development. Therefore, some students did not benefit from these discussions. We therefore realized that we needed to situate our intervention more explicitly within the levels of SRL development (Zimmerman, 2000) as we have done in the present discussion. Characteristics of effective SRL instruction that emerge from these examples of intervention research will be integrated into our intervention presented in the next section.

SRL IN A MATHEMATICS CLASSROOM: THE MACRO AND MICRO LEVELS

In this section, we integrate the literature on SRL phases and levels of development as well as the intervention literature discussed in the previous section into an educational intervention to support SRL and mathematical understanding. The intervention we are proposing reflects multiple principles and classroom practices that, when framed in terms of the phases of SRL (i.e., forethought, performance, and self-reflections) and situated within the levels of SRL development (i.e., observation, emulation, self-control, and self-regulation), makes the subprocesses of each phase explicit for students (Tables 2.1 and 2.2). We argue that teachers should be more explicit with modeling and discussion of mathematical thinking and strategic behavior during the early stages of learning and can slowly withdraw this support as students begin to take on the behaviors in a self-controlled or self-regulated manner.

On the macro, or lesson level, we use the SRL phases, which are depicted in Figure 2.1 by three large phase shapes, as a frame for thinking about the structure of a lesson. We propose that teachers should engage students in iterative cycles of SRL phases, which we term the micro level, within the larger phases of the lesson or macro level. Further, we forward the position that teachers' instructional moves or levels of support within the phases should take the students' SRL developmental level into consideration (Tables 2.1 and 2.2). For example, in early stages of SRL development the teacher must provide clear discussions of tasks and expectations as a model of task analy-

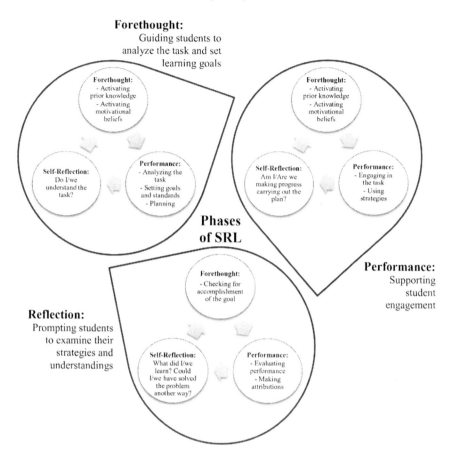

Figure 2.1 Selected behaviors associated with phases of SRL within a mathematics lesson: The macro and micro levels.

sis, but during later stages the teacher may engage students in whole-class discussion to ensure the students understand the task prior to engagement. These varying teacher behaviors at each of the levels of development are outlined in Table 2.2 and discussed in greater detail in the next section.

A contextual condition that supports this intervention is establishing classroom norms that encourage engagement with rich and complex tasks or problems often presented in a realistic context. Sociomathematical norms have been described by McClain and Cobb (2001) to include: (1) the expectation for explanation and justification of student reasoning; (2) a safe environment for contributing to the class discussion regardless of whether the contribution was judged to be invalid; (3) an expectation for students to listen to others' explanations and decide if they understand and agree; (4) frequent feedback and restatement of students' contributions from the teacher; (5) a student expectation to state any misunderstanding and ask clarifying questions; and (6) a student expectation to state any disagreement and justify why the explanation seemed invalid. Through establishment of these norms, students become comfortable with learning through the sharing and examination of students' solutions.

Macro or Lesson Level

On the macro level, a lesson within this intervention is segmented into three phases to provide a model for SRL behavior (Zimmerman, 2000): (1) setting up the task, which aligns with the forethought phase; (2) supporting student engagement in investigating a mathematical concept, which aligns with the performance phase; and (3) prompting students to analyze their thinking and products of their work to reveal, examine, and adjust student strategies and understanding, which aligns with the reflection stage.

Forethought Phase

During the forethought phase of a lesson, the teacher will introduce the task, problem, or concept, which implicitly or explicitly focuses the students' attention on a common learning goal for the class. The teacher will then carefully set up the task to support students' engagement with the content by conducting a task analysis, activating prior relevant knowledge, clarifying terms and concepts, and/or eliciting initial conjectures about ways of solving the problem. The teacher may provide more guidance and direction for the class during early encounters with the strategy or content by asking questions that elicit the task requirements from the students and support their understanding of the problem. At later developmental levels, the teacher may provide only task directions and expect students to analyze the task individually or in small groups. Each of these ways of setting up the task reflects the intersection of the teachers' needs to direct the students' activities and the developmental needs of the students within the class.

Performance Phase

During the performance phase of a lesson, teachers following this intervention will support student engagement in a variety of ways. Students' early attempts at mathematical processes, behaviors, and thinking are often performed initially within small groups where students support one another and the teacher monitors progress by asking probing questions that stimulate or direct the group's thinking. Students will be reminded that they will be expected to share their solutions. Following several minutes of individual work, the teacher may bring the students back to a whole-class discussion to provide a context for groups to discuss their initial understanding of the problems and strategies. Beginning with students' strategies and slowly building their repertoire through strategy instruction is a hallmark of intervention designed to impact SRL behaviors (e.g., Butler, 2003; Butler, Beckingham, & Lauscher, 2005).

This whole-class discussion provides opportunities for students to develop strategic behavior by observing the teacher's and classmates' regulated behaviors, engaging with strategic/regulated behaviors, and receiving teacher feedback and recognition. Such display of strategic behaviors also conveys implicit messages regarding what it means to be a self-regulated learner in this classroom and helps to develop classroom norms regarding acceptable behaviors. It is important to note, however, that small group work may not always be as effective as whole-group discussions, especially for students who are beginning to develop SRL behaviors.

(Self-)Reflection Phase

Finally, during the reflection phase at the end of a lesson, the teacher will bring the students back to a whole-class discussion and encourage them to reflect on their mathematical understanding and the behaviors that led to understanding and task completion. Students' strategic behaviors and solutions become objects of discourse for class examination, and students are then able to make individual judgments based on feedback from the teacher as well as classmates. Making students' thinking an object of classroom discourse provides students with models of SRL subprocesses for self-monitoring: self-observation, self-judgment, and self-reaction. Consistent uptake of correct and incorrect responses in a non-threatening and educative manner strengthens students' notions of and dispositions toward self-monitoring. Similar to the performance phase, whole-class discussions during the reflection phase of the lesson convey messages (implicitly as well as explicitly) regarding standards for self-regulated behavior. Additionally, teachers need to attend to students' attributions for successes and failures (Borkowski et al., 1988). Students must learn to make attributions that allow them to change behaviors and beliefs such that they attribute success to the use of a particular strategy and failure to lack of a strategy or to an ineffective strategy.

Micro or Within-Phase Level

The micro level of our intervention consists of individual episodes within a lesson phase that reflect smaller, local cycles of forethought, performance, and self-reflection. These episodes are depicted in Figure 2.1 as cycles within lesson phases. For example, during the performance phase at the macro level, the teacher will engage students in a whole-class discussion to examine progress toward reaching their class goal. In the course of this collective self-reflection during this micro-level cycle of SRL within the performance phase of the lesson, additional understanding of the task or concept may result. New goals for task completion will be set based on this analysis, and students would be encouraged to persist toward task completion. The teacher will again ask the class to work on the task in small groups based on new understandings. Thus, within a phase of a lesson, the class experiences iterative cycles of forethought, performance, and self-reflection.

Regardless of whether our conversation is at the macro (lesson) or micro (within a lesson) levels, the cyclical nature of SRL and the subprocesses of each phase (e.g., goal setting, strategic planning, self-instruction, etc.) are made explicit with and for students. The degree of explicitness needed beyond simple modeling, however, varies among students (Pape et al., 2003). Taking up students' mathematical thoughts, strategic behaviors, and questions for discussion increases the level of explicitness. By "take up for discussion" we mean allowing an individual's statements to direct the conversation as class members think about, examine, and discuss each other's ideas (i.e., these ideas become objects for examination within the class). This requires that classroom norms have been established such that individual students or the teacher might press a speaker to explain and justify his/her response to a question. In the next section we illustrate our intervention through two vignettes of mathematics classroom practice.

VIGNETTES OF SRL INSTRUCTION
IN THE MATHEMATICS CLASSROOM

In the following sections, we provide vignettes of lessons in two urban settings—a middle school mathematics classroom (Yetkin, 2006; Yetkin-Ozdemir, & Pape, 2011a, 2011b, 2012) and an Algebra I classroom in which classroom connectivity technology (CCT) was being implemented (Bell, 2008; Bell & Pape, 2012). The vignettes are provided for three purposes. Broadly, the vignettes (1) illustrate the nature of the teacher's role in promoting SRL, (2) portray the SRL skills and characteristics of students during these lessons, and (3) illustrate the cyclical nature of the intervention on both the macro and micro levels. The vignettes are snapshots of these teachers' classroom practices, however, and therefore do not depict how the teachers' behaviors differed in relation to the students' developmental levels of SRL because SRL develops over broader periods of time. We highlight both the lesson (macro) level as well as the micro level of our intervention within our discussions of these classes. Following these vignettes, and in Tables 2.1 and 2.2, we provide an overview of principles for instruction drawn from the theoretical discussion above as well as these two examples.

The first vignette, Mrs. Thompson's sixth-grade mathematics classroom, was developed from a case study exploring classroom practices supporting students' strategic competence and self-efficacy (Yetkin, 2006; Yetkin-Ozdemir, & Pape, 2011a, 2011b, 2012). Mrs. Thompson had been teaching sixth-grade mathematics for 15 years at the time of this study. She was familiar with SRL through a professional development program focused on NCTM standards and implications of SRL theory for classroom practice. Twenty-two 80-minute classroom observations were captured from December to March, and the vignette presented below is from a lesson that occurred at the beginning of the spring semester (toward the end of January).

The second vignette, Ms. Brenner's Algebra I classroom, took place within the *Classroom Connectivity for Mathematics and Science Achievement* (CCMS) project, which was an interdisciplinary professional development and research project examining the impact of CCT on Algebra I and physical science achievement (Owens, Abrahamson, Pape, Irving, & Demana, 2005). Ms. Brenner, who taught high school in a large urban area in the northeastern United States, was a mathematics coach in her fourth year of teaching. Ms. Brenner's classroom was videotaped for two consecutive days in each of two years as part of the CCMS project.

The vignette of Ms. Brenner's class, which occurred during the second year of the study, included the use of the Texas Instruments Navigator™ (Navigator; see Figures 2.2 and 2.3), which allowed Ms. Brenner to communicate wirelessly between her computer and hubs that connected to students' handheld graphing calculators. During the observation that formed the basis for the second vignette, Ms. Brenner was using the Activity Center, which allowed her to display a coordinate system and students to contribute individual points, equations and their graphs, or data lists to a shared workspace (Figure 2.3).

Our work to understand these two teachers' classes has been fueled by our realization that the instructional practices and interactional patterns in these classrooms were similar to the theoretical descriptions of classrooms that support SRL and mathematical understanding and contrasted significantly with the predominant interactions we observed in the national sample of Algebra I classrooms in the CCMS project (Pape et al., 2010). Teacher-led discourse and teacher non-instructional statements dominated the observed classroom interactions across these observations. Specifically, mathematics instruction was dominated by teacher-to-student questions that required short responses of known information. These low-level recitation questions elicited student-to-teacher mathematics statements that were typically four words long, and the accuracy of these statements were typically evaluated by the teacher through initiate-respond-evaluate (IRE)

Figure 2.2 Depiction of the TI Navigator™ within a classroom. Copyright 2008 by Texas Instruments, Inc. Adapted and reprinted with permission.

cycles. "This pattern of interaction points toward a disturbing reality. The students in these classrooms [within the national CCMS sample] are frequently asked to compute basic operations rather than to think mathematically, and teachers controlled the mathematical thinking" (Pape et al., 2010, p. 23). In the following vignettes, we provide details of these two classes in contrast to these typical interactional patterns and highlight the teacher behaviors that we theorize have an impact on SRL development and mathematical understanding.

Mrs. Thompson's Sixth-Grade Class

Mrs. Thompson usually began to orient her students to a lesson by writing "Today's agenda" on the board, which informed students about the daily activities and set common class-level goals for the lesson. For example, the agenda for one observed class session consisted of the problem of the day (POD), which would be followed by the new topic, perimeter of rectangles. In this initial phase of the lesson, Mrs. Thompson's effort to set class-level goals modeled goal setting as an important SRL behavior during the forethought phase. For the POD, students were provided with a data set and asked questions related to measures of central tendency:

Alicia's homework points: 10, 7, 8, 10, 9, 6, 10, 9

a) Find the mean, median, and mode for the set of math homework points.
b) Which measure of central tendency would be the best representative of the homework points?
c) How does the mean change if two of the 10's become 0's? Explain why this happens.

PODs involved concepts and skills that were previously taught and supported students' self-reflection on their understanding of the previous lesson. While the first part of the task (i.e., finding the mean, median, and mode) required routine procedures, the second and third parts required higher levels of understanding and strategic behavior.

Students worked on the POD individually for approximately 10 minutes, which provided an opportunity for students to engage in forethought and performance, and then engaged in whole-class discussion, which offered the students an opportunity for reflection on their individual work. Mrs. Thompson started the discussion by asking the students several questions, such as "What do the numbers represent?" and "Why do we need to find the mean, median, and mode?" Students' answers were recorded on the board and examined for differences, which provided the problem solvers an opportunity to make observations about their initial solution processes, realize any mistakes, and make adjustments to their work and understanding, which are important subprocesses of the performance and self-reflection phases of SRL (Zimmerman, 2000, 2002). The class work on this POD is an example of a micro level cycle of SRL. Mrs. Thompson asked questions that pressed her students to monitor their actions (i.e., Why do we need to order the data when we compute the median?) and provided support while they worked on the task as depicted below:

Mrs. T: What's the purpose of the median, why [do] they need to be in order?

S: Finding the middle number.

Mrs. T: What would be [the] purpose to find the middle number in the data that is not in order? Would that tell you anything?

S: No.

Mrs. T: Because you don't want just the middle number, you want, um, what are you looking for? If [these were] your homework scores, what would the middle tell you?

S: Average.

> **Mrs. T:** It's an average. It's another type of average, or measure of central tendency. So, we don't want just the middle of any random numbers, we want where the data falls toward the middle, the central tendency, the average.

Mrs. Thompson often pressed students to explain and justify their mathematical processes. She facilitated whole-class understanding by rephrasing and synthesizing ideas. Students were able to compare different ideas and evaluate them based on the goals for task completion. Each of these teacher practices made the SRL subprocesses of setting goals, monitoring outcomes in terms of these goals, and adjusting behavior according to this judgment of goal attainment explicit behaviors in this classroom.

Mrs. Thompson introduced the main learning activity, to compare the perimeters of two rectangles with the same area without using a standard unit of measurement, by asking students to show the perimeter of their classroom and how they would define and compute the perimeter. The class focused on the difference between perimeter and area and how they would measure the perimeter of the classroom using standard and nonstandard units of measurement. This initial discussion illustrated task analysis; activated students' prior knowledge of the concepts, terms, and notations they would use to complete the task; and was important in terms of orienting the students by negotiating a common understanding of the task.

Mrs. Thompson then asked students to fold an eight by 11-inch sheet of paper so that the shorter sides were bisected, which she termed "hotdog style." Subsequently she asked the students to fold a paper so that the longer sides were bisected, which she called "hamburger style." Students were asked to individually compare the perimeter of each of the resulting figures (the "hotdog" and "hamburger" half-sheets) without using a standard unit of measurement. This time of individual exploration of perimeter began the performance phase of the lesson. Mrs. Thompson explicitly indicated her expectation that they would share their findings and ideas during whole-class discussion and reminded the students that they could use words, drawings, and/or numbers when explaining their reasoning. For the next five minutes, students worked on the task individually while Mrs. Thompson walked around the room and observed them. She did not provide feedback related to students' strategies but clarified the task requirements as necessary depending on the SRL level of individual students. For instance, she focused one student's attention on the difference between standard and nonstandard units of measurements to facilitate his comprehension of the task. On the other hand, when another student, Nathan, asked whether the problem was related to area or perimeter, she wanted him to decide by himself, which illustrates a different level of support. Mrs. Thompson's guidance during this performance phase kept students on task and scaffolded their individual task analysis, strategy selection, strategy implementation, and problem solution, a micro cycle of SRL.

Next, Mrs. Thompson engaged the students in whole-class discussion, pressing them to talk about their thoughts and strategies, which provided a context for students' thinking to become objects for discussion and reflection within the performance phase of SRL. Michael shared his strategy of putting one figure on top of the other and comparing the width and length of the figures. While he was talking about his strategy, Mrs. Thompson probed his explanation by asking questions such as "What are you matching? What part of the rectangle are we talking about? Show us where the perimeter is?" By asking these questions, Mrs. Thompson not only clarified Michael's idea and facilitated communication among students but also pressed him to reanalyze the task in front of his classmates. This form of support could be particularly helpful for students at the observation level of SRL development or for those who need explicit modeling of task analysis. Michael's initial idea was that the rectangle's perimeter was greater when folded hotdog style, which he justified by comparing the figures' lengths. While he was comparing the width of the figures, however, he realized that the width of the figure was greater when the paper was folded in the hamburger style.

Having recognized the flaw in his strategy, Michael adjusted his thinking, which helped students to understand the importance of self-reflection as they examined their strategies and made adjustments to their behaviors and thinking to solve the problem. Mrs. Thompson commended Michael for his explanation and guided the discussion by asking Nathan, who had agreed with Michael's initial idea, to share his thinking:

> **Mrs. T:** So, you agree that hotdog has longer . . . these longer sides, so it has more perimeter than shorter sides. But now what about when you get to the width of both of them. How can you prove that? This is when Michael changed his mind. He believed that hot dog has longer sides . . . but then what about the width of these compared to the width of that? Can you prove that they're not the same? This one has more perimeter?

Here, by rephrasing Michael's idea, Mrs. Thompson helped students to communicate and facilitated the evaluation of the strategy (i.e., comparing the shorter and longer sides separately). This provided all students an opportunity to reflect on their own strategies in a public venue and make adjustments to their thinking.

Nathan suggested using estimation but he struggled to clarify his point. Mrs. Thompson turned to the class and asked, "What do you think about his strategy? Does anybody notice anything about the widths of these? If I put one [figure on] top of the other [figure]—[what is the] width of the hot dog compared to the width of the hamburger?" She also reminded students about the definition of perimeter "What is perimeter—just these two sides?" Even though an individual student suggested the strategy, Mrs. Thompson wanted all students to think about and evaluate it by taking into account the task requirements (i.e., the perimeter of a figure consists of all sides of the figure). Again, Mrs. Thompson orchestrated a conversation about the strategy the students were using in terms of the task goals.

At the end of the lesson, the class reviewed the activity by discussing the definition of perimeter and how to find the perimeter of a figure. During this part of the lesson, the class again engaged in self-reflection by summarizing and reflecting upon their learning. Mrs. Thompson commended and praised students and emphasized the importance of adjusting their thinking and strategies when needed: "One of the things that happened is you guys changed your minds. And sometimes, you think something initially, or you had a chance to think it through or hear somebody else's strategy, and then you can change." Mrs. Thompson acknowledged their ideas and strategic behaviors: "Did you hear what he said? He used a pen as a measuring stick. That's a good nonstandard unit of measure. . . . Now, Mike had a great strategy of using his pen as a nonstandard unit of measure." By praising students' performances and recognizing their strategic behaviors, Mrs. Thompson also helped students to personalize their strategies.

Ms. Brenner's Algebra I Class

Ms. Brenner also started mathematics classes with group problem-solving activities that required students to recall and apply previously learned concepts and explore mathematical relationships. A problem situation was introduced, and then small-group and whole-group work alternated—students iteratively worked together on solving the problems in small groups and then presented their emerging understanding and findings for whole-class discussion. Ms. Brenner set the context by explicitly stating expectations for student work, which made the goal-setting subprocess explicit for the class during this forethought phase of the lesson. She asked her students to work together in small groups to create equations to represent a problem situation and then solve the equation:

> Create and solve an equation for the following problem: A toy company spends $1,500.00 each day on plant costs plus $8.00 per toy for labor and materials. The toys sell for $12.00 each. How many toys must the company sell in one day to equal its daily costs?

Students worked together in small groups to analyze the task and discuss possible solutions. Task analysis and reviewing one's repertoire of strategies to solve a problem are important behaviors of the self-regulated student. During whole-class discussion, students shared their solution processes, which facilitated their observation of the efficacy of their behaviors. They were guided to explore and question one another's ideas for the purpose of deepening their understanding. During one such discussion, Ms. Brenner asked a student, Zara, to present her initial equation. Zara was reluctant to share because she thought her work might be incorrect, at which point Ms. Brenner took the opportunity to talk about talking about mathematical thinking (Cobb, Wood, & Yackel, 1993).

> **Ms. B:** Zara does not have confidence in her answer, but at the same time it gives us a lot to talk about, right? So even though you have an awareness that it's not the answer that you would prefer, maybe if you put it up there it would just give us [something to talk about].

These comments contributed to setting the norms for examination of both correct and incorrect answers and highlighted the importance of examining progress made toward solving a problem, which made the self-reflection phase of SRL explicit. Since Zara was still reluctant to display what she thought might be incorrect, Ms. Brenner continued the discussion by "making up" a student error in order to direct attention toward the mathematical reasoning required for writing the equation for the problem. The following student analysis and explanation of the error illustrates the ongoing teacher support for student engagement with mathematical reasoning. She pressed the students to examine the equation and explain the error.

> **Ms. B:** Now, I'm just making up this equation so we have something to talk about. Okay? What do you guys think? Eight-t plus twelve-t equals fifteen hundred. Is that going to work? Celia.
>
> **Celia:** That's what I did in the beginning, but then I changed it.
>
> **Ms. B:** Why did you change it? [*Pause*] Why won't this work? [*Pause*] Alana.
>
> **Alana:** Because they're not [spending] eight dollars per toy because twelve dollars per toy equals what they spent so the total amount they spend—they're saying that it's fifteen hundred plus eight for the toy and then that would become twelve dollars per toy.

Celia volunteered that she had set up the equation in the same way as Zara but had realized that she made a mistake. Her comment highlighted that other students often have to work through initial inaccurate reasoning, which requires self-observation and making adjustments when necessary. Ms. Brenner then pressed for the reasoning behind Celia's decision to change her work. Celia was not able to provide her reasoning at that time, but another student, Alana, presented her thoughts on *why* the hypothetical equation would not work. This discussion afforded the class an opportunity to take up Alana's mathematical thinking as an object of discourse and made the self-reflection phase of SRL explicit for the students. Within the whole-class discussions, students were encouraged to make their thinking processes available for public examination and to make recommendations related to others' mathematical thinking and strategic behavior.

Following the warm-up problem, students engaged in a task that addressed the new topic for the day. The objective of this lesson was for students to describe the effects of changing the coefficients, a, b, and c, of a quadratic equation in the form $y = ax^2 + bx + c$ on the position and shape of its graph. Ms. Brenner used the Activity Center component of the CCT to project a picture, which had a coordinate grid overlay, of a man on a basketball court crouched in position to shoot a free throw (see Figure 2.3). Students were instructed to work together in small groups to determine an equation that resulted in a graph that matched the basketball's trajectory through the hoop and then submit the equation to be projected over the image on the screen at the front of the class.

Students worked in small groups, formulating plans for accomplishing the task and sharing and negotiating mathematical ideas. Several times, students went up to the projection screen to determine the coordinates for key points needed to form an arch from the ball in the shooter's hands to the basket. Student groups submitted their equation, examined the projected parabola defined by their equation to see if they achieved the desired result, reanalyzed the task, made conjectures about changing coefficients to produce different results, tested modified equations, and so forth. Ms. Brenner conversed with student groups to check on their progress and supported their performance by strategically questioning them to focus and guide their work.

Reflection on small-group work also took place during whole-class discussion. The teacher paused the activity to draw students' attention to individual graphs, which were projected on the screen; the linked equations were visible in a portion of the Activity Center screen to the right of the coordinate plane. In Figure 2.3, we see an image of Ms. Brenner guiding students in a discussion of the group-submitted parabolas. During this guided reflection, students were asked to make conjectures about changes to each group's equation by describing how the position and shape of the parabola would change as the equation's coefficients were modified. Ms.

Figure 2.3   Ms. Brenner taking up a student solution for discussion.

Brenner took up the students' work and subsequent mathematical comments during these discussions so that everyone could benefit from each other's experience and make sense of the mathematics together. These discussions modeled the subprocesses essential during the performance and self-reflection phases of SRL.

> **Ms. B:** Can we all talk for a second?...This equation down here [*pointing to a parabola that did not match the trajectory of the ball*], what could the user do to make this equation a little closer up so that it's shooting from here and landing in here? What Edgar?
>
> **Edgar:** Make b bigger.
>
> **Ms. B:** Okay, so Edgar's suggesting that we make the b bigger. So this equation, try making the b bigger....
>
> **Ms. B:** What happened here?
>
> **Dianna:** The parabola has to be narrower.
>
> **Ms. B:** So how can they make the parabola more narrow?
>
> **S:** By putting a large number.
>
> **Ms. B:** By putting a larger number. Now, what is special about these parabolas? Which direction do they go?
>
> **S:** [Inaudible]
>
> **Ms. B:** So that means that they're what?
>
> **S:** Negative.
>
> **Ms. B:** They're negative, so the *absolute value* of the a-value is going to be bigger, correct?

Ms. Brenner accepted suggestions for making changes to the equations that would result in changing the parabolas (e.g., Make b bigger) or asked additional questions to elicit more specific responses (e.g., How can they make it narrower?). Repetition of the students' comments was not evaluative but served to re-voice the students' suggestions. Ms. Brenner followed up with questions that drew attention to the negative coefficient of the quadratic term in order to clarify that the students' use of the terms "large" and "bigger" were in reference to absolute value. The students still had to process the meanings of the suggestions, which involved cycling back through the steps of forethought, performance, and reflection (i.e., a local cycle of SRL on the micro level within a phase of the lesson on the macro level; Figure 2.1). They went back to working in their small groups to discuss new ideas, modify the coefficients of their equations, and resubmit their equations to test their progress toward matching the parabolic path of the basketball. Again, this illustrates a micro cycle of SRL within the performance phase of the lesson on the macro level.

DISCUSSION

While not evident in the vignettes due to their focus on one class observation each, the development of SRL occurs in levels (Zimmerman, 2000, 2002) that require varying degrees of modeling and support (see Tables 2.1 and 2.2). The observation level requires more detailed and elaborate teacher modeling of subprocesses such as task analysis and goal setting during the forethought phase of a lesson. Teachers may think aloud as they model strategic behavior, task persistence, and self-observation during the performance phase of the lesson. Finally, they may examine the effectiveness of the strategies they used to accomplish their goal and specifically connect strategic behavior to the accomplishment of goals when they model reflection on their progress toward task completion and discuss how they may adapt strategic behavior given their appraisal of goal attainment.

This degree of explicit scaffolding support is withdrawn as the students progress from the observation to the emulation level of SRL development. As they become more capable of engaging with mathematical tasks, students begin to imitate the teachers' modeled skills, behaviors, and ways of thinking mathematically. During the emulation stage, students still require careful guidance, which may be provided by the teacher or another student who has mastered the skills. Again this scaffolding varies depending upon which phase of SRL the teacher is intending to facilitate.

At the self-control and self-regulation levels, which may develop only in later grades, the teacher might simply provide the task with limited introduction. Students perform the task analysis, search for strategies to accomplish the task, implement their strategies, and finally reflect on goal attainment. At the self-regulation level, students are also able to adapt previously learned strategies to varying conditions. The teacher slowly decreases the level of support and guidance as the students gain competence in completing tasks.

The teacher's role then, at the macro or lesson level, is to provide varied instructional practices that focus on the three phases of SRL (i.e., forethought, performance control, and self-reflection; Zimmerman, 2000, 2002) while varying and adjusting the intensity of instructional support as students advance through Zimmerman's developmental levels of SRL. In addition, they must be aware that developmental levels are not fixed—an individual student may have different needs (e.g., appearing to regress in developmental level) depending on the content of the lesson. Teachers may therefore need to provide differential support at the micro level for students who are not yet able to engage in mathematical tasks in a self-regulated way. They may provide additional modeling to guide students through iterative cycles of SRL, moving back through subprocesses during the performance phase of the lesson. It is also important to note that students may be at different levels of SRL competence with regard to different phases (Butler, 1995, 1998). That is, while a student may be competent in analyzing task requirements, he or she may be at the observation level with regard to task engagement. Therefore, teachers must strive to set classroom norms and structure lessons for students at differential levels of SRL development with regard to different phases/processes of SRL competence (e.g., task analysis, self-monitoring, self-evaluation).

FUTURE RESEARCH

Mrs. Thompson's and Ms. Brenner's classrooms were chosen for discussion of SRL because their interactional patterns differed from the typical classroom we observed in a national study (Pape et al., 2010). Mrs. Thompson and Ms. Brenner explicitly created classroom contexts that supported strategic approaches to thinking and learning about mathematics; thus, they potentially supported the development of SRL. Although their classroom interactions are used to discuss the development of SRL, there are notable differences between the two classrooms. Some of the differences might be attributed to the age differences between the students (in this case, about three years, on average). We believe, however, that there may be other important aspects of the classroom contexts that contributed to the differences. Future longitudinal research might examine the ways in which teachers adjust levels of support as their students progress toward self-regulation. Furthermore, cross-sectional research might support the comparison of students' experiences and needs at different grade and age levels with this type of explicit strategy instruction. Continued research in this area is needed to provide teachers with greater detail about the needs of students at different developmental levels.

Future research might also be designed to investigate outcomes of different interactional patterns in the classroom. We would like to know more about how subtle variations might create differences in opportunities to learn mathematics and affect the development of SRL. In particular, we would like to more deeply understand the impact of CCT and the variations in the ways teachers use CCT on the differences we have observed among CCMS classrooms. During the initial segments of many of the lessons, teachers used features of the CCT to review content and monitor student understanding. We hypothesize that these opportunities for formative assessment supported the development of SRL and mathematical understanding because they provided students and the teacher with immediate feedback regarding students' knowledge. Unfortunately, we have also observed many lessons in which the teachers did all of the mathematical thinking. We believe that teacher control of the mathematical thinking limits students' development of both mathematical understanding and SRL behavior. Consequently, questions remain about the different ways that teachers choose to encourage and take up students' mathematical thinking, with and without CCT, and the impact on subsequent classroom interactions. To foster greater mathematical thinking within CCT classrooms, we have proposed several characteristics of effective CCT use (Pape et al., 2012). We anticipate examining these components in follow-up studies.

Finally, we are pursuing research projects to examine teachers' needs for professional development to implement the instructional practices we have described here by incorporating CCT as a tool. Teachers need varying levels of support to implement instructional practices that turn responsibility for mathematical thinking over to students. Students need significant opportunities to think mathematically as well as to construct positive dispositions toward learning mathematics and thinking mathematically. We are currently working with a group of teachers to implement these instructional sequences and investigating the impact of this intervention on student outcomes. We are interested in continuing our examination of professional development that is designed to have enduring and positive impacts on classroom teaching and learning.

CONCLUSION

Our proposed intervention consists of instructional practices that, when incorporated within lessons, the macro level framed using Zimmerman's (2000, 2002) three phases of SRL (i.e., forethought, performance, and self-reflection), make SRL subprocesses explicit for students who may begin to take on these behaviors. Factors that contribute to the effectiveness of the intervention include the tasks that are chosen, the norms that are set for classroom interactions, and the public sharing of student work for the purpose of exploring and discussing mathematical thinking.

While we emphasize that CCT is not required for fostering SRL behaviors, we forward the position that CCT can be an important tool for implementing mathematical instruction as depicted in this chapter. Within the CCMS study, the use of CCT for the public display of student work provided a context for shared responsibility for mathematical thinking and accountability for continued performance. As noted above, in typical classrooms students were not often given responsibility for their mathematical performance during instruction. In many cases the teacher demonstrated mathematical procedures while the students were called on to do the arithmetic within the procedures. We believe that this pattern of interaction limits students' development of mathematical understanding as well as SRL behavior. While there is still a great deal we need to learn about how to support teachers in relinquishing mathematical authority and opening up spaces for the examination of student mathematical constructions, explanations, and argumentation, consistent and ongoing long-term professional development holds potential for supporting teachers' needs to work toward constructing classrooms that support SRL.

REFERENCES

Bell, C. V. (2008). *Cultural diversity and white teacher scaffolding of student self-regulated learning in algebra classes.* Unpublished doctoral dissertation, The Ohio State University, Columbus, OH. Retrieved from http://etd.ohiolink.edu/

Bell, C. V., & Pape, S. J. (2012). Scaffolding students' opportunities to learn through social interactions. *Mathematics Education Research Journal.* doi:10.1007/s13394-012-0048-1

Borkowski, J. G., Weyhing, R. S., & Carr, M. (1988). Effects of attributional retraining on strategy-based reading comprehension in learning-disabled students. *Journal of Educational Psychology, 80,* 46–53. doi:10.1037/0022-0663.80.1.46

Butler, D. L. (1995). Promoting strategic learning by postsecondary students with learning disabilities. *Journal of Learning Disabilities, 28,* 170–190. doi:10.1177/002221949502800306

Butler, D. L. (1998). In search of the architect of learning: A commentary on scaffolding as a metaphor for instructional interactions. *Journal of Learning Disabilities, 31*(4), 374–385. doi:10.1177/002221949803100407

Butler, D. L. (2003). Structuring instruction to promote self-regulated learning by adolescents and adults with learning disabilities. *Exceptionality, 11,* 39–60. doi:10.1207/S15327035EX1101_4

Butler, D. L., Beckingham, B., & Lauscher, H. J. N. (2005). Promoting strategic learning by eighth-grade students struggling in mathematics: A report of three case studies. *Learning Disabilities Research & Practice, 20,* 156–174. doi:10.1111/j.1540-5826.2005.00130.x

Cobb, P., Boufi, A., McClain, K., & Whitenack, J. (1997). Reflective discourse and collective reflection. *Journal for Research in Mathematics Education, 28,* 258–277. doi:10.2307/749781

Cobb, P., Wood, T., & Yackel, E. (1993). Discourse, mathematical thinking, and classroom practice. In E. A. Foreman, N. Minick & C. A. Stone (Eds.), *Contexts for learning: Sociocultural dynamics in children's development* (pp. 91–119). New York, NY: Oxford University Press.

De Corte, E., Verschaffel, L., & Eynde, P. O. (2000). Self-regulation: A characteristic and a goal of mathematics education. In M. Boekaerts, P. Pintrich, & M. Ziedner (Eds.), *Handbook of self-regulation* (pp. 687–726). Orlando, FL: Academic Press. doi:10.1016/B978-012109890-2/50050-0

Dweck, C. S. (2000). *Self-theories: Their role in motivation, personality, and development.* Philadelphia, PA: Taylor & Francis.

Gee, J. P. (2008). A sociocultural perspective on opportunity to learn. In P. A. Moss, D. C. Pullin, J. P. Gee, E. H. Haertel, & L. J. Young (Eds.), *Assessment, equity, and opportunity to learn* (pp. 76–108). New York, NY: Cambridge University Press.

Gresalfi, M. S. (2009). Taking up opportunities to learn: Constructing dispositions in mathematics classrooms. *The Journal of the Learning Sciences, 18,* 327–369. doi:10.1080/10508400903013470

Gresalfi, M. S., Martin, T., Hand, V., & Greeno, J. (2009). Constructing competence: An analysis of student participation in the activity systems of mathematics classrooms. *Educational Studies in Mathematics, 70,* 49–70. doi:10.1007/s10649-008-9141-5

Hufferd-Ackles, K., Fuson, K. C., & Sherin, M. G. (2004). Describing levels and components of a math-talk learning community. *Journal for Research in Mathematics Education, 35,* 81–116. doi:10.2307/30034933

Kelly, S. (2009). The Black-White gap in mathematics course taking. *Sociology of Education, 82,* 47–69. doi:10.1177/003804070908200103

Kilpatrick, J., Swafford, J., & Findell, B. (2001). *Adding it up: Helping children learn mathematics.* Washington, DC: National Academy Press.

McClain, K., & Cobb, P. (2001). An analysis of development of sociomathematical norms in one first-grade classroom. *Journal for Research in Mathematics Education, 32,* 236–266. doi:10.2307/749827

National Council of Teachers of Mathematics. (2000). *Principles and standards for school mathematics.* Reston, VA: Author.

National Research Council. (1989). *Everybody counts: A report to the nation on the future of mathematics education.* Washington, DC: National Academy Press.

Owens, D. T., Abrahamson, L., Pape, S. J., Irving, K., & Demana, F. (2005). *Classroom connectivity in promoting mathematics and science achievement.* Columbus, OH: The Ohio State University.

Pape, S. J. (2005). Intervention that supports future learning: Developing self-regulated learners. In S. Wagner (Ed.), *PRIME: Prompt intervention in mathematics education* (pp. 77–98). Columbus, OH: Ohio Resource Center for Mathematics, Science, and Reading and Ohio Department of Education.

Pape, S. J., Bell, C. V., & Yetkin, I. E. (2003). Developing mathematical thinking and self-regulated learning: A teaching experiment in a seventh-grade mathematics classroom. *Educational Studies in Mathematics, 53,* 179–202. doi:10.1023/A:1026062121857

Pape, S. J., Bell, C. V., Owens, S. K., Bostic, J. D., Irving, K. E., Owens, D. T., . . . Silver, D. (2010, May). *Examining verbal interactions within connected mathematics classrooms.* Paper presented at the Annual Meeting of the American Educational Research Association, Denver, CO.

Pape, S. J., Irving, K. E., Bell, C. V., Shirley, M. L., Owens, D. T., Owens, S., . . . Lee, S. C. (2012). Principles of effective pedagogy within the context of connected classroom technology: Implications for teacher knowledge. In R. N. Ronau, C. R. Rakes, & M. L. Niess (Eds.), *Educational technology, teacher knowledge, and classroom impact: A research handbook on frameworks and approaches* (pp. 176–199). Hershey, PA: IGI Global. doi:10.4018/978-1-60960-750-0

Pape, S. J., & Smith, C. (2002). Self-regulating mathematics skills. *Theory into Practice, 41,* 93–101. doi:10.1207/s15430421tip4102_5

Pape, S. J., & Wang, C. (2003). Middle school children's strategic behavior: Classification and relation to academic achievement and mathematical problem solving. *Instructional Science, 31,* 419–449. doi:10.1023/A:1025710707285

Pólya, G. (1957). *How to solve it.* Garden City, NY: Doubleday. (Original work published 1945)

Porter, A. C., & Polikoff, M. S. (2011). Measuring academic readiness for college. *Educational Policy, XX,* 1–24. doi:10.1177/0895904811400410

Randi, J., & Corno, L. (2000). Teacher innovations in self-regulated learning. In M. Boekaerts, P. Pintrich, & M. Ziedner (Eds.), *Handbook of self-regulation* (pp. 651–685). San Diego, CA: Academic Press. doi:10.1016/B978-012109890-2/50049-4

Schoenfeld, A. H. (1985). *Mathematical problem solving.* Orlando, FL: Academic Press.

Schoenfeld, A. (1987). What's all the fuss about metacognition? In A. Schoenfeld (Ed.), *Cognitive science and mathematics education* (pp. 189–215). Hillsdale, NJ: Lawrence Erlbaum.

Schoenfeld, A. H. (1992). Learning to think mathematically: Problem solving, metacognition, and sense making in mathematics. In D. A. Grouws (Ed.), *Handbook of research on mathematics teaching and learning* (pp. 334–370). New York, NY: Macmillan.

Schoenfeld, A. H. (2002). Making mathematics work for all children: Issues of standards, testing, and equity. *Educational Researcher, 31,* 13–25. doi:10.3102/0013189X031001013

Schunk, D. H. (2001). Social cognitive theory and self-regulated learning. In B. J. Zimmerman & D. H. Schunk (Eds.), *Self-regulated learning and academic achievement* (2nd ed., pp. 119–144). Mahwah, NJ: Lawrence Erlbaum. doi:10.1007/978-1-4612-3618-4_4

Schunk, D. H., & Zimmerman, B. J. (1997). Social origins of self-regulatory competence. *Educational Psychologist, 32,* 195–208. doi:10.1207/s15326985ep3204_1

Thompson, L. R., & Lewis, B. F. (2005). Shooting for the stars: A case study of the mathematics achievement and career attainment of an African American male high school student. *The High School Journal, 88*, 6–18. doi:10.1353/hsj.2005.0011

Tuckman, B. W., & Kennedy, G. (2009, April). *Teaching learning and motivation strategies to enhance the success of first-term college students*. Paper presented at the annual meeting of the American Educational Research Association, San Diego, CA.

Verschaffel, L., & De Corte, E. (1997). Teaching realistic mathematical modeling in the elementary school: A teaching experiment with fifth graders. *Journal for Research in Mathematics Education, 28*, 577–601. doi:10.2307/749692

Verschaffel, L., De Corte, E., Lasure, S., Van Vaerenbergh, G., Bogaerts, H., & Ratinckx, E. (1999). Learning to solve mathematical application problems: A design experiment with fifth graders. *Mathematical Thinking and Learning, 1*, 195–229. doi:10.1207/s15327833mtl0103_2

Yackel, E., & Cobb, P. (1996). Sociomathematical norms, argumentation, and autonomy in mathematics. *Journal for Research in Mathematics Education, 27*, 458–477. doi:10.2307/749877

Yetkin, I. E. (2006). *The role of classroom context in student self-regulated learning: An exploratory case study in a sixth-grade mathematics classroom*. Unpublished doctoral dissertation, The Ohio State University, Columbus, OH. Retrieved from http://etd.ohiolink.edu/

Yetkin-Ozdemir, I. E., & Pape, S. J. (2011a). *The role of interactions between student and classroom context in developing adaptive self-efficacy in one sixth-grade mathematics classroom*. Manuscript submitted for publication.

Yetkin-Ozdemir, I. E., & Pape, S. J. (2011b). *The role of interactions between student and context in creating opportunities for developing strategic competence in a mathematics classroom*. Manuscript submitted for publication.

Yetkin-Ozdemir, I. E., & Pape, S. J. (2012). Supporting students' strategic competence: A case of a sixth-grade mathematics classroom. *Mathematics Education Research Journal, 24*(2), 153–168. doi:10.1007/s13394-012-0033-8

Zimmerman, B. J. (1989). A social cognitive view of self-regulated academic learning. *Journal of Educational Psychology, 81*, 329–339. doi:10.1037/0022-0663.81.3.329

Zimmerman, B. J. (1990). Self-regulating academic learning and achievement: The emergence of a social cognitive perspective. *Educational Psychology Review, 2*, 173–196. doi:10.1007/BF01322178

Zimmerman, B. J. (2000). Attaining self-regulation: A social cognitive perspective. In M. Boekaerts, P. Pintrich, & M. Ziedner (Eds.), *Handbook of self-regulation* (pp. 13–39). Orlando, FL: Academic Press.

Zimmerman, B. J. (2002). Achieving self-regulation: The trial and triumph of adolescence. In F. Pajares & T. Urdan (Eds.), *Academic motivation of adolescents* (Vol. 2, pp. 1–27). Greenwich, CT: Information Age.

Zimmerman, B. J. (2008). Investigating self-regulation and motivation: Historical background, methodological developments, and future prospects. *American Educational Research Journal, 45*, 166–183. doi:10.3102/0002831207312909

Zimmerman, B. J., & Martinez-Pons, M. (1986). Development of a structured interview for assessing student use of self-regulated learning strategies. *American Educational Research Journal, 23*, 614–628. doi:10.3102/00028312023004614

CHAPTER 3

SELF-REGULATED STRATEGIES DEVELOPMENT IN WRITING

Development, Implementation, and Scaling Up

Karen R. Harris, Steve Graham, and Tanya Santangelo

Since the 1980s, Harris, Graham, and their colleagues have conducted research on the writing of students in elementary through secondary grades. Much of this research has focused on four critical constructs and their importance in the development of writing ability: strategies, knowledge, will, and skills (Graham & Harris, 2012; Harris & Graham, 1999). We have examined these constructs and their importance in typical writing development and their role among struggling writers and those with writing disabilities. We have also focused our attention on the role of basic writing skills, such as handwriting, spelling, and sentence construction, in students' development as writers. Recently, we have been increasingly pulled into the policy arena as we have joined those making the case for why writing should be an integral part of school and educational reform. Throughout the past 30 years, a central focus has been development and refinement of an interven-

Applications of Self-Regulated Learning across Diverse Disciplines, pages 59–87
Copyright © 2013 by Information Age Publishing
All rights of reproduction in any form reserved.   **59**

tion for developing writing strategies, knowledge, will, and skills among school-age students.

In this chapter, we focus on the development of, and research base for, that intervention: Self-Regulated Strategy Development (SRSD). We begin by briefly looking at the importance of being able to compose effectively. Next, we turn to the relationship between the development of SRSD and the work of Barry Zimmerman; his scholarship has been, and continues to be, a critical influence on our work with SRSD. The evidence base for SRSD is then briefly summarized. We then present the implementation of SRSD in detail, describing actual SRSD instruction as it occurred in one teacher's classroom. Finally, we conclude this chapter with a discussion of future research and practice needs in terms of SRSD, with emphasis on the need for work in scaling up and sustaining SRSD instruction in schools.

IMPORTANCE OF WRITING AND IMPROVING WRITING INSTRUCTION

Students who struggle significantly with writing are at a terrible disadvantage, as they may not be able to draw on its power to support learning and development. Writing becomes an essential tool for both learning and showing what you know during the elementary school years and is one of the primary cornerstones on which content learning is built (Graham & Harris, 2011; Swedlow, 1999). Further, writing provides a powerful mechanism for communication, self-expression, and self-reflection and can be beneficial to students' psychological health and well-being (Graham, Harris, & MacArthur, 2004; Harris & Graham, in press; Smyth, 1998). Significant challenges with writing put students at risk for school failure and may impact their futures, as high-level literacy skills are required for most jobs that pay a living wage today, with this likely to become even more pronounced in the future (Berman, 2001; Kirsch, Braun, Yamamoto, & Sum, 2007).

We know, however, that despite its importance, writing is one of the most difficult academic areas for students to master. The majority of 4th, 8th, and 12th grade students failed to demonstrate mastery of the writing abilities needed at their grades levels in 1998, 2002, and 2007 (the latest date for which writing data is available) on the National Assessment of Educational Progress (NAEP). In 2007, only 6% of eighth-grade and 5% of twelfth-grade students scored at or above the proficient level in writing (Salahu-Din, Persky, & Miller, 2008). The majority of American students have significant difficulties with narrative, expository, and persuasive writing (Applebee, Langer, Mullis, Latham, & Gentile, 1994; Applebee, Langer, Jenkins, Mullis, & Foertsch, 1990). Not surprisingly, although most children begin school with a positive attitude toward composing, our students also demonstrate a deteriorating attitude toward writing (Applebee, Langer, & Mullis, 1986). SRSD was initially developed in response to the writing challenges faced by students with learning disabilities, but since 1985 it has been found to be an effective approach with both typical writers and those who struggle with writing (cf. Harris, 1982, 1986; Harris & Graham, 1985, 2009).

FOUNDATIONS FOR SRSD AND THE WORK OF BARRY ZIMMERMAN

As Harris and Graham (2009) explained, they began development of the SRSD approach to strategies instruction with several critical underlying premises. They argued that students who face significant and often debilitating academic difficulties would benefit from an integrated approach to instruction that deliberately and directly addressed their affective, behavioral, and cognitive characteristics, strengths, and needs. Further, they believed that many students often require more extensive, structured, and explicit instruction to develop skills, strategies (including academic, social, and self-regulation strategies), and understandings that their peers form more easily, with the level of explicit instruction needed dependent upon student needs. They argued earlier, and continue to believe, that no single theory of teaching or learning at this point in time addresses all of the challenges faced by learners, their teachers, and their schools. An additional premise, therefore, was the need to integrate multiple lines of research from multiple theoretical perspectives in order to develop powerful interventions for students who face significant academic challenges (Harris, 1982; Harris & Alexander, 1998: Harris & Graham, 1985).

A thoughtful, effective integration of diverse, validated approaches to learning, regardless of whether or not the theories and disciplines from which they originated are viewed by some as discordant (such as affective, behavioral, and cognitive approaches to teaching and learning), has been key to the development of SRSD. One critical area of research that has deeply influenced SRSD is the development and enhancement of self-regulation, an area to which Barry Zimmerman (cf. Zimmerman, 1997) has made major contributions.

Detailed descriptions of the evolution of SRSD over the past decades have been offered elsewhere (cf. Graham & Harris, 1989, 2009; Harris, 1982; Harris & Graham, 1992, 1999, 2009). Here, we note the initial foundations for SRSD and then explain how Zimmerman's work came to influence ours. Four theoretical and empirical sources provided the initial foundation for this model in the early 1980s (Harris & Graham, 2009):

1. Meichenbaum's (1977) cognitive-behavioral intervention model (particularly his emphasis on Socratic dialogue as well as stages of

intervention that involve interactive learning, modeling, scaffolding, and self-regulation components);

2. the work of Soviet theorists and researchers (including Vygotsky, Luria, and Sokolov) on the social origins of self-control and the development of the mind (this work contributed further to the self-regulation and modeling components of the SRSD model);

3. the work of Brown, Campione, and their colleagues on development of self-control, metacognition, and strategies instruction (cf. Brown, Campione, & Day, 1981; one critical aspect emphasized by Brown and her colleagues was "informed instruction," meaning that students should clearly understand what they are doing and why they are doing it, as well as the emphasis on metacognition); and

4. the work of Deshler, Schumaker, and their colleagues on the validation of acquisition steps for strategies among adolescents with learning disabilities (cf. Schumaker, Deshler, Alley, Warner, & Denton, 1982; their steps were also influenced by the work of Meichenbaum).

Early development of SRSD was also strongly influenced by important research on self-regulation conducted by behavioral researchers, who identified four efficacious procedures: self-instruction, self-determined criteria, self-assessment, and self-reinforcement (Harris, 1982; O'Leary & Dubey, 1979; Rosenbaum & Drabman, 1979). Each of these self-regulation procedures were integrated into our initial strategies instruction model; over time, how these self-regulation abilities are addressed in SRSD was refined due to several influences, including the work of Zimmerman and colleagues.

Thus, while Harris and her colleagues began looking at self-regulation through the work of behavioral researchers, the work of Zimmerman and his colleagues on self-regulation quickly became a critical influence on SRSD's development and subsequent research. One important example was the advance of a model of the development of self-regulatory abilities by Zimmerman and his colleagues, a model that emphasized four levels of development: observation, imitation, self-control, and self-regulation (cf. Schunk & Zimmerman, 1997). Zimmerman (1997, 1989) theorized that students are capable of self-regulating components of their learning behaviors, environment, and internal cognitive and affective processes. Working from a social cognitive perspective, Schunk and Zimmerman (1994) defined self-regulation as the "process whereby students activate and sustain cognitions, behaviors and affect, which are systematically oriented toward attainment of their goals" (p. 309). SRSD instruction, as will be seen in the description to come, involves the activation, management, and maintenance of cognitions, behaviors, and affect in support of the writer's goals.

Further, in 1997, Zimmerman and Reisemberg reviewed extant models of writing. They argued that although these models included the task environment and self-regulatory strategies, they focused on the role of cognitive processes in students' writing *competence*, as opposed to writer *performance* and its self-regulated development. They further argued that "explanations focusing on writing performance and its self-regulated development need to include the role of social, motivational, and behavioral processes as well as cognitive ones" (Zimmerman & Reisemberg, 1997, p. 75). Working from social-cognitive theory and self-regulation theory (Zimmerman, 1989), they proposed a model of writing composed of three fundamental forms of self-regulation: environmental, behavioral, and covert or personal. The authors argued that these triadic forms of self-regulation interact reciprocally via a cyclic feedback loop that allows writers to self-monitor and self-react to feedback about the effectiveness of specific self-regulatory techniques or processes.

From the 1980s to the present day, the work of Barry Zimmerman and his colleagues has influenced the form and components of SRSD instruction. Especially critical, their work further buttressed Harris and Graham's initial premise that effective intervention must focus on affect, behavior, and cognition, and helped in fleshing out the development of self-regulation abilities in the SRSD approach to writing instruction. While Schunk and Zimmerman (1997) reported on a model of the development of self-regulation, and SRSD is an instructional model, the two models both make the development of self-regulation a key objective to improving academic performance (cf. Zito, Adkins, Gavins, Harris, & Graham, 2007).

The work of Zimmerman and his colleagues on development of self-regulation has been critical to both the initial development and ongoing refinement of the stages of instruction in the SRSD approach. Finally, a critical and explicit goal in SRSD is the development of self-efficacy and attributions for effort and strategy use; the work of Zimmerman and his colleagues on self-efficacy has been a major foundation for this aspect of SRSD. The significant contributions to SRSD today made by Zimmerman and his colleagues can be seen throughout the following description of SRSD instruction.

SRSD INSTRUCTION

In this section, we provide an overview of the SRSD instructional model and process. First, we summarize several fundamental characteristics that facilitate success with SRSD. Next, we outline the six stages in the SRSD instructional framework. Lastly, we offer a case example that illustrates how SRSD was used to teach fourth grade students a persuasive writing strategy.

Space limitations preclude us from providing a comprehensive description of the SRSD instructional approach; however, interested readers can find detailed information about the instructional stages and process, a wide range of strategies, lesson plans, recommendations for evaluation, and other SRSD-related materials in existing, practitioner-oriented publications, such as Graham and Harris (2005), Harris and Graham (1996), and Harris, Graham, Mason, and Friedlander (2008), and on the website http://kc.vanderbilt.edu/projectwrite. Another excellent web-based resource for learning about strategies instruction, in general, and SRSD, in particular, is the IRIS Center: two free, interactive tutorials can be found at http://iris.peabody.vanderbilt.edu/pow/chalcycle.htm and http://iris.peabody.vanderbilt.edu/srs/chalcycle.htm. Finally, the video titled, *Teaching Students with Learning Disabilities: Using Learning Strategies* (Association for Supervision and Curriculum Development, 2002) shows SRSD being implemented in an elementary and a middle school classroom.

Characteristics of SRSD Instruction

Extensive research and practice that now spans several decades underscores that certain characteristics are essential to optimizing positive outcomes with SRSD; thus, they might be considered "non-negotiable" for SRSD implementation. Although some characteristics are common to other strategy instruction models, others are unique to SRSD and likely contribute to its comparative efficacy (a detailed discussion can be found in Harris, Graham, Brindle, & Sandmel, 2009).

First, with SRSD, students are provided with systematic and explicit instruction targeting the multiple domains that contribute to the development of writing competence: (a) writing strategies for specific genres (e.g., personal narrative, persuasive essay, expository report); (b) universal writing strategies (e.g., using powerful vocabulary, crafting engaging opening and closing sections); (c) self-regulation procedures that help manage the writing process and use of strategies (i.e., goal setting, self-monitoring, self-instructions, and self-reinforcement); and (d) relevant declarative, conditional, and procedural knowledge (that is, knowing what to do; how to do it; and when, where, and why to do it, respectively). The intensive and direct focus on developing writing processes and knowledge is a cornerstone of SRSD and has been shown to be particularly important for students who experience difficulty learning to write, including those with disabilities (e.g., Vaughn, Gersten, & Chard, 2000). SRSD further advocates the establishment of a predictable routine for writing, wherein students plan, draft, revise, edit, and publish their written products. Such consistency not only ensures that students have ample opportunities to apply what they learn, but also reinforces the notion that writing is a highly valued and meaningful activity.

Second, many developing writers—and especially those who experience difficulty learning to write—have needs that are not only cognitive, but also affective and behavioral in nature; each of these domains is, therefore, addressed with SRSD. For example, as part of SRSD, teachers deliberately and repeatedly help students develop self-regulation abilities, motivation, positive attitudes towards writing, and belief in themselves as capable writers. Numerous strategies are used to accomplish these goals. For instance, learning is constructed as an engaging, interactive, and collaborative process among teachers and students. This means teachers initially provide the necessary level of scaffolding and support to ensure that students learn the targeted knowledge and strategies, but then gradually and purposefully transfer responsibility for applying what is learned back to the students. To help students overcome negative perceptions and attitudes towards writing, SRSD is embedded in an affirming and supportive classroom environment where writing is genuinely valued and prioritized. Examples of how teachers achieve this goal include: projecting "contagious enthusiasm" during SRSD instruction; designing interesting, authentic, and appropriately-challenging writing projects; establishing an exciting and inspiring mood during writing time; consistently reinforcing the direct connection between students' effort and their trajectory of writing development; providing frequent constructive feedback that inspires students to improve their writing process and products; and creating multiple opportunities for positive peer interactions and support (for additional information about establishing the context for writing, see Santangelo & Olinghouse, 2009).

Third, SRSD instruction is individualized to optimize each student's writing development. More specifically, teachers use their knowledge of students' strengths and needs to differentiate both what and how they teach (see, for example, Sandmel et al., 2009). For example, a teacher might modify a strategy to make it more complex for some students, and simplified for others. Instruction is further individualized by having students establish personalized goals. The nature and frequency of support and feedback provided to students is also adjusted in response to their individual needs; in general, as students' academic and behavioral difficulties become more significant, SRSD instruction becomes more comprehensive, explicit, and scaffolded. Importantly, although SRSD is individualized, this does not necessitate the exclusive use of a one-to-one instructional format. As illustrated in the case study offered later in the chapter, when SRSD is used with a full class, there are times when it is both appropriate and beneficial for students to work together as a large group. At other times, teachers employ flexible grouping and have students work in small groups, pairs, or independently.

Fourth, students progress through SRSD instruction based on their individual levels of performance and rates of mastery. In other words, there is not a pre-established, standardized time-table for moving through the SRSD instructional stages; rather, each student advances from one stage to the next only after demonstrating he/she has met the criteria for doing so. Students are also provided with opportunities to re-visit an earlier stage, as needed. With this criterion-based approach, SRSD instruction ends for each student when he or she can independently apply and manage the targeted strategy and self-regulation procedures.

Because the ultimate goal of SRSD is for students to incorporate writing strategies and self-regulation procedures into their regular composing routine, a fifth characteristic is the infusion of multiple procedures that promote long-term maintenance (the desire and ability to continue using strategies after instruction ends) and generalization (appropriately and effectively applying strategies to other writing tasks and settings) throughout the stages of instruction. Examples of how teachers facilitate maintenance and generalization include: helping students understand the purpose and benefits of using a strategy; providing booster sessions to review, discuss, and support strategy use, as needed; facilitating students' critical consideration of when and how they should use a newly-learned strategy and then evaluating these experiences; exploring how to adapt a strategy for different writing tasks and settings; creating a variety of peer support opportunities that target generalization and maintenance; and bolstering strategy use through collaboration with other school professionals (e.g., other teachers and specialists), as well as family members.

Finally, SRSD is an ongoing and iterative process whereby students continually enhance their use of strategies and self-regulation procedures. Teachers lay the foundation for this developmental growth by helping students understand and appreciate the meaning and benefits of a particular strategy, along with its inherent limitations or weaknesses. Then, as students' writing improves, they are provided with opportunities to refine and expand previously learned strategies, as well as learn new strategies that are aligned with evolving writing goals and tasks.

The SRSD Instructional Process

The framework for SRSD instruction consists of six instructional stages:

1. *Develop background knowledge*—students are taught the knowledge and skills needed to learn and use the writing strategy and self-regulation procedures;

2. *Discuss it*—students are familiarized with the purpose, benefits, and steps in the strategy; self-regulation procedures such as self-instructions and self-monitoring are often introduced;

3. *Model it*—the teacher models how to use the strategy and self-regulation procedures, providing a running "think aloud" commentary to highlight internal thoughts and processes that support the writing process; students establish their personal goals and self-statements;

4. *Memorize it*—students memorize the strategy steps, mnemonic (if applicable), and their personal self-statements;

5. *Support it*—students practice using the writing strategy and accompanying self-regulation procedures with appropriate support that is faded out over time;

6. *Independent performance*—students use the writing strategy independently; self-regulation procedures are faded or modified, as appropriate; procedures to promote generalization and maintenance (e.g., peer partners, booster sessions) continue.

Whereas some instructional approaches and curricula are intended to be implemented in a regimented, uniform, and linear fashion, the six stages of SRSD represent a flexible set of guidelines that are intended to be thoughtfully re-sequenced, combined, modified, and revisited in response to students' and teachers' needs. The stages are also recursive, meaning that if a student or group of students did not quite master the targeted skills in a particular stage, they can be carried over into subsequent stages or, if appropriate, a stage can be repeated. Research has shown that outcomes associated with SRSD are dependent on implementing the essential aspects of each stage with integrity; there are, however, occasional instances when a stage—or part of a stage—is not necessary. For example, if a student already has ample background knowledge, the teacher might have him or her skip the second stage of instruction (develop background knowledge), or to participate in a different way—such as in the role of "co-teacher."

SRSD lessons typically last 20–45 minutes and occur three to five days a week, depending on the targeted student population and time available for instruction. The total time required for students to learn and independently apply a writing strategy and accompanying self-regulation procedures will, of course, vary; however, it often takes less time than teachers initially anticipate. With elementary-aged students, for instance, eight to 12 lessons conducted over a period of three to five weeks is often sufficient to reach independent performance (additional details by grade and genre can be found in Graham & Harris, 2003).

An Example of SRSD in Latrisha's Fourth Grade Classroom

In this section, we present a case study to illustrate one of the myriad implementation possibilities with SRSD. Specifically, we describe how Latrisha, a general education teacher, used SRSD to teach a persuasive writing strategy to her fourth grade students. Throughout the narrative, we offer examples of how to address individual students' needs by highlighting the experience of Bria—one of several students in Latrisha's classroom who has a learning disability and experiences significant difficulties with writing.

Planning

In preparation for an upcoming unit, Latrisha had each of her students write an opinion essay in response to the prompt, *Should children have to go outside for recess?*. This pre-assessment revealed that students were having difficulty expressing their opinions in thoughtful and convincing ways. Bria, for example, produced the following text (corrected for spelling and punctuation):

> No because kids need to be inside in storms and icky wet weather.
> Also to stay warm and cozy.
> Yes because it might be really hot.
> Also it might not be too cold.

In fact, only two students' compositions included all the basic genre elements (i.e., an introduction, reasons with supporting details, a conclusion)—the rest were incomplete, like Bria's. Latrisha was also aware that several students had negative attitudes towards writing and little confidence in their ability to compose, as instanced by Bria's teary proclamation, "I hate writing! I'm no good at it and I never want to do it again!"

Latrisha decided to teach a persuasive writing strategy to her entire class because each student's pre-assessment evidenced the need for improvement. She considered several validated strategies as options and ultimately selected one that was developmentally appropriate and flexible enough to meet her students' individual needs.

Stages 1 & 2: Discuss it and Develop Background Knowledge

Latrisha began SRSD instruction with a class meeting that allowed students to share what they already knew about persuasive writing (e.g., "The newspaper has a section for opinion letters." "It's kind of like a commercial to sell your idea.") and explore several foundational questions, including: What are the differences between facts and opinions?; What are the "key ingredients" in a good opinion paper?; and Why is it important to express your opinion in writing?. Throughout this discussion, a student volunteer recorded important ideas on chart paper so they could be displayed as a resource for the remainder of the year. Next, Latrisha explained they were going to "hit the Writer's Workshop pause button" for the next few days and use that block of time to learn a strategy that would help them write opinion essays that were more complete and "super-persuasive." Given that this was the class's first experience with strategy instruction, before Latrisha continued any further, she posed the question, "What is a strategy?" "It's something that helps you reach a goal."; "It's something that leads you through a task."; and "It's kind of like a trick for figuring out how to do something." are examples of responses that were generated and discussed. At this point in the lesson, each student received a TREE strategy handout (shown in Figure 3.1) and Latrisha familiarized them with "the basics," including the purpose and goals for learning the strategy, how the strategy works, the rationale for each strategy step, when and where the strategy should be used, and how they would learn the strategy. The lesson concluded with each student making a personal commitment to put forth his/her best effort to master the strategy.

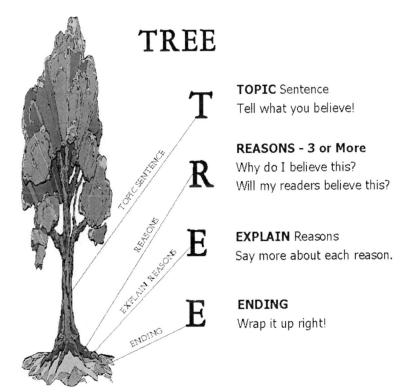

TREE

T

TOPIC Sentence
Tell what you believe!

R

REASONS - 3 or More
Why do I believe this?
Will my readers believe this?

E

EXPLAIN Reasons
Say more about each reason.

E

ENDING
Wrap it up right!

Figure 3.1   TREE strategy.

In the next lesson, students were given the opportunity to "dissect" a model opinion paper and determine whether it contained all eight parts of the TREE strategy. Knowing students would require different levels of support to successfully complete this activity, Latrisha had some work with peer partners and others—including Bria—work with her in a small group. After the class reconvened and discussed their analysis of the model text, Latrisha helped them "become detectives and sleuth out other great writing ideas," examples of which included the use of transition words, an introduction that "grabs the reader's attention," and "million dollar words" (words that help you reach the reader and say exactly what you mean; i.e., effective vocabulary). Finally, in small groups, students created a series of posters that described and illustrated how they could incorporate these characteristics of good writing into their own essays. These resources remained on display for the remainder of the school year and, as students identified new ideas, additional posters were created and added to what the class called the "Try this when you write!" gallery.

Latrisha began the third lesson with an introduction to the concept of self-monitoring and a demonstration of how students would use "rocket graphs" (shown in Figure 3.2) to track the completeness of their opinion essays before, during, and after strategy instruction. Working independently, students next identified how many parts of the TREE strategy they included in their pre-assessment essays and colored their first rocket, accordingly. During this initial self-monitoring activity, students received individualized support. For example, after observing that Bria was having difficulty analyz-

_____ Rockets

Figure 3.2 Rocket graphs.

ing her text in a systematic way, Latrisha scaffolded the process for her with verbal prompts (e.g., "First, let's see if you have a topic sentence—remember, that's a sentence that tells us what your opinion is.") and a graphic organizer. Additionally, even though Latrisha had emphasized students should not be disappointed if their pre-assessment essay didn't contain all (or even any!) of the parts in the TREE strategy when she introduced the self-monitoring activity, Latrisha was cognizant that Bria might still interpret her data negatively. Consequently, when Bria finished graphing and dispiritedly remarked, "My rocket is mostly empty," Latrisha had already sat down next to her and, through conversation, helped her realize, "If my essay already had all the parts, it would be silly to learn the strategy!"

Stage 3: Model It

During the next two lessons, Latrisha modeled how to write an opinion essay with the TREE strategy, following the same multi-step process students would be using: generate ideas and record them on a graphic organizer that corresponds with the eight parts in TREE; use those planning notes to write a first draft, revise and edit the text; and record final performance on the rocket graph. While modeling, she offered a running "think aloud" commentary to help students understand the internal thoughts, dialogue, and actions good writers use when they compose; in other words, she made the invisible, visible. For example, she used self-statements to help focus her attention ("What is the first thing I need to do?"), stay on task ("Don't think about other stuff—stay focused!"), monitor performance ("Will this introduction catch my reader's attention?"), cope with frustration ("I can do this. Take a deep breath and try again."), and reinforce effort ("Using the thesaurus paid off—those are some awesome words!"). As part of the model, Latrisha also covertly constructed several challenges she anticipated her students were likely to encounter when writing (e.g., writer's block, losing interest in the task, accidentally skipping a step in the strategy, not being able replace "boring words" with "super-duper" vocabulary) because this allowed her to show how each could be overcome. Once the model paper was finished, students reflected on the experience and decided the strategy should be modeled once more, before they tried to use it themselves. When Latrisha modeled the strategy a second time, she structured it such that students actively participated in the process.

At this point, the class focused on how self-statements can guide and enhance writing. They discussed different types of self-statements, considered the impact of positive versus negative messages, and also spent time unpacking the examples Latrisha integrated in the two models. Recognizing that students might have difficulty grasping this new and relatively abstract concept, Latrisha skeptically posed the question, "Do real people actually use self-statements?" and, after giving students a chance to discuss their responses, shared specific examples of her own self-statements, as well as those that reflect the writing process used by several of the students' favorite authors. "Did you know J. K. Rowling—the author of the Harry Potter series—makes her characters come alive by imagining exactly what each scene looks like?" Latrisha asked (e.g., Shapiro, 2000). "Therefore, she literally closes her eyes and asks herself questions such as: What would Harry be doing here? and What would Hermione be wearing?" With that foundation established, students next developed and recorded the self-statements they planned to use when writing.

Stage 4: Memorize It

To introduce the next lesson, Latrisha asked the class, "Why is it important to memorize the steps in TREE and your self-statements?", and used students' responses (e.g., "Because we won't always have the TREE paper, but still might want to use the strategy;" "Because if we don't have to keep looking up what to do and say to ourselves, we can focus more on our ideas.") to establish the purpose for this stage of instruction. Although most of the class memorized the information easily and quickly by playing games and quizzing each other, a few students (including Bria) needed additional time to practice—which Latrisha provided over the next several days.

Stage 5: Support It

At this point in the instructional process, Writer's Workshop resumed and students began using the TREE strategy and accompanying self-regulation procedures (e.g., goal setting, self-instructions, self-monitoring) to write opinion essays. Those who were ready to work without a high level of teacher support were given the option of writing their first paper independently or with a peer, assisted by Latrisha as needed. Bria and several other students who struggled with writing worked together as a "writing team" and composed their first essay collaboratively with Latrisha. This enabled Latrisha to closely monitor students' understanding and use of the strategy and to provide immediate feedback and guidance. As students continued to practice using the strategy, Latrisha adjusted the nature and intensity of support she provided in response to their individual needs. Bria, for instance, needed to see the second and third steps of the strategy modeled again and also required reminders and reinforcement to use her self-statements. As students' proficiency and confidence increased, assistance from Latrisha and other supports (e.g., self-statement and strategy reminder cards) were reduced and eventually eliminated. Latrisha also encouraged students who were still vocalizing their self-statements to say them "in their mind, instead of out loud."

Prior to SRSD instruction, as part of the established Writer's Workshop routine in the classroom, students shared their draft compositions with a peer partner so they could receive feedback about the strengths of the paper, as well as suggestions for improvement. At the beginning of Stage 5, the class decided to structure their peer response process to better align with the opinion essays they would be writing to practice TREE. This resulted in the creation of the following Guide for Peer Reviewers:

Step 1. Listen and read along as the author reads the essay.
Step 2. Tell the author what you liked best about the essay and
        why you liked it. (Remember you can pick more than one thing!)
Step 3. Tell the author what you found most persuasive and why.
Step 4. On your own, read the essay again and make notes: (a)
        Are all eight parts of TREE included?; (b) Is everything clear and
        logical?; (c) What could the author do to make the essay better?
Step 5. Share your suggestions with the author.

This five-step process was used each time a student drafted an opinion essay with TREE. In general, Latrisha allowed students to select their own peer response partners. However, to optimize the experience for students who struggled with writing, Latrisha strategically matched them with a more advanced peer until they reached Stage 6. For example, the first time Bria used the TREE strategy by herself, she produced the following rough draft (corrected for spelling and punctuation) in response to the prompt, *Should kids be paid to go to school?*:

> Listen up! Kids should get paid for going to school. My first reason is that they'll do their work better because if kids don't get paid, they won't do their work. Another reason is that kids work hard to learn. If kids really work hard to learn, they've earned cash. My last reason is that if kids are paid to go to school they can use the money to buy things that will help them learn better. They can buy pencils, paper, crayons, books, calculators and even more. This will be great for teachers too because they won't have to buy kids supplies like they do now. Now you know why kids need to be paid to go to school!

After listening to Bria read her essay (Step 1), her peer partner, Solomon, said, "I really liked the introduction because it caught me by surprise and made me pay attention to what came next. I also thought you did a good job using transition words because it helped me pick out each reason." (Step 2). He next told Bria, "To me, reason three is the most persuasive because it is something adults might actually believe and also because you gave specific ideas, so I knew exactly what kids could buy to help them learn more." (Step 3). After reading Bria's draft, Solomon wrote down the following notes (Step 4) and discussed them with Bria (Step 5):

A. I think so, but with reason one and two it's a little hard to pick out the reasons and the explanations.

B. I'm not sure what reason two means.

C. Say more about reason one and two. Change the ending so it includes the topic and reminds the reader why they should agree with your opinion.

With this feedback, Bria then made meaningful revisions to her essay.

Stage 6: Independent performance. Most students were able to use the TREE strategy and self-regulation procedures without assistance after writing three opinion essays—four in the case of Bria and a few other students. Henceforth, students composed independently, continuing to share their drafts with a peer partner and also receiving positive and constructive feedback from Latrisha. Once every student reached Stage 6, the class reflected on their experience learning the strategy, explored how the strategy and self-regulation procedures might be improved, and created a list of other opportunities to use the strategy, including the ways it could be adapted "to fit perfectly" in each instance. They also discussed how the self-regulation procedures would be beneficial in other contexts, generating examples such as "I can use a rocket graph to monitor if I practice piano for 30 minutes every day" and "I can use self-statements to help me get through my math homework—like, I might say to myself, 'This is really tough, but you can do it!'" Latrisha also had an individual conference with each student to explore and decide on next steps, such as new writing goals and whether it would be beneficial to continue using the rocket graph. To support maintenance over time, Latrisha periodically held "Strategy Session" mini-lessons as part of Writer's Workshop, tailoring the content of each to meet students' needs.

EMPIRICAL SUPPORT FOR SRSD

An essential aspect of any educational intervention is the empirical evidence showing that the practice consistently produces meaningful gains in the targeted area. In this section, we summarize the research that has been conducted to investigate the efficacy of SRSD. First, we provide a brief overview of the research on SRSD in writing, highlighting several overarching themes that have emerged from this work. Thereafter, we summarize several recent studies that have systematically reviewed the extant SRSD literature and that indicate that SRSD for writing is now considered an evidence-based practice.

An Overview of SRSD Research

Since the inaugural SRSD study was published in 1985 (Harris & Graham, 1985), Harris, Graham, and others have continued to develop and evaluate the model. To date, over 50 SRSD-related studies have been conducted (two detailed reviews of the SRSD database can be found in Graham & Harris, 2003 and Harris et al., 2009). The majority of these investigations feature SRSD as a writing intervention, but the SRSD instructional model has also been used in areas such as reading (e.g., Mason, 2004; Hagaman, Casey, & Reid, in press; Hagaman & Reid, 2008), math (e.g., Case, Harris, & Graham, 1992), and social skills (e.g., Schadler, 2011), and shown to be beneficial with each. Although Harris, Graham, and their colleagues have conducted many of the SRSD studies, independent researchers and practitioners have also conceptualized and implemented SRSD research (e.g., Anderson, 1997; Curry, 1997; Garcia-Sanchez & Fidalgo-Redondo, 2006; Glaser & Brunstein, 2007; Wong, Hoskyn, Jai, Ellis, & Watson, 2008). Moreover, many SRSD investigations have involved general and/or special education teachers implementing SRSD in their own classrooms (e.g., Danoff, Harris, & Graham, 1993; De La Paz, 1999; De La Paz & Graham, 2002; MacArthur, Schwartz, & Graham, 1991; Schadler, 2011).

Collectively, the extant literature provides solid evidence that SRSD is a highly effective intervention. For example, results from more than 40 SRSD writing studies document that the model consistently produces significant and meaningful gains in multiple areas: students' writing knowledge increases, their approach to writing is enhanced (e.g., effective use of planning and revising strategies), their writing self-efficacy is bolstered, and their written products improve in important ways (i.e., length, completeness, and quality) (for detailed reviews of SRSD outcomes see Graham & Harris, 2003; Graham, Kiuhara, McKeown, & Harris, 2011; Graham & Perin, 2007a, 2007b; Harris et al., 2009; Rogers & Graham, 2008). In fact, many struggling writers—including those with disabilities—experience such growth as a result of SRSD, their post-instruction performance is commensurate with that of their normally-achieving peers (e.g., Danoff et al., 1993; De La Paz, 1999; De La Paz, Owen, Harris, & Graham, 2000; MacArthur, Schwartz, Graham, Molloy, & Harris, 1996; Sawyer, Graham, & Harris, 1992). Research also shows that gains attributed to SRSD are typically maintained over time and generalized across settings, genres, and writing media (e.g., paper and pencil to word processor; see, for example, Graham & Harris, 2003; Harris et al., 2009).

An examination of the research on SRSD further reveals that the model is not only highly effective, but also notably versatile in terms of how, and with whom, it is implemented (e.g., Graham & Harris, 2003). SRSD has been used successfully with multiple instructional formats (i.e., one-to-one, pairs, small groups, whole class), in a variety of general and special education settings, and across different curricular contexts (e.g., incorporated into a process writing approach and used as a distinct writing intervention). Recent studies, such as Harris et al. (in press) and Little, Lane, Harris, Graham, Story, and Sandmel (2010), document that SRSD can also be successfully integrated into multi-tiered models of prevention and support. A three-tiered model for preventing the development of learning and behavior problems and responding effectively to existing concerns consists of interventions at Tier 1 (primary level; typically school or class wide, delivered by the classroom teacher), Tier 2 (secondary level; typically delivered in or outside of the classroom to small groups of students who are not responding adequately at Tier 1), or Tier 3 (tertiary level; typically highly intensive and individualized for students not responding adequately to Tier 1 and Tier 2 interventions). Research has shown that SRSD for writing has meaningful effects at all three tiers.

SRSD has proven to be effective with academically diverse students in second to twelfth grade, including students with disabilities (e.g., learning disabilities, speech and language disabilities, emotional and behavioral disorders, attention deficit hyperactivity disorder, autism spectrum disorders); students without disabilities who have, or are at risk for, learning and/or behavioral difficulties; and students who do not exhibit learning and/or behavioral challenges (e.g., Graham & Harris, 2003; Jacobson & Reid, 2010; Reid & Lienemann, 2006). Students who have participated in SRSD research are also diverse in terms of socio-economic status, race, ethnicity, and geographic location (e.g., rural, urban, and suburban settings across the United States).

Systematic Reviews of SRSD

Four recent meta-analyses offer additional support for the efficacy of SRSD and help situate it within the larger context of identifying evidence-based writing practices (an additional meta-analysis of single subject design writing intervention research that reports similar findings to those described next can be found in Rogers & Graham, 2008). Meta-analytic reviews are particularly relevant for interpreting intervention research because the resulting effect sizes indicate both statistical and practical significance. In group design studies, effect sizes of .80, .50, and .20 are typically interpreted as designating large, moderate, and small impacts, respectively (Lipsey & Wilson, 2001). With single subject research, a metric termed percentage of non-overlapping data points (PND) is used to determine effect sizes (Scruggs & Mastropieri, 2001). PND scores between 70% and 90%

suggest an intervention is effective, scores between 50% and 70% indicate uncertain effectiveness, and scores below 50% suggest little or no efficacy.

Graham and Harris (2003) conducted a meta-analysis of 18 group and single subject design studies that featured SRSD within the context of writing. For group design studies, the average weighted effect sizes were 1.47 for quality, 1.78 for genre elements, and ≥ 2.0 for length and story grammar. With single subject design studies, the percentages of PND for quality, genre elements, and story grammar were all above 90%. The authors also examined the differential effects of SRSD and determined that the overall robust and positive findings were consistent across student populations (e.g., students with learning disabilities, struggling writers, good writers; younger students, older students), strategies (e.g., planning, revising), genres (e.g., personal narrative, persuasive), and interventionists (e.g., graduate assistants, teachers). Moreover, the gains students experienced as a result of SRSD were maintained over time and generalized across genres.

Harris et al. (2009) conducted a meta-analysis of 15 true- and quasi-experimental SRSD writing studies to update and extend the results reported by Graham and Harris (2003). The average weighted effect size for writing quality at post-test was 1.20, with these gains showing maintenance over time (average weighted effect size = 1.23) and generalization to another genre (average weighted effect size = .80). Consistent with findings of Graham and Harris, Harris et al. found no statistically significant difference in outcomes among students who differed in writing ability (i.e., students who struggled with writing vs. students who represented full range of writing abilities) or grade level. Stated simply, SRSD had a strong, positive impact for all participating students.

Graham and Perin (2007a; see also 2007b) conducted a comprehensive meta-analysis of true- and quasi-experimental writing intervention research with adolescent students (i.e., grades 4–12). Using writing quality as the outcome variable, the authors calculated an effect size for 11 types of writing interventions and found explicit strategy instruction was the largest (average weighted effect size = .82). Within that category, there was a statistically significant difference between the effect sizes for studies that used SRSD (average weighted effect size = 1.14) and those that did not use SRSD (average weighted effect size = .62). Taken together, these findings suggest that strategy instruction is a generally effective writing intervention, but strategy instruction with SRSD produces distinctly larger gains.

Graham et al. (2011) also conducted a comprehensive meta-analysis of the true- and quasi-experimental writing intervention research, but the targeted population for this study was elementary-aged students (i.e., grades 1–6). Akin to the findings of Graham and Perin (2007a; 2007b), Graham et al. reported that explicitly teaching writing strategies yielded the greatest impact on writing quality (average weighted effect size = 1.02). Likewise, a statistically significant difference was found between the effect sizes for strategy instruction studies that used SRSD (average weighted effect size = 1.17) and studies that used an approach other than SRSD (average weighted effect size = .59).

A final evaluation by Baker, Chard, Ketterlin-Geller, Apichatabutra, and Doabler (2009) offers a complementary perspective to these four meta-analyses and renders additional support for SRSD. In this investigation, the quality of SRSD research conducted with students who had, or were at risk for, learning disabilities was systematically evaluated using criteria that designated multiple facets of methodological rigor. For this review, five SRSD group experimental studies were analyzed and each met the standard for high quality research. The average weighted effect size for this corpus of research was 1.22. Consequently, SRSD was designated an evidence-based practice for students with, or at risk for, learning disabilities. Based on the analysis of 16 single subject studies, SRSD was, again, found to be an evidence-based practice. Baker et al. (2009) summarized their findings by stating, "studies of SRSD in writing represent one of the most consistent efforts to explore the specific features of an instructional intervention, including systematic replications of research. The evidence suggests that if the approach is implemented with fidelity, schools can expect to see significant improvement in students' writing" (p. 315).

FUTURE RESEARCH AND PRACTICE NEEDS REGARDING SRSD

Writing development and effective writing instruction are based upon changes in students' knowledge, strategies, skills, and will (Harris & Graham, in press). Promoting students' academic competence and literacy requires a complex integration of skills, strategies, processes, and attributes (cf. Harris, 1982; Harris & Graham, 1996; Harris, Graham, & Mason, 2003; Tracy, Reid, & Graham, 2009). While SRSD makes an important contribution to teachers' instructional repertoires, it is not a complete writing curriculum. Much more work is needed to develop writing instruction across the grades that results in flexible, goal-directed, self-regulated writing (cf. Graham & Harris, 1994; Harris & Graham, in press; Harris et al., 2011).

For example, social cognitive theory and research point to the value of peer support and peer involvement in instruction, and greater attention is needed to the role of peers in SRSD instruction, including investigations of peers as cognitive models (cf. Harris, Graham, & Mason, 2006). Further, social cognitive theory further directs our attention to the role of parents in learning to write, and little research has been addressing contributions made outside of school instruction. Maintenance and generalization results have been promising in SRSD research, but much remains to be addressed here as well. We also believe that an important and intriguing focus for future research is the long-term results of SRSD in writing across the K–12 grade levels. No longitudinal research has been conducted; the longest studies have involved teaching two writing strategies within a single school year (Harris & Graham, in press). The relationships between writing and reading, and how effective instruction can enhance both, need further research (Graham & Hebert, 2010). Assessment issues also remain to be addressed (MacArthur, Graham, & Fitzgerald, 2006).

Researchers have also argued that a focus on how teachers become adept at, committed to, and supported in strategy instruction is needed, as is more work aimed at scaling up and sustaining this approach in our schools (Pressley & Harris, 2006). Harris, Graham, and their colleagues have recently begun to address in-service professional development in SRSD, and we turn now to this early research.

FINAL FOCUS: PROFESSIONAL DEVELOPMENT AND SCALING UP SRSD IN SCHOOLS

As we noted earlier, research has indicated that SRSD can be useful at all levels in three-tiered approaches to instruction and intervention. Most research, however, involves implementation of SRSD at Tiers 2 and 3 by trained research assistants, rather than classroom teachers, and researchers have not focused on the professional development provided to teachers. Harris, Graham, and their colleagues have recently reported on two studies to address this need. For over two decades they have been involved in professional development in SRSD (although they have not conducted research on such professional development), with their approach congruent with the theoretical base of, and elements in, the practice-based professional development approach (cf. Ball & Cohen, 1999; Grossman & McDonald, 2008).

In each of the initial two studies on professional development for general education teachers (Harris, Graham, & Adkins, 2011; Harris, Lane, et al., 2012), school-university partnerships had been established over several years, and the authors strove to create a meaningful learning community around SRSD with the teachers at the schools involved. Critical characteristics of the professional development were consistent with both research on effective professional development and the practice-based approach to professional development (Ball & Cohen, 1999; Desimone, 2009; Grossman & McDonald, 2008).

Practice-based professional development is focused on teacher development of understanding and skills regarding an effective educational practice, rather than more narrowly focusing on knowledge about a practice.

Both theory and research indicate that the following are important: (a) collective participation of teachers within the same school with similar needs; (b) basing professional development around the characteristics, strengths, and needs of the students in these teachers' current classrooms; (c) attention to content knowledge needs of teachers, including pedagogical content knowledge; (d) opportunities for active learning and practice of the new methods being learned, including opportunities to see examples of these methods being used and analyze the work; (e) use of the materials and other artifacts during professional development that are identical to those to be used in the classroom; and (f) feedback on performance while learning and before using these methods in the classroom so that understandings and skills critical in implementation are developed.

Each of these six critical characteristics was carefully addressed and incorporated in the professional development approach in these two studies. At each school, one or more grade level and/or genre specific writing teams for professional development and ongoing support were formed; teachers shared their students' current writing performance, strengths and needs; teachers read and discussed summaries of research and practice involving SRSD; teachers observed exemplars of SRSD instruction and participated in practice of the SRSD method and its stages (using the materials they would use in the classroom) until they met criteria for implementation in the classroom; and support was provided after initial professional development. Resources for intensive coaching after professional development were not available in either study, although observation and support once teachers began instruction were provided.

In the first study, Harris, Graham, and Adkins (2011) conducted a randomized controlled trial to investigate Tier 2 implementation of SRSD instruction in story writing by second grade teachers who collaborated in practice-based professional development. Teachers implemented strategies instruction in small groups in their classrooms; both control and intervention students were identified as struggling with writing. Integrity of strategies instruction and social validity were assessed among the participating teachers. Student outcomes assessed included inclusion of genre elements and story quality, generalization to personal narrative, and teacher perceptions of intrinsic motivation and effort for writing. Teachers implemented strategies instruction with high integrity; social validity was positive. Significant effects were found for inclusion of genre elements and story quality at both posttest and maintenance; effect sizes were large (.89 to 1.65). Intervention also resulted in significant generalization to personal narrative (effect sizes were .98 for elements and .88 for quality). Teachers reported significantly higher perceptions of both intrinsic motivation and effort (effect sizes were 1.09 and 1.07, respectively).

In the second study, Harris, Lane, Graham, et al. (2012) conducted a randomized controlled study involving 20 second and third grade teachers who participated in practice-based professional development in SRSD instruction in either story or opinion essay writing. These teachers worked in schools collaborating with a local university to implement an evidence-based, three-tiered model of prevention and supports targeting academic, behavioral, and social goals. The effects of intensive practice-based professional development and follow up support on the writing of second and third grade students in terms of quality, length, and inclusion of basic genre elements; integrity of SRSD instruction; and teacher and student judgments of the social validity of SRSD were investigated. Whole class (Tier 1) teacher implemented SRSD instruction resulted in significant and meaningful changes in student writing outcomes for both story and opinion essay writing. Teachers implemented SRSD with fidelity, and SRSD was viewed as socially valid by teachers and students.

While these two studies provide initial promise for a practice-based approach to professional development in SRSD, much more research is needed. Future research is needed to compare the intensive, initial practice-based professional development (followed by observations and support) implemented in these two studies to other professional development approaches, such as coaching. Further, in the second study Harris, Lane, Graham et al. (2012) noted that while all teachers implemented SRSD instruction adequately, two were not implementing it as enthusiastically or as well as the other 18 teachers. Future research needs to closely examine how to support all teachers in high levels of implementation and more closely follow individual teacher implementation. In both studies, it was not possible to investigate whether or not SRSD instruction in writing was sustained after the study was completed; anecdotal information, however, indicates that many of these teachers continued SRSD instruction into the next school year in both cases. Sustainability needs to be investigated in future studies. In both studies, teachers also indicated that they would be more able and willing to modify SRSD instruction now that they used SRSD once. Studies of how teachers adapt SRSD, both successfully and in unsuccessful ways, as well as larger scaling up studies, are needed.

CONCLUSION

In this chapter, we have focused on the challenges our students face in writing, and on SRSD as one intervention in composing. We looked at the importance of writing today and its critical role into the future. The influence of research and scholarship by Barry Zimmerman and his colleagues on research and practice involving SRSD was summarized. The influence of

Zimmerman and his colleagues on the initial and continuing development of SRSD, and on research on SRSD, has been substantial. The implementation of SRSD was then described in detail, including an example from one classroom. Limitations and future directions for research on SRSD were considered. Finally, we presented two studies on scaling up SRSD in schools using a practice-based professional development approach.

While some may be tempted to say that we now have a good understanding of SRSD and its introduction into schools, we believe that the research to date represents only a beginning. Much more remains to be addressed, as we have indicated. We look forward to the continuation of research regarding SRSD, and the continued influence of work by Barry Zimmerman and his colleagues in this area.

REFERENCES

Anderson, A. A. (1997). *The effects of sociocognitive writing strategy instruction on the writing achievement and writing self-efficacy of students with disabilities and typically achievement in an urban elementary school.* Unpublished doctoral dissertation, University of Houston, Houston, TX.

Applebee, A., Langer, J., Jenkins, L., Mullis, I., & Foertsch, M. (1990). *Learning to write in our nations' schools.* Princeton, NJ: Educational Testing Service.

Applebee, A., Langer, J., & Mullis, I. (1986). *The writing report card: Writing achievement in American schools.* Princeton, NJ: Educational Testing Service.

Applebee, A., Langer, J., Mullis, I., Latham, A., & Gentile, C. (1994). *NAEP 1992: Writing report card.* Washington, DC: US Government Printing Office.

Association for Supervision and Curriculum Development (Producer). (2002). *Teaching students with learning disabilities: Using learning strategies* (DVD). Available from http://shop.ascd.org

Baker, S. K., Chard, D., Ketterlin-Geller, L. R., Apichatabutra, C., & Doabler, C. (2009). Teaching writing to at-risk students: The quality of evidence for self-regulated strategy development. *Exceptional Children, 75,* 303–318.

Ball, D. L., & Cohen, D. K. (1999). Developing practice, developing practitioners: Toward a practice-based theory of professional education. In L. Darling-Hammond & G. Sykes (Eds.), *Teaching as a learning profession: Handbook for policy and practice* (pp. 3–31). San Francisco, CA: Jossey-Boss.

Berman, J. (2001, November). Industry output and employment projections to 2010. *Monthly Labor Review, 40,* 39–56.

Brown, A. L., Campione, J. C., & Day, J. D. (1981). Learning to learn: On training students to learn from texts. *Educational Researcher, 10,* 14–21.

Case, L. P., Harris, K. R., & Graham, S. (1992). Improving the mathematical problem solving skills of students with learning disabilities: Self-regulated strategy development. *Journal of Special Education, 26,* 1–19.

Curry, K. A. (1997). *A comparison of the writing products of students with learning disabilities in inclusive and resource room settings using different writing approaches.* Unpublished doctoral dissertation, Florida Atlantic University, Boca Raton, FL.

Danoff, B., Harris, K. R., & Graham, S. (1993). Incorporating strategy instruction within the writing process in the regular classroom: Effects on the writing of students with and without learning disabilities. *Journal of Reading Behavior, 25,* 295–319.

De La Paz, S. (1999). Self-regulated strategy instruction in regular education settings: Improving outcomes for students with and without learning disabilities. *Learning Disabilities Research & Practice, 14,* 92–106.

De La Paz, S., & Graham, S. (2002). Explicitly teaching strategies, skills, and knowledge: Writing instruction in middle school classrooms. *Journal of Educational Psychology, 94,* 291–304.

De La Paz, S. Owen, B., Harris, K. R., & Graham, S. (2000). Riding Elvis's motorcycle: Using self-regulated strategy development to PLAN and WRITE for a state writing exam. *Learning Disabilities Research & Practice, 15,* 101–109.

Desimone, L. M. (2009). Improving impact studies of teacher's professional development: Toward better conceptualizations and measures. *Educational Researcher, 38*(3), 181–199.

Garcia-Sanchez, J., & Fidalgo-Redondo, R. (2006). Effects of two types of self-regulatory instruction programs on students with learning disabilities in writing products, processes, and self-efficacy. *Journal of Learning Disabilities, 29,* 181–211.

Glaser, C., & Brunstein, J. (2007). Improving fourth-grade students' composition skills: Effects of strategy instruction and self-regulatory procedures. *Journal of Educational Psychology, 99,* 297–310.

Graham, S., & Harris, K. R. (1989). Improving learning disabled students' skills at composing essays: Self-instructional strategy training. *Exceptional Children, 56,* 201–216.

Graham, S., & Harris, K. R. (1994). The role and development of self-regulation in the writing process. In D. Schunk & B. Zimmerman (Eds.), *Self-regulation of learning and performance: Issues and educational applications* (pp. 203–228). Hillsdale, NJ: Lawrence Erlbaum Associates, Inc.

Graham, S., & Harris, K. R. (2003). Students with learning disabilities and the process of writing: A meta-analysis of SRSD studies. In H. L. Swanson, K. R. Harris, & S. Graham, (Eds.), *Handbook of learning disabilities* (pp. 323–344). New York, NY: Guilford Press.

Graham, S., & Harris, K. R. (2005). *Writing better. Effective strategies for teaching students with learning difficulties.* Baltimore, MD: Paul H. Brookes.

Graham, S., & Harris, K. R. (2009). Almost 30 years of writing research: Making sense of it all with *The Wrath of Khan. Learning Disabilities Research & Practice, 24,* 58–68.

Graham, S., & Harris, K. R. (2011). Writing and students with disabilities. In L. Lloyd, J. Kauffman, & D. Hallahan (Eds.), *Handbook of special education* (pp.422–433). London, UK: Routledge.

Graham, S., & Harris, K. R. (2012). The role of strategies, knowledge, will, and skills in a 30-year program of writing research (with homage to Hayes, Fayol, and Boscolo). In V.W. Berninger (Ed.), *Past, present, and future contributions of cognitive writing research to cognitive psychology* (pp. 177–196). New York, NY: Psychology Press.

Graham, S., Harris, K. R., & MacArthur, C. (2004). Writing instruction. In B. Wong (Ed.), *Learning about learning disabilities* (3rd ed., pp. 281–313). Orlando, FL: Academic Press.

Graham, S., & Hebert, M. (2010). *Writing to read: Evidence for how writing can improve reading.* Washington, DC: Alliance for Excellent Education. (Commissioned by the Carnegie Corp. of New York)

Graham, S., Kiuhara, S. A., McKeown, D., & Harris, K. R. (2011). *A meta-analysis of writing instruction for students in the elementary grades.* Manuscript submitted for publication.

Graham, S., & Perin, D. (2007a). A meta-analysis of writing instruction for adolescent students. *Journal of Educational Psychology, 99,* 445–476.

Graham, S., & Perin, D. (2007b). *Writing next: Effective strategies to improve writing of adolescents in middle and high schools—A report to the Carnegie Corporation of New York.* Washington, DC: Alliance for Excellent Education.

Grossman, P., & McDonald, M. (2008). Back to the future: Directions for research in teaching and teacher education. *American Educational Research Journal, 45,* 184–205.

Hagaman, J., Casey, K., & Reid, R. (in press). The effects of a paraphrasing strategy on the reading comprehension of young students. *Remedial and Special Education.*

Hagaman, J., & Reid, R. (2008). The effects of the paraphrasing strategy on the reading comprehension of middle-school students at-risk for failure in reading. *Remedial and Special Education, 29,* 222–234.

Harris, K. R. (1982). Cognitive-behavior modification: Application with exceptional students. *Focus on Exceptional Children, 15*(2), 1–16.

Harris, K. R. (1986). The effects of cognitive-behavior modification on private speech and task performance during problem solving among learning disabled and normally achieving children. *Journal of Abnormal Child Psychology, 14,* 63–76.

Harris, K. R., & Alexander, P. A. (1998). Integrated, constructivist education: Challenge and reality. *Educational Psychology Review, 10*(2), 115–127.

Harris, K. R., & Graham, S. (1985). Improving learning disabled students' composition skills: Self-control strategy training. *Learning Disability Quarterly, 8,* 27–36.

Harris, K. R., & Graham, S. (1992). Self-regulated strategy development: A part of the writing process. In M. Pressley, K. R. Harris, & J. Guthrie (Eds.), *Promoting academic competence and literacy in school* (pp. 277–309). New York, NY: Academic Press.

Harris, K. R., & Graham, S. (1996). *Making the writing process work: Strategies for composition and self-regulation.* Cambridge, MA: Brookline Books.

Harris, K. R., & Graham, S. (1999). Programmatic intervention research: Illustrations from the evolution of self-regulated strategy development. *Learning Disability Quarterly, 22,* 251–262.

Harris, K. R., & Graham, S. (2009). Self-regulated strategy development in writing: Premises, evolution, and the future. *British Journal of Educational Psychology* (monograph series), *6,* 113–135.

Harris, K. R., & Graham, S. (in press). "An adjective is a word hanging down from a noun": Learning to write and students with learning disabilities. *Annals of Dyslexia.*

Harris, K., Graham, S., & Adkins, M. (2011). *Tier 2, teacher implemented writing strategies instruction following practice-based professional development.* Manuscript submitted for publication.

Harris, K. R., Graham, S., Brindle, M., & Sandmel, K. (2009). Metacognition and children's writing. In D. J. Hacker, J. Dunlosky, & A. C. Graesser (Eds.), *Handbook of metacognition in education* (pp. 131–153). New York, NY: Routledge.

Harris, K. R., Graham, S., MacArthur, C., Reid, R., & Mason, L. (2011). Self-regulated learning processes and children's writing. In B. Zimmerman & D. H. Schunk (Eds.), *Handbook of self-regulation of learning and performance* (pp. 187–202). London, UK: Routledge Publishers.

Harris, K. R., Graham, S., & Mason, L. (2003). Self-regulated strategy development in the classroom: Part of a balanced approach to writing instruction for students with disabilities. *Focus on Exceptional Children, 35*(7), 1–16.

Harris, K. R., Graham, S., & Mason, L. (2006). Improving the writing, knowledge, and motivation of struggling young writers: Effects of self-regulated strategy development with and without peer support. *American Educational Research Journal, 43*(2), 295–340.

Harris, K. R., Graham, S., Mason, L. H., & Friedlander, B. (2008). *Powerful writing strategies for all students.* Baltimore, MD: Paul H. Brookes.

Harris, K. R., Lane, K. L., Driscoll, S., Graham, S., Wilson, W., Sandmel, K., Brindle, M., & Schatschneider, C. (in press). Tier one teacher-implemented self-regulated strategy development for students with and without behavioral challenges: A randomized controlled trial. *Elementary School Journal.*

Harris, K. R., Lane, K. L., Graham, S., Driscoll, S., Wilson, W., Sandmel, K., Brindle, M., & Schatschneider. (2012). Practice-based professional development for strategies instruction in writing: A randomized controlled study. *Journal of Teacher Education, 63(2),* 103–119.

Jacobson, L., & Reid, R. (2010) Improving the persuasive essay writing of high school students with ADHD. *Exceptional Children, 76,* 157–174.

Kirsch, I., Braun, H., Yamamoto, K., & Sum, A. (2007). *America's perfect storm: Three forces changing our Nation's future.* Princeton, NJ: ETS.

Lipsey, M., & Wilson, D. (2001). *Practical meta-analysis.* Thousand Oaks, CA: Sage Publications.

Little, M. A., Lane, K. L., Harris, K. R., Graham, S., Story, M., & Sandmel, K. (2010). Self-regulated strategy development for persuasive writing in tandem with schoolwide positive behavioral support: Effects for second-grade students with behavioral and writing difficulties. *Behavioral Disorders, 35,* 157–179.

MacArthur, C. A., Graham, S., & Fitzgerald, J. (Eds.). (2006). *Handbook of writing research.* New York, NY: Guilford Press.

MacArthur, C. A., Schwartz, S., & Graham, S. (1991). Effects of a reciprocal peer revision strategy in special education classrooms. *Learning Disabilities Research & Practice, 6,* 201–210.

MacArthur, C. A., Schwartz, S. S., Graham, S., Molloy, D., & Harris, K. (1996). Integration of strategy instruction into a whole language classroom: A case study. *Learning Disabilities Research & Practice, 11,* 168–176.

Mason, L. H. (2004). Explicit self-regulated strategy development versus reciprocal questioning: Effects on expository reading comprehension among struggling readers. *Journal of Educational Psychology, 96*, 283–296.

Meichenbaum, D. (1977). *Cognitive behavior modification: An integrative approach.* New York, NY: Plenum.

O'Leary, S. G., & Dubey, D. R. (1979). Applications of self-control procedures for children: A review. *Journal of Applied Behavior Analysis, 12*, 449–465.

Pressley, M., & Harris, K. R. (2006). Cognitive strategies instruction: From basic research to classroom instruction. In P. A. Alexander & P. Winne (Eds.), *Handbook of educational psychology* (2nd ed., pp. 265–286). New York, NY: MacMillan.

Reid, R., & Lienemann, T. O. (2006). Self-regulated strategy development for written expression with students with attention deficit hyperactivity disorder. *Exceptional Children, 73*, 53–68.

Rogers, L. A., & Graham, S. (2008). A meta-analysis of single subject design writing intervention research. *Journal of Educational Psychology, 100*, 879–906.

Rosenbaum, M. S., & Drabman, R. S. (1979). Self-control training in the classroom: A review and critique. *Journal of Applied Behavior Analysis, 12*, 467–485.

Salahu-Din, D., Persky, H., & Miller, J. (2008). *The nation's report card: Writing 2007* (NCES 2008–468). Washington, DC: National Center for Education Statistics, Institute of Education Sciences, U.S. Department of Education.

Sandmel, K. N., Brindle, M., Harris, K. R., Lane, K. L., Graham, S.,... Little, A. (2009). Making it work: Differentiating tier two self-regulated strategy development in writing in tandem with schoolwide positive behavioral support. *Teaching Exceptional Children, 42*(2), 22–33.

Santangelo, T., & Olinghouse, N. G. (2009). Effective writing instruction for students who have writing difficulties. *Focus on Exceptional Children, 42*(4), 1–20.

Sawyer, R. J., Graham, S., & Harris, K. R. (1992). Direct teaching, strategy instruction, and strategy instruction with explicit self-regulation: Effects on learning disabled students' composition skills and self-efficacy. *Journal of Educational Psychology, 84*, 340–352.

Schadler, C. (2011). *Teaching students with autism self-determination skills through the use of self-regulated strategy development.* Manuscript in preparation.

Schumaker, J. B., Deshler, D .D., Alley, G. R., Warner, M. M., & Denton, P. H. (1982). Multipass: A learning strategy for improving reading comprehension. *Learning Disability Quarterly, 5*, 295–304.

Schunk, D. H., & Zimmerman, B. J. (1994). *Self-regulation of learning and performance: Issues and educational applications.* Hillsdale, NJ: Lawrence Erlbaum Associates, Inc.

Schunk, D. H., & Zimmerman, B. J. (1997). Social origins of self-regulatory competence. *Educational Psychologist, 32*(4), 195–208.

Scruggs, T., & Mastriopieri, M. (2001). How to summarize single-participant research: Ideas and applications. *Exceptionality, 9*, 227–244.

Shapiro, M. (2000). *J. K. Rowling: The wizard behind Harry Potter,* New York, NY: St. Martin's Press.

Smyth, J. (1998). Written emotional expression: Effect sizes, out-come types, and moderating variables. *Journal of Consulting and Clinical Psychology, 66*, 174–184.

Swedlow, J. (1999). The power of writing. *National Geographic, 196*, 110–132.

Tracy, B., Reid, R., & Graham, S. (2009). Teaching young students strategies for planning and drafting stories. *Journal of Educational Research, 102,* 323–331.

Vaughn, S., Gersten, R., & Chard, D. J. (2000). The underlying message in LD intervention research: Findings from research syntheses. *Exceptional Children, 67,* 99–114.

Wong, B., Hoskyn, M., Jai, D., Ellis, P., & Watson, K. (2008). The comparative effects of two approaches in teaching sixth graders opinion essay writing. *Contemporary Educational Psychology, 33,* 757–784.

Zimmerman, B. (1989). A social cognitive view of self-regulated learning. *Journal of Educational Psychology, 81,* 329–339.

Zimmerman, B. J. (1997). Dimensions of academic self-regulation: A conceptual framework for education. In D. H. Schunk & B. J. Zimmerman (Eds.), *Self-regulation of learning and performance: Issues and educational applications.* (pp. 3–21). Hillsdale, NJ: Lawrence Erlbaum Associates, Inc.

Zimmerman, B., & Reisemberg, R. (1997). Becoming a self-regulated writer: A social cognitive perspective. *Contemporary Educational Psychology, 22,* 73–101.

Zito, J., Adkins, M., Gavins, M., Harris, K. R., & Graham, S. (2007). Self-regulated strategy development: Relationship to the social-cognitive perspective and the development of self-regulation. *Reading and Writing Quarterly, 23,* 77–95.

CHAPTER 4

APPLICATION OF CYCLICAL SELF-REGULATION INTERVENTIONS IN SCIENCE-BASED CONTEXTS

Timothy J. Cleary and Andju S. Labuhn

Over the past few decades, researchers have shown that self-regulation and motivation processes are key determinants of academic achievement for students across the developmental spectrum (DiPerna, Volpe, & Elliot, 2002; Eccles & Wigfield, 2002; Schunk, Pintrich, & Meece, 2008; Zimmerman & Schunk, 2011). In short, the literature demonstrates that students who effectively use self-regulatory processes tend to exhibit strong academic skills, such as math, reading, and writing (De Corte, Mason, Depaepe, & Verschaffel, 2011; Eccles & Wigfield, 2002; Fuchs, Fuchs, Prentice, Burch, Hamlett, Owen, & Schroeter, 2003; Graham & Harris, 2005; Guthrie, Wigfield, & Perencevich, 2004; Schunk & Swartz, 1993; Zimmerman, Bandura, & Martinez-Pons, 1992) and high levels of performance across many different types of academic tasks (Butler, 1998; Cleary, Platten, & Nelson, 2008; DiBenedetto & Zimmerman, 2010). The importance of these processes has also been conveyed by educators and other school-based personnel who

Applications of Self-Regulated Learning across Diverse Disciplines, pages 89–124
Copyright © 2013 by Information Age Publishing
All rights of reproduction in any form reserved.

work directly with children and adolescents struggling in school contexts. In a series of recent surveys, teachers and school psychologists reported self-regulation and motivation assessments and interventions to be critical areas of professional development interest and need (Cleary, 2009; Cleary, Gubi, & Prescott, 2010; Coalition for Psychology in Schools and Education, 2006; Grigal, Neubart, Moon, & Graham, 2003; Wehmeyer, Agran, & Hughes, 2000).

Many renowned scholars have contributed to this burgeoning field and increasing popularity of applying self-regulation principles to school contexts. However, in our opinion, Professor Barry Zimmerman represents one of the most influential theorists and researchers, particularly in terms of the applicability of his theoretical models to diverse fields and the ease with which researchers, practitioners, and laypersons can use these models to develop self-regulation interventions (Bonner, Zimmerman, Evans, Irigoyen, Resnick, & Mellins, 2002; Cleary & Zimmerman, 2004; McPherson & Zimmerman, 2002; Zimmerman & Kitsantas, 1996). Of particular importance to this chapter is to underscore the key role that one of Professor Zimmerman's models, the three-phase cyclical feedback loop, has played in the development and application of two self-regulation interventions to science-based contexts.

In recent years, researchers have emphasized the importance of linking self-regulation and science education, with many arguing that strategic and self-regulatory principles should be directly taught to students or infused into science education and curriculum (Millar & Osborne, 1998; Organisation for Economic Co-operation and Development, 2003; Peters & Kitsantas, 2010; Schraw, Crippen, & Hartley, 2006; Sinatra & Taasoobshirazi, 2011). According to Schraw et al. (2006), effective science instruction should not only increase learning, but should also help to nurture the motivation, strategic behaviors, and metacognitive skills needed to meet the ever increasing standards and demands of science education, particularly as students progress through the secondary school years. Hence, as much as students need to master complex scientific concepts, they also need to exhibit effective strategic thinking and metacognitive reflection in order to adapt and adjust when faced with learning, motivation, or other academic-related challenges—that is, they need to become autonomous, self-regulated learners. Although research in science education has focused on metacognition, some have argued that much less is known about how the broader concept of self-regulation can be applied to such contexts (Schraw et al., 2006). We intend to address this issue in detail.

In this chapter, we address four primary objectives. First, we provide an overview of Zimmerman's three-phase cyclical model and present two case scenarios to illustrate the nature and application of the model. We then discuss how this model served as the theoretical foundation and guiding framework for two self-regulation intervention programs targeting science achievement: (a) a classroom-based intervention program, henceforth called the Self-Regulated Learing (SRL) classroom intervention (Labuhn, Bögeholz & Hasselhorn, 2008a, 2008b) and (b) a small group or individual intervention program, called the Self-Regulation Empowerment Program (SREP; Cleary et al., 2008; Cleary & Zimmerman, 2004). The essential characteristics of these two intervention approaches will be examined, with particular emphasis placed on the implementation process in science classrooms or small group tutoring contexts. It is our hope that readers will gain a clear understanding and appreciation of the applicability of Zimmerman's cyclical phase model to the development and implementation of science-based intervention programs varying in instructional format, intensity, and comprehensiveness. After briefly reviewing studies examining the implementation and effectiveness of these interventions, we conclude the chapter by discussing educational implications and key areas to address in future research.

CYCLICAL NATURE OF SELF-REGULATION

According to Zimmerman (2000), *self-regulation* refers to "self-generated thoughts, feelings, and actions that are planned and cyclically adapted to the attainment of personal goals" (p. 14). He conceptualized self-regulation as an integration of motivational, behavioral, and metacognitive processes that collectively operate in a sequential fashion; that is, *prior* to (forethought), *during* (performance control), and *following* (self-reflection) learning or performance (see Figure 4.1). In preparation for a study session, sophisticated self-regulated learners exhibit strong forethought skills, such as seeking to understand the nature of task demands (*task analysis*), deciding upon the objectives or goals that they wish to attain (*goal-setting*), and selecting the tactics and strategies needed to reach their goals (*strategic planning*). The desire or impetus to initiate this regulatory process is not a fait accompli, but rather is determined by a set of forethought motivational beliefs, such as self-efficacy (Bandura, 1997), task interest and instrumentality (Eccles & Wigfield, 2002), and goal orientation (Pintrich, 2000). That is, students who feel more efficacious about performing well on a given task, perceive the task to be enjoyable and interesting, and appreciate and value academic activities that are challenging are more likely to engage in the cyclical feedback loop.

As these students engage in the performance phase or attempt to learn science concepts, they will often use one or more *self-control* strategies to sustain their motivation, such as self-talk or self-reinforcement, and will often rely on multiple strategies to maximize learning and recall of information (Schraw et al., 2006; Wolters, 2003; Zimmerman, 1989). In addition to the

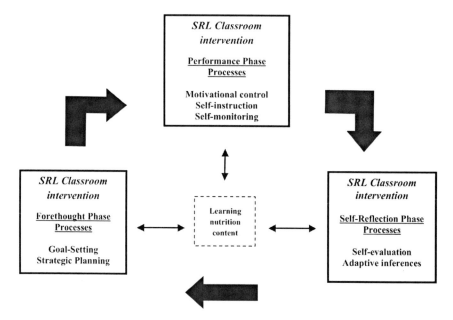

Figure 4.1 Cyclical phase self-regulation processes targeted by the SRL classroom intervention during classroom-based learning activities. Double arrowed lines indicate that all self-regulation processes are taught in relation to course content (nutrition).

use of these strategies, sophisticated regulators also use *self-observation* techniques to gather information about learning progress or areas of confusion, such as when students record the number of problems that they get correct on a practice quiz or write down the key terms that are vague or confusing to them during a study session. From an academic perspective, the performance phase is particularly important in the cyclical model because it is within this phase of the loop that students actively engage with curriculum or content and gather performance and behavioral information used to engage in self-reflection.

During the self-reflection phase, students determine whether they have attained success or not (*self-evaluation*), identify the key causal reasons or links to performance (*causal attributions*), and decide how best to improve performance when needed (*adaptive inferences*). Collectively, these reflection phase processes directly impact what students choose to do in order to sustain or improve their learning and performance on subsequent academic activities (Weiner, 1986; Zimmerman, 2000). The three-phase model is quite applicable to science contexts given that it clearly defines and integrates a set of regulatory processes, such as planning, monitoring, and evaluating, that directly relate to performing specific science tasks including conceptual change, inquiry, and problem-solving. Effective self-regulatory skills will not only enable learners to successfully engage in academic activities in general, they are also necessary to direct their learning efforts outside the science classroom, such as studying for unit exams and writing laboratory reports.

To more clearly delineate the nature of this theoretical model as it pertains to student preparation for a science unit exam and to underscore the key regulatory processes that are often targeted by science-based intervention programs, consider the following two case scenarios. Suppose that two students, Alison and Rebekah, both exhibit average intellectual and academic skills. They are enrolled in the same ninth-grade science class and were recently informed by their science teacher that they will be taking a major exam on the human circulatory system in approximately one week.

Upon being told about the upcoming exam, Rebekah immediately recorded the exam date in her assignment book and began to think about any major family or leisure activities that would interfere with her ability to study and prepare (planning, task analysis). Although Rebekah clearly wanted to get an A on the exam (outcome goal), she was more concerned with figuring out the best plan for mastering all science concepts to be covered on the exam (process goal). She also realized that she needed some guidance in terms of how to best prepare and thus decided to ask her teacher for clarification about specific types of information to be included on the exam as well as the exam format and structure (self-control, seeking social assistance). Based on these conversations as well as her own review and analysis of prior science exams, Rebekah identified that the exam would probably include a combination of multiple choice questions, diagrams, and an integrative essay question. As a result, she wanted to develop a study plan that was varied and comprehensive in nature (strategic planning). For example, to learn basic facts and details that are typically targeted in multiple choice questions, Rebekah planned to use index cards to learn at least eight key terms per night and to make a list of key facts for each component of the circulatory system. To prepare for the essay questions, Rebekah developed a graphic organizer to integrate the large quantity of information and to identify how different concepts relate together (strategic planning). Rebekah possessed a high level of confidence in using these strategies because of her success in using similar tactics in prior years as well as her observations of the success that her older brother exhibited using these strategies when taking the same course a couple years earlier (self-efficacy).

In order to effectively manage her time, Rebekah decided to make a study schedule and even include a couple of "optional study times" in her calendar that she could use if needed (self-control, time management). During the week of exam preparation, Rebekah used the strategies from her study plan (strategy use) but also recorded several topics and key terms that were confusing to her. Her use of this self-observation tactic enabled her to effectively seek out help from her teacher or a peer during subsequent classes (self-recording).

Rebekah received an A on the test and was quite pleased because she reached her outcome goal (self-evaluation). Interestingly, she found greater enjoyment in the realization that her level of preparation, particularly how her tracking of difficult or confusing problems and the use of the graphic organizer, impacted the quality of her learning (attributions). Rebekah also felt efficacious in her study approach and believed that preparing for her science exams in this way would be helpful to her as she progresses through high school and college. Although students like Rebekah are greatly respected and appreciated, educators tend to be most concerned with and devote much of their time and resources to helping students who struggle to succeed or who are disengaged or resistant to learning. Consider the case of Alison, who was one of Rebekah's classmates.

Upon learning about the science exam, Alison became nervous because she realized that she had performed poorly on her last few exams (self-reflection about prior performance). She realized that she needed to do well on one of the next couple of science exams or else she might be in danger of failing the course. At that moment, Alison reflected with a skeptical tone, "So how am I going to study for this exam?" (strategic planning). Unfortunately, she did not think about the exam again until her science teacher reminded the class about the test a couple of days before the exam.

Realizing that she had yet to begin studying, Alison told herself that she was going to review her notes as soon as she got home that night (self-control, self-talk). When she got home, she took out her science textbook and notebook. She read over her notes and looked at a couple of old homework assignments (learning strategy). After about 20 minutes, she took a break. An hour and a half later, she decided to look at the study guide developed by her teacher to identify the important areas to study (task analysis). She noticed that there were several unfamiliar concepts on the study guide and a few topics that she recalled from class lectures. Alison decided to begin refining her understanding of these more familiar topics by reading her notes several times, but unfortunately avoided the more difficult topics (self-control). She repeated this same general process the following night. After about 30 minutes on this second night of studying, Alison felt confident in her ability to pass the exam (self-efficacy) and thought to herself, "I think I really get this stuff now" (self-observation).

Upon receiving a 62 on the test, Alison rolled her eyes and shoved the exam in her binder. She fleetingly thought, "I try hard but I just can't seem to do the work." She lamented about how boring and ineffective her teacher was as an instructor (causal attributions) and began to think about how much she dislikes school (self-motivation beliefs). Unfortunately, Alison avoided thinking about her performance in science over the next few weeks until a couple of days before the next exam (adaptive inferences).

What is the key point of these case scenarios? From our perspective, it is important for educators to recognize that all students will engage in some form of regulatory thinking and action as they learn or reflect on performance. That is, the extent to which individuals self-regulate during learning is not an all-or-nothing phenomenon, nor is it a reflection of an enduring trait or characteristic of only successful learners. Rather, most students will use some method to learn, will make reflective judgments following performance, and will demonstrate various perceptions and beliefs about themselves as learners and the learning context. What is important, however, is the sophistication and quality of their strategic and cognitive engagement during learning and performance (Cleary & Zimmerman, 2001; DiBenedetto & Zimmerman, 2010; Ericsson & Charness, 1994; Graham & Harris, 2005; Wolters, 2003). Although both Rebekah and Alison exhibited some level of engagement in all three phases of the loop, Rebekah exhibited a high level of strategic thinking throughout the entire cycle of forethought, performance, and reflection. As predicted by Zimmerman's cyclical phase model, because Rebekah approached studying in a highly strategic way, implemented and monitored her use of various learning strategies, and reflected on her exam performance in relation to her strategic behaviors, she exhibited adaptive motivation and performance outcomes.

In contrast, Alison was more of a reactive type of learner who did not exhibit a high level of forethought in her approach to learning. Without a clear plan on how best to study for science exams, she simply relied on using simple rehearsal strategies to learn course content. In addition, because Alison rarely tracked or self-monitored her learning progress and behaviors during studying, she did not have access to information that would have helped her to adaptively or strategically reflect on her poor exam performance. When students are unaware of task demands, do not track the topics or concepts that confuse them, and have poor knowledge or skill in using learning strategies, they tend to display maladaptive motivation profiles characterized by avoidance, low effort, and self-defeating patterns of attributions (e.g., the teacher is the cause of poor performance) and efficacy beliefs (i.e., doubts about personal capabilities). The primary purpose of this chapter is to illustrate how two distinct interventions instill strategic, cyclical thinking in high school students as they learn science topics.

OVERVIEW OF SREP AND SRL CLASSROOM INTERVENTION

In this section we examine the link between Zimmerman's three-phase cyclical model of self-regulation and two science-based self-regulation intervention programs: (a) Self-Regulation Empowerment Program (SREP; Cleary et al., 2008; Cleary & Zimmerman, 2004) and (b) Self-Regulated Learning (SRL) classroom intervention (Labuhn et al., 2008a, 2008b). We also discuss the instructional characteristics and features of both programs.

Theoretical Foundation and Assumptions

The SREP and SRL classroom interventions are grounded in social-cognitive theory, with primary focus on Zimmerman's three-phase cyclical model. Accordingly, the goal of both programs is to optimize the academic achievement of academically at-risk students by facilitating their engagement in multiple iterations of the forethought, performance, and self-reflection phase processes. It should be noted that these programs were specifically customized for science but are quite applicable to other academic areas. Collectively, training in these regulatory processes guides students' selection, use, and refinement of learning strategies during task performance. That is, both intervention programs teach students how to proceed through the cyclical process of setting goals and strategic plans (forethought), using learning strategies and tracking learning progress (performance), and self-evaluating goal progress and reflecting on their performance at well-defined points throughout the intervention process.

The SREP and SRL classroom interventions are also highly contextualized in that intervention protocols are fully integrated with the specific curriculum administered in a particular school context. Thus, rather than training students to use a broad set of isolated skills across an array of domains, these interventions target self-regulation skills as they unfold and occur during learning and engagement within the science curriculum. This is a particularly important feature of the programs given that much research has shown that self-regulation can often vary across contexts and situational factors (Bong, 2005; Cleary & Chen, 2009; Hadwin, Winne, Stockley, Nesbit, & Woszczyna, 2001).

Both intervention programs also emphasize the importance of triadic reciprocality (Bandura, 1986). While it is assumed that social agents can directly impact students' personal processes and behaviors, it is also recognized that students' self-perceptions and approaches towards learning can impact how teachers or tutors perceive students as well as how they instruct or interact with those students. To briefly illustrate this point, although SREP tutors use modeling and direct strategy instruction to impact student behaviors and perceptions during training sessions, they are also taught to adapt or modify this instruction based on feedback and collaboration with students. In a sense, students and tutors act as collaborators, or reciprocal agents, during the process of selecting, practicing, and adapting the use of learning strategies.

Instructional Characteristics and Features

From our perspective, a wonderful aspect of Zimmerman's cyclical phase model is that it has been applied to many distinct domains and contexts (Bonner et al., 2002; Cleary, Zimmerman, & Keating, 2006; DiBenedetto & Zimmerman, 2010; McPherson & Zimmerman, 2002; Zimmerman & Kitsantas, 1996). The specific focus of this chapter, however, is to illustrate how his three-phase model was used to guide the development of two separate science-based self-regulation interventions that, although being similar in many respects, were distinct in terms of how they were implemented in school contexts. Thus, although the SREP and SRL classroom interventions were both applied to science-based contexts and focused on teaching students to engage in the three-phase cyclical loop, they can be distinguished with regard to their instructional intensity, implementation procedures, and contexts for learning (see Table 4.1).

TABLE 4.1 Instructional Characteristics of SREP and SRL Classroom Intervention

Instructional features	Self-Regulation Empowerment Program (SREP)	SRL Classroom Intervention
Instructional context	• Outside of science classroom setting • Before or after school tutoring program	• Science classroom settings • Within a curricular unit on nutrition
Duration/frequency of intervention	• Approximately 18 to 20 sessions • Two times per week • 40 to 50 minutes per session	• Eight sessions • Two times per week • 45 minutes per session

Instructional methods	• Administered by trained tutors
	• Instructional activities
	  – tutor-directed administration of standardized modules
	  – direct explanation
	  – modeling
	  – guided practice
	• Self-regulation worksheets/activities (students complete task analysis, goal-setting, strategic planning worksheets)
	• Self-regulation graph (students graph test grade goals, test grades, and strategic plans
	• Peer group discussions
		• Administered by trained science teachers
		• Instructional activities
		  – teacher-directed activities
		  – direct explanation
		  – modeling
		• Peer discussions (students discuss their experiences with course content and how self-regulatory processes can be applied to the different tasks)
		• Group work (groups of three to four students work on joint tasks)
		• Individual seatwork (students complete worksheets to apply self-regulatory processes to actual course content)

Instructional Context and Intensity

At a general level, the SREP and SRL classroom interventions can be distinguished using a response-to-intervention (RTI) framework. RTI is a school-based service delivery approach whereby different levels or tiers of interventions are provided to students based on the severity of their problems as well as their level of responsiveness to prior interventions (Marston, 2005; Tilly, 2008). At the broadest level, Tier I, interventions reflect universal design principles, and thus all students in the school are exposed to identical initiatives or programs.

At the next level, or Tier II, interventions are typically implemented at a classroom level, with all students within that classroom receiving the intervention. The SRL classroom intervention corresponds most closely with this level because it is implemented in typical science classrooms targeting the entire group of students. To date, the SRL classroom intervention has been implemented as part of instructional lessons targeting nutrition concepts within the regular science curriculum in German schools (Labuhn et al., 2008a, 2008b). The authors noted that they developed the content of the classroom-based lesson plans in close collaboration with a group of science teachers in order to enhance their perceptions and beliefs about the appropriateness and acceptability of the procedures. Enhancing the social validity or treatment acceptability of Tier II intervention is important because the teachers, rather than researchers or experimenters, are responsible for administering the intervention. The SRL classroom intervention consists of eight 45-minute sessions, administered over a period of approximately three weeks (i.e., two to three sessions per week). Although this program attempts to ensure that the needs of academically at-risk students are adequately addressed, its primary function is to provide a general or broad intervention for all students, regardless of competency or skill level.

As part of an RTI perspective, students who do not respond positively to a Tier II intervention are eligible to receive additional support services or Tier III interventions. SREP is an example of a Tier III program because it addresses the specific challenges and needs of individual students over an extended length of time. In comparison to the SRL classroom intervention, SREP is more intensive in that it is administered two times per week for approximately 10 weeks and provides a high level of support to address the needs, challenges, and concerns exhibited by individual students. It is also important to note that SREP was not designed to be a classroom intervention. Rather, it was developed to provide intensive tutoring or remedial assistance to individual or small groups of students outside of the general education context. SREP is typically administered as a before-school tutoring program with high school youth, although it can be incorporated into the typical schedule or routine of a school day (Cleary et al., 2008; Cleary & Zimmerman, 2004).

Instructional Methodology

Broadly speaking, the SRL classroom intervention incorporates a variety of activities, such as group work, peer-to-peer discussions, and individual seatwork, to give the students multiple opportunities to enhance their learning and to practice self-regulatory skills. Both group work and peer-to-peer discussions entail cooperative learning experiences with classmates. For example, during group work, students work collaboratively on a joint task in small groups of three or four students and are given the opportunity to share and discuss their work with classmates in order to obtain feedback and further guidance. During peer-to-peer discussions, students meet in dyads to discuss their experiences with course content and how self-regulatory processes can be applied to the different tasks and activities in the science course. These cooperative learning activities are supplemented with individual seatwork sessions whereby students are given the opportunity to identify, develop, and refine their individualized learning strategies used to enhance content knowledge of nutrition and to practice applying self-regulatory strategies, such as self-monitoring and self-evaluation, during learning.

Although these student work periods are a key aspect of the instructional model, it is important to note that science teachers are trained to use direct explanation and modeling when introducing new content-related concepts and basic ideas of self-regulatory processes. For most sessions, teacher-directed instruction is immediately followed by the aforementioned cooperative learning activities to facilitate student involvement and participation. Furthermore, each session adheres to three basic principles in order to support long-term effects and transfer. First, at the beginning of each lesson, the teacher takes up the topic of the previous lesson and discusses key aspects (both science and self-regulatory related) with the students. Second, at the end of each lesson, the students are asked to write down some take-home messages in their notebooks. Finally, during each session the teacher encourages students to apply their newly acquired competencies to other tasks, to their homework assignments and to other subjects.

The Self-Regulation Empowerment Program (SREP) shares many instructional features illustrated in the SRL classroom intervention. For example, SREP tutors use direct explanation and modeling when introducing cognitive strategies or procedures for setting goals, developing strategic plans, or self-monitoring performance processes and outcomes. In addition, given the small number of students in any particular group, peer discussion and interactions are facilitated and encouraged by SREP tutors. Finally, although SREP is a small group intervention program delivered outside of a general classroom context, SREP tutors collaborate extensively with teachers to ensure that the course content is directly infused into SREP instructional modules.

The SREP, however, possesses a variety of unique instructional characteristics and features. First, it utilizes a flexible standard protocol approach whereby tutors or coaches use a training manual (with scripts and activities) to guide all instruction and intervention activities (Cleary et al., 2008). This manual is broken down into several modules targeting self-regulation processes (e.g., goal-setting, task analysis, planning, self-reflection), specific learning strategies, or self-control strategies. It is important to note, however, that although SREP tutors adhere to these structured modules, they are encouraged to adapt the nature of the lessons or the specific learning strategies discussed during a session based on student feedback, interest, and input.

Another unique feature of SREP is that it involves individualized guided practice sessions to facilitate students' learning and refinement of cognitive strategies. According to Zimmerman (2000), after students observe a model demonstrate the use of a learning strategy, they need to be given frequent emulation or practice opportunities whereby they not only attempt to use the cognitive strategies in context but will also receive hints, reinforcement, and feedback from an expert or model. The use of these guided practice activities during SREP sessions is essential to not only help students refine and master their use of cognitive strategies but to also sustain students' motivation as they seek to further develop their skills. The individualized focus of the feedback provided during SREP is one of the most essential features in helping at-risk students develop personally relevant regulatory behaviors and thoughts during learning.

Coverage of Cyclical Loop

As indicated previously, both the SREP and SRL classroom interventions were grounded in Zimmerman's three-phase cyclical feedback loop. The SRL classroom intervention mirrored Zimmerman's three-phase cyclical process by purposively including preparatory, action-oriented, and self-reflective elements (see Figure 4.1). More precisely, the intervention successively focuses on goal-setting and planning (forethought phase), self-monitoring and motivational control (performance phase), and self-evaluation (self-reflection phase) to encourage subsequent strategic adaptations during future learning. Although these sub-processes are taught in sequence, students are encouraged to integrate these sub-processes to parallel the premise that self-regulation is a cyclical, feedback-oriented phenomenon. In terms of forethought training, students are encouraged to set specific, moderately challenging and personally meaningful goals and learn to differentiate realistic and unrealistic goals. They are also encouraged to consider *how* they will attain their personal goals and thus develop specific strategic plans.

Labuhn and colleagues highlight that motivational control is a key component of their intervention and occurs during both forethought and performance phases. Goal-setting serves as a motivational function in that it sets the benchmark that students hope to attain (Schunk & Swartz, 1993; Zimmerman, 2008a). As part of the strategic planning process, teachers help students identify specific self-control strategies that would specifically optimize their motivation and perseverance in the face of challenge. However, Labuhn and colleagues point out that these self-control conversations occur both before learning (development of plans) and during learning (actual use of tactics) in order to provide students with motivational feedback needed to sustain their efforts as they learn. To enhance personal learning outcomes, students not only need to plan and react to motivational states during studying, they also need to gather information about their behaviors and cognitions during learning. This is accomplished by having students engage in self-monitoring during learning. Self-monitoring refers to the deliberate attention placed on aspects of one's behavior, such as selectively attending to specific actions and cognitive processes, distinguishing them from others, and discriminating their outcomes as they occur or "on-line." By self-monitoring progress, students are increasingly able to generate information that can be used to directly adjust strategies and thereby considerably improve personal outcomes.

In terms of self-reflection, Labuhn and colleagues focus most directly on self-evaluation, which involves comparing one's own performance and self-monitored outcomes with a goal or standard (Winne & Hadwin, 1998). As part of the SRL classroom intervention, students are prompted to frequently examine whether they have reached their personal goals, to identify potential obstacles, and to infer how they could improve their results. That is, monitoring and evaluating the quality of learning enables students to search for ways to improve their knowledge and to develop new strategies. Taken together, the classroom intervention addresses self-regulatory processes from all three phases of the cyclical model. As the sub-processes are taught consecutively, the components become progressively more interrelated and finally cover the entire cyclical loop.

Although there is much overlap in content between the SREP and SRL classroom intervention, SREP provides more comprehensive coverage of the specific sub-processes embedded within the three-phase cyclical feedback loop (see Figure 4.2). This distinction is primarily due to differences in intervention intensity of the two programs and not the quality of the actual intervention. As previously discussed, the SREP includes more than double the number of sessions of the SRL classroom intervention, is administered over a longer period of time, and incorporates a highly individualized approach when working with students. In terms of forethought training, SREP tutors not only teach students to set goals and to develop strategic plans when studying for science tests, they also help students understand the specific demands and potential obstacles to studying (task analysis). Studying for exams is often an ambiguous and complex activity because it

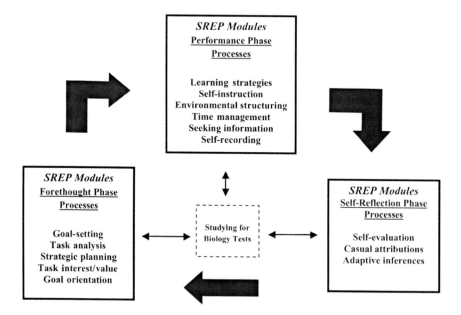

Figure 4.2   Cyclical phase self-regulation processes targeted by SREP training modules during studying activities. Double arrowed lines indicate that all self-regulation processes are taught in relation to biology course content and in preparation for biology tests.

necessitates the management of several factors that can either facilitate or inhibit the studying process. As part of forethought training, SREP tutors also model adaptive task values and mastery orientation beliefs, such as the importance of focusing on the process of learning and striving to optimize skills and competencies, and challenge students' maladaptive attributions and beliefs about learning or school (Ames, 1992; Weiner, 1986).

SREP instruction focuses most heavily on increasing students' repertoire of learning strategies and self-control strategies. Thus, SREP tutors model and provide guided practice in using concept maps, graphic organizers, and mnemonic devices, but also in implementing tactics to help enhance students' self-motivation, time management, or studying environments. Similar to the SRL intervention, the SREP was also developed based on the premise that in order for students to engage in effective self-evaluation and adaptive processes, they must generate information about their behaviors, cognition, or outcomes through self-observation techniques, such as self-recording. In this program, students are taught to self-record their exam grades, strategic plans, and studying or homework behaviors. This activity generates extensive feedback about how well they are improving and increases their awareness about their actual methods of studying and preparation. This feedback generation component in SREP underscores an essential premise of the cyclical feedback loop; that is, effective adaptation and regulation can only occur when students have access to self-monitored information or external feedback about prior performances (Zimmerman, 2000).

Finally, the SREP targets a comprehensive set of reflection phase processes: self-evaluation, causal attributions, adaptive inferences, and emotional reactions. That is, following each biology exam, SREP tutors administer the Self-Reflection module (see Table 4.1), which provides extensive training in how to make accurate self-evaluations and strategic attributions and adaptive inferences. That is, a key outcome of this module is having students reflect on whether their strategic plans lead to improve outcomes and to consider how such strategies can be modified to optimize future performance.

INTERVENTION PROCEDURES AND CASE EXAMPLES

In this section, we provide more extensive details regarding implementation procedures and processes to be followed when administering the SREP and SRL classroom intervention (see Table 4.2).

SRL Classroom Intervention

This intervention begins with two sessions on *goal-setting*, a key forethought phase process in the cyclical model. To introduce the idea of goal-setting and its function within the cyclical loop of SRL, the teacher and students discuss the purpose of goals as well as procedures for establishing moderately challenging and reasonable goals. The students are also asked to give examples for realistic and unrealistic goals and to discuss possible results of setting unattainable goals in small groups.

For each session, students are provided a worksheet on which they note their specific goals for the particular task. That is, at the top of each worksheet, it read, "Please take a look at today's tasks first. What is your goal for this work? Please describe your goal specifically!" For example, the third session of the science lesson unit was on nutrients and their function in the human body (Labuhn et al., 2008a). The science teacher gave students a worksheet with several paragraphs to read and then prompted them to answer 10 comprehension questions. The teacher reminded the students to first examine the task and then to think about a reasonable personal goal for the upcoming seatwork phase. The teachers also used cognitive modeling procedures to illustrate her thought process in determining a realistic goal and recording the goal on her worksheet. Throughout the interven-

TABLE 4.2   Overview of Core Characteristics of Cyclical Phase Training in SREP and SRL Classroom Intervention

Phase of training	Self-Regulation Empowerment Program (SREP)	SRL Classroom Intervention

Forethought training	• Addressed in four modules
	  – *Introduction*
	  – *Task analysis*
	  – *Goal-setting*
	  – *Strategic planning*
	• Modules are administered during first four to five sessions
	• SREP tutors cultivate adaptive self-efficacy, interest, value, and mastery goal beliefs throughout entire program
		• Addressed in sessions 1–2
		  – *Goal-setting*
		  – *Strategic planning*
		• Teachers encourage students to apply forethought phase processes throughout entire program

Performance training	• Addressed in a meta-module
	  – *Learning Strategies* (concept maps, mnemonic devices, and other learning tactics)
	• Students are also taught self-control strategies based on their individual needs
	• Modules are administered over approximately ten sessions
	• Students engage in self-recording during all sessions
		• Addressed in sessions 3–6
		  – *Motivational Control (entails planning and self-control processes)*
		  – *Self-monitoring*
		• Teachers encourage students to link newly acquired control/monitoring strategies to forethought phase processes

Self-reflection training	• Addressed in a single module
	  – *Self-reflection* (self-evaluation, attributions, and adaptive inferences)
	• Module is administered after every biology test (approximately three to four times during SREP)
		• Addressed in sessions 7–8
		  – *Self-evaluation*
		• Students are guided to refer back to their self-set goals and diagnose their performance for improvement (adaptive inferences)

tion, the teacher regularly referred to students' written personal goals and used these goals as self-evaluative standards against which to judge goal progress. That is, students were not only taught to set reasonable goals, but to also self-evaluate their goal-attainment, a fundamental aspect of the self-reflection phase of the cyclical loop.

After students had gained some experience with the process of goal-setting, the teacher introduced the topic of *motivational control* during the third lesson. In small groups, students discussed questions such as, "How can I motivate myself to study even if I really don't feel like it?" and "How can I stay focused on my task even if there are so many other interesting things to do?" Although both of these questions address student motivation, the former targets the motivation or impetus to act *prior* to learning or studying whereas the latter was designed to stimulate student thought and action *during* actual studying. The students were asked to think of personal self-instructions that they considered helpful in those situations prior to or during studying. For example, one girl, Hannah, who often struggled with procrastination, discussed this problem with her group and came up with the self-instruction "I start working right now and stay focused for thirty minutes." Her self-instruction not only included a clear idea of *when* she was going to start, but also the *time* she intends to work on the task. After the group discussion phase, the students wrote their personal self-instructions down in their notebooks to keep them in mind and to apply them in subsequent homework.

In the following lesson, students were asked to share their experiences with their self-instructions in small groups. If necessary, they made adaptations to improve self-motivation. In some instances, students were encouraged to be more precise in their statements and to directly relate their self-instruction to their personal goal for a certain task. For a student like Hannah, this appeared to be motivationally advantageous because a manageable amount of concentrated work in a reasonable time helped her aim toward her personal goal and made it less likely that she would put off studying or doing homework.

The classroom intervention then proceeded with two sessions on *self-monitoring*. To introduce the process of self-monitoring, the teacher suggested three central questions as helpful reminders during studying: (a) "What is my goal for this particular task?", (b) "Do I understand what I am doing?", and (c) "Am I making progress toward the goal?" The students were subsequently asked to discuss why monitoring the learning progress could improve the individual results and to think of an example. After this group discussion, the students were asked to apply the central questions to their own work in class. The teacher modeled the use of the three questions on a sample task to introduce the idea of "supervising oneself." The topic of this particular science lesson was the composition of healthy food. Working in small groups, the students were to plan a well-balanced breakfast, gathering information from various sources like several textbooks and worksheets. In the subsequent lesson, they shared their personal experiences with self-monitoring in class. Hannah, for example, found it helpful to ask herself from time to time whether she grasped the concepts, and, if not, she reread the passage. This was key self-monitored information that Hannah could use to subsequently self-evaluate and to adapt her strategy as needed in the future.

The final self-regulatory process that was included in the intervention was *self-evaluation*, a key process of self-reflection. In these sessions, the students were guided toward evaluating their own performance and diagnosing it for improvement. They were encouraged to ask themselves "What have I learned so far?", and "Have I successfully completed the task, and how can I improve the result?" (adaptive inference). The teacher modeled how to evaluate one's own performance critically by comparing the self-monitored outcomes with one's self-set goal. Students were then asked to practice self-evaluation using a biology quiz on proteins they worked on in that lesson. As one student, Dan, self-evaluated his progress, he realized that he wasn't able to successfully meet the requirements of the task. As a result, he thought about the reason for his failure and realized that he had neither studied the text on proteins nor memorized the figure from his textbook carefully enough. He therefore planned to catch up on reading and studying in the afternoon. Although Dan did make an error in not following the demands of the task, he exhibited ideal cognition and behavior from a self-regulation perspective. That is, he recognized his mistake and took the necessary steps to correct or fix it. This brief case example showed that self-monitoring can lead to effective self-evaluations, which can in turn lead to making successful adaptations regarding one's self-set goals, motivational states, or task strategies—in essence, illustrating Zimmerman's cyclical phase model in action.

SELF-REGULATION EMPOWERMENT PROGRAM

The SREP is administered by highly trained SREP tutors using a set of instructional modules. In this section, we will briefly describe these modules and provide case study examples to illustrate key implementation procedures. In a broad sense, the instructional modules are broken down into three general components: (a) foundational modules, (b) strategy modules, and (c) self-reflection modules (see Cleary et al., 2008 for more details). There are four foundational modules (i.e., introduction, task analysis, goal-setting, and strategic planning) that are administered in sequence. During this initial part of the program, which typically involves the first four or five sessions, participants are trained how to think and strategically prepare for upcoming biology exams. As part of the introduction module, the SREP tutor explains to students about the value of the SREP and self-regulation in general. The tutors also ask students to complete a couple of reflection activities in order to ascertain their primary attributions for their struggles and the quality of the strategies that they use to prepare for exams and to learn biology course material. The primary goal of the SREP tutor is to promote adaptive self-motivation and regulatory beliefs by modeling and conveying adaptive self-beliefs such as, "The use of learning strategies is the primary cause of good grades on biology tests"; "All students are capable of improving their test performance"; and "Science tests grades are important because they greatly affect your final report card grades, which will appear on your high school transcript."

Following this general introduction, students are administered modules to help them identify the key test demands, to set effective goals, and to develop a strategic plan. For example, as part of the task analysis module, students are asked to complete a form that requires them to record information germane to upcoming biology tests (format, content coverage, etc.) as well as the personal challenges or barriers that they experienced during previous biology exams. In short, the key purpose of this module is to increase students' awareness of the upcoming test characteristics as well as the areas of challenge that they need to consider prior to developing a study plan. This module is followed by goal-setting instruction, whereby students learn about the importance and meaning of outcome goals and process goals. As part of goal-setting directions, students are taught how to establish test grade goals and to plot their goals using the Self-Regulation Graph (See Figure 4.3).

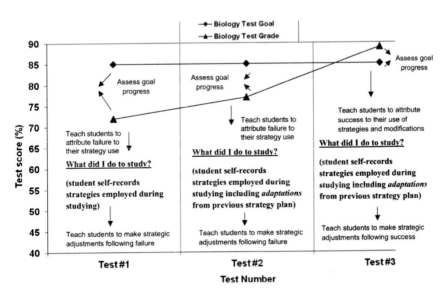

Figure 4.3 Example of the Self-Regulation Graph used to teach students to evaluate goal progress and to make strategic attributions and adaptive inferences. From "Effectiveness of the Self-Regulation Empowerment Program with urban high school students" by T. J. Cleary, P. Platten, & A. Nelson, 2008, *Journal of Advanced Academics*, *20*(1), p. 87. Copyright 2008 by Prufrock Press. Reprinted with permission.

The task analysis module addresses the questions, "What is required for the upcoming test?" and "Have I had any difficulties on previous tests?", whereas the goal-setting module helps student to examine, "What am I hoping to accomplish when studying and taking the upcoming test?" These two forethought processes are instrumental in helping to address the issue of, "How am I going to accomplish these goals regarding my test preparation and performance?" In other words, students need to learn about their personal goals and the nature of the task prior to developing a strategic plan. It is during the strategic planning module where students learn about the value of using specific learning strategies during test preparation and begin to explore the specific tactics and strategies that they need to use to optimize learning during the studying process. After a brief introduction to the value of strategic planning, students are asked to complete a worksheet delineating different areas that give them the most difficulty when studying or learning biology course materials, such as time management, memorization, motivation, and environmental structuring. This worksheet is then transformed into an initial strategic plan so that students collaborate with the SREP tutors about potential strategies that can be used optimize their regulatory and learning processes. Because students would not have received formal strategy instruction at this point in the SREP, they are not expected to complete a full strategic plan during this session. Rather, they are prompted and encouraged to add, modify, or delete strategies from their strategic plan during subsequent SREP sessions as they learn and master new strategies.

The majority of the SREP sessions involve learning strategy instruction. SREP tutors use explicit instruction, modeling, and guided practice activities to teach students an array of evidence-based strategies, such as graphic organizers and mnemonic devices, to enhance learning and recall of science content. For each learning strategy that is taught, tutors explain the purpose and value of the strategy, use behavioral and cognitive modeling techniques to demonstrate the use of the strategy, and provide students with multiple opportunities to practice using it in relation to biology course content. Although tutors use structured modules to guide their teaching of strategies, they are afforded the flexibility to modify or adapt the nature of these strategies to best meet student interests and needs (Cleary et al., 2008).

The first few strategy-training sessions are typically devoted to a single strategy. However, over the course of the training program, additional learning and or regulatory strategies are emphasized, if needed. In addition to tactics that directly enhance learning and recall of biology material, students often encounter self-control or environmental obstacles and challenges when studying. Thus, SREP also includes supplemental modules that target various self-control tactics to optimize student motivation and self-management during studying, including self-reinforcement, environmental structuring, seeking information/social support, self-instruction, and time management. These supplemental modules can be introduced at any point during SREP training, although they typically are presented after students identify a particular area as problematic to their learning. For example, in one study a student conveyed that she often struggled to learn key terms and had difficulty learning some concepts on which she had poor notes. In response, the SREP tutor used a seeking information module to introduce a variety of tactics that the student could use to seek out information from social and non-social sources. Interestingly, following this session, the student proactively asked her older siblings for assistance and decided to research different types of study tactics on the internet for learning and recalling information for her upcoming test on the circulatory system (Cleary & Platten, in press). Although this strategy was not a part of her initial strategic plan, it was included to address a problem that naturally arose during the intervention.

It is important to note that students often developed their own tactics during studying and brought them to SREP sessions to receive additional feedback from tutors and to share with their classmates. For example, during practice of using graphic organizers while studying at home, one student spontaneously developed a series of potential test questions to further guide his studying. He brought these questions into the following SREP session to ensure their appropriateness and to help teach "his method" of generating test questions to his peers (Cleary et al., 2008).

The final core instructional component of the SREP involves administering a comprehensive self-reflection module after each biology exam. The key goal of this module is to reinforce cyclical thinking in students by teaching them how to evaluate the effectiveness of their learning strategies and to consistently make strategic attributions and adaptive inferences. To accomplish this objective, SREP tutors employ a structured graphing procedure that facilitates reflection dialogue (see Figure 4.3). This graph is initially introduced during the goal-setting module and strategic planning modules when students are prompted to plot a personal test grade goal and their strategic plan used to prepare for each test. Following each biology exam, students plot their exam grades and check to make sure that they recorded their strategic study plan accurately. This graph is a critical component to teach self-reflection because it combines both process (e.g., strategy use) and outcomes. After completing the graph, students are then asked to address the three critical self-reflection phase questions: (a) Did you reach your goal? (self-evaluation), (b) What is the main reason why you reached/did not reach your goal? (causal attributions), and (c) What do you need to do to improve your next test score? (adaptive inferences). These task-specific questions are derived from a structured interval protocol called self-regulated learning (SRL) microanalysis (Cleary, 2011; DiBenedetto & Zimmerman, 2010). In short, this interview measures students' forethought, performance, and self-reflection phase processes as students engage in a particular activity or in a specific situation, such as when receiving a test grade back from their teacher. During the SREP reflection module, the tutors use the microanalytic questions to not only formatively track changes in students' judgments and reactions following success or failure, but to also use the information to engage students in a reflection dialogue and to potentially restructure or reframe maladaptive regulatory thinking.

Using the self-regulation graph as a reference point, SREP tutors engage the entire group in a reflective discussion. Regarding self-evaluation, tutors encourage students to evaluate their performance against two types of self-criteria: prior exam scores and/or mastery goals. Zimmerman (2000, 2008a) has argued that these types of self-evaluative standards are more adaptive than normative criteria because they direct students' attention and subsequent efforts to their own behaviors and strategy use, rather than to peer performance. After addressing the issue of how they performed, students are then asked to openly talk about attribution responses, or the factors that they believed contributed most strongly to their grades. Although many factors could have impacted their performance, students are encouraged to think about failure and success in terms of variables that are controllable, unstable, and internal, such as strategy use (Borkowski, Weyhing, & Carr, 1988; Cleary & Zimmerman, 2001; Clifford, 1986; Schunk et al., 2008). It is also important to note that because the self-regulation graph contains grade goals, actual test grades and their strategic plan, it becomes the key instructional tool through which students can visually see the causal connection between their strategy use and grades.

This type of attribution re-training is designed to teach students how to reflect specifically and strategically about test performance, which ultimately should impact the quality of their adaptation and modification of their science-based learning strategies prior to the next exam. For example, following an exam on the circulatory system, one student identified running out of time when taking the test and spending too much time studying for a narrow set of topics as the key causal factors impacting her exam performance (Cleary & Platten, in press). This led to an important reflective discussion during the SREP whereby the tutor, the student, and her peers talked about adaptive ways to alter or enrich her strategic plan prior to the next exam.

EFFECTIVENESS OF SREP
AND SRL CLASSROOM INTERVENTION

Given the variations in scope and format of the two intervention programs, the authors used different methodological designs to examine their effectiveness. For example, Labuhn and colleagues used a quasi-experimental design to examine the effectiveness of the classroom-based intervention, whereas Cleary and colleagues have used mixed model case study designs to provide an in-depth analysis regarding changes in students' science achievement and regulatory behaviors during training. In the following section, we briefly review these varying methodologies and offer a few key conclusions from this initial work.

SRL Classroom Intervention

Methodology and Design

Labuhn and colleagues used a quasi-experimental pretest–posttest design (see Figure 4.4) to evaluate the effectiveness of a classroom intervention for improving self-regulation and science achievement in high school students (Labuhn et al., 2008a, 2008b). Seven classes from a single school were randomly assigned to a training condition (four classes) or a control group (three classes). To control for confounding influences that might affect students' self-regulatory and knowledge development, the authors demonstrated that the groups were comparable across age, gender, migration background, and verbal competencies. All students from both the training and control groups received an identical set of eight lessons occurring over a three-week period. The lesson unit on the topic of nutrition was developed in collaboration with a group of science teachers. While all participating teachers received training on the instructional lessons prior to the intervention, only teachers in the experimental condition additionally received training on integrating self-regulation instruction and content instruction.

To examine the short-term and maintenance effects of this intervention, students' content knowledge and self-regulatory competencies were assessed at posttest and at six-month follow-up. The self-regulation measure (Perels, Gürtler, & Schmitz, 2005) was administered at pretest to serve as a control for initial group differences. The content knowledge measure was

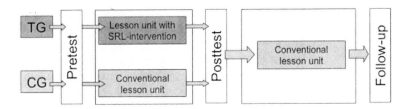

Figure 4.4 Research design used as part of the SRL classroom intervention. TG = Treatment group; CG = Control group.

a criterion-referenced test consisting of twelve multiple-choice questions and a cloze procedure, developed in collaboration with the science teachers. Transfer effects were examined during a subsequent unit that did not involve self-regulatory instruction. This lesson involved decision-making regarding socioscientific issues and did not relate to the nutrition unit (for more information about this topic, see Eggert & Bögeholz, 2010). The content knowledge test for this transfer unit was also co-constructed by science teachers and researchers.

Data Analysis and Results

The authors examined the short-term, maintenance, and transfer effects of the classroom intervention on student achievement and self-regulatory processes. Students who participated in the intervention improved their self-regulatory skills significantly from pretest to posttest, whereas students from the control group did not. These observed changes were stable over a period of six months.

The authors also examined whether the treatment and control groups differed in achievement or content knowledge at posttest and at six months follow-up on the nutrition unit. In contrast to the observed changes in self-regulation processes, there was no significant difference in content knowledge between training and control groups at posttest. However, the trained students showed significantly greater knowledge than the control group at follow up. This latter finding is compelling because it suggests that students from the SRL training group were better able to remember the material from the nutrition unit several months following the intervention than the controls. Although speculative, one may surmise that because students in the training group learned about the science content while engaging in multiple iterations of the self-regulatory cycle, they processed the information in a more meaningful way and therefore exhibited better long-term recall.

Finally, the authors examined whether students' acquisition of self-regulatory skills transferred to a different science lesson unit on decision-making on socioscientific issues. Students in the training group showed better results on a knowledge test following this unit than the control group. The authors reasoned that these results may have occurred because students from the SRL training group had intensive training in flexibly using strategies to address course content demands and thus may have applied these strategies and regulatory processes to the new content area.

Collectively, the results from this study suggest that a relatively brief intervention implemented within a regular classroom environment can promote sustainable improvements in students' use of regulatory processes and academic achievement. The key instructional factor was immersing students in a continuous cycle of regulatory thought and action across all science activities and tasks that they were expected to perform.

SREP: A Small Group/Individualized SRL Intervention

Methodology and Design

The SREP has been implemented in secondary school contexts, with recent studies targeting academically at-risk students enrolled at an urban school (Cleary & Platten, in press; Cleary et al., 2008). The basic objective of these initial case studies was to administer SREP to a group of ethnically diverse adolescents who displayed adequate science skills and prior achievement but who were failing or near failing science in their first year of high school. Students were also eligible to participate in the intervention studies if their high school teachers expressed concerns regarding their motivation and regulatory behaviors (homework completion and quality, interest, engagement) as measured by informal teacher ratings. Students who exhibited poor school attendance or who were diagnosed with a learning disability were not eligible to participate in these studies.

The authors used a mixed model research approach involving case studies embedded in a pretest-posttest design (Butler, 1998). As recommended by case study researchers, multiple assessment tools (e.g., self-report scales, teacher rating scales, self-regulated learning [SRL] microanalytic interview protocols, and field note observations) were used to evaluate changes in student motivation and self-regulation (Butler, 2011; Creswell, 2007). Such an approach allows researchers to establish convergence of data, thereby increasing the appropriateness of inferences made regarding students' self-regulation processes and how such processes may have impacted science achievement (Butler, 2011).

Although a case study design limits the extent to which one can draw causal inferences about intervention effectiveness, researchers have argued that internal validity of case research designs can be enhanced through various analytic tactics, such as pattern matching, explanation building, and addressing rival explanations (Creswell, 2007; Yin, 2009). As a result, Cleary and colleagues used several tactics to rule out maturational and historical factors and employed Zimmerman's three-phase cyclical model as the basis for explaining and understanding how changes in students' self-perceptions and strategic behaviors related to changes in their overall science achievement (see Cleary & Platten, in press; Cleary et al., 2008).

Data Analysis and Results

Cleary and colleagues have examined changes in students' achievement in biology exams, motivation beliefs, and regulatory behaviors following SREP (Cleary & Platten, in press; Cleary et al., 2008). In terms of achievement, the authors descriptively examined differences between the participants' pretest average biology exam scores to their average exam performance during the intervention. In order to establish normative based scores, the authors used classroom test average as a benchmark to evaluate the growth of students' exam scores. In general, in these studies, all participants showed an increase in exam performance, with an average z-score gain approximating .50. On a more practical level, although seven of the nine participants exhibited below average pretest exam scores (typically ranging from C– to D), five of those seven students surpassed the classroom average exam score during the intervention. Furthermore, Cleary et al. (2008) showed that on the biology final exam, which was administered about a month after SREP ended, four out of five students surpassed the class final exam average of 84, with two of the students earning 93 and 95, respectively.

In terms of evaluating changes in self-regulation processes, Cleary et al. (2008) and Cleary and Platten (in press) utilized a variety of assessment tools, including self-report scales, teacher rating scales, field note observations, work products, and structured microanalytic interviews. Student self-report data reflected student perceptions of their use of self-regulation strategies when studying or completing homework whereas teachers provided ratings of students' regulatory behaviors in the classroom. The self-report and teacher rating scales were quantitative in nature and were administered at both pretest and posttest. Pretest-posttest changes were evaluated using reliability change index (RCI; Jacobson, Follette, & Revenstorf, 1984). To supplement these traditional forms of assessment, the authors gathered qualitative data about students' regulatory behaviors and cognitions using field note observations, student work products, and microanalytic interviews during SREP sessions (Cleary, 2011; Cleary et al., 2008).

Although several important findings and implications emerged from these studies, a key point of emphasis was that using a multi-dimensional assessment approach allowed the researchers to obtain a more robust account of changes in students' regulatory and strategic behaviors and cognition. For example, Cleary et al. (2008) found statistically significant pretest-posttest changes across a self-report measure of strategy use and teacher ratings. Based on these findings one can accurately conclude that students' and teachers' global perceptions of student regulatory behaviors and engagement showed significant changes from pretest to posttest. However, can one reasonably infer that students actually used specific strategies in real time to deal with challenging content or environmental challenges when studying? Furthermore, does the use of self-report surveys and teacher rating scales adequately capture the essence of the dynamic, cyclical phase process of self-regulation as depicted by Zimmerman (2000)?

From our perspective, observations and other event forms of measurement, such as SRL microanalysis, are critical supplements to the more traditional measures of self-regulation. SRL microanalytic protocols are structured interviews that involve asking students to respond to contextualized questions targeting the different processes within the cyclical phase model as they perform a particular task or are placed in a specific academic situation (Cleary, 2011). In the SREP studies, the authors used reflection-phase microanalytic questions to examine students' attributions and adaptive inferences following each biology exam. Cleary et al. (2008) provided examples of students' self-initiated and proactive use of strategies and linked changes in these strategic behaviors to changes in actual exam performance. Cleary et al. (2008) noted,

> For example, after learning how to create general categories or summarizing questions as part of a concept map during a SREP session, Jamal spontaneously developed a series of questions that he perceived might appear on the next biology test when studying at home the following day. He proceeded to bring these questions into the subsequent SREP session to present to the group. Interestingly, SRC field notes revealed that Jamal's test performance following this self-initiated use of test question generation was the highest he had attained during the entire program. (pp. 93–94)

These latter observations are particularly important because they are consistent with a key premise of the cyclical feedback loop; that is, self-regulation is a proactive, self-initiated process whereby students adapt, modify, and supplement their repertoire of strategies to attain personal goals (Zimmerman, 2000). It is important to note that Jamal's decision to bring in his supplemental strategy of generating test questions sparked a reflective discussion with other SREP group members as a potential strategy for them to use for subsequent exams.

Field note observations and SRL microanalytic protocols were also used to demonstrate the cyclical relationship among self-reflection phase processes as predicted in Zimmerman's three-phase feedback model (Cleary & Platten, in press; Cleary et al., 2008). For example, based on the use of the results generated from a microanalytic protocol administered during the self-reflection module, one participant conveyed that her poor time management and organization skills were the key causal factors of her poor exam performance (attributions) (Cleary et al., 2008). This student subsequently revealed that she needed to change how much time she devoted to all parts of the study guide and to more carefully manage the time demands expected from her family (adaptive inferences). These metacognitive reactions were highly consistent with the student's subsequent behaviors and the strategies that she discussed with the SREP tutor prior to subsequent exams (Cleary et al., 2008). In short, attempting to capture shifts in students' strategic and regulatory processes as they occur *during* an intervention or during authentic tasks is a powerful way to supplement data generated from assessment tools administered at pretest and posttest, such as teacher and parent ratings and self-report scales.

IMPLICATIONS AND FUTURE RESEARCH DIRECTIONS

The primary objective of this chapter was to illustrate the application of Zimmerman's (2000) three-phase cyclical model as manifested in two science-based self-regulation interventions. Given that emergent service delivery models in education, such as response-to-intervention (RTI), stress the need for theoretically grounded and empirically-supported intervention programs that can be applied at both the classroom and individual level (Marston, 2005; Tilly, 2008), we have shown Zimmerman's model to be quite relevant to this objective, particularly as it relates to self-regulation embedded instruction in science contexts. The importance of the interventions presented in this chapter is also underscored given the recent data emerging from survey studies that educators and school-based practitioners expressed a strong need for professional development training in motivation and self-regulation interventions (Cleary et al., 2010; Cleary & Zimmerman, 2006; Wehmeyer et al., 2000).

Although more research is clearly needed to establish the SRL classroom intervention and the SREP as empirically-supported approaches in science contexts, these interventions show great promise. From our perspective, the most appealing aspect of these programs is their attempt to train students to think and act in cyclical, regulated ways as they learn science content. Across multiple domains, experimental research has shown that multiphase training in self-regulatory processes is more beneficial than single phase or no self-regulatory training (Cleary et al., 2006; Reid & Borkowski, 1987; Zimmerman & Kitsantas, 1997, 2002). In addition, although many applied intervention researchers do not all specifically reference Zimmerman's three-phase model as the key theoretical framework for their self-regulation interventions, the large majority of them emphasize training in multiple phase processes (Butler, 1998; Graham & Harris, 2005).

Another important issue for both practitioners and researchers is to not assume that transfer will spontaneously occur following an intervention. Pressley et al. (1990) indicated that transfer of self-regulated learning depends primarily on three factors: knowledge of self-regulation, confidence about using self-regulatory thinking, and skill in adapting the use of self-regulatory processes to a given situation. With regard to the latter point, researchers have shown that students with learning disabilities who received self-control and attributional training exhibited greater maintenance and generalizability of strategy use than single phase training and control conditions (Borkowski et al., 1988; Reid & Borkowski, 1987). More recently, Fuchs, Fuchs, Prentice, Burch, Hamlett, Owen, Hosp, and Jancek (2003) showed that in order to enhance the likelihood that students will transfer self-regulatory skills across academic contexts, teachers explicitly taught students abstraction and metacognitive strategies to analyze new problems, such as making connections to familiar problem structures. From our perspective, it would be interesting for researchers to examine whether training students to think and act in a complete cyclical loop, relative to single phase or two phase training, increases the quality and depth of transfer that occurs. It seems reasonable to hypothesize that students who receive training in the complete cyclical loop will likely be better able to flexibly and consistently apply their skills across multiple content areas.

It is important for self-regulation researchers to not only examine shifts in achievement and self-regulation, but to also consider the social validity of these interventions and the outcomes that they produce. Social validity has been described as a type of consumer satisfaction that involves three primary components: (a) social significance of goals, (b) social importance of outcomes, and (c) social acceptability of intervention procedures (Gresham & Lopez, 1996; Wolf, 1978). Although Labuhn and colleagues did not directly measure social validity in their studies, they noted that even though teaching self-regulatory processes during the lessons seemed to reduce the time available for the actual presentation of content knowledge, it did not take away time from students' actual learning. In addition, although students who participated in the SRL classroom intervention did not display significantly higher science achievement than the control group directly after the training period, they were better able to recall the learned material at follow-up (Labuhn et al., 2008a, 2008b). Given that teachers and school professionals sometimes raise concerns about the acceptability of infusing SRL and content-based instruction, these concerns may not be justified in all situations.

Cleary et al. (2008) and Cleary and Platten (in press) directly established the social validity of the SREP in two ways. First, they established the significance of goals by engaging in collaborative conversations with the biology teacher and school administrators. Improving biology exam grades was deemed to be a socially valid goal because exam grades had the greatest impact on students' final grades, which would subsequently appear on their high school transcripts. The other two components of social validity, social importance of effects and acceptability of procedures, were examined at post-test using a parent, teacher, and student questionnaire (see Cleary et al., 2008 for an illustration of the social validity questionnaire). From our perspective, future research should seek to further evaluate the circumstances under which self-regulation interventions are most appealing, useful, and influential from the perspective of educators and the students and parents who receive these interventions. In addition, it would be of great value for researchers to examine how SRL principles can be most easily and efficiently infused into the general science curriculum in a way that allows for frequent practice of content-related and self-regulatory skills.

Finally, researchers should consider alternative research designs and assessment approaches when examining the effectiveness of self-regulation intervention programs. Although group designs, such as experimental and quasi-experimental design, are ideal for enhancing the internal validity of a study, single participant research designs and case study designs can provide a more robust account of how self-regulatory processes unfold in authentic contexts to directly impact performance outcomes. That is, examining changes in individual students can provide a better understanding for how and why self-regulatory processes enhance achievement in science contexts (Butler, 1998; Creswell, 2007; Kratochwill & Levin, 2010; Yin, 2009). Case study projects are of particular relevance and importance to school-based practitioners because of their interest in seeing how and why changes in students' regulatory thoughts and actions will impact their subsequent motivation and achievement.

With regard to the measurement models used in research, given that self-regulation is believed to be a complex, dynamic, and cyclical process, it has become increasingly clear that one should adhere to a multi-dimensional assessment approach to adequately capture this process. Although self-report surveys have clearly been the most frequently used self-regulation measure (Cleary, 2009; Winne & Perry, 2000), researchers have advocated for greater use of event measures, such as think alouds, behavioral traces, direct observations, and microanalytic approaches. These latter approaches tend to measure self-regulatory behaviors and processes as they occur in real time in authentic contexts and often do not correspond with student self-report surveys (Winne & Jamieson-Noel, 2002; Winne & Perry, 2000; Zimmerman, 2008b). Using multiple assessment tools to establish convergence or divergence of data is important, but one must realize that the source of these discrepancies can reflect differences in the measurement tools, the informants or sources of data (i.e., students, teachers), or the targeted modalities (i.e., behavior, cognition). Thus, when selecting assessment tools to use in a research study or as part of school-based evaluations, it is important to not only consider using different types of measures, but to also gather information about multiple modalities of regulatory functioning (e.g., metacognition, strategy use, motivation beliefs) from multiple sources (e.g., students, teachers, parents).

CONCLUSION

In this chapter we underscored an important component of Professor Barry Zimmerman's legacy: that is, the flexibility and applicability of his three-phase cyclical model to academic contexts. Two distinct self-regulation interventions were developed to improve the motivation, self-regulation, and science achievement of high school students. Whereas the SRL classroom intervention has been incorporated as part of classroom-wide instruction, the SREP was developed to provide intensive, individualized or small group tutoring. Regardless of the focus of these particular interventions, we showed that it is possible to help students think and act in a regulated, cyclical manner and that such training can improve the science outcomes of these students. Although more research is clearly needed to further document the effectiveness of these two interventions, they are quite promising because of their strong theoretical foundation and intuitive appeal to practitioners.

We owe a debt of gratitude to Professor Barry Zimmerman for paving the way for our intervention work with his highly accessible theories and innovative insights into human behavior. We are also deeply appreciative of having been mentored by a man who has dedicated his personal and professional life to one of quality, genuineness, and integrity. He was clearly an exemplary model who has forever changed our lives.

REFERENCES

Ames, C. (1992). Classrooms: Goals, structures, and student motivation. *Journal of Educational Psychology, 84*(3), 261–271. doi:10.1037/0022-0663.84.3.261

Bandura, A. (1986). *Social foundations of thoughts and action: A social cognitive theory.* Englewood Cliffs, NJ: Prentice Hall.

Bandura, A. (1997). *Self-efficacy: The exercise of control.* New York, NY: Erlbaum.

Bong, M. (2005). Within-grade changes in Korean girls' motivation and perceptions of the learning environment across domains and achievement levels. *Journal of Educational Psychology, 97*(4), 656–672. doi:10.1037/0022-0663.97.4.656

Bonner, S., Zimmerman, B. J., Evans, D., Irigoyen, M., Resnick, D., & Mellins, R. D. (2002). An individualized intervention to improve asthma management among urban Latino and African-American families. *Journal of Asthma, 39*(2),167–179. doi:10.1081/JAS-120002198

Borkowski, J. G., Weyhing, R. S., & Carr, M. (1988). Effects of attributional retraining on strategy-based reading comprehension in learning-disabled students. *Journal of Educational Psychology, 80*(1), 46–53. doi:10.1037/0022-0663.80.1.46

Butler, D. (1998). The strategic content learning approach to promoting self-regulated learning: A report of three studies. *Journal of Educational Psychology, 90,* 682–697. doi:10.1037/0022-0663.90.4.682

Butler, D. (2011). Investigating self-regulated learning using in-depth case studies. In B. J. Zimmerman & D. H. Schunk (Eds.), *Handbook of Self-Regulation of Learning and Performance* (pp. 346–360). New York, NY: Routledge.

Cleary, T. J. (2009). School-based motivation and self-regulation assessments: An examination of school psychologists beliefs and practices. *Journal of Applied School Psychology, 25*(1), 71–94. doi:10.1080/15377900802484190

Cleary T. J. (2011). Emergence of self-regulated learning microanalysis: Historical overview, essential features, and implications for research and practice. In B.

J. Zimmerman & D. H. Schunk (Eds.), *Handbook of Self-Regulation of Learning and Performance* (pp. 329–345). New York, NY: Routledge.

Cleary, T. J. & Chen, P. (2009). Self-regulation, motivation, and math achievement in middle school: Variations across grade level and math context. *Journal of School Psychology, 47*(5), 291–314. doi:10.1016/j.jsp.2009.04.002

Cleary, T. J., Gubi, A., & Prescott, M. V. (2010). Motivation and self-regulation assessments: Professional practices and needs of school psychologists. *Psychology in the Schools, 47*(10), 985–1002. doi:10.1002/pits.20519

Cleary, T. J., & Platten, P. (in press). Examining the correspondence between self-regulated learning and academic achievement: A case study analysis. *Education Research International.*

Cleary, T. J., Platten, P., & Nelson, A. (2008). Effectiveness of the self-regulation empowerment program (SREP) with urban high school youth: An initial investigation. *Journal of Advanced Academics, 20,* 70–107.

Cleary, T. J. & Zimmerman, B. J. (2001). Self-regulation differences during athletic practice by experts, non-experts, and novices. *Journal of Applied Sport Psychology, 13*(2), 185–206. doi:10.1080/104132001753149883

Cleary, T. J. & Zimmerman, B. J. (2004). Self-regulation empowerment program: A school-based program to enhance self-regulated and self-motivated cycles of student learning. *Psychology in the Schools, 41*(5), 537–550. doi:10.1002/pits.10177

Cleary, T. J. & Zimmerman, B. J. (2006). Teachers' perceived usefulness of strategy microanalytic assessment information. *Psychology in the Schools, 43*(2), 149–155. doi:10.1002/pits.20141

Cleary, T. J., Zimmerman, B. J., & Keating, T. (2006). Training physical education students to self-regulate during basketball free-throw practice. *Research Quarterly for Exercise and Sport, 77,* 251–262.

Clifford, M. M. (1986). The effects of ability, strategy, and effort attributions for educational, business, and athletic failure. *British Journal of Educational Psychology, 56*(2), 169–179. doi:10.1111/j.2044-8279.1986.tb02658.x

Coalition for Psychology in Schools and Education. (2006). *Report on the teacher needs survey.* Washington, DC: American Psychological Association, Center for Psychology in Schools and Education. Retrieved from http://www.apa.org/ed/schools/coalition/teachers-needs.pdf

Creswell, J. W. (2007). *Qualitative inquiry and research design: Choosing among five approaches* (2nd ed.). Thousand Oaks, CA; Sage Publications.

De Corte, E., Mason, L., Depaepe, F., & Verschaffel, L. (2011). Self-regulation of mathematical knowledge and skills. In B. J. Zimmerman & D. H. Schunk (Eds.), *Handbook of Self-Regulation of Learning and Performance* (pp. 155–172). New York, NY: Routledge.

DiBenedetto, M. K. & Zimmerman, B. J. (2010). Differences in self-regulatory processes among students studying science: A microanalytic investigation. *The International Journal of Educational and Psychological Assessment, 5,* 2–24.

DiPerna, J. C., Volpe, R. J., & Elliot, S. N. (2002). Promoting academic enablers to improve student achievement: An introduction to the mini-series. *School Psychology Review, 31*(3), 293–297.

Eccles, J. S. & Wigfield, A. (2002). Motivational beliefs, values, and goals. *Annual Review of Psychology, 53*(1), 109–132. doi: 10.1146/annurev.psych.53.100901.135153

Eggert, S. & Bögeholz, S. (2010). Students' use of decision making strategies with regard to socioscientific issues—an application of the Rasch partial credit model. *Science Education, 94,* 230–258.

Ericsson, K. A. & Charness, N. (1994). Expert performance: Its structure and acquisition. *American Psychologist, 49*(8), 725–747. doi:10.1037/0003-066x.49.8.725

Fuchs, L. S., Fuchs, D., Prentice, K., Burch, M., Hamlett, C. L., Owen, R., . . . Jancek, D. (2003). Explicitly teaching for transfer: Effects on third-grade students' mathematical problem solving. *Journal of Educational Psychology, 95*(2), 293–304. doi: 10.1037/0022-0663.95.2.293

Fuchs, L. S., Fuchs, D., Prentice, K., Burch, M., Hamlett, C. L., Owen, R., & Schroeter, K. (2003). Enhancing third-grade students' mathematical problem solving with self-regulated learning strategies. *Journal of Educational Psychology, 95*(2), 306–315. doi:10.1037/0022-0663.95.2.306

Graham, S., & Harris, K. R. (2005). *Writing better: Effective strategies for teaching students with learning difficulties.* Baltimore, MD: Brookes. doi:10.1080/19404150509546791

Gresham, F. M. & Lopez, M. F. (1996). Social validation: A unifying concept for school-based consultation research and practice. *School Psychology Quarterly, 11*(3), 204–227. doi:10.1037/h0088930

Grigal, M., Neubart, D. A., Moon, S. M., & Graham, S. (2003). Self-determination for students with disabilities: Views of parents and teachers. *Exceptional Children, 70,* 97–112. Retrieved from http://cec.metapress.com/content/mg85l508408w/?p=2e0e81ddcbda4f4cb32eb1e24fdeaf19&pi=34

Guthrie, J. T., Wigfield, A., & Perencevich, K. C. (2004). Scaffolding for motivation and engagement in reading. In J. T. Guthrie, A. Wigfield, & K. C. Perencevich (Eds.), *Motivating reading comprehension: Concept-oriented reading instruction* (pp. 55–86). Mahwah, NJ: Lawrence Erlbaum Associates Publishers.

Hadwin, A. F., Winne, P. H., Stockley, D. B., Nesbit, J. C., & Woszczyna, C. (2001). Context moderates students' self-reports about how they study. *Journal of Educational Psychology, 93,* 477–487. doi:10.1037//0022-0663.93.3.477

Jacobson, N. S., Follette, W. C., & Revenstorf, D. (1984). Psychotherapy outcome research: Methods for reporting variability and evaluating clinical significance. *Behavior Therapy, 15(4),* 336–352. doi:10.1016/S0005-7894(84)80002-7

Kratochwill, T. R. & Levin, J. R. (2010). Enhancing the scientific credibility of single-case intervention research: Randomization to the rescue. *Psychological Methods, 15,* 122–144. doi:10.1037/a0017736

Labuhn, A. S., Bögeholz, S., & Hasselhorn, M. (2008a). Lernförderung durch Anregung der Selbstregulation im naturwissenschaftlichen Unterricht [Promoting learning through a classroom based intervention in science education]. *Zeitschrift für Pädagogische Psychologie, 22,* 13–24. doi:10.1024/1010-0652.22.1.13

Labuhn, A. S., Bögeholz, S., & Hasselhorn, M. (2008b). Selbstregulationsförderung in einer Biologie-Unterrichtseinheit–langfristige und differentielle Wirksamkeit [Long-term and differential effects of a classroom based intervention to promote self-regulated learning in science education]. *Zeitschrift für Entwicklungspsychologie und Pädagogische Psychologie, 40,* 167–178. doi:10.1026/0049-8637.40.4.167

Marston, D. (2005). Tiers of intervention in responsiveness to intervention: Prevention outcomes and learning disabilities identification patterns. *Journal of Learning Disabilities, 38*, 539–544. doi:10.1177/00222194050380061001

McPherson, G. A. & Zimmerman, B. J. (2002). Self-regulation of musical learning: A social cognitive perspective. In R. Colwell & C. Richardson (Eds.), *The new handbook of research on music teaching learning* (pp. 327–347). New York, NY: Oxford University Press.

Millar, R. & Osborne, J. F. (Eds.). (1998). *Beyond 2000: Science education for the future.* London: King's College London.

Organisation for Economic Co-operation and Development (OECD). (2003). *The PISA 2003 assessment framework. Mathematics, reading, science and problem solving knowledge and skills.* Paris: Author.

Perels, F., Gürtler, T., & Schmitz, B. (2005). Training of self-regulatory and problem-solving competence. *Learning and Instruction, 15*, 123–139. doi:10.1016/j.learninstruc.2005.04.010

Peters, E. E. & Kitsantas, A. (2010). Self-regulation of student epistemic thinking in science: The role of metacognitive prompts. *Educational Psychology, 30*(1), 27–52. doi:10.1080/01443410903353294

Pintrich, P. R. (2000). The role of goal orientation in self-regulated learning. In M. Boekaerts, P. R. Pintrich, & M. Zeidner (Eds.), *Handbook of self-regulation* (pp. 451–502). San Diego, CA: Academic Press. doi:10.1016/B978-012109890-2/50043-3

Pressley, M., Woloshyn, V., Lysynchuk, L. M., Martin, V., Wood, E., & Willoughby, T. (1990). A primer of research on cognitive strategy instruction: The important issues and how to address them. *Educational Psychology Review, 2*, 1–58. doi:10.1007/BF01323528

Reid, M. K. & Borkowski, J. G. (1987). Causal attributions of hyperactive children: Implications for teaching strategies and self-control. *Journal of Educational Psychology, 79*(3), 296–307. doi:10.1037/0022-0663.79.3.296

Schraw, G., Crippen, K. J., & Hartley, K. (2006). Promoting self-regulation in science education: metacognition as part of a broader perspective on learning. *Research in Science Education, 36*, 111–139. doi:10.1007/s11165-005-3917-8

Schunk, D. H., Pintrich, P. R., & Meece, J. L. (2008). *Motivation in education: Theory, research, and applications* (3rd ed.). Upper Saddle River, NJ: Pearson Prentice Hall.

Schunk, D. H. & Swartz, C. W. (1993). Goals and progress feedback: Effects on self-efficacy and writing achievement. *Contemporary Educational Psychology, 18*(3), 337–354. doi:10.1006/ceps.1993.1024

Sinatra, G. M. & Taasoobshirazi, G. (2011). Intentional conceptual change. The self-regulation of science. In B. J. Zimmerman & D. H. Schunk (Eds.), *Handbook of Self-Regulation of Learning and Performance* (pp. 203–216). New York, NY: Routledge.

Tilly, W. D. (2008). The evolution of school psychology to science-based practice: Problem-solving and the three-tiered model. In A. Thomas & J. Grimes (Eds.), *Best Practices in School Psychology* (5th ed.). Bethesda, MD: National Assocation of School Psychologists.

Wehmeyer, M. L., Agran, M., & Hughes, C. A (2000). National survey of teachers' promotion of self-determination and student-directed learning. *The Journal of Special Education, 34*, 58–68. doi:10.1177/002246690003400201

Weiner, B. (1986). *An attributional theory of motivation and emotion.* New York, NY: Springer Verlag.

Winne, P. H. & Hadwin, A. F. (1998). Studying as self-regulated learning. In D. J. Hacker, J. Dunlosky, & A. C. Graesser (Eds.), *Metacognition in educational theory and practice* (pp. 279–306). Hillsdale, NJ: Erlbaum.

Winne, P. H. & Jamieson-Noel, D. L. (2002). Exploring students' calibration of self-reports about study tactics and achievement. *Contemporary Educational Psychology, 28*, 259–276. doi:10.1016/S0361-476X(02)00006-1

Winne, P. H. & Perry, N. E. (2000). Measuring self-regulated learning. In M. Boekaerts, P. R. Pintrich & M. Zeidner (Eds.), *Handbook of self-regulation.* (pp. 531–566). San Diego, CA US: Academic Press.

Wolf, M. M. (1978). Social validity: The case for subjective measurement or how applied behavior analysis is finding its heart. *Journal of Applied Behavior Analysis, 11*(2), 203–214. doi:10.1901/jaba.1978.11-203

Wolters, C. A. (2003). Regulation of motivation: Evaluating an underemphasized aspect of self-regulated learning. *Educational Psychologist, 38*(4), 189–205. doi:10.1207/S15326985EP3804_1

Yin, R. K. (2009). *Case study research design and methods* (4th ed.). Thousand Oaks, CA; Sage Publications.

Zimmerman, B. J. (1989). A social-cognitive view of self-regulated academic learning. *Journal of Educational Psychology, 81(3)*, 329–339. doi:10.1037/0022-0663.81.3.329

Zimmerman, B. J. (2000). Attaining self-regulation: A social cognitive perspective. In M. Boekaerts, P. R. Pintrich & M. Zeidner (Eds.), *Handbook of self-regulation* (pp. 13–39). San Diego, CA: Academic Press.

Zimmerman, B. J. (2008a). Goal setting: A key proactive source of academic self-regulation. In D. H. Schunk & B. J. Zimmerman (Eds.), *Motivation and self-regulated learning: Theory, research, and applications.* (pp. 267–295). Mahwah, NJ: Lawrence Erlbaum Associates Publishers.

Zimmerman, B. J. (2008b). Investigating self-regulation and motivation: Historical background, methodological developments, and future prospects. *American Educational Research Journal, 45*(1), 166–183. doi:10.3102/0002831207312909

Zimmerman, B. J., Bandura, A., & Martinez-Pons, M. (1992). Self-motivation for academic attainment: The role of self-efficacy beliefs and personal goal setting. *American Educational Research Journal, 29*, 663–676. doi:10.3102/00028312029003663

Zimmerman, B. J. & Kitsantas, A. (1996). Self-regulated learning of a motoric skill: The role of goal setting and self-monitoring. *Journal of Applied Sport Psychology, 8*, 69–84. doi:10.1080/10413209608406308

Zimmerman, B. J. & Kitsantas, A. (1997). Developmental phases in self-regulation: Shifting from process goals to outcome goals. *Journal of Educational Psychology, 89*(1), 29–36. doi:10.1037/0022-0663.89.1.29

Zimmerman, B. J. & Kitsantas, A. (2002). Acquiring writing revision and self-regulatory skill through observation and emulation. *Journal of Educational Psychology, 94*(4), 660–668. doi:10.1037/0022-0663.94.4.660

Zimmerman, B. J. & Schunk, D. H. (2001). *Self-regulated learning and academic achievement: Theory, research, and practice.* New York, NY: Springer-Verlag Publishing.

Zimmerman, B. J. & Schunk, D. H. (2011). *Handbook of self-regulation of learning and performance.* New York, NY: Routledge.

CHAPTER 5

CYCLICAL FEEDBACK APPROACHES FOR ENHANCING ACADEMIC SELF-REGULATION IN POSTSECONDARY MATHEMATICS CLASSROOMS

Adam Moylan

A highly important and recurring dilemma for postsecondary education in the United States concerns the widespread remedial education needs of students attempting to attain college-level competency in core academic areas such as mathematics. The significance of finding effective ways to assist the many students who struggle to attain college-level competence in mathematics or other basic skills cannot be understated, and has become a major policy issue for the preparation of the workforce for careers in science, technology, engineering, and mathematics (STEM) professions (e.g., President's Council of Advisors on Science and Technology, 2012). Developmental education is a field grounded in developmental psychology and learning theories that encompasses research and practice intend-

Applications of Self-Regulated Learning across Diverse Disciplines, pages 125–152
Copyright © 2013 by Information Age Publishing
All rights of reproduction in any form reserved.

ed to foster the academic skill development in students through a variety of means, including coursework, tutoring, and counseling/advisement (Boylan, 1999; National Association for Developmental Education, 2012). The skills that are deemed necessary to succeed in higher education are broad and include consideration of students' cognitive, motivational, and affective development.

One specific problem area in developmental education concerns the large numbers of students who find themselves repeating the developmental coursework that serves as a gateway to further study, and the increased motivational and financial costs associated with the delays lead to major problems in postsecondary achievement and persistence. Students who enter college with the poorest math skills have been found to be at the greatest risk for not achieving successful remediation (Bahr, 2008). When faced with repeated occurrences of failed attempts to attain sufficient levels of competence in mathematics, students' self-efficacy (Bandura, 1997) can be lowered, and thus have a negative motivational impact on their academic persistence and choices in pursuit of an education (Pajares, 1996; Zimmerman, 1995). In addition, financial costs can escalate for students as they retake remedial and lower level courses and extend the amount of time it takes to complete what is designed to be a two- or four-year degree. Increased educational loans and delays in entering the workforce or in attaining higher levels of income can be major burdens and obstacles in the pursuit of a postsecondary degree.

These issues in developmental education have been faced by community colleges and other postsecondary institutions for decades (Tinto, 1998). However, with the recent surges in community college enrollment due to economic recession there is increased pressure to develop appropriate solutions (Taylor, Fry, Wang, Dockterman, & Velasco, 2009). The good news is that when students in developmental education do attain college-level competencies, long-term indicators of achievement, such as graduation or transfer, are equal to their peers in non-developmental education. Yet, the bad news is that effective remediation programs are often not available to or utilized by a large majority of students (Bahr, 2008).

The difficulties experienced by many developmental education students can be viewed, in part, as problems in self-regulation. Self-regulation is a key component of effective mathematics learning and adaptive mathematical competence (De Corte, Mason, Depaepe, & Verschaffel, 2011). In particular, many students who repeatedly experience failed attempts often are stuck in reactive or maladaptive cycles of self-regulatory thought and action. These problems in regulation result in students not being able to systematically adapt and improve their learning or performance efforts. By not having the motivation and/or skills to take personal responsibility for learning or performance, academically at-risk learners tend to focus primarily on the outcomes of their efforts, which typically results in reactive or maladaptive approaches to undesirable progress (Zimmerman, 2005).

Self-regulated learning has been described as a cyclical feedback process (Zimmerman, 2000), whereby learners acquire feedback about the implementation of learning methods and outcomes to reflect on goal progress and to inform decisions about subsequent planning for learning. Zimmerman's (2000) model of self-regulation involves three cyclical phases:

(a) *forethought phase*, which encompasses motivational beliefs and task-analysis processes that precede efforts to perform, learn or problem solve;

(b) *performance phase*, which entails self-observation (i.e., metacognitive monitoring, self-recording) and self-control processes (i.e., self-instruction, attention focusing, task strategies); and

(c) *self-reflection phase*, which involves self-judgments and self-reactions after attempts to learn, problem solve, or perform.

An underlying component of this cyclical model is the central role that feedback plays in enabling students to effectively self-regulate their learning (Hattie & Timperley, 2007). As defined by Hattie and Timperley (2007), feedback is broadly conceived as information about performance or understanding provided by external sources (e.g., teacher, peer, book) and/or internal sources (e.g., self, experience). Effective feedback helps learners plan, monitor, and reflect on their learning and performance efforts. In the classroom, support for learners can involve providing feedback to help them: (1) *prepare* for educational endeavors, (2) *monitor* their efforts during such endeavors, and (3) *self-reflect* after such endeavors. Although feedback is an extremely important aspect of learning and can have a strong positive influence on it, learners often do not inherently recognize its value. Factors having to do with the nature of tasks, the context in which they are embedded, and personal characteristics of the learners can mediate the effectiveness of feedback (Shute, 2008). Learners who actively seek and use feedback to their advantage are empowered to advance in their academic pursuits (or other learning or performance efforts), while learners who do not actively engage with or avoid feedback on their learning and performance efforts tend to struggle in their achievements and have diminished self-efficacy, task interest, and self-satisfaction (Zimmerman, 2000). The self-regulatory intervention highlighted in this chapter focused specifically on providing different forms of feedback in order to help struggling students re-conceptualize how they interpret and perceive academic errors (Zimmerman & Moylan, 2009; Zimmerman & Schunk, 2008).

A learner can derive feedback from multiple social sources, including from teachers and peers, as well as from classroom assessments or their own monitoring or assessment of performance (Hattie & Timperley, 2007). Errors during learning or performance are an important source of feedback about progress and the effectiveness of one's approaches to the task. Yet the educational value of attending to and learning from one's mistakes is commonly overlooked or underappreciated by many students and teachers (Hattie & Timperley, 2007). In fact, students often need effective feedback to prevent them from engaging in maladaptive self-evaluation and self-reflection. For example, for many struggling learners, there is a tendency to attribute the cause for errors and poor achievement to a stable lack of ability or a fixed trait or perhaps to external factors in the educational environment that are difficult to control. These types of attributions are problematic because they tend to be resistant to change and are not under the student's control. Such situations can undermine students' motivation because they often lead to inaction, a lack of effort, or avoidance of the task (Zimmerman, 2011). Effective feedback should help these students to attribute their failures or struggles to their level of effort or their choice or implementation of strategies (e.g., Schunk & Cox, 1986). This type of feedback pertains to the process of problem solving or learning, whereas progress feedback informs about the correctness of approaches to problem solving or learning. Feedback that conveys progress in performing or learning a task indicates to the student a personal capability for learning, which increases their self-efficacy (Schunk, 1989). When students are encouraged to think about performance in terms of behaviors that they can control, they will become more empowered to identify or learn new strategies or to adapt their use of current strategies. Proactive engagement in feedback cycles can thus bring a learner to systematically and progressively greater levels of achievement.

In this chapter, I describe a self-regulatory intervention developed to help academically at-risk college-level learners improve their achievement and basic competencies at the postsecondary level (Zimmerman & Moylan, 2009; Zimmerman, Moylan, Hudesman, White, & Flugman, 2011). This intervention was based on Zimmerman's three-phase feedback model of self-regulation. Highlighted in this chapter are: (1) the essential components and features of the self-regulation intervention, particularly as it pertains to the provision of frequent feedback and instruction in self-reflective error analysis; and (2) how the distinguished theoretical and research work of Barry Zimmerman can be applied to help address particularly vexing learning or motivation challenges in developmental education contexts. In addition, consideration of potential future research in self-regulatory interventions will be shared to conclude the chapter.

INTERNAL SOURCES FOR POOR AND REACTIVE
ACADEMIC SELF-REGULATION

Being underprepared at the postsecondary level typically involves deficits in domain-based knowledge and skills as well as problems in self-regulation or management. Common problems in self-regulation include the following:

- *Insufficient metacognitive awareness about one's own competence at a specific task.* Students who struggle academically tend to overestimate their knowledge and skills, which can lead to insufficient effort or a distorted sense of how they need to try to succeed, such as the amount or quality of study preparation enacted for an upcoming test.
- *Erroneous judgments about one's learning efforts.* Poor self-regulators frequently are inaccurate in their self-perceptions of their approaches to learning, such as their use of strategies.
- *Maladaptive attributions to uncontrollable, external sources, and or fixed personal traits.* Rather than adaptively attributing one's mistakes to specific choices or implementations of strategies, which can be improved in subsequent attempts to learn, poor self-regulators exhibit a tendency to attribute errors to factors that they have less control over, such as the actions of others or placing blame on a permanent lack of ability.
- *Inefficient use of errors to adapt learning or performance strategies.* Despite receiving feedback about gaps in learning and performance, struggling students can often continue to make the same mistakes. These students fail to improve their use of strategies or select ones that are more effective.

Concerns are widespread in developmental education about the prevalent, and sometimes severe, gaps between self-perceptions and actual competence among learners struggling to achieve academically. The correspondence between these self-perceptions and actual behavior is described in the literature as calibration (Yates, 1990), and is an issue that has received considerable attention in education (Bol & Hacker, 2001; Hacker, Bol, & Bahbahani, 2008; Pieschl, 2009; Ramdass & Zimmerman, 2011b; Winne & Jamieson-Noel, 2002). Optimistic self-perceptions are instrumental to successful endeavors; however, excessively inaccurate self-perceptions can hinder the strategic, flexible use of feedback (Schunk & Pajares, 2004), as well as performance (Bandura, 1997). Problems in calibration are a pervasive issue among learners of all ages and across diverse educational contexts (Dunning, 2004). The tendency for learners is to be overconfident (Pajares & Miller, 1994), and overconfidence has been found to be associated with lower performance outcomes (e.g., Bol & Hacker, 2001; Klassen, 2006). In contrast, self-regulated learners are characterized as being well-calibrated (Ramdass & Zimmerman, 2011b; Stone, 2000; Zimmerman, 1990). A dynamic interplay of both metacognitive and motivational factors is believed to influence the accuracy of self-beliefs and judgments (Ehrlinger & Mitchum, 2010; Zimmerman & Moylan, 2009). A key aspect of this chapter is to argue that the inclusion of both metacognitive and motivational processes and beliefs in Zimmerman's (2000) model of academic self-regulation provides a compelling framework for the development of strategies to enhance calibration and overall self-regulation among underprepared learners through the cyclical use of feedback. In the following section, this cyclical feedback model is delineated further.

ZIMMERMAN'S SUBPROCESSES OF PROACTIVE SELF-REGULATED LEARNING

Proactive self-regulated learners are effortful and persistent in their pursuit of goals, and skilled at acquiring and using feedback to adapt and revise their strategic planning towards increasingly challenging performance criteria (Zimmerman, 2000; Zimmerman & Moylan, 2009). Zimmerman's (2000) model of academic self-regulation is characterized as a dynamic feedback loop that involves a forethought phase, performance control phase, and a self-reflection phase. Important subprocesses are described within each cyclical self-regulation phase. The following are five subprocesses of the forethought phase that can be productive for math learners:

1. *Reviewing prior performance.* When faced with a new learning task, valuable information can be acquired by carefully considering feedback from past performances. Students can be encouraged to review their prior strategies, thoughts and affective reactions, and outcomes to help identify strengths and weaknesses to aid in setting a course of action.
2. *Conducting a task analysis.* Tasks are made more manageable by dividing the overall task into smaller steps. The process of conducting a task analysis can specify each individual step and delineate any order to those steps. Subsequently, in the performance control phase, this breakdown of the task can be used as a checklist for implementing and monitoring one's learning or performance efforts.
3. *Setting goals.* Explicitly identifying desired attainments and how they will be attained is more functional than having vague notions of what an individual wants to achieve. Goals direct one's attention towards performance and can increase levels of effort and sustain persistence over time. It is also advantageous to develop specific goals that are

challenging but reasonable. In stating learning goals, students can specify a start and end date for their practice, specific strategies to be used, and a measure and criterion for progress or success.

4. *Selecting strategies.* Self regulated learning (SRL) requires the thoughtful selection and implementation of specific strategies. When a particular strategy does not work, an effective self-regulator will use feedback to investigate whether they are properly implementing the strategy and seek alternative strategies when necessary, since particular strategies are not effective for all individuals and in all situations.

5. *Motivational beliefs.* A core contribution of the social cognitive perspective on self-regulation is the explanation of the role that motivational beliefs play in the regulation of learning and performance (Bandura, 1986, 1997). The self-efficacy and outcome expectancy beliefs that learners hold are central determinants of the goals that learners set, the choices they make, the amount of effort they exert, and the persistence they display in the face of setbacks or errors (Bandura, 1986, 1997; Pajares, 1996; Zimmerman, 1995). Self-efficacy is an expectancy belief about the level of ability one can use to reach designated levels of performance, while outcome expectancy beliefs pertain to the judgments about the likely outcomes of one's efforts (Bandura, 1997).

The performance phase of SRL involves *self-observation* and *self-control* of one's goal-directed behaviors and enactment of planned strategies from the forethought phase. Self-observation strategies include self-monitoring and self-recording, which are important in determining goal progress and systematically implementing strategies. Strategic problem solvers will self-monitor their metacognition—that is, they will observe their thinking during performance to keep themselves on track. Keeping written records of learning performance (e.g., diaries/logs, graphs, or checklists) can be an effective means of self-monitoring because it provides feedback on behaviors and progress towards process goals. These internal sources of performance feedback, as well as feedback from external sources (e.g., feedback provided by the teacher in the form of written comments or a grade on a math quiz), provide essential information that is used for self-reflection about performance and goal progress. Self-regulated learners also use a variety of ways to exert self-control over their learning and performance. These approaches include help-seeking (e.g., acquiring additional feedback from the teacher), self-instruction (e.g., self-verbalizing steps in a task or motivational self-talk), and environmental structuring strategies (e.g., choosing a quiet, comfortable location to study that is free from distractions).

Self-reflection phase processes involve self-judgments and self-reactions to one's performance. From the agentic perspective (Bandura, 1997, 2008), a critical determinant of the self-regulated use of performance information lies with the self-reflective judgments and reactions of the individual. *Self-evaluating* goal achievement and strategy use involves students determining whether they achieved their goals by comparing actual progress to desired outcomes. Students also make *attribution judgments* about the reasons for their successes or failures.

Causal attributions that learners make are important sources of motivation for self-regulated learning (Schunk, 2007), and when learners attribute the causality for outcomes to controllable, modifiable sources, they will tend to examine their choice and use of strategies to identify what works and what does not work. Certainly, it is important for students to accurately perceive the environmental constraints in which they perform and to be aware when external factors have considerable influence on one's efforts and outcomes. However, it is even more important that students feel empowered to direct and control their learning efforts.

A critical feature of the self-reflection phase of SRL involves the decisions about the maintenance or adaptation of strategies. These reflections can then inform decisions about what strategies to continue, adapt, or replace with new ones. When causal attributions are made to controllable, changeable strategies, this increases the likelihood of learners engaging in desirable adaptive cycles of self-regulation, rather than becoming stuck in cycles of repeating their errors and feeling that desired learning outcomes are beyond their control. These proactive self-regulators are therefore empowered to adapt their strategies in subsequent, cyclical attempts to achieve goals. However, as previously explained, underprepared college students in developmental education often get stuck in reactive cycles of self-regulation whereby they do not strategically adjust their efforts to learn despite receiving feedback about unwanted outcomes implying that their methods were unsuccessful. As noted earlier, such reactive learners tend to attribute the cause for undesirable outcomes to either unchangeable, stable personal limitations (i.e., fixed inability) or to external sources, such as the teacher's actions or the inherent difficulty of a particular math problem, for example. What happens in these situations is that the learner fails to make appropriate adaptations to forethought phase processes during the next self-regulatory cycle.

FEATURES AND IMPLEMENTATION OF A MATHEMATICS CLASSROOM INTERVENTION

From a self-regulatory perspective, errors can be viewed as opportunities for learning. That is, they present the learner with a source of direction or guidance for self-regulating learning. This is contrary to the way many students and teachers think about academic mistakes. For many individuals, it is more common to think of errors, especially repeated errors, as indicators of personal imperfection. It is important to recognize that errors can be analyzed to reveal different ways to achieve desired outcomes. For instance, in solving mathematics problems, the particular choice of strategy used may have increased the likelihood of making computational errors. Effective self-regulators will investigate where errors are made so that they can take corrective actions to make progress towards their goals. Academically at-risk students who gets stuck in self-regulatory cycles that do not yield academic progress show a tendency to avoid identifying and reflecting on errors. As a result, they either do not respond to errors at all or respond in maladaptive ways. This commonly encountered problem in developmental education contexts was a factor driving the design of the self-regulatory intervention program.

A self-regulatory intervention in mathematics, which was based on Zimmerman's cyclical model of self-regulation, was developed to assist academically at-risk college students to become effective strategic learners of mathematics. The program evolved over many years of development and implementation by Barry Zimmerman and an array of researchers, students, and educators and was part of a larger agenda to apply the ideas provided in the widely influential research-to-practice guide written by Zimmerman, Bonner, and Kovach (1996). The academic challenges confronting undergraduates, especially in developmental education, were viewed through the lens of Zimmerman's (2000) dynamic feedback model of academic self-regulation, and thus informed the development of the self-regulatory interventions, including how they were adapted over time in response both to an evolving understanding of the classroom contexts, and to changes in those contexts. Although this intervention program necessitated a number of features to address an array of interrelated academic issues, the core components involved a formative assessment process whereby feedback was provided to students to optimize their learning and self-reflection, rather than to emphasize the instructors' summative purposes for assessment (Shute, 2008). More specifically, there were several components of the SRL intervention that can be categorized across three broad dimensions: (a) an adaptive classroom culture, (b) instructional methodologies, and (c) a feedback system.

Creating an Adaptive Classroom Culture

An essential aspect of supporting instructional and assessment change in the classroom was to discuss self-regulation concepts and teachers' beliefs and practices. Thus, training involved explaining self-regulatory cycles in academics as well as other domains, such as health behavior change (e.g., weight management). It also involved discussing self-regulatory cycles using Zimmerman's social cognitive model of self-regulation (Zimmerman, 2000). Teachers and tutors were referred to as "SRL coaches" to highlight the importance of supporting the development of strategic metacognition and motivation. Typically, a simpler model of self-regulation was used by the SRL coaches that represented the three phases of SRL as "plan it" (forethought), "practice it" (performance), and "evaluate it" (self-reflection). The key was for teachers and students alike, to use ongoing cycles of planning, practicing, and evaluating. It was also a practice to conceptualize these three phases in terms of what happens before, during, and after learning cycles.

In negotiating and creating strategies with teachers to foster improved SRL in the classroom, it was necessary to challenge beliefs about learning, the purposes for assessment, and the limitations of time and pace of instruction. The teachers who enacted these SRL interventions served as testimony that time limitations were not an absolute barrier to making effective shifts in practices so that students could engage in more improved cycles of self-regulated learning.

Models of SRL can be used to identify ways to support the three phases of academic self-regulation for students. For example, to train mathematics teachers how to support students in forethought processes, we focused on teaching about strategic instruction. We highlighted four features of strategic instruction that were to be followed by teachers of developmental and introductory level mathematics courses (see Table 5.1). These four features were derived from a social cognitive model of how self-regulation is developed (Schunk & Zimmerman, 1997). The first feature of strategic instruction involved modeling specific strategies during each step of the problem solving process with multiple exemplars. This feature particularly related to the modeling phase of how self-regulatory skill is acquired. The second component entailed teachers also explicitly writing down the math strategies or procedures in a clear, concise method. This second feature enabled students to emulate the key features of the problem-solving process during practice, the second phase of the developmental SRL model. The third feature of strategic instruction involved teachers providing ongoing encouragement for students to write down the strategies themselves. This feature fostered a means for students to exhibit self-control over the problem-solving process by monitoring their enactment of strategies via the written checklist. Lastly, the fourth component entailed teachers guiding students in monitoring their use of strategies during the process of solving math problems.

In our work with teachers, we encouraged them to think about students in terms of being "error detectives" during this process of embracing and learning from math errors. Thus, in the classroom, while working to solve problems or reviewing problems together as a class at the blackboard,

TABLE 5.1   Four Features of Strategic Instruction

Feature	Description
Modeling of strategies with multiple exemplars	Teacher and peer modeling in classroom of how to approach different types of math tasks Providing multiple examples of strategy use to demonstrate adjustments for variations in the math tasks Using cognitive modeling: articulation of the thinking process while modeling Using coping modeling: demonstrating the making, detection, and correction of errors
Providing explicit, concise strategy steps	Listing the essential features of the strategy to focus learners' attention during observational learning and facilitate retention
Students write down strategy steps	Writing down specific steps to facilitate learning and commit to memory of the strategy Writing strategy steps produced tools/checklists to be used to self-monitor their implementation of strategies
Guidance for student monitoring of strategy use	Teacher providing strategic support to learners during classroom practice with monitoring the problem solving process and evaluating the accuracy of solutions Teacher coaching the identification, adaptation, implementation, and evaluation of strategies

the "error detectives" would verbalize aloud both the act of implementing problem solving strategies and the process of recognizing an error and making adjustments. Teachers also were able to increase practice and feedback by having students discuss their problem solving solutions and errors with their peers in small groups or one on one.

Instructional Strategies

Coping modeling (Bandura, 1997; Schunk, Hanson, & Cox, 1987) can have advantages over mastery modeling in the development of self-regulatory competence for a particular task because it shows the process of making errors, identifying them, and then making strategic adjustments while performing the task, rather than performing flawlessly (Kitsantas, Zimmerman, & Cleary, 2000). We encouraged teachers to purposefully make errors during strategic modeling of solving math problems and to gradually correct them and shift to mastery. These occasions introduced opportunities for students to learn how to deal with task-specific difficulties during math problem solving. Modeling the gradual acquisition of skill has been shown to increase novice learners' self-efficacy and performance in mathematics (Schunk et al., 1987) as well as in other domains such as the acquisition of athletic skill (Kitsantas et al., 2000). Additional features of the strategic instruction involved teaching all aspects of problem solving and thinking aloud during modeling to share thoughts with observers.

As part of the self-regulatory intervention, instructors not only verbalized math and self-regulatory strategies in the classroom but also wrote them down. When strategies were written on the chalkboard, students were encouraged to write down the strategies in their notebooks. Other methods for providing written strategies involved creating pocket-sized cards with a specific math or SRL strategy (see Figure 5.1), as well as listing a strategy on a chart to be used in the classroom. Emphasis was on helping students to become strategic learners, rather than bombarding them with many different lists of strategy procedures. Skilled self-regulators carefully select which strategies they are going to use, are skilled in seeking help with finding new ones, and are also flexible in how they adapt them to varying contexts. The steps for self-reflecting on math errors from quizzes and tests were provided in the self-reflection tool.

In the intervention, teachers were encouraged to break up didactic instruction in math into short segments and to provide continual opportunities in class for students to actively apply and practice new knowledge. In the classroom, students solved mathematics problems from previous homework and quizzes on the classroom chalkboards and analyzed strategies and answers in class discussion. By doing so, the classroom practice provided timely performance feedback from the teacher, tutor, and peers.

Steps for Successful Math Problem Solving	
Plan:	What type of problem is this?
Select a Strategy:	Which strategies will you use?
	What kind of solution do you expect?
Implement Your Strategy:	Are you monitoring your strategy use as you do the problem?
	Are you checking to see if you are getting the results you expect at each step?
Evaluate Your Strategy:	Have you been an error detective and checked for your common mistakes (e.g., sign errors) or other computational mistakes?
	Have you compared your answer with your estimate to see if your answer makes sense?
	What is your plan if your answer isn't correct?

Figure 5.1   Example strategy pocket card for mathematics problem solving. This figure depicts an example of steps or tips about mathematics problem solving that were provided to students on a "pocket card" to serve as an aid for self-monitoring during problem solving.

Feedback System

A chief source of difficulty in learning environments for poor self-regulators is a lack of feedback that could facilitate adaptive self-regulation for learning and performance improvements. The application of a dynamic, cyclical model of self-regulated learning (Zimmerman, 2000) to the classroom entailed timely and ongoing performance feedback. That is, it was necessary for students to have continuous feedback to help them strategically plan, monitor, and reflect on their learning progress in math. This feedback was provided across several authentic classroom activities, such as frequent quizzing and testing, through homework, and exercises that entailed students making metacognitive judgments and engaging in self-reflection (see Table 5.2 for an overview). A brief description of the five chief elements of the cyclical feedback system follows.

Ongoing Quizzes

Frequent quizzing is an approach to learning that has been widely touted as an effective mechanism for learning (Hattie & Timperley, 2007; Pashler

TABLE 5.2   Cyclical Feedback System

Components	Feedback characteristics
Recurrent quizzes	Students were administered frequent in-class quizzes involving the same types of math problems contained on tests. These instructor-graded quizzes provided students with information about their learning gaps and ability to perform under test-like situations.
Daily homework	Continual homework assignments assured timely practice of math problems outside of instruction that involved newly and previously learned math content. Graded feedback largely consisted of only an indication of right or wrong (because of time constraints), but students also received process-related feedback when they demonstrated their homework problem solving in front of the classroom.
Frequent testing	Higher-stakes tests were periodically administered to provide graded feedback about cumulative learning.
Metacognitive monitoring	Quizzes and tests involved students making self-efficacy judgments prior to solving individual math problems and self-evaluations of performance immediately afterwards.
Self-reflection process	Students used feedback from corrected assessments (e.g., quizzes) and completed self-reflection forms to generate further feedback about their math problem solving efforts. Furthermore, students could receive further feedback pertaining to the completion of the self-reflection forms.

et al., 2007). The origins of the present self-regulatory intervention were grounded in providing frequent feedback for students and instructors via quizzes every two to three classes. These classroom quizzes gave students opportunities to practice performing in test-like, yet low-stakes situations.

Daily Homework

Because a great amount of content had to be fit into a single semester, the pace of instruction and learning that students and teachers faced made it extra important to proactively address any areas of difficulty. Daily homework provided students with ongoing opportunities for practicing mathematics problem solving, preparing for quizzes, and identifying areas for improvement. The instructors reviewed and provided corrective feedback on homework assignments. Students also demonstrated their work on the classroom chalkboard and received feedback from the teacher and peers to adjust their methods and solutions when necessary. In addition to its enhancement of students' achievement, homework was viewed as an important strategy to develop their self-regulatory competence (Ramdass & Zimmerman, 2011a). Systematic homework assignments provide progress feedback for students to help them self-monitor their achievement and provide information for self-reflection. Feedback about progress, as well as the practice and motivation that is exercised in completing homework, can increase students' self-efficacy for learning and responsibility for learning (Kitsantas & Zimmerman, 2009; Zimmerman & Kitsantas, 2005).

Frequent Testing

The assessment system also involved periodic tests to demonstrate learning and further assess any deficiencies to date. Features of this assessment system paralleled mastery learning approaches (Zimmerman & DiBenedetto, 2008), whereby: (1) assessment revolved around specific math competencies and accompanying feedback about strategy use and the accuracy of solutions, (2) students were provided with extra time for learning, and (3) there were repeated opportunities for students to demonstrate learning. Such approaches have been associated with high math self-efficacy, high self-satisfaction with math learning progress, and high personal standards for success (Zimmerman & DiBenedetto, 2008).

Instructors and tutors diligently provided elaborate feedback as much as possible when grading assignments and assessments. This meant that besides marking problems right or wrong, or providing the amount of points earned on a particular problem, students would receive an indication of where errors had occurred during problem solving. A written explanation of strategic errors also provided insights for students. This level of detailed error feedback was not always a possibility given time constraints, and so students were sometimes provided with a simple indication of whether an answer or step in problem solving was right or wrong. The frequent homework, quizzing, and testing in the SRL classrooms also supported the goal of engaging students in continual, deliberate practice of new and formerly acquired knowledge and skills. Feedback derived from external sources came via teacher or tutor feedback on graded homework or quizzes, while students' active engagement in completing homework and quizzes was an internal source of feedback on progress in mathematics.

Metacognitive Judgments

A key feature of the self-regulatory intervention was for students to report their self-efficacy beliefs prior to solving problems and then self-evaluate their performance after attempting a problem. One way of operationalizing this in the classroom was to have students rate their task-specific self-efficacy and self-evaluation on quizzes and tests. These judgment ratings were written right alongside each problem so that when students analyzed their performances on quizzes and tests at a later date, they had information about their calibration immediately before and after solving or attempting to solve discrete mathematics tasks. Thus, another way students could become better "error detectives" was for them to use this self-efficacy and self-evaluation information as a source for learning about their awareness about errors. By systematically analyzing the strength of their confidence as well as its congruence with actual performance, students were metacognitively engaged in their thinking about math and in a position to become better regulators of that thinking. Explicit classroom discussions about self-efficacy and self-evaluation were important ways for students to become aware, gain control over their self-judgments, and enhance sources of achievement motivation.

Self-Reflective Error Analysis

Emphasis thus far has been placed on ongoing, frequent feedback for the benefit of both teachers and students. However, another level of support was needed to help students make linkages in performance and subsequent adjustments to their approaches to learning mathematics. Feedback alone, and even corrective feedback about their performances, was not always sufficient, and students often stubbornly repeated the same types of errors over time. For the assessment system to be more effective in helping students to progress, it was necessary to enhance students' skills in learning from their errors. Over time, the team of researchers and educators developed tools and procedures for students to acquire explicit support in analyzing their errors and implementing new or improved strategies in problem solving.

To facilitate students making adaptive changes in problem solving that would foster achievement, a self-reflection process was enacted that involved students using a tool to analyze their math errors and to practice solving similar types of problems. Some of the specifics of the self-reflection process changed over time, but core elements are embodied in the example tool shown in Figure 5.2. In the example self-reflection tool, it can be seen that students were prompted to think about what they had done to prepare for the type of math problem they were correcting. Students were also prompted to consider the accuracy of their prior self-efficacy beliefs specific to the math task they were correcting and to write out what had gone wrong in their attempts to solve the problem. The next step on the tool had students attempt to solve the same problem again, while also writing down the new or revised steps or strategies. The subsequent step involved students attempting a similar but new math problem to practice their new methods again. Lastly, additional prompts for students to consider their self-efficacy about solving these problems were intended to help students be more accurate in their self-perceptions about math competencies.

The structured self-reflection process involved students deliberately attending to the three phases of SRL to correct errors for a specific type of mathematics problem. Therefore, although much emphasis of this intervention was on enhancing self-reflection processes among students, this was accomplished by encouraging students to attend to processes and self-motivational beliefs from each of the forethought, performance, and self-reflection phases. It was deemed important for students to reflect on what occurred before, during, and after their problem solving attempts.

Another important element of the intervention was that students received ongoing support from the teachers and tutors with using the self-reflection tools. This was important because the self-reflection process was not intuitive and required a considerable amount of effort. Students received support from the instructors, tutors, and, to a lesser extent, peers in progressing from more superficial analyses of their errors to more sophisticated, deeper analyses of their math problem solving. To help incentivize student engagement in the process of analyzing and correcting their math errors, extra grade points were awarded to students for revising their math errors with the self-reflection tool. The quality of students' self-reflections was scored by assessing the accuracy and depth of explanations as well as how much of the tool was completed. Any extra points that students earned were used to offset prior poor achievement scores. Students can be slow to understand the benefits of engaging in the self-reflection process, and they have many other academic responsibilities competing for their time and effort, so we felt it was helpful to include these small rewards for their effort and persistence in analyzing their math errors. It is important to understand that the offering of incentives alone was not deemed enough to influence improved calibration (e.g., Ehrlinger, Johnson, Banner, Dunning, &

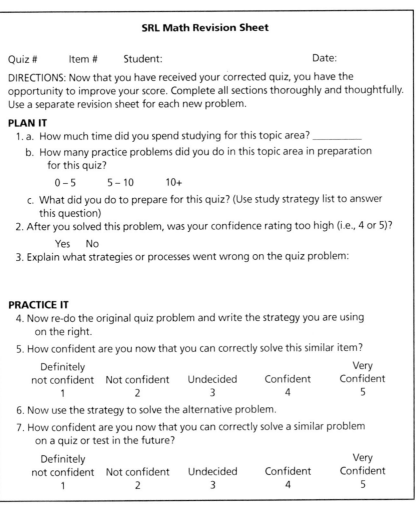

SRL Math Revision Sheet

Quiz #   Item #   Student: Date:

DIRECTIONS: Now that you have received your corrected quiz, you have the opportunity to improve your score. Complete all sections thoroughly and thoughtfully. Use a separate revision sheet for each new problem.

PLAN IT

1. a. How much time did you spend studying for this topic area? _____

   b. How many practice problems did you do in this topic area in preparation for this quiz?

      0 – 5   5 – 10   10+

   c. What did you do to prepare for this quiz? (Use study strategy list to answer this question)

2. After you solved this problem, was your confidence rating too high (i.e., 4 or 5)?

      Yes   No

3. Explain what strategies or processes went wrong on the quiz problem:

PRACTICE IT

4. Now re-do the original quiz problem and write the strategy you are using on the right.

5. How confident are you now that you can correctly solve this similar item?

Definitely not confident	Not confident	Undecided	Confident	Very Confident
1	2	3	4	5

6. Now use the strategy to solve the alternative problem.

7. How confident are you now that you can correctly solve a similar problem on a quiz or test in the future?

Definitely not confident	Not confident	Undecided	Confident	Very Confident
1	2	3	4	5

Figure 5.2   Example math self-reflection tool for systematic correction and learning about math errors. This figure illustrates an instrument used to support students with learning from specific mathematics errors. After receiving feedback from the teacher about performance on specific math problems, students would use the form to (a) self-reflect about their preparations before performance, (b) correct the error and write down an explanation of the correction, and (c) practice their adjustments on another similar problem. Adapted from "Enhancing self-reflection and mathematics achievement of at-risk urban technical college students" by B. J. Zimmerman, A. Moylan, J. Hudesman, N. White, & B. Flugman, 2011, *Psychological Test and Assessment Modeling, 53*, p 160. Copyright (2011) by Pabst Science Publishers. Adapted with permission.

Kruger, 2008). It was, however, the intention to engage students metacognitively, motivationally, and behaviorally in the process of self-reflecting about the mathematics learning and performance.

EFFECTIVENESS OF SELF-REGULATORY INTERVENTION PROGRAM

Empirical evidence suggests that the SRL intervention described in this chapter helped struggling college-aged students improve their mathematics achievement and calibration of metacognition (Zimmerman et al., 2011). Zimmerman and colleagues (Zimmerman et al., 2011) studied the effectiveness of the intervention at a four-year college in developmental and introductory level mathematics classrooms. The semester-long intervention was integrated into six developmental math classrooms and 12 introductory math classrooms with an equal number of intervention and control classrooms. Each student was randomly assigned to either the intervention group or control group. The control classrooms used regular instructional methods, which were monitored by conducting periodic classroom observations. Student achievement on periodic examinations and a final examination and problem-specific self-efficacy and self-evaluation were the primary dependent variables in the study. The mathematics instructors jointly created the examinations. Self-efficacy was assessed on examinations by students rating how confident they were to solve each math problem before they attempted to solve the problem. Similarly, self-evaluation was assessed on examinations by students judging how confident they were that they had solved the problem correctly after each attempt. The influence of the SRL intervention on student calibration of self-efficacy beliefs and self-evaluative judgments with actual math performance was also investigated.

Findings from this study indicated that students in classrooms using the SRL intervention program outperformed their peers in conventional classrooms on multiple tests of math performance, including both instructor-developed tests and standardized, high-stakes tests. In addition, the evidence suggested that the SRL intervention also helped the students become more calibrated in their metacognitive self-judgments made immediately before and after their math problem solving attempts. The accuracy of their self-efficacy and self-evaluation predicted math achievement at the end of the course. Other research has shown external incentives to yield similar calibration improvements among poor performing college students (Hacker et al., 2008). Furthermore, greater engagement in the math error self-reflection process was associated with improved calibration and math achievement. Overall, task-specific self-efficacy beliefs of the forethought phase and self-evaluation judgments of the self-reflection phase were significantly correlated with test performance during the semester and at the end. That is, higher levels of self-efficacy for solving individual math problems predicted better math performance both on proximal problem solving as well as on distal, end-of-the semester examinations. Likewise, higher post-performance self-evaluative judgments were positively associated with proximal and distal math achievement. Unexpectedly, the SRL intervention did not lead to higher self-efficacy or self-evaluation. It was speculated that the failure to find a measured improvement in self-efficacy and self-evaluation might have been influenced by the tendency of this low-performing group of students to be overconfident in their self-judgments.

Interventions focused on enhancing feedback can yield large effects (Hattie & Timperley, 2007). An array of recent intervention research has been conducted to improve math learners' self-regulation in primary, secondary, and postsecondary levels (Labuhn, Zimmerman, & Hasselhorn, 2010; Moylan, 2009; Ramdass & Zimmerman, 2008, 2011). A common finding in this body of research is that feedback provided to learners can effectively improve calibration. Clearly, teachers can devise methods for improving feedback in approaches to instruction and assessment, thus providing opportunities for students to become more accurate in their self-judgments and in better control of their academic attainments.

EDUCATIONAL IMPLICATIONS

Busy practitioners require help in translating theory and research to practice. For instructors, the process of making meaningful, significant improvements for the most difficult problems can be arduous and long. However, the intervention based on Zimmerman's cyclical feedback model of self-regulated learning that was described in this chapter provides some initial ideas for practical, feasible changes to address cognitive, metacognitive, and motivational issues faced by instructors and their students. The many experienced mathematics teachers who contributed to this intervention found that the SRL model and its implications for practice resonated with their understanding of the particular learning issues they faced with their students, as well as gave them new insights on how to improve their efforts.

Given the complex, dynamic nature of self-regulated learning, models that attempt to describe it can also be rather complex. Yet, more basic levels of understanding of SRL models, such as Zimmerman's, can give practitioners some practical conceptual ideas to constructively frame instruction and learning issues they face. Specifically, there are some fundamental aspects of SRL shared across various theoretical models (Zimmerman & Schunk, 2001). One fundamental aspect of SRL is that it is viewed as a multidimensional process that includes sub-processes occurring before, during, and after learning. Although seemingly a simple idea, this concept has important, potentially powerful implications for instruction and the way that learning is supported and managed for students. It is important to consider these different phases of learning to develop a more nuanced understanding of learning issues and how to remediate them.

Perhaps the other most central aspect of SRL is that it is viewed as a cyclical feedback loop (Zimmerman, 2000). Zimmerman has explained that the nature of self-regulation involves an ongoing process or series of processes that entail the acquisition and use of feedback to make successive adaptations in the pursuit of learning goals. Viewing learning through this lens can empower instructors and students to devise ways for improving effort, persistence, and attainment. Teachers can help students focus on aspects of learning or performance that they do have control over, helping them to avoid self-defeating thoughts or passivity so that they can strive for and attain higher academic achievements. Self-regulatory interventions can be particularly powerful in this regard and can help build students' academic self-efficacy (Zimmerman et al., 1996).

A key theme that emerged from the math intervention work of Zimmerman and his colleagues is that the enhancement of self-regulatory competence in math can be approached through explicit, systematic structuring of the classroom assessment process. The cyclical feedback system based on Zimmerman's cyclical model of academic self-regulation (Zimmerman, 2000) was used to identify methods to improve learners' self-reflection processes, including the accuracy of their self-assessments and resultant strategies that were implemented to improve their mathematics achievement. This work emphasized how a structured feedback process was embedded in an overall milieu of embracing mathematical errors and utilizing guided practice to help students develop more accurate understandings of their mathematical knowledge and skill, as well as give them the tools to enhance their self-regulation.

Particularly for students who have a long history of poor academic achievement in a domain, the acquisition of assessment feedback can be entirely viewed as a negative or even punishing experience. Yet, teachers can help students learn, or perhaps relearn, to use feedback for positive, constructive purposes by deliberately explaining and creating classroom processes that support these purposes. Assessment practices designed to support learning and performance can explicitly address the metacognitive, motivational, and behavioral aspects of self-regulation. Without teacher efforts towards these goals, many students will not appreciate the uses and benefits of academic feedback. Instructional mechanisms that support active, accurate, and constructive self-assessment are needed across the educational spectrum. Zimmerman and colleagues demonstrated examples of unconventional approaches to assessment being integrated into challenging college math courses in the context of enhancing self-regulated learning cycles (Zimmerman et al., 2011). Teachers used a formative assessment system of highly frequent homework, quizzing, and examinations that included students making judgments about their ability to solve specific mathematical problems both before and after math performance (metacognition). They also supported the adaptive use of feedback from classroom performance assessments to analyze their math errors. Students were coached on how to use a self-reflection tool to learn to make cyclical adjustments (behavior), and they were encouraged to do so by awarding bonus grade points (motivation).

Embracing a process to encourage and support self-reflection about math errors was difficult for both students and teachers. Other researchers have found similar challenges (e.g., Perels, Gürtler, & Schmitz, 2005). Students faced difficulties not only learning about challenging mathematics tasks, but also in learning about themselves as learners and how to better manage their approaches to academics. For instance, they had to develop a greater self-awareness of their habits in math learning in general and of their attempts to perform specific types of math tasks. Self-motivation to persevere in systematic error analysis was also difficult for many students. Teachers were challenged by rethinking and shifting the way they approached instruction, as well as in using the SRL framework in assessment. For example, teachers' use of coping model techniques whereby they deliberately made math errors during a demonstration of problem solving so that they could show students how they found such errors and then made adjustments was counter to their habits of avoiding errors. While these endeavors can be difficult, they are also vital to deep levels of learning (Zimmerman et al., 1996), especially for students who enter college without a strong background of success and preparation in academics (Bembenutty, 2011). It is important to realize that relatively brief training programs in SRL have yielded positive effects on variables such as self-efficacy, effort, math problem solving competence, and achievement (e.g., Perels et al., 2005; Stoeger & Ziegler, 2008).

FUTURE DIRECTIONS FOR RESEARCH

Although there is an impressive body of scholarly work that has amassed over three decades of theory and research in self-regulation (Zimmerman & Schunk, 2011), there continue to be important research directions for future study of self-regulation in applied contexts, as articulated in the chapters throughout this book. In this chapter, intervention strategies based on Zimmerman's theoretical and empirical work were applied in an attempt to address particularly difficult academic challenges that are faced by many undergraduates who enter higher education without sufficient competence in math and an extensive history of negative outcomes associated with their past attempts to learn.

Future self-regulatory intervention research should continue to target and assess a number of key self-regulation processes in higher education math settings and other applied settings. These targeted areas for interventions include enhanced self-efficacy about self-regulated learning, deeper self-knowledge about learning, more adaptive problem solving skills, attitudes that errors or setbacks are opportunities for learning rather than indices of fixed ability, and attributions to more controllable causes, like the selection and adaptation of strategies. There is also a need for better understanding about the ways learners' beliefs can be influenced by instructional techniques to increase calibration (Hacker et al., 2008). This line of research could include additional investigations of self-beliefs about ability and intelligence (Dweck & Master, 2008) and their influence on calibration.

Continued classroom research is warranted to advance understanding about calibration and how it becomes enhanced (Hacker et al., 2008), particularly for the benefit of academically at-risk students. Limitations on controls of threats to internal validity by studying calibration interventions in developmental education classrooms, for example, are balanced by the gains in understanding of how interventions can be practically applied in complex learning environments. A great deal of exciting research in naturalistic contexts is also being performed with the aid of computer-based instruction to study the metacognitive, motivational, and behavioral features of self-regulation (e.g., Azevedo, Moos, Johnson, & Chauncey, 2010; Graesser & McNamara, 2010; Perry & Winne, 2006). Computer-based learning environments can offer greater variable control in line with that attained in laboratory-based research. In addition, these methodologies have the advantage of including real-time measures of self-regulated learning as it occurs (Perry & Winne, 2006; Zimmerman, 2008).

As stated earlier, the need for remedial education in mathematics is widespread and a highly important issue for retention in college and advancement in STEM fields. Recently, the problem and its potential solutions or remedies have received increased attention from major foundations. With the support of these foundations—including the Melinda and Bill Gates Foundation and the Hewlett Packard Foundation—the Carnegie Foundation for the Advancement of Teaching is heading efforts to implement programs at scale to improve mathematics achievement (Carnegie Foundation for the Advancement of Teaching, Retrieved July 6, 2011 from http://www.carnegiefoundation.org/developmental-math). The empirical and theoretical contributions of Zimmerman and his colleagues provide an example of how a cyclic model of self-regulated learning (Zimmerman et al., 1996) can serve as a productive framework for teams of researchers and teachers in creating innovative, effective strategies for the classroom.

CONCLUSIONS

This chapter covered several essential themes for classroom learning that have been highlighted in the theoretical and research work of Barry Zimmerman and are likely to be among some of his most significant contributions. The themes revolved around applying self-regulated learning to enhance academically at-risk learners' calibration of perceived self-efficacy and self-evaluation, and enabling them to learn and achieve important academic milestones. For many college students who experienced substantial struggles in mathematics, Zimmerman's self-regulatory intervention program was a means towards viewing the analysis of errors as a key component of the learning process. This perspective, which was new for many students, was fostered by a deliberate, systematic change in the way the assessment process was enacted in college mathematics classrooms. To help under-prepared college students succeed in challenging remedial and entry-level mathematics courses, the self-regulatory intervention in essence involved using errors during mathematics problem solving as a source for learning, and this practice was supported by a cyclical feedback system that involved highly frequent homework, quizzes, and tests, as well as a self-reflection tool and other instructional activities.

Esteem and affection for the insightful theoretical and research work of Barry Zimmerman about self-regulation of learning are widely shared by researchers and educators alike. To those who have had the honor and joy to know him personally, it is obvious that his stature in education is not only due to his intellect, but also to his own infectious enthusiasm for SRL and its widespread applications. Clearly, the powerful ideas that have informed and emerged from Zimmerman's classroom interventions will continue to reverberate for a long time to come.

NOTES

This chapter reviews a project spearheaded by Barry J. Zimmerman and his colleagues John Hudesman and Bert Flugman, to which the author contributed. The work was supported in part by the Institute of Education Sciences, U.S. Department of Education, R305H060018, and the Fund for Postsecondary Education, U.S. Department of Education, P116B060012 and P116B010127 to the City University of New York. The opinions expressed are those of the author and do not represent views of the U.S. Department of

Education. I wish to express my gratitude to the many researchers, teachers, students, and administrators who participated in this project. I also thank the editors of this volume for their assistance in preparing this manuscript.

REFERENCES

Azevedo, R., Moos, D. C, Johnson, A. M., & Chauncey, A. D. (2010). Measuring cognitive and metacognitive regulatory processes during hypermedia learning: Issues and challenges. *Educational Psychologist, 45,* 210–223. doi:10.1080/004 61520.2010.515934

Bahr, P. R. (2008). Does mathematics remediation work? A comparative analysis of academic attainment among community college students. *Research in Higher Education, 49,* 420–450. doi:10.1007/s11162-008-9089-4

Bandura, A. (1986). *Social foundations of thought and action: A social cognitive theory.* Englewood Cliffs, NJ: Prentice-Hall.

Bandura, A. (1997). *Self-efficacy: The exercise of control.* New York, NY: Freeman.

Bandura, A. (2008). Toward an agentic theory of the self. In H. W. Marsh, R. G. Craven, & D. M. McInerney (Eds.), *Self-processes, learning, and enabling human potential: Dynamic new approaches* (pp. 15–49). Charlotte, NC: Information Age.

Bembenutty, H. (2009). Three essential components of college teaching: Achievement calibration, self-efficacy, and self-regulation. *College Student Journal, 43,* 562–570.

Bembenutty, H. (2011). New directions for self-regulation of learning in postsecondary education. *New Directions for Teaching and Learning,* 117–124. doi: 10.1002/tl.450

Bol, L., & Hacker, D. J. (2001). A comparison of the effects of practice tests and traditional review on performance and calibration. *The Journal of Experimental Education, 69,* 133–151. doi:10.1080/00220970109600653

Boylan, H. R. (1999). Demographics, outcomes, and activities. *Journal of Developmental Education, 23,* 2–6.

De Corte, E., Mason, L., Depaepe, F., & Verschaffel, L. (2011). Self-regulation of mathematical knowledge and skills. In B. J. Zimmerman & D. H. Schunk (Eds.), *Handbook of self-regulation of learning and performance* (pp. 155–172). New York, NY: Routledge.

Dunning, D. (2004). Flawed self-assessment: Implications for health, education, and the workplace. *Psychological Science in the Public Interest, 5,* 69–106. doi:10.1111/ j.1529-1006.2004.00018.x.

Dweck, C. S., & Master, A. (2008). Self-theories motivate self-regulated learning. In D. H. Schunk & B. J. Zimmerman (Eds.), *Motivation and self-regulated learning: Theory, research and applications* (pp. 31–51). New York, NY: Lawrence Erlbaum Associates.

Ehrlinger, J., & Mitchum, A. (2010). How beliefs in the ability to improve influence accuracy in and use of metacognitive judgments. In A. M. Columbus (Ed.), *Advances in psychology research* (Vol. 69, pp. 229–238). New York, NY: Nova Science Publishers.

Ehrlinger, J., Johnson, K., Banner, M., Dunning, D., & Kruger, J. (2008). Why the unskilled are unaware: Further explorations of (absent) self-insight among the incompetent. *Organizational Behavior and Human Decision Processes 105,* 98–121. doi:10.1016/j.obhdp.2007.05.002

Graesser, A., & McNamara, D. (2010). Self-regulated learning in learning environments with pedagogical agents that interact in natural language. *Educational Psychologist, 45,* 234–244. doi:10.1080/00461520.2010.515933

Hacker, D. J., Bol, L., & Bahbahani, K. (2008). Explaining calibration accuracy in classroom contexts: The effects of incentives, reflection, and explanatory style. *Metacognition and Learning, 3,* 101–121. doi:10.1007/s11409-008-9021-5

Hattie, J., & Timperley, H. (2007). The power of feedback. *Review of Educational Research, 77,* 81–112. doi:10.3102/003465430298487

Kitsantas, A., & Zimmerman, B. J. (2009). College students' homework and academic achievement: The mediating role of self-regulatory beliefs. *Metacognition Learning, 4,* 97–110. doi:10.1007/s11409-008-9028-y

Kitsantas, A., Zimmerman, B. J., & Cleary, T. (2000). The role of observation and emulation in the development of athletic self-regulation. *Journal of Educational Psychology, 92,* 811–187. doi:10.1037//0022-0663.92.4.811

Klassen, R. M. (2006). Too much confidence? The self-efficacy of adolescents with learning disabilities. In F. Pajares & T. Urdan (Eds.), *Self-efficacy beliefs of adolescents* (pp. 181–200). Greenwich, CT: Information Age Publishing.

Labuhn, A., Zimmerman, B. J., & Hasselhorn, M. (2010). Enhancing students' self-regulation and mathematics performance: The influence of feedback and self-evaluative standards. *Metacognition Learning, 5,* 173–194. doi:10.1007/s11409-010-9056-2

Moylan, A. R. (2009). *Enhancing self-regulated learning on a novel mathematical task through modeling and feedback.* Unpublished doctoral dissertation, City University of New York, New York, NY. Retrieved from ProQuest Dissertations and Theses. (Accession Order No. AAT 3354667).

National Association for Developmental Education. (2012). About developmental education. Springfield, IL: Author. Retrieved from http://www.nade.net/AboutDevEd.html

Pajares, F. (1996). Self-efficacy beliefs in academic settings. *Review of Educational Research, 66,* 543–578. doi:10.2307/1170653

Pajares, F., & Miller, D. (1994). Role of self-efficacy and self-concept beliefs in mathematical problem solving: A path analysis. *Journal of Educational Psychology, 86,* 193–203. doi:10.1037//0022-0663.86.2.193

Pashler, H., Bain, P., Bottge, B., Graesser, A., Koedinger, K., McDaniel, M., & Metcalfe, J. (2007). *Organizing instruction and study to improve student learning (NCER 2007-2004).* Washington, DC: National Center for Education Research, Institute of Education Sciences, U.S. Department of Education.

Perels, F., Gürtler, T., & Schmitz, B. (2005). Training of self-regulatory and problem-solving competence. *Learning and Instruction, 15,* 123–139. doi:10.1016/j.learninstruc.2005.04.010

Perry, N. E., & Winne, P. H. (2006). Learning from learning kits: gStudy traces of students' self-regulated engagements with computerized content. *Educational Psychology Review, 18,* 211–228. Doi:10.1007/s10648-006-9014-3

Pieschl, S. (2009). Metacognitive calibration—an extended conceptualization and potential applications. *Metacognition and Learning, 4,* 3–31. doi:10.1007/s11409-008-9030-4

President's Council of Advisors on Science and Technology. (Feb., 2012). *Report to the President: Engage to excel: Producing one million additional college graduates with degrees in science, technology, engineering, and mathematics.* Retrieved February 18, 2012, from http://www.whitehouse.gov/sites/default/files/microsites/ostp/pcast-executive-report-final_feb.pdf

Ramdass, D., & Zimmerman, B. J. (2008). Effects of self-correction strategy training on middle school students' self-efficacy, self-evaluation, and mathematics division learning. *Journal of Advanced Academics, 20,* 18–41. doi:10.4219/jaa-2008-869

Ramdass, D., & Zimmerman, B. J. (2011a). Developing self-regulation skills: The important role of homework. *Journal of Advanced Academics, 22,* 194–218. doi:10.1177/1932202X1102200202

Ramdass, D., & Zimmerman, B. J. (2011b). The effects of modeling and social feedback on middle school students' math performance and accuracy judgments. *The International Journal of Educational and Psychological Assessment, 7,* 4–23. Retrieved from http://tijepa.books.officelive.com/Documents/A2_V7_1_TI-JEPA.pdf

Schunk, D. H. (1989). Self-efficacy and achievement behaviors. *Educational Psychology Review, 1,* 173–208. doi:10.1007/BF01320134

Schunk, D. H. (2007). Attributions as motivators of self-regulated learning. In D. H. Schunk & B. J. Zimmerman (Eds.), *Motivation and self-regulated learning: Theory, research, and applications* (pp. 245–266). Mahwah, NJ: Lawrence Erlbaum Associates.

Schunk, D. H., & Cox, P. D. (1986). Strategy training and attributional feedback with learning disabled students. *Journal of Educational Psychology, 78,* 201–209. doi:10.1016/j.cedpsych.2005.05.003

Schunk, D. H., Hanson, A. R., & Cox, P. D. (1987). Peer model attributes and children's achievement behaviors. *Journal of Educational Psychology, 79,* 54–61. doi:10.1037//0022-0663.79.1.54

Schunk, D. H., & Pajares, F. (2004). Self-efficacy in education revisited: Empirical and applied evidence. In D. M. McInerney & S. Van Etten (Eds.), *Big theories revisited: Vol. 4. Research on sociocultural influences on motivation and learning* (pp. 115–138). Greenwich, CT: Information Age.

Schunk, D. H., & Zimmerman, B. J. (1997). Social origins of self-regulatory competence. *Educational Psychologist, 32,* 195–208. doi:10.1207/s15326985ep3204_1

Shute, V. J. (2008). Focus on formative feedback. *Review of Educational Research, 78,* 153–189.

Stoeger, H., & Ziegler, A. (2008). Evaluation of a classroom based training to improve self-regulation in time management tasks during homework activities with fourth graders. *Metacognition and Learning, 3,* 207–230. doi:10.1007/s11409-008-9027-z

Stone, N. J. (2000). Exploring the relationship between calibration and self-regulated learning. *Educational Psychology Review, 12,* 437–475. doi:10.1023/A:1009084430926

Taylor, P., Fry, R., Wang, W., Dockterman, D., & Velasco, G. (2009). *College enroll-ment hits all-time high, fueled by community college surge.* Washington, DC: Pew Research Center. Retrieved from http://pewsocialtrends.org/files/2010/10/college-enrollment.pdf

Tinto, V. (1998, January). *Learning communities and the reconstruction of remedial edu-cation in higher education.* Paper presented at the Replacing Remediation in Higher Education Conference, Stanford University, Palo Alto, CA.

Winne, P. H., & Jamieson-Noel, D. (2002). Exploring students; calibration of self reports about study tactics and achievement. *Contemporary Educational Psychol-ogy, 27,* 551–572. doi:10.1016/S0361-476X(02)00006-1

Yates, J. F. (1990). *Judgment and decision making.* Englewood Cliffs, NJ: Prentice-Hall.

Zimmerman, B. J. (1990). Self-regulated learning and academic achievement: An overview. *Educational Psychology, 25,* 3–17. doi:10.1207/s15326985ep2501_2

Zimmerman, B. J. (1995). Self-efficacy and educational development. In A. Bandura (Ed.), *Self-efficacy in changing societies* (pp. 202–231). New York, NY: Cambridge University Press. doi:10.1017/CBO9780511527692.009

Zimmerman, B. J. (2000). Attaining self-regulation: A social cognitive perspective. In M. Boekaerts, P. R., Pintrich, & M. Zeidner (Eds.), *Handbook of self-regulation* (pp. 13–39). San Diego, CA.: Academic Press. doi:10.1016/B978-012109890-2/50031-7

Zimmerman, B. J. (2005). Enhancing students' academic responsibility and achieve-ment: A social-cognitive self-regulatory account. In R. J. Sternberg & R. Sub-otnik (Eds.), *Optimizing student success in school with the other three Rs: Reasoning, resilience, and responsibility* (pp. 179–197). Greenwich, CT: Information Age.

Zimmerman, B. J. (2008). Investigating self-regulation and motivation: Historical background, methodological developments and future prospects. *American Educational Research Journal, 45,* 166–183. doi:10.3102/0002831207312909

Zimmerman, B. J. (2011). Motivational sources and outcomes of self-regulated learning and performance. In B. J. Zimmerman & D. H. Schunk (Eds.), *Hand-book of self-regulation of learning and performance* (pp. 155–172). New York, NY: Routledge.

Zimmerman, B. J., Bonner, S., & Kovach, R. J. (1996). *Developing self-regulated learn-ers: Beyond achievement to self-efficacy.* Washington, DC: American Psychological Association. doi:10.1037/10213-000

Zimmerman, B. J., & DiBenedetto, M. K. (2008). Mastery learning and assessment: Implications for students and teachers. *Psychology in the Schools, 45,* 206–216. doi:10.1002/pits.20291

Zimmerman, B. J., & Kitsantas, A. (2005). Students' perceived responsibility and completion of homework: The role of self-regulatory beliefs and processes. *Contemporary Educational Psychology, 30,* 397–417. doi:10.1016/j.cedpsych.2005.05.003

Zimmerman, B. J., & Moylan, A. (2009). Self-regulated learning: Where motivation and metacognition intersect. In D. J. Hacker, J. Dunlosky, & A. C. Graesser (Eds.), *Handbook of metacognition in education* (pp. 299–315). New York, NY: Routledge.

Zimmerman, B. J., Moylan, A., Hudesman, J., White, N., & Flugman, B. (2011). Enhancing self-reflection and mathematics achievement of at-risk urban technical college students. *Psychological Test and Assessment Modeling, 53*, 108–127.

Zimmerman, B. J., & Schunk, D. H. (Eds.). (2001). *Self-regulated learning and academic achievement: Theoretical perspectives* (2nd ed.). Mahwah, NJ: Lawrence Erlbaum Associates.

Zimmerman, B. J., & Schunk, D. H. (2008). Motivation: An essential dimension of self-regulated learning. In D. H. Schunk & B. J. Zimmerman (Eds.), *Motivation and self-regulated learning: Theory, research, and applications* (pp. 1–30). Mahwah, NJ: Erlbaum.

Zimmerman, B. J., & Schunk, D. H. (2011). *Handbook of self-regulation of learning and performance.* New York, NY: Routledge.

CHAPTER 6

THE TRIUMPH OF HOMEWORK COMPLETION THROUGH A LEARNING ACADEMY OF SELF-REGULATION

Héfer Bembenutty

Homework is an essential component in most educational settings (Bembenutty, 2011; Cooper, Steenbergen-Hu, & Dent, 2012; Dettmers, Trautwein, Ludtke, Kunter, & Baumert, 2010). Good (1926), provided an early definition of homework as: "school assignments to be completed out of regular school hours at the residence of a pupil" (p. 285). According to Cooper et al. (2012), *homework* refers to tasks assigned to students by school teachers that are meant to be carried out during non-instructional time. Homework is associated with better retention of factual knowledge, increased understanding, better critical thinking and information processing, learning during leisure time, and acquiring better study habits and skills (Kitsantas & Zimmerman, 2009; Cooper et al., 2012). Homework also is associated with students' greater self-direction, self-discipline, better time organization, and more independent problem solving (Cooper, 2001). Research has produced a vast amount of empirical work supporting its effectiveness,

Applications of Self-Regulated Learning across Diverse Disciplines, pages 153–196
Copyright © 2013 by Information Age Publishing
All rights of reproduction in any form reserved.

in particular at the middle and high school levels (Cooper et al., 2012) as well as at the college level (Bembenutty, 2010; Kitsantas, Cheema, & Ware, 2011). Therefore, homework continues to be an instructional activity that is important in most educational settings ranging from elementary school to college education.

In his meta-analysis examining the association between homework and academic achievement, Cooper (1989) found that high school students who have done homework had higher academic performance than students who did not do homework. Teachers assign homework for a variety of purposes. For instance, Strang (1968) recommended that homework should be given to meet students' needs and to extend their class work. Cooper (2001) suggested that homework can serve as a means of improving students' learning and achievement in schools. Cooper and Valentine (2001) reported that homework has positive causal effects on enhancing retention of information, increasing understanding of course material, increasing study skills, and increasing independence and responsibility.

Although homework is assigned for multiple educational purposes, Zimmerman and his associates (Kitsantas & Zimmerman, 2009; Ramdass & Zimmerman, 2011; Zimmerman, Bonner & Kovach, 1996; Zimmerman & Kitsantas, 2005) have suggested that from the social cognitive theory (Schunk, 2012), in addition to conveying academic knowledge to students, homework is a process that prompts students to engage in self-initiated, independent, and self-directed learning. He contends that homework could promote self-regulation of learning. *Self-regulation of learning* refers to learners setting goals, maintaining motivation, and controlling their actions, beliefs, and behaviors in order to attain important academic goals (Zimmerman, 2008). If homework is to be understood as an important academic task influenced by social, cultural, and educational elements, then the relationship between homework and achievement needs to be examined through the lens of the self-regulatory processes that guide learners to manage distractions in light of competing alternatives, to sustain motivation and remain task-focused and self-reflective in order to get the best of their study time and to secure successful task completion. According to Zimmerman (Ramdass & Zimmerman, 2011; Zimmerman & Kitsantas, 2005), self-regulated learners are those who, during homework completion, engage in self-directed learning by motivating themselves, avoiding distractions, setting specific goals, monitoring their progress, and evaluating the outcomes of their efforts.

While previous models of homework primarily focused on homework as a task to convey knowledge acquisition (e.g., Keith & Cool, 1992), most current models point out that students' engagement in self-regulation, such as how self-regulated learners will proactively engage in homework rather than passively complete it. To this end, contemporary models (e.g., Dumont et al., 2012; Walker & Hoover-Dempsey, 2001; Xu & Corno, 1998, 2003; Xu, Coasts, & Davidson, 2012) attempt to assess homework by including in their models self-regulated constructs such as self-monitoring, help-seeking, and emotional, attentional, and environmental controls. However, Zimmerman's self-regulation model of homework completion offers an important alternative to current trends in research on homework. From Zimmerman's perspective, a comprehensive self-regulation approach should focus on specific cyclical and controllable processes and beliefs before, during, and after homework completion, such as how students select, self-monitor, and self-evaluate their homework activities. To assess and improve students' self-regulation of homework completion, Zimmerman, Bonner, and Kovach (1996) developed a learning academy model that frames teaching and learning as a self-regulated learning process. According to Zimmerman et al., a *learning academy* provides "a performance context where standards, personal goals, and a sense of self-efficacy are mutually valued and can emerge as students watch expert models' and peers' self-directed practice" (p. 9). An important component of the learning academy is its behavioral focus on learning methods with cyclic properties while learners progress toward mastering their own learning. In the learning academy model, teachers shift responsibility for learning and homework processes to students until they become independent, self-directed, self-assessed, self-monitored, self-evaluated, and in control of their homework tasks. In the learning academy model, teachers serve as models and coaches who provide the appropriate social and individual support to students while they develop as self-regulated learners.

Despite how relevant self-regulation of learning is to successful homework completion, current trends in the literature suggest that it is important to consider how the homework process could be evaluated and enhanced through the lens of a learning academy. It is vital to understand the homework process in the light of students' needs to engage in goal setting and planning; enacting study tactics and strategies; implementing, monitoring, and evaluating strategies; and making decisions and adjustments. Nevertheless, new directions from the social cognitive perspective suggest that this path is an important one that deserves further investigation, new directions, and interventions. Thus, this chapter will first provide an overview of the purpose, effects, and importance of homework in our current educational system. Second, it will discuss the major components of Zimmerman's learning academy model of self-regulatory training as it applies to homework. Third, it will describe intervention programs that used Zimmerman's learning academy model of self-regulatory training. Fourth, it will report the implementation and effectiveness of a self-regulatory intervention program consistent with Zimmerman's learning academy model in which pre-service teachers used homework logs to enhance the learning experience of their students. The specific components of the intervention approach, the implementation procedures, and how educators can apply the same principles in their classrooms will be discussed with case data to illustrate the essential aspects of implementing the self-regulation intervention and the effectiveness of such interventions. Fifth, the chapter will conclude with suggestions for future research and a discussion of educational implications on how to enhance the quality of homework from a learning academy perspective.

HISTORICAL ROOTS, PURPOSES, AND EFFECTS OF HOMEWORK

The concept of homework has been defined as including academic tasks assigned by teachers to be done by students outside of the instructional time (Bembenutty, 2011; Cooper et al., 2012). However, homework can also be conceptualized as using learners' self-initiated study time in order to master specific academic skills.

Historical Roots

During the 20th century, the debate about the usefulness, purpose, and utility of homework was a consistent one (Alleman et al., 2010; Cooper, 2001; Vatterott, 2009). According to Cooper (2001) and Vatterott (2009), the debate fluctuates from some asking to abolish it completely and others to increase it. The debate takes cycles ranging from 15 to 30 years in favor of, or against homework. In the United States, concerns about homework are certainly influenced by historical events. As Cooper (2001) observed, in the early 20th century, homework was considered a favorable educational tool when it was construed as a way to discipline children's minds with activities such as repetition in math to increase memory retention. During that period, memorization of facts was emphasized because the mind was considered a muscle.

As Cooper (2001) observed, by the 1940s, homework opposition developed with an emphasis on problem-solving ability in our educational system; it challenged the function of homework as a way to enhance memorization. At that point, the focus was on promoting learners' self-initiative and interest. Concerns also focused on whether homework interfered with students pursuing personal and non-academic activities. However, during the time as the Russians advanced their technological skills, Americans were concerned about their students' technological abilities to compete at that level. Thus, homework was again considered as a way to increase knowledge and technological skills to compete against the educational system of Russians (Alleman et al., 2010; Cooper, 2001; Vatterott, 2009). During the 1960s, homework was again considered detrimental to students' achievement and mental health, and its value was again questioned with arguments such as that it interferes with children's opportunities for creative activities and social experiences. During the 1980s, the general public was in favor of homework with arguments such as that our nation was at risk and needed a fundamental reform, which could be benefited by pushing for more research. During the 1990s, the increase of state test assessments resulted in teachers assigning more homework in order to meet the states' expectations.

These trends continued until the end of the 20st century (Alleman et al., 2010; Cooper, 2001; Cooper et al., 2012). At the end of the 20st century, massive media attention on the debate of homework was led by educators and scholars who were concerned about the use of homework. The leaders at this point were Kralovec and Buell (Buell, 2004; Kralovec & Buell, 2000) who called for ending homework suggesting it disrupts families, overburdens children, and limits learning. Similarly, Bennett and Kalish (2006) presented a case against homework by arguing that homework hurts children. Likewise, Kohn (2006) argued against homework and called its benefit a myth and claimed that homework has detrimental effects. Contemporary trends on homework in the 21st century continue to affirm and challenge the effect of homework. These oppositions to homework drastically contrasted with solid, rigorous, and empirical research findings (e.g., Xu & Corno, 1998; Kitsantas & Zimmerman, 2009; Zimmerman & Kitsantas, 2005) and research syntheses (Cooper, 2001; Cooper, Robinson, & Patall, 2006; Patall, Cooper, & Robinson, 2008) supporting the positive effects and benefits of homework for learners, a point that will be discussed next.

Homework's Purposes and Effects

In order to understand the function of homework in our educational system, it is important to consider its purpose and effects. According to Cooper (1989), homework serves as a means of improving students' learning and achievement in schools. Earlier, Lee and Pruitt (1979) provided a taxonomy of homework purposes, which involved practice, preparation, extension, and creativity. *Practice* refers to those homework assignments designed to enhance skills and material covered in class. *Preparation* refers to homework designed to ready learners for future learning activities. *Extension* refers to those homework assignments designed to increase the transfer and application of course materials to other aspects and situations. *Creative* refers to homework that requires critical thinking and cognitive engagement on the part of the learners.

Cooper (2001; Cooper et al., 2012) observes that in addition to instructional purposes, homework has been used for noninstructional purposes, such as parent-child communication, fulfilling directives, punishment, and community relations. Cooper (2001; Cooper et al., 2012) observes that homework can be used to increase skill areas such as reading, writing, and memory or retention and that homework could be focused on individual students or group of students. Homework can also be given to students as a choice, compulsory or voluntary, and it can be done independently, in groups, or assisted by parents, siblings, and peers. Epstein (1988) provides a comprehensive taxonomy of the purposes of homework, which includes increased responsibility, self-confidence, and time management. Epstein construed homework as a meaning consistent with students achieving self-regulation of learning. Thus, the purpose of homework can include enhancing students' self-regulation.

Before returning to consider homework as a way to enhance self-regulation of learning among students, it is important to discuss the effects of homework on academic achievement. Cooper et al. (2012) examined the positive and negative effects of homework. According to Cooper, immediate positive academic effects of homework on students include that it provides opportunities to review and practice class materials, to prepare for larger projects or subsequent classes, and to provide curriculum enrichment. The positive and long-term academic effects include increasing students' learning autonomy, improving attitudes toward school, development of study habits and skills, and increasing independence. According to Cooper, positive nonacademic effects include that homework develops students' character, improves psychological well-being, fosters practice of time management skills, provides practice resisting distractions and temptations, and keeps students away from unsafe environments after school. These effects of homework in particular are consistent with the self-regulation of learning approach.

Cooper and his associates have conducted several syntheses on the effectiveness of homework on academic achievement (Cooper, 1989; Cooper et al., 2006). They reported a positive relationship between the amount of homework done by students and their academic achievement ($d = 0.60$), which suggests that students benefited by doing homework. They conclude that doing homework "can cause improved academic achievement" (p. 483). With regard to nonacademic effects of homework, Cooper observed that homework has positive effects on students' motivation, affect, emotion, and behavior; however, it is important to examine the role that students and teachers play in homework effectiveness.

BARRIERS TO SUCCESSFUL HOMEWORK COMPLETION: STUDENTS' AND TEACHERS' ROLES

Although some of the purposes of assigning homework include increased responsibility, self-confidence, and time management (Bembenutty, 2011; Cooper et al., 2012; Dettmers et al., 2010), often students are mere passive agents in the pursuit, process, and evaluation of homework completion (Zimmerman et al., 1996). The mere definition of homework delineated by Cooper implies that homework is a task assigned by teachers and completed by students. A traditional scenario in the elementary, middle, and high school classrooms is one in which homework is written on the board when students enter the classroom, students copy the assignment, do it at home, and return it the next day (Kohn, 2006). Infrequently, specific feedback is provided to students or the homework is not discussed in class (Alleman et al., 2010). Students who did not understand the homework can move on with the course material without their individual gaps being addressed. At the college level, sometimes homework assignments are written on the syllabi and students are expected to master them on their own (Zimmerman, 2002). How to approach homework and specific strategies and processes are not frequently discussed in class.

Often students have a limited voice and autonomy about the selection of homework assignments (Warton, 2001) and they infrequently initiate homework study to master tasks not directly assigned by the teacher (Zimmerman, 2002). Students' negative reaction toward homework reflects their apathy to this instructional tool, which frequently results in diminishing creativity, loss of interest, low returns on effort, low time investment, physical fatigue, and poor attitudes (Cooper et al., 2012). Frequently, students use phrases, such as, "I hate homework" or "This homework is driving me crazy" (Buell, 2004; Kralovec & Buell, 2000). They also engage in a maladaptive behavior, such as procrastination, cheating, plagiarism, self-handicapping, and under or over-regulation (Bembenutty, 2011).

At this time of an explosion of knowledge through the Internet and media, there are students who approach homework in a passive way and view homework as unrelated to their lifelong learning (Alleman et al., 2010). Many students do not feel that homework is an important process of which they should be in control (Bembenutty, 2011; Warton, 2001) and that will help them to acquire independence and self-directed learning. Frequently, students do not know that they can be empowered in the homework process by engaging in peer modeling, peer feedback, setting short and long-term goals, engaging in self-monitoring, self-observation, and self-judgment or seeking help from appropriate social sources (Zimmerman et al., 1996). When attending classes, learners place little effort on understanding lectures and instruction or do not write clear homework instructions or deadlines on their weekly planners (Alleman et al., 2010). Although students frequently experience difficulty in approaching homework, teachers play a significant role in how students approach homework and in the effectiveness of homework (Bembenutty, 2011).

Most teachers see significant benefit from assigning homework (Alleman et al., 2010) and do laudable work with regard to dispensing knowledge and academic skills to the students under their supervision (Bruce, 2012). However, traditionally, homework is often considered an adjunct activity unrelated to the curriculum and course standards. Homework is not often embedded in the curriculum at the college level; it is often assigned at the last few minutes of class instruction (Alleman et al., 2010). At the college level, some instructors consider that students are adults and mature learners and if they have questions or concerns about the homework, they should seek help. During regular and daily class instruction, some educators dedicate limited time to promoting acquisition of learning strategies, such as goal setting, planning, selection of strategies, self-monitoring, and self-reflection (Zimmerman et al., 1996).

Frequently, traditional classrooms do not directly involve explicit training on goal setting, assessment of motivation, and reflection of post-performance outcomes (Zimmerman et al., 1996). Frequently, feedback is not provided and when it is, it often includes general statements such as "Great!" or "Good job!" Unfortunately, these kinds of classroom settings are not a social environment designed to empower students with the social, personal, and educational skills that could results in students' capacity to self-regulate their social climate, independence, and self-directed learning. These trends on teachers' approaches to homework and instruction call for new patterns of instruction focused on learning academies where learners are empowered with competent beliefs and self-regulatory skills, where learning through homework comes naturally and eliminates distractions and competing demands in favor of acquiring self-regulation of learning.

In sum, this section considered the definition, positive and negative effects of homework, and the roles of students and teachers in the homework process. Although homework has some negative effects, it has significant positive effects on students' academic achievement, and it also has positive effects on students' nonacademic endeavors. An examination of the role of students and teachers with regard to homework suggests that there is a need for students to be empowered with self-regulatory skills in order to master the skills intended by each homework assignment. However, it was also uncovered that the classroom climates led by teachers are often limited in their efforts to promote methods of learning that will result not only in knowledge acquisition but in long-term and independent self-regulated learning. This call for a performance context where standards, personal goals, and high level of efficacy beliefs are developed leads next to a discussion of the important roles that the learning academy model could include to facilitate learning and effectiveness of homework under the grounds of self-regulation of learning proposed by Zimmerman and his associates.

LEARNING ACADEMY MODEL OF SELF-REGULATION

The significant theoretical, empirical, and practical contributions of Zimmerman's research to cognition, motivation, and behavior have had an indelible impact on current theory and applications to homework instruction and practice. He has demonstrated that learners can control their cognition and behavior to attain academic goals, select appropriate learning strategies, and monitor and evaluate their academic progress. Zimmerman proposes that through effective homework instruction, learners can be empowered to become *smart learners* (Zimmerman et al., 1996). Zimmerman developed an innovative instructional procedure sustained by solid theoretical approaches that could be used in and outside of the classroom for learners to empower themselves with self-regulatory learning strategies, appropriate motivational beliefs, and academic knowledge and skills while doing homework.

A General View of the Learning Academy Model

Zimmerman provides an instructional model for teaching essential study skills during homework and studying. To this end, he developed a learning academy model of self-regulation. *Learning academy* refers to a "form of school designed to improve performance as well as impart established knowledge through expert and peer modeling, direct social feedback for performance efforts, and practice routines involving specific goals and methods of self-monitoring" (Zimmerman et al., 1996, p. 140). The learning academy is characterized by four cyclical phases: (a) self-monitoring and evaluation, (b) planning and goal setting, (c) strategy implementation and monitoring, and (d) strategic-outcome monitoring (see Figure 6.1). He put forth the notion that empowered learners are intrinsically motivated and highly self-efficacious. *Self-efficacy* is an important motivational component of self-regulation and refers to individuals' beliefs in their capabilities to learn or perform a specific task successfully (Bandura, 1997).

Before continuing to Zimmerman's learning academy model, it is important to observe that this model is different from his cyclical phases of self-regulation (Zimmerman, 1998, 2000, 2008). In the latter model, during the *forethought phase*, learners generate goals, engage in task analysis, strategic planning, and self-motivational beliefs, such as self-efficacy, intrinsic

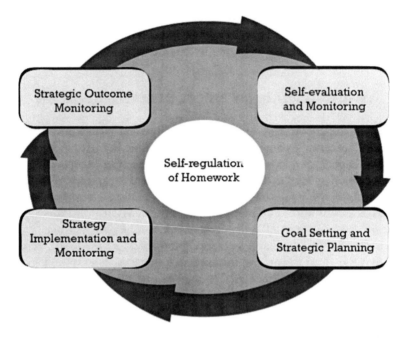

Figure 6.1 Learning Academy Model of self-regulatory training.

motivation, and outcome expectancy. During the *performance phase*, learners initiate actions to enact self-control and self-observation during performance. During the *self-reflection phase*, learners engage in self-judgment and self-reaction to task completion. The three-phase model intends to address the interrelated and cyclical processes of the structure of the self-regulatory systems, which describe the process that precedes efforts to act, actions and behaviors while executing those efforts, and the processes that influence learners' reactions after performance. These processes are cyclical because they dramatically influence subsequent actions. However, the three-phase model is not prescriptive, and it is general in scope. By contrast, the academy model is prescriptive and specific to a particular task a learner has at hand. Zimmerman developed the academy model before the three-phase model, and as such, the three-phase model encompasses the comprehensive structure of the elements that were not fully delineated in the academy model. These two models are not in opposition to each other; rather, they complement each other with the academy model highlighting the specific steps of task completion while the three-phase model highlights the processes that take place during task completion. For more details about the three-phase model, readers could see the chapter written in this volume by Schunk and Usher.

With regard to the academy model, Zimmerman envisions that classrooms can be converted into learning academies where students enhance their self-efficacy beliefs; engage in peer learning and modeling; are active agents, producers and products of social environments; and have an effect on their environment. From this perspective, Zimmerman envisions teachers and educators as self-regulatory coaches or consultants. His learning academy model of self-regulatory training is an effective model that can help learners and educators reach their academic and professional goals. One of the most serious classroom problems reported by teachers is their students' lack of motivation to do homework, and that when it is submitted the quality is often below their teacher's expectations (Gilbertson & Sonnek, 2010; Jones & Jones, 2010). The academy model provides an alternative to current trends of homework patterns.

Four Steps of the Learning Academy Model

Zimmerman's enduring impact on the field of educational psychology is reflected in his vision of learning academies where learners are conceived as active agents who sustain self-efficacy beliefs, enact mastery experiences, and learn through social interactions and modeling. In this model, students learn to set personal goals and establish standards of progress and outcomes. Further, in the learning academy, learners engage in self-regulation by observing and emulating expert models and by self-directing action, behavior, and practice.

The academy model is the result of the understanding that often learners (a) do not complete homework assignments, (b) do not know how to self-direct their own learning process, (c) do not know how to generate thoughts, feelings, and actions to attain academic success, (d) do not know how to set goals, (e) lack reading, writing, and computational skills, (f) lack effective test preparation, and (g) lack self-beliefs about their capabilities to perform designed tasks.

The learning academy model is based on four fundamental roles of teachers:

- Teachers can provide *modeling*. Teachers can model the same self-regulatory processes they expect students to master.
- Teachers can provide *encouragement* to students in such a way that students can pursue appropriate learning avenues.
- Teachers can teach *task and strategy analysis*. Teachers can help students develop and implement effective learning strategies and provide opportunities for students to engage in task analysis and pursue strategic goals.

- Teachers can help students engage in *outcome checking and strategy refinement*. After students complete a learning task, teachers assist them in shifting their attention to evaluate their progress based on predetermined standards.

The learning academy model provides an instructional frame for helping learners get the most out of their homework and study time. Zimmerman provides a model based on middle-school learners, because during this period homework becomes an important task in creating responsibility and self-management in school. The learning academy is an instructional model that describes the different roles that teachers can play in helping the students learn and empower themselves with self-regulatory learning skills. Concomitantly, the academy model can be construed as a learning model that describes steps and processes that learners can follow to enhance their homework processes when limited teaching instruction is provided. Therefore, in the following section, the roles of the teachers and students in the academy model are both described (see Table 6.1).

Step 1: Self-Evaluation and Monitoring

The first step involves students' judgments of their competence and effectiveness from observation of teachers and peers and from self-recording of tasks and previous performance. The role of the teacher is to provide guidelines, offer clear instructions and feedback, provide daily assignments to develop skills and encourage frequent assessment, highlight students' academic progress, and to facilitate peer evaluation and task monitoring. The role of the students includes evaluation of their capabilities and skills to complete the assignments. The learners monitor how closely and how well they complete the task by checking their records, comparing assignments with peers, and by redoing the assignment if necessary all according to the guidelines provided by the teacher.

During the first step of self-regulated learning training, for instance, social studies teachers assist middle school students in examining their preparation to conduct an in-depth study of the specific aspects of particular cultures in similar and different places, times, conditions, and contexts. The students judge their competence to perform that task and monitor their progress.

Step 2: Goal Setting and Strategic Planning

The second step focuses on learners setting specific and short-term goals, and choosing learning strategies that could help them attain those goals. The role of the teachers is to teach the students how to evaluate their tasks; to assist learners in identifying specific and short-term goals; to model and teach the use of learning strategies; to provide opportunities for the

TABLE 6.1 Learning Academy Model of Self-Regulated Training with Applications to Teachers and Students

Learning Academy Model of Self-Regulated Training	Description of the Subprocesses of Learning Academy Model	Teacher's Tasks to Enhance Acquisition of the Self-Regulatory Skills	Student's Tasks to Acquire Self-Regulatory Skills	Examples of Collaboration between Teachers and Students in Middle-School Social Studies Classes
• Self-evaluation and monitoring	• Students judge their competence and effectiveness from observation of teachers and peers and from self-recording of tasks and previous performances.	• Teachers provide guidelines and feedback. • Teachers offer clear instructions and feedback. • Teachers provide daily assignments to develop skills and frequent assessments. • Teachers identify the students' academic progress. • Teachers facilitate peer evaluation and task monitoring.	• Students evaluate their competencies and skills to complete the tasks. • Students monitor how close and how well they complete the task by checking their record. • Students compare assignments with peers and the guidelines provided by the teacher. • Students redo assignments if it is necessary according to the guidelines teacher provided.	• Teachers assist learners to examine their preparation to conduct an in-depth study of the specific aspects of particular cultures in similar and different places, times, conditions, and contexts. • Learners judge their competence to perform their task.
• Goal setting and strategic planning	• Students assess and set specific and short-term goals and choose learning strategies that could help them to attain the goals.	• Teachers teach how the students could evaluate their tasks. • Teachers assist in identifying specific and short-term goals. • Teachers model and teach the use of learning strategies. • Teachers provide opportunities for the students to identify when, where, with whom, and how they will complete the homework.	• Students evaluate the tasks and set specific and short-term goals. • Students set goals and choose learning strategies. • Student identify when, where, with whom, and how they will complete the homework.	• Teachers provide opportunities for students to understand the differences in historical perspectives and the recognition that interpretations are influenced by individual experiences, societal values, and cultural traditions. • Students use mnemonic devices, index cards, and teachers are available for consultation when the students need help.

(continued)

TABLE 6.1 Learning Academy Model of Self-Regulated Training with Applications to Teachers and Students (Cont.)

Learning Academy Model of Self-Regulated Training	Description of the Subprocesses of Learning Academic Model	Teacher's Tasks to Enhance Acquisition of the Self-Regulatory Skills	Student's Tasks to Acquire Self-Regulatory Skills	Examples of Collaboration between Teachers and Students in Middle-School Social Studies Classes
• Strategy-implementation monitoring	• Students carry out and implement the learning strategies and monitor the learning goals and academic progress.	• Teachers serve as important social sources of feedback. • Teachers provide self-monitoring tools and homework logs for students to monitor their progress. • Teachers recommend appropriate environmental settings where tasks could be more effectively completed and assess the progress of the students.	• Students execute a plan of action to attain the goals while monitoring their progress toward task completion. • Students work on their homework by implementing the pre-selected strategies and by checking their progress. • Students seek help from teachers and peers if it is necessary. • Students select appropriate social relations and control the environment. • Students monitor their strategies.	• Teachers provide self-monitoring forms to students for them to keep track of how the government addresses human needs, changes over time, promotes social conformity, and influences cultures.
• Strategic-outcome monitoring	• Students evaluate the effectiveness of their academic outcomes and strategies with the standards and goals they previously established for themselves.	• Teachers assess the progress of the students. • Teachers provide feedback about the outcomes. • Teachers make suggestions for continued use of effective strategies or for using new ones. • Teachers help students to understand the cyclical process of task completion. • Teachers provide feedback about the progress made by the students and the self-efficacy level they have achieved.	• Students engage in self-assessment, self-examination, and self-reflection of how well the task was completed. • Students check whether they have made significant progress toward task completion. • Students examine what was not completed or was completed unsatisfactorily. • Students check their academic progress with the standards they set for themselves and with the feedback teachers provided to them.	• Teachers assist students relating their personal experiences to happenings in other environmental contexts such as the current economic status of the USA. • Students make a list of the tasks completed and compare it with the standards they set for themselves. • Students evaluate their improvement and whether their efforts would lead to satisfactory performance on the course.

students to identify when, where, with whom, and how they will complete the homework; and to teach how to use learning strategies.

To illustrate, middle school students could have a social studies homework assignment about understanding and appreciating differences in historical perspectives, and developing the recognition that interpretations are influenced by individual experiences, societal values, and cultural traditions. To complete the task, students will set specific goals about how much they will complete by specific deadlines, determine where and with whom they will complete the assignment, and select a range of appropriate strategies (e.g., develop a mnemonic device, divide the assignments in several parts, create index cards with important vocabulary words, consult with a tutor or a peer, and seek help from the teacher) in order to do the particular task on hand.

Step 3: Strategy Implementation and Monitoring

During the third step, students carry out and implement the learning strategies and monitor the learning goals and academic progress. That is, learners execute a plan of action to attain their goals while monitoring their progress toward task completion. During this step, teachers and tutors are important social sources of feedback to secure enactment of tasks.

The role of the teacher is to be available to provide feedback to secure students' enactment of tasks, provide self-monitoring tools and homework logs for students to self-monitor their progress and check the progress of the identified strategies, and recommend appropriate environmental settings where tasks could be more effectively completed. Teachers also assess the progress of the students.

The responsibilities of the students include executing a plan of action to attain their goals while monitoring their progress toward task completion. They also work on their homework by implementing the pre-selected strategies, checking their progress, and seeking help from teachers and peers if it is necessary. Students select appropriate social relations and control the environment while monitoring their implementation of strategies. For an illustration from a social studies middle school classroom, teachers provide self-monitoring forms to students for students to keep track of how the government addresses human needs, promotes social conformity, and influences cultures.

Step 4: Strategic Outcome Monitoring

The last step encompasses engaging in self-assessment, self-examination, and self-reflection of how well the task is completed. It involves an evaluation of the effectiveness of their strategies within the standards and goals previously established. During this step, teachers assess the progress of students and provide feedback about the outcomes. Teachers also make suggestions for continuing to use effective strategies or for using new ones and help students understand the cyclical process of task completion by reviewing the cyclical self-regulatory process. Teachers provide feedback about the progress made by the students and the self-efficacy levels they have achieved.

The responsibilities of the students include determining whether they have made significant progress toward task completion. They examine what is not completed or completed unsatisfactorily. Learners compare their academic progress with the standards they set for themselves and with the feedback teachers provided to them. For example, learners may be asked to complete a homework assignment relating their personal experiences to happenings in other environmental contexts such as the current economic status of the U.S. and the influence of the Tea Party in American politics. They would make a list of the tasks completed and would compare it with the standards they had set for themselves and with the feedback provided by the teachers. They would evaluate how much improvement they made on their understanding of the homework assignment and whether their efforts would lead to satisfactory performance in their social studies course.

According to Zimmerman, students' engagement in this cyclical process of self-regulation would result in effective time management, which would enhance their self-efficacy beliefs. As a consequence of this proactive and self-directed learning experience, learners would believe that they could effectively complete tasks in the future under similar conditions. They would feel capable of completing their work. At the same time, this cyclical process would allow learners to self-monitor and self-evaluate their own self-efficacy beliefs. Ratings of self-efficacy beliefs about homework assignments are also important because learners can react appropriately and make adjustments based on the standards they have. Learners can compare their scores on homework with their level of self-efficacy beliefs. Graphing these scores could enhance self-regulatory reactions conducive to increased performance. Figure 6.2 displays a cartoon, drawn by Robert A. Reidel, a social studies teacher, depicting the interaction between a teacher and a student in a social studies class within the frame of the learning academy model.

Self-Recording During the Learning Academy Self-Regulatory Training

In the learning academy model, teachers provide forms to students for them to self-monitor their learning process. One of such forms is a homework time log for students to monitor their homework learning process and time. On the homework log, students report the following information: (1) the homework assignment for that day or week, (2) the time when the homework assignment is started, (3) the time when the homework assign-

Figure 6.2 Cartoon depicting the interaction between a teacher and a student within the frame of the Learning Academy Model.

ment is completed, (4) the amount of time spent on the homework assignment, (5) where the homework assignment is completed, (6) with whom the homework assignment is completed, (7) whether there were distractions during the homework completion, and (8) the degree of self-efficacy about the effectiveness of homework completion. The homework log serves as feedback that students can use to judge their learning progress.

By using the homework log, students can monitor whether the time spent on task produced the expected outcomes, whether where and with whom the task was completed increased performance, and whether distractions influenced task completion. For instance, if students conclude that doing homework in the living room with the television on interferes with their task completion, then they may select a different place to study such as at their desks in their bedrooms. Similarly, if learners find that studying alone is not conducive to satisfactory outcomes, they can select study partners who can contribute to task completion. Further, if students discover that while they do homework the telephone rings with calls from friends, they could decide to turn off the telephone until the assignment is done.

Based on students' reported information in the homework logs, teachers can suggest changes in the students' use and management of strategies and places of work. Teachers can provide feedback, assist in monitoring the students' progress, and assist in setting realistic goals. Teaches can also assist students in setting regular study periods, assist in choosing a regular study area, help with prioritizing tasks, assist with avoiding distraction, and help students engaging in self-reward of academic successes. Finally, teachers can change students' focus from a reactive attitude about homework to a proactive attitude, and gradually move the students from a monitoring dependency on the teacher to a students' self-directed homework completion.

To illustrate the use of the homework log, Zimmerman described a girl, Maria, who did her homework with her friend and spent most of the time talking about boyfriends and gossiping (Zimmerman et al., 1996). Clearly, Maria had academic problems and was deficient in the use of learning strategies and had low self-efficacy about her capabilities to complete her assignments satisfactorily. However, with assistance from her teacher, Maria understood that in order to complete her mathematics problems she would need to avoid social distractions, monitor her academic progress, use effective learning strategies, spend more time on task, and elect to do her assignments in the library where her friends would not distract her. She started prioritizing goals (e.g., social goals versus academic goals). Thus, Maria decided to take a proactive and self-directed action to achieve homework completion. She started to improve her work and skills. However, she suffered several setbacks such as getting initially low grades on her assignments because now that she did the assignments alone, she needed to learn new strategies. However, eventually Maria increased her math homework scores, increased her self-efficacy beliefs, and used effective learning strategies.

An important step in Maria's determination to improve her skills was that she plotted her self-efficacy beliefs against her quiz scores over a period of time. A visual display of self-efficacy beliefs contrasted with academic performance could serve as a catalyst that begins with an assessment and evaluation, followed by an attribution, and ending with an adaptation with modification of future action and homework plans and selection of strategies in a cyclical process. Intervention studies support the effectiveness of graphing performance in contrast to motivational beliefs. For instance, following Zimmerman's academy model, Campillo and Pool (1999) report that graphed self-efficacy estimates along with writing scores on quizzes helped at risk college students become more accurate in monitoring their writing performance and selection of learning strategies. Similarly, and once again applying Zimmerman's academy model, Hanlon and Schneider (1999) reported that during an intervention designed to increase at risk students' mathematics proficiency through self-efficacy training, comparing their self-efficacy judgments to their mathematics quiz scores helped students to identify short-term goals and engage in self-monitoring. Maria also engaged in time management, and she discovered that after five weeks, her level of self-efficacy beliefs corresponded with her quiz scores. Her use of the homework log enhanced her self-monitoring and self-evaluation skills, which resulted in desirable academic outcomes.

The case of Maria leads to the discussion of actual interventions following Zimmerman's conceptualization of the learning academy model. Researchers have designed learning interventions consistent with the learning academy model in order enhance the learning experience of students at all levels of the learning stratification.

INTERVENTIONS SUPPORTING THE LEARNING ACADEMY MODEL OF SELF-REGULATORY TRAINING

Zimmerman's learning academy model of self-regulatory training as applied to homework has been successfully implemented among elementary, middle, high school, and college students. These interventions support the basic principles of the model such as that during the self-evaluation and monitoring step, teachers effectively provide self-monitoring forms to students containing guidelines that learners could follow to assess their studying progress. Teachers give daily or weekly assignments for which students set goals and engage in strategic planning. Students also evaluate their progress after receiving initial feedback from the teachers. Students establish a plan of action and self-monitoring and implement appropriate learning strategies while the teacher monitors the enactment of the new strategies. Students also monitor outcomes and refine strategies while the teacher continues to monitor learners' use of the new strategies, assist learners in refining their strategies if it is necessary, and check their self-confidence.

An Elementary School Intervention

Following Zimmerman's learning academy model of self-regulatory training, Stoeger and Ziegler (2008) reported on an intervention study of classroom-based training of self-regulated learning with fourth grade students attending German public schools. The goal of the intervention was to train homework behavior with a focus on time management. Specifically, the aim was to improve time management skills among fourth grade students. The researchers planned the intervention at this grade level because after this grade students move to secondary education with multiple teachers, and they wanted to provide an intervention targeting the students' self-regulatory skills and self-efficacy to prevent a drop in motivation after transferring to a different school system. Randomly, students were assigned to either a training group or a control group. Students in the training group received five weeks of training on self-regulation during normal classroom instruction and homework activities.

The intervention with the students was conducted over a five-week period. The intervention included self-evaluation and monitoring of homework behavior for the subject of mathematics. Using homework logs, the students reported their learning behaviors, when and for how long they studied, whether they took breaks, what types of distractions were present, whether they studied alone or with partners, and where these activities took place.

Each week the students were given homework logs in the form of tables with spaces for entries. The training followed the four steps identified by Zimmerman: self-evaluation and monitoring, goal setting and strategic planning, strategy implementation and monitoring, and strategic outcome monitoring. The results of the training suggest that it was effective. The students in the training group reported improved time management skills and self-reflection of their own learning in comparison to the control group. The self-efficacy of the students increased over the course of the training. The training group also reported increased motivation, willingness to exert effort, interest, and learning goal orientation, whereas helplessness decreased. With regard to performance on math exercises and quizzes, the training group showed no immediate performance growth, but their relative gains won through the training were significant in comparison to the control group. Stoeger and Ziegler concluded that the results of training confirmed the effectiveness of the learning academy model developed by Zimmerman and his colleagues and that the training developed by Zimmerman can be used in classroom settings.

A High School Intervention

In terms of high school students, Cooper, Horn, and Strahan (2005) designed an intervention program implementing Zimmerman's learning academy model of self-regulatory training with special attention to students' engagement in homework completion. The purpose of the investigation was to examine the responses of students and teachers to an intervention designed to improve the quality of assignments and enhance the motivation of 42 high school students. The purpose of the intervention was to promote higher levels of self-regulation. Seven English teachers met weekly with the researchers for three months. The teachers developed an intervention to promote higher levels of student involvement in lessons and homework assignments. The researcher assisted teachers in providing higher-order reasoning questions to the students, assigning homework and quizzes, reviewing students' responses, and planning instructional strategies. The intervention included observations, anecdotal notes, and interviews. The researchers had two specific questions: (1) how did participating teachers promote self-regulation and higher level reasoning? and (2) how did students respond to teachers' efforts of promoting self-regulation and higher level reasoning?

The researchers observed and interviewed the students and their teachers. Each of the teachers implemented the program in one of their classes within a school located in the Piedmont triad of the Carolinas. Using Zimmerman's homework logs, teachers examined students' self-regulatory behavior. On the logs, students reported the date that the assignments were completed, when, where, and with whom the assignments were completed, the presence of any distractions, and their level of self-efficacy.

The results of the intervention indicated that some students completed the homework logs without prompting. In addition, teachers reported that although the homework logs seemed like a chore at the time for the students and the teachers, the logs helped students self-monitor, assess, and ultimately improve their grades. Four teachers reported that teaching self-regulation strategies helped their students and that students responded to the teachers' efforts to help them to be self-regulated. With regard to goal setting, the students' most frequent performance goal was to obtain high grades, but they also reported mastery goals such as reading a book that they may not have read otherwise and becoming better readers. Some students reported a preference for completing assignments alone, whereas others preferred seeking help from instructors, small group discussion, or whole class reading and answering questions. The researchers concluded that the students demonstrated greater awareness of self-regulation and goal setting at the completion of the intervention.

A Technical College Intervention

Following Zimmerman's learning academy model, Bembenutty (2009, 2010) conducted an intervention to improve the self-regulatory skills of academically at-risk college students enrolled in a New York City college. The students were participating in a semester-long training seminar on self-regulation. Fifty-eight students were enrolled in an introductory mathematics course concurrently with an introduction to college life course. Students were all members of underrepresented minority groups. The focus of the program was to help college students become active agents in their own learning process by engaging in self-evaluation, goal setting, self-monitoring, self-adjustment, and effective learning strategies.

Students were assessed on their self-efficacy beliefs for learning math, willingness to delay gratification, intrinsic interest in the math course, outcome expectancies, and use of self-regulatory strategies. Students were given four homework logs developed by Zimmerman for two weeks. On the homework logs, students recorded their math homework assignments, goals for that day, where, when, and with whom the homework was completed, the presence of distractions, and their level of homework satisfaction.

After coding the homework logs (see Bembenutty, 2009 for the coding procedure), correlational analyses were conducted. The frequency of not reporting homework was inversely related to homework completion. Reporting general goals was significantly related to self-efficacy for learning. The association between reporting general goals and setting specific goals approached statistical significance. Time management accuracy was positively related to homework completion and midterm grade, and approaching a significant level of association with delay of gratification. Level of satisfaction with the effectiveness of their study time was positively and significantly related to their final course grades and self-efficacy. Based on the findings those students who effectively completed the homework logs, engaged in time management, displayed higher self-efficacy beliefs and satisfaction with the homework outcomes avoided distractions, and obtained higher midterm and final course grades. Bembenutty concluded that the findings of this study were consistent with and supported the effectiveness of Zimmerman's learning academy model of self-regulatory training.

A Private College Intervention

Bembenutty and White (2012) conducted a study applying Zimmerman's learning academy model of self-regulation among 133 college students enrolled in a religious private college in New York. The students were predominantly from underrepresented groups in higher education. On average, the students lacked study skills, had difficulty managing their time effectively, and lacked academic problem solving skills. The students were given homework logs during six weeks, in which they needed to record their homework activities in relation to a specific project in their classes. Students were enrolled in 12 different classes with nine different instructors. The instructors administered and collected the homework logs every week.

Of particular interest in the intervention were college students' self-reported homework practices and beliefs as well as their entries into weekly homework logs. In the homework logs, students reported the amount of homework completed per week, frequency of doing homework, general or specific homework goals, time management, study partners, distractions, and level of satisfaction with homework completion. This intervention had two primary objectives: (1) to examine the association between motivational beliefs, use of self-regulatory and help-seeking strategies, delay of gratification, and homework practices and (2) to examine whether differences in motivational beliefs, use of self-regulatory and help-seeking strategies, delay of gratification, and homework practices separately accounted for unique variance on final course grade and satisfaction with homework completion.

In this intervention, the process of effective homework completion started with students setting goals and planning strategies, implementing and monitoring strategies, and monitoring outcomes; it ended with self-evaluation. With regard to the first objective, the findings revealed that frequency of reporting specific homework goals in the homework log was related to final course grade and self-efficacy, whereas frequency of *not* reporting homework was negatively related to final course grade. Reporting avoiding distraction and having a high level of satisfaction with the homework outcomes as indicated in the homework log were positively related to final course grade. Number of homework assignments recorded was positively related to course final grade, homework outcome expectancy, and adaptive help-seeking. The results supported the effectiveness of Zimmerman's learning academy model of self-regulatory training. With regard to the second objective, the findings revealed that self-efficacy beliefs, use of learning strategies, and help seeking separately accounted for unique variance on final course grade and satisfaction with homework completion.

A College Intervention in an Educational Psychology Class

Wong (2005) conducted an intervention to improve students' approach to learning educational psychology and also to improve their self-efficacy in the subject topics. Twenty-five students enrolled in the first year of an undergraduate program in education participated in this intervention in Malaysia. She followed the four steps recommended by Zimmerman with slightly different terms but with equal meaning: (1) initial reflection on the situation, (2) planning for improvement, (3) enacting the plan and observing how it works, and (4) reflections. The intervention was implemented over a period of eight weeks. At the beginning and end of the intervention, an achievement test was administered to the students about five topics related to educational psychology. Self-efficacy was assessed and the students maintained written reflections at the beginning and end of the intervention. Students were given instruction and guidance in carrying out the four steps in the cyclical model, and the educator monitored the implementation of the tasks.

At the end of the intervention, the students' self-efficacy increased. An examination of the written reflections revealed that the students acquired a significant level of awareness and that they benefited from the intervention and obviated higher academic performance. Wong concluded that applying the principles of the learning academy model of self regulated learning (SRL) enhanced students' attainment in educational psychology and raised the self-efficacy in the participants.

In sum, how are these previous interventions supporting Zimmerman's learning academy model? The procedures and methods utilized in these interventions are consistent with Zimmerman's theoretical approaches. Administering a weekly homework log with visual display of the estimates of motivational beliefs and academic performance serves as a way for learners to check their academic status, level of academic proficiency, effectiveness of strategies selected, and adjustment of plans and goals for subsequent tasks. The outcomes of the intervention suggest that the students improved their accuracy in evaluating their performance and eventually became better calibrated on their judgments. Similarly, keeping records of these processes served to facilitate self-monitoring of performance, which increased their academic performance.

As these interventions suggest, there is an increasing interest in students' proactive and self-directed learning from the framework of self-regulated learning. Findings from the above discussed interventions and other consistent interventions continue to support Zimmerman's learning academy model. For instance, Chen (2011) conducted an intervention with Taiwanese college students to develop their academic self-regulatory skills. Similarly, Dembo and Seli (2004) in California, as part of a learning-to-learn course, conducted individual case studies and successfully followed Zimmerman's academy model over a period of six weeks. Stoeger and Ziegler (2005) conducted a self-regulated learning program for underachieving gifted mathematics elementary students. Shih, Kao, Chang, and Chen (2010) conducted a study with students learning English. Both supported the effectiveness of Zimmerman's learning academy model. As these interventions suggest, in the learning academy model, students are expected to be independent and to take full responsibility for their learning. Students are also expected to exhibit self-monitoring control and self-evaluation of their homework activities. Zimmerman's model of self-regulatory training has emerged as an appropriate theoretical and practical framework that serves to describe and delineate the learning experience of students in general, and those academically at-risk in particular. Homework logs or dailies have been effective tools used to implement the academy model when students are doing homework.

AN INTERVENTION CONSISTENT WITH THE LEARNING ACADEMY MODEL AMONG PRE-SERVICE TEACHERS

In this section, I will describe the implementation and effectiveness of a self-regulatory, non-experimental intervention modeled after Zimmerman's learning academy model among pre-service teachers. Pre-service teachers were trained to design homework logs following Zimmerman's learning academy model in order for them to enhance the learning experiences of their own students. The participants of this intervention were pre-service teachers teaching 7th to 12th grade middle and high school students. The specific components of the intervention approach, the implementation procedures, and case data will be discussed. The targets of this intervention were not the 7th to 12th grade students, but the teacher candidates. The work of the students is examined only as a way to understand how teacher candidates were able to understand the process of self-regulation as it relates to homework.

Description of Teacher Candidates and Classroom Setting

Teacher Candidates

Twenty-seven social studies student teachers who enrolled in an undergraduate or graduate educational psychology class during their student teaching participated in the intervention program. Teacher candidates were pursuing an initial teaching certification and were taking their last education class while teaching in middle or high school classrooms under the mentorship of a cooperating teacher and college field supervisor. Students were teaching in urban schools in New York. Teacher candidates were responsible for the instruction of one or two of the following social studies classes: Social Studies, American History, Economics, World History, and Law.

Educational Setting

The educational psychology course was taught by a tenured faculty member with training in self-regulation. The course covered the traditional topics of educational psychology such as cognitive development, behavioral theories, constructivist theories, cognitive theories, classroom management, and instructional strategies. However, the instructor included direct instruction based on self-regulation theory in the curriculum. For instance, for the end-of-the-semester portfolio, students were required to include an entire unit containing lesson plans that addressed how they would enhance the self-efficacy of the students, promote self-regulation, promote multicultural differences, and help students delay gratification. Teacher candidates were required to provide evidence of how they implemented self-regulation in the class as indicated in the unit, lesson plans, and 7th to 12th grade students' performance.

Components of the Intervention

For this intervention, teacher candidates knowledgeable about Zimmerman's learning academy model were assigned to create a homework log that they could give to their 7th to 12th grade students (at least to one of their students) so that the students could try to improve their homework process for a week (including a weekend). The homework logs include the students' self-assessment *before* doing the homework, *during* the homework activities, and *after* the homework was completed. Teacher candidates were asked to identify at least one component of self-regulation to be the target in the homework log. Consequently, the specific self-regulation of learning components varied across teacher candidates. In this regard, the only requirement was that they needed to target at least one self-regulatory component, such as self-efficacy, goal setting, help-seeking, self-monitoring or use of a strategy. They were also informed that they could use or adapt Zimmerman et al.'s (1996) homework log. Since the teachers were supervised by a cooperating teacher, they were instructed to ask permission from their cooperating teachers to give the homework log to the entire class (or at least to one of their students).

Unit of Analysis

As mentioned above, the precise nature of the intervention was to improve teacher candidates' ability to enhance and assess the homework self-regulation of their 7th to 12th grade students by focusing on at least one of the self-regulatory components while using a homework log. Thus, the unit of analysis was the teacher candidates. In other words, the intervention was designed to improve teacher candidates' awareness and skills of implementing self-regulation of homework among their students. The assessment tool used to improve teacher candidates' awareness and skills was their administration of a homework log to their students. Although the discussion will include how the 7th to 12th grade middle and high school students responded to the homework log and display self-regulatory skills, the target is not the students; rather, the unit of analysis is the teacher candidates.

Teacher Candidates' Tasks

As part of the college assignment, the teacher candidates were instructed to: (1) describe the student(s) (e.g., age, grade level, sex, class in which she or he was enrolled, and level of academic performance), (2) justify the selection of the components of the homework log and their purposes, (3) analyze the homework log in relation of the quantity and quality of homework submitted, (4) indicate what could be done differently in the future if they have to assign a homework log to their students, and (5) provide the original homework log used by the students.

Teacher Candidates' Analysis of the Homework Logs: General Findings

Twenty-seven teacher candidates submitted their homework reports to the instructor with the original homework logs completed by their students. Most of the teacher candidates opted to give the logs only to one or two students in their classes. Teacher candidates analyzed the homework logs submitted to them by their students. As the general findings described next suggest, teacher candidates were able to understand and help their students acquire self-regulatory skills.

Homework Assignments

Most of the assignments written by the students were prescribed by the teacher candidates. The assignments reflect more general (e.g., "Study for quiz") than specific goals (e.g., "One paragraph of Jewish Ghetto"). This suggests that about 75% of the teacher candidates were unable to train their students on the importance of setting specific goals. However, others were able to do so.

Time Management

Time management was computed by comparing the amount of time students expected the homework would take and the actual time to be completed. Although the discrepancy between expected time and actual time of homework completion is affected by the students' abilities and the level of difficulty of the homework assignments, most students were calibrated in their estimation of time. Specifically, 95% of the teacher candidates were able to train their students on the importance of calibrating and managing their time in order to successfully complete homework assignments.

Settings where Homework was Completed

All of the 7th to 12th grade students reported that they completed their homework at home (e.g., bedroom or living room), in the library, or at a tutor's home. For each homework assignment, students indicated in the homework log where they completed the assignment. Looking at the homework logs across time in relation to the students' self-satisfaction with the homework performance and the teacher grading of the homework suggests that the selection of study place was quite appropriate for these students considering the homework across time (i.e., selection of study places during the week). This suggests that through feedback, 95% of the teacher candidates were able to help their students to understand the importance of selecting appropriate environmental settings in order to successfully complete homework assignments.

Help-Seeking during Homework Completion

Teacher candidates were able to identify that 95% of the students reported that they completed their homework assignments alone, while 5% reported that they sought help from their parents, peers, or the Internet. The students who studied alone were also those whose homework assignments were graded satisfactory by the teachers. These findings suggest that teacher candidates were able to understand the importance of help-seeking as a self-regulatory strategy that could help students during the process of homework completion.

Distractions

In the teacher candidates' report, candidates were able to identify students' distraction while completing homework assignments. Students reported a high presence and frequency of distractions during homework completion. The most frequent distractions were family members, television, computer, text messages, Facebook, Internet, music, and telephone. However, more successful students often reported that they did not have distractions, and this was related to their level of satisfaction with homework performance. Since the immediate targets of this intervention are the teacher candidates, it is obvious that they were able to understand that distractions during homework could interfere with effective homework completion.

Level of Satisfaction with Homework Performance

Level of satisfaction refers to how satisfied the students were with the quality of their homework completion. By analyzing their students' homework logs, teacher candidates understood that students with more frequent distractions also reported lower levels of satisfaction with the quality of homework completed than students with fewer distractions. Nevertheless, teacher candidates observed that about 60% of the students reported a moderate to high level of satisfaction with the quality of homework completed.

Summary of This Subsection

The purpose of this intervention was to improve pre-service teachers' awareness and skills to design homework logs following Zimmerman's academy model in order for them to enhance the learning experience and self-regulation of their own students. The effectiveness of the intervention is understood based on how well the teacher candidates were able to construct effective homework logs targeting self-regulatory skills, and their ways to interpret those skills reported by their students.

In the summary report to the college instructor, each teacher candidate evaluated their students' homework logs. These reports provide evidence that the teacher candidates understood the process of self-regulation as it applies to homework. For instance, they were able to connect their students' time management, ability to seek help, ways of coping with distractions, level of calibration, and environmental control with the grades obtained on the homework and students' level of satisfaction with the homework completed. To understand this process with more detail, a case illustrating the implementation of the intervention is presented next.

AN INDIVIDUAL CASE ILLUSTRATING THE
IMPLEMENTATION OF THE INTERVENTION

Marie, one of the teacher candidates, administered the homework log to two students enrolled in her 11th grade U.S history class. As Figure 6.3 displays, Student 1, Tanya, received mostly A grades and performed very well in class. As Figure 6.4 displays, Student 2, Kvetlana, was assigned mostly B and C grades, participated in class, and was an average student. Marie assigned the homework logs to these students for them to self-regulate their homework completion over the period of a week, including the weekend. Marie created a homework log of eleven columns (see Figure 6.3 and Figure 6.4). The first non-numbered column was the day of the week to help students keep track of the days of the week and help them to remember what assignment they needed to do.

In Column 1 (Homework Assignment), students reported their general or specific assignments. Tanya did not record entries in this column during

Day of the Week	1 Homework Assignment	2 Estimation of Time Needed	3 Self-confidence assessment (Before doing homework; 1–10)	4 Time Started	5 Self-confidence assessment (During the homework; 1–10)	6 Time Completed	7 Self-confidence assessment (After the homework is completed; 1–10)	8 Strategy used to complete the assignment	9 Distraction	10 Level of satisfaction with the assignment completed (1–10)
Saturday										
Sunday										
Monday	Page 398 textbook, answer question	10 minutes	10	4:50	9	5:02	10	Notes	TV	10
Tuesday	Castle learning	25 minutes	9	5:10	9	6:18	9	Notes	TV	8
Wednesday	Focus question	15 minutes	10	6:02	10	6:22	10	Notes	TV	10
Thursday	Focus question	10 minutes	8	7:00	9	7:30	9	Worksheets	Facebook	10
Friday										

Figure 6.3 Homework log of Tanya.

Day of the Week	1 Homework Assignment	2 Estimation of Time Needed	3 Self-confidence assessment (Before doing homework; 1–10)	4 Time Started	5 Self-confidence assessment (During the homework; 1–10)	6 Time Completed	7 Self-confidence assessment (After the homework is completed; 1–10)	8 Strategy used to complete the assignment	9 Distraction	10 Level of satisfaction with the assignment completed (1–10)
Saturday	Essay	10 minutes	8	5:30	7	6:00	8	The DBQ	Computer	8
Sunday	Essay	5 minutes	8	6:10	6	6:20	9	The DBQ	Computer	8
Monday	Read p. 398; answer the following question: Do you know what it was?	15 minutes	6	3:30	6	3:35	8	The textbook	My sister and parents	8
Tuesday	Complete castle learning for Unit 1 & 2	2 hours	5	5:30	4	6:30	8	Castle learning	Facebook and game	9
Wednesday	Answer focus question	5 minutes	6	5:43	7	5:50	9	Knowledge of castle site	Nothing	9
Thursday	Answer focus question	10 minutes	5	5:30	6	5:40	8	The notes	Mon and family	9
Friday	Was US involving a mistake?	10 minutes	5	3:45	6	3:55	8	The notes	nothing	8

Figure 6.4 Homework log of Svetlana.

the weekend beginning on Friday and reported only general goals. Kvet-lana reported general and specific goals, but mostly general goals. At this level, the teacher goal was to help both students to set specific goals rather than general goals, and to identify practical and realistic goals given the students' strengths and limitations. During the week, the teacher provided feedback about the kind of goals identified by the student in relation to the outcome obtained for that particular assignment. The teacher functions as a coach during this process.

Column 2 (Estimation of Time Needed) was designed to help students manage their time. Students approximated the amount of time they would need for the assignment to self-regulate their time. Column 2 is related to Column 4 (Time Started) and Column 6 (Time Completed). Tanya was less calibrated in assignment of the time required to complete the assignment than Kvetlana. During this process, the teacher provided feedback to the students about whether the expected time and actual time needed to complete the homework matched. The goal of the teacher was to make the students calibrated between their expected time, skills, quality of the assignment, and their actual time.

Column 3 (Self-confidence Assessment *Before* Doing the Homework) was related to Column 5 (Confidence *During* Homework) and Column 7 (Confidence *After* the Homework Was Completed). The teacher candidate explained that these three columns would help the students and the teacher to see how confident or motivated students were before, during, and after working on the homework and whether and how the confidence changed across time. Tanya sustained high levels of confidence across the three phases of homework completion. In contrast, Kvetlana started with somewhat moderate levels of confidence but increased across time. The interaction between the teacher and the students at this level is to assist the students to calibrate their levels of self-efficacy. To accomplish this, the teacher questions the students about their beliefs and how they increased or decreased during the process of homework completion. If the students were estimating their self-efficacy level with over-confidence or under-confidence, the teacher used verbal prompts, questioning, and modeling to bring the student back to a calibrated level. The teachers often encountered resistance from the students who overestimated their ability level. For instance, overconfident students made statements, such as, "That is the way in which I learn. I do not need to change my strategies." Underconfident students made statements, such as, "Estimating and monitoring of my work do not help me to learn. I do not need to plan my work."

Column 8 asked students to report the strategies used to complete the homework. Marie intended to examine what techniques or strategies students used to complete the assignment believed that "students and the teachers can reflect back and evaluate whether or not the strategies used were efficient and what could be done in the future to improve." Tanya used only notebooks and worksheets as strategies to complete the homework, while Kvetlana used a variety of strategies such as the textbook and notes. When the teacher identified that the students used effective strategies, the teacher praised the students with specific feedback about the strategy used.

According to the teacher candidate, Column 9 (Distraction) was "used to document the distractions students encountered while working on their assignments." The teacher candidate observed that by using this column, "students can reflect back on this entry in the future and control the distractions they encountered while working on their homework so that they are more efficient in the future." Tanya and Kvetlana experienced similar distractions (e.g., Facebook). However, for Tanya, television was a distraction twice, while Kvetlana reported no distractions on two different days, but considered family members to be frequent distractions. The role of the teacher at this level is to help the students to maintain a high level of motivation in spite of distractions and to suggest ways to avoid future distractions.

Column 10 (Level of Satisfaction with the Assignment Completed) was done after the assignment was completed. The teacher candidate stated: "Students rate themselves on how satisfied they are with their completed work. Students can reflect on this entry and change certain aspects of their homework procedures in order to improve their satisfaction rating at the end of the assignment." Overall, Tanya rated herself as more satisfied than Kvetlana on the quality of the homework completed. At this point, the interaction between the teacher and the students is to help the students to become aware of the level of agreement between their satisfaction and the grade obtained and to reflect on the other elements contained in the homework that could explain positive or negative outcomes of the homework efforts.

Teacher Candidate's Reflection of the Intervention with Tanya and Kvetlana

Marie, the teacher candidate, observed that Tanya "exceeded the estimated time she set for herself. She completed all the assignments and got full points for each assignment. However, Tanya was absent on Friday and missed the homework assigned for that day." The teacher candidate reflected that Tanya used strategies that helped her on her homework and that in the future she could finish on time by eliminating the distractions she encountered.

The teacher candidate observed that Kvetlana "did not exceed the estimated time she set for herself. She completed all her assignments and got full points for almost all her assignments." Marie observed that Student 2 could have still used more sources such as handouts and the internet to do research. Marie asserted that in the future, Kvetlana could finish the assignments by eliminating the distractions, that her confidence increased across time, and that she was satisfied with the quality of the homework completed.

Marie concluded that in the future, she "would assign a homework log for the entire month instead of just one week, so that I can analyze several weeks of entries instead of just one week." Marie also indicated that in the future, she would provide students with "feedback on their progress and advice on what they can do to improve their self-regulation skills on future assignments" each week. Derived from this intervention is the point that self-monitoring is an important self-regulatory skill that teachers can impart to their students so that they can become independent, self-directed, and autonomous learners.

To recapitalize this section, the bottom line is that interventions to assess the effectiveness of homework are warranted, and when they have been done, they produced positive and promising outcomes. The theoretical ground delineated by Zimmerman and the examples he presented represent clear guidelines for teachers and students alike in order to facilitate learning and teaching. The learning academy model put forth by Zimmerman has proved to be effective across different populations of students, classroom settings, academic contexts, and educational levels. An essential component in the learning academy model is the process of self-monitoring. Future research on homework should consider the importance of self-monitoring for achieving self-regulation, and this point will be further discussed in the next section.

WHERE ARE WE GOING FROM HERE? FUTURE RESEARCH

This section provides an overview of the status of empirical support for the learning academy model and highlights what might be useful to expand on in research on self-regulation of homework. The status of empirical support for the academy model is solid. International empirical studies have been conducted with learners at different developmental levels. All findings support Zimmerman's theoretical grounds. However, future research on homework conducted under the academy model should consider expanding its frontiers. First, it should focus more on self-monitoring as an invaluable tool for obtaining academic self-regulation during homework completion. Zimmerman has advocated for strengthening observable behavior as well as assessment of beliefs related to self-regulation (Cleary & Zimmerman, 2004, 2006; Zimmerman, 2008; Zimmerman & Labuhn, 2012; Zimmerman & Paulsen, 1995). Self-monitoring tools can be used to support self-regulatory behavior among learners (Schmitz & Perels, 2011), and self-monitoring is one of Zimmerman's hallmarks, which could be applied to understanding and assessing students' homework. Self-monitoring is particularly important during homework completion where students work independently on their assignments without the direct supervision of teacher (Zimmerman & Paulsen, 1995).

Second, it is clear that Zimmerman's learning academy model considers the contexts in which learning takes place. Skills acquisition in an academic context is not separate from where learners are with regard to their culture, language proficiency, family traditions, ethnicity, and socio-economic status. Future research should make an effort to consider these contextual factors that could explain learners' homework performance. For instance, imagine that Maria, the middle school student described above, is a homeless learner. She may not be able to conduct a social studies homework designed to evaluate a webinar speech by a Wall Street magnate about how the U.S. economy is affecting current trends in women's employment if she does not have the necessary socio-economic resources to conduct that task.

Third, derived from Zimmerman's learning academy model is the importance of conducting research that is not only based on students' self-reported data at a sole time. In the example of Maria, data that could be obtained from Maria's homework performance over a long period of time could reflect the generalization of her behavior patterns across time and circumstances.

Fourth, Zimmerman (2008) invites researchers to consider other methods of assessing learning and performance that could be used to assess homework performance in the academy model. Specifically, Zimmerman (2008) invites researchers to conduct research on self-regulation using computer trace to assess changes on psychological processes during learning and to use think-aloud protocols for students to report about thoughts and cognitive processes while learning. In addition to using logs, he also suggests using study diaries, which could facilitate a cyclical analysis of context, and using direct observations and qualitative measures such as portfolios. Zimmerman also advocates for microanalysis of context in sequential phases and task specific. These five methods could all be helpful to assess students' homework motivation and performance.

Fifth, although conducting research using surveys and questionnaires are legitimate ways to obtain information about students' homework processes, researchers should consider complementing those methods with interviews, dialogic inquiries, creativity processes (such as drawing and painting), art performance, and role-playing. These methods should be triangulated with multiple methods of causal inferences, such as class level and group level (Trautwein, Lüdtke, Schnyder, & Niggli, 2006), and with experimental and control groups.

Sixth, all research on self-regulation of homework should consider inherited factors in learning, such as students' characteristics (e.g., ability, motivation, and study habits), subject matter, and grade level (Cooper, 2001). Likewise, this line of research could include total amount and frequency of homework assigned and the purpose of the homework (Cooper, 2001).

Seventh, effective homework interventions need to consider in a cyclical fashion administering weekly homework logs to students. These logs will empower students to take control of their learning and self-direct their efforts. In a similar vein, providing graphs or asking learners to graphs their motivational beliefs in contrast with their weekly performance should serve as a "reality check" about their learning proficiencies (Campillo & Pool, 1999; Hanlon & Schneider, 1999). These self-monitoring processes should help to enhance students' capabilities to judge their learning progress and to determine new courses of action in the event of disappointing outcomes.

Eighth, from Zimmerman's learning academy model it is derived that teachers play a crucial role in students' learning. That is why teachers' characteristics, such as self-efficacy for teaching, multicultural awareness, classroom management skills, knowledge of the content, and use of teaching strategies and skills are vital to the students' successful adoption of self-regulated learning approaches. In a similar vein, teachers' written feedback on homework, grading policies and procedures, testing approaches, and use of class instruction and discussion need to be well orchestrated with the students' characteristics. These perspectives are highlighted by Rebecca Mieliwocki, who received the 2012 USA National Teacher of the Year from President Barack Obama. Mieliwocki states,

> What I do have are the qualities that some of the best teachers have. I have an absolute passion for my work. I have a bottomless well of belief in my students and their potential. I have a thirst for getting better at what I do every single day. And I have a warm and welcoming heart for all students and the unique gifts that they bring to my classroom. (Bruce, 2012, para. 6)

Educational Implications: Academic Delay of Gratification and Homework Behavioral Contracts

Derived from Zimmerman's theory and research, in this section, academic delay of gratification and homework behavioral contracts are offered as practical educational applications and as important determinant factors to the triumph of homework completion.

Academic Delay of Gratification

For the learning academy model to work successfully and comprehensively, students need to be able to defer immediate gratification. *Academic delay of gratification* refers to learners' willingness to postpone immediately available rewards and impulses for the sake of reaching more important and valuable academic rewards and goals, such as completing an important homework assignment in spite of declining a very tempting invitation by friends to attend a party (Bembenutty & Karabenick, 1998, 2004). On this point, Zimmerman (1998) observed, "Naïve self-regulators remain dependent on others or must generate extraordinary personal motivation to delay gratification until distant goals are achieved" (p. 6). Zimmerman (1990) further contended that "during academic studying, students must sacrifice immediate recreational time for the possible eventual rewards of high marks. Their willingness to make this sacrifice demands both self-confidence in one's ability to learn and then personal resolve to delay gratification" (p. 12). In a consistent vein, Wigfield, Klauda, and Cambria (2011) propose that delay of gratification is most relevant while students are monitoring their task performance.

In order for students to be fully capable of self-regulation, they need to be able to delay gratification for the sake of mastering academic tasks and homework assignments. Bembenutty and Karabenick (1998, 2004) have presented evidence supporting the important association between delay of gratification and motivational, cognitive, and self-regulatory components of academic achievement. An effective educational experience is inconceivable if students are unable to delay gratification. However, what is also inconceivable is classroom instruction and homework processes for which educators are not themselves trained as students on research about delay of gratification.

A teacher could provide the best self-monitoring forms and homework logs to students, but if the teachers do not integrate the importance of promoting delay of gratification into their daily curricula, the best and most skilled learners could eventually succumb to immediately available gratification. For instance, they would be distracted by tempting media and technology such as text messages, Facebook, Twitter, LinkedIn, and chat rooms while attempting to complete homework. It is imperative that delay of gratification be included in every lesson and every homework assignment. Teachers are invited to consider ways to promote students' willingness to delay gratification. Providing self-monitoring forms with which students can monitor when, where, with whom, and at what time task assignments are completed will serve as an initial step toward enacting delay of gratification during homework completion (Bembenutty, 2009).

Bembenutty (2009) sought to examine the roles of motivational beliefs and self-regulatory processes on predicting homework completion and academic achievement among college students. The investigation was conceptualized under the umbrella of Zimmerman's (2000) model of self-regulation. A path analysis revealed that students who reported completing their homework assignments indicated that they (a) used diverse and effective self-regulatory learning strategies, (b) were willing to delay gratification for the sake of long-term academic goals, (c) were more motivated as indicated by their high self-efficacy, outcome expectancy, and intrinsic interest, and (d) obtained higher grades than students who did not successfully complete their homework assignments. These results provide support for Zimmerman's self-regulatory processes in relation to homework practices and engagement.

In the field of self-regulation and homework research, wrong ideas about self-regulation and homework have propagated. For instance, the idea that self-regulation is a martyrdom with complete deprivation often dominates thinking, when indeed self-regulation is a celebration of our empowerment and agentic control of our behavior, cognition, and environment. With regard to learners, self-regulation should reflect passion for learning. With regard to teachers, self-regulation is first, a passion for learning and then a passion for teaching. Passion for teaching is reflected in the words William James (1899) addressed to teachers:

> In teaching, you must simply work your pupil into such a state of interest in what you are going to teach him that every other object of attention is banished from his mind; then reveal it to him so impressively that he will remember the occasion to his dying day; and finally fill him with devouring curiosity to know what the next steps in connection with the subject are. (pp. 9–10)

The call from James is also a call for learners to have passion while engaging in academic tasks and homework, as he said, "... that every other object of attention is banished from his mind." In the painting displayed in Figure 6.5, an art teacher, John Riveaux, portrays the challenges that students often experience while attempting to do homework and that to successfully complete the homework, students need to remain task-focused over time.

Homework Behavioral Contract

Behavioral contracts for homework completion should facilitate self-regulation of learning and increase the quality of the homework submissions. A *behavioral contract* is an agreement between the student and the teacher, and sometimes it involves parents, peers or other school officials. A contract has the following basic components (Jones & Jones, 2010):

- The teacher and the student should identify the problem with the homework. Recognizing the problem is usually not a challenge for the teacher because teachers should keep track of the quantity and quality of homework submissions.
- The teacher and the student should find reasons why they are having difficulties with the homework. The teacher asks questions such

Figure 6.5 Painting depicting a student's willingness to delay gratifcaition while doing homework. In this painting, a student is centered and levitating to convey an affirmation to be disciplined and ability to delay gratification while studying and doing homework. The books are symbols of academic rigor and study. The background represents a parade of distractions, from sports, movies, a carousel, marshmallows, and a loud marching band. These are symbols of the distractions of life and its temptations that students often experience while attending to do homework assignments. Emotionally one wonders, as a good student, "Is life passing me by?" The symbol of the universal serial bus (USB) port is what makes this latest piece consistent with an awareness of the ubiquitous presence of distracting technology. The student will need to engage in self-regulation and delaying gratification in order to successfully complete his homework.

as, "Is the homework too easy or too challenging for the student? Does the student have to sit for a long time at her desk?"

- The teacher and the student develop a plan to help the student better her homework and reach her full potential in class.

- The teacher and the student identify reinforcements and consequences if the homework is or is not completed. The responsibilities of the teacher and the student need to be clearly delineated, and both need to agree on them.
- The teacher and the student check on the progress of the plan periodically and amend it if it necessary.

CONCLUSION

Zimmerman's seminal work on self-regulation and motivation has had a profound effect on education and psychology as well as in other fields such as sports, health, and music. Learning from and collaborating on research with Zimmerman has been exciting and rewarding. In this chapter, I have provided an overview of the major components of Zimmerman's learning academy model of self-regulatory training as it applies to homework. I also described intervention programs that have used Zimmerman's self-regulatory training and described the implementation and effectiveness of the intervention program in which pre-service teachers used homework logs following Zimmerman's model to enhance the learning experiences of their 7th to 12th grade students.

The data support that if teachers adopt the learning academy model of self-regulatory training, they will be able to empower learners with life-long tools that will foster human agency, self-regulation of motivation through anticipatory and self-reaction mechanisms, exercise of self-control, and delay of gratification. From Zimmerman's work on self-regulation, it is evident that the cultivation of self-efficacy and self-regulation through proximal and specific goals leads to the acquisition of knowledge and skills that will have a lasting effect at the personal level as well as in our educational system, in homework in particular.

REFERENCES

Alleman, J., Brophy, J., Knighton, B., Ley, R., Botwinski, B., & Middlestead, S. (2010). *Homework done right: Powerful learning in real-life situations.* Thousand Oaks, CA: Corwin Press.

Bandura, A. (1997). *Self-efficacy: The exercise of control.* New York, NY: Freeman.

Bembenutty, H. (2009). Self-regulation of homework completion. *Psychology Journal, 6*(4), 138–153.

Bembenutty, H. (2010). Homework completion: The role of self-efficacy, delay of gratification, and self-regulatory processes. *The International Journal of Educational and Psychological Assessment, 6*(1), 1–20. Retrieved from http://tijepa. books.officelive.com/Documents/A1_V6.1_TIJEPA.pdf

Bembenutty, H. (2011). Meaningful and maladaptive homework practices: The role of self-efficacy and self-regulation. *Journal of Advanced Academics, 22*(3), 448–473. doi:10.1177/1932202X1102200304

Bembenutty, H. & Karabenick, S. A. (1998). Academic delay of gratification. *Learning and Individual Differences, 10,* 329–346. doi:10.1016/S1041-6080(99)80126-5

Bembenutty, H. & Karabenick, S. A. (2004). Inherent association between academic delay of gratification, future time perspective, and self-regulated learning. *Educational Psychology Review, 16*(1), 35–57. doi:10.1023/B:EDPR.0000012344.34008.5c

Bembenutty, H. & White, M. (2012, April). *Academic performance and satisfaction with homework completion among college students: Do self-efficacy, self-regulation, help seeking, and class context make a difference?* Paper presented during the annual meeting of the American Educational Research Association, Vancouver, Canada.

Bennett, S. & Kalish, K. (2006). *The case against homework: How homework is hurting children and what parents can do about it.* New York, NY: Three Rivers Press.

Bruce, M. (2012, April, 24). *Obama honors National Teacher of the Year.* Retrieved from http://abcnews.go.com/blogs/politics/2012/04/obama-honors-national-teacher-of-the-year/

Buell, J. (2004). *Closing the book on homework: Enhancing public education and freeing family time.* Philadelphia, PA: Temple University Press.

Campillo, M. & Pool, S. (1999, April). *Improving writing proficiency through self-efficacy training.* Paper presented at the annual meeting of the American Educational Research Association, Montreal, Canada.

Chen, P. (2011). Guiding college students to develop academic self-regulatory skills. *Journal of College Teaching and Learning, 8*(9), 29–33.

Cleary, T. J. & Zimmerman, B. J. (2004). Self-regulation empowerment program: A school-based program to enhance self-regulated and self-motivated cycles of student learning. *Psychology in the Schools, 41,* 537–550. doi:10.1002/pits.10177

Cleary, T. J. & Zimmerman, B. J. (2006). Teachers' perceived usefulness of strategy microanalyic assessment information. *Psychology in the Schools, 43,* 149–155. doi:10.1002/pits.20141

Cooper, H. (1989). *Homework.* New York, NY: Longman.

Cooper, H. (2001). *The battle over homework: Common ground for administrators, teachers, and parents* (2nd. ed.). Thousand Oaks, CA: Corwin Press.

Cooper, J. E., Horn, S., & Strahan, D. B. (2005). "If only they would do their homework": Promoting self-regulation in high school English classes. *The High School Journal, 88*(3), 10–25. doi:10.1353/hsj.2005.0001

Cooper, H., Robinson, J. C., & Patall, E. A. (2006). Does homework improve academic achievement? A synthesis of research 1987–2003. *Review of Educational Research, 76,* 1–62. doi: 10.3102/00346543076001001

Cooper, H., Steenbergen-Hu, S., & Dent, A. L. (2012). Homework. In K. R. Harris, S. Graham, & T. Urdan (Eds.), *APA Educational Psychology Handbook* (Vol. 3, pp. 475–495). Washington, DC: American Psychological Association. doi:10.1037/13275-019

Cooper, H., & Valentine, J. C. (2001). Using research to answer practical questions about homework. *Educational Psychologist, 36*(3), 143–153.

Dembo, M. H. & Seli, H. P. (2004). Students' resistance to change in learning strategies courses. *Journal of developmental Education, 27*(3), 2–11.

Dettmers, S., Trautwein, U., Ludtke, O., Kunter, M., & Baumert, J. (2010). Homework works if homework quality is high: Using multilevel modeling to predict the development of achievement in mathematics. *Journal of Educational Psychology, 102*(2), 467–482. doi:10.1037/a0018453

Dumont, H., Trautwein, U., Lüdtke, O., Neumann, M., Niggli, A., & Schnyder, I. (2012). Does parental homework involvement mediate the relationship between family background and educational outcomes? *Contemporary Educational Psychology, 37*(1), 55–69.

Epstein, J. L. (1988). *Homework practices, achievements, and behaviors of elementary school students*, Report No. 26. Washington, DC: Office of Educational Research and Improvement.

Gilbertson D., & Sonnek. R (2010). Interventions for homework problems. In G. G. Peacock, R. A. Ervin, E. J. Daly III, & K. W. Merrell (Eds.), *Practical handbook of school psychology: Effective practices for the 21st century* (pp. 353–370). New York, NY: Guilford Press.

Good, W. R. (1926). Opinions on homework for elementary school pupils. *Elementary School Journal, 27*(122), 8–25.

Hanlon, E. H. & Schneider, Y. (1999, April). *Improving math proficiency through self-efficacy training*. Paper presented at the annual meeting of the American Educational Research Association, Montreal, Canada.

James, W. (1899). *Talks to teachers on psychology and some of life's ideals*. Retrieved from http://www.ttrb.ac.uk/viewArticle2.aspx?contentId=11037

Jones, V. & Jones, L. (2010). *Comprehensive classroom management: Creating communities of support and solving problems* (9th ed.). Boston, MA: Allyn & Bacon.

Keith, T. Z. & Cool, V. A. (1992). Testing models of school learning: Effects of quality of instruction, motivation, academic coursework, and homework on academic achievement. *School Psychology Quarterly, 3*, 207–226.

Kitsantas, A., Cheema, J., & Ware, H. (2011). The role of homework support resources, time spent on homework, and self-efficacy beliefs in mathematics achievement. *Journal of Advanced Academics, 22*(2), 312–341.

Kitsantas, A. & Zimmerman, B. J. (2009). College students' homework and academic achievement: The mediating role of self-regulatory beliefs. *Metacognition Learning, 4*, 97–110. doi:10.1007/s11409-008-9028-y

Kohn, A. (2006). *The homework myth : Why our kids get too much of a bad thing*. Cambridge, MA: Da Capo Life Long.

Kralovec, E. & Buell, J. (2000). *The end of homework: How homework disrupts families, overburdens children, and limits learning*. Boston, MA: Beacon Press.

Lee, J. F. & Pruitt, K. W. (1979). Homework assignments: Classroom games or teaching tools? *Clearing House, 53*, 31–35.

Patall, E. A., Cooper, H., & Robinson, J. C. (2008). The effects of choice on intrinsic motivation and related outcomes: A meta-analysis of research findings. *Psychological Bulletin, 134*, 270–300.

Ramdass, D. & Zimmerman, B. J. (2011). Developing self-regulation skills: The important role of homework. *Journal of Advanced Academics, 22*(2), 194–218.

Schmitz, B. & Perels, F. (2011). Self-monitoring of self-regulation during math homework behaviour using standardized diaries. *Metacognition Learning, 6,* 255–273. doi:10.1007/s11409-011-9076-6.

Schunk, D. H. (2012). Social cognitive theory. In K. R. Harris, S. Graham, & T. Urdan (Eds.), *APA Educational Psychology Handbook* (Vol. I, pp. 101–123). Washington, DC: American Psychological Association. doi:10.1037/13273-005

Shih, K., Kao, T., Chang, C., & Chen, H. (2010). Development and evaluation of a self-regulatory-learning-cycle-based system for self-regulated learning. *Educational Technology & Society, 13*(1), 80–93.

Stoeger, H. & Ziegler, A. (2005). Evaluation of an elementary classroom self-regulated learning program for gifted mathematics underachievers. *International Education Journal, 6*(2), 261–271.

Stoeger, H. & Ziegler, A. (2008). Evaluation of a classroom based training to improve self-regulation in time management tasks during homework activities with fourth graders. *Metacognition in Learning, 3,* 207–230. doi:10.1007/s11409-008-9027-z

Strang, R. (1968). *Guided study and homework: What research says to the teacher?* Series No. 8. Washington, DC: Association of Classroom Teachers of the National Education Association.

Trautwein, U., Lüdtke, O., Schnyder, I., & Niggli, A. (2006). Predicting homework effort: support for a domain-specific, multilevel homework model. *Journal of Educational Psychology, 98,* 438–456. doi:10.1037/0022-0663.98.2.438.

Vatterott, C. (2009). *Rethinking homework: Best practices that support diverse needs.* Alexandria, VA: Association for Supervision and Curriculum Development.

Walker, J. M. T. & Hoover-Dempsey, K. V. (2001, April). *Age-related patterns in student invitations to parental involvement in homework.* Paper presented at the annual meeting of the American Educational Research Association, Seattle, WA.

Warton, P. M. (2001). The forgotten voices in homework: Views of students. *Educational Psychologist, 36*(3), 155–165.

Wigfield, A., Klauda, S. L., & Cambria, J. (2011). Influences on the development of academic self-regulatory processes. In B. J. Zimmerman & D. H. Schunk (2011). *Handbook of self-regulation and performance* (pp. 33–48). New York, NY: Routledge

Wong, M, S. L. (2005). Exploring the effects of a cyclical model of self-regulated learning in learning educational psychology. *Jurnal Penyelidikan MPBL 6,* 11–21.

Xu, J., Coasts, L. T., & Davidson, M. L. (2012). Promoting student interest in science: The perspectives of exemplary African American teachers. *American Educational Research Journal February, 4,* 124–154.

Xu, J. & Corno, L. (1998). Case studies of families doing third-grade homework. *TeachersCollege Record, 100*(2), 402–436.

Xu, J. & Corno, L. (2003). Family help and homework management reported by middle school students. *Elementary School Journal, 103*(5), 503–517.

Zimmerman, B. J. (1990). Self-regulated learning and academic achievement: An overview. *Educational psychologist, 25*(1), 3–17.

Zimmerman, B. J. (1998). Developing self-fulfilling cycles of academic regulation: An analysis of exemplary instructional models. In D. H. Schunk & B. J. Zimmerman (Eds.), *Self-regulated learning: From teaching to self-reflective practice* (pp. 1–19). New York, NY: Guilford Press.

Zimmerman, B. J. (2000). Attaining self-regulation: A social cognitive perspective. In M. Boekaerts, P. R. Pintrich, & M. Zeidner (Eds.), *Handbook of self-regulation* (pp. 13–39). San Diego, CA: Academic Press.

Zimmerman, B. J. (2002). Achieving self-regulation: The trial and triumph of adolescence. In F. Pajares & T. Urdan (Eds.), *Adolescence and Education* (Vol. 2, pp.1–27). Greenwich, CT: Information Age.

Zimmerman, B. J. (2008). Goal setting: A key proactive source of academic self-regulation. In D. H. Schunk & B. J. Zimmerman (Eds.), *Motivation and self-regulated learning: Theory, research, and applications* (pp. 267–295). New York, NY: Lawrence Erlbaum Associates.

Zimmerman, B. J., Bonner, S., & Kovach, R. (1996). *Developing self-regulated learners: Beyond achievement to self-efficacy.* Washington, DC: American Psychological Association. doi:10.1037/10213-000

Zimmerman, B. J. & Kitsantas, A. (2005). Homework practices and academic achievement: The mediating role of self-efficacy and perceived responsibility beliefs. *Contemporary Educational Psychology, 30,* 397–417. doi:10.1016/j.cedpsych.2005.05.003

Zimmerman, B. J. & Labuhn, A. S. (2012). Self-regulation of learning: Process approaches to personal development. In K. R. Harris, S. Graham, & T. Urdan (Eds.), *APA Educational Psychology Handbook* (Vol. I, pp. 399–425). Washington, DC: American Psychological Association. doi:10.1037/13273-014

Zimmerman, B. J. & Paulsen, A.S. (1995). Self-monitoring during collegiate studying: An invaluable tool for academic self-regulation. *New Directions for Teaching and Learning, 63,* 13–27. doi:10.1002/tl.37219956305

CHAPTER 7

HELPING COLLEGE STUDENTS BECOME MORE STRATEGIC AND SELF-REGULATED LEARNERS

Claire Ellen Weinstein and Taylor W. Acee

Theory and research on learning strategies within cognitive educational psychology and both strategic and self-regulated learning have suggested that humans can improve their learning and create more meaningful and retrievable memories by using learning strategies to actively process the information they are trying to learn (Mayer & Alexander, 2011; Paris & Paris, 2001; Weinstein & Mayer, 1986; Woolfolk, 2009). VandenBos (2007) defines a learning strategy as "a mental or behavioral strategy used to facilitate learning, such as forming a mental image, organizing items, searching for existing associations, or practicing retrieval" (p. 530). Researchers and educators who focus on strategic and self-regulated learning, two highly related but distinct conceptions, also generally agree that learning strategies involve the proactive and planful use of cognition, metacognition, motivation, affect, and behavior to facilitate learning and the successful performance of complex cognitive tasks, such as critical thinking and problem solving (see

Applications of Self-Regulated Learning across Diverse Disciplines, pages 197–236
Copyright © 2013 by Information Age Publishing
All rights of reproduction in any form reserved. **197**

Zimmerman & Schunk, 2011). Contemporary theory and research place learning strategies within interactive and dynamic models of strategic and self-regulated learning that emphasize the importance of students taking more responsibility for their own learning (Pintrich, 2000, 2004; Weinstein, Acee, & Jung, 2010; Weinstein, Husman, & Dierking, 2000; Zimmerman, 2000, 2011). Fostering both strategic and self-regulated learning is essential for developing lifelong learners who can survive and thrive in diverse educational settings and workplace training environments.

The exploding enrollments in higher education in the United States, as well as the large percentage of new and continuing students who are not academically ready to succeed and thrive in college-level classes (Aud et al., 2011), has led to broader definitions of what it means to be *college ready* (Conley, 2007) and an increasing focus on strategic and self-regulation interventions to help students succeed in their studies (Weinstein, Acee, & Jung, 2011). A recent national report on the high school graduating class of 2010 suggested that, based on American College Testing (ACT) score benchmarks, only 43% of the students were prepared to take college algebra, and only 66% were prepared to take college English composition (ACT, 2010).

In order to help students develop basic skills necessary to succeed in college, institutions often require them to take developmental education (DE) courses in reading, writing, and/or mathematics before they can enroll in credit-bearing college courses (Arendale, 2010). Although teaching students basic content knowledge and skills in reading, writing, and math is necessary, research suggests that these courses alone are insufficient to help students who are underprepared for college-level work succeed academically (Bailey, 2009; Conely, 2007). National data indicate that 36% of entering college students enroll in at least one DE course (Aud et al., 2011), and the passing rates in these courses are dismal (Parsad, Lewis, & Greene, 2003; Russell, 2008). Consequently, policymakers in Washington have identified the improvement of DE courses as a major national challenge, especially for two-year colleges, because they have much higher enrollments of students who are underprepared for college-level work (Russell, 2008). One method for helping these students that has been gaining popularity in higher education is to integrate study skills, learning strategies, and other areas within strategic and self-regulated learning content into various facets of post-secondary institutions (e.g., learning assistance centers, tutoring and mentoring programs, and faculty development).

Among the many areas his work has influenced, Barry J. Zimmerman has had a profound effect on theory, research, and applications related to the self-directed use of learning strategies among college students. His model of self-regulated learning (SRL; Zimmerman, 2000, 2011) highlights cyclical phases and self-regulatory processes that underlie students' intentional selection, implementation, and evaluation of learning strategies. Barry's early research in this area helped to define SRL processes related to learners' motivation, metacognition, and behavior, and established relationships between SRL processes and academic performance (Zimmerman, 1986a, 1989, 2008, 2011; Zimmerman & Bandura, 1994; Zimmerman & Martinez-Pons, 1986, 1988). His pioneering work on SRL has helped to lay a solid foundation for current research on college students' intentional use of learning strategies and the development of applications for teaching students to use learning strategies. Zimmerman's model of SRL has also greatly influenced Weinstein's Model of Strategic Learning (MSL; Weinstein et al, 2010; Weinstein et al., 2000) and many of the applications she uses in her strategic learning course to teach college students how to choose and use a wide range of learning and self-regulation strategies effectively. The genealogy of her model began in the mid 1970s (Weinstein 1975, 1978) and has undergone a number of transformations. In the more recent versions of the model, part of the added emphasis on the self-regulation component was clearly influenced by Zimmerman's (2000, 2011) model.

In this chapter, we discuss the progression of learning strategies research in educational psychology and the development of interactive dynamic models of strategic and self-regulated learning. We describe Weinstein's MSL, compare it to Zimmerman's model of self-regulated learning, and discuss the utility of these models for helping students survive and thrive in postsecondary educational settings. We also overview types of interventions and initiatives designed to help foster college students' strategic and self-regulated learning and describe Weinstein's strategic learning course and several of the applications developed by Weinstein and her colleagues to help students become more strategic learners.

Finally, we end on a personal note from the senior author about a dear and wonderful friend, colleague, mentor and teacher … Barry Zimmerman.

LINKING STRATEGIC AND SELF-REGULATION INTERVENTIONS WITH ZIMMERMAN'S THEORY AND RESEARCH

Reflecting on Zimmerman's work and its importance to incredibly diverse fields in education, psychology, sports, and medicine, it is astounding in its conceptual, empirical and applied scholarship. In addition, this work has had profound influences on the work of so many researchers and practitioners, expanding his impact geometrically. This is no less true for the work the senior author and her colleagues and many of her graduate students have completed over the years. Although the development of the MSL predates the development of Zimmerman's work in self-regulation, it is an evolving model and has incorporated a number of his ideas about self-regulatory processes and strategies.

Our specific research focus related to Zimmerman's work has been in the area of learning strategies and the continuing development of the self-regulation component of the MSL (Weinstein et al., 2010; Weinstein et al., 2000), an assessment of strategic learning, the Learning and Study Strategies Inventory (LASSI; Weinstein, Palmer, & Schulte, 2002; Weinstein, Schulte, & Palmer, 1987), and the development of models for implementing strategic learning interventions in college contexts. A full description of Zimmerman's (2000, 2011) model of self-regulation is beyond the scope of this chapter; however, we will briefly compare Weinstein's MSL and Zimmerman's model of self-regulation and discuss how learning strategies fit within Zimmerman's model. Then, we will go on to describe Weinstein's MSL, assessment instruments, and interventions in more detail.

Weinstein's MSL (see Figure 7.1 as well as Weinstein et al., 2010; Weinstein et al., 2000) and Zimmerman's model of self-regulation (2000, 2011) are complementary; they just differ in scope and emphasis. Both models emphasize factors that learners can intentionally use or modify to improve their learning, such as students' attitudes, beliefs, goals, and their use of strategies related to information processing, comprehension monitoring, motivation regulation, goal-setting, self-observation, and self-reflection. Zimmerman's model is centered on the cyclical process of self-regulation and the various self-regulatory processes and strategies learners can use to manage their motivation, metacognition, and behavior. Weinstein's model emphasizes interactions among the skill, will, self-regulation, and academic environment components of strategic learning and the importance of developing and using a repertoire of strategies related to each component. Weinstein's model is an emergent model of strategic learning (i.e., successful learning is what emerges in the interaction of skill, will, and self-regulation elements within an academic and classroom environment much like a gestalt), and Zimmerman's model is a cyclical process model of self-regulation that is situated within a social-cognitive perspective that emphasizes reciprocal interactions among personal, environmental, and behavioral factors.

Students' use of cognitive learning strategies is an important aspect of both strategic and self-regulated learning. The skill component of the MSL is strongly focused on cognitive learning strategies and differentiates the following forms of strategy knowledge:

- declarative knowledge—knowing about a variety of learning strategies,
- procedural knowledge—knowing how to effectively and efficiently use a variety of learning strategies
- conditional knowledge—knowing when and under what circumstances it may be useful to use particular learning strategies

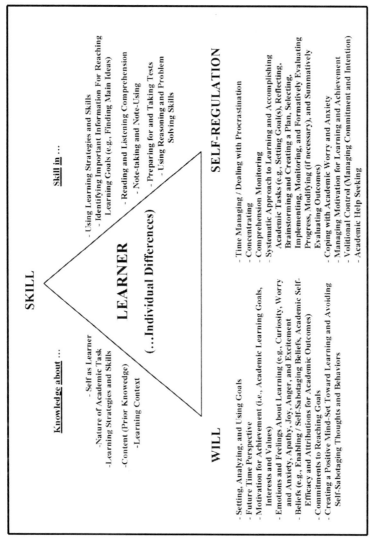

Figure 7.1 Model of strategy learning. © C. E. Weinstein, 2006.

Zimmerman's model of self-regulation addresses students' use of cognitive learning strategies to successfully complete learning tasks. Zimmerman's (2000, 2011) model of self-regulation highlights three cyclical phases of self-regulation (i.e., forethought, performance, and self-reflection) and subprocesses of self-regulation that fall under each phase. The *forethought phase* involves subprocesses related to task analysis and self-motivation beliefs; the *performance phase* concerns subprocesses related to self-control and self-observation; and the *self-reflection phase* addresses subprocesses related to self-judgment and self-reaction.

Strategic planning is an important subprocess of the forethought phase in Zimmerman's model. Strategic planning involves learners setting intentions for using specific study methods and learning strategies to help reach their goals. For example, a college student studying for a quiz covering material in a textbook chapter in her history course may generate a strategic plan to use the following learning strategies: (a) generate a written summary of each section of the chapter, (b) create a concept map of the important information discussed in the chapter, and (c) generate and answer possible quiz questions. According to Weinstein's MSL, students' declarative knowledge of different types of learning strategies, in addition to their conditional knowledge about which learning strategies would be particularly effective on the task at hand, play important roles in generating a successful strategic plan. Students' actual use of learning strategies comes into play during the performance phase of self-regulation.

Task strategies, imagery, self-instruction, and attention focusing are types of self-control subprocesses identified in the performance phase of Zimmerman's model. Some of these subprocesses, particularly task strategies and imagery, correspond to learning strategies that are discussed under the skill component of Weinstein's MSL (e.g., information processing strategies, selecting main ideas, note-taking, and test-taking strategies). During the performance phase, students' procedural knowledge and skill at effectively and efficiently implementing learning strategies and other task strategies is particularly important. For example, most college students know that note-taking is an important strategy to incorporate into their strategic plans to learn and remember information for their courses. However, students do not necessarily know how to take useful notes that include active processes such as generating examples, relating new information to prior knowledge, and summarizing. Knowing what to do is particularly important in the forethought phase, whereas knowing how to do it is essential in the performance phase. Zimmerman's model suggests that through self-observation (e.g., metacognitive monitoring and self-recording), students can become aware of their needs and refine their procedural knowledge of learning strategies as they implement them on a task. Similarly, Weinstein's model highlights comprehension monitoring and self-testing as important metacognitive strategies that involve setting up check points to assess the extent to which successful learning occurred and, if necessary, making modifications to improve students' strategic approaches.

The self-evaluation sub-process of the self-reflection phase in Zimmerman's model involves students reflecting on their performance and learning from their successes and mistakes. Students can generate new knowledge and modify their existing knowledge about the effectiveness of different study methods and learning strategies for different content areas and different academic tasks. This information can then be used during future strategic planning, hence the cyclical nature of self-regulation. Research on self-regulation and learning strategies has suggested strong associations among motivation, self-regulation, use of learning strategies, and performance (Pintrich & De Groot, 1990). For example, there is evidence that using learning strategies mediates the relationships between motivational constructs (e.g., self-efficacy and goal orientations) and performance (Al-Harthy, Was, & Isaacson, 2010; Diseth, 2011; Fenollar, Román, & Cuestas, 2007; Sins, van Joolingen, Savelsbergh, & van Hout-Wolters, 2008).

LEARNING STRATEGIES

The following section addresses the progression of learning strategies research and links it to Zimmerman's theory and research. The progression reveals the importance of using learning strategies for academic success.

Progression of Learning Strategies Research

Human's desire to understand the world around them, remember information important for their survival, and teach this information to their children can be traced back to prehistoric times. For instance, some anthropologists believe that cave drawings were in part used to keep track of animal migrations and seasonal weather patterns, and to teach culture and safety to children. However, it was not until the 1970s that researchers began systematically investigating strategies that humans could use to more effectively learn and remember information. Early research on cognitive learning strategies showed that learning and memory could be enhanced through the use of rehearsal, elaboration, and organizational strategies on basic and complex tasks (Weinstein & Mayer, 1986). For example, Weinstein (1975, 1978) found that students could be trained to use general learning strategies that were not tied to a specific subject area, and that the use of these strategies could enhance learning on free-recall, paired-associate, and reading comprehension tasks. Groundbreaking work, such as Wittrock's (1974) theory of generative learning, which suggested that active cognitive processing could lead to more meaningful learning, and Flavell's (1979) work on metacognition that highlighted the importance of thinking about and regulating one's own thinking, challenged mainstream views within psychology at the time that posited that learners were passive receptacles of knowledge, and that academic ability was a developmental phenomenon that could not be modified through the active use of strategies. As research on cognitive learning strategies grew, findings showed that students were not likely to use learning strategies on their own in non-experimental learning contexts (Pressley & McCormick, 1995; Zimmerman, 2008). It became clear that teaching students to use cognitive learning strategies was necessary but not sufficient to make lasting impacts on learning and performance. Researchers and practitioners had to also take into account the interaction of cognitive, metacognitive, motivational, affective, and behavioral factors (Weinstein et al., 2010). As Zimmerman (2008) pointed out, "an early defining moment in research on self-regulation was a symposium at the American Educational Research Association annual meeting in 1986 that was published in a special issue of *Contemporary Educational Psychology* (Zimmerman, 1986b). It sought to integrate under a single rubric research on such processes as learning strategies, metacognitive monitoring, self-concept perceptions, volitional strategies, and self-control" (p. 167). Current models of strategic and self-regulated learning highlight how these factors reciprocally interact to influence learning and performance over time. Cognitive learning strategies are thus one important component within both strategic and self-regulated learning. In the next section we discuss Weinstein's MSL.

Model of Strategic Learning

The MSL (Weinstein et al., 2010; Weinstein et al., 2000) includes four major components with a number of elements in each one (see Figure 7.1). The four major categories, or components, are: skill (e.g., cognitive learning strategies, study skills, and reasoning skills), will (e.g., achievement motivation, positive affect toward learning, and self-efficacy for learning), self-regulation (e.g., time management, comprehension monitoring, strategic planning, and help-seeking), and the academic environment (e.g., nature of the academic task, teachers' expectations and beliefs, and available resources). The model emphasizes both direct effects and interactions among these components and their individual elements in specific academic environments and learning contexts.

An underlying concept of the MSL is that learners need to be aware of elements from all four major components of the model: skill, will, self-regulation, and the academic environment. It is the interactions among elements from all four areas that are crucial to strategic learning, transfer of learning, and ultimately, students' academic success, retention and graduation.

Skill Component

There are a number of different elements within the skill component. All of these elements are important in and of themselves, but for students to be able to reach their academic goals they must also be aware of how these elements interact. For purposes of description, some of these elements will be individually highlighted. For a complete listing of the elements in all four categories refer to Figure 7.1.

There are five types of knowledge within the skill component that can help students become more effective and efficient learners. *Knowledge of self* as a learner is important because it is a key step toward developing self awareness as a learner and metacognitive awareness (a critical feature of strategic and self-regulated learning) and the ability to think strategically about learning (Weinstein et al., 2000; Winne, 2011; Zimmerman & Moylan, 2009). This includes knowing one's strengths and weaknesses as a learner and one's attitude, motivation and anxiety level towards learning. Knowledge of self as a learner provides crucial information to learners about areas where they may not need to improve as well as areas where they might anticipate difficulties in a given learning context so that they can work to avoid or minimize potential problems. For example, knowing that he does not like science courses and has had difficulty taking science exams in the past can alert a student to the potential benefits of participating in a study group or finding out about the availability of science tutors at a college learning center. Students need to reflect and think about their answers to a number of questions, such as: What are my preferences? What are my strengths? What are my weaknesses? What are my interests and talents? What are my current study habits and practices? Knowing about themselves as learners helps students orchestrate the resources they need to accomplish the studying and learning activities necessary for academic success. It is important to note that management of resources refers not only to external resources such as how often a student goes to see a tutor, or the amount of reading they must complete, but also how they orchestrate their personal resources, such as their cognitive strategies, emotions, feelings, and time management. The management of external and internal resources is even more important in online learning environments because students must take even more responsibility for scheduling and doing the work (Bol & Garner, 2011; Winters, Greene, & Costich, 2008).

Knowledge of academic tasks, the second category, includes understanding what is required to successfully complete a given academic task (e.g., reading text on a computer, writing a term paper, taking an essay test, taking notes, participating in online chats, and giving an oral presentation), including the steps to be taken and how much time will be required to complete the task (Weinstein et al., 2000; Winne, 2011). This type of knowledge helps to clarify what learners need to think about and do in order to reach a desired outcome.

Knowledge about strategies and skills for acquiring, integrating, thinking about, and applying new learning is the third category. Learning and thinking strategies and skills are the tools we use to meet our learning goals. They help us to generate meaning, monitor our learning progress, and store new information in ways that facilitate future recall or application (Paris & Paris, 2001).

Learning strategies can take a variety of forms ranging from simple paraphrasing to complex content analysis (Pintrich, 1999; Weinstein & Mayer, 1986). The common factor underlying each of these forms is the active involvement of the student. Active cognitive involvement is crucial for meaningful learning. Students cannot be passive and expect to reach their learning goals. We build meaning and memories by actively engaging the material we are trying to learn and by using learning strategies to help guide this active engagement. Strategic learners have a variety of different strategies available so that they can generate strategies for different learning goals, or to use when a learning problem occurs.

The simplest forms of learning strategies involve repetition or review, such as reading over a difficult section of text, or repeating an equation or rule. A bit more complexity is added when we try to paraphrase or summarize in our own words the material we are studying. Other strategies focus on organizing the information we are trying to learn by creating some type of scheme for the material—for example, creating an outline of the main events and characters in a story, making a time line for historical occurrences, classifying scientific phenomena, or separating foreign vocabulary into parts of speech are all organizational strategies. Some learning strategies involve elaborating on, or analyzing, what we are trying to learn to make it more meaningful and memorable. For example, using analogies to access relevant prior knowledge, comparing and contrasting the explanations offered by two competing scientific theories, and thinking about the implications of a policy proposal are examples of elaboration strategies.

Students need a repertoire of learning approaches, strategies, and methods that they can use and adapt to a variety of academic as well as everyday learning situations (Weinstein et al., 2010). There are two major reasons why students need to develop a repertoire of studying and learning strategies and skills: first, learners need to know about a variety of strategies and methods for learning before they can make mindful decisions about their preferences or the methods that seem to be most effective for them; and, second, when students encounter academic difficulties, it is important for them to have a set of tools that they can use to resolve the problems.

The fourth area of knowledge necessary for the development of learning expertise is *knowledge about content*, often referred to as prior knowledge. It is easier for individuals to learn something new about a subject when they already know something about it (Hailikari & Nevgi, 2010). Part of the reason for this is that we already have an existing knowledge base that we can use to help us acquire the new information, to help us understand it, and to help us integrate it. Activating prior knowledge and integrating it with new information can help to increase learning and make the new knowledge more memorable (Acuna, Rodicio, & Sanchez, 2011; Wetzels, Kester, & van Merrienboer, 2011).

Knowledge about the learning context is the last knowledge element under the skill component. Students need to know about present or future contexts in which they could use what they are trying to learn now (Husman, Derryberry, Crowson, & Lomax, 2004; Husman & Hilpert, 2007). Students can improve their learning and motivation by identifying and internalizing the importance or utility value of what they are trying to learn for helping them to meet their personal, social, academic, or occupational goals (Acee & Weinstein, 2010). Students must value the outcomes of learning enough to translate their motivation into action.

Will Component

The second major component in the model is the will component. It is not enough for students to know how to study and learn new material; they must also want to do it. Motivation has been defined as "the process whereby goal-directed activity is instigated and sustained" (Schunk, Pintrich, & Meece, 2008, p. 378) and as "a person's willingness to exert physical or mental effort in pursuit of a goal or outcome" (VandenBos, 2007, p. 594). Motivation has many elements and interacts with and results from many factors (see Eccles & Wigfield, 2002; Schunk, Pintrich, & Meece, 2008) such as value perceptions and expectancy beliefs (Eccles et al., 1983; Wigfield & Eccles, 2000), attribution beliefs (Weiner, 1985, 2000), goal orientations (Dweck & Leggett, 1988; Elliot, 1999; Elliot & Murayama, 2008), goal properties (Acee, Cho, Kim, & Weinstein, 2012; Austin & Vancouver, 1996; Locke & Latham, 2002), and future time perspective (Husman et al., 2004; Husman & Hilpert, 2007). Setting, analyzing, and using goals are central elements of motivation. Wanting to reach learning goals becomes a driving force that can be used to help generate and maintain motivation as well as the thoughts and behaviors necessary to accomplish the goals. The specific topics listed under the will component in Figure 7.1 are discussed in more detail in a number of the chapters in this volume.

Self-Regulation Component

The self-regulation of thoughts, beliefs, and actions in the model focuses on the self-management aspects of learning (Pintrich, 2000, 2004; Zimmerman, 2000, 2011; Zimmerman & Schunk, 2011). Strategic learners manage their skill and will factors in light of the demands and resources in their learning environment through self-regulation (Weinstein et al., 2010). Essentially, self-regulation involves awareness, reflection, and control of relevant factors in order to achieve a desired outcome (Winne, 2011).

Strategic learners regulate on a macro level and on a micro level. Regulation on a macro level involves broad, often multistep, processes that have a wide domain of applicability. For example, learning about what time management is, how to do it, and when to use it is a macro level of self-regulation. It can be applied in a wide variety of settings and for a wide variety of academic tasks. A micro level of self-regulation involves using specific processes or methods related to a specific task such as monitoring your use of time during a chemistry exam. The macro level of regulation, when combined with other categories and elements from the MSL, helps students to select or create the specific self-regulation strategies they will use to accomplish a specific goal associated with a specific task. Thus, micro level strategies have a narrower domain of applicability. Micro level strategies are the real-time applications of macro level broad strategies from all of the components of the MSL.

The self-regulation component of the model of strategic learning has many commonalities with Zimmerman's model of self-regulation. There are many macro level processes related to planning, implementing, and evaluating that correspond to Zimmerman's phases of forethought, performance, and self-regulation. There are also micro level processes related to generating awareness, reflecting, and exercising control for specific academic tasks that correspond with processes involved in the performance phase of Zimmerman's model.

Time management is one of the major elements of self-regulation and refers to the learner's use of time resources in the pursuit of learning tasks and goals (Weinstein et al., 2000). Self-regulation of time use involves the monitoring and control of time management to help attain a desired learning outcome, is amenable to training, and has been found to correlate positively with academic behaviors and success (Ramdass & Zimmerman, 2011; Stoeger & Ziegler, 2008).

Another major element of self-regulation is the use of a systematic approach to learning and accomplishing academic tasks. This systematic approach to learning involves eight steps that are essential for self-regulated learning (Weinstein et al., 2000) and corresponds to the cyclical phases of self-regulation outlined in Zimmerman's (2000, 2011) model of self-regulation. The first step is to set a goal for the desired outcome, such as a specific grade in a course, performance on an assessment instrument or proficiency in performing a specific academic task. To be most effective, the goal needs to correspond to the generally accepted characteristics of a useful goal, in other words, specific, measurable, challenging, realistic, and with a specific start and completion date (Acee et al., 2012; Locke & Latham, 2002).

The second step is to reflect on the learning task at hand to clearly identify the specific task requirements, consider these requirements in terms of the learner's level of skill and will, and determine how the task relates to the learner's goals. Strategic learners also reflect on other relevant external contextual factors, such as the resources available to help them achieve the desired outcome, the expectations of the instructor, and the social support upon which they can draw.

Having reflected on all these factors, the strategic learner moves to the third step by developing a plan, which includes brainstorming several potential strategies for achieving the desired outcome in the given situation. In the fourth step the learner selects from potential strategies those that appear to be most effective and efficient in achieving the outcome desired. The learner then actively implements (fifth step) the chosen strategies and monitors and formatively evaluates (sixth step) how well the strategies have been implemented by conducting an ongoing evaluation of the effectiveness of each strategy as it is being used. If the results are satisfactory, the learner continues following the plan. If they are not, the strategic learner modifies or replaces the strategies (seventh step) and then monitors and evaluates the results of the changes. If necessary, the learner may even decide to modify the learning goal, itself. Finally, when the learning task has been completed, successfully or unsuccessfully, the self-regulated learner performs the eighth and last step, which is a summative evaluation of the effectiveness and efficiency of the learning strategies applied and the outcome achieved for use as a future reference when similar learning tasks arise. This step contributes to both avoiding unsuccessful approaches in the future and to increasing cognitive efficiency by helping the learner build up a set of useful approaches for similar learning tasks in the future. Strategic learners also know ways to monitor and manage their level of stress, motivation, concentration and their own comprehension. To monitor and manage their comprehension, students need to know how to use self-assessment or self-testing to determine whether they are meeting their learning goals. There are many forms of self-assessment. It can be as simple as paraphrasing while reading or as complex as trying to teach new information or skills to someone else. Other forms of monitoring include trying to apply new knowledge, transforming it into another form such as a diagram or outline, and summarizing it. Each of these activities is designed to help students see if they really understand what they are studying and learning. Often, students believe that they understand but they do not test themselves to confirm or deny this belief. When they are wrong—that is, when they have only the *illusion of knowing*, students think that they have reached their achievement goals and do not realize that they have not.

An expert learner can also generate fix-up strategies when problems in their comprehension arise. Fix-up strategies are the approaches and methods that students use to help remedy a learning problem. These methods can range from very simple activities such as rereading a confusing text section, to trying to reason through a problem-solving method, to going to a tutor for help, to teaming with someone else who is taking the same course in order to study difficult sections together. Each of these activities is designed to help solve a learning or comprehension problem. It is important that students have a repertoire of fix-up strategies so that they can deal with a variety of academic problems that might occur.

Academic Environment Component

The MSL also includes elements in the learning or academic environment that are external to the learner. These are represented in the outside boundaries of the model and include: the resources available to the learner; instructor expectations; nature of the learning activity, assignment, project or test, and time constraints; and the nature of the social context and the level of social support available to them.

Available resources refers to any materials or learning aids that the learner can use in acquiring knowledge, such as workbooks, reading materials, computers, reference materials, diagrams, examples and case studies. Available resources also include campus resources such as instructors' office hours, labs, tutors, learning skills centers, teaching assistants, and advisors.

The *teacher expectations* element refers to the expectations held by an instructor (and/or course developer). These expectations could include the skill level of students, what tasks the students should be able to perform, and what teaching methods are appropriate for the students. The extent to which the teacher's or course developer's expectations match or do not match the learner's abilities/needs can have a major impact on the acquisition and retention of information and subsequent transfer. If the teacher's expectations exceed the learner's ability, the learner may not be able to acquire the information and may be less motivated to put forth the effort to learn or utilize the subject matter. If the teacher's expectations are below the learner's ability, the learner may become bored or place less value on the subject matter and subsequently experience less motivation to learn or utilize the subject matter (Tsiplakides & Keramida, 2010; Woolley, Strutchens, Gilbert, & Martin, 2010).

The *nature of the learning activity*, assignment, project, or test, and time constraints, refers to the specific tasks and task requirements the learners must do in order to acquire the new information and use their new knowledge and skills. This might include listening to a lecture, taking notes, role-playing, demonstrating proficiency, writing a paper or taking a timed test. The nature of a specific task assigned in a class will interact with the learner's levels of skill, will and self-regulation to help determine the degree of learning success (Weinstein et al., 2010; Winne, 2011). If the task calls for an activity for which a learner lacks skill or motivation, he or she may have difficulty in performing that activity or may seek to avoid it altogether. In addition, the time constraints within which the course material is delivered, or other time constraints that may be impacting the learner (e.g., outside deadlines not related to the course) affect the learning outcomes. If the class time is limited, students may not be able to practice using the knowledge acquired in the program. The learner might also be overwhelmed if a large amount of information is presented in a short period of time, especially if his or her learning strategies and skills are limited.

Social context/support refers to the support learners receive from peers, fellow students, family, and student support personnel at their institution. This might include roommates and other students with whom the learner could study and share class experiences and advice from siblings or parents. Modeling, beliefs of peers and family members, and supportive or antagonistic views towards school or a particular course can also affect participants' motivation to accept or reject course content and the level of participation in the class exhibited by the learner (Rosenthal & Bandura, 1978; Schunk, 1987; Schunk et al., 2008).

All of these external factors interact with the internal factors associated with the skill, will and self-regulation components of the model. The concept of strategic learning comes out of systems theory and Gestalt psychology (Blunden, 2011; Humphrey, 1924). In this sense, the model is a dynamic system where change in one factor can produce changes in other factors. As in all systems, it is important to consider all factors. Strategic learners try to be aware of and control as many of these factors as possible so that new knowledge can be acquired, retained, integrated with existing knowledge, and ultimately transferred as needed. This model helps students examine the impact of changes in one factor on other strategic learning factors. For example, students' knowledge about themselves as learners helps them to identify task characteristics that may be particularly problematic for them. Identifying these potential problems helps them to think about the learning strategies and study skills they know that might help address these particular problems. When students can think about what they have already studied in an area, it may help them to create more meaning for the new material so that they can successfully complete the task.

Using the MSL, Weinstein and her associates developed a diagnostic/prescriptive self-report measure of strategic learning. The LASSI was designed to assess students' awareness and use of elements from the skill, will and self-regulation components of the MSL (academic environment elements were not addressed because they are not directly under students' control). LASSI has been used in varying contexts at approximately 70% of colleges and universities in the United States and has been translated into more than 25 languages. There is also a high school version that is used in many summer transition programs as well as in high schools. After discussing the LASSI in the next section, we will discuss a strategic learning course that was also developed using the MSL that incorporates the LASSI into the pre and post course assessment measures.

ASSESSMENT OF STRATEGIC AND SELF-REGULATED LEARNING IN COLLEGE CONTEXTS

Three widely used and highly related assessments of strategic and self-regulated learning have been developed—Zimmerman and Martinez-Pons' (1986, 1988) self-regulated learning interview scale (SRLIS), Weinstein et al.'s (1987, 2002) LASSI 2nd edition, and Pintrich, Smith, Garcia, and McKeachie's (1991) Motivated Strategies for Learning Questionnaire (MSLQ). Each of these instruments was originally developed in the 1980s and overlap in their content domains. All of them use a classification system that fits well with the three defining self-regulated learning criteria related to motivational, metacognitive, and behavioral factors (Zimmerman, 2008). The differences are more in nomenclature, processes that are emphasized, and the nature of the self-report procedures used. For example, the SRLIS interview is a prospective self-report measure and both the LASSI and MSLQ are retrospective instruments. Motivation is a critical component in each assessment, but it is broken down into a number of subscales on the MSLQ and only one global scale on the LASSI. The SRLIS interview codes anxiety responses as a form of self-evaluations reactions, while on the LASSI there is a separate scale for anxiety. The MSLQ includes anxiety as a subscale under motivation. Although all of these assessments offer important information about college students' strengths and vulnerabilities as strategic self-regulated learners, the LASSI has been used in the intervention to be described in detail in the next section, so a more detailed account of it will be presented next.

The LASSI (Weinstein, Palmer, & Schulte, 2002) is a 10-scale, 80-item assessment of students' use of learning and study strategies related to skill, will and self-regulation components of the Model of Strategic Learning (Weinstein & Palmer, 2002). Students respond to each item using a Likert-type scale from 1 to 5 where 1 is not at all typical of me, 2 is not very typical of me, 3 is somewhat typical of me, 4 is fairly typical of me, and 5 is very much typical of me. The 10 scales are: Anxiety, Attitude, Concentration, Information Processing, Motivation, Selecting Main Ideas, Self Testing, Study Aids, Test Strategies, and Time Management. Research has repeatedly demonstrated that these factors contribute significantly to success in college and can be learned or enhanced through educational interventions (Albaili, 1997; Cano, 2006; DeRoma, Bell, Zaremba, & Abee, 2005; Mireles, 2010; Mireles, Offer, Ward, & Dochen, 2011; Proctor, Prevatt, Adams, Hurst, & Petscher, 2006). The Cronbach's alpha coefficients for all ten scales range from a low of .73 to a high of .89 (Weinstein & Palmer, 2002). Weinstein and her colleagues developed a metacognition scale for the LASSI, but it correlated at .7 and above with every other LASSI scale, suggesting that metacognition is foundational to many elements of strategic and self-regulated learning.

The LASSI can be used as: (a) a diagnostic measure to help identify areas in which students could benefit most from educational interventions; (b) a basis for planning individual prescriptions for both remediation and enrichment; (c) a means for instructors to use for examining individual students' scores and class trends to help make decisions about instruction, assignments, and so on; (d) an evaluation tool to assess the degree of success of strategic learning intervention courses or programs; and, (e) an advising/counseling tool.

Strategic learners can benefit from declarative, procedural and conditional knowledge and skills in each of the categories of the LASSI scales. They also need to know how to pick and choose among the various elements within and across categories to help them reach specific learning goals and objectives. For example, a student experiencing high anxiety about an upcoming essay test will need to use anxiety-coping or reduction strategies even before creating a study plan or selecting learning strategies to use when reading the assigned chapters in his textbook. The next section will highlight the individual LASSI scales and the component of the MSL that they are most related to conceptually.

LASSI Scales Most Related to the Skill Component of Strategic Learning

The LASSI scales most related to the skill component of strategic learning are: Information Processing, Selecting Main Ideas, and Test Strategies (Weinstein & Palmer, 2002). These scales examine students' learning strategies, skills and thought processes related to identifying, acquiring, and constructing meaning for important new information, ideas and procedures, and how they prepare for and demonstrate their new knowledge on tests or other evaluative procedures.

The Information Processing Scale assesses how well students' can use imagery, verbal and visual elaboration, organization strategies, and reasoning processes as learning strategies to help learn new information and skills and to build bridges between what they already know and what they are trying to learn and remember. Do students try to summarize or paraphrase their class reading assignments? Do they try to relate what is being presented in class to their prior knowledge? The Selecting Main Ideas Scale assesses students' skill at identifying important information for further study from less important information and supporting details. Can students identify the key points in a lecture? Can they decide what is important to underline in a textbook? The Test Strategies Scale assesses students' use of both test preparation and test taking strategies. Do they know how to study for tests in different types of courses? Do students review their answers to essay questions?

LASSI Scales Most Related to the Will Component of Strategic Learning

The LASSI scales related to the will component of strategic learning are: Anxiety, Attitude, and Motivation. These scales measure the degree to which students worry about their academic performance, their receptivity to learning new information, their attitudes and interest in college, and their diligence, self-discipline, and willingness to exert the effort necessary to successfully complete academic requirements. The Anxiety Scale assesses the degree to which students worry about school and their academic performance. Do students worry so much that it is hard for them to concentrate? Are they easily discouraged by low grades? The Attitude Scale assesses students' attitudes and interests in college and achieving academic success. How clear are students about their own educational goals? Is school really important or worthwhile to them? The Motivation Scale assesses students' diligence, self-discipline, and willingness to exert the effort necessary to successfully complete academic requirements. Do they stay up-to-date in class assignments? Do students easily give up in difficult classes?

LASSI Scales Most Related to the Self-Regulation Component of Strategic Learning

The LASSI scales related to the self-regulation component of strategic learning are: Concentration, Self-Testing, Study Aids, and Time Management. These scales measure how students manage, or self-regulate and control, the whole learning process through using their time effectively, focusing their attention and maintaining their concentration over time, checking to see if they have met the learning demands for a class, an assignment, or a test, and using study supports such as review sessions, tutors or special features of a textbook. The Concentration Scale assesses students' ability to direct and maintain their attention on academic tasks. Are students easily distracted? Can they direct their attention to school tasks? The Self Testing Scale assesses students' use of reviewing and comprehension monitoring techniques to determine their level of understanding of the information or task to be learned. Do the students review before a test? Do they stop periodically while reading to review the content? The Study Aids Scale assesses students' creation and use of support techniques, materials or resources to help them learn and remember new information. Do students complete practice exercises? Do they create or use organizational aids? The Time Management Scale assesses students' use of time management principles and tactics for academic tasks. Are students well organized? Do they anticipate scheduling problems?

Strategic and Self-Regulated Learning Interventions

Strategic and self-regulated learning interventions come in many different forms, can be more or less intensive, and may serve various student populations within postsecondary institutions (e.g., students underprepared in mathematics and/or literacy, students who are on academic probation, students who are not experiencing extreme difficulty but need additional learning support). Learning centers sometimes offer voluntary workshops and/or provide handouts on strategic and self-regulated learning. Academic advisors, tutors, and supplemental instructors may incorporate formal and informal instruction on strategic learning. The metacurriculum approach involves teaching strategic and self-regulated learning within a credit-bearing college course (e.g., Economics, Chemistry) or a developmental education course in mathematics, reading, or writing. For example, Mireles (2010) and Mireles et al. (2011) designed and evaluated an intensive five-week summer bridge program that was focused on a developmental education mathematics course that incorporated strategic learning workshops, problem solving strategies, mandatory tutoring, collaborative learning, and an algorithmic instructional technique that uses modeling, practice, transition, and independence. Results from this study showed significant improvements on all ten of the LASSI scales from the beginning to the end of the program. In another study, DeCorte and Masui (2004) integrated ten 90-minute sessions focusing on metacognitive and self-regulatory skills training into an undergraduate economics course and found that, compared to students in the control and comparison groups, students in the intervention group were more likely to use metacognitive and self-regulatory strategies in their economics course, had higher exam scores and course success rates, and were more likely to transfer their learning to a statistics course that was not tied to the intervention.

There are also online self-regulated learning resources for college students such as gStudy (Winne et al., 2006), which is a shell that provides students with tools (e.g., highlighting, annotation, questioning, explaining, planning, goal setting, making connections, and reviewing) and an adaptable artificial intelligence system to facilitate self-regulatory processes. Weinstein's online set of modules, Becoming a Strategic Learner: LASSI Instruction Modules (Weinstein, Woodruff, & Awalt, 2002) uses text, graphics, and activities to teach students important concepts, strategies, and applications aligned with the 10 scales of the LASSI. These modules are used in the learning strategies course we discuss in this section.

Courses in strategic and self-regulated learning, often referred to as learning-to-learn or learning frameworks courses, tend to be one of the more intensive, comprehensive, and powerful methods for fostering strategic and self-regulated learning, particularly when paired with a content course that incorporates a metacurriculum. Unlike basic study skills courses that teach students isolated learning skills, courses in strategic and self-regulated learning teach students theory related to learning, cognition, motivation, and self-regulation; applications of learning strategies and self-regulatory processes on authentic academic tasks; and strategies for transferring their learning across academic domains. Although postsecondary institutions have offered courses to help students study and learn since the 1920s, courses in strategic and self-regulated learning, or learning frameworks courses, did not emerge until the 1970s (Hodges & Agee, 2009; Maxwell, 1997). Based on her model of strategic learning, Weinstein was among the first developers of a successful postsecondary credit-bearing strategic learning course, which was established in 1977 (this course and research on its effectiveness will be described below).

Description of a Strategic Learning Course at the University of Texas at Austin

As we stated in the introduction, the specific applied focus of this chapter is on an example of a semester-long course in strategic learning. Implementing strategic and self-regulated learning courses can be a powerful way to help students become more strategic and self-regulated learners (e.g., Hodges, Dochen, & Sellers, 2001; Hofer & Yu, 2003; McKeachie, Pintrich, & Lin, 1985; Weinstein et al., 1998).

Based on the MSL and incorporating the use of the LASSI as a diagnostic/prescriptive measure, the course at the University of Texas at Austin (UT) called EDP310 has been found to be extremely successful at helping students become more strategic and self-regulated learners who persist to graduation at higher levels than their peers. For example, in one study (Weinstein et al., 1998), UT first-year students were tracked for five years in order to compare graduation rates of students who took the course to those students who did not (the general student population). Students who did not take the course had a five-year graduation rate of 55%, which was typical for UT students at that time. Students who took the course, in either the first or second semester of their first year and did not drop out or fail the course due to excessive absences, had a graduation rate of 71%. This was true despite these students having significantly lower verbal and math SAT scores than students who did not take the EDP310 course. These results are even more marked because most students who took the course were required to take it by advisors or counselors because they were on academic probation, and many students reported having low motivation for the course. We have repeated this with statistical control groups and waiting-list control groups and found similar results. In addition, unpublished internal evaluations of our course have shown that students improve an average of 24 to 28 percentile points on Brown, Fishco, and Hanna's (1993) Nelson-Denney reading test. What follows is a description of the course, including an overview of the course structure, course content and the instructional methods used in this course.

EDP310 (Individual Learning Skills) is a graded, three-credit course offered through the department of educational psychology at UT that meets 50 minutes a day, three days a week, for 15 weeks. This is a multi-section course with nine to 16 sections of the course offered each semester, depending on the academic budget. EDP310 is a coordinated course with a common curriculum and common assessments across all sections. Weinstein coordinates the course with the help of two graduate assistant coordinators and multiple instructors. The co-coordinators and instructors are all advanced doctoral students and are typically in the Learning, Cognition, Motivation and Instruction concentration in the department of educational psychology at UT. The students who are selected to teach the sections undergo a rigorous interview process and must have completed a doctoral-level course in college teaching methods as well as a graduate course in college student learning and retention. In addition, all new instructors undergo six full days of training prior to each semester (one day for experienced instructors). Additional training takes place during the weekly two-hour staff meetings and after two separate teaching observations during each semester.

This course is technically a voluntary elective and so is not required for any major or degree plan at UT. However, as noted above, a large proportion of the students in the course are required to take it because they are either predicted to be at-risk for low achievement or are already on academic probation. Consequently, many of these students do not want to be in the course and have low motivation for participation. Although many places are reserved for first-year students, other students may take EDP310 because they have been placed on academic probation after their first year of school, want to improve their college performance, or, rarely, are preparing for graduate school. Course enrollment data from 2005 show the following demographic breakdown: female (58%), male (42%); first year (29%), sophomore (42%), junior (20%), and senior (9%); African American (5%), Asian (20%), Caucasian (48%), Hispanic (23%), and Native American (3%). These figures were representative of the UT population at that time. There are currently nine sections of the EDP310 course with a maximum of 28 students in each section. The faculty coordinator and two graduate student assistant coordinators together develop course content and structure, as well as determine which assessments to use each semester in the course. They also help with course administration and the training of new teachers. Assistant coordinators must have served for at least two semesters as an instructor in the course.

The MSL is used to select and organize the course content. Topics are selected from all four components, but the emphasis is on the skill, will and self-regulation components. In addition to the elements from the model, several traditional study skills topics are included such as academic notetaking. A recent version of the EDP310 schedule of course topics and assignments can be found in the Appendix. Students are taught about the MSL and the core theoretical ideas behind each variable in the model. Students are also taught skills, strategies and approaches that they can use to improve in each area. They are guided in using these strategies in a variety of academic situations that they encounter in their other classes. EDP310 is a blended delivery course, with much content being delivered through the Becoming a Strategic Learner Online modules (Weinstein, Woodruff, & Awalt, 2002) in addition to in-class instruction that emphasizes application, modeling, small-group work and whole-class discussions. A set of readings and handouts are also used.

The MSL is used as the organizing framework for the entire course. Students receive a highly abbreviated version at the beginning of the course. As the course progresses, new concepts and strategies are integrated into the MSL so by the last quarter of the semester students are using the entire model and the constellation of components to address learning tasks and problems. Instruction is based on a metacognitive model of awareness, reflection and taking control or action. The assessments, instructional materials, instructional practices and the teachers help students become aware of the different topic areas that foster strategic learning, help them reflect on their strengths and weaknesses in these areas, and then teach them ways they can help themselves to improve and be more effective and efficient in reaching their academic and occupational goals. There are clear relation-ships between this approach and Zimmerman's model of self-regulation. Although EDP310 was created in 1975, prior to the publication of Zimmer-man's model and his early work on self-regulation (Zimmerman, 1986a; Zimmerman & Martinez-Pons, 1986), it is an evolving course and a number of the changes in processes, instruction, and content have been greatly in-fluenced by his work. We have also used Zimmerman's work to improve our emphasis on pre-, during-, and post-task processes and strategies.

There are a number of different types of classes that are taught in EDP310. Please refer to Table 7.1 for a summary of the types of classes taught, the metacognitive processes emphasized in each class type, and the categories of strategy knowledge emphasized in each type of class. The three types of classes are: context classes, content classes without an associated online module and content classes with an associated online instructional module. Context classes provide declarative (what) and procedural (how) knowledge about the frame of reference, structure, scaffolding, classroom climate, course objectives, instructor expectations and student/instructor contracts for EDP310. Examples of context classes include introducing and analyzing the syllabus, using ice breakers to build community, using struc-tured discussions to provide autonomy support, and providing students with decision-making opportunities on the course process and assignments. Content classes with no associated instructional modules are those classes that must rely solely on readings and in-class instruction for learning the content. For example, note-taking strategies are not included at the pres-ent time in any of the on-line modules. Therefore, during class, instructors must provide instruction on the rationale for this topic, basic information on potentially useful note-taking strategies (declarative knowledge), how to use them and develop one's own strategies (procedural knowledge), and conditional knowledge of when a particular strategy may or may not be use-ful for a given task. In contrast to this, the third category of type of classes is content classes with an online instructional module component.

EDP310 is a blended course. Part of the instruction takes place in class and part of it takes place via a series of ten online modules that correspond to the ten scales of the LASSI but also have extensive additional material. These interactive online instructional modules also use a metacognitive model and emphasize awareness, reflection and control using informative presentation and an extensive series of reflections and activities designed to provide declarative, procedural and conditional knowledge about the types of control strategies students can use across a variety of content areas and learning and performance tasks. Each module is designed to help students reflect on their knowledge relating to one area and to understand why they may need to improve in that area. The modules also provide material for students to study and activities that guide them in applying the material

TABLE 7.1 Types of Classes in Weinstein's Strategic Learning Course (EDP310)

	Context Classes	Content Classes Without an Online Module	Content Classes With an Online Module	
			Will Topics	Skill and Self-Regulation Topics
Topics	For example: • Completing Pre- and Post-assessments • Course Overview • Course Syllabus and Expectations • Community Building • Autonomy Support • Academic Environment	For example: • Model of Strategic Learning • The Systematic Approach • Assessment Feedback and Reflection • Student Reflections • Content Overviews and Band-aid Strategies	Anxiety Attitude Motivation	Concentration Information Processing Selecting Main Ideas Self-Testing Study Aids Test Taking Time Management
Metacognitive Processes Emphasized				
Awareness	e.g., Taking Pre-assessments	e.g., Content Overview Days	✓	
Reflection	e.g., Learning Autobiography	e.g., Feedback and Reflection on Pre-test Scores	✓	
Control	e.g., Using Course Syllabus and Expectations	e.g., Using the Systematic Approach		✓
Types of Strategy Knowledge Emphasized				
Declarative Knowledge	✓		✓	
Procedural Knowledge	✓	✓	✓	✓
Conditional Knowledge		✓	✓	✓

Note: ✓ = Emphasized metacognitive process or emphasized type of strategy knowledge.

they are learning and practicing using new or enhanced learning strategies. For each module, students are required to take notes on the content, complete selected activities, and write one or two paragraphs that integrate the module topic with material they learned in other modules and the MSL. Each module takes approximately two and a half to four hours to complete, depending on the topic and a student's prior knowledge and experience with the topic content. Students' responses to the reflections and activities can be captured online or printed so they are available to the instructor in whichever form they prefer. We also save some of the activities for in-class small group work, pair-and-share work, and discussions. Classes with an associated online instructional module do not have to focus on declarative knowledge, although it is reviewed through teacher and student-led discussions (and evaluated through short-answer quizzes at the beginning of any class on a new topic). This allows class time to focus more on honing procedural knowledge and conditional knowledge.

Although a variety of teaching methods is used in EDP310, perhaps the most important method for learning effective strategy use is guided practice with feedback. It is critical that students are able to practice using strategic learning methods across a variety of academic tasks and contexts. It is also important that they receive feedback from their instructor and classmates that can help them improve both their understanding and use of these methods. For this reason, students taking EDP310 are required to take at least one other course at the same time so they can apply the strategies they are learning in the EDP310 course.

Pre-assessments given to students at the beginning of the semester are used in EDP310 to help build student and instructor awareness of students' strengths and weaknesses related to strategic and self-regulated learning. This can help students and their instructors identify where students most need to concentrate their efforts. EDP sections have up to 28 students in each class, and this makes it difficult to individualize instruction. The assessments help to identify areas where students can individualize the curriculum to focus on the material that will be most helpful for them. This is also accomplished through learning logs, small papers, reflections, progress analyses and other assignments and activities. The pre-assessments and post-assessments (same instruments) also provide feedback for evaluating and modifying the course. The post-assessments help students to evaluate their progress and develop action plans for what they are going to do to keep developing their strategies and skills in the future. For example, the pre-LASSI helps students to become aware of their strengths, as well as those areas in which they need to improve in order to help foster academic success during the current semester while they are taking EDP310. The post-LASSI helps them to assess areas in which they still need to improve. The LASSI is used in conjunction with measures of goal orientation, help seeking, and reading comprehension. Additional measures are often added to help develop curriculum or evaluate the coordinators' and instructors' success in reaching course goals. The course also includes three exams that are used to assess and provide feedback on students' learning of course content. Finally, students complete other assignments such as writing a learning biography, a series of short papers on their progress or problems impeding their progress, and a capstone project based on the application of what they are learning to another course.

FUTURE RESEARCH DIRECTIONS IN STRATEGIC LEARNING

As the definitions of academic preparedness for higher education and training continue to evolve, so will the need for further research into the cognitive, metacognitive, motivational, emotional, and behavioral variables that both contribute to (e.g., positive motivation for learning) and detract from (e.g., high anxiety) strategic and self-regulated learning. A more in-depth understanding of these variables, individually and in combination, will also lead to more accurate and useful conceptual models that can be used as the basis for both broad (e.g., generalizable learning strategies such as the use of elaboration) and content-specific (e.g., elaboration strategies for learning algebra equations) strategies and skills interventions at all levels of education. In addition, future research also needs to focus on adapting these interventions to individual student strengths and problem areas. Current applications attempt to account for these individual differences, but more systematic and effective guidelines are needed.

Further work is also needed in the area of assessment of strategic and self-regulated learning. The continued development of generic assessments like Zimmerman and Martinez-Pons's (1986, 1988) SRLIS, Pintrich et al.'s (1991) MSLQ and Weinstein, Palmer, & Schulte's (2002) LASSI will help us to more accurately screen college students to help identify areas of strengths and weaknesses so that general prescriptions can be derived. However, in addition to broad-level diagnostic/prescriptive measures, we will also need further development of measures for content-specific learning and online measures of self-regulation such as computer traces, think-aloud protocols, diaries of studying, direct observation, and microanalyses (Zimmerman, 2008). While it is true that any generalizable strategy becomes content-specific when applied to a topic area, there are still subsets and special cases of generalizable strategies that are useful for learning in specific content areas such as math, foreign language learning or history. This area has not yet been systematically explored.

Another area that needs systematic study and expansion is the duration and evaluation of interventions. Currently, most research interventions take place in laboratory settings rather than actual courses or programs in colleges and universities. One primary underlying problem is the lack of cooperation between and among researchers and higher education institutions. More elaborate interventions are needed, as well as extended time for follow-ups to gauge both the success and endurance of the results of higher education interventions. We have been fortunate to be able to do five-year follow-ups on students for several semesters of our EDP310 course, but there are few studies of this duration.

Educational Implications of Current and Future Work in Strategic Learning

The educational implications of work in strategic learning for college access, success and attainment of individual and societal educational goals are enormous. Programs are being developed or expanded for high school students and summer transition, or bridge, programs for graduating seniors and/or for students who are considered to be underprepared for college-level work. These programs not only facilitate student access to higher education but they also enhance student success and retention. For example, in Texas, the Higher Education Coordinating Board (THECB) has been funding a number of different approaches to summer transition programs and evaluating the effects of various components and their contributions to success in college-level coursework for students with low entry scores on measures such as ACT's Compass assessment, the College Board's Accuplacer assessment, and Pearson Education's Texas Higher Education Assessment (THEA; see the THECB website, www.thecb.state.tx.us, for more information on these efforts and the reports documenting the outcomes of these ongoing projects). In addition, many colleges and most community colleges have some form of developmental education focusing on math, reading, writing, personal development and learning strategies. The characteristics of these programs vary greatly, and a more comprehensive view of strategic and self-regulated learning is still needed.

Strategic and self-regulated learning can also be taught in a number of different contexts in higher education. For example, as part of the Cognitive Learning Strategies Project at the University of Texas at Austin, college faculty are trained in the use of a metacurriculum—teaching students *how* to learn the content in their courses as well as *what* to learn. Workshops are also conducted for student support personnel, tutors, counselors, mentors and advisors. Most college learning centers have more modern versions of study skills classes and workshops, often targeting specific courses with higher than average drop-out or failure rates. There are also a number of textbooks and self-help books available for students to use to improve their strategic and self-regulated learning (e.g., Nist-Olenjnik & Holschuh, 2011; Sellers, Dochen, & Hodges, 2011; VanderStoep & Pintrich, 2007). Online materials, such as Lucy Macdonald's HowToStudy.org and Becoming a Strategic Learner: The LASSI Online Instructional Modules (Weinstein, Woodruff, & Awalt, 2002) are also available for individual or academic contexts.

In the future, it will be even more important to not only have online materials available for students but to also develop materials specifically for elearning. As more and more colleges are turning to elearning and blended courses (including both online and face-to-face components) like the EDP310 strategic learning course we described earlier, it will be more and more important to address the additional self-regulation needs of these students. The number of students who take one or more online classes that drop out or fail to achieve a passing grade is very high (Hachey, Wladis, & Conway, 2009; Patterson, & McFadden, 2009). At least part of this can be attributed to the additional need for well-developed self-regulation processes and skills in a population that is often lacking effective strategies and skills. Results using a version of the LASSI for online learning contexts have supported these needs.

There is also a need for greater cooperation among researchers, practitioners, college administrators, and college institutional researchers. Much of the applied research in our field is proprietary and cannot be published. Particularly in community college contexts, there is little pressure to publish, and often the results are not readily available in a published form or even presented at conferences (Simpson, 2002). This makes it difficult to cite studies that fall under institutional research but which have important implications for strategic and self-regulated learning (a difficulty we had in citing references for many of our own findings). A partnering of these different stakeholders could enrich theory, research and application, further helping numerous students gain access to higher education, thrive in academic environments, and reach their educational and occupational goals.

CONCLUSION

As the need for some type of postsecondary education is increasing, the preparation of many students transitioning into higher education is often inadequate. Projections of American workforce needs now and in the future emphasize the need for highly skilled employees and employers who can adjust to the rapidly changing technological world and global economy. Mastering one content area or skill set is rarely sufficient for today's jobs and careers, and on-the-job learning and continuing education will become even more necessary over time. Staying on the forefront of innovation will involve educating people to become life-long strategic and self-regulated learners who can self-manage their own learning and skill development and generate motivation to reach their goals. It is therefore critical that postsecondary education institutions implement a variety of initiatives aimed at helping students to become more strategic and self-regulated learners. The theories, research and applied work in strategic and self-regulated learning provide promising foundations for the further development of effective interventions to meet these needs because they provide evidence that students can proactively improve how they study and learn, making academic success more likely. Models of strategic and self-regulated learning, like the two discussed in this chapter, provide conceptual frameworks for researchers, educators, and students to use to organize many factors that influence learning and performance, and target those factors that students can modify to exercise control over how and what they learn to enhance their chances of academic success.

Zimmerman's model of self-regulation offers a framework of cyclical phases and key processes involved in self-regulating one's use of learning strategies, motivation, metacognition, affect, and behaviors in the pursuit of learning and achievement goals. Similarly, Weinstein's MSL organizes a constellation of factors that impact students' learning and provides a framework for guiding students in developing and using a repertoire of learning strategies related to their skill, will, and self-regulation that they can use to improve their learning and achievement across diverse learning environments. As we reviewed in this chapter, many successful postsecondary interventions have been derived from or influenced by Zimmerman's model of self-regulation and Weinstein's MSL. Opportunities to expand applied work in this area are growing rapidly with increased national and local attention and funding from policy-makers, professional organizations, and foundations to better serve students who are academically underprepared. The success of this movement will partly depend on the effective implementation of strategic and self-regulated learning content and instruction across various facets of an institution, including learning support centers and programs, course-based and non-course-based interventions, online and hybrid interventions, advising and counseling programs, and professional development for faculty and staff. Although a number of interventions currently exist, from short workshops to intensive three-credit courses, more research and development is needed in this area, and the best is yet to come!

Finally, we want to emphasize that more research and development work needs to address the needs of elementary, middle school, and high school students. It is projected that 25% of today's ninth graders will not complete high school—we must do better!

FINAL COMMENT—A PERSONAL NOTE
FROM CLAIRE ELLEN WEINSTEIN

We all know that Barry's work has had a profound influence on research and applied efforts in so many fields, but not everyone is aware of the profound effects he has had on his students, colleagues, friends and generations of students and medical patients who have benefited from his insightful theories, creative research, and constant efforts to positively impact their success and the quality of their lives. His awards are legendary, ranging from an outstanding contributions award from the American Lung Association for his work in medicine compliance for patients with long-term chronic diseases such as asthma (first non-physician to win the award) to his Thorndike Award for career achievement in educational psychology from the Division of Educational Psychology of the American Psychological Association. However, perhaps Barry's greatest achievement is the warmth, concern, assistance, and support he offers to colleagues and friends. Barry is a great mentor who genuinely cares about his students and colleagues. For Barry, his work has been and is a magnificent obsession, and I am honored, proud, and delighted to call him my friend. L'chaim, Barry!

REFERENCES

ACT. (2010). *ACT profile report—National: Graduating class of 2010*. Retrieved from http://www.act.org/newsroom/data/2010/pdf/profile/National2010.pdf?utm_campaign=cccr10&utm_source=profilereports&utm_medium=web

Acee, T. W., Cho, Y., Kim, J., & Weinstein, C. E. (2012). Relationships among properties of college students' self-set academic goals and academic achievement. *Educational Psychology: An International Journal of Experimental Educational Psychology, 32,* 681–698. DOI:10.1080/01443410.2012.712795

Acee, T. W. & Weinstein, C. E. (2010). Effects of a value reappraisal intervention on statistics students' motivation and performance. *Journal of Experimental Education, 78,* 487–512. doi:10.1080/00220970903352753

Acuna, S. R., Rodicio, H. G., & Sanchez, E. (2011). Fostering active processing of instructional explanations of learners with high and low prior knowledge. *European Journal of Psychology of Education, 26,* 435–452.

Albaili, M. A. (1997). Differences among low-, average- and high-achieving college students on learning and study strategies. *Educational Psychology, 17,* 171–178.

Al-Harthy, I. S., Was, C. A., & Isaacson, R. M. (2010). Goals, efficacy, and metacognitive self-regulation: A path analysis. *International Journal of Education, 2,* 1–20.

Arendale, D. (2010). *Access at the crossroads: Learning assistance in higher education.* San Francisco, CA: Jossey-Bass. doi:10.1002/aehe.3506

Aud, S., Hussar, W., Kena, G., Bianco, K., Frohlich, L., Kemp, J., & Tahan, K. (2011). *The condition of education 2011* (NCES 2011-033). Washington, DC: U.S. Department of Education, National Center for Education Statistics.

Austin, J. T. & Vancouver, J. B. (1996). Goal constructs in psychology: Structure, process, and content. *Psychological Bulletin, 120*(3), 338–375.

Bailey, T. (2009). Challenge and opportunity: Rethinking the role and function of developmental education in community college. *New Directions for Community Colleges, 2009* (145), 11–30. doi:10.1002/cc

Blunden, A. (2011). Vygotsky's idea of a Gestalt and its origins. *Theory & Psychology, 21*, 457–471.

Bol, L. & Garner, J. K. (2011). Challenges in supporting self-regulation in distance education environments. *Journal of Computing in Higher Education, 23*, 104–123. doi:10.1007/s12528-011-9046-7

Brown, J. I., Fishco, V. V., & Hanna, G. (1993). *The Nelson-Denny reading test.* Itasca, IL: The Riverside Publishing Company.

Cano, F. (2006). An in-depth analysis of the Learning and Study Strategies Inventory (LASSI). *Educational and Psychological Measurement, 66*, 1023–1038.

Conley, D. T. (2007). *Redefining college readiness.* Eugene, OR: Educational Policy Improvement Center.

De Corte, E. & Masui, C. (2004). The CLIA-model: A framework for designing powerful learning environments for thinking and problem. *European Journal of Psychology of Education, 19*, 365–384.

DeRoma, V. M., Bell, N. L., Zaremba, B. A., & Abee, J. C., (2005). Evaluation of a college transition program for students at-risk for academic failure. *Research & Teaching, 21*, 20–33.

Diseth, A. (2011). Self-efficacy, goal orientations and learning strategies as mediators between preceding and subsequent academic achievement. *Learning and Individual Differences, 21*, 191–195.

Dweck, C. S. & Leggett, E. L. (1988). A social-cognitive approach to motivation and personality. *Psychological Review, 95* (2), 256–273. doi:10.1037/0033-295X.95.2.256

Eccles, J. S. & Wigfield, A. (2002).Motivational beliefs, values and goals. *Annual Review of Psychology, 53*, 109–132. doi:10.1146/annurev.psych.53.100901.135153

Eccles, J. S., Adler, T. F., Futterman, R., Goff, S. B., Kaczala, C. M., Meece, J. L., et al. (1983). Expectancies, values, and academic behaviors. In J. T. Spence (Ed.), *Achievement and achievement motivation* (pp. 75–146). San Francisco, CA: W. H. Freeman.

Elliot, A. J. (1999). Approach and avoidance motivation and achievement goals. *Educational Psychologist, 34* (3), 169–189.

Elliot, A. J. & Murayama, K. (2008). On the measurement of achievement goals: Critique, illustration, and application. *Journal of Educational Psychology, 100*, 613–628. doi:10.1037/0022-0663.100.3.613

Fenollar, P., Román, S., & Cuestas, P. J. (2007). University students' academic performance: An integrative conceptual framework and empirical analysis. *The British Journal of Educational Psychology, 77*, 873–891. doi:10.1348/000709907X189118

Flavell, J. H. (1979). Metacognition and cognitive monitoring: A new area of cognitive-developmental inquiry. *American Psychologist, 34*(10), 906–911.

Hachey, A. C., Wladis, C. W., & Conway, K. M. (2009). Is the second time the charm? Investigating trends in online reenrollment, retention and success. *The Journal of Educators Online, 9*, 1–25.

Hailikari, T. K. & Nevgi, A. (2010). How to diagnose at-risk students in chemistry: The case of prior knowledge assessment. *International Journal of Science Education, 32*, 2079–2095. doi:10.1080/09500690903369654

Hodges, R. & Agee, K. S. (2009). Program management. In R. F. Flippo & D. C. Caverly (Eds.), *Handbook of College Reading and Study Strategy Research* (2nd ed., pp. 351–378). New York, NY: Routledge.

Hodges, R. B., Dochen, C. W., & Sellers, D. (2001). Implementing a learning framework course. In J. L. Higbee & P. L. Dwinell (Eds.), *NADE Monograph: 2001 A Developmental Odyssey* (pp. 3–13). Warrensburg, MO: National Association for Developmental Education.

Hofer, B. K. & Yu, S. L. (2003). Teaching self-regulated learning through a "learning to learn" course. *Teaching of Psychology, 30*, 30–33.

Humphrey, G. (1924). The psychology of the gestalt: Some educational implications. *Journal of Educational Psychology, 15*, 401–412.

Husman, J., Derryberry, P. W., Crowson, M. H., & Lomax, R. (2004). Instrumentality, task value, and intrinsic motivation: Making sense of their independent interdependence. *Contemporary Educational Psychology, 29*, 63–76. doi:10.1016/S0361-476X(03)00019-5

Husman, J. & Hilpert, J. (2007). The Intersection of students' perceptions of instrumentality, self-efficacy, and goal orientations in an online mathematics course. *Zeitschrift für Pädagogische Psychologie, 21*, 229-239. doi:10.1024/1010-0652.21.3.229

Locke, E. A. & Latham, G. P. (2002). Building a practically useful theory of goal setting and task motivation: A 35-year odyssey. *American Psychologist, 57*(9), 705–717. doi:10.1037//0003-066X.57.9.705

Maxwell, M. (1997). *Improving student learning skills: A new edition.* Clearwater, FL: H&H publishing.

Mayer, R. E. & Alexander, P. A. (Eds.). (2011). *Handbook of research on learning and instruction.* New York, NY: Routledge.

McKeachie, W. J., Pintrich, P. R., & Lin, Y. G. (1985). Teaching learning strategies. *Educational Psychologist, 120*, 53–160.

Mireles, S. V. (2010). Developmental mathematics program: A model for change. *Journal of College Reading and Learning, 40*, 81–90.

Mireles, S. V., Offer, J., Ward, D. D., & Dochen, C. W. (2011). Incorporating study strategies in developmental mathematics/college algebra. *Journal of Developmental Education, 34*, 12–41.

Nist-Olenjnik, S. & Holschuh, J. P. (2011). *College rules!: How to study, survive, and succeed in college* (3rd ed.). New York, NY: Ten Speed Press.

Paris, S. G. & Paris, A. H. (2001). Classroom applications of research on self-regulated learning. Educational Psychologist, 36, 89–101.

Parsad, B., Lewis, L., & Greene, B. (2003). *Remedial Education at Degree-Granting Postsecondary Institutions in Fall 2000.* Washington, DC: National Center for Education Statistics. Retrieved from http://nces.ed.gov/pubs2004/2004010.pdf

Patterson, B., & McFadden, C. (2009). Attrition in online and campus degree programs. *Online Journal of Distance Learning Administration, 12*(2). Retrieved from http://www.westga.edu/~distance/ojdla/summer122/patterson112.html.

Pintrich, P. R. (1999). The role of motivation in promoting and sustaining self-regulated learning. *International Journal of Educational Research, 31*, 459–470.

Pintrich, P. R. (2000). The role of goal orientation in self-regulated learning. In M. Boekaerts, P. R. Pintrich, & M. Zeidner (Eds.), *Handbook of self-regulation* (pp. 452–502). San Diego, CA: Academic Press.

Pintrich, P. R. (2004). A conceptual framework for assessing motivation and self-regulated learning in college students. *Educational Psychology Review, 16*(4), 385–407. doi:10.1007/s10648-004-0006-x

Pintrich, P. R. & De Groot, E. V. (1990). Motivational and self-regulated learning components of classroom academic performance. *Journal of Educational Psychology, 82*, 33–40. doi:10.1037/0022-0663.82.1.33

Pintrich, P. R., Smith, D. A., Garcia, T., & McKeachie, W. J. (1991). *A manual for the use of the motivated strategies for learning questionnaire (MSLQ)* (Technical Report No. 91-B-004). Ann Arbor, MI: National Center for Research to Improve Postsecondary Teaching and Learning.

Pressley, M. & McCormick, C. B. (1995). *Advanced educational psychology: For educators, researchers, and policymakers.* New York, NY: HarperCollins.

Proctor, B. E., Prevatt, F., Adams, K., Hurst, A., & Petscher, Y. (2006). Study skills profiles of normal-achieving and academically-struggling college students. *Journal of College Student Development, 47*, 37–51. doi:10.1353/csd.2006.0011

Ramdass, D. & Zimmerman, B. J. (2011). Developing self-regulation skills: The important role of homework. *Journal of Advanced Academics, 22*, 194–218.

Rosenthal, T. L. & Bandura, A. (1978). Psychological modeling: Theory and practice. In S. L. Garfield & A. E. Bergin (Eds.), *Handbook of psychotherapy and behavior change: An empirical analysis* (2nd ed., pp. 621–658). New York, NY: Wiley.

Russell, A. (2008). Enhancing college student success through developmental education. *American Association of State Colleges and Universities—Policy Matters: A Higher Education Policy Brief.* Retrieved from http://www.aascu.org/uploadedfiles/aascu/content/root/policyandadvocacy/policypublications/pmaug08.pdf

Schunk, D. H. (1987). Peer models and children's behavioral change. *Review of Educational Research, 57*, 149–174.

Schunk, D. H., Pintrich, P. R., & Meece, J. L. (2008). *Motivation in education: Theory, research, and applications* (3rd ed.). Upper Saddle River, NJ: Prentice Hall.

Sellers, D., Dochen, C. W., & Hodges, R. W. (2011). *Academic transformations: The road to college success* (2nd. ed.). Boston, MA: Prentice Hall.

Simpson, M. L. (2002). Program evaluation studies: Strategic learning delivery model suggestions. *Journal of Developmental Education, 26*, 2–10.

Sins, P. H. M., van Joolingen, W. R., Savelsbergh, E. R., & van Hout-Wolters, B. (2008). Motivation and performance within a collaborative computer-based modeling task: Relations between students' achievement goal orientation, self-efficacy, cognitive processing, and achievement. *Contemporary Educational Psychology, 3*, 58–77. doi:10.1016/j.cedpsych.2006.12.004

Stoeger, H. & Ziegler, A. (2008). Evaluation of a classroom based training to improve self-regulation in time management tasks during homework activities with fourth graders. *Metacognition and Learning, 3*, 207–230. doi:10.1007/s11409-008-9027-z

Tsiplakides, I. & Keramida, A. (2010). The relationship between teacher expectations and student achievement in the teaching of English as a foreign language. *English Language Teaching, 3*, 22–26.

VandenBos, G. R. (Ed.). (2007). *APA dictionary of psychology.* Washington, DC: American Psychological Association.

VanderStoep, S. W. & Pintrich, P. R. (2007). *Learning to learn: The skill and will of college success* (2nd ed.). Boston, MA: Prentice Hall.

Weiner, B. (1985). An attributional theory of achievement motivation and emotion. *Psychological Review, 92* (4), 548–573.

Weiner, B. (2000). Intrapersonal and interpersonal theories of motivation from an attributional perspective. *Educational Psychology Review, 12*(1), 1–14.

Weinstein, C. E. (1975). *Learning of elaboration strategies.* Unpublished doctoral dissertation, University of Texas at Austin, Austin, TX.

Weinstein, C. E. (1978). Elaboration skills as a learning strategy. In H. F. O'Neil, Jr. *Learning Strategies* (pp. 31–55). New York, NY: Academic Press.

Weinstein, C. E., Acee, T. W., & Jung, J. H. (2011). Self-regulation and learning strategies. *New Directions for Teaching & Learning, 2011*(126), 45–53. doi:10.1002/tl.443

Weinstein, C. E., Acee, T. W., & Jung, J. H. (2010). Learning strategies. In B. McGaw, P. L. Peterson, & E. Baker (Eds.), *International encyclopedia of education* (3rd ed., pp. 323–329). New York, NY: Elsevier.

Weinstein, C. E., Hanson, G. R., Powdrill, L., Roska, L. A., Dierking, D., Husman, J., & McCann, E. (1998). The design and evaluation of a course in strategic learning. In J. Higo & P. Dwindle (Eds.), *Developmental education: Meeting diverse student needs.* Chicago, IL: National Association of Developmental Education.

Weinstein, C. E., Husman, J., & Dierking, D. R. (2000). Self-regulation interventions with a focus on learning strategies. In M. Boekaerts, P. Pintrich, & M. Zeidner (Eds.), *Handbook of self-regulation* (pp. 724–747). San Diego, CA: Academic Press.

Weinstein, C. E. & Mayer, R. E. (1986). The teaching of learning strategies. In M. Wittrock (Ed.), *Handbook of research on teaching* (3rd ed., pp. 315–327). New York, NY: Macmillan.

Weinstein, C. E. & Palmer, D. R. (2002). *User's manual for those administering the learning and study strategies inventory* (2nd ed.). Clearwater, FL: H & H Publishing.

Weinstein, C. E., Palmer, D. R., & Schulte, A. (2002). *The learning and study strategies inventory* (2nd ed.). Clearwater, FL: H & H Publishing.

Weinstein, C. E., Schulte, A., & Palmer, D. R. (1987). *The learning and study strategies inventory.* Clearwater, FL: H & H Publishing.

Weinstein, C. E., Woodruff, T., & Awalt, C. (2002). *Becoming a strategic learner: LASSI instructional modules.* Clearwater, FL: H & H Publishing.

Wetzels, A. J., Kester, L., & van Merrienboer, J. J. G. (2011). Adapting prior knowledge activation: Mobilisation, perspective taking, and learners' prior knowledge. *Computers in Human Behavior, 27*, 16–21. doi:10.1016/j.chb.2010.05.004

Wigfield, A. & Eccles, J. S. (2000). Expectancy-value theory of achievement motivation. *Contemporary Educational Psychology, 25*(1), 68–81. doi:10.1006/ceps.1999.1015

Winne, P. H. (2011). A cognitive and metacognitive analysis of self-regulated learning. In B. J. Zimmerman & D. H. Schunk. *Handbook of self-regulation of learning and performance* (pp. 15–32). New York, NY: Taylor & Francis.

Winne, P. H., Nesbit, J. C., Kumar, V., Hadwin, A. F., Lajoie, S. P., Azevedo, R., et al., (2006). Supporting self-regulated learning with gStudy software: The learning kit project. *Technology, Instruction, Cognition and Learning, 3*, 105–113.

Winters, F. I., Greene, J. A., & Costich, C. M. (2008). Self-regulation of learning in computer-based learning environments: A critical analysis. *Educational Psychology Review, 20*, 429–444. doi:10.1007/s10648-008-9080-9

Wittrock, M. C. (1974). Learning as a generative process. *Educational Psychologist, 11*(2), 87–95.

Woolfolk, A. (2009). *Educational psychology* (11th ed.). Boston, MA: Prentice Hall.

Woolley, M. E., Strutchens, M. E., Gilbert, M. C., & Martin, W. G. (2010). Mathematics success of Black middle school students: Direct and indirect effects of teacher expectations and reform practices. *The Negro Educational Review, 61*, 41–59.

Zimmerman, B. J. (1986a). Becoming a self-regulated learner: Which are the key subprocesses? *Contemporary Educational Psychology, 11*, 307–313.

Zimmerman, B. J. (Ed.). (1986b). Special issue on self-regulated learning [Special issue]. *Contemporary Educational Psychology, 11*, 305–427.

Zimmerman, B. J. (1989). A social cognitive view of self-regulated academic learning. *Journal of Educational Psychology, 81*(3), 329–339.

Zimmerman, B. J. (2000). Attaining self-regulation: A social cognitive perspective. In M. Boekaerts, P. R. Pintrich, & M. Zeidner (Eds.), *Handbook of self-regulation* (pp. 13–39). San Diego, CA: Academic Press.

Zimmerman, B. J. (2008). Investigating self-regulation and motivation: Historical background, methodological developments, and future prospects. *American Educational Research Journal, 45*(1), 166–183. doi:10.3102/0002831207312909

Zimmerman, B. J. (2011). Motivational sources and outcomes of self-regulated learning and performance. In B. J. Zimmerman & D. H. Schunk, *Handbook of self-regulation of learning and performance* (pp. 49–64). New York, NY: Taylor & Francis.

Zimmerman, B. J. & Moylan, A. R. (2009). Self-regulation: Where metacognition and motivation intersect. In D. J. Hacker, J. Dunlosky, & A. C. Graesser (Eds.), *Handbook of Metacognition in Education* (pp. 299–316). New York, NY: Taylor & Francis.

Zimmerman, B. J. & Bandura, A. (1994). Impact of self-regulatory influences on writing course attainment. *American Educational Research Journal, 31*, 845–862. doi:10.3102/00028312031004845

Zimmerman, B. J. & Martinez-Pons, M. (1986). Development of a structured interview for assessing students' use of self-regulated learning strategies. *American Educational Research Journal, 23*, 614–628.

Zimmerman, B. J. & Martinez-Pons, M. (1988). Construct validation of a strategy model of student self-regulated learning. *Journal of Educational Psychology, 80*, 284–290.

Zimmerman, B. J. & Schunk, D. H. (Eds.). (2011). *Handbook of self-regulation of learning and performance*. New York, NY: Taylor & Francis.

APPENDIX: Course Topic Outline for EDP310 Course, Fall Semester 2011

Date	Preparation	Topic(s)	To Be Handed in at the Start of Class	Assigned in Class
Aug. 24, Wed.		Course Introduction		
Aug. 26, Fri.	Read: *"Top Ten List for Longhorn Success"*	Pre-Assessments: LASSI and Goal Orientation Top Ten List for Longhorn Success		
Aug. 29, Mon.	Read: Syllabus, Course Schedule, Assignment Descriptions	Course Expectations: Blackboard & Online Modules Assignment Descriptions Quality of Assignments Participation Communication with Instructor		Learning Autobiography
Aug. 31, Wed.		Pre-Assessments: Nelson Denny Help Seeking		
Sept. 2, Fri.		*Community Building*		
Sept. 5, Mon.		NO CLASS: Labor Day		
Sept. 7, Wed.	Read: *"Model of Strategic Learning"*	Model of Strategic Learning Why is the model important? What are the components?		Information Processing & Self-Testing Integrative Assignment

Date	Reading	Topic		
Sept. 9, Fri.		"Content Overview" Day 1 / Information Processing / Self-Testing / Motivation / Attitude	Learning Autobiography	
Sept. 12, Mon.		"Content Overview" Day 2		
Sept. 14, Wed.		"Content Overview" Day 3		
Sept. 16, Fri.		Model of Strategic Learning Recap		
Sept. 19, Mon.	Read: "Information Processing Reading"	Information Processing for Acquiring Knowledge	Information Processing & Self-Testing Integrative Assignment	
Sept. 21, Wed.		Information Processing for Acquiring Knowledge		
Sept. 23, Fri.	Read: "Self-Testing Reading"	Information Processing for Acquiring Knowledge / Self-Testing		Motivation & Attitude Integrative Assignment
Sept. 26, Mon.		Self-Testing		
Sept. 28, Wed.	Read: "Systematic Approach"	Systematic Approach		
Sept. 30, Fri.	Read: "Types of Knowledge"	Types of Knowledge		

APPENDIX: Course Topic Outline for EDP310 Course, Fall Semester 2011 (continued)

Date	Read	Systematic Approach	Integrative Assignment	Integrative Assignment
Oct. 3, Mon.		Systematic Approach		
Oct. 5, Wed.	Read: "Goals, Goal Orientation Reading"	Motivation	Motivation & Attitude Integrative Assignment	
Oct. 7, Fri.	Read: "Attitude Reading"	Motivation Attitude		Time Management & Anxiety Integrative Assignment
Oct. 10, Mon.		Attitude		
Oct. 12, Wed.		Exam 1 Review		
Oct. 14, Fri.		Exam 1		
Oct. 17, Mon.	Read: "Academic Environment Reading"	Academic Environment Components Strategies		
Oct. 19, Wed.	Read: "Academic Help-Seeking Reading"	Academic Help-Seeking Types of Help-Seeking Situational Analyses Exam 1 Feedback		Study Aids & Test-Taking Strategies Integrative Assignment
Oct. 21, Fri.		Time Management	Time Management & Anxiety Integrative Assignment	

Date	Read	Topic		
Oct. 24, Mon.		Procrastination		Concentration & Selecting Main Ideas Integrative Assignment
Oct. 26, Wed.	Read: *"Anxiety Reading"*	Anxiety		
Oct. 28, Fri.		Coping with Anxiety		
Oct. 31, Mon.		Study Aids	Study Aids & Test-Taking Strategies Integrative Assignment	
Nov. 2, Wed.		Study Aids / Test-Taking Strategies		
Nov. 4, Fri.		Test-Taking Strategies		
Nov. 7, Mon.		Concentration	Concentration & Selecting Main Ideas Integrative Assignment	
Nov. 9, Wed.	Read: *"Reading Strategies Reading"* *"Note-taking Reading"*	Reading, Listening & Note-Taking Strategies		
Nov. 11, Fri.		Selecting Main Ideas		
Nov. 14, Mon.		Exam 2 Review		

APPENDIX: Course Topic Outline for EDP310 Course, Fall Semester 2011 (continued)

Date	Topic		Assignment
Nov. 16, Wed.	Exam 2		Capstone Assignment
Nov. 18, Fri.	Post-Assessments: LASSI and Goal Orientation		
Nov. 21, Mon.	Post-Assessments: Nelson Denny Help Seeking Exam 2 Feedback		
Nov. 23, Wed.	Individual Projects Day		
Nov. 25, Fri.	NO CLASS: Thanksgiving Break		
Nov. 28, Mon.	Integration Day		
Nov. 30, Wed.	Integration Day		
Dec. 2, Fri.	Where will you go from here? Also discuss other online resources	Capstone Assignment	

CHAPTER 8

HELP SEEKING AS A SELF-REGULATED LEARNING STRATEGY

Stuart A. Karabenick and Jean-Louis Berger

Barry J. Zimmerman has long recognized that self-regulated learning (SRL) may, and in fact often does, involve others who help learners by providing the resources (e.g., information and skills) they need to be successful. As he stated recently when describing the development of research on SRL, "Although SRL was viewed as especially important during personally directed forms of learning...it was also deemed important in social forms of learning, such as seeking help from peers, parents, and teachers" (Zimmerman, 2008, p. 167). This view had its origins more than two decades previously when Zimmerman and Martinez-Pons (1988) concluded that "self-regulated students were not passive learners but actively sought out information and assistance when needed...one of the most widely emphasized characteristics of self-regulated learners (Zimmerman, 1986), and our data support its theoretical importance" (p. 289). This perspective was reinforced in a subsequent publication (Zimmerman & Martinez-Pons, 1990). Other researchers shared the self-regulatory perspective on help seeking at the time, providing evidence that students who seek help when neces-

Applications of Self-Regulated Learning across Diverse Disciplines, pages 237–261
Copyright © 2013 by Information Age Publishing
All rights of reproduction in any form reserved.

sary are more likely to use other strategies as well (Karabenick & Knapp, 1991). Zimmerman's and Schunk's inclusion of help seeking in subsequent volumes devoted to SRL (Newman, 1994, 2008) has reinforced this view.

Described in more detail subsequently, *help seeking* can be defined as the process of seeking assistance from other individuals or other sources that facilitate accomplishing desired goals, which in an academic context may consist of completing assignments or satisfactory test performance. There is now substantial agreement that seeking help can be considered a form of behavioral (Pintrich & Zusho, 2002) or social self-regulation (e.g., Newman, 1994; Zimmerman, 2008) that is included in the set of tools used by cognitively, behaviorally, and emotionally engaged learners (Butler, 1998, 2006; Karabenick, 1998, 2003, 2004; Karabenick & Newman, 2006; Nelson-Le Gall & Resnick, 1998; Newman, 2000; Skinner & Zimmer-Gembeck, 2007; Zusho, Karabenick, Bonney, & Sims, 2007).

Nelson-Le Gall (1981, 1987) and others (e.g., Ames, 1992; Gross & Mc-Mullen, 1983) set the stage by altering the conception of help seeking as an act of dependency (Beller, 1955; Winterbottom, 1958). Essential to changing its status was Nelson-Le Gall's identification and explication of *instrumental* help seeking. By obtaining the assistance just necessary to overcome difficulties, such as asking for explanations or hints rather than direct help (labeled *executive* help seeking), instrumental help seeking can serve to increase learning and understanding and decrease the need for help and thus subsequent dependency on others (Nelson-Le Gall, 1981, 1985; Nelson-Le Gall, Gumerman, & Scott-Jones, 1983). As a consequence of being proactive and generally beneficial to the learning process, instrumental help seeking is also referred to as *adaptive, strategic, appropriate,* and *autonomous* (Bembenutty, 2006; Butler, 1998; Karabenick, 1998; Karabenick & Newman, 2006, 2009, 2010; Nelson-Le Gall, 1981; Newman, 2008; Ryan, Patrick, & Shim, 2005; White, 2011).

Seeking help that involves others either directly or indirectly renders it unique among self-regulated learning strategies. The student-teacher interaction is a prime example of an extended relationship with multiple instances of bids for assistance and responses to those requests. Even technology-mediated help seeking can be social when the presence of others is real, imagined or even implied (Karabenick, 2010). By contrast, social interactivity is not inherently a component of such cognitive strategies as rehearsal and elaboration, although it could be (e.g., reciting a poem to others). Metacognitive planning, monitoring, and regulating also need not involve interactions with others, although they could in some instances, such as when taking into consideration information from other learners when determining one's own level of comprehension (Karabenick, 1996) or working collaboratively to solve math problems (i.e., socially shared metacognition; Iiskala, Vauras, Lehtinen, & Salonen, 2011). One consequence of the social-interactive nature of help seeking is that it renders the process susceptible to a host of influences to which other forms of self-regulated learning are relatively immune.

The purpose of the present chapter is to describe the help-seeking process and the person and situation influences on that process, especially perceived costs that decrease the likelihood that learners will seek help when needed. The long observed and documented underuse of needed help seeking (e.g., Dillon, 1988; Good, Slavings, Harel, & Emerson, 1987) points to the need for interventions that render it more likely to benefit students. With that background, we then outline the features of several potential interventions that are designed to facilitate learners' adaptive help seeking—that is, seeking help in ways that are proactive and generally beneficial to the learning process. Both sections will include ways that Zimmerman's work informs and is consistent with the development and use of help seeking as part of the self-regulatory process, which includes task analysis, self-motivation beliefs, self-control, self-observation, self-judgment, and self-reaction (Zimmerman, 1989, 2000).

THE HELP-SEEKING PROCESS

Help-seeking process models include a series of stages and decision points that govern if and when learners seek help (e.g., Gross & McMullen, 1983; Karabenick & Newman, 2009; Nelson-Le Gall, 1981). As shown in the first column of Table 8.1, these stages and decision points are to: (1) determine whether there is a problem, (2) determine whether help is needed/wanted, (3) decide whether to seek help, (4) decide on the type of help (goal), (5) decide whom to ask, (6) solicit help, (7) obtain help, and (8) process the help received. An example of an optimal sequence would be the following: a student attempting to complete a math assignment cannot solve a problem even after hours of trying, determines she cannot do so without help, wants to know the general approach to solving this type of problem, realizes that her classmate probably knows how, calls her friend who provides that information, and uses the help to solve the problem. It should be emphasized that the stages and decisions may not occur in the order specified by these models, and especially that learners may not be mindful of the steps involved. Rather, in most instances, the process probably involves a combination of automatic and controlled cognitive and motivational processing that may begin at various points. For example, students' awareness may begin with the decision to seek help, and the assessment of available resources (for example, teachers or other students) could occur before as well, after weighing the costs and benefits that determine that decision. Automatic-

TABLE 8.1   Stages of the Help-Seeking Process and Three-Phase Model of SRL

Stages of the Help-Seeking Process	Processes of Self-Regulation	SRL Phase in the Zimmerman Model
1 Determine whether there is a problem	Task analysis	Forethought
2 Determine whether help is needed/wanted		
3 Decide whether to seek help	Strategic planning	
4 Decide on the type of help (goal)		
5 Decide whom to ask		
6 Solicit help	Self-control	Performance
7 Obtain help		
8a Process the help received—judge or evaluate it	Self-judgment: self-evaluation	Self-Reflection
8b Process the help received—react to it	Self-reaction: self-satisfaction and adaptive inference	

ity may occur when seeking help is well-understood and practiced to the extent that the act takes place with minimal or no conscious deliberation.

Zimmerman's model of self-regulated learning (Zimmerman, 2000) offers a cyclical and procedural micro-explanation of self-regulation that fits the use of strategic help seeking and may even provide more details than the models described above. Specifically, the eight-step model described here can be successfully mapped onto Zimmerman's SRL model (see Table 8.1, columns entitled "SRL Phase in the Zimmerman model" and "Processes of Self-regulation"). Stages 1 to 5 of the help-seeking process are part of the forethought phase, as processes setting the stage for action and influencing the effort and decision to act. Motivational self-beliefs are most influential in this phase. Stages 6 and 7 pertain to the performance phase, including processes occurring during action and affecting attention. Finally, Stage 8 (process the help received) is part of the self-reflection stage, as it involves the processes that occur after performance of the action and affect how learners respond to the experience. We further divide Stage 8 into two sub-stages. Stage 8a involves processing the help received, judging whether it adequately addresses the learner's help-seeking goals (e.g., for answers or hints). Stage 8b involves reacting to the answer to the previous judgment—how satisfied one is and implications for subsequent help seeking. In cyclic fashion, this last stage influences processes in the forethought phase the next time a student seeks help, such as whether to ask for help at all and whether the processing in Stage 8 suggests variations in whom and how one asks for help.

Further correspondences are notable in terms of cognitive processes. Determining whether there is a problem and whether help is needed and wanted are examples of task analysis processes, whereas Stages 3 to 5 (decide whether to seek help, the type of help, and whom to ask) relate to what Zimmerman calls the *strategic planning* processes. Four types of self-motivation beliefs are considered as activated during the forethought phase in Zimmerman's SRL model. With respect to help seeking, these include: self-efficacy (belief that one can marshal the resources to seek the desired help); outcome expectations (beliefs that doing so will result in the desired outcome); task value (e.g., help-seeking's benefits and costs); and goal orientation (e.g., whether knowledge or skill development or demonstration are more important). Each of these beliefs may influence the performance phase. In the case of help seeking, self-motivation beliefs would thus affect both the propensity to seek help and the type of help targeted. The relations between goal orientation (or achievement goals) and help seeking are the most studied of the associations between motivation and help seeking (see below).

The two stages of the performance phase (solicit and obtain help) are part of general self-control strategies applicable across contexts and situations. In their framework of SRL, Zimmerman and Moylan (2009) describe help seeking as a social form of information seeking. Even if these stages of the process are largely dependent on others, and may therefore seem at first glance the opposite of self-control, they require knowledge of what to ask, when to ask and whom to ask. Thus, they reflect a form of self-regulated learning.

It is pertinent how the last stage of the help-seeking process (i.e., process the help received) can be examined using Zimmerman's model. Manifested here are both self-judgment, which is the self-evaluation of one's own performance and self-reaction, and the degree of perceived (dis)satisfaction and inferences about "how one needs to alter his or her self-regulatory approach during subsequent efforts to learn or perform" (Zimmerman, 2000, p. 23). During this last stage, the student makes such self-evaluative judgments as "Does the help I received provide me with the information I needed?" This judgment consists of comparing the outcome of help seeking with one's goal (Stage 4); that is, a monitoring process. Moreover, two processes of self-reaction may take place. First, a certain level of self-satisfaction is experienced, which encourages or discourages further demands for help. The congruence between the type of help sought by the student and the form of help provided by the teacher or a peer is one type of satisfaction. For example, asking for expedient help and receiving help in that form is a source of self-satisfaction, which increases the probability of seeking the same type of help in the future. Second, adaptive or defensive inferences can lead students to alter their use of help seeking toward appropriate strategies for learning. In the case of what Zimmerman calls defensive inferences, students protect themselves from future dissatisfaction and negative affect by avoiding seeking help the next time it would be needed. These self-reaction processes feed back to the first stage of the help-seeking model. In sum, applying Zimmerman's model of SRL to help-seeking stages as they have been identified in prior research highlights the dynamic and cyclical feature of this self-regulatory strategy. We now turn to the stages of the help-seeking process in more detail, including relevant empirical evidence.

HELP-SEEKING NEED, BEHAVIOR, AND INTENTIONS

Calibrating the extent of learners' need for help is essential when they confront a learning impasse or are faced with less than desired levels of performance, and it would be intuitive that greater need translates into higher levels of help seeking. That relation does exist at the range between low and moderate levels of need; however, the monotonic relation between need and help seeking breaks down at very high need levels, providing evidence for the maxim that those who need help the most are least likely to seek it. The result is a non-monotonic (inverted U-shaped) relationship between need and help seeking, which for college students was most frequent in the C+ to B– GPA range (Karabenick & Knapp, 1988a). One interpretation of the low probability of help seeking among those who very much need it is that students may be too discouraged to take advantage of available help, considering it hopeless. Another reason, to be elaborated subsequently, is that these students are too threatened by displays of their ignorance. Contributing as well could be their lack of help-seeking skills, which the present chapter seeks to address.

This non-monotonic relationship illustrates an important point: that the level of need cannot be inferred directly from behavior. Instead, it must either be known through independent evidence (e.g., previous levels of performance on similar tasks), be independently assessed, or experimentally manipulated by, for example, inducing failure experiences (Newman, 2000). The non-monotonic relationship also illustrates the difference between help-seeking behavior and help-seeking intentions. *Intentions* refer to the likelihood of seeking help contingent on the need for help. Such conditional statements have become the standard in research on help seeking, which has consistently found that, as just discussed, more adaptively motivated students are not more likely to seek help but rather are more likely to seek help if needed (Karabenick & Knapp, 1991; Karabenick & Newman, 2010).

Knowledge about the need for help is essential when responding to requests for assistance, which often take the form of questions or when students fail to ask for needed help. It is generally possible to infer the need for help from requests, although help can be sought for reasons other than need, such as for purposes of ingratiation or impression management (e.g., demonstrating mastery of the material). Not asking questions, however, is more ambiguous because it may signify the lack of perceived need but also the possibility that learners, often students in classrooms, lack the knowledge to even formulate a question (e.g., Renkl, 2002) or are too embarrassed or perceive that their teacher is not receptive to questions (Karabenick & Sharma, 1994).

HELP-SEEKING GOALS

As noted at the outset, defining learners' help-seeking goals was an essential step in recognizing that seeking help can be a self-regulated learning strategy, as in the performance phase of Zimmerman's model of self-regulation that incorporates help seeking as a social strategy for gaining needed assistance from an appropriate source (Zimmerman & Campillo, 2003). In addition to the distinction between instrumental and executive help-seeking goals, that are considered more versus less adaptive forms of help seeking, respectively, Butler (1998) identified three help-seeking orientations: (a) autonomous—focused on understanding and increased competency; (b) ability-focused—concerned with not appearing incompetent; and (c) expedient orientation (similar to executive help seeking). Furthermore, Ryan et al. (2005) proposed that help seeking can be characterized as appropriate, dependent or avoidant. Newman (2008) has designated an adaptive help-seeker as one who begins by accurately assessing that help is necessary, formulates an appropriate request for help, understands the best resources available, designs strategies for successful requests, and productively processes the help received to his or her mastery of the material or the ability to solve problems. In other words, an adaptive help-seeker is someone who negotiates the help-seeking process in an ideal manner, for maximum short- and long-term benefits.

HELP SEEKING AND ACHIEVEMENT GOAL ORIENTATIONS

Achievement goal orientations—students' goals or approaches to learning—have been consistently linked to help seeking (Butler & Neuman, 1995; Karabenick, 2004; Karabenick & Newman, 2009, 2010; Newman, 2007; Ryan, Hicks, & Midgley, 1997). Mastery oriented students (who focus on understanding) are more likely to seek instrumental help, not as threatened by help seeking, less likely to avoid seeking help and less likely to seek expedient/executive help. In contrast, students with performance-approach (who focus on performing better than others) and performance-avoid orientations (who are concerned about performing worse than others) to learning and performance are more threatened by help seeking, are more likely to avoid seeking instrumental help and more likely to seek help for expedient reasons (Karabenick, 2003; Ryan & Pintrich, 1997).

Goal orientations are considered important predictors of strategic planning in Zimmerman's model. First, goal orientation as a forethought process enhances efforts to learn or the quality of learning effort, which are manifest in the association between goal orientation and type of help seeking cited above. Zimmerman also assumes that students with a mastery goal orientation will engage in superior self-reflection processes more so than will students with a performance goal orientation (Zimmerman & Moylan, 2009). Accordingly, the way students process the help they receive may differ as a function of their goal orientation. If we consider instrumental help seeking as leading to deep learning, and expedient help seeking as leading to surface learning, then the model provides a procedural and theoretical explanation of how achievement goals affect help seeking. It thus supports the empirical relationship observed between mastery goals and instrumental help seeking on the one hand and between performance goals and expedient help seeking on the other.

INFLUENCES OF THE LEARNING CONTEXT

According to the social cognitive model of SRL (Zimmerman, 2000), founded on Bandura's social cognitive learning theory (Bandura, 1986), person, environment, and behavior reciprocally influence each other. Accordingly, the environment is seen as exerting potential influences at each phase of the help-seeking process. For instance, classroom context (environment) may affect strategy selection (i.e., behavior in the forethought phase) by favoring or restraining requests for help from the teacher or from other students.

Typically assessed by students' aggregated perceptions of their classes' achievement goal structure, there is evidence that younger students in elementary and middle school classes that are more mastery focused (i.e., having an emphasis on understanding and improvement) are less likely to avoid seeking needed help (Ryan, Gheen, & Midgley, 1998; Turner et al., 2002). The influence of perceived classroom performance goal structure (i.e., an emphasis on ability and inter-student comparisons) begins in middle school and persists during the high school years (Karabenick, Zusho, & Kempler, 2005; Ryan, et al., 1998), whereas the influence of mastery goal structure diminishes by the time students reach college (Karabenick, 2004).

In addition to research on goal structure, classes in which middle and high school students perceived higher levels of support (using a composite measure that combines perceived teacher support for student collaboration and student questioning, teacher fairness and respect and caring) were found more likely to seek adaptive help (Karabenick et al., 2005). Consistently, students in classes with teachers they perceive as more supportive are more likely to have questions, are less inhibited to ask them, and are thus more likely to ask questions when necessary (Karabenick & Sharma, 1994; see also Kozanitis, Desbiens, & Chouinard, 2007). Help-seeking skills are not only affected by the environment; they can be actively promoted by various forms of interventions.

RECOMMENDED INTERVENTIONS TO PROMOTE ADAPTIVE HELP SEEKING

Accumulated evidence and understanding of the help-seeking process and the approach to SRL by Zimmerman and colleagues provides the basis for interventions to increase the likelihood of adaptive help seeking. Improving adaptive help seeking would require a comprehensive approach, which includes that learners possess a set of help seeking relevant competencies and resources (Karabenick & Dembo, 2011; Karabenick & Newman, 2009). Based on diverse lines of research, listed in the second column of Table 8.2 are the

TABLE 8.2   Primary Resources/Competencies at Each Stage of the Help-Seeking Process

| | Resources/Competencies | | | |
Stage	Cognitive	Affective-Emotional	Contextual	Social
1 Determine whether there is a problem	X			
2 Determine whether help is needed/wanted	X	X		
3 Decide whether to seek help		X	X	
4 Decide on the type of help (goal)	X	X		
5 Decide whom to ask		X		X
6 Solicit help	X	X	X	X
7 Obtain help	X	X	X	
8 Process the help received	X			

Note: Adapted from Karabenick, S. A., & Dembo, M. (2011). The self-regulation of seeking help: Theory, research and application. *New Directions for Teaching and Learning, 126,* 37.

four classes of competencies and resources needed at each stage of the help-seeking process (some of which are important at more than one stage).

Cognitive competencies include the understanding of when help is needed and how to ask questions. *Social competencies* include knowledge of those who can best help under different conditions and having the skills to approach those resources in a socially desirable manner. *Affective-emotional resources* include the beliefs and emotions that allow learners to cope with difficulty and concerns about being perceived as inadequate or incompetent. *Contextual and interpersonal resources* include the ability to work collaboratively. This includes knowing the rules of teacher-learner engagement and understanding expectations from teachers, peers and parents. Table 8.3 presents possible interventions corresponding to each set of competencies and resources. The interventions proposed here have been adapted from numerous instructional procedures to improve learning and interpersonal behavior, but most have not been used or studied in relation to help-seek-

TABLE 8.3 Interventions Related to Needed Resources/Competencies in Help Seeking

Interventions	Resources/Competencies			
	Cognitive	Affective-Emotional	Contextual	Social
Goals/Objectives to Monitor Performance (stage 1)	X			
Academic Language Scripts (stages 6 and 7)	X			
Task/Goal Analysis (stages 1 and 2)	X			
Error Analysis (stage 8)	X			
Creating Mastery Learning Environments (stage 3)		X	X	
Establishing and Explaining classroom Norms for Help Seeking (stages 4 and 5)		X		
Cognitive Behavior Systems (stages 4, 5 and 6)			X	
Social Skills Training (stages 6 and 7)				X
Technological Context (all stages)	X	X	X	X

Note: Adapted from Karabenick, S. A., & Dembo, M. (2011). The self-regulation of seeking help: Theory, research and application. *New Directions for Teaching and Learning, 126,* 33–43.

ing behaviors. In brief, it is proposed that learners would be more likely to seek help if they had a better idea of what they did not know and how to access help to overcome those impediments to learning and performance.

COGNITIVE COMPETENCIES

Researchers have indicated that metacognition, which consists of knowledge about one's knowledge (Flavell, 1979), and more generally that involves planning, monitoring and regulating cognition, is an important factor in academic success. There are inter-individual differences between students in how aware they are of their own knowledge. This awareness is of utmost importance in the process of self-regulation. As Tobias and Everson (2009) suggest, "if students fail to differentiate what they know or have learned previously from what they do not know or need to learn (or relearn), they are not expected to engage more advanced metacognitive strategies, such as evaluating their learning in an instructional setting, or employing more efficient learning and study strategies" (pp. 107–108). Empirical evidence shows, for example, that students who are the most accurate in their metacognition (i.e., who are the most aware of their own knowledge) seek help more effectively—that is, when it is needed the most (Tobias & Everson, 2002). In contrast, those who are less accurate ask for help not only when it is really needed but also when it is not. The following are instructional strategies designed to improve metacognitive skills.

Goals/objectives to help monitor performance. Accurate self-monitoring is a necessary condition for more adaptive help seeking (Tobias, 2006). Although learners may realize they have a problem in an academic area, it is critical they understand what competencies they have failed to master. Increasing the accuracy of self-monitoring may be as simple as providing students with an outline for each unit of instruction that includes a concise statement of the goals or objectives, followed by an example of the goal and the location in assigned material where the standard is discussed. This could help students determine what they know and do not know and contribute to more accurate monitoring of their progress by allowing them to determine more precisely if and where help is needed.

Zimmerman's model (Zimmerman & Moylan, 2009) includes two processes that aim to improve knowledge about one's own knowledge: metacognitive monitoring and self-judgment, taking place respectively during the performance and self-reflection phases. Metacognitive monitoring consists of informally tracking one's performance, processes and outcomes. Self-judgment refers to comparing one's own performance with a standard or a goal. Both processes can help students better identify what they know and do not know and thus formulate tailored requests for help.

Academic language scripts. Structured oral language practice routines can provide structured scripts to help learners improve their literacy skills (e.g., Levy & Dutro, 2008), and in the process also improve their skills for seeking and receiving help. The simple technique of "pair and share" can be used as a forum for learners to practice those skills. Consider the following dialogue when Learner A states: "I am having difficulty solving problem 3; can you help me?" Followed by Learner B's "Yes, watch how I go through each step." Despite its simplicity, observations suggest that such public pronouncements and dialogue can be very effective. Newman (2008) identified a number of questions learners usually have about help seeking in the classroom. These include issues related to several forethought self-regulatory processes such as: What should I ask? (task analysis) Whom should I ask? How shall I formulate my question? and Which of my friends is most likely to know the answer? (all strategic planning processes). Therefore, the student's questions could be seen as evidence of lack of SRL skills that might be trained. These issues can also be practiced during such dialogues.

Task/goal and error analysis. Making explicit the knowledge (i.e., pre-skills and new knowledge) required to learn and to perform a task (Dick, Carey, & Carey, 2009) can help learners understand their need for help, which is sustaining the initial process of task analysis according to Zimmerman's terminology. For the instructor, this means asking "What is it I want my learners to do?" and "What do they need to know to do it?" Once the ultimate objective emerges, the instructor works backward to delineate which capabilities learners must acquire to reach that objective. Whereas task or goal analysis is used for instructional design by communicating the necessary knowledge or steps needed to complete a task to learners, the information also can be used to help them monitor their level of understanding, which is the linchpin of the help-seeking process. The analysis of errors can also assist in the adaptive use of help seeking, including during the last stage of the process. Thus, after giving help, instructors can guide learners through the process of how they arrived at their incorrect answers by orally describing each step taken when attempting to solve a problem. A review of the errors, followed by attempts to solve new problems, can further illuminate why errors occurred and help learners process the help they receive.

AFFECTIVE-EMOTIONAL RESOURCES

Cognitive behavior systems. Since research on help seeking indicates that for many learners there is a personal cost of seeking help, these learners would benefit from a process to help them deal with beliefs that contribute to those costs. Rational emotive behavioral therapy (Ellis, 1998), cognitive therapy (Beck, 1995), and cognitive behavior modification (Meichenbaum

& Goodman, 1971) are among the cognitive behavioral systems used to change attitudes, emotions and beliefs that are often associated with help seeking, which can serve as models for that process. Rational emotive therapy, for example, can help learners develop greater awareness of their own emotional states and how those states vary over time. Students can also learn to detect the automatic thoughts and identify beliefs that underlie their thought processes that influence their emotions. Third, they can evaluate and dispute their automatic thoughts and beliefs. Finally, the process focuses on eliminating the maladaptive thoughts and beliefs and replacing them with more positive beliefs and statements.

As with academic scripts and sharing dialogues discussed previously, the process of verbalizing maladaptive thoughts and replacing them with more adaptive ones could be beneficial. It should be noted that the process would have to be modified for younger learners. Consider the following example: A (activating event)—Phil receives a failing grade on his history examination and decides he needs help; B (the irrational or helpless belief that follows the event)—"My teacher will think I am dumb if I ask for help"; C (consequence)—Phil feels helpless and anxious, decides not to ask for help, and believes that he will not succeed in the class; D (disputing irrational beliefs)—"Ok. I did poorly on this exam. Everyone needs help at one time or another. Giving help is what instructors do. They may even think that I'm smart if I ask for help when I need it. I'm going to do something about my low test scores;" E (new effect)—"I still feel disappointed that I didn't do well, but I now have a plan to do better in the future, which includes going to seek assistance when I don't understand something. I can be a good student!" In reference to Zimmerman's model, this type of intervention primarily targets strategic planning processes and self-control. In contrast, the task/goal and error analysis form of intervention fosters the task analysis process. Therefore the two forms of intervention can be seen as complementary.

CONTEXTUAL RESOURCES

Creating mastery learning environments. Since studies have demonstrated that learners are more likely to seek adaptive help in mastery-oriented classrooms, it follows that instructors can influence learners' goal orientations by establishing a culture or climate that emphasizes mastery over performance goals—that is, different achievement goal structures (Karabenick & Newman, 2009). According to the TARGET framework (e.g., Ames, 1992; Maehr & Anderman, 1993), the six areas of instruction that can lead to a more mastery goal oriented classroom are: the type of *task* that learners are asked to do, the degree of *autonomy or authority* learners are allowed in classroom activities, how learners are *recognized* for their outcomes, *grouping* practices, *evaluation* procedures, and the scheduling of *time* for completing activities. In essence, emphasizing mastery focuses learners on the task and improvement while de-emphasizing performance-focused reasons for learning, especially interpersonal comparisons with peers. Such a shift in the classroom goal structure decreases the focus on inability, and thus the cost of error and its implied lack of ability that may be revealed by asking for help.

In reference to Zimmerman's model, creating a mastery or performance learning environment would not only affect self-regulatory processes in the forethought and performance phases but also in the self-reflection phase. In fact, with such a change in the classroom goal structure, students would process the help they receive quite differently. In a mastery-oriented classroom, the help received would be expected to be instrumental for improved learning, which should encourage subsequent requests for help. Furthermore, the help received would be judged satisfactory since it does not display one's weakness, especially in comparisons with other students.

Establishing and explaining classroom norms for help seeking. Establishing certain norms can contribute to decreasing the cost of help seeking that is often perceived in classrooms. It is important that instructors discuss the rules and procedures they wish to establish early in a course, and perhaps, use scenarios to discuss different situations that will occur. For example, some instructors want to be interrupted for questions during a presentation, while others may want learners to wait until they are finished speaking (Karabenick & Sharma, 1994; Kozanitis et al., 2007). Some instructors may allow students to work collaboratively during class periods, whereas others only allow collaborative work outside of class. It is important for instructors to discuss classroom rules and procedures to help learners understand how they might proceed in obtaining help, as well as the types of help resources available in the classroom and when to access them.

SOCIAL COMPETENCIES—SOCIAL SKILLS TRAINING

Asking and receiving help requires a number of important social skills that some learners have not mastered. This lack of knowledge prevents learners from positive interaction with peers and limits their requests for assistance. An intervention by Goldstein and McGinnis (1997) for improving learners' prosocial skills includes a number of skills that could be useful when applied to the help-seeking process. Such social competencies would be important, for example, when focused on starting a conversation, asking a question, asking for help, helping others, dealing with embarrassment, responding to failure, and numerous others skills. For example, the following are suggested steps to teach the skill of asking a question (trainer notes in parentheses; Goldstein & McGinnis, 1997, p. 71):

1. decide what you would like to know more about (ask about something you don't understand);
2. decide whom to ask (think about who has the best information on a topic);
3. think about different ways to ask your question and pick one way (think about wording; raise your hand);
4. pick the right time and place to ask your question (wait for a pause; wait for privacy); and
5. ask your question.

This procedure—termed skillmastering—includes four components: *modeling* (having someone show you the skill), *role-playing* (trying out the skill yourself), *feedback* (having someone tell you how well you did), and *transfer* (trying the skill when, where and with whom you really need to use the skill). To improve these skills, learners view videos, complete homework assignments, practice using the skill, and receive feedback on their behavior. This approach is congruent with the application of Zimmerman's social cognitive perspective of help seeking as a self-regulatory skill. Zimmerman (2000) describes the development of a self-regulatory skill or strategy as a four-step process that begins with observation of a model (vicarious experience) to emulation (imitation of the model), self-control (display of the strategy under structured conditions), and finally the ultimate goal of self-regulation (adaptive application of the strategy in changing conditions). The model supports the benefits of strategic modeling as exemplified in the Goldstein and McGinnis (1997) prosocial skills intervention.

TECHNOLOGICAL CONTEXT TO SUPPORT HELP SEEKING

Any intervention designed to facilitate adaptive help seeking must take into consideration the advantages afforded by these systems and more recent advances in social media. In fact, we propose that technology is so pervasive that, depending on the application involved, it can affect all stages of the help-seeking process and involve all competencies. The variety of information and communications technology (ICT) systems capable of supporting help seeking has considerably expanded since their potential impact was first systematically discussed (Keefer & Karabenick, 1998). They are variously categorized by their functions, such as computer-mediated communication (CMC), intelligent learning environments (ILE), learning and course management systems (LMS, CMS: e.g., Blackboard), and the pervasive and accelerating presence of iPads in education (e.g., e-books). Kitsantas and Dabbagh (2010) have suggested these could be considered different manifestations of integrative learning technologies (ILT) that facilitate SRL and provide additional supportive evidence for the applicability of Zimmerman's approach to the process.

Reducing the cost of seeking help is arguably a major affordance of technology. Seeking help with the aid of such technology-mediated helping resources typically requires less effort and, given the potential for anonymity, can be less threatening. Asynchronous computer-mediated communication (CMC; e.g., email, online discussions, texting, social networking sites) has the additional advantage of providing time for reflection (even if brief) that is not possible with synchronous CMC media (e.g., chat, voice, video). As demonstrated some time ago, help delivered by an intelligent system increased (approximately doubled) the rate of help seeking compared to a condition in which same information was ostensibly provided by a remote person via the same computer interface (Karabenick & Knapp, 1988b). Kitsantas and Chow (2007) supported several hypotheses about the preferences for and influences on the help seeking of college students enrolled in distance, distributed, and traditional classes. As predicted, students in courses with an online computer component reported feeling less threatened by and more likely to seek help. Students in general also reported the use of CMC (email) to be the most effective way to seek help. More recent research has also confirmed the advantages of seeking help in a CMC context (Puustinen, Volckaert-Legrier, Coquin, & Bernicot, 2009).

Variations of the Cognitive Tutor and its companion Help Tutor are based on models of the adaptive help-seeking process (Aleven, McLaren, & Koedinger, 2006; Aleven, Stahl, Schworm, Fischer, & Wallace, 2003). Because the purpose of ILEs is to increase knowledge and understanding rather than simply to provide answers, learners are allowed (and even encouraged) to select different types of help (e.g., answers or hints consisting of explanations). Consistent with some of the innovations described previously, recent innovations have been designed to increase help seeking by providing instruction regarding the help-seeking process and by having students practice help seeking and other self-regulatory skills prior to performance sessions (Roll, Aleven, McLaren, & Koedinger, 2007).

One of the apparent downsides of these innovations consists of evidence that students excessively use expedient help (i.e., gaming the system) by opting for direct hints rather than indirect instrumental help (e.g., access to a glossary of definitions). Although such behavior would be considered maladaptive from the perspective promoted in the help-seeking literature, a more benign alternative explanation is possible. This explanation proposes that acquiring direct hints in some instances may be desirable and adaptive. In the approach adopted by many medical students (Yudelson et al., 2006), for example, direct hints are considered self-instructional; that is, hints are considered another form of useful information. In other words, it is not simply the type of help requested and received that is important but also, in the self-regulation of help seeking, how that help functions and how it is processed. New developments in this area are in process to elaborate models that account for such tendencies.

One of the major consequences of these technologies is the availability of archived information that can be mined to track learners' interactions with each other, with instructors, and with ILEs (Winne et al., 2006; Wood & Wood, 1999; also Mäkitao-Siegl, Kohnle, & Fischer, 2010). As described subsequently, Winne and colleagues have championed the traces left by learners as more valid evidence of SRL than are self-reports. Synchronous and asynchronous communication systems used in classes, as well as during non-class times, can expand opportunities to track the student learning process to more completely understand help seeking and other forms of SRL. In just one example, Puustinen and Bernicot (2009) analyzed the linguistic form of students' anonymous online requests for academic assistance, finding a high incidence of demanding, insistent and impatient requests that can emerge under those conditions.

Technology also raises an important issue for Zimmerman's and other models of SRL. If we assume that seeking help involves social interactivity, then ILEs and other intelligent systems pose conceptual challenges to the very definition of help seeking (Keefer & Karabenick, 1998), which is assumed to set it apart from other forms of SRL. If help seeking is by definition a social-interactive process, then how would we construe seeking help from artificial intelligence systems? Leaving aside the complex issue of artificial life forms (e.g., applying the Turing Test), it would be important to consider intelligent systems as a channel for social influence. Social influence can exist when the presence of others is real (e.g., a teacher in a classroom), imagined (e.g., "What would your mother think?"), or implied (e.g., someone will know that I sought help). Given that definition, ILEs can be examined to determine the degree to which a system is *implicitly social* (Karabenick, 2011).

According to this criterion, what is critical is whether others are imagined or implied when learners consider seeking help. Knowing (or suspecting) that the use of learning systems such as gSTUDY (Winne et al., 2006) leaves traces—traces left behind by interactions with such systems, as well as those captured by online information resources (e.g., Google or social media tracking)—for example, could alter how learners construe access to help provided by the system. Thus whether ILEs (and information searching) influence help seeking depends on how "social" they are perceived to be, on the perceived costs and benefits of seeking and not seeking help (Karabenick & Knapp, 1988b), and on the motivation-related characteristics of the learning contexts in which such artificial systems are embedded (Schofield, 1995). Zimmerman and colleagues have identified help seeking as a form of social self-regulation (Zimmerman, 2008). The comprehensive view of what can be considered social in the foregoing analysis, therefore, expands the contexts to which their model can be applied to include technologically enhanced help seeking even when that social influence is not readily apparent.

IMPLICATIONS AND FUTURE DIRECTIONS FOR HELP-SEEKING RESEARCH AND INTERVENTIONS

We have reviewed the person and context variables that influence students' help seeking, the important resources and competencies needed to seek and obtain help, and some intervention strategies that might develop some of the resources and competencies. Although these are guides based on current knowledge, translational research is needed to turn existing theory and empirical evidence into pedagogical practice to promote adaptive help seeking. For example, it is known that learners do not always experience and follow the help-seeking stages in the order specified by the models, or that they are even mindful of all of those stages. Studies are required to explicate how students negotiate these stages, especially whether person and situation variables and development level mediate or moderate the process. Influences that are found may also have implications for the optimal ways to improve self-regulated help seeking. Other issues include whether all stages have equal impact on help seeking. In other words, are all stages necessary and sufficient to seek and obtain help? What stages play the most influential role in seeking or impeding help seeking? A series of investigations is warranted to explore these questions, their implications for understanding more about the help-seeking process, and the effectiveness of each of the recommended interventions based on that knowledge.

This work must especially take into consideration the presumption that older students have the self-regulatory skills required for effective learning. Considerable research (Simpson, Hynd, Nist, & Burrell, 1997) and experience suggest otherwise, however, including that many students lack the competencies required for adaptive help seeking. There is substantial evidence that more successful than less successful students have acquired key self-regulatory skills. Although study skills texts and courses (Dembo & Seli, 2008; Weinstein, Husman, & Dierking, 2000) are designed to remediate these deficiencies, they have rarely focused on help seeking. The competencies and interventions described here should be considered in the future.

Furthermore, instructors often stress the importance of seeking needed help (e.g., approaching teaching assistants or the instructor or even learning with other students; see Barkley, Cross, & Major, 2005 for a description of various collaborative learning techniques). Yet, such suggestions are rarely accompanied by information about the help-seeking process, which is suggested by research on the advantages of collaboration to improve learning (e.g., Barkley, Cross, & Major, 2005; Webb, Ing, Kersting, & Nemer, 2006). Although Barkley, Cross and Major (2005) introduced such simple procedures as *pair-share* as a discussion technique in collaborative learning, they did not include the language scripts to help students improve their discussion techniques and help-seeking behavior. It is highly suggested that K–12 teachers and college instructors use instructional time to provide students with the appropriate information that could reap important benefits in both the short term as well as help-seeking skills relevant for life-long learning, especially given an information environment that increasingly places demands for such skills.

CONCLUSION

It is evident that help-seeking research and development fits well within the approach to SRL pioneered by Zimmerman and colleagues. As shown in Table 8.1, forethought, performance and self-reflection phases of the model map on to stages in the help-seeking process, which reinforces the conclusion that successful learning and performance are more likely when SRL includes adaptive help seeking. Moreover, Zimmerman's model suggests further research on a procedural view of help seeking. For instance, the relation between goal orientation and help seeking is well explored, whereas the way in which this strategy relates to other self-motivation beliefs acting in the forethought phase has still to be explored. How do self-efficacy, task value, and outcome expectation articulate with goal orientation in influencing the performance and self-reflection phases of help seeking? After help is received, how does the self-reflection processes feedback on further forethought processes? Accordingly, studies adopting a micro and longitudinal perspective on help seeking would provide information on the dynamic of self-regulated help seeking. Coming full circle, such work may even inform Zimmerman's model, which as we stressed at the outset, was seminal for the initial establishment of help seeking as an SRL strategy.

ACKNOWLEDGMENTS

The authors wish to thank Kara Makara and Fani Lauermann for their helpful comments on a previous version of this chapter, and to Glen Raulerson, Pat Cotter and Pam MacInnis-Weir. The chapter was prepared while the first author was supported by a grant from the U. S. National Science Foundation: DUE-0928103.

REFERENCES

Aleven, V., McLaren, B., & Koedinger, K. (2006). Toward computer-based tutoring of help-seeking skills. In S. A. Karabenick & R. S. Newman (Eds.), *Help seeking in academic settings: Goals, groups and contexts* (pp. 259–296). Mahwah, NJ: Lawrence Erlbaum Associates.

Aleven, V., Stahl, E., Schworm, S., Fischer, F., & Wallace, R. M. (2003). Help seeking and help design in interactive learning environments. *Review of Educational Research, 73*(2), 277–320. doi:10.3102/00346543073003277

Ames, C. (1992). Classrooms, goals, structures, and student motivation. *Journal of Educational Psychology, 84*(3), 261–271. doi:10.1037/0022-0663.84.3.261

Bandura, A. (1986). *Social foundations of thought and action: A social cognitive theory.* Englewood Cliffs, NJ: Prentice Hall.

Barkley, E. F., Cross, K. P., & Major, C. H. (2005). *Collaborative learning techniques: A handbook for college faculty.* San Francisco, CA: Jossey-Bass.

Beck, J. S. (1995). *Cognitive therapy: Basic and beyond.* New York, NY: Guilford.

Beller, E. K. (1955). Dependency and independence in young children. *The Journal of Genetic Psychology: Research and Theory on Human Development, 87*(1), 25–35. doi: 10.1080/00221325.1955.10532913

Bembenutty, H. (2006, April). *Preservice teachers' help seeking tendencies and selfregulation learning.* Paper presented at the annual meeting of the American Educational Research Association, San Francisco, CA.

Butler, R. (1998). Determinants of help seeking: Relations between perceived reasons for classroom help-avoiding and help-seeking behaviors in an experimental context. *Journal of Educational Psychology, 90*(4), 630–644. doi:10.1037/0022-0663.90.4.630

Butler, R. (2006). An achievement goal perspective on student help seeking and teacher help giving in the classroom: Theory, research, and educational implications. In S. A. Karabenick & R. S. Newman (Eds.), *Help seeking in academic settings: Goals, groups, and contexts* (pp. 15–44). Mahwah, NJ: Erlbaum.

Butler, R., & Neuman, O. (1995). Effects of task and ego achievement goals on help-seeking behaviors and attitudes. *Journal of Educational Psychology, 87*(3), 261–271. doi:10.1037/0022-0663.87.2.261

Dembo, M., & Seli, H. (2008). *Motivation and learning strategies for college success: A self-management approach* (3rd ed.). New York, NY: Taylor and Francis.

Dick, W., Carey, L., & Carey, J. O. (2009). *The systematic design of instruction* (7th ed.). Columbus, OH: Merrill.

Dillon, J. T. (1988). The remedial status of student questioning. *Journal of Curriculum Studies, 20*(3), 197–210. doi:10.1080/0022027880200301

Ellis, A. (1998). *How to control your anxiety before it controls you.* New York, NY: Citadel Press.

Flavell, J. H. (1979). Metacognition and cognitive monitoring: A new area of cognitive-developmental inquiry. *American Psychologist, 34*(10), 906–911. doi:10.1037/0003-066X.34.10.906

Goldstein, A., & McGinnis, E. M. (1997). *Skill streaming the adolescent* (Revised ed.). Champaign, IL: Research Press.

Good, T. L., Slavings, R. L., Harel, K. H., & Emerson, H. (1987). Student passivity: A study of question asking in K–12 classrooms. *Sociology of Education, 60*(3), 181–189. Retrieved February 2, 2012, from http://www.jstor.org/stable/2112275

Gross, A. A., & McMullen, P. A. (1983). Models of the help seeking process. In B. M. DePaulo, A. Nadler, & J. D. Fisher (Eds.), *New directions in helping: Vol. 2. Help seeking* (pp. 45–70). San Diego, CA: Academic Press.

Iiskala, T., Vauras, M., Lehtinen, E., & Salonen, P. (2011). Socially shared metacognition of dyads of pupils in collaborative mathematical problem-solving processes. *Learning and Instruction, 21*(3), 379–393. doi:10.1016/j.learninstruc.2010.05.002

Karabenick, S. A. (1996). Social influences on metacognition: Effects of colearner questioning on comprehension monitoring. *Journal of Educational Psychology, 88*(4), 689–703. doi:10.1037/0022-0663.88.4.689

Karabenick, S. A. (1998). Help seeking as a strategic resource. In S. A. Karabenick (Ed.), *Strategic help seeking: Implications for learning and teaching* (pp. 1–11). Mahwah, NJ: Lawrence Erlbaum Associates.

Karabenick, S. A. (2003). Seeking help in large college classes: A person-centered approach. *Contemporary Educational Psychology, 28*(1), 37–58. doi:10.1016/S0361-476X(02)00012-7

Karabenick, S. A. (2004). Perceived achievement goal structure and college student help seeking. *Journal of Educational Psychology, 96*(3), 569–581. doi:10.1037/0022-0663.96.3.569

Karabenick, S. A. (2011). Classroom and technology-supported help seeking: The need for converging research paradigms. *Learning and Instruction, 21*(2), 290–296. doi:10.1016/j.learninstruc.2010.07.007

Karabenick, S. A., & Dembo, M. (2011). The self-regulation of seeking help: Theory, research and application. *New Directions for Teaching and Learning, 126*, 33–43.

Karabenick, S. A., & Knapp, J. R. (1988a). Help-seeking and the need for academic assistance. *Journal of Educational Psychology, 80*(3), 406–408. doi:10.1037/0022-0663.80.3.406

Karabenick, S. A., & Knapp, J. R. (1988b). Effects of computer privacy on help seeking. *Journal of Applied Social Psychology, 18*(6), 461–472. doi:10.1111/j.1559-1816.1988.tb00029.x

Karabenick, S. A., & Knapp, J. R. (1991). Relationship of academic help seeking to the use of learning strategies and other instrumental achievement behavior in college students. *Journal of Educational Psychology, 83*(2), 221–230. doi:10.1037/0022-0663.83.2.221

Karabenick, S. A., & Newman, R. S. (Eds.). (2006). *Help seeking in academic settings: Goals, groups, and contexts.* Mahwah, NJ: Erlbaum.

Karabenick, S. A., & Newman, R. S. (2009). Seeking help: Generalizable self-regulatory process and social-cultural barometer. In M. Wosnitza, S. A. Karabenick,

A. Efklides, & P. Nenniger (Eds.), *Contemporary motivation research: From global to local perspectives* (pp. 25–48). Göttingen, Germany: Hogrefe & Huber.

Karabenick, S. A., & Newman, R. S. (2010). Seeking help as an adaptive response to learning difficulties: Person, situation, and developmental influences. In E. Baker, P. L. Peterson & B. McGraw (Eds.), *International encyclopedia of education.* (3rd ed, pp. 653–659). Amsterdam: Elsevier.

Karabenick, S. A., & Sharma, R. (1994). Perceived teacher support of student questioning in the college classroom: Its relation to student characteristics and role in the classroom questioning process. *Journal of Educational Psychology, 86*(1), 90–103. doi:10.1037/0022-0663.86.1.90

Karabenick, S. A., Zusho, A., & Kempler, T. M. (2005, August). *Help seeking and perceived classroom context.* Paper presented at the biennial meeting of the European Association for Research on Learning and Instruction, Nicosia, Cyprus.

Keefer, J. A., & Karabenick, S. A. (1998). Help seeking in the information age. In S. A. Karabenick (Ed.), *Strategic help seeking: Implications for learning and teaching.* (pp. 219–250). Mahwah, NJ: Erlbaum.

Kitsantas, A., & Chow, A. (2007). College students' perceived threat and preference for seeking help in traditional, distributed, and distance learning environments. *Computers and Education, 48*(3), 383–395. doi:10.1016/j.compedu.2005.01.008

Kitsantas, A., & Dabbagh, N. (2010). *Learning to learn with integrative learning technologies: A practical guide for academic success.* Charlotte, NC: Information Age Publishing.

Kozanitis, A., Desbiens, J-. F., & Chouinard, R. (2007). Perception of teacher support and reaction towards questioning: Its relation to instrumental help-seeking and motivation to learn. *International Journal of Teaching and Learning in Higher Education, 19*(3), 238–250. Retrieved February 2, 2012, from http://www.isetl.org/ijtlhe/pdf/IJTLHE238.pdf

Levy, E., & Dutro, S. (2008). *Constructing mean: Explicit language for content instruction.* San Clemente, CA: E. L. Achieve.

Maehr, M. L., & Anderman, E. M. (1993). Reinventing schools for early adolescents: Emphasizing task goals. *The Elementary School Journal, 93*(5), 593–610. Retrieved February 2, 2012, from http://www.jstor.org/stable/1001830

Makitalo-Siegl, K., Kohnle, C., & Fischer, F. (2011). Computer-supported collaborative inquiry learning and classroom scripts: Effects on help-seeking processes and learning outcomes. *Learning and Instruction, 21*(2), 257–266. doi:10.1016/j.learninstruc.2010.07.001

Meichenbaum, D., & Goodman, J. (1971). Training impulsive children to talk to themselves: A means of developing self-control. *Journal of Abnormal Psychology, 77*(2), 115–126. doi:10.1037/h0030773

Nelson-Le Gall, S. (1981). Help-seeking: An understudied problem-solving skill in children. *Developmental Review, 1*(3), 224–246. doi:10.1016/0273-2297(81)90019-8

Nelson-Le Gall, S. (1985). *Help seeking behavior in learning. Review of research in education* (Vol. 12, pp. 55–90). Washington, DC: American Educational Research Association.

Nelson-Le Gall, S. (1987). Necessary and unnecessary help-seeking in children. *Journal of Genetic Psychology, 148*(1), 53–62.

Nelson-Le Gall, S., Gumerman, R. A., & Scott-Jones, D. (1983). Instrumental help-seeking and everyday problem-solving: A developmental perspective. In De-Paulo, B. M., Nadler, A., & Fisher, J. D. [Eds.], New directions in helping, 265-281. New York, NY: Academic Press.

Nelson-Le Gall, S., & Resnick, L. (1998). Help seeking, achievement motivation, and the social practice of intelligence in school. In S. A. Karabenick (Ed.), *Strategic help seeking: Implications for learning and teaching* (pp. 39–60). Hillsdale, NJ: Erlbaum.

Newman, R. S. (1994). Academic help seeking: A strategy of self-regulated learning. In D. H. Schunk & B. J. Zimmerman (Eds.), *Self-regulation of learning and performance: Issues and educational applications.* (pp. 283–301). Hillsdale, NJ: Erlbaum.

Newman, R. S. (2000). Social influences on the development of children's adaptive help seeking: The role of parents, teachers, and peers. *Developmental Review, 20*(3), 350–404. doi:10.1006/drev.1999.0502

Newman, R. S. (2008). The motivational role of adaptive help seeking in self-regulated learning. In D. H. Schunk, & B. J. Zimmerman (Eds.), *Motivation and self-regulated learning: Theory, research, and applications* (pp. 315–337). Mahwah, NJ: Erlbaum.

Pintrich, P. R., & Zusho, A. (2002). The development of academic self-regulation: The role of cognitive and motivational factors. In P. R. Pintrich & J. S. Eccles, (Eds.), *Development of achievement motivation: A volume in the educational psychology series* (pp. 249–284). San Diego, CA: Academic Press.

Puustinen, M., & Bernicot, J. (2009, August). *The form and the function of French students' technology-mediated requests for help: The complementary contribution of two theoretical approaches.* Paper presented at biennial meeting of the European Association for Research on Learning and Instruction, Amsterdam.

Puustinen, M., Bernicot, J., & Bert-Erboul, A. (2011). Written computer-mediated requests for help by French-speaking students: An analysis of their forms and functions. *Learning and Instruction, 21*(2), 281–289. doi:10.1016/j.learninstruc.2010.07.005

Puustinen, M., Volckaert-Legrier, O., Coquin, D., & Bernicot, J. (2009). An analysis of students' spontaneous computer-mediated help seeking: A step toward the design of ecologically valid supporting tools. *Computers and Education, 53*(4), 1040–1047. doi:10.1016/j.compedu.2008.10.003

Renkl, A. (2002). Worked-out examples: Instructional explanations support learning by self-explanations. *Learning and Instruction, 12*(5), 529–556. doi:10.1016/S0959-4752(01)00030-5

Roll, I., Aleven, V., McLaren, B., & Koedinger, K. (2007, August). *Modeling and tutoring help seeking with a cognitive tutor.* Paper presented at the biennial meeting of the European Association for Research on Learning and Instruction, Budapest.

Ryan, A. M., Gheen, M., & Midgley, C. (1998). Why do some students avoid asking for help? An examination of the interplay among students' academic efficacy, teachers' social-emotional role, and classroom goal structure. *Journal of Educational Psychology, 90*(3), 528–535. doi:10.1037/0022-0663.90.3.528

Ryan, A. M., Hicks, L., & Midgley, C. (1997). Social goals, academic goals, and avoiding help in the classroom. *Journal of Early Adolescence, 17*(2), 152–171. doi:10.1177/0272431697017002003

Ryan, A. M., Patrick, H., & Shim, S. O. (2005). Differential profiles of students identified by their teacher as having avoidant, appropriate or dependent help-seeking tendencies in the classroom. *Journal of Educational Psychology, 97*(2), 275–285. doi:10.1037/0022-0663.97.2.275

Ryan, A. M., & Pintrich, P. R. (1997). Should I ask for help? The role of motivation and attitudes in adolescents' help seeking in math class. *Journal of Educational Psychology, 89*(2), 329–341. doi:10.1037/0022-0663.89.2.329

Schofield, J. W. (1995). *Computers and classroom culture*. Cambridge, MA: Cambridge University Press.

Simpson, M. L., Hynd, C. R., Nist, S. L., & Burrell, K. I. (1997). College academic assistance programs and practices. *Educational Psychology Review, 9*(1), 39–87. doi:10.1023/A:1024733706115

Skinner, E. A., & Zimmer-Gembeck, M. J. (2007). The development of coping. *Annual Review of Psychology, 58*, 119–144. doi:10.1146/annurev. psych.58.110405.085705

Tobias, S. (2006). The importance of motivation, metacognition, and help seeking in web-based learning. In H. F. O'Neil & R. S. Perez (Eds.), *Web-based learning: Theory, research, and practice* (pp. 203–220). Mahwah, NJ: Erlbaum.

Tobias, S., & Everson, H. T. (2002). *Knowing what you know and what you don't: Further research on metacognitive knowledge monitoring* (College Board Rep. No. 2002–03). New York, NY: College Board.

Tobias, S., & Everson, H. T. (2009).The importance of knowing what you know. In D. J. Hacker, J. Dunlosky & A. C. Graesser (Eds.), *Handbook of metacognition in education* (pp. 107–127). New York, NY: Routledge.

Turner, J. C., Midgley, C., Meyer, D. K., Gheen, M., Anderman, E. M., Kang, Y., & Patrick, H. (2002). The classroom environment and students' reports of avoidance strategies in mathematics: A multimethod study. *Journal of Educational Psychology, 94*(1), 88–106. doi:10.1037//0022-0663.94.1.88

Webb, N. M., Ing, M., Kersting, N., & Nemer, K. M. (2006). Help seeking in cooperative groups. In S. A. Karabenick & R. S. Newman (Eds.). *Help seeking in academic settings: Goals, groups, and contexts* (pp. 45–88). Mahwah, NJ: Erlbaum.

Weinstein, C. E., Husman, J., & Dierking, D. R. (2000). Self-regulation interventions with a focus on learning strategies. In M. Boekaerts, P. R. Pintrich, & M. Zeidner (Eds.), *Handbook of self-regulation* (pp. 727–747). San Diego, CA: Academic Press.

White, C. M. (2011). Predicting success in teacher certification testing: The role of academic help seeking. *The International Journal of Educational and Psychological Assessment, 7*(1), 24–44. Retrieved from http://tijepa.books.officelive. com/Documents/A3_V7_1_TIJEPA.pdf

Winne, P. H., Nesbit, J. C., Kumar, V., Hadwin, A. F., Lajoie, S. P., Azevedo, R., et al. (2006). Supporting self-regulated learning with gStudy software: The learning kit project. *Technology, Instruction, Cognition and Learning, 3*(1/2), 105–113.

Winterbottom, M. R. (1958). The relation of need for achievement to learning experiences in independence and mastery. In J. W. Atkinson (Ed.), *Motives in fantasy, action, and society* (pp. 453–478.). New York, NY: Van Nostrand.

Wood, H. A., & Wood, D. J. (1999). Help seeking, learning, and contingent tutoring. *Computers and Education, 33*, 153–169. Retrieved February 3, 2012, from https://www.tlu.ee/~kpata/haridustehnoloogiaTLU/tutoring.pdf

Yudelson, M., Medvedeva, O., Legowski, E., Castine, M., Jukic, D., & Crowley, R. S. (2006, December). *Mining student learning data to develop high level pedagogic strategy in a medical ITS.* Paper presented at the Workshop on Educational Data Mining at The Twenty-First National Conference on Artificial Intelligence (AAAI 2006), Boston, MA. Retrieved February 3, 2012 from https://www.aaai.org/Papers/Workshops/2006/WS-06-05/WS06-05-011.pdf

Zimmerman, B. J. (1989). A social cognitive view of self-regulated academic learning. *Journal of Educational Psychology, 81*(3), 329–339. doi:10.1037/0022-0663.81.3.329

Zimmerman, B. J. (2000). Attaining self-regulation. A social cognitive perspective. In M. Boekaerts, P. R. Pintrich, & M. Zeidner (Eds.), *Handbook of self-regulation* (pp. 13–39). San Diego, CA: Academic Press.

Zimmerman, B. J. (2008). Investigating self-regulation and motivation: Historical background, methodological developments, and future prospects. *American Educational Research Journal, 45*(1), 166–183. doi:10.3102/0002831207312909

Zimmerman, B. J., & Campillo, M. (2003). Phases and subprocesses of self-regulation. In J. E. Davidson & R. J. Sternberg (Eds.), *The nature of problem solving* (pp. 233–262). New York, NY: Cambridge University Press.

Zimmerman, B. J., & Martinez-Pons, M. (1988). Construct validation of a strategy model of student self-regulated learning. *Journal of Educational Psychology, 80*(3), 284–290. doi:10.1037/0022-0663.80.3.284

Zimmerman, B. J., & Martinez-Pons, M. (1990). Student differences in self-regulated learning: Relating grade, sex, and giftedness to self-efficacy and strategy use. *Journal of Educational Psychology, 82*(1), 51–59. doi:10.1037/0022-0663.82.1.51

Zimmerman, B. J., & Moylan, A. R. (2009). Where metacognition and motivation intersect. In D. J. Hacker, J. Dunlosky, & A. C. Graesser (Eds.), *Handbook of metacognition in education* (pp. 299–315). New York, NY: Routledge.

Zusho, A., Karabenick, S. A., Bonney, C. R., & Sims, B. (2007). Contextual determinants of motivation and help seeking in the college classroom. In R. P. Perry, & J. C. Smart (Eds.), *The scholarship of teaching and learning in higher education: An evidence-based perspective* (pp. 611–660). New York, NY: Springer.

CHAPTER 9

UTILIZING CALIBRATION ACCURACY INFORMATION WITH ADOLESCENTS TO IMPROVE ACADEMIC LEARNING AND PERFORMANCE

Peggy P. Chen and Paul D. Rossi

Researchers have been interested in studying metacognition for the past several decades; this interest has grown disproportionally compared with other areas of educational research (de Bruin & van Gog, in press). In particular, this mounting interest in metacognition research has been concerned with how to improve students' self-monitoring and self-regulation in the classroom. *Metacognition* has been defined in multiple ways but was originally described as one's knowledge and understanding of his or her own cognitive processes, and later expanded to include psychological aspects such as knowing one's and others' motives, emotions, and motor skills (Flavell, 1979, 1987). Major theorists conceptualize metacognition similarly, including facets such as metacognitive knowledge, monitoring, and

Applications of Self-Regulated Learning across Diverse Disciplines, pages 263–297
Copyright © 2013 by Information Age Publishing
All rights of reproduction in any form reserved.

control (Dunlosky & Metcalfe, 2009; Nelson & Narens, 1990). *Metacognitive monitoring*, a particular aspect of metacognition, refers to how people judge and assess their understanding of any ongoing cognitive activity (Dunlosky & Metcalfe, 2009). For example, when a student reads a novel, she may monitor the accuracy of her learning by assessing the extent of her comprehension of text, by rereading sections or pausing to question her understanding. In educational contexts, students frequently engage in cognitive monitoring processes, such as judging whether they are solving problems correctly, assessing the extent to which they are approaching completion of the task at hand, and estimating how well they have learned the material.

This chapter focuses on one type of metacognitive monitoring, *calibration*, which has been studied more frequently in educational contexts than any other metacognitive process. It has been defined as the metacognitive monitoring judgment of one's current knowledge or skill with respect to a task, and the comparison of that knowledge level to actual task performance (Hacker, Bol, & Keener, 2008). Calibration is one of the most evident links between metacognition and self-regulation. Zimmerman's (2000) cyclical three-phase self-regulatory model is connected with calibration in that the mechanisms that underlie calibration share the same features of several subprocesses of Zimmerman's self-regulatory model—components such as self-observation, self-evaluation, and self-reaction. Zimmerman's model is comprehensive in explaining students' self-directive learning behaviors, their motivations, and their metacognitive processes. We capitalize on the full breadth of Zimmerman's model, as well as its connections to metacognition and calibration, in our design of an intervention program to help academically at-risk high school students pass high-stakes tests.

In any learning context, students are constantly engaged in metacognitive processes to a certain degree. For example, a student who is preparing for the verbal section of a standardized test may recognize the difficulty of learning vocabulary based solely on a flashcard technique, and may choose to apply the more effective approach of generating imagery based on personal associations to help her recognize the meanings of more words. Furthermore, this student might use an awareness of her own vocabulary level to inform her decision to spend more time studying unfamiliar words rather than familiar words. However, academically at-risk students may not be as metacognitively aware of their own level of knowledge, or how to best adapt their study approach to meet the demands of a particular learning task. Such students are more likely to persist in employing a suboptimal strategy, either because their perception of what they know is inaccurate or because of low motivation to modify their study behaviors. These two examples illustrate that students may differ in terms of their metacognitive awareness and that such differences can have considerable effects on academic performance.

Calibration is particularly important to educational contexts because it can act as the basis for subsequent studying decisions. The accurate monitoring of one's knowledge or skill level, as well as realistic predictions and evaluations of one's performance, typically result in higher performance in the classroom, especially in high-stakes learning or testing situations. For example, a well-calibrated student with a childhood interest in chemistry may spend time reviewing a vocabulary list of words that will appear on an upcoming high-stakes science test. Based on her prior exposure, the student may confidently judge that she will score at least 90% on the exam, and indeed, her performance bears out her prediction. With this highly-calibrated student, high confidence is coupled with high performance. However, in a different subject such as Algebra II, this same student may exhibit high calibration in a different way—low confidence and lower performance. In this context, she considers herself lacking in knowledge or skill for a particular topic and indeed does poorly on tests. However, she at least knows she does not know the material. The difference is that higher-calibrated students are more likely to exert more effort when they know that they do not know something. Depending on their motivation, they will take steps to change their performance, and the strategies they employ will likely be more adaptive and effective because they will be based on accurate knowledge.

This positive relationship between calibration and student achievement has been well documented (Bol, Riggs, Hacker, Dickerson, & Nunnery, 2010; Chen, 2003; Pajares & Graham, 1999). The higher achievement of better-calibrated learners is due to the greater likelihood that students are basing their study strategy decisions on more accurate assessments of both what they know and what they do not know. Research also indicates that these well-calibrated students are less likely to grossly overestimate their capabilities to perform a task successfully, be more critical in task analysis, and choose and implement strategies effectively. They also utilize feedback information to evaluate themselves, have well-developed metacognitive skills, and make necessary adjustments for subsequent learning events (Hacker, Bol, & Bahbahani, 2008; Stone, 2000; Zimmerman, 2008). Thus, highly-calibrated learners (from K–12 to college, and in various content areas) consistently achieve at higher levels in academic endeavors than poorly-calibrated learners (Bol & Hacker, 2001; Chen & Zimmerman, 2007). Poorly-calibrated students may, for example, overestimate their knowledge of material on an upcoming test, and therefore terminate their studying behaviors earlier than students with the same knowledge level who more accurately assess their content knowledge; the former group of students is more likely to underperform on a test relative to the latter group. The consequences of poor calibration are clear in that students with poor academic performance may not graduate or even move to the next grade level, severely limiting their chances for higher education and employment opportunities. In sum, calibration, a metacognitive monitoring process, can serve as the foundation on which students can judge their current competency and evaluate performance outcomes in given learning situations. Such accurate monitoring processes subsequently influence the extent to which a student will put forth effort, use strategies, and positively adapt behaviors to be successful in accomplishing learning goals and completing tasks. Importantly, the research discussed in this section clearly demonstrates the positive impact of accurate calibration and student academic performance.

Although calibration is not a subprocess termed in his self-regulated learning (SRL) model, Zimmerman has explicitly discussed the importance of the metacognitive monitoring process, specifically the subprocess of self-observation in the performance phase as well as self-evaluation in the self-reflection phase. The conceptual underpinnings of the calibration processes closely correspond to these two subprocesses in Zimmerman's SRL model. The higher achievement of better-calibrated students derives from better self-monitoring and more accurate feedback mechanisms by which they garner information about their skills and knowledge level. These more accurate evaluations become the basis for effective study decisions made in subsequent phases of the cycle. In this chapter, we discuss the link between metacognition and self-regulation, highlighting Zimmerman's (2000) three-phase model of self-regulation, which was used as the basis for a school-based calibration intervention. We begin the chapter by discussing various theoretical models of metacognition and how calibration processes specifically relate to these frameworks. We then provide an overview of calibration accuracy research, with a particular focus on the effects of calibration interventions implemented in classroom settings. The key goals of this chapter, however, are to describe the connection between calibration and selected processes within Zimmerman's (2000) three-phase model of self-regulation, such as self-observation (metacognitive monitoring) and self-reflection (self-evaluation), and to underscore how this model served as the basis for developing a calibration intervention program to improve the academic learning and performance of at-risk high school students. We conclude the chapter by detailing the importance of calibration in Zimmerman's three-phase model along with recommendations for future research.

METACOGNITION WITH A FOCUS ON CALIBRATION

The term *metacognition* was first introduced by Flavell in the 1970s (Flavell, 1979, 1987). The concept was both broad and "fuzzy" at the time it was developed (Brown, 1987). To clarify the concept, a number of notable psychologists such as Flavell, Nelson, and Narens developed different models to illustrate the nature of this construct. Flavell (1979, 1987) originally defined *metacognition* as one's knowledge and cognition about anything cognitive, but later expanded the definition to include anything psychological, including knowing one's and others' motives, emotions, and motor skills. In his model, metacognition consists of two components: *metacognitive knowledge* (an individual's knowledge of or beliefs about his or her cognition as well as anything psychological) and *metacognitive experience* (an individual's conscious cognitive as well as affective experiences that vary in complexity and duration of time). Flavell (1979, 1987) subdivided each component of the model into various factors or variables. The metacognitive knowledge component can be divided into *person* variables (one's beliefs about self and others as cognitive beings), *task* variables (information available and derived from the event or situation during one's cognitive engagement), and *strategy* variables (one's knowledge about strategies or procedures that could permit one to achieve goals). These variables interact among each other and then affect an individual's course of actions and outcomes. For example, John may believe that he is not as good in math as his best friend (a *personal* component of metacognitive knowledge). Rather than take shortcuts (one possible *strategy*) on solving quadratic equations (*task*) for a homework assignment, which is his friend's approach, John may decide to follow every step of the procedures demonstrated by his math teacher (an alternate *strategy*). In this example, he based his decision on a combination of these aspects of his metacognitive knowledge. In effect, by recognizing that the task involves complex and multiple steps as well as knowing some shortcuts for it, John prefers those strategies that he is sure will accomplish his desired goal, as opposed to risking failure with the shortcut strategy.

As for the second component, Flavell (1987) describes metacognitive experiences as "conscious experiences that are cognitive and affective...hav[ing] to do with some cognitive endeavor or enterprise, most frequently a current, ongoing one" (p. 24). For example, a student who is baffled by dense class readings may suddenly feel anxious about her lack of comprehension and want to ask her teacher for assistance. This experience of not comprehending the material and feeling the need to understand a complex cognitive undertaking (e.g., reading) is considered a metacognitive experience. Students can encounter metacognitive experiences in learning situations at any time (before, during, or after), particularly when they think problems are too difficult to solve, readings are too complex to decipher, details are too hard to remember, and so on. Flavell's (1979, 1987) model of metacognition was particularly important because it provided the groundwork for future research in this area.

In the 1990s, researchers developed another dynamic theoretical framework of metacognition, with several structural components (Nelson, 1996; Nelson & Narens, 1994). First, they divided cognitive processes into two levels: object-level and meta-level. The object-level consists of cognition (e.g., "This is a two-digit multiplication problem"), while the meta-level consists of metacognition, or cognition of the object-level (e.g., "Which strategy should I use to obtain the correct solution with the least number of steps?"). The second component of the model concerns information flow between the two levels. According to Nelson and Narens (1994), the meta-level is active and regulatory, and acquires information from the object-level via *monitoring*. Monitoring informs an individual about (or provides a higher-order representation of) the state of the cognitive level. Via monitoring, the individual may also gain information about content knowledge, skills, or strategies at the cognitive level. Additionally, the meta-level sends information via *controlling* or *control actions* to the object-level. In other words, by exercising control, an individual can use his or her knowledge at the meta-level or metacognitive level to regulate or direct what to do or not to do at the object-level or cognitive level. Throughout the course of cognitive activity, these two processes simultaneously operate to deliver both information (monitoring) and directives (control) between the object- and meta-levels. Nelson and Narens' model is also goal-driven; the meta-level contains within it both goals and ways of regulating the object-level to accomplish these goals. As Nelson (1996) states, "the meta-level accomplishes goals by communicating back and forth with the object-level" (p. 106).

Nelson and Narens (1994) elaborated on their metacognitive framework by defining various monitoring-related and control-related constructs or processes occurring within the three stages of learning or information processing: *acquisition, retention,* and *retrieval* (Nelson & Narens, 1994; see also Hacker, Bol, & Keener, 2008). Recalling our earlier example, John's assessment of the difficulty of solving quadratic equations occurred during an *acquisition* phase of learning and is specifically considered an "ease-of-learning" monitoring process. During this same phase, his choice to follow the teacher's strategy (not his friend's) is considered to be a control process, namely *strategy selection*. During the *retention* phase of learning, students execute processes relevant to maintaining their knowledge. For example, while studying at home for an upcoming test on quadratics, John, from our prior example, might make a judgment-of-learning (a monitoring process) as to whether or not he had successfully memorized the teacher's strategy. Depending on whether or not he felt his knowledge was adequate, he might cease or continue to study (a control process).

During the *retrieval phase,* either while self-testing or during an actual test, students will make confidence judgments about their answers to determine whether they have answered the questions correctly. Adapting Nelson and Narens' (1994) three-stage model, Hacker, Bol, and Keener (2008) specifically propose that *calibration,* a monitoring process, is the level of alignment between one's perception of performance and actual performance.

Calibration may occur both prior to retrieval (prediction judgments) and/ or after retrieval (postdiction judgments). Calibration likewise informs control processes. In our example, John would make such predictive judgments immediately prior to taking the actual test or attempting to answer a given question. If John perceives that a question is too difficult, he might not risk trying his friend's strategy and rely on a more methodical approach. Postdiction judgments, such as whether or not to check his work after solving a question, would also inform his control processes during the test.

Collectively, these models of metacognition provide a useful framework for understanding the nature of information processing when one engages in any cognitive activity. In particular, the monitoring and controlling processes of Nelson and Narens' model show that people are self-regulated and goal-driven in their cognitive and metacognitive capacities and processing. One metacognitive construct, calibration, is deeply informed by this interchange of the underlying psychological processes of monitoring (i.e., regulating information flow from object-level to meta-level) and controlling (i.e., when meta-level modifies ongoing object-level activities). A graphic illustration and detailed discussion of these metacognition models are presented in Nelson and Narens' (1990, 1994) work; the distinguishing characteristics of prediction and postdiction judgments (i.e., calibration) are highlighted in Hacker, Bol, and Keener (2008). The following section highlights the construct of calibration and its relation to metacognition in more detail.

THE NATURE AND CHARACTERISTICS OF CALIBRATION

Calibration is the extent of agreement or accuracy between one's judgment of performance and one's corresponding actual performance (Hacker, Bol, & Keener, 2008; Nietfeld, Cao, & Osborne, 2005). Researchers interested in measuring calibration have examined learners' judgments prior to and/ or following task performance. In terms of performance prediction, the learner makes judgments about his or her current state of knowledge and skills and then compares those judgments with certain objective criteria such as task complexity. However, calibration judgments can also be targeted after the individual has performed the learning task. In this situation, the learner attempts to evaluate the extent to which he or she met the performance criteria. Both of these *pre* and *post* "performance" judgments are considered types of calibration as well as monitoring processes. Calibration is considered a monitoring process because it entails a judgment of learning, made prior to or after retrieval of the particular skills or knowledge. As Hacker, Bol, and Keener (2008) suggest, a *prediction judgment* is a *prospective* monitoring process (i.e., the judgment is made prior to the targeted performance task) that comes after acquisition and retention but before retrieval in a learning situation. A *postdiction judgment* is a *retrospective* monitoring process (i.e., the judgment is made after the targeted performance task) that occurs after a learning or performance situation.

In the calibration literature, many researchers have focused on how learners make their prediction and/or postdiction judgments during learning or testing situations (Bol & Hacker, 2001; Bol, Hacker, O'Shea, & Allen, 2005; Hacker, Bol, & Bahbahani, 2008; Nietfeld et al., 2005). Other researchers have focused on calibration in terms of the accuracy of students' self-efficacy beliefs as they correspond to actual performance; for these studies, calibration of self-efficacy beliefs is itself a prediction judgment or prospective monitoring process (Brannick, Miles, & Kisamore, 2005; Chen & Zimmerman, 2007; Klassen, 2002, 2007; Pajares & Graham, 1999). Similarly, in a later section of this chapter, we present an intervention designed to assist academically at-risk high school students in passing high-stakes tests; the students' prospective monitoring processes were assessed by measuring calibration of self-efficacy beliefs. Thus far, we have conceptually defined calibration as both prediction and postdiction judgments. For the purposes of our intervention and to establish how the participants used calibration accuracy information, we now turn to discussing how this construct has been measured by researchers.

MEASURING CALIBRATION ACCURACY

Literature on measuring metacognitive judgments provides guidance on different ways of specifically measuring calibration accuracy. According to Schraw (2009), the main interest in measuring metacognitive judgments is to examine the extent of agreement between learners' confidence judgments and their corresponding performance. Further, Schraw divided measures of judgments into two major categories: absolute accuracy and relative accuracy. Absolute accuracy indices show the extent to which a confidence judgment corresponds to performance outcome, such as the number or percentage of items answered correctly. These indices indicate confidence levels and performance outcomes on a criterion task, such as a test question (item-level) or set of test questions (global-level). Relative accuracy indices indicate the relationship between a confidence judgment or a set of confidence judgments and performance outcomes. With relative accuracy, one can measure the "consistency of a set of students' confidence judgments relative to a set of performance outcomes rather than the degree to which each confidence judgment is precise on an item-to-item-basis" (Schraw, 2009, p. 419). In other words, relative accuracy evaluates the consistency of judgments (Schraw, 2009), while absolute accuracy targets the precision of judgments.

Most studies on calibration, especially in the educational context, have used some form of absolute accuracy index. Bol et al. (2005) offer an example of a simple absolute accuracy measure of calibration assessed at the global level. In their research, students were asked to predict or postdict confidence before or after an examination (e.g., "What percentage of questions do you think you will get correct?" and "Now that you have completed the final, what percentage of questions do you think you got correct?"). Once the students' performances were assessed, the overall test scores were then subtracted from the students' prediction and postdiction scores. If a student predicted 80% on an exam but earned 60%, she would receive a difference score of +20, indicating overconfidence. On the other hand, if a student predicted 60% and earned 70%, he would receive a difference score of -10, indicating underconfidence. In the above examples, the student with a -10 difference score would be considered more accurate than the student who was overconfident by +20. Difference scores that are closer to zero indicate greater accuracy (Hacker, Bol, & Keener, 2008), and the positive or negative sign indicates over- and underconfidence, respectively. These absolute accuracy measures of calibration can be computed locally (single question predictions) or globally (overall test score predictions). Because absolute accuracy measures are mostly used in educational contexts and because they give a precise match between judgment and performance specifically for a particular local item or globally for a set of questions, the intervention that will be described later in this chapter employed absolute accuracy measures (global- and local-level item-specific measures).

EVOLUTION OF CALIBRATION RESEARCH
TO CLASSROOM INTERVENTIONS

In this section, we briefly review research detailing the effects of calibration intervention programs in learning or classroom contexts and discuss how these findings guided the development of our intervention program based on Zimmerman's model of self-regulation. Studies have consistently shown that lower-achieving students (both children and adults) make poor calibrations and gross overestimations of their academic skills and knowledge, compared with their higher-achieving counterparts (Bol et al., 2005; Klassen, 2002, 2007; Pajares & Graham, 1999). In other words, lower-achieving students lack metacognitive monitoring skills and tend to grossly miscalculate their knowledge and skill levels to complete tasks successfully. Such naïve optimism about performance can be detrimental to student learning and achievement. Poor calibrators are inaccurate in assessing their own capabilities or they misjudge task difficulty and, in turn, are less likely to persist and exert effort on challenging tasks or to seek assistance from teachers, peers or other resources.

Early studies on calibration stemmed from learning, memory, and metacognition research, and were conducted mostly with adults in laboratory settings (specifically, college students) rather than in natural environments, such as classrooms (Hacker, Bol, & Keener, 2008). Such poor ecological validity minimized the generalizability of research results and thus offered minimal practical educational implications, particularly for classroom contexts. In recent years, however, several calibration studies have been conducted in classroom settings. Interestingly, the findings have often differed depending on the measure's level of specificity (i.e., confidence ratings at the local or item level or confidence ratings at the test or global level) as well as on the research design and various focuses of the interventions (e.g., providing participants with feedback, teaching learners monitoring skills or providing guidelines to students about tracking their learning progress). Studies have consistently shown that college students' achievement levels influence their calibration accuracy, with high-achieving students being better calibrated or more accurate than lower-achieving students (Bol & Hacker, 2001; Hacker, Bol, & Bahbahani, 2008). Similar findings were observed with upper elementary school students and middle school students (Bol, Riggs, Hacker, Dickerson, & Nunnery, 2010; Huff & Nietfeld, 2009). However, Nietfeld et al. (2005) found no correlation between students' calibration accuracy and achievement levels (when calibration was measured globally after performance). Although research on calibration has mostly demonstrated a positive relationship between students' achievement and calibration accuracy, the more pertinent question is whether students' calibration can be improved through an intervention that also improves achievement.

In college classroom settings, Flannelly (2001) studied nursing students' calibration (particularly bias judgments) and found that the experimental group that received feedback on its confidence judgments and performance improved significantly in accuracy, compared with the control group, which received no feedback. Although Flannelly's study used a one-shot intervention (students were given the answer key after a single practice test), results showed that feedback alone can reduce students' judgment bias. To show improvement of calibration accuracy over time, Nietfeld, Cao, and Osborne (2006) found that undergraduate students who received monitoring exercise and feedback throughout a semester improved their calibration accuracy, compared with a control group. These researchers further found that higher calibration and greater change in calibration accounted for unique variance in students' final test scores.

Using a pretest-posttest experimental design, Huff and Nietfeld (2009) found that incorporating an explicit monitoring intervention improved both calibration accuracy and reading comprehension performance in fifth grade students. Walck and Bol (under review) examined both group and individual calibration in high school biology classes. Students who were provided calibration guidelines (used to make prospective judgments when studying for tests) were more accurate and had higher test scores than those who were not given them, indicating that calibration guidelines positively influence students' calibration and performance. Although Flannelly's (2001) study did not include explicit teaching of monitoring calibration accuracy to the participants, it showed that improvement in accuracy (i.e., reduced confidence bias) was mainly the result of receiving feedback. The interventions that also showed positive effects on students' calibration accuracy included elements such as providing feedback, explicitly teaching monitoring skills, using calibration monitoring exercises, and providing guidelines to students on how to track their progress (Huff & Nietfeld, 2009; Nietfeld et al., 2006; Walck & Bol, under review).

Unfortunately, other studies on calibration accuracy training have shown less positive results. For example, Bol et al. (2005) found that undergraduate students using a number of practice tests over one semester showed no significant change in calibration accuracy. Similarly, Nietfeld et al. (2005) found that monitoring accuracy remained unchanged over three tests that covered the course materials used during one semester. However, these authors did not deliberately teach students how to reflect on or use their accuracy information to improve calibration. Even though the studies reviewed thus far vary in their research designs, the mixed findings about the effectiveness of calibration accuracy seem to be related to whether study interventions included explicit instruction on how to monitor calibration accuracy.

We used this prior research to aid in the planning and development of our calibration intervention program. However, we also used Zimmerman's (2000) three-phase cyclical model as a guide because its cyclical and recursive nature made it ideal for integrating feedback into our intervention and because it linked well with many of the intervention components reported in prior calibration research. For instance, Huff and Nietfeld (2009) employed self-regulation techniques such as self-monitoring to improve comprehension, and provided more focused strategy-based feedback relevant to the particular content domain. As self-monitoring elements, these would be most effective when added as modifications to the performance phase of Zimmerman's model. Furthermore, participants in Nietfeld et al. (2006) were administered monitoring worksheets tied to the content discussed during the week and given feedback on the accuracy of their calibration. Whereas the first aspect of the treatment condition of this study would also be applicable to a performance phase modification, the feedback element would be most useful if administered during the self-reflection phase. The use of calibration guidelines in Walck and Bol (under review) during home study was also shown to be effective, and would be instrumental as a performance phase modification. We have sought to integrate components of these successful treatments (Flannelly, 2001; Huff & Nietfeld, 2009; Nietfeld et al., 2006; Walck & Bol, under review) with Zimmerman's cyclical self-regulation model in developing our intervention targeting lower-achieving students who face high-stakes testing and learning situations.

ZIMMERMAN'S SELF-REGULATED
LEARNING (SRL) MODEL

Academic self-regulation has been defined as a deliberate and proactive process that learners use to acquire academic skills by setting goals, selecting and implementing strategies, sustaining self-motivation, self-monitoring, and making necessary adjustments to successfully attain or master desired outcomes (Zimmerman, 2008). Self-regulated learners are active and efficient in managing their own behaviors, learning environment, motivation, and metacognitive and cognitive processes through continuous monitoring and strategy use (Greene & Azevedo, 2007). Accordingly, highly self-regulated learners continuously and mindfully repeat, adapt, and modify these processes and behaviors during academic endeavors. Research has documented that effective self-regulated learners engage in proactive processes such as analyzing tasks, setting proximate goals, and selecting appropriate strategies to complete a task at hand. Further, highly self-regulated learners monitor and exert self-control while engaging in a learning task. These individuals then self-evaluate and make adjustments during as well as after completing the task. Such cognition, behaviors, and motivation thereby provide learners with continuous feedback as they undertake any new learning endeavors (Schunk, 2001; Zimmerman, 2002, 2008). Not only is accurate self-observation and self-evaluation important for successful self-regulation, but it also reflects the relevance of accurate calibration as well as the interplay between monitoring and control processes. These processes generate information with which learners may modify their beliefs, behaviors, and/or strategies in successive phases of the cycle.

For decades, Zimmerman has written extensively about self-regulated learning, and we focus exclusively on his three-phase dynamic feedback loop model (Zimmerman, 2000). The self-observation and self-judgment subprocesses of Zimmerman's (2000) three-phase self-regulated learning (SRL) model are especially important to this chapter's focus on calibration. This model consists of three phases: forethought, performance, and self-reflection. Within each phase of SRL, learners are guided by their own motivational beliefs to engage in various metacognitive processes and actions. The *forethought phase* entails two major subprocesses—*task analysis* and *self-*

motivational beliefs—which precede learning or performance. Specifically, this phase involves learners engaging in task analysis processes such as goal setting (e.g., prioritizing immediate goals in order to reach distal goals successfully) and strategic planning (e.g., selecting or creating appropriate strategies to guide one's cognition and metacognition in order to execute a task at hand). According to Zimmerman (2000), initiating these two metacognitive processes (goal setting and strategic planning) depends on the learners' self-motivational beliefs such as self-efficacy beliefs, outcome expectancies, task interests, and goal orientation. These beliefs not only influence learners' goal setting and strategic planning during the forethought phase, but they also influence subprocesses during the performance phase. In the forethought phase, self-regulated learners are self-motivated and likely have higher self-efficacy (i.e., beliefs in their confidence to successfully execute a task at hand) and outcome expectancy (i.e., knowledge and awareness of different outcomes). They also show task interest or valuing (i.e., intrinsic interest in the task) and tend to adopt a specific learning goal orientation (i.e., reasons for engaging in the task in order to achieve academically).

The second phase of Zimmerman's (2000) model is the *performance phase*, which consists of two major subprocesses: *self-control* and *self-observation*. While learning or solving tasks, highly self-regulated learners are more likely than less self-regulating individuals to engage in self-control by using metacognitive strategies (e.g., task strategies that are developed to target a particular component of the task, and imagery in which forming mental pictures adds to learning); managing time better; setting self-consequences to motivate learning; structuring the learning environment to enhance learning and complete tasks; and seeking help or information (Wolters, 2003). Furthermore, self-regulated students are likely to control their performance progress through self-observation processes, such as metacognitive monitoring (i.e., covertly and mentally tracking learning progress and performance outcomes) and self-recording (i.e., overtly and deliberately recording and tracking learning progress and performance outcomes; Zimmerman, 2011). These self-observation processes in Zimmerman's SRL model are especially important to this chapter's focus on calibration because in this performance phase of the cycle, learners are most directly engaged with the content and learning tasks. During this phase, they also modify their time of study, monitor their learning progress, and select study strategies based on their judgments or assessments of what they know and do not know or how well they are doing on the tasks at hand. The accuracy of information generated during the performance phase then feeds back to the learner, who then evaluates the effectiveness of his or her learning performance. Calibration, which is a type of metacognitive awareness, is important from a regulatory perspective because it provides information or feedback derived from comparing the monitoring of one's perception of performance with the actual performance. In our later description of an intervention that employs calibration strategies, we discuss in detail how calibration feedback functions within the context of Zimmerman's cyclical model.

The third phase of Zimmerman's (2000) cyclical SRL model is the *self-reflection phase*. This phase involves two major categories of responses to learning or performance: *self-judgments* and *self-reactions*. Self-judgments entail evaluating one's own performance against a standard and making causal attributions to the outcomes; therefore, accurate calibration is the *sine qua non* of effective self-judgment. Awareness of the gap between a standard of performance and actual performance affects one's attributions of learning outcomes. Calibration that is made post-performance (i.e., postdiction) has a comparative function that relates one's assessment of performance to the actual outcome of that performance. Another key component of the self-reflection phase is self-reaction, which refers to the learners' level of satisfaction or dissatisfaction and their adaptive or defensive reactions to the outcomes. Whether learners engage in further learning and proceed again to the forethought phase depends on these self-reactions. Research has shown that effective self-regulated learners engage in proactive forethought processes, monitor and self-control during performance, and self-evaluate and make adjustments during self-reflection. According to Zimmerman's theoretical model, this self-evaluation feeds back to the forethought phase and continues the cycle of self-regulation as learners engage in new tasks (Schunk, 2001; Zimmerman, 2000, 2008). Self-reactions may affect calibration ability in that learners who experience negative self-reactions to a performance outcome may not properly "feed-forward" that information into the next iteration of the cycle. Therefore, they may not properly modify their pretest assessment of their own knowledge and adopt new study strategies.

It is important to note that the three phases of Zimmerman's cyclical model are described in terms of a feedback loop. According to Zimmerman (2000), self-regulation is considered cyclical because feedback from a previous phase is utilized to make adjustments for the current phase; as a result of any adjustments made, such information then "feeds-forward" to the next phase. In addition, feedback is a critical component of learning, which is crucial for guiding student learning and providing motivation (Shute, 2008). To be effective, feedback information should be non-evaluative, supportive, timely, and specific. In particular, feedback should address the accuracy of students' responses to problem tasks that may contain particular errors and misconceptions (Shute, 2008) in order for them to bridge the gap between their present understanding of learning tasks or performance and the level of understanding that they aim to possess (Hattie & Timperley, 2007). According to Hattie and Timperley (2007), feedback to close this gap should address the following three questions: "where am I going?" (what direction has been set or what are the learning goals?), "how am I going?" (what strategies do I need to adopt to get there?) and "where to next?" (what subsequent goals follow from the previous goal?). Feedback also has a regulatory function (Hattie & Timperley, 2007), and as posited in Zimmerman's model, feedback generated from any given phase forms the basis for motivation, behavior, cognition, and metacognition in a subsequent phase.

The connection between Zimmerman's model and calibration is implicit, yet they overlap in substantial ways, particularly with respect to self-observation (metacognitive monitoring) and self-reflection (self-evaluation). In the next section, we present an intervention with a focus on calibration, discuss its implementation, and indicate where and how we integrated feedback relative to the processes within Zimmerman's cyclical model.

DESIGN AND IMPLEMENTATION OF THE INTERVENTION

In this section, our goal is to present a calibration intervention to assist at-risk high school students in passing high-stakes tests. First, we present the context of the intervention by describing the background of the particular summer program in which it was initially conducted. Second, we discuss the goals of the intervention for both the students and their tutors. Third, we discuss several components of the intervention, including opportunities for students to make confidence judgments (self-efficacy), receive calibration accuracy information, and self-reflect on the feedback. We also illustrate how tutors engaged in calibration exercises to estimate the tutees' performance as well as their own level of confidence that their students can answer correctly. We conclude by discussing how the intervention was implemented during a five-week summer program.

Our calibration intervention was developed specifically for an intensive summer remedial program and was designed to incorporate cyclical calibration monitoring as students learn academic content. For over a century, New York State has required its 9th and 10th grade high school students to pass the Regents examinations—end-of-year high-stakes tests that evaluate skills in core areas such as integrated algebra (IA) and living environment (LE). Each year, many New York City high school students fail these classes and cannot pass these Regents exams with the required passing scaled score of 65 (rather than reporting raw scores on these exams, converted or scaled scores are used and reported for the purpose of comparing results over time among examinees or among test forms). Intensive all-day summer programs offer additional instructional support so that some members of this struggling population will pass Regents exams in these subjects by the end of the program. A unique feature of the program was that it employed peer tutors in the classrooms to help students on a daily basis. The first author provided feedback to both the students and their tutors on each student's weekly calibration information. The intervention targeted both math (IA) and science (LE). In addition to taking weekly practice tests, students were taught to use self-regulated monitoring strategies (e.g., calibration accuracy) and received both formative and summative feedback to engage them in cyclical, regulatory thinking over the course of five weeks.

GOALS OF THE INTERVENTION

This intervention was designed to improve the metacognitive awareness and skills of both tutors and students. Regarding students, the primary goal of the intervention was to help students become more calibrated (i.e., improve their monitoring accuracy of their own knowledge and skills) by using feedback to identify their strengths and weaknesses with respect to key ideas within each content area (LE and IA). By increasing student awareness of their cognitive processes, knowledge, and skill levels, it was assumed that we would be able to work more effectively toward meeting desired learning goals. In addition, as predicted by Zimmerman's (2000) three-phase cyclical model, enhancing students' metacognitive awareness (i.e., performance) would further help students adapt and modify learning strategies, and assist them in making adjustments to improve their academic performance (i.e., reflection).

With respect to the tutors, the intervention components were developed to help them improve their calibration, specifically in terms of their awareness of each tutee's strengths and weaknesses in key ideas within each content area. In other words, tutors were asked to make confidence judgments about their tutees' knowledge and evaluate the accuracy of these judgments. Via feedback, tutors monitored their own ongoing knowledge of each student's skill levels, and focused on the particular skills and knowledge areas that each student needed to develop. In addition, tutors monitored their tutees' overall performance on the practice tests to ascertain the progress towards a score goal (i.e., passing the Regents with at least a score of 65). Another aspect of the intervention allowed tutors to compare their confidence about teaching each key idea to a particular tutee with the tutee's actual score for each key idea. Such feedback provided tutors with a mechanism to monitor their teaching effectiveness according to each student's needs. As a result, tutors were encouraged to reflect on their current teaching strategies and effectiveness as well as to adjust and modify their strategies to better serve their students. Similar to the intervention for students, tutors received continuous feedback on their confidence in teaching as well as their students' performance.

COMPONENTS OF THE INTERVENTION

The intervention design was guided by the theoretical framework of a social cognitive model of *academic self-regulation*, particularly Zimmerman's three-phase model (Bandura, 1997; Schunk & Meece, 2006; Zimmerman, 2008). This framework highlights several specific ways in which calibration judgments can be used as *formative feedback* and incorporated cyclically over successive iterations of the model. As Shute (2008) defines it, formative feedback is "information communicated to the learner that is intended to modify his or her thinking or behavior for the purpose of improving learning" (p. 154). This concept is related to the purpose and goals of feedback. According to Hattie and Timperley (2007), the purpose of feedback is to decrease the gap between learners' current understanding, as reflected in their performance, and a future performance goal; to be effective, feedback must target the learners' appropriate skill level. Formative feedback can be either *outcome-* or *process-based* (Butler & Winne, 1995); outcome feedback derives from a student's performance results on a criterion task, whereas process feedback is concerned with how a student performs that task. In the present intervention, both types of feedback were employed to encourage students to self-regulate more effectively.

The components of this intervention consisted of: (1) eliciting self-efficacy judgments pertaining to key ideas within each content area (LE and IA); (2) gathering students' overall predictions of their performance on practice tests; (3) assessing knowledge and skill levels via multiple practice Regents tests; and (4) providing feedback on students' calibration judgments. Each component corresponded to a particular subprocess in each phase of Zimmerman's cyclical model: self-efficacy judgments (motivational beliefs) and test score predictions corresponded to self-motivation (forethought phase), taking practice tests offered opportunities for self-control (performance phase), and feedback on calibration accuracy corresponded to self-evaluation (self-reflection phase).

Judgments of self-efficacy. The inclusion of self-efficacy judgments in the intervention had three treatment benefits. First, through the act of making self-efficacy judgments, students were provided with an opportunity to examine their self-motivational beliefs. According to Zimmerman and Labuhn (2012), proactive learners draw heavily on their self-efficacy beliefs during the forethought phase; thus, we included this component as a way to encourage proactive learning by promoting greater self-assessment of one's confidence levels. Second, the self-efficacy judgment component collected information that could be compared with performance scores in order to compute calibration scores and provide calibration feedback to students after each practice test was completed and scored. Third, we asked students to self-evaluate their confidence levels for specific key ideas within each content area (LE or IA). By structuring the intervention in this way, we followed Bandura's (1997) suggestion that self-efficacy judgments are most useful when related to specific types of tasks. With this in mind, we asked students to make specific self-efficacy judgments for multiple "key ideas" within each content area. For example, the seven key ideas for LE are: (1) similarities and differences among living and nonliving things, (2) genetic inheritance, (3) change over time, (4) reproduction and development, (5) dynamic equilibrium, (6) interdependence and dependence on physical environment, and (7) impact of humans on the environment. Appendix A presents an example sheet of self-efficacy judgments that was distributed to students in the program; for each key idea, students rated their confidence in their ability to answer a sample question. The sample questions in Appendix A are for illustration purposes only and are not the actual items used in the intervention. The items in Appendix A illustrate the types of questions aligned with particular key ideas. For the intervention, the questions used to help students to render their self-efficacy judgments were actual released Regents questions from prior years.

Estimation of practice test scores. Similar to the self-efficacy judgments for each key idea, this component asked students to make a global self-efficacy judgment with respect to their overall performance on the upcoming practice test. This provided an opportunity for students to make an overall summative evaluation, as opposed to an evaluation for each key idea of how they would perform on a test. In addition, this overall judgment was compared with students' scaled test scores to derive an overall calibration accuracy score for each student. An example of this component is included at the end of Appendix A.

Practice Regents exams. This component of the intervention provided students with multiple opportunities to practice taking full-length NYS Regents exams, consisting of items previously released by the NYS Regents Board and made available to the general public. Since these at-risk students had not yet passed the Regents prior to this program, multiple administrations of practice tests were necessary for them to acclimate to the upcoming official exam. According to Zimmerman and Labuhn's (2012) description of the performance phase of the cyclical model, metacognitive monitoring involves mental tracking of one's performance processes and outcomes. Because these were at-risk students, we helped them monitor their performance by grouping the items according to key ideas along with their self-efficacy judgments corresponding to those key ideas, to help them better identify learning gaps. Presenting information in this way helped students track their performance relative to their self-efficacy judgments, not only for the overall content domain but also for the specific knowledge areas within that domain.

It is important to note that in any intervention, practice tests alone are not enough to ensure that performance or calibration accuracy will improve, especially when practice test questions can take substantially different forms from those on the actual test (Bol & Hacker, 2001). For this reason, we offered more substantive ways to use feedback from test results so that both students and tutors could learn to monitor their performance and perceived capabilities (i.e., self-efficacy) more accurately and, thus, improve them. Once the practice tests were scored, the self-efficacy judgment component, the estimation of the overall score, and the performance on the practice test were all incorporated into the feedback component of the intervention to illustrate calibration accuracy.

Calibration feedback to students. The purpose of feedback during this intervention, when conceptualized in terms of Zimmerman's model, was to provide calibration accuracy information during the performance and self-evaluation phases of the cycle. This information helped students monitor their learning progress throughout the five weeks of the program. Weekly feedback was included in the intervention to help students develop better self-monitoring skills and accurately assess their knowledge and learning. The goal was for learners to use the weekly feedback to decrease their learning gap by directing their study efforts toward improving particular sets of skills and knowledge.

After the practice tests were scored, the students were presented with a customized one-page feedback sheet of results (see Appendix B) that included their mock Regents score, as well as their estimate of their overall score which they provided prior to the test. For each key idea, students' earlier self-efficacy ratings were also indicated next to the number of items they answered correctly in that category; thus, they could compare their confidence judgments with their actual performance in each area. Additionally, sample questions representing each key idea were also provided on a separate sheet in order to cue students to the content knowledge or skills assessed by the questions, and to help students interpret their performance on the different ideas of the Regents tests.

The rationale for organizing the feedback sheet by key idea was to allow students to compare their self-efficacy judgments with their actual performance, and thereby monitor their calibration accuracy by key concept. In addition to identifying the accuracy of their predictions and performance, students were provided opportunities to reflect on prior study approaches and evaluate the strengths and weaknesses of their content knowledge. To encourage self-reflection, students were asked the following questions: (1) "You saw your overall score on the mock Regents; to what extent did you use the results to change how you study?" and (2) "You saw your scores for each key idea on the mock Regents; to what extent did you change how you study by focusing on specific key ideas that need improvement?" With respect to Zimmerman's model, these questions provided opportunities for students to self-reflect on how they would adapt and modify the study tactics they employed during the performance phase. This self-reflection aided planning during the upcoming learning cycle.

Frequent assessment and feedback are important tools that provide students with opportunities to develop better self-monitoring skills and to assess their knowledge and learning more accurately. In addition, students receiving frequent feedback may increase their calibration accuracy. Zimmerman, Moylan, Hudesman, White, and Flugman (2011) found that calibration training of college students in remedial math improved their calibration accuracy and self-efficacy beliefs over the course of a semester, as measured by item-by-item self-efficacy judgments collected over successive examinations. Similarly, Nietfeld et al. (2006) found that intervention groups of undergraduates who received monitoring exercise and feedback improved their calibration accuracy over one academic semester, compared to the control group.

Calibration feedback for tutors. Another goal of the intervention was to encourage tutors to reflect on their own teaching effectiveness, much as students were encouraged to develop better self-monitoring skills and calibration. Similarly, frequent instances of feedback were included as a way to help tutors develop better self-monitoring skills for their teaching and assess their knowledge of their tutees more accurately. In terms of Zimmerman's model, the purpose of this feedback for the tutors was similar to that for the students—to provide continuous calibration accuracy information to help tutors better monitor their teaching and their tutees' knowledge and understanding of content materials. Tutors were also given an opportunity to consider how they might adapt their teaching strategies during the self-reflection phase.

This goal was accomplished by giving each tutor the opportunity to make judgments about how well each student would perform for each key idea and then compare those judgments with actual outcomes. Prior to each practice test, the tutors predicted how well each of their students would perform on representative questions for each key idea (see Appendix C). At the same time, they also predicted each student's overall score across content domain. After the tests were scored, the tutors received the same performance feedback that each student received—performance on each key idea as well as overall score. The tutors' feedback also included their weekly confidence judgments of how effectively they taught the key idea to each student, which allowed them to assess the calibration accuracy of their teaching effectiveness (Appendix D).

The last component of the intervention for tutors was to encourage the evaluation of the effectiveness of their teaching/tutoring strategies. To accomplish this goal, days after the tutors had seen the students' performance results and worked with their tutees in the key areas needing the most instruction, they were encouraged to self-evaluate by responding to the following two questions: (1) "You saw each tutee's overall score on the mock Regents; to what extent did you use the results to change how you planned your next tutoring sessions?" and (2) "You saw each tutee's scores for each key idea on the mock Regents; to what extent did you change how you tutor by focusing on specific key idea(s) that need improvement?"

Each of the above intervention components—self-efficacy judgments, practice tests, and feedback information—was designed to function in an integrated way to improve calibration for both tutors and students, particularly according to key ideas for each content area. Targeting key ideas where students are most overconfident also addresses the "hard-easy" effect—that is, the students' tendency to approach difficult items with overconfidence and easy items with underconfidence (Hacker, Bol, & Keener, 2008). Since this effect may influence students to "allocate the least amount of time to difficult material that is, ironically, most in need of additional study effort due to their unrealistic confidence judgments" (Hacker, Bol, & Keener, 2008, p. 439), teaching students to focus primarily on key areas where they are overconfident during their study is one way to confront this issue directly. Once students have identified these specific areas to study and with their tutors' guidance, together they can co-construct advantageous learning methods that are appropriate to the task and environmental setting (Zimmerman & Moylan, 2009).

In the next section, we discuss how these intervention components were implemented in a specific classroom setting for at-risk students in a summer program. We also discuss how tutors and students used calibration feedback effectively over the course of a self-regulation cycle, at specific points corresponding to the phase dimensions of Zimmerman's (2000) model.

IMPLEMENTATION OF THE INTERVENTION

In our discussion of the implementation, we demonstrate how different components of the intervention can be incorporated into the context of a program curriculum. The directors of the summer program had allotted a certain number of weeks to assist at-risk students to improve their content knowledge and ultimately pass the Regents exams. Structured to correspond to the program's five-week schedule, the implementation of the intervention components also built in enough time for the timely scoring of practice tests and the preparation of feedback materials.

Figure 9.1, which is referenced throughout this section, graphically depicts how the intervention was implemented and how different components for both students and tutors aligned with particular subprocesses of Zimmerman's three-phase model (Zimmerman, 2008; Zimmerman & Moylan, 2009). Each week of the five-week program corresponds to one complete iteration of the three-phase cycle: forethought, performance, and self-reflection.

Classes ran Monday through Thursday and lasted five hours each, for a total of about 20 hours of instruction per week. Approximately 90 students worked with about 25 peer tutors, who were close in age and grade levels to their tutees, but who had successfully passed the Regents and were considered above average students in either the IA or LE content areas. Four classes (two IA and two LE) contained about 20 to 25 students; within each class, two classroom teachers provided daily instruction and supervised six peer tutors, each of whom worked with three to five students. Tutors were assigned to work with the same students over the course of the five weeks.

Key ideas were taught during all weeks of the program; however, teachers and tutors may have selected one or two key ideas to focus on each week, based on their students' needs. The tutors worked with the students on practice problems, teacher-assigned questions, homework questions, or specific questions from the students. Both the teachers' instruction and

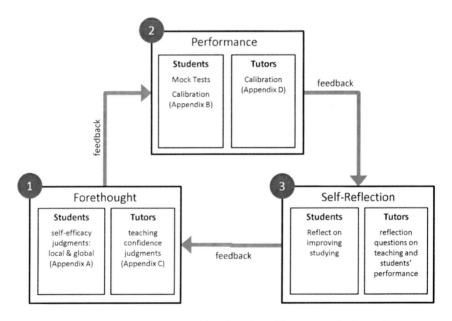

Figure 9.1 Components of intervention based on Zimmerman's three-phase model of self-regulation.

the structure of the tutoring groups were developed by the program and remained unaffected by our intervention. We did not dictate any aspect of the classroom curriculum/instruction beyond the intervention; all such aspects were left to the teachers' discretion. Our integration of the components into the curriculum of the program posed minimal disruption of classroom instruction or tutoring sessions. Aside from the weekly practice tests, which took three hours each week, each of the other intervention components took about 30 minutes to conduct.

As indicated earlier, the intervention components of this program were aligned with the specific subprocesses of each of the three phases of Zimmerman's model. Since the program began on a Wednesday, our intervention components corresponding to the forethought phase were implemented on every Wednesday of the five weeks. On the first Wednesday, students rendered both their item-specific and global self-efficacy judgments (see Appendix A). Simultaneously, tutors made judgments about each tutee's knowledge level of the same items and estimated each tutee's overall upcoming practice Regents scores (see Appendix C). On Thursday, during the performance phase, a full-length three-hour practice Regents test was given to students. On Friday and over the weekend, the tests were scored, and individualized calibration feedback was prepared. The tutors' own calibration information was also derived from a comparison of their students' performance outcomes with the tutors' confidence judgments of teaching effectiveness.

When students returned to class the following Monday, they were given the test results as well as calibration feedback sheets (Appendix B), each of which included their performance outcomes compared with their self-efficacy judgments. The tutors also received their tutees' performance outcomes as well as calibration feedback related to their accuracy in assessing their tutees' current knowledge level (Appendix D). On that Monday, both tutors and tutees took time to review their calibration feedback information, after which they were encouraged with brief verbal instructions to incorporate that information into either their studying or teaching approach. This period included a comprehensive review of all key ideas assessed by the mock Regents test, as well as any particular key ideas that both tutors and students decided to focus on. On Wednesday, students were presented with self-reflection questions, to assess how their approaches to study may have changed over the previous three days as a result of the calibration feedback they received. To encourage self-reflection, students were asked the following questions: (1) "You saw your overall score on the mock Regents; to what extent did you use the results to change how you study?" and (2) "You saw your scores for each key idea on the mock Regents; to what extent did you change how you study by focusing on specific key ideas that need improvement?" Similarly, after reviewing each tutee's performance outcomes and their earlier confidence judgments of teaching, the tutors reflected on the extent to which they modified their teaching strategies during that period to improve their tutees' performance for each key idea. The cycle began anew when, on that same Wednesday, students and tutees again gave their self-efficacy judgments for the next mock test that Thursday.

These intervention components for both students and tutors were repeated during the remaining four weeks. In the final (fifth) week of the program, however, students were not given a practice test, but rather took the official Regents test in the content domain for which they needed a passing score. Not including the practice tests, the amount of class time related to the intervention totaled about an hour per week, 30 minutes each for judgments of self-efficacy and reflection on calibration accuracy feedback.

Providing feedback throughout this five-week program was the main goal of the intervention—and is at the core of Zimmerman's cyclical phase model of SRL. The purpose of the weekly feedback was to continuously assist students in monitoring their calibration accuracy by comparing their predictions and actual performances by key concepts as well as by overall test score. Students could then use the feedback to monitor and reflect on how to study and decide which key topics needed more work during each upcoming week. Similarly, the weekly feedback was designed to encourage tutors in monitoring their students' performance outcomes according to key ideas and to improve tutors' methods of teaching their students more effectively. As noted by Zimmerman and Labuhn (2012), feedback is a key element of SRL models because it provides learners with repeated opportunities to review their efforts and to develop certain skills or knowledge through various stages of self-directed learning.

FUTURE RESEARCH DIRECTIONS

Zimmerman's SRL model is a very powerful framework that can guide design of programs to improve students' self-directedness in challenging learning situations. However, most research has only examined specific subprocesses rather than the entirety (i.e., all subprocesses) of the model. Since this intervention was mostly based on the first author's work with a summer program, this initial work was similarly focused on a particular subset of subprocesses of Zimmerman's model: self-motivation beliefs (self-efficacy), metacognitive monitoring (particularly calibration judgments), and self-evaluation. Future research should investigate the relationship between monitoring accuracy and other specific processes of Zimmerman's self-regulation model that were not addressed in the current intervention. For instance, a student's motivational beliefs, such as goal orientation or outcome expectancy (forethought phase subprocesses), may substantially influence his or her calibration accuracy. Particular performance phase subprocesses may also have an effect on calibration accuracy. These include the selection of specific task strategies such as employing imagery as a memorization technique, or using attention-focusing to screen out distractions and concentrate on a task. Ultimately, we suggest fully testing this intervention in regular classrooms and during the academic school year, in particular focusing on the intricate interrelationship of the subprocesses in Zimmerman's SRL model as they influence calibration accuracy.

Furthermore, future studies of calibration accuracy should be conducted in authentic classroom settings and contextualized to improve ecological validity. We also suggest that future studies employ mixed-method designs to test the effects of calibration accuracy training on more academically diverse student populations. As indicated by Hacker, Bol, and Keener (2008), most classroom-based studies of calibration accuracy are dominated by quantitative studies; employing qualitative research tools such as interviews, open-ended responses or think-aloud may provide richer explanations for students' discrepancies between their confidence judgments and their actual performance.

Any intervention study that seeks to improve students' calibration accuracy and self-regulated learning should also examine the long-term effects on students' learning and performance. Currently, the long-term effects of calibration training are not well documented; most studies in the literature are limited to a semester and do not measure students' long-term metacognitive skill development (Nietfeld et al., 2006). As a consequence, longitudinal studies are needed to determine whether students, on their own, will continue to monitor and improve their calibration accuracy post-intervention. Future research should determine whether the calibration accuracy monitoring skills learned in one educational context transfer to other educational contexts. Will students who improve their calibration in a mathematics course also improve their accuracy in other domains of study? Will students with improved calibration skill in reading also apply this metacognitive skill to improve performance in science?

The components of this intervention that sought to improve the calibration skills of the tutors should also be investigated more fully. Peer tutors, who work with their tutees to improve students' performance, present a unique opportunity for research. Because peer tutors are both teachers and learners, it is critical for them to improve their calibration not only as learners but also with respect to their teaching effectiveness. Peer tutors who improve their monitoring of tutees' knowledge and skills, and become more effective in teaching their tutees, may concurrently improve their monitoring of their own learning. Research in this area could prove instrumental in designing more robust interventions for school environments that employ peer tutoring for at-risk students.

Finally, and perhaps most importantly, however, any intervention that is designed to improve calibration accuracy should include explicit monitoring training for students while providing repeated feedback. Nietfeld et al. (2006) found that undergraduate students who received monitoring training exercises improved their calibration accuracy compared to their counterparts without training. Similarly, Huff and Nietfeld (2009) and Walck and Bol (under review), both of whom included monitoring training in their studies, also showed improved calibration accuracy in learners. Merely presenting a learner with feedback information is not enough to teach him or her how to monitor confidence judgments and performance—elements which form the basis of calibration accuracy.

CONCLUSION

This chapter focused on utilizing Zimmerman's three-phase cyclical self-regulated learning model to improve academically at-risk students' metacognitive awareness, particularly calibration accuracy, in classroom settings with high-stakes accountability. Calibration, a metacognitive construct, reflects the underlying psychological processes of monitoring and controlling. Following Zimmerman's three-phase SRL model with a focus on the metacognitive process of self-monitoring and self-evaluation, the cyclical and feedback nature of this model afforded the students in the summer program opportunities to continue exercising their learning and skills through multiple iterations. We designed an intervention to improve at-risk students' chances to learn, relearn, and ultimately pass high-stakes tests. In addition, the intervention engaged tutors to reflect on their own tutoring effectiveness and knowledge of their students' needs; by doing so, they could ultimately assist their students to master the content materials and pass the tests.

Although this intervention was specifically implemented in an intense summer program and used living environment and integrated algebra content to illustrate the processes that students would undergo in Zimmerman's three-phase model, we believe teachers can tailor this intervention to complement a regular academic timeframe and/or the particular content being studied. Overall, this intervention was designed to complement, not replace, instruction or curriculum; educators are encouraged to modify the length and iterations of this SRL intervention in order to meet their students' needs and curriculum demands. Teachers who utilize peer tutors in their classroom can also engage peer tutors in the calibration process, to monitor the effectiveness of tutoring strategies.

This five-week summer intervention utilized ongoing feedback to target learning difficulties across the three phases and particular subprocesses of Zimmerman's SRL model—a framework that emphasizes self-monitoring and structured feedback to improve calibration accuracy judgments, accuracy of self-evaluation, and adaptation of learning strategies during learning. Because the cyclical and recursive qualities of Zimmerman's model make it highly conducive for implementing both outcome and process feedback, it served as an ideal framework for our efforts to structure improvement in at-risk students' SRL behaviors (particularly calibration accuracy monitoring), and in knowledge and specific content area skills. Our implementation was one attempt to apply Zimmerman's (2000) cyclical three-phase model of self-regulation, which, in our opinion, will continue to guide interventions designed to improve students' self-directedness in diverse learning contexts.

APPENDIX A

FORM: Living Environment _____ Student ID: _____

Confidence Level for Living Environment Questions

Directions: The purpose of this survey is for you to know how confidently you believe you can correctly answer or solve questions representing each key idea. Please circle only one number for each scale. DO NOT ANSWER or SOLVE the questions.

[LE questions for key ideas 1, 2, 3, 4, and 7 omitted for space considerations]

LE Question 5: Dynamic equilibrium

The hypothalamus, an area in the brain, regulates body temperature. When overall body temperature drops, it signals muscles to shiver, which warms your body. What type of feedback mechanism is this an example of?

DO NOT SOLVE OR ANSWER

How confident are you that you can answer the above question correctly?

1	2	3	4	5	6	7
Not at all			*Somewhat*			*Completely*
confident			*confident*			*confident*

LE Question 6: Interdependence and dependence on physical environment

A dugong is a large water-dwelling herbivore, endangered because of fatalities related to hunting and commercial fishing. If dugongs became extinct, what would be the likely result for certain producer plants throughout their habitat?

DO NOT SOLVE OR ANSWER

How confident are you that you can answer the above question correctly?

1	2	3	4	5	6	7
Not at all			*Somewhat*			*Completely*
confident			*confident*			*confident*

Overall Confidence Level of Living Environment Mock Exam

Directions: For tomorrow's mock Regents exam, what score do you think you will get? (circle *one* number on a scale of 0 to 100)

0 5 10 15 20 25 30 35 40 45 50 55 60 65 70 75 80 85 90 95 100

APPENDIX B

LIVING ENVIRONMENT Student Mock Regents Score Report

Student ID: _____

Student's Name: _____

This page of the report shows your performance on the mock Regents test that you took last week. Please keep this page of results and use it to help guide your studies.

Living Environment: Key Ideas (Standard 4)	Number of multiple choice items correct	Number of open-ended item points earned	Your confidence BEFORE you took the test*						
			1 Not at all confident	2	3	4 Somewhat confident	5	6	7 Completely confident
Similarities & differences among living and nonliving things	___ out of 8	___ out of 2							
Genetic inheritance	___ out of 5	___ out of 3							
Change over time	___ out of 5	NA							
Reproduction and development	___ out of 4	___ out of 6							
Dynamic equilibrium	___ out of 5	___ out of 7							
Interdependence and dependence on physical environment	___ out of 4	___ out of 8							
Impact of humans on the environment	___ out of 3	___ out of 6							

Living Environment: Total test	Number of multiple choice items correct	Number of open-ended item points earned**	Scale Score	The scale score you predicted BEFORE you took the test
TOTAL TEST	___ out of 34	___ out of 45		

* BEFORE you took last week's mock Regents, you rated sample items in each key idea area according to how CONFIDENT you were that you would answer similar questions correctly.

** The total points for open-ended items include a number of dimensions not linked to the stated standards under the enumerated points.

Keep this Weekly Mock Exam Results Page for Your Information.

APPENDIX C

FORM: *Living Environment Tutor*   Tutor ID: _____

                                            Tutor's Name: _____

Part 1: How Each Tutee Will Do on the Living Environment Questions

Directions: Judge how each tutee is likely to do on each Living Environment question by answer the corresponding rating scale ranging from 1 to 7. Please circle only one number for each scale.

[Judgments for key ideas 1, 2, 3, 4, and 7 omitted due to space considerations]

Question 5: Dynamic equilibrium

The hypothalamus, an area in the brain, regulates body temperature. When overall body temperature drops, it signals muscles to shiver, which warms your body. What type of feedback mechanism is this an example of?

DO NOT ANSWER THE QUESTION

a. How confident are you that _____(name of tutee 1)_____ can answer the above question correctly?

1	2	3	4	5	6	7
Not at all confident			*Somewhat confident*			*Completely confident*

b. How confident are you that _____(name of tutee 2)_____ can answer the above question correctly?

1	2	3	4	5	6	7
Not at all confident			*Somewhat confident*			*Completely confident*

c. How confident are you that _____(name of tutee 3)_____ can answer the above question correctly?

1	2	3	4	5	6	7
Not at all confident			*Somewhat confident*			*Completely confident*

Question 6: Interdependence and dependence on physical environment

A dugong is a large water-dwelling herbivore, endangered because of fatalities related to hunting and commercial fishing. If dugongs became extinct, what would be the likely result for certain producer plants throughout their habitat?

DO NOT ANSWER THE QUESTION

a. How confident are you that _____(name of tutee 1)_____ can answer the above question correctly?

1	2	3	4	5	6	7
Not at all			*Somewhat*			*Completely*
confident			*confident*			*confident*

b. How confident are you that _____(name of tutee 2)_____ can answer the above question correctly?

1	2	3	4	5	6	7
Not at all			*Somewhat*			*Completely*
confident			*confident*			*confident*

c. How confident are you that _____(name of tutee 3)_____ can answer the above question correctly?

1	2	3	4	5	6	7
Not at all			*Somewhat*			*Completely*
confident			*confident*			*confident*

Part 2: How each tutee will do on the test overall

Directions: Judge how each tutee is likely to score on tomorrow's mock Regents exam.

1. On tomorrow's mock Regents exam, what score do you think _____(name of tutee 1)_____ will get? (circle *one* number on a scale of 0 to 100)

0   5   10   15   20   25   30   35   40   45   50   55   60   65   70   75   80   85   90   95   100

2. On tomorrow's mock Regents exam, what score do you think _____(name of tutee 2)_____ will get? (circle *one* number on a scale of 0 to 100)

0   5   10   15   20   25   30   35   40   45   50   55   60   65   70   75   80   85   90   95   100

3. On tomorrow's mock Regents exam, what score do you think _____(name of tutee 3)_____ will get? (circle *one* number on a scale of 0 to 100)

0   5   10   15   20   25   30   35   40   45   50   55   60   65   70   75   80   85   90   95   100

APPENDIX D

LIVING ENVIRONMENT Tutor Feedback Report

Tutor ID: _____

Tutor's Name: _____

This report shows the performance of the students in your group of tutees. Please keep the first pages with your results and those of your tutees, and use them to help guide your tutoring.

Your Tutee's Results: Student Name: _____

Living Environment: Key Ideas (Standard 4)	Number of multiple choice items correct	Number of open-ended item points earned	Your confidence BEFORE you took the test*						
			1 *Not at all confident*	2	3	4 *Somewhat confident*	5	6	7 *Completely confident*
Similarities & differences among living and nonliving things	____ out of 8	____ out of 2							
Genetic inheritance	____ out of 5	____ out of 3							
Change over time	____ out of 5	NA							
Reproduction and development	____ out of 4	____ out of 6							
Dynamic equilibrium	____ out of 5	____ out of 7							
Interdependence and dependence on physical environment	____ out of 4	____ out of 8							
Impact of humans on the environment	____ out of 3	____ out of 6							

Living Environment: Total test	Number of multiple choice items correct	Number of open-ended item points earned	Scale Score	The scale score you predicted BEFORE you took the test (first week NA)
TOTAL TEST	____ out of 40	____ out of 45		

* BEFORE last week's mock Regents, you rated items in each key area according to how CONFIDENT you were teaching your tutees.

Keep this Weekly Mock Exam Results Page for Your Information.

REFERENCES

Bandura, A. (1997). *Self-efficacy: The exercise of control.* New York, NY: Freeman.

Bol, L. & Hacker, D. (2001). A comparison of the effects of practice tests and traditional review on performance calibration. *Journal of Experimental Education, 69,* 133–152. doi:10.1080/00220970109600653

Bol, L., Hacker, D. J., O'Shea, P., & Allen, D. (2005). The influence of overt practice, achievement level, and explanatory style on calibration accuracy and performance. *The Journal of Experimental Education, 73,* 269–290. doi:10.3200/JEXE.73.4.269-290

Bol, L., Riggs, R., Hacker, D. J., Dickerson, D., & Nunnery, J. (2010). The calibration accuracy of middle school students in math classes. *Journal of Research in Education, 21,* 81–96. Retrieved from http://www.eeraonline.org/journal/v20n2.cfm

Brannick, M. T., Miles, D. E., & Kisamore, J. L. (2005). Calibration between student mastery and self-efficacy. *Studies in Higher Education, 30,* 473–483. doi:10.1080/03075070500160244

Brown, A. (1987). Metacognition, executive control, self-regulation and other more mysterious mechanisms. In F. Weinert & R. Kluwe (Eds.), *Metacognition, motivation, and understanding* (pp. 65–116). Hillsdale, NJ: Lawrence Erlbaum.

Butler, D. L. & Winne, P. H. (1995). Feedback and self-regulated learning: A theoretical synthesis. *Review of Educational Research, 65*(3), 245–281. doi:10.3102/00346543065003245

Chen, P. P. (2003). Exploring the accuracy and predictability of the self-efficacy beliefs of seventh-grade mathematics students. *Learning and Individual Differences, 14*(1), 77–90. doi:10.1016/j.lindif.2003.08.003

Chen, P. & Zimmerman, B. (2007). A cross-national comparison study on the accuracy of self-efficacy beliefs of middle-school mathematics students. *Journal of Experimental Education, 75*(3), 221–244. doi:10.3200/JEXE.75.3.221-244

de Bruin, A. B. H. & van Gog, T. (in press). Improving self-monitoring and self-regulation: From cognitive psychology to the classroom. *Learning and Instruction.* doi:10.1016/j.learninstruc.2012.01.003

Dunlosky, J. & Metcalfe, J. (2009). *Metacognition.* Thousand Oaks, CA: Sage Publications, Inc.

Flannelly, L. T. (2001). Using feedback to reduce students' judgment bias on test questions. *Journal of Nursing Education, 40,* 10–16.

Flavell, J. H. (1979). Metacognition and cognitive monitoring. *American Psychologist, 34,* 906–911. doi:10.1037/0003-066X.34.10.906

Flavell, J. H. (1987). Speculations about the nature and development of metacognition. In F. Weinert & R. Kluwe (Eds.), *Metacognition, motivation, and understanding* (pp. 21–29). Hillsdale, NJ: Lawrence Erlbaum. doi:10.1016/S0885-2014(87)90104-3

Greene, J. A. & Azevedo, R. (2007). The theoretical review of Winne and Hadwin's model of self-regulated learning: New perspectives and directions. *Review of Educational Research, 77,* 334–372. doi:10.3102/003465430303953

Hacker, D. J., Bol, L., & Bahbahani, K. (2008). Explaining calibration accuracy in classroom contexts: The effects of incentives, reflection, and explanatory style. *Metacognition and Learning*, *3*(2), 101–121. doi:10.1007/s11409-008-9021-5

Hacker, D. J., Bol, L., & Keener, M. C. (2008). Metacognition in education: A focus on calibration. In J. Dunlosky & R. Bjork (Eds.), *Handbook of memory and metacognition* (pp. 429–455). Mahwah, NJ: Lawrence Erlbaum.

Hattie, J. & Timperley, H. (2007). The power of feedback. *Review of Educational Research*, *77*, 81–112. doi:10.3102/003465430298487

Huff, J. D. & Nietfeld, J. L. (2009). Using strategy instruction and confidence judgments to improve metacognitive monitoring. *Metacognition Learning*, *4*, 161–176. doi:10.1007/s11409-009-9042-8

Klassen, R. M. (2002). A question of calibration: A review of the self-efficacy beliefs of students with learning disabilities. *Learning Disability Quarterly*, *25*, 88–103. doi:10.2307/1511276

Klassen, R. M. (2007). Using predictions to learn about the self-efficacy of early adolescents with and without learning disabilities. *Contemporary Educational Psychology*, *32*, 173–187. doi:10.1016/j.cedpsych.2006.10.001

Nelson, T. O. (1996). Consciousness and metacognition. *American Psychologist*, *51*, 102–116. doi:10.1037/0003-066X.51.2.102

Nelson, T. O. & Narens, L. (1990). Metamemory: A theoretical framework and new findings. In G. H. Bower (Ed.), *The psychology of learning and motivation* (pp. 125–173). New York, NY: Academic Press. doi:10.1016/S0079-7421(08)60053-5

Nelson, T. O. & Narens, L. (1994). Why investigate metacogntiion? In J. Metcalfe & A. P. Shimamura (Eds.), *Metacognition: Knowing about knowing* (pp. 1–25). Cambridge, MA: MIT Press.

Nietfeld, J. L., Cao, L., & Osborne, J. W. (2005). Metacognitive monitoring accuracy and student performance in classroom. *The Journal of Experimental Education*, *74*, 7–28.

Nietfeld, J. L., Cao, L., & Osborne, J. W. (2006). The effect of distributed monitoring exercises and feedback on performance, monitoring accuracy, and self-efficacy. *Metacognition and Learning*, *1*, 159–179. doi:10.1007/s10409-006-9595-6

Pajares, F. & Graham, L. (1999). Self-efficacy, motivation constructs, and mathematics performance of entering middle school students. *Contemporary Educational Psychology*, *24*, 124–139. doi:10.1006/ceps.1998.0991

Schraw, G. (2009). Measuring metacognitive judgments. In D. J. Hacker, J. Dunlosky, & A. C. Graseer (Eds.), *Handbook of metacognition in education* (pp. 415–429). New York, NY: Routledge.

Schunk, D. H. (2001). Teaching elementary students to self-regulate practice of mathematical skills with modeling. In D. H. Schunk & B. J. Zimmerman (Eds.), *Self-regulated learning: From teaching to self-reflective practice* (pp. 137–159). New York, NY: Guilford.

Schunk, D. H. & Meece, J. L. (2006). Self-efficacy development in adolescence. In F. Pajares & T. Urdan (Eds.), *Self-efficacy beliefs of adolescents* (pp. 71–96). Greenwich, CT: Information Age Publishing.

Shute, V. J. (2008). Focus on formative feedback. *Review of Educational Research*, *78*, 153–189. doi:10.3102/0034654307313795

Stone, N. J. (2000). Exploring the relationship between calibration and self-regulated learning. *Educational Psychology Review, 12,* 437–475. doi:10.1023/A:1009084430926

Walck, C. C. & Bol, L. (under review). The effect of individual or group guidelines on the calibration accuracy and achievement of high school biology students.

Wolters, C. A. (2003). Regulation of motivation: Evaluating an underemphasized aspect of self-regulated learning. *Educational Psychologist, 38,* 189–205.

Zimmerman, B. J. (2000). Attaining self-regulation: A social cognitive perspective. In M. Boekaerts, P. R. Pintrich, & M. Zeidner (Eds.), *Handbook of self-regulation* (pp. 13–39). San Diego, CA: Academic Press.

Zimmerman, B. J. (2002). Achieving self-regulation: The trial and triumph of adolescence. In F. Pajares & T. Urdan (Eds.), *Academic motivation of adolescents* (pp. 1–27). Greenwich, CT: Information Age Publishing.

Zimmerman, B. J. (2008). Investigating self-regulation and motivation: Historical background, methodological developments, and future prospects. *American Educational Research Journal, 45,* 166–183. doi:10.3102/0002831207312909

Zimmerman, B. J. (2011). Motivational sources and outcomes. In B. J. Zimmerman & D. H. Schunk (Eds.), *Handbook of self-regulation of learning and performance* (pp. 49–64). New York, NY: Routledge.

Zimmerman, B. J. & Labuhn, A. S. (2012). Self-regulation of learning: Process approaches to personal development. In K. R. Harris, S. Graham, & T. Urdan (Eds.), *APA educational psychology handbook* (Vol. 1, pp. 399–425). Washington, DC: American Psychological Association. doi:10.1037/13273-014

Zimmerman, B. J. & Moylan, A. R. (2009). Self-regulation: Where metacognition and motivation intersect. In D. J. Hacker & J. Dunlosky (Eds.), *Handbook of metacognition in education* (pp. 299–315). New York, NY: Routledge.

Zimmerman, B. J., Moylan, A. R., Hudesman, J., White, N., & Flugman, B. (2011). Enhancing self-reflection and mathematics achievement of at-risk urban technical college students. *Psychological Test and Assessment Modeling, 53,* 141–160. Retrieved from http://www.psychologie-aktuell.com/index.php?id=204

TRAINING METACOGNITIVE SKILLS IN STUDENTS WITH AVAILABILITY AND PRODUCTION DEFICIENCIES

Marcel V. J. Veenman

Metacognition is cognition about cognition (Flavell, 1979). It comprises two components: knowledge about one's cognitive system and exercising control over one's cognitive system (Brown, 1987; Schraw & Dennison, 1994). The first component, *metacognitive knowledge*, pertains to descriptive knowledge about the interplay among person characteristics, task characteristics, and strategy characteristics (Flavell, 1979). For instance, learners may know that they are having difficulties with math and, therefore, that they should practice a lot with math exercises. Having metacognitive knowledge at one's disposal, however, does not guarantee that this knowledge is actually used for the regulation of learning behavior (Veenman, Van Hout-Wolters, & Afflerbach, 2006; Winne, 1996). Metacognitive knowledge may be incorrect or incomplete (e.g., the learner may over or underestimate math difficulties), the learner may fail to see the usefulness for applying that knowledge in a particular situation (e.g., during homework), or the

Applications of Self-Regulated Learning across Diverse Disciplines, pages 299–324
Copyright © 2013 by Information Age Publishing
All rights of reproduction in any form reserved.

299

learner may lack the skills for doing so (e.g., math problem-solving skills). From a motivational viewpoint, learners may also show a lack of interest because the outcome of task performance is valued as low or even negative (Zimmerman, 2000).

The second component, *metacognitive skills*, refers to the execution of skills that are required for the control over and regulation of one's learning behavior. Orientation, goal setting, planning, monitoring, evaluation, and recapitulation are manifestations of those skills (Veenman, 2011a). Metacognitive skills directly shape learning behavior, and, consequently, they affect learning outcomes. In line with results from an extensive review study (Wang, Haertel, & Walberg, 1990), Veenman (2008) estimated that metacognitive skillfulness accounts for about 40% of variance in learning outcomes for a broad range of tasks and domains. Thus, proficient utilization of metacognitive skills is essential to learning competency.

Some researchers have equated self-regulation with metacognitive skills (Brown & DeLoache, 1978; cf. Veenman, 2007). According to self-regulated learning (SRL) theory, however, self-regulation is more broadly defined as the management of cognitive, metacognitive, motivational, and affective processes (Zimmerman, 1994). Metacognitive skillfulness, then, is constrained to the metacognitive regulation of cognitive processes. This chapter addresses the instruction and training of metacognitive skills. Metacognitive instruction not only pertains to skill acquisition, it also involves inciting learners to utilize their skills whenever appropriate. Self-regulation is a matter of skill and will (Zimmerman, Greenberg, & Weinstein, 1994). That statement signifies Zimmerman's seminal work on the role of motivation in SRL. Although the main focus of this chapter is on metacognitive skills, the motivation of learners for applying those skills cannot be ignored. First, instructional principles will be discussed. One of these principles acknowledges the role of motivation for inciting the execution of metacognitive skills. Examples of successful training programs will be presented to signify the importance of the principles. Next, a program for metacognitive instruction in mathematics will be described in detail, along with procedures for implementing such a program. This program represents the self-regulatory cycle of Zimmerman's (2000, 2008) model. Finally, it will be argued that assessment of metacognitive skills is prerequisite to successful metacognitive instruction.

GENERAL PRINCIPLES OF METACOGNITIVE INSTRUCTION AND TRAINING

There are three essential principles for effective instruction of metacognitive skills: (a) embedding instruction in the learning context, (b) informed training, and (c) prolonged training (Veenman et al., 2006). According to the first principle, *embedded instruction*, metacognitive instruction should be embedded in a specific learning context to ensure connectivity between metacognitive processes and task demands. The integration of strategy training with the instruction of content matter has been advocated in general (e.g., Glaser, 1984; Perkins & Salomon, 1989), as well as specifically for the training of metacognitive skills (Bransford, Sherwood, Vye, & Rieser, 1986; Veenman, Elshout, & Busato, 1994; Volet, 1991).

Embedded instruction enables the learner to link up conditional knowledge of *which* metacognitive skill is required *when* during task performance with the specific characteristics of the task (Veenman, 2011a). For instance, goal setting may be triggered by different task characteristics for text studying (e.g., keywords or a theme presented in the text), than for problem solving (e.g., the discrepancy between what is given and what is asked for). The learner has to recognize and appreciate the relevant conditions for applying an appropriate metacognitive skill in a given learning situation. Studies that failed to embed metacognitiveon instruction in a learning context (e.g., De Jong & Ferguson-Hessler, 1984; Stoutjesdijk & Beishuizen, 1992) invariably lacked training effects. For instance, Stoutjesdijk and Beishuizen (1992) presented a sheet with metacognitive instructions to learners prior to studying a text, without further instructions during text studying. Merely presenting metacognitive instructions in a handout prior to task performance did not result in the acquisition of metacognitive skills by the learners, nor did it result in improved text comprehension. In the same vein, study-skill lessons in schools do not make sense if they are isolated from teaching content (Zimmerman et al., 1994). Instruction of metacognitive skills should be given hands and feet in a learning context.

The second principle, *informed training* (Campione, Brown, & Ferrara, 1982), entails that learners should be informed about the usefulness and benefits of applying metacognitive skills. Learners must be motivated to initiate self-regulated learning at the onset of the task (Zimmerman, 1994). If expectancies of success are low or if the use of metacognitive skills is not appraised properly, then the learner will shy away from adopting these skills. Under those circumstances, any metacognitive instruction will fall on stony grounds. Learners, however, should also be motivated to exert the extra effort needed during the acquisition of skills (Veenman, 2011a).

When learners are not capable of spontaneously utilizing metacognitive skills, the execution of the instructed skills initially requires extra effort and occupies working-memory space. This may result in a temporary cognitive overload of working memory, especially if the task at hand is demanding. In fact, task performance may be temporarily impaired due to the effort expenditure needed for skill acquisition (Puntambekar & Stylianou, 2005). Consequently, learners may be inclined to abandon the instructed skills, unless they appreciate *why* the application of metacognitive skills eventually facilitates their performance on the task. Here self-motivation beliefs are crucial to sustained execution of trained skills. Ultimately, through the smooth application of metacognitive skills, learners should experience the positive cognitive, motivational, and behavioral consequences of their efforts, and hence develop a sense of competence and control (Zimmerman & Tsikalas, 2005). The principle of informed training has practical implications for teachers. Teachers tend to give implicit instruction rather than explicit instruction. That is, they spontaneously use examples of metacognitive activity as part of their lessons, but they often do not explain the metacognitive nature of these activities and the ultimate benefit of using the underlying skills. Veenman, De Haan, and Dignath (2009) observed the lessons of secondary-school teachers from various disciplines, and they concluded that 96% of metacognitive instruction was given implicitly and only 4% was explicit. By doing so, teachers unintentionally disregard the principle of informed instruction. With explicit instruction, teachers may focus the students' attention to how they can effectively improve their performance.

The third principle, *prolonged training*, is meant to guarantee the smooth and maintained application of metacognitive skills. As a rule, the longer the duration of the training, the better the results of training are (Dignath & Büttner, 2008). The time needed for metacognitive instruction, however, may depend on the number of skills instructed, the complexity of skills that need to be acquired, and the competency level of the individual learner (Veenman, 2011a). The training period may be relatively short for attaining mastery of a limited number of skills, for the training of rather simple and straightforward skills with concrete activities (e.g., note-taking or checking calculations), or for skills for which the learner has some metacognitive proficiency in other tasks or domains. On the other hand, the acquisition process will be quite extensive for complex skills that need to be built up from scratch, through modeling and practice of *how* to employ the skills (Anderson, 1996; Veenman, 2011a; Zimmerman, 2000). It may take the learner a year or more to establish a consistent and enduring repertoire of metacognitive skills, especially for learning-disabled students (Pressley & Gaskins, 2006).

Veenman (1998, Veenman et al., 2006) captured these three principles in the WWW&H rule (what to do, when, why, and how) for the full instruction and training of metacognitive skills. The value of attending to *what, when, why,* and *how* in metacognitive instruction has been acknowledged in the past (Borkowski, Carr, & Pressley, 1987; Brown, 1978; Schraw, 1998; Zimmerman, 1994). They serve as the landmarks of metacognitive functioning. Explicit instruction of WWW&H is crucial to the learner for making associations between situational characteristics (that is, conditions for action) and potential metacognitive actions in the initial phase of skill acquisition (Veenman, 2011a).

An additional fourth principle of metacognitive instruction pertains to the reattribution of poor self-regulatory beliefs in students with learning disabilities or students suffering from fear of failure (Veenman, 1998). This principle clearly marks the need of supportive self-motivation beliefs for the instigation of metacognitive activity, as endorsed by Zimmerman (2000, 2008). According to Borkowski, Estrada, Milstead, and Hale (1989), students with learning disabilities often believe that they cannot influence their performance on a task. They have developed a low self-efficacy and expect to fail on the task, which may result in learned helplessness. A reattribution training, in which they are taught that they *can* be in control of their performance, particularly by applying metacognitive skills, can break through this helplessness. Maladaptive attributions of performance to lack of ability should be rationalized to attributions with controllable factors, such as effort exertion, seeking help, and so on. Cognitive-behavioral training or rational-emotive training may be helpful techniques to this purpose.

Not all learners, however, are alike in their need for metacognitive instruction. Learners with poor metacognitive behavior may suffer from either an availability deficiency or a production deficiency (Veenman, Kerseboom, & Imthorn, 2000; Veenman, Kok, & Blöte, 2005). Learners with an availability deficiency do not have metacognitive skills at their disposal. For instance, they do not know how to plan their actions. In fact, they may not adequately know what planning is and when it should be deployed. Thinking aloud during task performance revealed that poor learners often equate planning with "doing something" on the spot, which misses out the utility of thinking ahead and sequencing actions (Veenman & Elshout, 1991). These learners, who are devoid of metacognitive skills, need to be instructed and trained from scratch, that is, fully according to the WWW&H rule. Learners with a production deficiency, on the other hand, have metacognitive skills at their disposal but they do not spontaneously execute the available skills for some reason (Brown & DeLoache, 1978; Flavell, 1976). For instance, they do not know when to plan or monitor their actions, they do not recognize the relevance of those skills for a particular task, or test anxiety may prevent them from doing so (Veenman et al., 2000). Apparently, these learners need not be fully trained in *how* to handle metacognitive skills, as they are capable of skillful behavior under other circumstances. A deficiency in the production of available skills means that they run short of knowledge about *when* or *why* skills should be applied in this particular learning context. Therefore, metacognitive instruction could be limited to these two components of the WWW&H rule. For instance, production-deficient learners could be provided with cues or prompts during task performance, which remind them of skill application. Merely providing cues to availability-deficient learners neither affects their metacognitive behavior, nor results in enhanced performance (Connor, 2007; Muth, 1991; Veenman et al., 2000, 2005).

EXEMPLARY TRAINING PROGRAMS

Pressley and Gaskins (2006) developed a teaching method in a special benchmark school for students with very low reading ability. Throughout the day, teachers of all school disciplines addressed the students with a broad array of metacognitive reading instructions. They incessantly explained, modeled, and prompted the use of reading-comprehension strategies, such as determining the purpose for reading, grasping the theme and main ideas of the text, making predictions about further developments in the text, relating new information to prior knowledge, monitoring understanding through self-questioning, resolving incomprehension by re-reading or by consulting additional information sources, summarizing the text, and reviewing the reading process. Instruction explicitly addressed when and how strategies are to be used. After spending four to eight years at the benchmark school, most students returned to regular education with above-average scores on a national reading test.

In a classroom program on time management (Zimmerman et al., 1994), university students were instructed for one semester to become strategic learners through goal setting, task analysis, managing plans for learning, time management, practical skills for note taking and preparing for tests, using feedback, and coping with stress and frustration. Initially, time management had been taught as a separate course, but strategy use did not appear to maintain well. In later years, the time-management course was introduced at the beginning of the semester, and further taught integrated with the semester curriculum. Students could practice and apply the skills with other courses in the semester. Embedding the time-management course in the curriculum made the grade point average at the end of the semester go up about half a point (on a four-point scale).

In a study of Azevedo, Greene, and Moos (2007), undergraduate students studied the blood circulatory system with hypermedia. Half of the students received metacognitive prompts from a human tutor during their work in the hypermedia environment. These prompts encouraged them to set learning goals, activate prior knowledge, plan time and effort, monitor comprehension and progression towards the learning goals, and apply strategies such as summarizing, hypothesizing, and drawing diagrams. The prompted group was more engaged in self-regulatory activities and showed higher gains in content knowledge from pretest to posttest, relative to the control group without prompts. Moreover, the prompted group attained a higher level of sophistication in their mental model of the circulatory system.

IMPROVE (Kramarski & Mevarech, 2003; Mevarech & Fridkin, 2006) is a training program in which learners address themselves with metacognitive questions during mathematics problem solving. These self-questions pertain to understanding the nature of the problem, activating prior knowledge, planning solution steps, and evaluating outcomes. In a study of Mevarech and Fridkin (2006), pre-college students who failed on a math entry test for university followed a 50 hours math course. The group receiving IMPROVE training enhanced their math knowledge and reasoning from pretest to posttest significantly more than the control group did. Kramarski and Mevarech (2003) further showed that IMPROVE training in a cooperative setting of small workgroups yielded better math results, relative to individualized IMPROVE training.

This is just a selection of highlights; there are more studies that report positive outcomes of metacognition training (e.g., Brown & Palincsar, 1987; Masui & de Corte, 1999; Mettes, Pilot, & Roossink, 1981; Van Luit & Kroesbergen, 2006; Veenman et al., 1994; Volet, 1991; Zohar & Ben-David, 2008; see also Dignath & Büttner, 2008, for an overview). What these studies have in common is that they promote the execution of proper metacognitive activities at the right time within the context of a given task, through informed training. In conclusion, any successful instructional program for metacognitive skills abides with the aforementioned three principles and the WWW&H rule. Next, one program for the instruction and training of metacognitive skills will be discussed in more detail.

INSTRUCTION AND TRAINING OF METACOGNITIVE SKILLS IN MATHEMATICS

During the last two decades, a group of mathematics teacher-trainers and educational psychologists in the Netherlands developed a remedial-teaching aid for math teachers in late primary and early secondary school. This resulted in a loose-leaflet publication (Duinmaijer, Van Luit, Veenman, & Vendel, 1997–2011) with a package of diagnostic and remedial instruments that is now widely used in the Netherlands. Students with math problems are first tested with diagnostic tests for subdomains in math in order to make an inventory of the specific math problems they have. Subsequently, individual process diagnosis is used for assessing the nature of math problems, that is, for mapping precisely what knowledge or skill components are either missing or incorrectly applied. Finally, a whole range of general or more math-specific remedial instruments is provided. One of the general remedial instruments pertains to the training of metacognitive skills (Veenman, 1998, 2000). A core element in this instrument is the step-by-step action plan of metacognitive activities (see Table 10.1) that learners can apply

TABLE 10.1   Step-by-step Action Plan for Metacognitive Planning

Forethought phase:

1) Thoroughly read the entire problem text

   1a) Underline important words in the problem text

   1b) Write down what is relevant in the problem text, and what is irrelevant (in a two-column diagram)

2) Try to make a drawing of the problem

3) Write down in your own words what you need to know (what is asked for)

4) Write down what you already know (what is given in the text)

5) Do you have a clue about what the outcome roughly would be?

6) Set out a plan for how you are going to solve the problem

   6a) Think of which numbers you need to solve the problem

   6b) Think of which steps you need to take to solve the problem

   6c) Think of which step to take first, and which step next

Performance phase:

7) Carry out your plan step-by-step

8) Write down everything you do, step-by-step

9) In the mean time, monitor yourself to make sure that you are still on the right track: Do you still think that you will find the right answer with your plan?

   9a) If you think so, continue with your plan

   9b) If you do not think so, think of a new plan (go back to step 6)

10) If you have found the answer, write down the answer as completely as possible

Self-reflection phase:

11) Check your calculations

   11a) Does your answer correspond to what you initially thought it should be (in step 5)? If not, check and see whether you have made a calculation mistake by recalculating the problem

   11b) Try and calculate the solution in a different way (go back to step 6)

12) Look back to the question: Did you find the answer to that question?

13) If everything tallies, then give the complete answer

14) Look back to how you solved the problem

   14a) What went well?

   14b) What went wrong and why?

Note: Adapted from Veenman, M. V. J. (2000). Materiaal voor leerlingen, algemeen: metacognitieve werkkaarten. [Materials for students, general: Metacognitive worksheets.]. In A. F. Duinmaijer, J. E. H. van Luit, M. V. J. Veenman, & P. C. M. Vendel, (Eds.), *Hulp bij leerproblemen; Rekenen-wiskunde* (pp. G0050.1-13). Zoetermeer: Betelgeuze.

while solving math problems, in particular more complex word problems. All steps of the action plan are printed on separate cards, along with a drawing depicting the intended activity.

    The composition of this action plan is based on the self-regulatory cycle of a forethought phase, a performance phase, and a self-reflection phase

(Kitsantas & Zimmerman, 2006; Zimmerman, 2000, 2008; Zimmerman & Tsikalas, 2005). Zimmerman's model is a prescriptive model of adequate self-regulatory behavior for performing learning tasks in general. According to Zimmerman, learners should prepare themselves before actually engaging in the execution of a task. In this *forethought phase*, learners should set goals and plan their strategic behavior. They also have to manage their motivational beliefs, such as their self-efficacy and interest for the task at hand. When learners enter the *performance phase*, they should exert control over their task performance through self-instruction of appropriate strategies and monitoring the execution of those strategies (cf. Veenman, 2011a), but also through volitional control of focusing attention and maintaining motivation to complete the task. Finally, in the *self-reflection phase*, learners should evaluate and reflect upon their learning outcomes, but also they should adequately attribute success or failure in a way that is effective to future performance. This process is cyclic because learners may get stuck during the performance phase, or their self-reflection may result in renewed attempts to achieve an adequate outcome. In fact, learners would then reenter the forethought phase with a new perspective on task performance (that is, reorientation; Veenman, 2011a), while orchestrating their motivation to pursue task performance. Zimmerman's distinction in cyclic phases is reminiscent of process cycles of task-analysis, execution, and evaluation in the literature on problem solving (cf. Newell & Simon, 1972; Schoenfeld, 1987). Although motivational beliefs and appraisals are intrinsically part of Zimmerman's cyclical model, the focus here is on metacognitive self-regulation.

In the forethought phase, task analysis represents the metacognitive activities of goal setting and strategic planning. Activities in the forethought phase (Steps 1 to 6 in Table 10.1) are preparatory to actual task performance (Veenman, 2011a). In Step 1, learners are urged to read and analyze the entire problem text first. Poor learners are inclined to read only bits and pieces of the problem text, which often leads to incomplete or flawed representations of the problem. Making a drawing in Step 2 may help the learner to concretize the problem. It is important to verify whether the drawing made really relates to the math problem. Especially, young children (8–11 years) may invest effort in making lovely drawings (for instance, of a smiling sun) that do not support the understanding of the problem (Van Essen & Hamaker, 1990). Steps 3 and 4 ask the learner to summarize what is given and what is asked for in the problem text, thus initiating the formation of a goal structure by contrasting the initial state with the goal state. Estimation of the outcome in Step 5 provides a (subjective) criterion for monitoring progress towards the goal and for evaluating the answer. As some children tend to exaggerate their estimates, the remedial teacher should keep an eye on whether these estimates are realistic.

Finally, Step 6 refers to the planning of problem-solving activities for attaining the goal. Planning activities consists of identifying the required actions and, subsequently, organizing the selected actions into an orderly sequence. Poor learners tend to plan only one step ahead. After execution of that step, they take on planning the next step (Elshout, Veenman, & Van Hell, 1993). With fragmented planning, the learner runs the risk of leading the problem-solving process astray. The learner may lose sight of the ultimate goal, while necessary intermediate steps, like converting units, may be omitted. Although full planning is cognitively demanding, it clears the path for the performance phase.

Self-control and self-observation (or monitoring) are metacognitive activities in the performance phase, represented by Steps 7 to 10. The main focus in this phase is on the systematic execution of a plan and the monitoring of progress towards the goal (Veenman, 2011a). Step 7 reminds learners to stick to their plan. Poor learners tend to generate a chaotic pattern of problem-solving activities, stumbling from one unsuccessful operation into the other (Elshout, 1988). When they get stuck, this chaotic pattern of activities hinders them from retracing their problem-solving steps in search for an error made. A clear path, on the other hand, allows you to reverse your steps. Writing down every step taken (Step 8) also facilitates such a clear path. During the execution of a plan, learners should ask themselves now and again whether their plan brings them closer to solving the problem (Step 9). If not, in particular when they are drifting away from their goal, learners should reorient by returning to the forethought phase. This is the first main recursive loop in the self-regulation cycle. Once an answer is obtained and the goal seems to be reached, the answer needs to be fully written down (Step 10), including quantities and units (hours or minutes, kilometers or meters). Poor learners tend to jot down a single number. A complete answer, however, provides an adequate entry to the self-reflection phase.

The self-reflection phase (Steps 11 to 14) pertains to activities of self-judgment and adaptive responses. The metacognitive function of these activities is to evaluate and interpret the outcome, and to learn from one's course of action for future occasions through reflection (Veenman, 2011a). Evaluation takes two separate shapes: establishing that the answer is mathematically correct (Step 11), and reviewing the outcome of calculations as an answer to the question in the problem statement (Step 12). A negative evaluation should result in either retracing the executed problem-solving procedure or reorientation by returning to the forethought phase. This is the second main recursion loop in the self-regulation cycle. Unfortunately, young children (under 14 years) tend to skip evaluation before delivering the answer (Van der Stel & Veenman, 2010). The children's eagerness to produce an answer is likely due to their impulsiveness and the immaturity of the pre-frontal cortex at that age (Crone, 2009). Therefore, Steps 11 and

12 force learners to make an explicit halt and to reconsider their outcomes before the full answer is given in Step 13. Metacognitively speaking, the task is not yet completed. Step 14 prompts learners to recapitulate the way they solved the problem and to reflect on errors made. Again, these reflection activities rarely occur spontaneously in the problem-solving behavior of young children (Van der Stel & Veenman, 2010). The payback of investing effort into reflection is a clear memory trace of procedures for solving similar problems in the future, which may prevent the learner from making the same mistakes over and over again.

Though this action plan is especially designed for problem solving in mathematics, it could be easily adapted to problem solving in other science domains, such as physics (cf. Elshout et al., 1993; Mettes et al., 1981). Moreover, a similar action plan could be devised for text studying. Many metacognitive skills are overlapping for problem solving and text studying, although the practical implementation of steps may differ for both types of tasks (Van der Stel & Veenman, 2010). In the Appendix, a specimen of an action plan for text studying is given, based on the detailed analysis of text studying processes by Pressley and Afflerbach (1995). It should be noted that Pressley and Afflerbach discern some 150 different activities that are relevant to constructive reading. The number of steps included in an action plan for the metacognitive instruction, however, should be limited for practical reasons.

The self-regulatory process is cyclic because the feedback from self-observations (monitoring) and self-judgments (evaluation) may lead to renewed orientation in the forethought phase (Cleary & Zimmerman, 2001). When the problem-solving process runs ashore, these feedback loops offer the learner a way out, rather than ending up with a "sudden death" of the problem-solving process, with no answer to the problem, and with dissatisfaction. In order to regenerate the motivation for making yet another attempt, however, the learner should learn to deal with the frustration of getting stuck in a functional way (Zimmerman, 2000). Through experiencing that repeated cycles of self-regulation might yield a positive outcome, the learner can protect feelings of self-efficacy from harmful effects of initial failure. This is relevant to students with learning disabilities in particular because they are inclined to give up due to low self-efficacy and low outcome expectancies (Zimmerman, 2000).

IMPLEMENTATION OF THE METACOGNITIVE ACTION PLAN

The action plan in Table 10.1 describes *what* metacognitive activities to do *when* while solving math problems. There is a normative element present in the prescribed path from forethought through performance to self-reflection. One obviously needs to set a goal before one can even think of evaluating the attainment of that goal. In fact, metacognitive activities are interdependent. Good orientation, goal setting, and planning in the forethought phase leads to more self-control and better monitoring in the performance phase, which in turn improves the conditions for evaluation and reflection in the self-reflection phase (Veenman, Elshout, & Meijer, 1997; Veenman et al., 2005; Veenman & Spaans, 2005). The action plan as such, however, does not provide information about *how* to execute metacognitive skills: how to distinguish relevant from irrelevant information, how to design a plan (though sub-steps 6a to 6c are helpful), how to monitor progression towards the goal, how to check calculations, how to reflect on the problem-solving process. Neither does the action plan explain to the learner *why* it is relevant to pursue these activities.

Simply presenting a flowchart on the classroom wall or providing a stack of cards depicting the metacognitive action plan will not suffice for learners with an availability deficiency. These learners need to be fully instructed and trained to use the action plan through modeling and scaffolding (Brown & Palincsar, 1987; Kramarski & Mevarech, 2003; Veenman, 1998, 2011a). During metacognitive modeling, the remedial teacher first demonstrates the metacognitive steps from the action plan cards, while explaining each step to the learner according to the WWW&H rule. In this initial phase of skill acquisition, some intangible steps need to be concretized and made applicable to the learner. For instance, learners are told that planning means to subdivide a complex problem into smaller parts, which need to be tackled one by one in a specific order. Next, the learner starts to enact the steps, while being guided by verbal support of the teacher. For example, the teacher can scaffold the learner's actions for Step 14a and 14b with the following questions: Was your drawing correct? Was your plan correct? What calculation errors did you make? Can you calculate your answer in a more efficient way? With further practice the learner should become a more independent actor and scaffolding is slowly faded out. First the teacher refrains from providing verbal support, unless necessary. Next, the learner tries to apply the steps without the cards, although the stack of cards remains available for consultation. Finally, the learner should be able to apply the steps smoothly without external aid. In fact, this modeling and scaffolding procedure follows Zimmerman's socio-cognitive model of skill acquisition (Zimmerman, 2000). At the observation level, the learner first induces the major features of the skill by watching the model (i.e., the remedial teacher) executing skillful behavior. Next, at the emulation level, the learner starts to enact the skill by imitating the model, while being corrected by the remedial teacher. Through further practice, the learner reaches the self-controlled level where the skill is independently enacted without the model. Finally, at the self-regulated level, the learner can apply the skill in a flexible way, adapted to situational requirements. From the observational level to the self-regulated level, scaffolding by the model (and the cards) is slowly faded out.

It is obvious that this entire modeling and scaffolding procedure requires a substantial time investment from the remedial teacher. For learners with severe math limitations, this long-term investment pays off (Van Luit & Kroesbergen, 2006). Math learning-disabled students often are deficient in a broad array of metacognitive skills, and one cannot expect to remediate these deficiencies without time and effort. Other learners with math problems, however, may be deficient in more specific areas. Take, for instance, a learner who primarily has problems with planning activities. Even if only planning is poor, then the entire problem-solving process is likely to derail. In that case, not all steps of the action plan need to be trained; modeling and scaffolding should focus on planning steps first. On the one hand, such a limited remedial training requires less investment of time and effort from the teacher. On the other hand, it will demand more diagnostic skills of the remedial teacher. In the assessment of specific metacognitive deficiencies, the teacher should be competent in distinguishing major from subsidiary problems. Moreover, once poor planning is remediated, the teacher needs to verify whether the learner is capable of proficiently executing the other metacognitive skills. Either a deficiency that was masked by the massive planning problems will now come to light (and needs to be further addressed), or remediation of planning problems may have resolved related deficiencies. We will return to the assessment issue later.

Learners with a production deficiency know the *what*, *when*, *why*, and *how* of metacognitive skills under normal circumstances. There are task situations, however, in which they do not produce the available skills. The complexity of the task at hand may overwhelm them and they cannot see the forest for the trees. Or test anxiety may evoke worrying thoughts that block the execution of skills in working memory (Veenman et al., 2000). As said, they have to be reminded when to apply skills and why to do so by cueing or prompting the use of metacognitive skills. Extensive modeling and scaffolding of how to perform the skills is not needed, which means that substantially less investment of time and effort is demanded from the remedial teacher. What do we know about the effects of cueing?

In two studies the effect of metacognitive cueing was investigated. Veenman et al. (2005) asked 41 secondary-school students (12 to 13 years old) to solve two series of three mathematical word problems. Problems of the first series were solved without further instruction (non-cued). During the second series (cued), participants were provided with six metacognitive cues on cards (representing Steps 3, 4, 6, 9, 11, and a combined Step 12 & 13). Participants were told to use these cues when solving the second series of problems, but they were not instructed how to do so. Thus, the cues merely served as a reminder for applying metacognitive skills. Thinking aloud and systematical observation were used to assess the metacognitive activities of participants. Cueing significantly improved the level of metacognitive activity, as well as performance on the math problems. Closer inspection of the metacognition data revealed that metacognition not only improved on cued activities, but also on activities (e.g., Steps 5 and 14) that were *not* addressed by the six cues.

Using the same method, Veenman et al. (2000) asked 20 high test-anxious and 10 low-anxious secondary-school students (12 to 13 years old) to solve the two series of math problems with/without cueing. Overall, low-anxious participants displayed a higher level of metacognitive activity and math performance than test-anxious participants did. There was also a positive main effect of cueing on metacognitive activity and math performance for both groups. Low-anxious participants, however, profited more from cueing than test-anxious participants did. Closer inspection of the metacognition data for test-anxious participants revealed that 60% improved due to cueing, whereas 40% did not improve or even got worse. The latter group without positive cueing effect was assumed to suffer from an availability deficiency. In conclusion, cueing without further instruction or training may alleviate production deficiencies, but it may be even detrimental to students with an availability deficiency.

ASSESSMENT OF METACOGNITIVE SKILLS

Before exposing learners to metacognitive instruction, one needs to ascertain that they indeed suffer from metacognitive deficiencies. Other factors, such as lack of domain-specific knowledge and skills, need to be excluded as the main cause of poor task performance. Moreover, one needs to diagnose precisely which metacognitive skills are flawed or missing. For the assessment of metacognitive skills, often self-report instruments (in particular questionnaires, such as the MSLQ; Pintrich & De Groot, 1990) are used because they are easy to administer either prior or retrospective to task performance. Self-report instruments, however, may suffer from validity problems (see Veenman, 2011a, 2011b, for a full discussion). In a nutshell, self-reports need to be reconstructed from memory by the learner and, consequently, these self-reports could be subject to memory failure, distortion, and interpretive reconstruction. In a review study, Veenman (2005) has shown that self-reports of metacognitive strategy use hardly correspond to actual metacognitive behavior in a task situation. People simply do not actually do what they have reported beforehand, and they fail to adequately report afterwards what they have done. Moreover, questionnaires may not supply sufficiently detailed information about flawed or missing skills for diagnostic purposes.

Perhaps questionnaires reflect the learner's state of metacognitive knowledge about the cognitive system, but they may not represent the learner's actual metacognitive regulatory behavior (Veenman, 2011a, 2011b).

Zimmerman and Martinez-Pons (1986, 1988) have developed an interview instrument called the self-regulated learning interview schedule (SRLIS) as an alternative to questionnaire measures. They ask students to describe their use of self-regulated learning strategies in six hypothetical learning contexts that are realistic in nature (i.e., classroom situation, studying at home, writing assignment, math assignment, preparing for and taking a test, and completing homework when poorly motivated). Spontaneous self-reports of students are scored on 14 categories of self-regulated learning strategies, and these SRLIS scores have been validated against teacher ratings ($r = .70$). The advantage of SRLIS over questionnaires is that the information gathered is far more detailed and not narrowed down to fixed items. Duinmaijer et al. (1997–2011) adopt a similar approach for the diagnosis of metacognitive deficiencies in math problem solving, albeit with real math problems. From the results of a math test, the remedial teacher selects an item that is problematic to the learner. Immediately after a new attempt to solve the math problem, the learner is asked to report how the problem was tackled. If necessary, the learner is addressed with additional questions to clarify the WWW&H of reported activities. Thus, an inventory of reported metacognitive activities is made up, from which the learner's missing activities can be inferred. Though interview techniques are practical diagnostic instruments for remedial teachers, one should be aware of the limitations (Veenman, 2003). Interviews are retrospective self-reports, which makes them vulnerable to the memory-reconstruction problems described earlier. Moreover, asking questions may provoke social-desirable answers, or even prompt the report of activities that actually never occurred (Veenman, 2011b). In general, the more concrete and elaborated reports are, the more reliable they are. These issues have to be verified during further stages of remedial teaching. In case of doubts about the self-reports, the remedial teacher can also resort to on-line observations.

On-line measurements, obtained from observations or thinking aloud, allow for a valid and detailed description of metacognitive skills that are actually employed during task performance (Veenman, 2011a, 2011b). The learner is asked to perform a problematic task while thinking aloud, that is, while verbalizing ongoing thoughts without giving interpretations. The session is either recorded on tape and analyzed afterwards, or concurrently scored by the remedial teacher according to a codebook. For instance, the action plan in Table 10.1 can also be used as codebook for scoring metacognitive skills in math (Veenman et al., 2000, 2005). A zero is given for each step that is absent or incorrectly done, one point is awarded to each step that is partly executed but not completed, and two points are given for each complete and correct step. As some steps need to precede others, the remedial teacher also has to take into account whether steps are performed in the right order and at the right time (respecting the cyclic nature of self-regulation). This scoring procedure maps precisely which metacognitive skills the learner can produce spontaneously, and which skills are (partly) missing. Next, a similar task is given to the learner, while the remedial teacher cues the missing or incomplete steps. The metacognition scoring on this second task distinguishes availability versus production deficiencies in the learner for the cued steps. Obviously, this diagnostic procedure is time-consuming and labor-intensive, but the outcome provides a clear point of departure for further remedial teaching.

ASSESSMENT AFTER METACOGNITIVE INSTRUCTION AND TRAINING

After remedial instruction and training, effectiveness of the intervention is often only evaluated by improved task performance. Many studies fail to report the effects of metacognitive instruction on the actual metacognitive behavior (Veenman, 2007). In order to account for instructional effectiveness, a causal chain of instruction leading to improved metacognitive behavior and, thus, leading to enhanced learning outcomes should be established. When the mediating metacognitive behavior is not assessed, instructional effects on learning outcomes could equally be attributed to various confounding variables, such as extended time-on-task due to compliance with the instructions or enhanced motivation due to extra attention. Thus, to ensure that lasting effects are attained, it is imperative that the learner's metacognitive skills are re-assessed after instruction and training.

DIRECTIONS FOR FUTURE RESEARCH

In remedial teaching, instruction and training is often given on a one-to-one individual basis. For learners with severe metacognitive deficiencies, an individual approach is required to address their specific difficulties, not only because their lack of metacognitive skills often goes hand-in-hand with other task- or domain-specific learning problems, but also to repair idiosyncratic errors during the acquisition of metacognitive skills (Veenman, 1998). Teachers in the study of Pressley and Gaskins (2006) are successful, partly because they adapt the metacognitive instruction to the specific needs of individual students.

For learners with milder metacognitive deficiencies, collaborative learning in small groups may be an appropriate alternative to individualized training. In the successful program of reciprocal teaching (Brown & Palincsar, 1987), students collaboratively study a text in a small group, while the teacher models and scaffolds the use of metacognitive skills. Group discussions with students as alternate chairs appear to be instrumental to skill acquisition and learning performance. In the same vein, Molenaar, Van Boxtel, and Sleegers (2010) show that small groups of elementary-school students, who collaboratively write an essay with metacognitive scaffolds, exhibit more metacognitive activities during group discussions relative to groups without scaffolding. In general, metacognitive instruction in a collaborative-learning setting yields better results than either direct metacognitive instruction only, or collaborative learning only (Brown & Palincsar, 1987; Kramarski & Mevarech, 2003; Manlove, Lazonder, & De Jong, 2007). The surplus value of providing metacognitive instruction during collaborative learning is that learners actively discuss the application of metacognitive skills while performing the task. Not much is known, however, about the effects of metacognitive instruction in a collaborative setting for students with severe metacognitive deficiencies.

With the introduction of computers in education, computer-based learning environments (CBLEs) have also been used for the assessment of metacognitive deficiencies and for metacognitive instruction (Veenman, 2007; Winters, Greene, & Costich, 2008). Recently, Zimmerman (2008; cf. Bembenutty, 2008) drew attention to the potential of diagnosing self-regulation activities with on-line registration in computer logfiles. During task performance in a CBLE, all activities of the learner are traced and logged as events in a back-up file (Winne, 2010; Veenman, Wilhelm, & Beishuizen, 2004). Obviously, the task should lend itself to a computerized version, or otherwise the ecological validity of assessments would be compromised. Tracing events, however, is restricted to the learner's concrete, overt behavior without metacognitive deliberations. In fact, the metacognitive nature of learner activities has to be inferred by the researcher (Veenman, in press). That is not an easy ride. A selection of relevant metacognitive activities has to be made through a rational analysis of the computerized task, and this selection has to be subsequently validated against other on-line measures (e.g., observations or thinking aloud). The advantage of logfile registration, however, is that assessment is minimally intrusive to the learner, and that it can be administered to large groups at the same time (Veenman et al., 2006).

CBLEs are particularly useful for presenting metacognitive cues or prompts to learners with a production deficiency (Veenman et al., 1994). By tracing the activities of learners in the CBLE, cues or prompts can be appropriated to the phase of task performance. For instance, cues for goal setting or planning are given at the onset of the task, monitoring cues are repeatedly presented during task performance, and evaluation cues are offered upon task completion. Merely cueing or prompting with CBLEs, however, is not always successful (cf. Winters et al., 2008), presumably because learners with an availability deficiency need additional modeling and scaffolding. To that purpose, many CBLEs provide a fixed array of metacognitive scaffolds based on step-by-step action plans (e.g., Elshout et al., 1993; Kapa, 2001; Kramarski & Hirsch, 2003; Manlove et al., 2007; Teong, 2003). Though these programs reveal positive overall effects of scaffolding, not all learners profit equally. Especially metacognitive deficient learners are less capable of taking advantage of fixed scaffolding without further help (Elshout et al., 1993). They may not see the relevance of metacognitive activities (i.e., the *why*) and simply skip them. They may not notice the relation between task characteristics and actions (i.e., the relation between *when* and *what*), which is embedded in scaffolds. The learning paradox (Bereiter, 1985) here is that learners need to have a certain level of metacognitive skillfulness in order to profit from metacognitive scaffolds. Fixed scaffolds cannot resolve this learning paradox for metacognitive deficient learners. Hence, human tutors are used to provide additional instruction and support in a CBLE (Azevedo et al., 2007). Scarcely out of the egg are attempts of adapting metacognitive scaffolds to the learner's needs through an intelligent tutoring system, so far with mixed results (Puntambekar & Stylianou, 2005; Roll, Aleven, McLaren, & Koedinger, 2007; Winters et al., 2008).

CONCLUSION

The learner who goes cautiously, goes safely and goes far. Thus, metacognitive instruction is meant to motivate learners to think and look before they leap, to keep on thinking while they are acting, and to look back and re-think afterwards. And, it is meant to make them do so in a progressive cyclic way. This adage should be appealing to Zimmerman, who studied self-regulation not only in academic learning situations, but also in sports (Cleary & Zimmerman, 2001; Kitsantas & Zimmerman, 2006). One may get people to act more thoughtfully when you provide them with the necessary metacognitive skills, as well as with the incentives for utilizing those skills.

Before initiating instruction and training, the scope and nature of the learner's metacognitive deficiencies should be assessed. With interview and thinking-aloud techniques, information is gathered about which metacognitive skills are deficient or not, but also about whether deficient skills are available but not produced, or not available at all. Establishing the latter has consequences for the instruction and training of metacognitive skills. An availability deficiency needs to be remediated through full-blown modeling and scaffolding of metacognitive activities in the self-regulatory cycle of Zimmerman, according to the WWW&H rule. Learners with a production deficiency, on the other hand, merely need to be reminded of *when* and *why* to utilize their metacognitive skills. Informed cueing or prompting metacognitive skills during task performance may suffice to undo their production deficiency. In addition to evaluating learning performance, metacognitive skillfulness should be re-assessed after metacognitive instruction in order to verify the nature of training effects. If metacognitive instruction works out well, learners may be incited to tread where they have not gone before.

APPENDIX
**Step-by-step Action Plan for Metacognitive Training
in Text Studying**

1. Thoroughly read the entire assignment to set your reading goal:
   a. To what purpose are you going to read the text?
   b. After reading, are you expected to answer multiple-choice or open-ended questions on a test, to give a presentation, or to write a paper?
2. Read the title and scan all paragraph headings in the text
3. Write down in your own words what the main topic of the text is
4. Write down what you already know about the topic (prior knowledge)
5. Do you have a clue about what conclusion the text is heading for?
6. Set out a plan for how you are going to read the text:
   a. Think of which parts of the text you are going to read and in what order
   b. Think of which parts of the text you are going to pay extra attention to
   c. Think of which parts of the text you are going to ignore because they are not relevant to your reading goal
7. Start reading, while carrying out your plan
8. Make notes by paraphrasing main ideas of the text:
   a. Explicitly, look for relations between ideas
   b. Look for consistencies/inconsistencies between ideas
9. In the mean time, monitor your comprehension of the text:
   a. If you do not understand the meaning of a word, consult a dictionary or infer the word meaning from its context
   b. If you do not understand the meaning of a paragraph, re-read the paragraph, read back to find previous information, or read on to find additional information
   c. Check if your overall comprehension of the text is in line with your reading goal and reading plan (if not, go back to step 1 or step 6)
10. Try to integrate main ideas into a cohesive summary of the text
11. Evaluate your summary:
    a. Does your summary correspond to what you initially thought the conclusion should be (in step 5)? If not, check and see what the discrepancy is between the two
    b. Formulate your own questions about the text to test your comprehension

12. Look back to the assignment: Did you attain your reading goal?
13. If everything tallies, then memorize your summary.
14. Look back to how you have studied the text:
    a. What went well?
    b. What went wrong and why?

REFERENCES

Anderson, J. R. (1996). *The architecture of cognition*. Mahwah, NJ: Erlbaum.

Azevedo, R., Greene, J. A., & Moos, D. C. (2007). The effect of a human agent's external regulation upon college students' hypermedia learning. *Metacognition and Learning, 2*, 67–87. doi:10.1007/s11409-007-9014-9

Bembenutty, H. (2008). The last word. An interview with Barry J. Zimmerman: Achieving self-fulfilling cycles of academic self-regulation. *Journal of Advanced Academics, 20*, 174–193.

Bereiter, C. (1985). Toward a solution of the learning paradox. *Review of Educational Research, 55*, 201–226. doi:10.3102/00346543055002201

Borkowski, J. G., Carr, M., & Pressley, M. (1987). "Spontaneous" strategy use: Perspectives from metacognitive theory. *Intelligence, 11*, 61–75.

Borkowski, J. G., Estrada, M. T., Milstead, M., & Hale, C. A. (1989). General problem-solving skills: Relations between metacognition and strategic processing. *Learning Disability Quarterly, 12(4)*, 57–70. doi:10.2307/1510252

Bransford, J., Sherwood, R., Vye, N., & Rieser, J. (1986). Teaching thinking and problem solving. *American Psychologist, 41*, 1078–1089.

Brown, A. L. (1978). Knowing when, where, and how to remember: A problem of metacognition. In R. Glaser (Ed.), *Advances in instructional psychology* (Vol. I, pp. 77–165). Hillsdale, NJ: Erlbaum.

Brown, A. (1987). Metacognition, Executive control, self-regulation, and other more mysterious mechanisms. In F. E. Weinert & R. H. Kluwe (Eds.), *Metacognition, Motivation and Understanding* (pp. 65–116). Hillsdale, NJ: Erlbaum.

Brown, A. L. & DeLoache, J. S. (1978). Skills, plans, and self-regulation. In R. S. Siegel (Ed.), *Children's thinking: What develops?* (pp. 3–35). Hillsdale, NJ: Erlbaum.

Brown, A. L. & Palincsar, A. S. (1987). Reciprocal teaching of comprehension skills: a natural history of one program for enhancing learning. In J. D. Day & J. G. Borkowski (Eds.), *Intelligence and exceptionality: New directions for theory, assessment, and instructional practices* (pp. 81–131). Norwood, NJ: Ablex.

Campione, J. C., Brown, A. L., & Ferrara, R. A. (1982). Mental retardation and intelligence. In R. J. Sternberg (Ed.), *Handbook of human intelligence* (pp. 392–490). Cambridge: Cambridge University Press.

Cleary, T. J. & Zimmerman, B. J. (2001). Self-regulation differences during athletic practice by experts, non-experts, and novices. *Journal of Applied Sport Psychology, 13*, 185–206. doi:10.1080/104132001753149883

Connor, L. N. (2007). Cueing metacognition to improve researching and essay writing in a final year high school biology class. *Research in Science Education, 37*, 1–16.

Crone, E. A. (2009). Executive functions in adolescence: Inference from brain and behavior. *Developmental Science, 12*, 1–6. doi:10.1111/j.1467-7687.2009.00918.x

De Jong, T. & Ferguson-Hessler, M. G. M. (1984). Strategiegebruik bij het oplossen van problemen in een semantisch rijk domein: electriciteit en magnetisme. [The use of strategy in solving problems in a semantically rich domain: Electricity and magnetism]. *Tijdschrift voor Onderwijsresearch, 9*, 3–15.

Dignath, C. & Büttner, G. (2008). Components of fostering self-regulated learning among students. A meta-analysis on intervention studies at primary and secondary school level. *Metacognition and Learning, 3*, 231–264. doi:10.1007/s11409-008-9029-x

Duinmaijer, A. F., Van Luit, J. E. H., Veenman, M. V. J., & Vendel, P. C. M. (1997–2011). *Hulp bij leerproblemen; Rekenen-wiskunde [Help with learning disabilities; Mathematics].* Zoetermeer: Betelgeuze.

Elshout, J. J. (1988). Intelligentie en goed beginnen. [Intelligence and good novice behavior.] In G. Kanselaar, J. L. Van Der Linden, & A. Pennings (Eds.), *Begaafdheid. Onderkenning en beïnvloeding* (pp. 46–54). Amersfoort: Acco.

Elshout, J. J., Veenman, M. V. J., & van Hell, J. G. (1993). Using the computer as help tool during learning by doing. *Computers & Education, 21*, 115–122. doi:10.1016/0360-1315(93)90054-M

Flavell, J. H. (1976). Metacognitive aspects of problem solving. In L. B. Resnick (Ed.), *The nature of intelligence* (pp. 231–235). Hillsdale, NJ: Erlbaum.

Flavell, J. H. (1979). Metacognition and cognitive monitoring: A new area of cognitive-developmental inquiry. *American Psychologist, 34*, 906–911.

Glaser, R. (1984). Education and thinking. The role of knowledge. *American Psychologist, 39*, 93–104. doi:10.1111/j.1745-3992.1994.tb00561.x

Kapa, E. (2001). A metacognitive support during the process of problem solving in a computerized environment. *Educational Studies in Mathematics, 47*, 317–336.

Kitsantas, A. & Zimmerman, B. J. (2006). Enhancing self-regulation of practice: The influence of graphing and self-evaluative standards. *Metacognition and Learning, 1*, 201–212. doi:10.1007/s11409-006-9000-7

Kramarski, B. & Hirsch, C. (2003). Using computer algebra systems in mathematical classrooms. *Journal of Computer Assisted Learning, 19*, 35–45. doi:10.1046/j.0266-4909.2003.00004.x

Kramarski, B. & Mevarech, Z. R. (2003). Enhancing mathematical reasoning in the classroom: The effects of cooperative learning and metacognitive training. *American Educational Research Journal, 40*, 281–310. doi:10.3102/00028312040001281

Manlove, S., Lazonder, A. W., & De Jong, T. (2007). Software scaffolds to promote regulation during scientific inquiry learning. *Metacognition and Learning, 2*, 141–155. doi:10.1007/s11409-007-9012-y

Masui, C. & de Corte, E. (1999). Enhancing learning and problem solving skills: Orienting and self-judging, two powerful and trainable learning tools. *Learning and Instruction, 9*, 517–542. doi:2048/10.1016/S0959-4752(99)00012-2

Mettes, C. T. C. W., Pilot, A., & Roossink, H. J. (1981). Linking factual and procedural knowledge in solving science problems: a case study in a thermodynamics course. *Instructional Science, 10*, 333–361.

Mevarech, Z. & Fridkin, S. (2006). The effects of IMPROVE on mathematical knowledge, mathematical reasoning and meta-cognition. *Metacognition and Learning, 1*, 85–97. doi:10.1007/s11409-006-6584-x

Molenaar, I., Van Boxtel, C. A. M., & Sleegers, P. J. C. (2010). The effects of scaffolding metacognitive activities in small groups. *Computers in Human Behavior, 26*, 1727–1738. doi:10.1016/j.chb.2010.06.022

Muth, K. D. (1991). Effects of cuing on middle-school students' performance on arithmetic word problems containing extraneous information. *Journal of Educational Psychology, 83*, 173–174.

Newell, A. & Simon, H. A. (1972). *Human problem solving*. Englewood Cliffs, NJ: Prentice-Hall.

Perkins, D. N. & Salomon, G. (1989). Are cognitive skills context-bound? *Educational Researcher, 18(1)*, 16–25. doi:10.2307/1176006

Pintrich, P. R. & De Groot, E. V. (1990). Motivational and self-regulated leaning components of classroom academic performance. *Journal of Educational Psychology, 82*, 33–40. doi:10.1037/0022-0663.82.1.33

Pressley, M. & Afflerbach, P. (1995). *Verbal protocols of reading: The nature of constructively responsive reading*. Hillsdale, NJ: Erlbaum.

Pressley, M. & Gaskins, I. (2006). Metacognitive competent reading is constructively responsive reading: How can such reading be developed in students? *Metacognition and Learning, 1*, 99–113. doi:10.1007/s11409-006-7263-7

Puntambekar, S. & Stylianou, A. (2005). Designing navigation support in hypertext systems based on navigation patterns. *Instructional Science, 33*, 451–481.

Roll, I., Aleven, V., McLaren, B. M., & Koedinger, K. R. (2007). Designing for metacognition – applying cognitive tutor principles to the tutoring of help seeking. *Metacognition and Learning, 2*, 125–140. doi:10.1007/s11409-007-9010-0

Schoenfeld, A. H. (1987). *Cognitive science and mathematics education*. Hillsdale, NJ: Erlbaum.

Schraw, G. (1998). Promoting general metacognitive awareness. *Instructional Science, 26*, 113–125.

Schraw, G. & Dennison, R. S. (1994). Assessing metacognitive awareness. *Contemporary Educational Psychology, 19*, 460–475. doi:10.1006/ceps.1994.1033

Stoutjesdijk, E. & Beishuizen, J. J. (1992). Cognitie en metacognitie bij het bestuderen van informatieve tekst. [Cognition and metacognition during the study of informative texts.] *Tijdschrift voor Onderwijsresearch, 17*, 313–326.

Teong, S. K. (2003). The effects of mathematical training on mathematical word-problem solving. *Journal of Computer Assisted Learning, 19*, 46–55.

Van der Stel, M. & Veenman, M. V. J. (2010). Development of metacognitive skillfulness: A longitudinal study. *Learning and Individual Differences, 20*, 220–224. doi:10.1016/j.lindif.2009.11.005

Van Essen, G. & Hamaker, C. (1990). Using self-generated drawings to solve arithmetic word problems. *Journal of Educational Research, 83*, 301–312.

Van Luit, J. E. H. & Kroesbergen, E. H. (2006). Teaching metacognitive skills to students with mathematical disabilities. In A. Desoete & M. V. J. Veenman (Eds.), *Metacognition in mathematics education* (pp. 177–190). New York, NY: Nova Science Publishing.

Veenman, M. V. J. (1998). Kennis en vaardigheden; Soorten kennis een vaardigheden die relevant zijn voor reken-wiskunde taken. [Knowledge and skills that are relevant to math tasks]. In A. F. Duinmaijer, J. E. H. van Luit, M. V. J. Veenman, & P. C. M. Vendel, (Eds.), *Hulp bij leerproblemen; Rekenen-wiskunde* (pp. G0501.1–6). Zoetermeer: Betelgeuze.

Veenman, M. V. J. (2000). Materiaal voor leerlingen, algemeen: metacognitieve werkkaarten. [Materials for students, general: Metacognitive worksheets.]. In A. F. Duinmaijer, J. E. H. van Luit, M. V. J. Veenman, & P. C. M. Vendel, (Eds.), *Hulp bij leerproblemen; Rekenen-wiskunde* (pp. G0050.1–13). Zoetermeer: Betelgeuze.

Veenman, M. V. J. (2003). Problemen bij bevraging van metacognitieve activiteiten. [Problems with inquiry after metacognitive activities.] In A. F. Duinmaijer, J. E. H. van Luit, M. V. J. Veenman, & P. C. M. Vendel (Red.), *Hulp bij leerproblemen: Rekenen-wiskunde* (pp. G0051.1–5). Zoetermeer: Betelgeuze.

Veenman, M. V. J. (2005). The assessment of metacognitive skills: What can be learned from multi-method designs? In C. Artelt & B. Moschner (Eds), *Lernstrategien und Metakognition: Implikationen für Forschung und Praxis* (pp. 75–97). Berlin: Waxmann.

Veenman, M. V. J. (2007). The assessment and instruction of self-regulation in computer-based environments: A discussion. *Metacognition and Learning, 2*, 177–183. doi:10.1007/s11409-007-9017-6

Veenman, M. V. J. (2008). Giftedness: Predicting the speed of expertise acquisition by intellectual ability and metacognitive skillfulness of novices. In M. F. Shaughnessy, M. V. J. Veenman, & C. Kleyn-Kennedy (Eds.), *Meta-cognition: A recent review of research, theory, and perspectives* (pp. 207–220). Hauppage, NY: Nova Science Publishers.

Veenman, M. V. J. (2011a). Learning to self-monitor and self-regulate. In R. Mayer & P. Alexander (Eds.), *Handbook of research on learning and instruction* (pp. 197–218). New York, NY: Routledge.

Veenman, M. V. J. (2011b). Alternative assessment of strategy use with self-report instruments: A discussion. *Metacognition and Learning, 6*, 205–211. doi:10.1007/s11409-011-9080-x

Veenman, M. V. J. (in press). Assessing metacognitive skills in computerized learning environments. In R. Azevedo & V. Aleven (Eds.), *International handbook of metacognition and learning technologies.* New York/Berlin: Springer.

Veenman, M. V. J., De Haan, N., & Dignath, C. (2009). *An observation scale for assessing teachers' implicit and explicit use of metacognition in classroom settings.* Paper presented at the 13th Biennial Conference for Research on Learning and Instruction, EARLI, Amsterdam.

Veenman, M. V. J. & Elshout, J. J. (1991). Intellectual ability and working method as predictors of novice learning. *Learning and Instruction, 1*, 303–317.

Veenman, M. V. J., Elshout, J. J., & Busato, V. V. (1994). Metacognitive mediation in learning with computer-based simulations. *Computers in Human Behavior, 10*, 93–106.

Veenman, M. V. J., Elshout, J. J., & Meijer, J. (1997). The generality vs. domain-specificity of metacognitive skills in novice learning across domains. *Learning and Instruction, 7*, 187–209.

Veenman, M. V. J., Kerseboom, L, & Imthorn, C (2000). Test anxiety and metacognitive skillfulness: Availability versus production deficiencies. *Anxiety, Stress, and Coping, 13,* 391–412.

Veenman, M. V. J., Kok, R., & Blöte, A. W. (2005). The relation between intellectual and metacognitive skills at the onset of metacognitive skill development. *Instructional Science, 33,* 193–211.

Veenman, M. V. J. & Spaans, M. A. (2005). Relation between intellectual and metacognitive skills: Age and task differences. *Learning and Individual Differences, 15,* 159–176. doi:10.1016/j.lindif.2004.12.001

Veenman, M. V. J., Van Hout-Wolters, B. H. A. M., & Afflerbach, P. (2006). Metacognition and Learning: Conceptual and methodological considerations. *Metacognition and Learning, 1,* 3–14. doi:10.1007/s11409-006-6893-0

Veenman, M. V. J., Wilhelm, P., & Beishuizen, J. J. (2004). The relation between intellectual and metacognitive skills from a developmental perspective. *Learning and Instruction, 14,* 89–109. doi:10.1016/j.learninstruc.2003.10.004

Volet, S. E. (1991). Modeling and coaching of relevant metacognitive strategies for enhancing university students' learning. *Learning and Instruction, 1,* 319–336.

Wang, M. C., Haertel, G. D., & Walberg, H. J. (1990). What influences learning? A content analysis of review literature. *Journal of Educational Research, 84,* 30–43.

Winne, P. H. (1996). A metacognitive view of individual differences in self-regulated learning. *Learning and Individual Differences, 8,* 327–353.

Winne, P. H. (2010). Improving measurements of self-regulated learning. *Educational Psychologist, 45,* 267–276. doi:10.1080/00461520.2010.517150

Winters, F. I., Greene, J. A., & Costich, C. M. (2008). Self-regulation of learning with computer-based learning environments: A critical analysis. *Educational Psychology Review, 20,* 429–444. doi:10.1007/s10648-008-9080-9

Zimmerman, B. J. (1994). Dimensions of academic self-regulation: A conceptual framework for education. In D. H. Schunk & B. J. Zimmerman (Eds.), *Self-regulation of learning and performance. Issues and educational implications* (pp. 3–21). Hillsdale, NJ: Erlbaum.

Zimmerman, B. J. (2000). Attainment of self-regulation: A social cognitive perspective. In M. Boekaerts, P. Pintrich, & M. Zeidner (Eds.), *Handbook of self-regulation, research, and applications* (pp. 13–39). Orlando, FL: Academic Press.

Zimmerman, B. J. (2008). Investigating self-regulation and motivation: Historical background, methodological developments, and future perspectives. *American Educational Research Journal, 45,* 166–183. doi:10.3102/0002831207312909

Zimmerman, B. J., Greenberg, D., & Weinstein, C. E. (1994). Self-regulating academic study time: A strategic approach. In D. H. Schunk & B. J. Zimmerman (Eds.), *Self-regulation of learning and performance. Issues and educational implications* (pp. 181–199). Hillsdale, NJ: Erlbaum.

Zimmerman, B. J. & Martinez-Pons, M. (1986). Development of a structured interview for assessing students' use of self-regulated learning strategies. *American Educational Research Journal, 23*(4), 614–628. doi:10.3102/00028312023004614

Zimmerman, B. J. & Martinez-Pons, M. (1988). Construct validation of a strategy model of student self-regulated learning. *Journal of Educational Psychology, 80*(3), 284–290. doi:10.1037/0022-0663.80.3.284

Zimmerman, B. J. & Tsikalas, K. E. (2005). Can computer-based learning environments (CBLEs) be used as self-regulatory tools to enhance learning? *Educational Psychologist, 40*, 267–271. doi:10.1207/s15326985ep4004_8

Zohar, A. & Ben-David, A. (2008). Explicit teaching of meta-strategic knowledge in authentic classroom situations. *Metacognition and Learning, 3*, 59–82. doi:10.1080/09500690802162762

CHAPTER 11

LEARNING TECHNOLOGIES AND SELF-REGULATED LEARNING

Implications for Practice

Anastasia Kitsantas, Nada Dabbagh, Faye C. Huie, and Susan Dass

Decades of research stemming from Zimmerman's (1989) seminal article regarding the social cognitive view of self-regulated learning has generated a notable amount of research regarding how self-regulation operates within the traditional classroom and across different disciplines. With the introduction of new learning technologies, the traditional classroom is no longer the only option by which students can enroll in a course. In fact, the growth rate for enrollment in online courses in higher education contexts continues to outpace overall enrollment with more than one in four higher education students taking at least one course online in an academic year (Allen & Seaman, 2010). It is projected that by 2014, over 10 million people will engage in some type of online learning (Flores, 2010). Although research regarding how students can self-regulate their learning within an *on-*

Applications of Self-Regulated Learning across Diverse Disciplines, pages 325–354
Copyright © 2013 by Information Age Publishing
All rights of reproduction in any form reserved.

line or blended learning context is generally limited (Hodges, 2005), Zimmerman (i.e., 2008) argued that technology-oriented learning environments could be a powerful medium through which students can develop their self-regulation skills.

According to Zimmerman, *self-regulated learning* refers to behaviors that a student uses to construct knowledge and acquire skill without reliance on others (i.e., teachers, parents, or peers). A self-regulated student is described as a metacognitively, behaviorally, and motivationally active participant in her or his own learning process (Zimmerman, 1989). Students who are skilled self-regulated learners have high levels of confidence in their ability to successfully complete certain tasks (e.g., self-efficacy beliefs) (Zimmerman & Kitsantas, 2005), set process oriented goals, monitor their progress, and self-evaluate their performance.

Although it is important for instructors at all levels to teach students how to become independent self-regulated learners, the focus of this chapter is on how post-secondary instructors can use learning technologies to encourage students to engage in independent learning. Specifically, this chapter will address how self-regulated learning can be supported in online or blended learning environments and how learning technologies have the potential to enhance and support student self-regulation. Additionally, a scenario will be described to illustrate how college instructors can promote and support self-regulatory processes while teaching with technology.

LEARNING TECHNOLOGIES IN ONLINE AND BLENDED LEARNING ENVIRONMENTS

There are many terms in the literature that describe online and blended learning. In this context, online learning is defined as a learning experience that is delivered exclusively online via Internet or web-based technologies and devices synchronously or asynchronously with no physical face-to-face interactions (Dabbagh & Bannan-Ritland, 2005). Blended learning combines online and classroom delivery methods and is also known as hybrid learning or a course for which 30 to 80% of course content and events are delivered online (Dabbagh & Bannan-Ritland, 2005). Online and blended learning are supported by learning technologies comprised of web tools, software applications and platforms, and mobile devices that integrate technological and pedagogical features of the Internet and the web (Kitsantas & Dabbagh, 2010). Examples include course and learning management systems (e.g., Blackboard, Moodle); asynchronous and synchronous communication tools (e.g., discussion boards, chat sessions, web conferencing); social media tools (e.g., blogs, microblogs, wikis); social networking platforms (e.g., Facebook and LinkedIn); cloud computing technologies such as

Google Apps; virtual worlds (e.g., Second Life, Active Worlds); and mobile technologies that enable anytime, anywhere learning such as digital audio players (e.g., iPods), wireless tablets, netbooks, e-readers (e.g., Kindle) and smartphones (e.g., iPhone and Blackberry). Higher education institutions acknowledge that online and blended learning delivery models are critical and strategic for continued growth and competitiveness. Furthermore, The Speak Up initiative of Project Tomorrow, a national nonprofit organization dedicated to the empowerment of student voices in education, revealed that online and blended learning were perceived as enablers for "a greater personalization of the learning process" (Project Tomorrow, 2011, p. 9) by the student and as facilitators for socially-based learning that provided opportunities for students to collaborate with peers and experts.

Examining the types of technologies students adopt and use to meet their learning needs can provide valuable insights for educators on how to design engaging and empowering online and blended learning experiences. For example, the 2010 Pew Internet and American Life Project (Zickuhr, 2010) examined generational differences in online activities and found that while 79% of all American adults (18 and older) use the Internet for a variety of online activities, Millennials (also known as Generation Y or those born between 1977 and 1994), which make up 30% of the total adult population (about 80 million), account for 35% of Internet use. The Pew project also revealed that Millennials and teens are the most active participants in the web's social services such as social networking, text messaging, online gaming, blogging, visiting a virtual world, or watching a video online. In fact, the social sphere of a typical undergraduate college student (ages 18 to 24 years) includes an average of 87 email contacts, 146 cell phone contacts, 438 friends on social networks, and only 29% of the participants in one survey ($n = 144$) preferred face-to-face communication (O'Malley, 2010).

It is clear that high school and college students are more connected than ever before and that technology, particularly wireless or mobile technology, is enabling this anytime, anywhere connectivity. Research also revealed that overall, students are leveraging emerging technologies for learning without the support or assistance of their teachers or schools and that these students have their own vision of how learning should take place in the 21st century—a vision that emphasizes learning as socially-based, un-tethered and digitally-rich—and value the potential for mobile learning (Project Tomorrow, 2011).

While colleges and universities are busy acquiring enterprise learning technologies such as course and learning management systems (e.g., Blackboard) to facilitate anytime, anywhere access to courses and learning activities and experimenting with social networking platforms to accommodate the younger generational cohorts (Dabbagh & Reo, 2011), a critical pedagogical intervention, self-regulated learning, is being overlooked. Given the generational trends in technology use and students' vision of how learning should take place in the 21st century, it is becoming increasingly important to train students to organize their learning experiences for optimum benefit and to encourage learner control over the learning process. However, this can only be achieved if learning technologies are leveraged to cultivate self-regulated and independent learning (Kitsantas & Dabbagh, 2010; McLoughlin & Lee, 2008). Below we review research regarding the use of learning technologies to support student self-regulated learning in online and blended learning environments. We focus on and organize the review on Zimmerman's three phased cyclic model of self-regulated learning. We also discuss the role of the college instructor in using learning technologies to engage students in self-regulated learning and present a scenario to demonstrate how a college instructor can use different learning technologies to support student self-regulated learning in a blended course.

RESEARCH ON SELF-REGULATED LEARNING IN ONLINE AND BLENDED LEARNING ENVIRONMENTS

Self-regulated learning involves several key processes (Zimmerman & Schunk, 2008) embedded within three cyclically sustained phases (Zimmerman, 2000). These three phases include forethought, performance, and self-reflection. They are cyclically interrelated in a self-oriented system of feedback where learners continually adjust self-regulated strategies to meet current or new demands to optimize learning. This cycle of learning enhances motivation, in part because it reinforces the beliefs of the learner in his or her ability to effectively control aspects of the learning experience toward a desired outcome. Figure 11.1 depicts Zimmerman's model.

The *forethought phase* consists of two distinct subcategories that include: (1) task analysis sub-processes of goal setting and strategic planning and (2) motivational beliefs such as self-efficacy, task interest, and goal orientation. Two of the key self-regulatory processes that successful learners use are goal setting and planning.

Goal setting and planning. Goal setting is defined as the process through which students set different goals to help guide their learning behaviors. Specifically, goal setting allows learners to aim their learning efforts to achieve a certain outcome or level of proficiency. Different goals have different characteristics or dimensions, such as attainability, specificity, and difficulty. For example, students who typically attain their goals tend to adopt goals that are proximal as opposed to distal (Latham & Seijts, 1999) and process-oriented as opposed to outcome oriented (Zimmerman & Kitsantas, 1997).

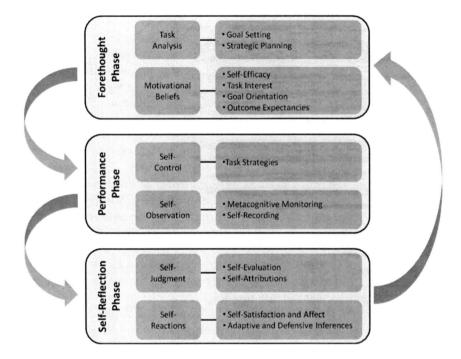

Figure 11.1 Zimmerman's model of self-regulated learning.

A number of studies have examined the role of goal setting in online learning (Conway & Sharkey, 2002; Hu & Gramling, 2009). For example, Hu and Gramling examined the different self-regulatory learning strategies that online learners most often engaged in and their perceptions about which strategies were most useful. A series of interviews and open-ended questionnaires administered to 12 undergraduate students revealed that students felt that goal setting was one of the most effective strategies utilized. The discussion board and assignments were the primary online tools that helped students set goals and allowed them to focus and organize their work. Similarly, Kitsantas and Dabbagh (2004) confirmed that collaborative and communication tools embedded within course management systems, such as WebCT, can be used to promote and support student goal setting. Other studies showed that online learning itself can facilitate the use of goal setting and planning (Conway & Sharkey, 2002; Lynch & Dembo, 2004). Specifically, Conway and Sharkey (2002) found that the nature of course delivery prompted students to set goals on what they needed to learn, what they needed help on, and the goals they needed to set to accomplish tasks. Similarly, Lynch and Dembo (2004) suggest that although self-regulation is an important skill for students to develop, if online courses were designed properly, the very nature of the course can help students regulate their learning with little effort. For example, Terry and Doolittle (2006) provide suggestions on how to enhance students' self-regulatory processes, including goal setting and time-management strategies in online learning settings. The suggestions include using calendar features to provide automated reminders and notices about upcoming project due dates and exam dates.

Self-efficacy beliefs. Research studies have also focused on student motivational beliefs, which constitute an important component of the forethought phase. One motivation construct, self-efficacy, has received considerable attention in online and blended learning. Self-efficacy is a context specific construct, defined as one's belief in his or her ability to successfully accomplish a certain goal (Bandura, 1986). Student academic learning self-efficacy is informed by a variety of sources, with mastery and vicarious experiences being the most powerful (Bandura, 1986). In online learning, self-efficacy can be examined across several different areas or activities, such as Internet self-efficacy (e.g., confidence in one's ability to *use* the Internet; Lynch & Dembo, 2004), online technologies self-efficacy (e.g., confidence in one's ability to effectively use online tools like email, discussion boards, downloading files; Miltiadou & Hu, 2000), and self-efficacy for learning in an online class (e.g., confidence in one's ability to excel academically in an online or blended class; Artino & McCoach, 2008). These different types of self-efficacy beliefs are certainly related but hold features that are unique to each construct. In online or blended learning, the different types of self-efficacy beliefs are important to consider in the context of self-regulated learning.

Research findings show that students who are more efficacious and satisfied with their online learning ability and course experience are more likely to report a stronger preference for online courses (Artino, 2010). In addition, students who report high self-efficacy beliefs in blended learning environments show higher levels of achievement. For example, using Zimmerman's model of self-regulation as a theoretical framework, Lynch and Dembo (2004) investigated which self-regulatory processes (intrinsic goal orientation, self-efficacy for learning, self-efficacy for Internet use, time management, and help-seeking) were most predictive of student academic achievement in a sample of 94 undergraduate students enrolled in a blended course. Specifically, 75% of the course was held online while 25% was face-to-face. The results revealed that out of the five self-regulatory processes, self-efficacy for learning was the only variable related to student academic achievement.

Other researchers (Spence & Usher, 2007) found that self-efficacy for self-regulated learning (e.g., confidence in one's ability to effectively engage in self-regulated learning processes) matters more than computer self-efficacy with regards to achievement. Specifically, they compared how college students enrolled in traditional face-to-face and online remedial math classes differed on various aspects of self-efficacy—math self-efficacy, grade self-efficacy (how efficacious is the student in attaining a certain grade in the course), and computer self-efficacy (how efficacious is the student in using a computer successfully)—and how it influenced engagement and achievement. Students who enrolled in the online course reported higher computer self-efficacy and engagement than students enrolled in the traditional course. Additionally, students in the traditional math course had higher grade self-efficacy and ultimately achieved higher final grades than students in the online math course. However, when mathematics grade self-efficacy was entered as a covariate, differences in achievement between the two groups of students no longer persisted. In other words, as long as students have high mathematics grade self-efficacy, students are likely to achieve at a high level, regardless of whether the course is online or traditional face-to-face learning. This suggests that regardless of the learning environment (traditional or online), the most important predictor of achievement is self-efficacy beliefs in mathematics.

Some researchers (Hodges, Stackpole-Hodges, & Cox , 2008; Matuga, 2009) argue that the online or blended learning environment must be properly designed to foster student self-regulation and motivation in order to positively enhance student motivational beliefs. Lack of training on how students can self-regulate learning can be detrimental to both achievement and self-efficacy beliefs. However, it is important to reiterate that self-regulation is a learned skill, and ultimately, students need to learn how to self-regulate their learning, whether in a face-to-face classroom or online learning environment.

The performance phase of Zimmerman's model includes two subcategories referred to as self-control and self-observation. While the forethought phase emphasized different motivational beliefs prior to engaging in the learning task, the performance phase represents the action phase, where the learner employs different strategies to engage in the learning process.

Self-control strategies. Self-control strategies refer to the different strategies that the student can engage in to most effectively learn. Highly self-regulated learners not only use various strategic approaches to learn such as imagery, attention focusing, environmental structuring, and task strategies, but they also strategically select the strategies that are most effective for the specific task. However, students who are less self-regulated tend to use superficial strategies such as memorization and rehearsal and do not analyze the task to select the most effective and efficient learning strategy (Kitsantas, 2002). Limited research provides some evidence that online learning environments can be designed to train students to become self-regulated learners. Yang (2006) showed that online learning environments can be designed to increase college student strategic use of different learning strategies (e.g., elaboration, summarization, and organization and self-instruction).

Self-monitoring. A key process of the second subcategory, self-observation, is self-monitoring, which refers to a student's cognitive tracking of progress. A number of studies have examined self-monitoring processes in online and blended learning contexts (Cho, Demei, & Laffey, 2010). For example, Geddes (2009) showed that first semester freshmen students were more likely to monitor their performance using the online gradebook feature in Blackboard than by asking the instructor or peers. Gradebook monitoring was also a positive predictor of final course grades and was associated with students who reported higher levels of learning and performance goal orientations as opposed to performance-avoidance goal orientations. Additionally, monitoring in an asynchronous learning environment has been shown to predict different social outcomes such as sense of community and social presence. Specifically, a study by Cho, Demei, and Laffey (2010) showed that the more active students were in monitoring their social environments, the more likely they were to experience stronger social connectedness within their courses. Overall, these findings suggest that online monitoring tools should be provided and updated often by the instructor to allow students to effectively and efficiently monitor their learning and experience a sense of connectedness.

Self-reflection, the final phase of Zimmerman's model, includes the subcategories of self-judgment and self-reactions. Within this phase, the learner evaluates his or her performance, usually in comparison to a personal or self-imposed standard or a goal. These evaluations are then utilized by the learner to influence the forethought phase of subsequent efforts. *Self-judgment* refers to how students judge or evaluate their own learning outcomes, and *self-reaction* refers to different affective and inferential reactions to those outcomes. Students engage in this phase after they have completed the learning task allowing them to reflect on their performance, make purposeful attributions, and ultimately inform the types of goals they set in the future. Researchers have also investigated how self-regulatory processes in the self-reflection phase operate within online or blended course environments.

In terms of self-evaluation, Campbell (2009) investigated whether the use of an online journal influenced students' ability to self-reflect and evaluate their learning and academic goals. The online journal included personalization tools that allowed the adolescent students to change various aspects of the journal based on their preferences and personality. The results revealed that online journaling was an important activity that allowed students to reflect on their learning goals more often, helped students with setting future goals, and served as a private outlet for students to record their feelings.

Similar findings were also shown with online tutorials that included self-evaluative prompts on undergraduate bioscience students' learning (Hejmadi, 2007). Specifically, Hejmadi found that the availability of the online materials coupled with different self-evaluation aspects contributed to student achievement. In fact, students were able to test their understanding of the different topics, which helped them better focus their learning. Research evidence also indicates that online activities such as reflecting on learning experiences, reviewing peers' reflections, engaging in online discussions regarding differences in experiences, and creating online learning portfolios helped students to self-reflect on their own learning as well as engage in future goal setting, planning, and management related activities (Morgan, Rawlinson, & Weaver, 2006). Correspondingly Terry and Doolittle (2006) suggest that instructors should provide materials for students to organize and check-off their work and accomplishments and frequently provide feedback to help them form adaptive self-evaluative judgments about their learning outcomes. The authors also suggest that instructors should provide checklists, organizers, and goals to students in order to scaffold the online learning process. Indeed, instructors' scaffolding process should be regularly implemented and monitored to help students effectively engage in self-regulated learning.

Overall, research suggests that different processes of self-regulated learning such as goal setting (Hu & Gramling, 2009), self-efficacy (Hodges et al., 2008), task strategies (Lynch & Dembo, 2004), and self-monitoring (Cho et al., 2010) can be supported in online and blended learning environments. In fact, online learning may be a stronger context for enhancing student self-regulated learning than more traditional learning contexts. However, self-regulation is a complex construct that is methodologically difficult to capture comprehensively, especially in the context of online and blended learning. In addition, some researchers (e.g., Lynch & Dembo, 2004) argue that instructors by default embed a number of self-regulatory strategies in the design of online courses (e.g., time and environment management and help-seeking strategies), which reduces students' need to engage in these processes on their own volition. For example, instructors are usually available online three times a week and provide feedback immediately to the students. In the next section, we outline how different learning technologies can be utilized to enhance student self-regulated learning in online and blended environments.

THE ROLE OF THE INSTRUCTOR IN USING LEARNING TECHNOLOGIES TO SUPPORT SELF-REGULATED LEARNING

As discussed earlier, research evidence shows that certain web tools embedded in course and learning management systems (CMS/LMS) can support different processes of self-regulated learning (Dabbagh & Kitsantas, 2004). These tools include: collaborative and communication tools (e.g., email, discussion boards, chat, group tools), content creation and delivery tools (e.g., syllabus tool, assignment tool, resource tool), administrative tools (tools to manage students and student information), learning tools (tools that allow students to personalize their learning experience such as course glossary, image databases, and search engines), and assessment tools (e.g., quiz generation tool). The instructor plays a key role in terms of directing students to use these tools effectively in online or blended learning. For example, the instructor must be mindful of how he or she provides goals and evaluation criteria (e.g., rubrics, feedback). If the standards are too high or the criteria are confusing, then students' levels of self-efficacy will most likely decrease. In fact, some researchers (Barnard-Brak, Paton, & Lan, 2010; Dabbagh & Kitsantas, 2009) argue that because self-regulation is a learned skill that is primarily acquired through the guidance of a more experienced individual, development of the self-regulatory skills is unlikely without a thoughtful and deliberate design of the course to actually include components aimed at improving student self-regulation.

In order to empirically investigate the role of the instructor in developing self-regulation in a blended learning context, Dabbagh and Kitsantas (2009) examined how experienced instructors used an LMS to support student self-regulated learning and whether they had intentionally designed activities to enhance student self-regulated learning. The findings showed that experienced online instructors used specific LMS tools to support specific self-regulatory processes. For example, content creation and delivery tools were used to enhance student goal setting by 25% of instructors, and administrative tools were used to support time planning and management by 84% of instructors. While this study further confirmed that different LMS tools can support specific processes of self-regulation, it also revealed that instructors did not always intentionally use these tools to support student self-regulation.

Excelling in an online course relative to face-to-face courses may entail greater self-sufficiency and independence (Kramarski & Dudai, 2009; Kramarski & Mizrachi, 2006). That is, perhaps instructors of an online course are more inclined to provide students with more structured guidance on certain tasks. As previously suggested, instructors should be trained and informed about the different ways that learning technologies can be used to support student self-regulation in online and blended learning contexts (see Table 11.1 for a summary of these results).

Researchers have also attempted to develop learning systems designed to engage students in self-regulation using Zimmerman's approach, with such efforts producing promising results. For example, Schober, Wagner, Reimann, and Spiel (2008) investigated the effectiveness of a blended learning system designed to introduce and familiarize psychology undergradu-

TABLE 11.1 Mapping Self-Regulatory Strategies to LMS Tools

Self-regulation processes	LMS tools category	Examples of instructors' role	Examples of students' use
Goal setting	Collaborative and communication tools	• Help students set goals	• Students use e-mail to communicate goals to instructor and receive feedback
Task strategies	Content creation and delivery tools	• Help students interact meaningfully with course content	• Students use audio and video to view and process learning content (e.g., download or create a podcast or webcast)
Self-monitoring	Learning tools	• Help students monitor progress	• Students use online journaling to self-record time spent studying
Self-evaluating	Assessment tools	• Help students evaluate their learning	• Students use online journaling to reflect on their learning and receive feedback from others
Time planning and management	Collaborative and communication tools	• Help students manage time more effectively	• Students use the online course calendar to prioritize assignments and manage activities

ate students on research methods and evaluation. The system attempted to integrate teaching both content (i.e., research methodology in psychology) and learning skills (i.e., self-regulation). Self-regulated learning components were designed around Zimmerman's three-phase model. The program first guided students to plan their learning and set various learning goals to achieve (forethought phase). Second, the program instructed students on the different strategies to use while accomplishing the goals (performance phase). Finally, the program prompted students to evaluate their learning based on feedback provided by the instructor (self-reflection phase). The authors evaluated the system based on how successfully it was able to teach students research methods as well as how well it enhanced self-regulated learning. The authors compared the performance and self-regulation of students who enrolled in the online course with self-regulated training to the performance and self-regulation of students who enrolled in the online course without self-regulated training. The results showed that both groups of students had achieved at similar levels in terms of their factual knowledge (memorization/lower level knowledge); however, students in the online learning plus self-regulated training course had achieved higher than students who only enrolled in online learning without self-regulated training in terms of their complex logical knowledge (e.g., solving problems and comprehension).

In summary, research shows that if designed properly, learning technologies can support and promote self-regulated learning in online and blended learning environments. In fact, a certain level of self-directedness must be practiced by the student due to the limited face-to-face interaction with the instructor (Kramarski & Mizrachi, 2006) and a variety of learning technologies can be used to support student self-regulated learning (Campbell, 2009; Cho et al., 2010; Kramarski & Michalsky, 2009; Lynch & Dembo, 2004). Therefore, to incorporate different elements of self-regulated learning in online and blended learning environments (e.g., metacognitive guidance by the instructor, offering different learning strategies) specific learning technologies or tools must be used systematically to support the specific self-regulatory process (Dabbagh & Kitsantas, 2004, 2005, 2009; Kitsantas & Dabbagh, 2010). Although the research reviewed above provides initial evidence regarding the role of learning technologies in supporting self-regulated learning in online learning, research has yet to comprehensively investigate how elements from Zimmerman's three phased self-regulation model should be incorporated in blended and online courses. Below we describe a scenario designed to illustrate how an instructor can deliberately use learning technologies to support specific processes of self-regulated learning in a blended course.

A SCENARIO ON HOW INSTRUCTORS CAN USE LEARNING TECHNOLOGIES TO PROMOTE SELF-REGULATED LEARNING IN A BLENDED COURSE

To illustrate how self-regulated processes can be embedded in a blended course, we describe a scenario in an upper level undergraduate economics course. In blended courses, an instructor typically meets at a scheduled time (e.g., every other week) in the classroom and also uses one or more learning technologies to support instruction. In this scenario, an LMS and 3D virtual worlds are used to organize and support online instruction and interaction. We first describe features associated with each learning technology and then describe the actual scenario.

LMS and Virtual World Descriptions

An LMS can support online learning and interaction through collaboration and communication tools, content creation and delivery tools, administrative tools, learning tools, and assessment tools as described earlier in this chapter (refer to Table 11.1). Examples of such tools for the LMS Blackboard are shown in Figure 11.2. However, not all LMS tools are necessarily used

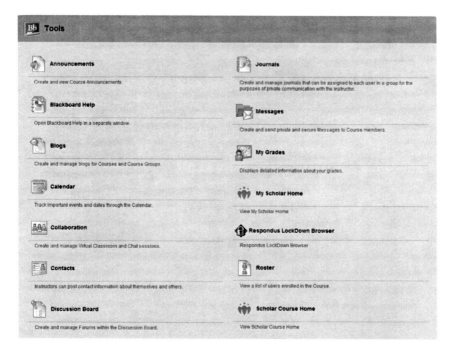

Figure 11.2   Example features in Blackboard, a learning management system.

in an online or blended course. For example, an instructor may opt to post a simple document file of the course calendar instead of using the LMS's built-in calendar tool. When specific LMS tools are not used in a course, they should be "hidden" from the student's view so as not to confuse them. The LMS allows instructors to hide or show the link to a tool enabling the customization of the LMS for a particular teaching context.

In an LMS, students are usually presented with the course content and activities in a folder system of web pages. On the course home page, students are presented with the course menu, which contains links to content, activities, and tools. For example, the course menu may include a link to Discussion Boards, which is a collaborative and communication tool. Other LMS collaborative and communication tools include an email system, a chat feature, and social media tools such as blogs and wikis. Content creation and delivery tools are also in place for instructors to create and upload the course syllabus, assignments, rubrics, and resources and for students to submit assignments, track their contributions, and receive instructor feedback.

A 3D virtual world is a learning technology that allows individuals, represented by avatars, to communicate, collaborate, and create artifacts in an online "world" with a sense of presence and awareness that promotes rich, immersive learning experiences (Dass, Dabbagh, & Clark, 2011). Many types of virtual worlds exist, offering role-play games, procedural training and simulation, and socialization. Some virtual worlds are freely accessible by the public (e.g., Second Life, Active Worlds, or OpenSim) while others are private and accessible only by privileged members (e.g., university developed virtual worlds).

Similar to using browsers such as Firefox or Safari to access the Internet, a viewer is used to access online virtual worlds. Once the viewer is downloaded (e.g., Second Life or Imprudence), you can log into a virtual world on the Internet, create an avatar, and begin exploring. Like a browser, viewers have built-in functionalities. The Second Life viewer supports communication through in-world email, text chat, and voice over Internet using a microphone, usually a headset. A search feature is included to locate areas and activities in the virtual world (e.g., a dance or an auction), controls to move your avatar, a map system to locate and teleport to different areas, and a camera to take snapshots of places visited.

From an educational perspective, a virtual world can be designed to set aside areas for lecture, socialization, resources, collaboration, and assignment submittal. The lecture area, for example, may contain stadium style seating with a lectern and projector board, where students can attend lectures and presentations as a group (see Figure 11.3). A single-story, single-room structure could be created as a private place for instructor office hours complete with a desk and chairs as visual cues for the intended purpose of the office, student-instructor discussions. A series of lakeside hous-

Figure 11.3 Lecture area in a virtual world.

es could be used to visually separate content perhaps based on topic (see Figure 11.4). A coffee shop area can also be created for socializing to improve student collaboration through an increased sense of community and belonging to ultimately open up channels of help-seeking. Virtual worlds use billboards similar to the real world in that they provide information on a large surface visible to multiple people simultaneously. Administrative

Figure 11.4 Modularized content represented by lakeside houses in a virtual world.

materials such as course syllabus, calendar, and rubrics could be posted to billboards in the main area as a visual cue of the course events and expectations whenever students arrive "in-world."

Scenario Description

In this scenario, six economic concepts are taught in the course using a variety of instructional strategies. In general, each concept can be reviewed using lecture slides, virtual world field trips, role-play activities, and group discussions of the role-play activities and assigned readings. The overarching course objective is to allow students to learn intermediate level microeconomic concepts through role-play activities so students can ultimately discuss the concepts from a firsthand, experience-based perspective. The 3D virtual world allows the students to freely interact with each other to experience an economic concept such as common goods and public defense. The role-play activities are conducted in the university's private online 3D virtual world while the virtual world field trips are conducted in the publicly accessible Second Life virtual world.

The virtual world field trips would require students in small groups to jointly observe a specified location in Second Life in relation to the current economic concept under study. In addition to jointly visiting the Second Life field trip location, each group can discuss the current readings before class and summarize their significant findings to be discussed with the class as a whole. Individual assignments may include participating in a discussion forum using the LMS, preparing a 500-word paper per economic concept, and a 10-page final paper on an economic topic of their choosing.

Next, we describe how course instructors can use the different learning technologies to support Zimmerman's model. It should be noted that the focus here is demonstrating how instructors can use learning technologies to enhance student self-regulation, not to review strategies on how this can also be accomplished in a face-to-face learning environment.

Applying Zimmerman's Model of Self-Regulation Using Learning Technologies

For each phase of Zimmerman's model, we describe how an LMS and a virtual world can support self-regulation processes.

Forethought Phase

The forethought phase occurs before students begin engaging in a learning activity. During this phase, students begin to identify the goals and strategies appropriate for the tasks and hold certain motivational beliefs such as self-efficacy. Therefore, instructors should deliberately design the course using the LMS to support student goal setting as well as select activities that would support both goal setting and self-efficacy.

Task Analysis

As described earlier, the LMS uses a folder system and linked web pages to create areas designated for specific activities to help focus students' attention to course expectations as a prompt for goal setting and strategic planning. The content associated with each economic concept can be collocated to support a student's planning and goal setting. The course menu can include links to the course syllabus, course calendar, and rubrics. Students can download and print the syllabus and rubrics since these items are typically electronic files, and they can use them to set personal expectations. Students can also access the course calendar to manage their time. Students are not only encouraged to add the course assignments to their personal calendars but to also schedule the time they will focus on the course readings and assignments. This calendar activity can encourage students to set proximal as opposed to distal learning goals. Due to the nature of the LMS, students can repeatedly explore these course links and tools to plan how to best support their learning.

Using the LMS, instructors can also upload various documents that would support student learning and task completion. For example, rubrics for each instructional activity such as the papers and the electronic discussion forums can provide a mechanism for students to plan and subsequently self-assess their performance. Exemplar papers from prior students can also be uploaded in a designated area in the LMS. The exemplars, combined with the assignment rubrics, support students in setting mastery type goals as well as serve as a vicarious source of self-efficacy.

The assignment submittal area in the LMS can be designed to specifically support student time management and develop content self-efficacy. Each assignment, such as the paper for each economic concept, can be listed chronologically according to due date. This list can be especially useful for struggling students who may need more scaffolding through explicit assignment tracking. Once an assignment is submitted, it can be automatically removed from the list. Not only does this diminishing list serve as an assignment tracking mechanism, but it can also provide students with a sense of accomplishment throughout the semester and allow them to directly attribute their performance to their effort.

Motivational Beliefs

As noted previously in the chapter, students' motivational beliefs such as self-efficacy and task value play a critical role in influencing student actions and learning. Self-efficacy is an important prerequisite to implementing effective strategies to attain specific goals. Instructors can deliberately address different forms of student self-efficacy. In this scenario, an instructor can target student self-efficacy for content and for different technologies, the LMS and the virtual worlds.

Specifically, an instructor can emphasize the technology-based skills as part of the learning objectives to draw students' attention to the importance of these skills for successful performance. Since virtual worlds are a relatively new technology to many students, a robust orientation class should be given to familiarize the students with the basic skills to effectively use the inherent virtual world features. This provides the foundation to developing self-efficacy using the virtual worlds. Skills can include moving the avatar through walking and flying, and using communication tools and teleports. Where appropriate, an instructor should compare the virtual world skills to skills used in other, more familiar technologies to scaffold students to the new technology. For example, a teleport can be explained as being similar to changing website browser locations but instead of going to another 2D website, the avatar goes to another 3D virtual world location. Similarly, text chat can be compared to cell phone text messaging.

As the students master the basics of virtual world features, the instructor should continue to include additional instructions for more complex activities that would allow the students to experience and adjust to the virtual learning environment gradually. For example, once students learn how to use voice chat, they can first practice with groups of two, increasing to groups of four, that is, the size of their small groups. In a two-person discussion, the conversation simply goes back and forth. As the group size increases, different communication skills become necessary to ensure all voices are heard. The speaker may purposely pause while explaining their thoughts to allow others an opportunity to comment before moving forward with the conversation. Alternatively, the speaker may ask group members for their opinions before moving forward. Additionally, technical support should be readily available throughout the course to alleviate technical difficulties and increase technology self-efficacy.

An orientation class can also be given to familiarize the students with the technology-based skills associated with the LMS. Although many students may be familiar with using an LMS, instructors have great latitude customizing the LMS for their particular courses. Specifically, instructors should tailor and design the LMS to the specific needs of the course. Therefore, it is important to help students develop a strong sense of efficacy to navigate throughout the system to easily locate certain resources. To do so, an instructor should design an activity to familiarize the students with the system, such as a scavenger hunt to practice the required LMS skills for the course and to prompt the students to explore all areas of the course in the LMS.

Areas for the scavenger hunt can include the place for course content, announcements, discussions, administrative, mail, roster, and chat. For example, to complete the hunt, students can be required to successfully accomplish different tasks such as uploading documents and participating in an online discussion forum. The directions emailed from the instructor would prompt the students to complete a series of tasks such as introducing themselves to the next person in the class roster in an email and copying the instructor. Such tasks require the students to locate the class roster and create an email within the LMS. Another scavenger hunt task can require the students to download a file from the course content area and upload it in the assignment submittal area. This scavenger hunt activity prompts students to practice several common technology skills required for the course.

Additionally, students may be asked to identify why they are taking the course and then use the discussion forum to post their reasons. The instructor can then participate in the discussion forum to align class goals with personal expectations. This activity serves multiple purposes: it provides personal relevancy to improve intrinsic motivation and task value; familiarizes the students with the functionality and protocols to group discussions; and fosters a sense of community to develop positive peer interactions, which opens up channels of peer help-seeking. These orientation tasks allow students to develop their self-efficacy about the LMS tools as well as familiarize themselves with the course expectations. While the face-to-face class discussions can promote peer-to-peer relationships, it is the built-in mail, roster, and instant text messaging that provide a readily available mechanism to support communication, collaboration, and peer help-seeking outside the classroom.

Although technology self-efficacy is certainly important to how students perform in a blended learning environment, what may be even more critical is a student's content self-efficacy. Specifically, depending on the task, an instructor can modularize the course into several sections to provide manageable task assignments. As a result, students will likely have more mastery experiences, resulting in a stronger self-efficacy for future tasks and assignments. An instructor can also provide students with examples of past projects as a model for their own assignments. Providing students with more manageable tasks along with exemplars from past students will inform the mastery and vicarious sources of self-efficacy. Additionally, the steps taken to ensure students have strong technology self-efficacy combined with content self-efficacy will most likely positively influence student overall self-efficacy and ultimately their performance level.

An instructor can also foster student motivational beliefs by using the virtual world role-play activities to increase student participation. Specifically, for this scenario, an instructor can design an activity to teach students about the social and economic concepts associated with creating public goods and services such as a fire department. Each student can be assigned a house on an island subject to hurricane damage. In this activity, each student earns money at a rate commensurate with the amount of damage their house has; the lower the damage, the higher the earning rate. An instructor can also provide different resources in virtual worlds such as weather stations, which can provide 100% protection if manned properly, that is, manned with three or four students depending on the weather station; fewer students means less percentage protection. An instructor can also design the "in-world" role-playing activity to provide the students with additional choices with different consequences. For example, students can choose to remain in their house to individually protect against a hurricane but at a reduced earning rate. Subsequent repair time reduces the time available to earn money. Each student can make the choice of uniting to protect their houses, perhaps taking turns to man a weather station, or individually protecting their houses. These decisions, affected by personal trust, mutual goals, and sense of public good, ultimately determine the earnings for each student. To motivate student participation, the highest individual earnings from past courses can be posted on a virtual world billboard to act as both motivation and as a goal. On this "wall of fame" the student avatar, amount of earnings, and the strategies used to incur these earnings may prove helpful and serve as an incentive to continue participation.

In summary, we presented several techniques used to promote self-regulated learning in the forethought phase, including the design of the LMS and the virtual world activities used to develop content and technology self-efficacy. Next we address how learning technologies can support the performance phase in this blended course.

Performance Phase

In this phase, students self-control and self-observe their performance during the learning activity. Instructors create activities and feedback mechanisms that prompt and support these self-employed student activities. To illustrate, we describe how instructors can design one activity to provide multiple prompts for students to self-monitor and self-assess.

During this phase of learning, instructors should encourage students to use different task strategies such as imagery by requiring them to conduct Second Life field trips where they observe economic concepts in practice. In an auctioning activity, for example, the students can visit a designated Second Life auction site in their small group allowing them to develop a mental model of how to participate in a particular type of auction. Here, they would review information on items for bid and then watch the auction progress. As part of the assignment, instructors should direct the students to theorize the different bidding strategies being employed based on the assigned readings.

Finally, students can share their findings from the field trips individually in a discussion forum in the LMS. The forum can be open for a week for the students to post their notes as well as comment on other posts such as providing different interpretations for different outcomes. The forum provides a visual reminder of the activity and also promotes full group participation. As more notes are posted, the students may begin to self-assess what they learned in comparison to what the field trip offered as related to the economic concept, thus promoting self-monitoring. Since the virtual world is always available, students can return to the field trip site to validate peer findings. The instructor can monitor the discussion in the LMS and post notes as feedback to scaffold student understanding and ensure completeness of information. This type of activity encourages students to take notes, summarize their findings, reflect on what they learned, and evaluate and compare their observations and experiences with their peers.

For this discussion forum, instructors should also provide a concise rubric indicating performance measures such as each post length (e.g., two paragraphs), frequency (e.g., posts should be spread across the week), number of entries (e.g., 5), and quality of postings (e.g., use references from readings or substantiate with personal observation at field trip site). Instructors can also use the rubrics to help guide student's thinking and approach to the field trip activity. Additionally, specifying the minimum number of posts can help develop students' effort regulation and time management whereas emphasizing post quality prompts students to employ task strategies (e.g., summarization, elaboration, and rehearsal). The LMS can automatically track the students' number of posts so they can easily self-monitor their performance.

Many LMSs provide a secure, built-in means for students to freely access their grades. As part of orientation, students should be directed to familiarize themselves with this area so they can monitor their efforts and performance throughout the semester. Since the LMS also allows instructors to comment on graded assignments, the instructor should also provide feedback and guidance so that students can continue to improve their performance through self-monitoring activities throughout the semester.

In summary, for the performance phase in this blended course, instructors should use a variety of techniques to promote self-regulated learning: imagery based on the field trip activity, a discussion forum as a means to self-monitor and self-evaluate, and a concise rubric to guide performance expectations. In the next subsection, we address the self-reflection phase.

Self-Reflection Phase

Having accomplished the learning activities, instructors should specifically instruct students to reflect on their performance to inform subsequent learning efforts and ultimately self-regulate their learning. We present two examples of how instructors of this blended course can support this phase of Zimmerman's model. In the first example, an instructor could deliberately design activities of similar nature for each economic concept that allows the students to assess performance consistently throughout the course. In the second example, an instructor could provide prompts for a semester-long paper to support adaptive causal attributions.

Since the course is modular in nature, instructors should develop similar type activities for each of the six concepts to provide a natural mechanism for the students to periodically self-assess performance according to each type of activity and then identify new task strategies as appropriate for improvement. To promote this self-assessment, instructors should email each student after all assignments and activities for the first economic concept have been completed, graded, and returned to students. Instructors should request each student email their assessment of their progress, the task strategies and on-line tools they felt were effective, those that were ineffective, and how they might change these strategies and tools based on their self-assessment. For example, some students may have found it advantageous to take personal notes on the readings while others may have found it beneficial to discuss the Second Life field trip assignment with their small group to identify economic concepts they expected to see, and hence become more prepared as to what they might look for during the virtual field trip. Instructors should collect the self-assessment information from all students and post them to the LMS discussion forum to allow students to comment or ask how a particular strategy or tool was used. Although the students could post their self-assessments directly to the LMS discussion forum, emailing instructors maintains anonymity and allows the students to initially self-reflect on their learning independent of others. Depending on student progress, instructors should decide whether to continue this process after each course module.

Furthermore, interim grading and instructor comments that focus on mastery and process related goals provide the basis for the students to reflect and re-direct their efforts for improvement. For example, the rubric for the week-long discussion forum allows the students to recognize (e.g., by comparing and contrasting progress against criteria) that performance is attributable to self-controlled effort and/or selection of effective strategies as opposed to an external, uncontrollable event such as luck.

Additionally, the individual paper due for each economic concept may provide the students a means to exhibit their level of mastery for which the instructor should provide feedback. Instructors should design the assignments to explicitly draw from the readings, field trip, and role-play activities so students can articulate their understanding of the concept. The semester long paper is typically a broader topic and a longer paper than those due on each economic concept. As such, instructors should divide the assignment into several manageable tasks such as topic selection, paper outline, draft, and final paper. These manageable tasks should be due across the semester, each providing a foundation for the next submittal. Instructors should provide feedback for improvement, focusing the comments on students' progress or way of thinking about the economics concept and avoiding comments that refer to student ability levels or luck. The final product becomes indicative of the interim feedback and continued effort. As a result the students will more likely attribute their performance to their strategy use and semester long effort.

In the self-reflection phase, we showed how instructors can deliberately design similar activities using learning technologies for each economic concept so that students can assess performance consistently throughout the course. We also showed how incremental assignments can be used to prompt the students to maintain effort and make adaptive attributions to performance.

Scenario Summary

This scenario with suggested learning technologies use demonstrated how Zimmerman's three phase self-regulation model can be incorporated into the design of an upper level undergraduate economics course to promote student self-regulated learning in a blended learning environment. A variety of learning technologies were used to achieve this goal: an LMS that consists of multiple tools, a publicly accessible virtual world (i.e., Second Life), and a private virtual world (i.e., one created by the university). In the forethought phase, an instructor may deliberately design the layout of the LMS and the private virtual world to support student goal setting, time management, and task strategies; activities can also be developed to support both content and technology self-efficacy. In the performance phase, self-regulated learning can be supported through imagery from the field trip activities, postings can be used as a means to self-monitor and self-observe performance, and administrative materials such as a rubric can be provided as a guide to expectations. In the self-reflection phase, instructors can deliberately provide repeated activities for each economic concept so students could asses, re-select, and apply new strategies to improve performance. Additionally, incremental assignments should be assigned to prompt the students to maintain effort and attribute performance to effort rather than ability or luck. These strategies, summarized in Table 11.2, are by no means the only strategies that can be used to promote self-regulated learning processes in blended or online courses. Many other examples and technologies could support Zimmerman's three phase model for self-regulated learning. Although this scenario demonstrated how the model can be integrated with relative ease in a blended course, it is important to note that each instructor should tailor and design the blended or online learning environment to the specific needs of his or her class.

TABLE 11.2 Example SRL Processes with LMS Technologies and Virtual World

SRL Process	Instructional Examples	Instructor Initiated Activities	Student Initiated Activities
Goal Setting and Planning	• Modularize course content	• Instructor breaks course into discrete topics, leveraging the 3D space in the virtual world and using a folder system in the LMS	• Students work on manageable sized topic areas
	• Conduct a scavenger hunt	• Instructor introduces course expectations by having students visit the different content and activity areas (e.g., the assignment submittal area)	• Students visit each online area to recognize course expectations and activities
	• Provide project planning guidance	• Instructor provides suggestions on how to subdivide long term assignments into manageable tasks	• Students integrate suggestions into personal calendar
Task Strategies	• Prompt students to identify and use task strategies and online learning tools	• Instructor prompts and posts strategies and tools for alternative ways of learning	• Students assess a variety of strategies to adopt in their learning
Self-Efficacy: Technology	• Practice skills used in course	• Instructor has students practice course-required skills during scavenger hunt	• Students perform skills until mastered
Self-Efficacy: Content	• Provide assignment tracking	• Instructor lists all assignments chronologically; uses an automated diminishing list in the LMS	• Students use the list to stay on task
	• Provide exemplars of past papers/projects	• Instructor uses the exemplars to convey expectations to students	• Students see how past students have excelled in the course and can model their projects after the exemplars
Imagery	• Conduct an activity that replicates previously viewed actions	• Instructor conducts an in-world or in-class activity for students to emulate an activity such as the Second Life auction	• Students use their observations as a model to use in the class activity
Attention Focusing	• Create compartmentalized student activity areas	• Instructor creates separate, distinct locations to access the content and activities for each economic concept	• Students access visibly different online areas to accomplish certain activities

(continued)

TABLE 11.2 Example SRL Processes with LMS Technologies and Virtual World (continued)

SRL Process	Instructional Examples	Instructor Initiated Activities	Student Initiated Activities
Time Management	• Create course calendar	• Instructor creates a simple online calendar of class activities, topics, and assignments by date	• Students repeatedly review for upcoming events to plan their activities; can merge with personal calendar
Self-Monitor	• Assign interim deliverables for semester long paper	• Instructor provides a printable calendar as a checklist to remind students to review the assignment submittal area to ensure all assignments are submitted	• Students review or print the calendar and visit the assignment submittal area to ensure all assignments submitted
Self-Evaluation	• Provide a means to evaluate assignment submittals	• Instructor provides timely feedback on interim assignments geared toward the final product	• Students examine how their cumulative and ongoing effort supported their overall paper
	• Begin a class discussion reviewing a class activity	• Instructor assigns students to review a Second Life location as related to the current topic and post their findings online	• Students post their findings while self-assessing their understanding and completeness
Help-Seeking	• Open peer-to-peer communication channels	• Instructor opens a class discussion where students can post questions and provide peer support	• Students learn about and potentially identify with fellow students to open avenues for help-seeking
	• Provide multiple means for peer-to-peer communication	• Instructor provides and uses multiple means for communication to open up help-seeking channels such as email, chat, and socialization areas and uses novel methods such as using voice over IP for small group work	• Students use communication methods of their choosing
	• Hold instructor office hours	• Instructor creates office hours whether in a virtual world or for an online synchronous discussion	• Students take advantage of instructor office hours

FUTURE RESEARCH

Further research is needed in online and blended learning environments, particularly using experimental studies to identify which self-regulation skills are most critical to student performance and how they can be supported. Future studies should use more methodologically sound approaches to assess self-regulation constructs. Specifically, Zimmerman (2008) suggests that although there is growing popularity of merging technology with self-regulation, there is a need to further refine the methods used to investigate the role of self-regulation in online or blended learning environments.

Overall, research shows that processes under each individual phase of self-regulation may have a positive influence on student academic achievement in online or blended courses. However, the studies reviewed in this chapter may indicate that stronger methodological approaches are necessary to uncover more conclusive evidence regarding the link between self-regulation and online learning (Hodges et al., 2008; Kitsantas & Dabbagh, 2010). Additionally, new research has shown that social media in particular have pedagogical affordances that can help support and promote student self-regulated learning by enabling the creation of personal learning experiences that empower students with a sense of personal agency in the learning process (Dabbagh & Kitsantas, 2011). Dabbagh and Kitsantas used Zimmerman's model to develop a cyclical three-level pedagogical framework that can guide faculty in scaffolding student self-regulation skills using social media. The three levels of this framework are based on the cognitive affordances that social media technologies enable and include: (1) personal information management, (2) social interaction and collaboration, and (3) information aggregation and management. There is strong evidence suggesting that students engage in self-regulated learning skills when using social media to create personal and social learning experiences. However, this framework has not been empirically tested; hence, research studies are needed to examine its effectiveness in motivating and empowering students to create personal and social learning environments that can help them achieve desired learning outcomes.

Finally, measuring self-regulation in the online context is a challenge in itself in terms of automating different measurements during ongoing learning. Specifically, technology has made drastic improvements in terms of teaching and tutoring students; however, how to measure the effects of an online learning environment on self-regulated learning needs to be further explored (Schraw, 2010). One potential method is the microanalytic approach, where self-regulation is measured both qualitatively and quantitatively in terms of context-specific real-time responses (Cleary, 2011).

CONCLUSION AND EDUCATIONAL IMPLICATIONS

This chapter focused on how learning technologies can be used to support student self-regulated learning processes in blended and online learning contexts. It is clear from this review that more systematic empirical research is needed to further examine what self-regulatory processes successful students are using and what learning technologies instructors can use to teach and support student self-regulation in these types of teaching and learning contexts. In addition, a scenario illustrating how Zimmerman's three-phase self-regulation model can be integrated into a blended course was provided.

There are several educational implications associated with using learning technologies to support student self-regulated learning. As the educational technology field continues to advance and new technologies continue to emerge, there is a growing concern about how well instructors are trained and motivated to actually use these technologies to foster student self-regulation. Professional development programs should be designed to assist instructors in how to use these technologies to support student self-regulation. For example, instructors should negotiate the technologies that they provide with the students and present students with different options that can help them meet the demands and learning goals of the course and explore their own interests in a more meaningful and personalized manner. Additionally, the content and the approach that instructors take to teaching should be more process as opposed to outcome driven. Ultimately, students should decide based on feedback from the instructor which technologies to use to accommodate their own technology preferences, learning needs, and social habits.

In closing, Barry Zimmerman's theory on self-regulated learning has had a substantial impact on how research has been conceptualized and conducted in relation to teaching in blended and online learning environments. As the field begins to evolve with the emergence of new learning technologies, we predict that his groundbreaking theory and research in self-regulation will continue to play a significant role in understanding the nature of learning in online and blended learning contexts for many years to come.

REFERENCES

Allen, I. E., & Seaman, J. (2010). Class differences: Online education in the United States, 2010.[Report]. Retrieved from http://sloanconsortium.org/publications/survey/pdf/class_differences.pdf

Artino, A. R., Jr. (2010). Online or face-to-face learning? Exploring the personal factors that predict students' choice of instructional format. *Internet and Higher Education, 13*, 272–276.

Artino, A., R., Jr., & McCoach, D. (2008). Development and initial validation of the Online Learning Value and Self-Efficacy Scale. *Journal of Educational Computing Research, 38*(3), 279–303. doi:10.2190/EC.38.3.c

Bandura, A. (1986). *Social foundations of thought and action: A social cognitive theory.* Englewood Cliffs, NJ: Prentice-Hall.

Barnard-Brak, L., Paton, V. O., & Lan, W. Y. (2010). Profiles in self-regulated learning in the online learning environment. *International Review of Research in Open and Distance Learning, 11*(1), 61–80.

Campbell, C. (2009). Middle years students' use of self-regulating strategies in an online journaling environment. *Educational Technology & Society, 12*(3), 98–106.

Cho, M. H., Demei, S., & Laffey, J. (2010). Relationships between self-regulation and social experiences in asynchronous online learning environments. *Journal of Interactive Learning Research, 21*(3), 297–316. doi:2010-18783-001

Cleary, T. J. (2011). Emergence of self-regulated learning microanalysis: Historical overview, essential features, and implications for research and practice. In B. J. Zimmerman and D. H. Schunk (Eds.), *Handbook of self-regulation of learning and performance* (pp. 329–345). New York, NY: Routledge.

Conway, J. J., & Sharkey, R. R. (2002). Integrating on campus problem based learning and practice based learning: Issues and challenges in using computer mediated communication. *Nurse Education Today, 22*(7), 552–562.

Dabbagh, N., & Bannan-Ritland, B. (2005). *Online learning: Concepts, strategies, and application.* Upper Saddle River, NJ: Prentice Hall, Inc.

Dabbagh, N., & Kitsantas, A. (2005). The role of Web-based pedagogical tools in supporting student self-regulation in distributed learning environments. *Instructional Science, 25,* 24–37.

Dabbagh, N., & Kitsantas, A. (2004). Supporting self-regulation in student-centered web-based learning environments. *International Journal of e-Learning, 2*(4), 40–47. doi:2005-06641-005

Dabbagh, N. & Kitsantas, A. (2009). Exploring how experienced online instructors use integrative learning technologies to support self-regulated learning. *International Journal of Technology in Teaching and Learning, 5*(2), 154–168.

Dabbagh, N., & Kitsantas, A. (2011). Personal learning environments, social medial, and self-regulated learning: A natural formula for connecting formal and informal learning. *Internet and Higher Education, 15,* 3–8.

Dabbagh, N., & Reo, R. (2011). Impact of Web 2.0 on higher education. In D. W. Surry, T. Stefurak, & R. Gray (Eds.), *Technology integration in higher education: Social and organizational aspects* (pp. 174–187). Hershey, PA: IGI Global.

Dass, S., Dabbagh, N., & Clark, K. (2011). Using virtual worlds: What the research says. *Quarterly Review of Distance Education, 12*(2), 95–112.

Flores, J. (2010). Moving ahead academically in 2010. *Media Planet, Online Learning 3rd Edition, June 2010.* Retrieved from http://www.usdla.org/assets/pdf_files/Online_Education_USAT_Final.pdf

Geddes, D. (2009). How am I doing? Exploring on-line gradebook monitoring as a self-regulated learning practice that impacts academic achievement. *Academy of Management Learning & Education, 8*(4), 494–510. doi:2010-00338-002

Hejmadi, M. V. (2007). Improving the effectiveness and efficiency of teaching large classes: Development and evaluation of a novel e-resource in cancer biology. *Bioscience Education e-Journal, 4*(2), 215–255.

Hodges, C. B. (2005). Self-regulation in web-based courses: A review and the need for research. *Quarterly Review of Distance Education, 6*(4), 375–383.

Hodges, C. B., Stackpole-Hodges, C. L., & Cox, K. M. (2008). Self-efficacy, self-regulation, and cognitive style as predictors of achievement with podcast instruction. *Journal of Educational Computing Research, 38*(2), 139–153. doi:10.2190/EC.38.2.b

Hu, H., & Gramling, J. (2009). Learning strategies for success in a web-based course: A descriptive exploration. *Quarterly Review of Distance Education, 10*(2), 123–134.

Kitsantas, A. (2002). Test preparation and test performance: A self-regulatory analysis. *Journal of Experimental Education, 70*(2) 101–113.

Kitsantas, A., & Dabbagh, N. (2004). Promoting self-regulation in distributed learning environments with web-based pedagogical tools: An exploratory study. [Special Issue]. *Journal on Excellence in College Teaching, 15*(1&2), 119–142.

Kitsantas, A., & Dabbagh, N. (2010). *Learning to learn with Integrative Learning Technologies (ILT): A practical guide for academic success.* Greenwich, CT: Information Age Publishing.

Kramarski, B., & Dudai, V. (2009). Group-metacognitive support for online inquiry in mathematics with differential self-questioning. *Journal of Educational Computing Research, 40*(4), 377–404. doi:10.2190/EC.40.4.a

Kramarski, B., & Michalsky, T. (2009). Investigating pre-service teachers' professional growth in self-regulated learning environments. *Journal of Educational Psychology, 101*(1), 161–175.

Kramarski, B., & Mizrachi, N. (2006). Online discussion and self-regulated learning: Effects of instructional methods on mathematical literacy. *Journal of Educational Research, 99*(4), 218–230. doi:10.3200/JOER.99.4.218-231

Latham, G. P., & Seijts, G. H. (1999). The effects of proximal and distal goals on performance on a moderately complex task. *Journal of Organizational Behavior, 20,* 421–429. doi:10.1002/job.70

Lynch, R., & Dembo, M. (2004). The relationship between self-regulation and online learning in a blended learning context. *International Review of Research in Open and Distance Learning, 5*(2), 1–16.

Matuga, J. M. (2009). Self-regulation, goal orientation, and academic achievement of secondary students in online university courses. *Educational Technology & Society, 12*(3), 4–11.

McLoughlin, C., & Lee, M. J. W. (2008). Personalized and self regulated learning in the Web 2.0 era: International exemplars of innovative pedagogy using social software. *Australasian Journal of Educational Technology, 26*(1), 28–43.

Miltiadou, M., & Yu, C. H. (2000, October). *Validation of the Online Technologies Self-Efficacy Scale (OTSES).* Paper presented at the AECT International Convention, Denver, CO. Retrieved from http://www.eric.ed.gov/PDFS/ED445672.pdf

Morgan, J., Rawlinson, M., & Weaver, M. (2006). Facilitating online reflective learning for health and social care professionals. *Open Learning, 21*(2), 167–176. doi:10.1080/02680510600715594

O'Malley, G. (2010, February 22). Social studies: Study reports students access an average of 14.3 screens, have potential to reach 671. *Online Media Daily*. Retrieved from http://www.mediapost.com/publications/?fa=Articles.show Article&art_aid=122938

Project Tomorrow. (2011). The new 3 E's of education: Enabled, engaged, empowered—How today's students are leveraging emerging technologies for learning. Irvine, CA: author. Retrieved from http://www.tomorrow.org/speakup/pdfs/SU10_3EofEducation_Students.pdf

Schober, B., Wagner, P., Reimann, R., & Spiel, C. (2008). Vienna E-Lecturing (VEL): Learning how to learn self-regulated in an Internet-based blended learning setting. *International Journal on E-Learning, 7*(4), 703–723. doi:2008-14478-007

Schraw, G. (2010). Measuring self-regulation in computer-based learning environments. *Educational Psychologist, 45*(4), 258–266. doi:10.1080/00461520.2010.515936

Spence, D. J., & Usher, E. L. (2007). Engagement with mathematics courseware in traditional and online remedial learning environments: Relationship to self-efficacy and achievement. *Journal of Educational Computing Research, 37*(3), 267–288. doi:10.2190/EC.37.3.c

Terry, K. P., & Doolittle, P. (2006). Fostering self-regulation in distributed learning. *College Quarterly, 9*(1). Retrieved from http://www.senecac.on.ca/quarterly/2006-vol09-num01-winter/terry_doolittle.html

Yang, Y. (2006). Effects of embedded strategies on promoting the use of self-regulated learning strategies in an online learning environment. *Journal of Educational Technology Systems, 34*(3), 257–269.

Zickuhr, K. (2010, December 16). Generations 2010: Pew internet and American life project. Washington, DC: Pew Research Center. Retrieved from http://www.pewinternet.org/Reports/2010/Generations-2010.aspx

Zimmerman, B. J. (1989). A social cognitive view of self-regulated academic learning. *Journal of Educational Psychology, 81*(3), 329–339. doi:10.1037/0022-0663.81.3.329

Zimmerman, B. J. (2000). Attaining self-regulation: A social-cognitive perspective. In M. Boekaerts, P. R. Pintrich, & M. Zeidner (Eds.), *Handbook of self-regulation* (pp. 245–262), San Diego, CA: Academic Press.

Zimmerman, B. J. (2008). Investigating self-regulation and motivation: Historical background, methodological developments, and future prospects. *American Educational Research Journal, 45*(1), 166–183. doi:10.3102/0002831207312909

Zimmerman, B. J., & Kitsantas, A. (1997). Developmental phases in self-regulation: Shifting from process goals to outcome goals. *Journal of Educational Psychology, 89*, 29–36. doi:10.1037/0022-0663.89.1.29

Zimmerman, B. J., & Kitsantas, A. (2005). The hidden dimension of personal competence: Self-Regulated learning and practice. In A. J. Elliot & C. S. Dweck (Eds.), *Handbook of competence and motivation* (pp. 204–222). New York, NY: Guilford Press.

Zimmerman, B. J., & Schunk, D. H. (2008). Motivation: An essential dimension of self-regulated learning. In D. H. Schunk & B. J. Zimmerman (Eds.), *Motivation and self-regulated learning: Theory, research, and applications* (pp. 1–30). New York, NY: Lawrence Erlbaum Associates.

CHAPTER 12

SELF-REGULATION INTERVENTIONS AND THE DEVELOPMENT OF MUSIC EXPERTISE

Gary E. McPherson, Siw G. Nielsen, and James M. Renwick

Every year, millions of children around the world begin learning a musical instrument. Very few of these learners understand the dedication needed to acquire expertise at the highest levels, with many starting their learning for the expressed purpose of just having fun with their friends or family members (McPherson & Zimmerman, 2011). Only weeks after starting, however, a number of demotivating influences start to emerge as young learners come to realize the commitments necessary to acquire sufficient skill for music performance to remain personally satisfying (McPherson, Davidson, & Faulkner, 2012).

In both formal and informal musical contexts it is self-evident that learning a musical instrument requires a great deal of effort and independent learning. Whether learners practice covering songs from an mp3-player, use YouTube to learn ukulele, or are involved in formal instrumental tuition, a number of self-regulatory tools need to be acquired to help them

Applications of Self-Regulated Learning across Diverse Disciplines, pages 355–382
Copyright © 2013 by Information Age Publishing
All rights of reproduction in any form reserved.

take control of their own learning and progress effectively (McPherson & Zimmerman, 2002, 2011). Whereas learners in sports can rely on their coaches to provide them with informative feedback and well-defined tasks in their training, many music learners, especially when they are practicing independently at home, must either themselves assume much of the responsibility for their own achievement or rely on peers or their parents to help shape their learning. In this situation, knowledge of how to manage this "freedom"—in terms of the quantity of time devoted to learning as well as the quality of effort invested—emerges as a principal factor influencing performance levels (Barry & Hallam, 2002; Pintrich, 1995). To understand these and various other processes involved in learning a musical instrument, researchers in music education have drawn on Barry J. Zimmerman's work on self-regulated learning to help shape their research agendas (Bartolome, 2009; Leon-Guerrero, 2008; Miksza, 2006; Nielsen, 2004; Renwick, McCormick, & McPherson, 2011), which they have used as a useful perspective from which to study the many varied aspects of music learning (cf. McPherson & Zimmerman, 2002; Schunk & Zimmerman, 1998).

The purpose of this chapter is to explain the types of interventions that we believe impact positively on music learners' self-regulation, based on research we have undertaken with beginning, intermediate and advanced level music learners. Our chapter begins with a short description of Zimmerman's (2000) triadic forms of self-regulation that Nielsen (2001) has applied to study various musical processes in intermediate and advanced level musicians. We use her model of cyclical self-regulation as a means of explaining how these processes unfold and can come under conscious control during the act of practicing and performing music. This provides the backdrop for a detailed explanation of the psychological dimensions of musical self-regulation that McPherson and Renwick (2001) have applied to frame their studies of beginning and intermediate level musicians who are learning a musical instrument. Using these dimensions of musical self-regulation allows us to document the types of interventions we have found to be most useful for helping students develop into efficient, self-regulated musicians. These include interventions that encourage learners to maintain their concentration and develop the self-motivation to persist with their learning, adapt suitable learning strategies that will facilitate their learning, plan and manage the time they have available for practicing and devoting attention to music, enhance their own behaviors as they choose, modify and react to feedback while learning, shape the physical setting in which they practice and engage in music, and connect socially with parents, teachers and peers in ways that will enhance and enrich their musical learning. Our chapter concludes by defining the main types of research issues that can be used to set a meaningful agenda for the coming decade of research on self-regulated music learning. These ideas are based on the previous four decades of pioneering work by Barry J. Zimmerman, whose research has served as our model and will continue to do so.

SELF-ORIENTED FEEDBACK LOOPS

According to Zimmerman (2000), self-regulation from a social-cognitive perspective refers to "self-generated thoughts, feelings, and actions that are planned and cyclically adapted to the attainment of personal goals" (p. 14). Certain actions and processes are applied by music learners to master various aspects of their music engagement, which is why Zimmerman (2000) highlights the role of personal agency in planning their use cyclically. From a social cognitive perspective the music learner's personal agency to act on his or her social setting and structures is important (Zimmerman, 1989). As such, Zimmerman (1989) links personal, behavioral, and environment self-regulated processes together (see Figure 12.1). For example, music learners need self-oriented feedback in order to (a) use strategies that are appropriate for the task and the setting (behavioral feedback loop), (b) decide how much and what kind of instruction they need or when they might choose more challenging tasks (environmental feedback loop), and (c) "keep on track" both cognitively and affectively during learning and performance (covert feedback loop; cf. Lehmann, Sloboda & Woody, 2007).

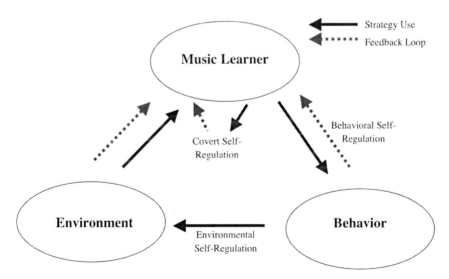

Figure 12.1 Triadic forms of musical self-regulation. Adapted from: B. J. Zimmerman (1989). A social cognitive view of self-regulated academic learning. *Journal of Educational Psychology, 81*, p. 330. © 1989 American Psychological Association.

Applying this work to studying music processes, Nielsen (2001) has proposed a model of cyclical self-regulation in music that is based on her analyses of the learning strategies of advanced music students. The value of this model is that it demonstrates the extensive self-regulatory skills that advanced students are able to apply as they strive to optimize their learning of specific musical challenges.

In Figure 12.2, the solid black arrows depict the problem to be solved, the musician's strategy use, the performance of the piece, and the level of self-evaluation of the performance. In her work, Nielsen has shown that when the musicians evaluate the success of their performance in terms of making progress, they tend to focus on a new problem (the full grey arrows in the model). At other times when they evaluate their performance as unsuccessful but believe in the value of the chosen strategy for solving the musical problem, they increase their effort and continue using the same strategy (the light grey dotted arrows). In situations where the musicians

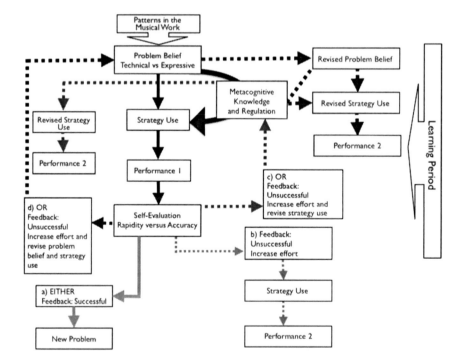

Figure 12.2   Cyclic self-regulation of learning strategies during practice, showing the basic first step and all four alternative problem-solving activities to follow it. From "Self-Regulating Learning Strategies in Instrumental Music Practice," by S. G. Nielsen, 2001, *Music Education Research, 3*, p. 155. © 2001 Taylor & Francis Ltd. Reprinted with permission.

evaluate their performance as unsuccessful and do not feel that the strategy being used is appropriate to the identified problem, they again search their metacognitive knowledge, revise the strategy and continue problem solving (the darker grey dotted arrows). A fourth option (shown with black dotted arrows) occurs when they evaluate an unsuccessful performance and realize that the nature of the original problem they have been trying to correct is not improving. In such situations they need to revise their strategy. An example would be when a technically secure performance plan is chosen for a difficult section because it is considered safer for an upcoming performance than a less reliable one that unduly extends the musician musically or expressively. In optimal practice conditions each of these ways of working are mediated through sophisticated metacognitive knowledge and self-regulation.

A FRAMEWORK FOR STUDYING SELF-REGULATED LEARNING IN MUSIC

Zimmerman (1998a, 1998b) does not view self-regulation as a fixed characteristic, such as a personality trait, ability or stage of development, but rather as a context-specific set of processes that students draw upon as they promote their own learning. McPherson and Zimmerman (2002, 2011) have described these processes as affecting one or more of six dimensions of musical self-regulation (see Table 12.1). Each dimension derives from a scientific question that can be used to underpin research on the socializing

TABLE 12.1   Dimensions of Musical Self-Regulation

Dimensions	Socialization Processes		Self-Regulation Processes
Motive	Vicarious or direct reinforcement by others	→	Self-set goals, self-reinforcement and self-efficacy
Method	Task strategies are modeled or guided socially	→	Self-initiated covert images and verbal strategies
Time	Time use is socially planned and managed	→	Time use is self-planned and managed
Behavior	Performance is socially monitored and evaluated	→	Performance is self-monitored and evaluated
Physical environment	Environments are structured by others	→	Environments are structured by self
Social	Help is provided by others	→	Help is sought personally

Note: Table adapted from McPherson, G. E. & Zimmerman, B. J. (2011). Self-regulation of musical learning: A social cognitive perspective on developing performance skills (pp. 130–175). In R. Colwell & P. Webster (Eds.), *MENC handbook of research on music learning. Volume 2: Applications.* New York: Oxford University Press.

processes that facilitate the development of the self-regulatory processes. By providing the basis for studying key processes involved in efficient musical learning as well as identifying strategies that help optimize music learning, Table 12.1 has proven invaluable for defining our research over the past decade and especially McPherson's 14-year longitudinal study involving 157 young Australian music learners (McPherson et al., 2012).

Motive

To learn a musical instrument, a child must be able to concentrate and move through different tasks in the face of many potential distractions (McPherson & Zimmerman, 2002, 2011). On any normal day, music learners can be distracted by a noisy work environment, intrusions by others and a host of personal factors, such as inappropriate practice strategies, confusion and changing interests and goals. Maintaining concentration requires a great deal of volition and personal self-motivation. As shown in Table 12.1, vicarious or direct reinforcement by others enables music learners to develop the types of self-regulatory processes needed for them to develop the self-motivation to persist under various conditions.

Children bring to their music learning clear expectations about how hard they are prepared to work based on their initial interests and motivation to commence learning (McPherson et al., 2012). This is why we encourage the music educators we train to understand the role of children's motivational beliefs, to be able to assess their presence, and to know how they might facilitate them. Understanding why some children are sufficiently self-motivated to take charge of their own learning while others lack the determination and commitment to achieve at even a mediocre level is therefore of special interest to us as music education researchers, particularly given the nature of music learning, which is often valued for leisure and recreation rather than seen as indispensable for daily life and beneficial for future employment (McPherson & Zimmerman, 2011; Robinson, 2011).

In many Western countries, one widespread system of providing an incentive to practice a musical instrument is observed when parents or teachers provide extrinsic rewards, such as stickers or pocket money, to a child for undertaking a set number of minutes' work on his or her instrument. Extensive research (Deci, Koestner, & Ryan, 1999) has shown that such rewards can undermine children's motivation to engage in musical behavior for its own intrinsic rewards, such as enjoying their increasing mastery of a skill, or feeling the emerging pulse of a dance piece as their performance becomes more fluent. Hence, interventions need to carefully control for the influence of such motivational climates both at school and at home.

Another prevalent characteristic of music learning in traditional, expertise-oriented music training is the high level of control over curricular material that the teacher imposes on the learning situation. While children learning to read their native tongue will typically be given carefully sequenced learning material in the early stages, as skill develops and personal interests emerge, teachers may be likely to encourage students to read books they choose themselves. In most formal musical training, however, teachers typically base their teaching on the view that the development of a "correct" technique requires a high level of teacher-centered repertoire choice. Our case study (Renwick & McPherson, 2002) of an adolescent clarinetist involved with a school wind ensemble showed a twelvefold increase in persistence and the spontaneous adoption of far more sophisticated learning strategies when the young player was practicing music she had chosen herself out of an emerging personal interest, compared with far less self-regulated behavior when practicing teacher-assigned tasks.

Such issues related to the undermining effect of controlling socializer behavior prompt wider considerations of how parents and teachers can foster self-motivation through a more autonomy-supportive approach (Renwick & Reeve, in press). For instance, one technique that has been found to enhance students' effort and engagement is the provision of a rationale to a child for why he or she should undertake an uninteresting activity. As an example, a teacher might help a student to see how practicing scales will be useful to learning how to improvise in a range of musical keys. Direct interventions of this type help learners of all abilities understand how the more mundane parts of practice can lead to opportunities to apply newly emerging skills in interesting and creative ways.

Method

The dimension of method allows us to contextualize the types of skills, knowledge and understandings that allow music learners to choose or adapt one approach over another. This dimension focuses on the "how" of practicing and performing music, and seeks to clarify the task specific strategies that musicians use to enhance their own musical abilities. As depicted in Table 12.1, task strategies related to rehearsing and performing music are often modeled or guided socially, and with exposure to quality teaching and increasing experience become increasingly self-initiated (McPherson & Zimmerman, 2011). In terms of the efficiency and effectiveness of these processes during musical practice, we know that at their highest level self-regulated musicians are methodical in the way they approach their learning and ability to "spontaneously invent increasingly advanced strategies to improve their performance" (Nielsen, 1999, p. 275).

Various studies in music have attempted to map out the sophistication of students' skills as they acquire musical abilities. These studies show that distinct changes occur as expertise develops (Barry & Hallam, 2002; Gruson, 1988; Hallam, 1994; Miksza, 2007) but that over 90% of the practice time of young learners is spent simply playing through a piece from beginning to end, without adopting a specific strategy to improve performance (McPherson & Renwick, 2001). Many beginners seem unaware of where they are going wrong because they have not developed their abilities to monitor and identify errors in ways that would allow them to compare the performance they are seeking to achieve with the unfolding "live" performance (Barry & Hallam, 2002). Slowly, as their skills develop, they begin to respond to errors using a musical "stutter" as they stumble over and correct individual notes (Williamon & Valentine, 2000). Then, as their growing awareness of larger structures develops, they begin to repeat slightly larger units of note patterns until they are able to focus their attention on identifying and improving difficult sections (Gruson, 1988). Young musicians tend, therefore, to focus on getting the notes correct before paying more attention to rhythm, other technical aspects of their playing, and finally to the expressive dimensions of musical performance (Barry & Hallam, 2002).

In contrast, advanced musicians are more likely to use a range of different learning strategies during their music practice as opposed to one particular type (Nielsen, 2002). The most important of these include rehearsal strategies where students focus their effort on sections of the music that have not yet been mastered, elaboration strategies where they vary their interpretation or the speed of a passage so that it can be performed under different conditions, organization strategies such as keeping track of what is to be learned in a practice diary or ordering practice to focus on mastering challenges first before playing for pleasure, and critical thinking strategies that involve experimenting with different technical or musical ways of performing a work in order to form a more sophisticated interpretation. Of these four categories of learning strategies, Nielsen (2002, 2004) has found that students tend to use rehearsal strategies (e.g., "I select important technical and musical parts and repeat these over and over again"), elaboration strategies (e.g., "I try to develop musical ideas by making connections between alternative interpretations from listening to music and from lessons"), and critical thinking strategies (e.g., "I often find myself questioning technical solutions and interpretations on my main instrument to decide if they work"), more often than organization strategies (e.g., "When I practice, I go through the music and try to find the most important musical ideas").

Some interesting instrument-specific differences have also been found. For example, singers tend to use elaboration strategies to a greater degree than instrumentalists, probably because their practice typically involves memorizing both lyrics and music (Ginsborg, 2002). Certain instrumentalists, such as string players, employ rehearsal and elaboration strategies to a lesser extent than other instrumentalists. Such results indicate that the demands inherent in playing different instruments may also affect what strategies advanced students use in their learning, in addition to time on task (Jørgensen, 1997). A number of other studies have addressed the individual diversity in the use of learning strategies by advanced students and musicians (e.g., Chaffin, Imreh, & Crawford, 2002; Ginsborg, 2002; Hallam, 2001; Miklaszewski, 1989).

Intervention processes for developing more self-regulated approaches to practice are many and varied. Over the past decade and a half, much has been achieved in understanding the cognitive strategies that young learners apply when performing music visually (sight-reading, performing rehearsed repertoire), aurally (playing from memory and by ear), and creatively (improvising). Because young learners do not always understand how to think in sound, they need to be exposed to interventions that encourage them to think musically. For example, when sight-reading music notation for the first time, we believe that students benefit from explicit, teacher-led instruction in mental strategies so that they learn to think and reflect on their own performance. As an example, during the first year of learning McPherson (2005) found that only 25% of students examined the first measure before commencing to play, only 23% and 45% respectively took note of the key signature and time signature, only 17% established a correct tempo for their performance, and only an alarming 5% took time to scan the music to identify obstacles before commencing to perform examples drawn from a standardized measure of sight-reading ability. Similar results were evident for the other measures. For example, students who maintained a practice diary in which they made notes about what and how to practice performed significantly better than their peers on rehearsed repertoire at the end of the first, second and third year of learning. Likewise, students who focused on repertoire that had to be learned before finishing their practice with pieces they could already play (as compared to the other way around) also performed significantly better across each of the first three years of their learning (McPherson, 2005).

For the aural and creative skills of performing from memory, by ear and by improvising, there was a clear positive relationship between the quality of the cognitive strategy used to prepare for a performance and actual performance (cf. McPherson & Renwick, 2011). Coding responses according to whether the cognitive strategy represented either a conceptual (independent of the instrument), kinesthetic (some physical connection to the instrument) or musical (connection between instrument and sound) approach proved a powerful means of understanding why some students struggled with their learning while others thrived. For example, the types of conceptual strategies the children employed when studying the musical notation before it was then covered and they were asked to perform it from memory were typically independent of the instrument they were playing and how the melody would sound. These involved thinking about the contour of the melody and whether it went up or down, or the letter names of individual notes (e.g., "I was trying to say it and get it stuck in my mind"; "I kept looking at it and saying the names of the notes over and over").

Kinesthetic strategies involved chanting the rhythm or pitch with rough contour while fingering the melody through on the instrument, either in sections or from beginning to end. Student in this category most often chanted the rhythm of the musical example they were trying to memorize without any sense of pitch while trying to think about how it would be fingered on their instrument.

Musical strategies were demonstrated by children who were able to link the sound of the melody to instrumental fingerings by mentally rehearsing as they studied the example in addition to processing the notation holistically by working from the beginning to the end of the piece in the same way the piece would eventually be performed. These students displayed the most highly developed capacity to coordinate their eyes, ears and hands (e.g., "I was singing it through while I was playing it on my instrument"). Most often, students who were categorized as adopting a musical strategy mentally rehearsed the music by singing the melody inwardly or out aloud while fingering it through on their instrument. They often kept doing this over and over until the music was covered and were asked to perform the melody back, exactly as it had been notated in the example.

Understanding musical progress involves much more than simply examining the relationship between the amount of practice time and levels of expertise. As we watched the children develop across their first three years of learning and analyzed their responses, we saw ample evidence that better players possessed more sophisticated strategies for playing their instrument very early in their development and that these players were the ones who went on to achieve at the highest level (McPherson, 2005). Importantly, these were the players who knew when and how to apply their strategies (especially when asked to complete the more challenging musical tasks), possessed the general understanding that their performance was tied to the quality of their effort (particularly effort expended in employing appropriate strategies to complete individual tasks), and were able to coordinate these actions to control their own playing (McPherson et al., 2012). In this sense the high achievers on each of the five aspects of performing music were those children who were in the beginning stages of developing their abilities to monitor and control their playing in the manner suggested by the *deliberate practice* literature (Ericsson, Krampe, & Tesch-Römer, 1993) where the emphasis is on continually stretching oneself to take on more challenging levels in order to master increasingly difficult skills.

One of the clear implications of our research is that music teachers need to recognize the importance of reacting perceptively to their students' performance errors by analyzing why they might occur and trying to understand what the student is thinking, especially when introducing a new skill. In our view, helping children to adopt regulatory strategies that encourage them to reflect on what they are doing, how they are doing it, and to consider alternative approaches to performing would go a long way to improving various forms of music instruction.

Also relevant is the devising of appropriate interventions for more developed players. One aspect of this line of research seeks to encourage learners to reduce a task to its essential parts so that the parts can be reorganized meaningfully. This has been the focus of Nielsen's (1999, 2001) research where learning strategies have been explored with two advanced organists to determine how to acquire the competence necessary to select relevant problem areas through visual examination of the score and by playing through larger parts of the piece or the entire piece at a tempo close to the final tempo. These problem areas were defined as "working areas" by the students and were given separate attention in their practice. With the aim of joining parts of the piece as a whole, the students played parts in different segments, played segments in different tempi and interspersed short and long segments, all according to the segments' complexity. This research shows that advanced music students often subdivide the more complex parts of a piece into smaller units that are repeated separately, and more often, and in more different segments, than less complex parts (Chaffin et al., 2002; Miklaszewski, 1989). Both musicians also developed exercises based on difficult parts of the piece and tested out different solutions to a problem when the chosen solution no longer worked as a whole (Nielsen, 1999).

Similar strategies have been found in a case study of two advanced jazz students (Nielsen, 2010). The students practiced jazz tunes by prominent jazz players, and in their first learning period of solo formulation on these tunes, they chose to learn pre-played solos on these tunes. With this task in mind, the jazz students selected a repertoire of appropriate strategies that included strategies to spot technically advanced passages in the pre-played solo and strategies that joined these passages of the pre-played solo together as a whole. For example, learning the solo by ear, one student used an mp3-player to explore very small details of the solo in a repetitive manner, and to move between listening to and practicing very short segments of the solo, before she tried to play increasingly longer segments in tempo. Although both students in a very intensive and detailed manner used these kinds of strategies in learning their pre-played solos, they also used other strategies such as making small improvisations over technically advanced passages in the solos.

A means of framing all of the above comments is to consider Zimmerman's view, which asserts that self-regulation has social origins and shifts to self sources in a developmental sequence involving four distinct dimensions: observation, emulation, self-control, and self-regulation (Zimmerman, 2000; Schunk & Zimmerman, 1997, 2003). This view proposes that learners who follow the sequence will learn more effectively and in a more self-regulated way. Reinterpreted for music, this would mean that a novice learner would acquire skill most efficiently when exposed to effective teaching, social modeling, task structuring, and encouragement (Schunk & Zimmerman, 2003). At this observational level, young musicians might be able to induce features of learning strategies from observing models—such as their teacher or other students. They will need to practice, however, in order to fully integrate the skills they are learning into their behavioral repertoires. Improvements during practice occur when learners have opportunities to observe models that provide guidance, feedback, and social reinforcement and that respond to the students' needs to refine aspects of the skill they are attempting to master. During this process, strategies and feedback are based on the learner's efforts to imitate a desired model. This means that skills (such as a hand coordination problem on piano) should be initially acquired cognitively through observing (including listening to) a model.

Learners move to the emulative level once they are able to perform at an approximate level to the model they are trying to imitate. To follow our example, at this stage the hand coordination skill a pianist was trying to master would not be at the same level as his or her teacher's demonstrations, but would nonetheless exhibit the basics of the skill, though the hand coordination and speed of performance may not yet be fully automatic or consistent. At the observational and emulative stages, learning is primarily social. Self-control emerges at the third stage when learners start to adopt strategies independently while performing transfer tasks, even though their use of these strategies, though internalized, is affected by representational standards that they attempt to duplicate (Schunk & Zimmerman, 2003). To expand our example further, the pianist would now be able to perform the musical passage independently, having mastered the basic physical skills required to perform this technique on the piano, but would still rely on aural images of modeled performances and other internalized representations plus self-reinforcement processes. Self-controlled efforts at this level involve practicing the skill in solitary but structured contexts, such as working through similar examples in other repertoire. When the skill becomes automatized, the learner can practice varying it (e.g., for speed and dynamics) according to changing contexts (e.g., an etude or sonata). At this point the learner shifts to personal outcomes as the criterion to modulate the skill, such as one's personal reaction or an audience's reactions. Self-regulated learning at this fourth level occurs when learners respond to differing personal and situational conditions by modifying learning and performing strategies and making adjustments depending on differing situations. Running in parallel, self-set goals and perceptions of self-efficacy motivate students to achieve.

Time

Self-regulated students are able to plan and manage their time more efficiently than unregulated learners (Zimmerman, 1994, 1998a), so understanding how a learner's use of time moves from being socially planned and managed to self-planned and managed has also been of interest to us as music researchers.

It is self-evident that young musicians' practice becomes increasingly more efficient as they develop their skills on an instrument. We saw this in our studies of young learners where 73% (range 57–82%) of the first year students' videotaped home practice, measured from the first to the last note of each practice session, was spent playing their instrument. This rose to 84% (range 76–90%) by year three, suggesting that these learners were beginning to use their time more efficiently. However, there were also large differences between students. The majority of the students' playing time was spent on learning musical *repertoire* (Year 1: 84%; Year 3: 93%). *Technical work* (scales and arpeggios) took up the remainder. Interestingly, the rest of these musicians' practice time (Year 1: 27%; Year 3: 16%) was spent on non-playing activities such as looking for printed music, talking or being spoken to, daydreaming, responding to distractions and expressing frustration. Less than 6% of non-practicing time was spent resting (McPherson & Renwick, 2001).

Research on academic subjects shows that many poorly self-regulating children actively avoid studying or use less time than allocated (Zimmerman, Greenberg, & Weinstein, 1994). This was also true in our analysis of beginners' practice (McPherson & Renwick, 2001). The least efficient learner spent around 21% of his total practice sessions talking with his mother about his practice tasks and expressing displeasure at his repeated failure to perform correctly, while others were seen to call out to a parent to ask when they would be allowed to stop practicing.

This line of research is in line with other work dealing with "formal" and "informal" aspects of home practice (Sloboda & Davidson, 1996). In these studies, drawn from various levels of music training, high achieving musicians have been shown to undertake significantly greater amounts of "formal" practice, such as scales, pieces and technical exercises, than their less successful peers. However, they also report more "informal" practice, such as playing their favorite pieces by ear or improvising. These "informal" ways of practicing are theorized to contribute to musical success because highest achieving students are able to find the right balance between freedom and discipline in their practice. When considered with other findings (e.g., McPherson & McCormick, 1999), results such as these suggest that students who are more cognitively engaged while practicing not only tend to do more practice, but enjoy learning their instrument more and are also more efficient with their learning. Consequently, helping students to achieve a balance between practicing to improve (or to please their teacher) as compared to practicing for pleasure is an important means of helping young musicians develop the motivational resources needed for them to develop into self-regulated learners and satisfied musicians.

Musicians also need to be able to pace and manage the use of their time, and it is not unusual to find that even young musicians will increase the quantity and quality of the time they spend practicing in the weeks leading up to a significant performance such as a music recital or examination (Hallam, 2001; Sloboda & Davidson, 1996). Hence, the intervention techniques we recommend focus on developing in learners a closer understanding of their use of time in the practice session. While research in the behaviorist tradition (Madsen & Geringer, 1981) has explored the use of devices to monitor distraction and attentiveness, we believe the modern social-cognitive emphasis on self-regulation is a more powerful means for helping teachers understand how, for instance, self-monitoring of time use can help their learners understand the close connection between time on particular tasks and the proximal development of fluency. For example, in our own teaching practice we have found that it is more effective to maintain an emphasis on mastery by asking beginning instrumentalists to practice difficult sections of a work they are learning until they can play it accurately three times in a row, and to spend time in lessons asking students when they think a predetermined criterion of mastery has been reached. This crucial element of self-monitoring and self-assessment in musical self-regulation where the emphasis is on encouraging students to monitor the process and master skills is for us far more effective than the tendency of many music teachers, including those in our studies (McPherson, Davidson & Faulkner, 2012), who typically recommend to their students that they practice for a set period of time each day.

Behavior

Self-regulated learners notice when they do not understand something or when they are having difficulty learning a particular skill (Thomas, Strage, & Curley, 1988). Consequently, the ability to choose, modify and react to feedback is central to the process of self-regulation (Zimmerman, 2000).

As inferred in other sections of this chapter, students' performance can be socially monitored and evaluated by knowledgeable others (e.g., teachers and parents) but needs to become self-monitored and evaluated to be truly self-regulating (McPherson & Zimmerman, 2011).

The principal means by which students monitor and control their performance is via the thoughts they have about what they know and do not know, and the thoughts they have about regulating their own learning (Shuell, 1988). Self-regulated learners develop along both dimensions by becoming more aware of their abilities to remember, learn and solve problems, and by developing more strategic efforts to manage their cognitive activities when learning, thinking, and problem-solving (Bruning, Schraw, Norby, & Ronning, 2004). Accordingly, we believe that interventions should aim to help musicians become more aware of how much time they will need to learn a new piece, different strategies that will help them perform correctly, and what they need to do in order to improve their playing (Barry & Hallam, 2002). But awareness of this type is not sufficient; unless students also learn to monitor and control their own cognitive processes they are unlikely to become effective learners (Bruning et al., 2004; see also Miksza, 2006, 2007). Good teaching practice therefore encourages students to describe what goes on in their minds, using probing questions that seek to encourage them to make themselves aware of how they want a particular musical phase to sound, and how they can monitor and control their own thinking to make their performance sound the way they feel makes most musical sense (Pogonowski, 1989).

Our own use of retrospective think-aloud protocols with students practicing (Nielsen, 1997; Renwick, McPherson, & McCormick, 2008) are ways of helping teachers and the students gain insight into such cognitive and metacognitive processes (Woody, 1999/2000). Perhaps the most important metacognitive skill, however, is the ability to make accurate assessments of one's own strengths and weaknesses (Hallam, 1997, 2001), in order to respond to different performance situations and to draw on a range of strategies that can be used to overcome the various technical and expressive problems encountered when playing music. Although there seems to be considerable variability among musicians, experts seem more able to construct a viable interpretation of a work while at the same time mastering the notes and planning ahead. In contrast, young learners often show little evidence of specific performance preparation and are often too reliant on their teachers to evaluate how effectively they are learning. Consequently, they often need to be guided on how to focus their concentration and attention on the music rather than their feelings about how they are doing (Hallam, 2001). The use of self-guiding speech can be particularly effective in developing fluency to perform, particularly as accuracy increases (Hallam, 1997).

To frame all of the above, we have used Zimmerman's (2000) comments about the four general criteria that people use to evaluate themselves: mastery, previous performance, normative, and collaborative. Mastery criteria involve the use of a graduated sequence from easy to hard. We see this type of mastery orientation in graded music examinations or instrumental method books that are carefully structured and sequenced according to increasing difficulty. The use of such process goal hierarchies predisposes a learner to adopt mastery criteria when self-evaluating because the sequential order of the sub-goals provides a ready index of mastery. A young musician will know, for example, that repertoire at the front of a book is easier than pieces toward the back of the book, and also that book one is easier than book two. Previous performance or self-criteria involves comparing one's current level of achievement with earlier levels. The benefit of this type of evaluation is that it highlights learning progress resulting from repeated practice.

Whereas mastery and previous performance evaluations involve judging changes in one's own performance, normative criteria involve comparing one's own progression with the progress of others. We see this in music in various ways, and especially when we make comparisons of our own playing with other members of an ensemble. The main drawback of this type of self-evaluation is that it focuses learners' attention on social factors such as how well they are doing in comparison with their peers. Normative criteria also tend to emphasize negative aspects of functioning, such as when an ensemble loses a music competition despite having improved in comparison with their previous efforts. Finally, collaborative criteria are relevant to group activities. In some ways the role of a trumpet player in an ensemble is distinctly different from that of a flutist because each instrument fulfills a different function in the ensemble. The criteria of success for trumpet performance are different than those used for other sections of an ensemble, and how well a flute player can work cooperatively with the rest of the ensemble becomes the ultimate criterion of success. Reviews on these four evaluative standards (Covington & Roberts, 1994; Zimmerman, 2000) suggest that mastery criteria enhance motivation and achievement more than normative criteria.

Physical Environment

Self-regulated learners understand how the physical environment can affect their learning and will actively seek to structure and control the setting where their learning takes place (Zimmerman, 1998a). Children come to realize the importance of these skills every time a teacher demonstrates good posture or a mother turns off the television so that her son or daughter is not distracted during practice.

Some students have little control over the setting where they can practice, especially in situations where an instrument is large or unable to be moved. For example, placing a piano in a family room close to a television can cause tension, especially if one child wishes to practice at the same time that another wants to relax in front of the television. From analyzing practice videos (McPherson & Renwick, 2001) we have become aware that many instrumentalists choose a wide variety of locations when practicing. Some of the students we studied appeared in different rooms on different days, suggesting that they were consciously choosing an appropriate place to practice depending on the family situation for that particular day. While this might enable them to obtain help from other family members whenever needed, it also meant that they were more likely to be distracted by others members of the family, pets or even the television. Additional data obtained from child and parent interviews supported our conclusion that the physical environment was mostly well equipped with a music stand and an appropriate chair. However, even from the initial stages of learning an instrument distinct differences between children were noticeable. Some displayed clearly desirable behaviors by holding their instrument correctly while seated or standing with a straight back and appropriate playing position, in contrast to others who were much less consistent with their posture. In one practice video, a young learner even sat cross-legged on his pillow with the bell of his instrument resting on his bed. From the first day they took their instruments home to practice, the children differed markedly in the way they structured their environments (see further, Austin & Berg, 2006; Pitts, Davidson, & McPherson, 2000), with the result that many students displayed clear maladaptive behaviors in the way they structured their physical environment and held their instrument.

Social Factors

Understanding the social factors that impact on learning involves examining the subtle distinction between help that is provided by others, in contrast to help that is sought personally. Obviously, parental support is vital, especially in the early months of learning when young learners often need to be reminded to practice.

McPherson and Davidson (2002) reported a large drop in reminders from parents of the 157 grades three and four beginning band students who were involved in their longitudinal study. Importantly, they concluded that very early in their learning the mothers made an assessment of their child's ability to cope with practice, as well as their own capacity to devote energy into regulating their child's practice through continual reminders and encouragement to practice. This variability in parental involvement resulted in wide differences in the children's motivation to continue learning their instruments (McPherson & Davidson, 2002, 2006; Pitts et al., 2000; see also, Zdzinski, 1996). Based on the mothers' comments and reports of practice reminders, we have even gone so far as suggesting that some mothers gave up on their children as potential musicians much earlier than the children came to feel the same way (McPherson & Davidson, 2002). Results such as these show how the socializing processes of direct reinforcement can act positively or negatively on a young learner's ability to develop the self-confidence needed to sustain musical involvement, and parallel work by other researchers showed that highly successful learners often have parents who display intense interest in their child's learning and systematically supervise their practice (Lehmann, 1997; Sosniak, 1985). Such intense interest helps young music learners to gradually build the confidence, motivation and persistence that eventually distinguish them as performers (Sosniak, 1987, 1990).

Another study (Davidson, Sloboda, & Howe, 1995/1996; Sloboda & Davidson, 1996) of 257 English students (aged eight to 18) varying widely in musical achievement and commitment shows that high achieving student musicians tend to have parents who actively support their child's practice, especially during the initial stages. They supported their child's practice with verbal reminders to practice, encouragement, moral support, and in some cases direct supervision, and their involvement was most evident in the early stages of development when their child's ability to self-regulate his or her own learning was least evident. Then, as each child's developing self-motivation started to increase and he or she became increasingly autonomous in lessons and practice, the parents, many of whom did not have a musical background themselves, started to withdraw their direct involvement even though they still maintained a high level of moral support for their child's increasing involvement with music. In contrast, low achieving student musicians tended to receive little parental support during their early years, but during their teenage years, parental pressure to motivate practice and attend lessons increased markedly (Davidson, Howe, Moore, & Sloboda, 1996; see also Davidson, Howe, & Sloboda, 1997; Davidson et al., 1995/1996; Sloboda & Davidson, 1996).

Because decisions on when and for how long to practice (or even what instrument to learn and how to become involved in music learning) are often negotiated within the home environment, it is of paramount importance that educators understand the subtle dynamics of the home environment and how this can promote or undermine children's motivation to learn an instrument. The model shown in Figure 12.3, influenced by the research of Pomerantz, Grolnick and Price (2005), helps us to frame such parent–child dynamics for the music educators we train. Using this model, we devise discussions and intervention exercises that encourage our trainees to first focus on what they might do to shape the goals (i.e., values, beliefs, attitudes, as-

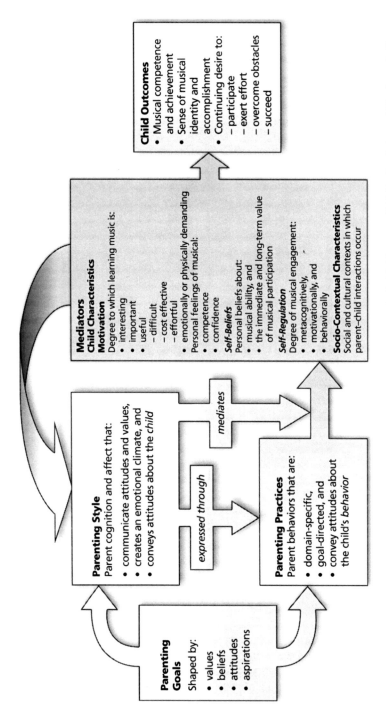

Figure 12.3 Parent–child interactions in children's musical learning. From G. E. McPherson (2009), *Psychology of Music*, p. 4. Copyright 2009 by Sage Publishing. Reprinted with permission.

pirations) of their students' parents so that they will understand the important role parents play in their children's learning. We spend time discussing the importance of how parents communicate attitudes and values to their children about how music is valued, and create the type of emotional climate that helps define the domain-specific and goal-directed behaviors and attitudes that help their offspring maintain their motivation, believe in their own abilities as they develop musical competence, gain a sense of their own musical identity, and maintain their desire to continue learning. As these same dimensions are relevant for understanding teaching, we have found this approach to be particularly useful also as a precursor for then focusing our music education trainees on discussions surrounding appropriate teacher–child interactions. Substituting "parenting" with "teaching" and "parent" with "teacher" in each of the three boxes on the left hand side of Figure 12.3 reconceptualizes the figure for dimensions that we believe are also appropriate for defining some of the more important teacher–child interactions.

The relationship between student and teacher can be intense, thereby affecting the developing musicians' conceptualization of themselves and their musical goals. As students mature and become more competent players, they start to differentiate more and more between the professional and personal qualities of their teachers, such that they may feel, for example, that their teacher is condescending and strict, but also a brilliant player (Sloboda & Davidson, 1996). It appears from various strands of research that the most important quality of a child's first teacher is to be able to communicate well and to pass on a love of music (McPherson & Davidson, 2006). Teachers who display these qualities are more likely to increase motivation because their students perceive learning as something that is fun and enjoyable. Later, after the child has started to develop skill on the instrument, the externally reinforced support received from parents and teacher develops into an intrinsic desire to learn that is focused more on improving and extended skills. Self-motivation of this sort means that students perceive learning as something that they can control themselves, with subsequently less need to rely on the external reinforcement provided by either their parents or teacher (Sloboda & Davidson, 1996).

The influence of siblings and peers is possibly just as important as that of teachers, given Davidson, Howe and Sloboda's (1997) comments that older siblings often take on the role of a teacher for their younger brother or sister, although rivalry and personality conflict between siblings can also hinder or stimulate a young child's musical development. Likewise, the influence of peers and older role models whom a student may strive to emulate have received virtually no attention from music researchers, although it is highly likely in certain instances that their impact might be profound. Even asking advice from another player in the ensemble can indicate a readiness to seek information that can benefit one's performance.

FUTURE MUSIC INTERVENTION RESEARCH

We have shown in this chapter how music research that has enthusiastically adopted Zimmerman's conceptualization of self-regulated learning has made a significant impact on our understanding of musical development. Nevertheless, research that applies self-regulated learning theory in music has been limited by a few key factors: (a) it is predominantly descriptive or correlational, (b) because of the complexity of reliably analyzing musical behavior it is based on very small samples, and (c) it has most often focused on highly teacher-centered learning situations and/or highly well-structured problem-solving tasks involving the "correct" performance of a notated score.

Building on the work of Barry J. Zimmerman and those who have been influenced by his scholarship, there is ample reason to feel confident that the next decade of research into self-regulated music learning will extend on this foundation. Among the most important lines of enquiry is research into the relative importance of motivational and behavioral components of self-regulated learning (e.g., Pintrich & De Groot, 1990; Renwick et al., 2011). This research would need to clarify the necessary duration of interventions, as early intervention music studies (e.g., Kenny, 1993) that have failed to create performance improvements may have been too brief. Studies would also profitably investigate the most effective level of instrument-specificity in an intervention intended to enhance self-regulatory skills. For instance, would violinists most usefully work in a group with their specialist teacher, or might they learn more by comparing learning strategies with players of non-string instruments? To what extent could generic skills in self-regulated musical learning transfer to the intense dynamic of the one-to-one lesson that characterizes much advanced music training?

Readers of this chapter who are experts in domains other than music may recognize many of the learning strategies we describe (e.g., planning, self-recording, and self-consequating; Zimmerman & Martinez-Pons, 1990). Many students are taught such generic self-regulatory skills at school and may or may not generalize what they have learned to their music-learning behavior. Future intervention studies in musical self-regulated learning therefore need to look at when strategies that young people learn at school in domains outside of music are effective, and when strategies that are inherently musical are necessary.

We are not aware of large sample research studies investigating the motivating effect of student choice and personal interest in music literature being taught or learned, but clearly the power of the case study we examined earlier in this chapter suggests this is an area that would clearly benefit from further attention (Cordova & Lepper, 1996). A related area that awaits self-regulated learning researchers is the emerging area of "informal" learning, which is the spontaneous learning approach typical of many popular musicians and is increasingly being trialed in school settings (Green, 2008). Here, students are given minimal guidance from the teacher, working on solving ill-structured musical problems cooperatively in groups of friends, and have considerable freedom in their choice of learning material.

Finally, very little research attention in music has focused on the ways in which some children and not others will structure their environment to ensure more effective learning. Based on our research, it appears that the physical environment is more important than previously imagined in children's musical development and that much more work is needed to tease out the types of interventions that would enable learners to become more self-regulated in the ways they assist their learning through structuring their physical environment.

Possessing highly refined self-regulatory skills is one thing, but it is an entirely different matter to "apply them persistently in the face of difficulties, stressors, or competing distractions" (Zimmerman, 1995, p. 219). In music, an area of learning that is particularly challenging for learners of all ages, difficulties, stressors and competing distractions are among the main reasons why so very few music learners continue active participation as instrumentalists and vocalists well into their adult lives. Consequently, as music research evolves and music pedagogy follows, researchers will find ample material beyond the areas highlighted here from which to study the self-regulated development of the musical mind.

CONCLUSIONS

This chapter has used self-regulation theory as a means of contextualizing some of the specific interventions that we have found to facilitate the development of school age learners – especially those in the beginning and intermediate stages of musical development. Among the most important interventions our research has uncovered are teacher-led instruction in mental strategies that prompt learners to use task-appropriate strategies when performing music and help scaffold learners to higher levels of functioning. Such procedures are especially needed in music because many instrumental lessons tend to be dominated by teacher statement-oriented behavior in which interactions consist largely of comments by the teacher about how a task should be accomplished with very few questions asked of the student (Hepler, 1986; Weerts, 1992). For example, Rostvall and West (2003) show that instrumental teachers tended to talk to their students in short utterances related to the previous or upcoming action about how the music should be performed in preference to performing and demonstrating it to them. In doing so, these teachers provided their students with "few opportunities to listen and form mental representations of the melodies they were going to learn" (p. 218). A variety of evidence in both individual and group lessons shows that this type of direct instruction results in a decrease in student attentiveness at all age levels (Kostka, 1984; Price, 1989; Spradling, 1985; Witt, 1986).

Given this evidence, we encourage the music teachers we train to recognize the importance of helping their students react perceptively to performance errors so that they are able to analyze why they might occur. Understanding what students are thinking is especially important when they are introduced to a new skill. Asking pupils to reflect on what they are doing, how they are doing it, and to consider alternative approaches to performing would in our opinion go a long way to improving music instruction, especially for children who find their learning frustrating and difficult and who typically fall behind or do not survive the first few months or years of learning.

In closing, all three authors pay homage to Barry J. Zimmerman for his insightful research over the past four decades. His work has shaped our thinking and others in music in ways that he could never have imagined possible. We are deeply indebted for his contribution to scholarship in expanding conceptions of what it means and implies to be a self-regulated learner. Barry's wisdom will continue to shape our thinking and our understandings of how young people and adults learn music all around the world.

REFERENCES

Austin, J. R. & Berg, M. H. (2006). Exploring music practice among sixth-grade band and orchestra students. *Psychology of Music, 34,* 535–558. doi:10.1177/0305735606067170

Barry, N. H. & Hallam, S. (2002). Practice. In R. Parncutt & G. E. McPherson (Eds.), *The science and psychology of music performance: Creative strategies for teaching and learning* (pp. 151–165). New York, NY: Oxford University Press.

Bartolome, S. J. (2009). Naturally emerging self-regulated practice behaviors among highly successful beginning recorder students. *Research Studies in Music Education, 31,* 37–51. doi:10.1177/1321103X09103629

Bruning, R. H., Schraw, G. J., Norby, M. M., & Ronning, R. R. (2004). *Cognitive psychology and instruction* (4th ed.). Upper Saddle River, NJ: Merrill.

Chaffin, R., Imreh, G., & Crawford, M. (2002). *Practicing perfection: Memory and piano performance.* Mahwah, NJ: Erlbaum.

Cordova, D. I. & Lepper, M. R. (1996). Intrinsic motivation and the process of learning: Beneficial effects of contextualization, personalization, and choice. *Journal of Educational Psychology, 88,* 715–730. doi:10.1037/0022-0663.88.4.715

Covington, M. V. & Roberts, B. (1994). Self-worth and college students: Motivational and personality correlates. In P. R. Pintrich, D. R. Brown & C. E. Weinstein (Eds.), *Student motivation, cognition, and learning: Essays in honor of Wilbert J. McKeachie* (pp. 157–187). Hillsdale, NJ: Erlbaum.

Davidson, J. W., Howe, M. J. A., Moore, D. G., & Sloboda, J. A. (1996). The role of parental influences in the development of musical performance. *British Journal of Developmental Psychology, 14*, 399–412. doi:10.1111/j.2044-835X.1996. tb00714.x

Davidson, J. W., Howe, M. J. A., & Sloboda, J. A. (1997). Environmental factors in the development of musical performance skill over the life span. In D. J. Hargreaves & A. C. North (Eds.), *The social psychology of music* (pp. 188–206). Oxford: Oxford University Press.

Davidson, J. W., Sloboda, J. A., & Howe, M. J. A. (1995/1996). The role of parents and teachers in the success and failure of instrumental learners. *Bulletin of the Council for Research in Music Education, 127*, 40–44.

Deci, E. L., Koestner, R., & Ryan, R. M. (1999). A meta-analytic review of experiments examining the effects of extrinsic rewards on intrinsic motivation. *Psychological Bulletin, 125*, 627–668. doi:10.1037/0033-2909.125.6.627

Ericsson, K. A., Krampe, R. T., & Tesch-Römer, C. (1993). The role of deliberate practice in the acquisition of expert performance. *Psychological Review, 100*, 363–406. doi:10.1037/0033-295X.100.3.363

Ginsborg, J. (2002). Classical singers learning and memorising a new song: An observational study. *Psychology of Music, 30*, 58–101. doi:10.1177/0305735602301007

Green, L. (2008). *Music, informal learning and the school: A new classroom pedagogy.* Aldershot, UK: Ashgate.

Gruson, L. M. (1988). Rehearsal skill and musical competence: Does practice make perfect? In J. A. Sloboda (Ed.), *Generative processes in music: The psychology of performance, improvisation, and composition* (pp. 91–112). Oxford: Clarendon Press.

Hallam, S. (1994). Novice musicians' approaches to practice and performance: Learning new music. *Newsletter of the European Society for the Cognitive Sciences of Music, 6*, 2–9.

Hallam, S. (1997). Approaches to instrumental music practice of experts and novices: Implications for education. In H. Jørgensen & A. C. Lehmann (Eds.), *Does practice make perfect? Current theory and research on instrumental music practice* (pp. 89–107). Oslo: Norges musikkhøgskole.

Hallam, S. (2001). The development of expertise in young musicians: Strategy use, knowledge acquisition and individual diversity. *Music Education Research, 3*, 7–23. doi:10.1080/14613800020029914

Hepler, L. E. (1986). *The measurement of teacher/student interaction in private music lessons, and its relation to teacher field dependence/field independence.* Unpublished doctoral dissertation, Case Western Reserve University, Cleveland, OH. Retrieved from Proquest Dissertations and Theses (UMI No. AAT 8627848).

Jørgensen, H. (1997). Time for practising? Higher level music students' use of time for instrumental practising. In H. Jørgensen & A. C. Lehmann (Eds.), *Does practice make perfect? Current theory and research on instrumental music practice* (pp. 123–139). Oslo: Norges musikkhøgskole.

Kenny, W. E. (1993). *The effect of metacognitive strategy instruction on the performance proficiency and attitude toward practice of beginning band students.* Unpublished doctoral dissertation, University of Illinois at Urbana-Champaign, Urbana, IL. Retrieved from Proquest Dissertations and Theses (UMI No. AAT 9305576)

Kostka, M. J. (1984). An investigation of reinforcement, time use and student attentiveness in piano lessons. *Journal of Research in Music Education, 32,* 113–122. doi:10.2307/3344978

Lehmann, A. C. (1997). The acquisition of expertise in music: Efficiency of deliberate practice as a moderating variable in accounting for sub-expert performance. In I. Deliège & J. A. Sloboda (Eds.), *Perception and cognition of music* (pp. 161–187). Hove, England: Psychology Press.

Lehmann, A. C., Sloboda, J. A., & Woody, R. H. (2007). *Psychology for musicians: Understanding and acquiring the skills.* Oxford: Oxford University Press.

Leon-Guerrero, A. (2008). Self-regulation strategies used by student musicians during music practice. *Music Education Research, 10,* 91–106. doi:10.1080/14613800701871439

Madsen, C. K. & Geringer, J. M. (1981). The effect of a distraction index on improving practice attentiveness and musical performance. *Bulletin of the Council for Research in Music Education, 66–67,* 46–52.

McPherson, G. E. (2005). From child to musician: Skill development during the beginning stages of learning an instrument. *Psychology of Music, 33,* 5–35. doi:10.1177/0305735605048012

McPherson, G. E. (2009). The role of parents in children's musical development. *Psychology of Music, 37,* 91–110. doi:10.1177/0305735607086049

McPherson, G. E. & Davidson, J. W. (2002). Musical practice: Mother and child interactions during the first year of learning an instrument. *Music Education Research, 4,* 141–156. doi:10.1080/14613800220119822

McPherson, G. E. & Davidson, J. W. (2006). Playing an instrument. In G. E. McPherson (Ed.), *The child as musician: A handbook of musical development* (pp. 331–351). Oxford: Oxford University Press.

McPherson, G. E., Davidson, J. W., & Faulkner, R. (2012). *Music in our lives: Redefining musical development, ability and identity.* Oxford: Oxford University Press.

McPherson, G. E. & McCormick, J. (1999). Motivational and self-regulated learning components of musical practice. *Bulletin of the Council for Research in Music Education, 141,* 98–102. Retrieved from http://www.jstor.org/stable/40318992

McPherson, G. E. & Renwick, J. M. (2001). A longitudinal study of self-regulation in children's musical practice. *Music Education Research, 3,* 169–186. doi:10.1080/14613800120089232

McPherson, G. E. & Renwick, J. M. (2011). Self-regulation and mastery of musical skills. In B. J. Zimmerman & D. H. Schunk (Eds.), *Handbook of self-regulation of learning and performance* (pp. 234–248). New York, NY: Routledge.

McPherson, G. E. & Zimmerman, B. J. (2002). Self-regulation of musical learning: A social cognitive perspective. In R. Colwell & C. Richardson (Eds.), *The new handbook of research on music teaching and learning* (pp. 327–347). New York, NY: Oxford University Press.

McPherson, G. E. & Zimmerman, B. J. (2011). Self-regulation of musical learning: A social cognitive perspective on developing performance skills. In R. Colwell & P. Webster (Eds.), *MENC handbook of research on music learning. Volume 2: Applications* (pp. 130–175). New York, NY: Oxford University Press.

Miklaszewski, K. (1989). A case study of a pianist preparing a musical performance. *Psychology of Music, 17,* 95–109. doi:10.1177/0305735689172001

Miksza, P. (2006). An exploratory investigation of self-regulatory and motivational variables in the music practice of junior high band students. *Contributions to Music Education, 33*(2), 9–26.

Miksza, P. (2007). Effective practice: An investigation of observed practice behaviors, self-reported practice habits, and the performance achievement of high school wind players. *Journal of Research in Music Education, 55*, 359–375. doi:10.1177/0022429408317513

Nielsen, S. G. (1997). Verbal protocol analysis and research on instrumental music practice. In A. Gabrielsson (Ed.), *Proceedings of the third triennial ESCOM Conference* (pp. 183–188). Uppsala, Sweden: Uppsala University.

Nielsen, S. G. (1999). Learning strategies in instrumental music practice. *British Journal of Music Education, 16*, 275–291.

Nielsen, S. G. (2001). Self-regulating learning strategies in instrumental music practice. *Music Education Research, 3*, 155–167. doi:10.1080/14613800120089223

Nielsen, S. G. (2002). Musical practice in the conservatoires: Strategies advanced students use in self-regulated learning. In I. M. Hanken, S. G. Nielsen & M. Nerland (Eds.), *Research in and for higher music education: Festschrift for Harald Jørgensen* (pp. 69–84). Oslo: Norwegian Academy of Music.

Nielsen, S. G. (2004). Strategies and self-efficacy beliefs in instrumental and vocal individual practice: A study of students in higher music education. *Psychology of Music, 32*, 418–431. doi:10.1177/0305735604046099

Nielsen, S. G. (2010, September). *Learning pre-played solos: Two case studies.* Paper presented at the the Student Ownership Conference, Royal Academy of Music, Stockholm, Sweden.

Pintrich, P. R. (1995). Understanding self-regulated learning. In P. R. Pintrich (Ed.), *Understanding self-regulated learning* (pp. 3–12). San Francisco, CA: Jossey-Bass Publishers.

Pintrich, P. R. & De Groot, E. V. (1990). Motivational and self-regulated learning components of classroom academic performance. *Journal of Educational Psychology, 82*, 33–40. doi:10.1037/0022-0663.82.1.33

Pitts, S. E., Davidson, J. W., & McPherson, G. E. (2000). Developing effective practice strategies: Case studies of three young instrumentalists. *Music Education Research, 2*, 45–56. doi:10.1080/14613800050004422

Pogonowski, L. (1989). Metacognition: A dimension of musical thinking. In E. Boardman (Ed.), *Dimensions of musical thinking* (pp. 9–19). Reston, VA: Music Educators National Conference.

Pomerantz, E. M., Grolnick, W. S., & Price, C. E. (2005). The role of parents in how children approach achievement: A dynamic process perspective. In A. J. Elliot & C. S. Dweck (Eds.), *Handbook of competence and motivation* (pp. 259–278). New York, NY: Guilford.

Price, H. E. (1989). An effective way to teach and rehearse: Research supports using sequential patterns. *Update, 8*, 42–46.

Renwick, J. M., McCormick, J., & McPherson, G. E. (2011). *An investigation of self-determined motivational beliefs and self-regulated practising behaviours.* Manuscript submitted for publication.

Renwick, J. M. & McPherson, G. E. (2002). Interest and choice: Student-selected repertoire and its effect on practising behaviour. *British Journal of Music Education, 19*, 173–188. doi:10.1017/S0265051702000256

Renwick, J. M., McPherson, G. E., & McCormick, J. (2008, July). *Effort management, self-monitoring and corrective strategies in the practising behaviour of intermediate instrumentalists: Observations and retrospective think-aloud protocols.* Paper presented at the International Society for Music Education world conference, Bologna, Italy.

Renwick, J. M. & Reeve, J. (in press). Supporting motivation in music education. In G. E. McPherson & G. Welch (Eds.), *The Oxford handbook of music education.* New York, NY: Oxford University Press.

Robinson, K. (2011). *Out of our minds: Learning to be creative* (2nd ed.). Southgate, Chichester, UK: Capstone.

Rostvall, A. -L. & West, T. (2003). Analysis of interaction and learning in instrumental teaching. *Music Education Research, 5*, 213–226. doi:10.1080/14613800032000126319

Schunk, D. H. & Zimmerman, B. J. (1997). Social origins of self-regulatory competence. *Educational Psychologist, 32*, 195–208.

Schunk, D. H. & Zimmerman, B. J. (Eds.). (1998). *Self-regulated learning: From teaching to self-reflective practice.* New York, NY: Guilford Press.

Schunk, D. H. & Zimmerman, B. J. (2003). Self-regulation and learning. In W. M. Reynolds & G. E. Miller (Eds.), *Handbook of psychology: Educational psychology* (pp. 59–78). Hoboken, NJ: John Wiley & Sons.

Shuell, T. J. (1988). The role of transfer in the learning and teaching of music: A cognitive perspective. In C. Fowler (Ed.), *The Crane symposium: Toward an understanding of the teaching and learning of music performance* (pp. 143–167). Potsdam, NY: Potsdam College of the State University of New York.

Sloboda, J. A. & Davidson, J. W. (1996). The young performing musician. In I. Deliège & J. A. Sloboda (Eds.), *Musical beginnings: Origins and development of musical competence* (pp. 171–190). Oxford: Oxford University Press.

Sosniak, L. A. (1985). Learning to be a concert pianist. In B. S. Bloom (Ed.), *Developing talent in young people* (pp. 19–67). New York, NY: Ballantine Books.

Sosniak, L. A. (1987). The nature of change in successful learning. *Teachers College Record, 88*, 519–535.

Sosniak, L. A. (1990). The tortoise, the hare, and the development of talent. In M. J. A. Howe (Ed.), *Encouraging the development of exceptional skills and talent* (pp. 477–506). Leicester, England: The British Psychological Society.

Spralding, R. L. (1985). The effect of time out from performance on attentiveness and attitude of university band students. *Journal of Research in Music Education, 33*, 123–127. doi:10.2307/3344732

Thomas, J. W., Strage, A., & Curley, R. (1988). Improving students' self-directed learning: Issues and guidelines. *The Elementary School Journal, 88*, 313–326. Retrieved from http://www.jstor.org/stable/1001959

Weerts, R. (1992). Research on the teaching of instrumental music. In R. Colwell (Ed.), *Handbook of research on music teaching and learning* (pp. 577–583). New York, NY: Schirmer Books.

Williamon, A. & Valentine, E. (2000). Quantity and quality of musical practice as predictors of performance quality. *British Journal of Psychology, 91,* 353–376. doi:10.1348/000712600161871

Woody, R. (1999/2000, December/January). Getting into their heads. *American Music Teacher, 49,* 24–27.

Witt, A. C. (1986). Use of class time and student attentiveness in secondary instrumental music rehearsals. *Journal of Research in Music Education, 34,* 34–42. doi:10.2307/3344796

Zdzinski, S. F. (1996). Parental involvement, selected student attributes, and learning outcomes in instrumental music. *Journal of Research in Music Education, 44,* 34–48. doi:10.2307/3345412

Zimmerman, B. J. (1989). Models of self-regulated learning and academic achievement. In B. J. Zimmerman & D. H. Schunk (Eds.), *Self-regulated learning and academic achievement: Theory, research, and practice* (pp. 1–25). New York, NY: Springer.

Zimmerman, B. J. (1994). Dimensions of academic self-regulation: A conceptual framework for education. In D. H. Schunk & B. J. Zimmerman (Eds.), *Self-regulation of learning and performance: Issues and educational applications* (pp. 3–21). Hillsdale, NJ: Erlbaum.

Zimmerman, B. J. (1995). Self-efficacy and educational development. In A. Bandura (Ed.), *Self-efficacy in changing societies* (pp. 202–231). New York, NY: Cambridge University Press.

Zimmerman, B. J. (1998a). Academic studying and the development of personal skill: A self-regulatory perspective. *Educational Psychologist, 33,* 73–86. doi:10.1037/0022-0663.91.2.241

Zimmerman, B. J. (1998b). Developing self-fulfilling cycles of academic regulation: An analysis of exemplary instructional models. In D. H. Schunk & B. J. Zimmerman (Eds.), *Self-regulated learning: From teaching to self-reflective practice* (pp. 1–19). New York, NY: Guilford Press.

Zimmerman, B. J. (2000). Attaining self-regulation: A social cognitive perspective. In M. Boekaerts, P. R. Pintrich & M. Zeidner (Eds.), *Handbook of self-regulation* (pp. 13–39). San Diego, CA: Academic Press.

Zimmerman, B. J., Greenberg, D., & Weinstein, C. E. (1994). Self-regulating academic study time: A strategy approach. In D. H. Schunk & B. J. Zimmerman (Eds.), *Self-regulation of learning and performance: Issues and educational applications* (pp. 181–199). Hillsdale, NJ: Erlbaum.

Zimmerman, B. J. & Martinez-Pons, M. (1990). Student differences in self-regulated learning: Relating grade, sex, and giftedness to self-efficacy and strategy use. *Journal of Educational Psychology, 82,* 51–59. doi:10.1037/0022-0663.82.1.51

CHAPTER 13

IMPLEMENTATION OF SELF-REGULATION INTERVENTIONS IN PHYSICAL EDUCATION AND SPORTS CONTEXTS

Marios Goudas, Athanasios Kolovelonis, and Irini Dermitzaki

Current theoretical approaches of learning focus on how students can self-direct their own learning to become self-regulated learners (Zimmerman & Schunk, 2001). Self-regulated learning emphasizes the agentic role that students have in the process of learning and refers to "self-generated thoughts, feelings, and actions that are planned and cyclically adapted to the attainment of personal goals" (Zimmerman, 2000, p. 14). Self-regulated learning involves cognitive, metacognitive, motivational, affective, and volitional processes (Boekaerts, 1996; Efklides, 2005). In particular, self-regulatory skills and strategies can be cognitive, metacognitive, and affective or motivational (Dermitzaki, 2005) and they influence students' achievements (Dermitzaki, Leondari, & Goudas, 2009). Students who use such self-regulatory skills are more likely to learn more, be successful in school, and become lifelong learners compared to their peers who lack such skills (Zimmerman, 2000).

Applications of Self-Regulated Learning across Diverse Disciplines, pages 383–415
Copyright © 2013 by Information Age Publishing
All rights of reproduction in any form reserved.   **383**

Therefore, the development of self-regulated learners is a challenge presented to educators interested in promoting effective learning.

The development of self-regulation facilitates the achievement of high levels of learning and performance in motor and sport skills (Zimmerman & Kitsantas, 2005). Reviewing studies examining self-regulation in sports and physical education, Crews, Lochbaum, and Karoly (2001) found that different theoretical approaches had been adopted, and self-regulation had been used as an "umbrella" term rather than a strategy or a set of strategies. In fact, the literature on self-regulation in the physical domain is far from systematic and consistent theoretically and methodologically (Crews et al., 2001; Gould & Chung, 2004). Therefore, a coherent theoretical background to guide self-regulation research in sports and physical education is necessary. Zimmerman's theory and models of self-regulated learning are suitable for understanding self-regulation development because they consider the collective impact of personal, behavioral, and environmental influences on self-regulated learning (Petlichkoff, 2004). Next, we briefly present these models, and we describe how they have influenced research in sports and physical education.

Zimmerman (2000) has proposed that self-regulatory processes and associated motivational beliefs interact in three cyclical phases: forethought, performance, and self-reflection. The forethought phase precedes students' engagement in a task and includes task analysis (e.g., strategic planning, goal setting) and motivational beliefs (e.g., self-efficacy). In this phase students set personal goals and plan how to attain these goals. The performance phase involves self-observation and self-control processes that students use during learning to attain their goals. During this phase students perform the task, self-observe their performance, and use self-control strategies to facilitate the attainment of their goals. The self-reflection phase involves processes that follow learning efforts and includes self-judgment (e.g., causal attribution) and self-reaction (e.g., satisfaction). This view of self-regulation is cyclical in that processes, beliefs, and self-reflections in each phase can affect efforts to learn during subsequent phases (Cleary & Zimmerman, 2001). Moreover, Zimmerman (2000) has proposed that students' self-regulatory skills develop through four sequential levels, namely, observation, emulation, self-control, and self-regulation. First, students watch a model perform the skill (observation level) and then they practice the skill, receiving social feedback (emulation level). Next they self-direct their practice setting process goals and self-monitoring their performance (self-control level). Finally, they can use and adopt the skill in changing environmental conditions focusing of performance goals (self-regulation level). The sequential experience of these four levels results in optimal learning (Zimmerman & Kitsantas, 2005). For a comprehensive description of these models see Zimmerman (2000).

Zimmerman's models are appropriate frameworks for designing, implementing and evaluating self-regulated learning interventions in sports and physical education contexts (Petlichkoff, 2004). They describe the process of self-regulated learning (i.e., the cyclical model of self-regulation) and provide an instructional approach for developing self-regulatory skills (i.e., the four-level training model). In particular, Zimmerman's theory and models delineate self-regulated learning as a process, rather than an aptitude, that can occur in virtually any context (Zimmerman, 2000). Therefore, these models can be used to explain students' efforts to regulate their learning in educational contexts in general and in physical education in particular. They include not only self-regulatory strategies but also motivational beliefs, such as self-efficacy. Moreover, according to these models, the development of self-regulated learning is based not only on self sources but also on social support (Zimmerman, 2000). Social cognitive views emphasize the role of socializing agents (e.g., teachers) in the development of self-regulated learning. Thus, a physical educator can play a significant role in promoting his or her students' self-regulated learning. Another advantage of Zimmerman's models is that they include processes and techniques that are common in sports (e.g., goal setting, modeling, feedback). This can facilitate the introduction and the implementation of these models in the sport and physical education domains. Moreover, these models propose that students can use various self-control techniques during performance. In sport and physical education settings various performance enhancement techniques such as self-talk are used. The incorporation of such techniques can make these models quite suitable for use in sport and physical education domains.

Developing students' self-regulatory skills can facilitate learning and performance in physical education. Thus, investigating the development of students' self-regulation is of great interest (Petlichkoff, 2004). Zimmerman's models and theory can guide such research in physical education. These models largely influenced our research program examining the development of self-regulated learning of motor and sport skills in physical education. In particular, the framework in our research was the cyclical model and the four-level training model of self-regulated learning development (Zimmerman, 2000). The social cognitive view emphasizes the role of both social (e.g., modeling, social feedback) and self (e.g., self-observation) sources on the development of self-regulated learning. That is, self-regulatory processes can be acquired from and sustained by social and self sources of influence (Zimmerman, 2000). Moreover, we focused on fifth and sixth grade elementary students from coeducational physical education classes because self-regulation research in earlier ages is limited (Petlichkoff, 2004).

The aim of this chapter is to present recent research findings regarding the development of self-regulated learning of motor and sport skills in physical education and sport contexts. This research used Zimmerman's models as theoretical background and provided evidence regarding the effectiveness of these models in the contexts of sports and physical education. Moreover, this chapter aims to offer practical suggestions regarding the use of processes and techniques for enhancing self-regulated learning in sports and physical education. These suggestions can be a useful guide for coaches and physical educators to help their students to enhance self-regulated learning. We also present an instructional approach of teaching motor and sport skills based on the four-level training model of self-regulated learning development (Zimmerman, 2000). We illustrate this instructional approach with a hypothetical case scenario to help coaches and physical educators comprehend key issues in implementing this approach. Finally, reflecting on theory and previous research, we provide suggestions for future research focusing on improving the instructional approach.

SELF-REGULATED LEARNING RESEARCH IN PHYSICAL EDUCATION

In this section we present our research implemented in physical education settings. The purpose of our research program was to expand Zimmerman's original studies examining the four-level process of self-regulation development. First, we describe the four-level training model in more detail and present how we built on previous research findings and theory to design our research program. Next, we describe our main intervention and the modifications developing our research program. Then, we present our research findings and discus them with reference to theory and previous research.

The Four-Level Training Model

According to the four-level training model (Zimmerman, 2000) students develop their self-regulatory skills through four sequential levels, namely, observation, emulation, self-control, and self-regulation. First, students watch a model perform the skill (observation level) to cognitively acquire the performance standards. Then they practice the skill while receiving social feedback (emulation level), which includes performance information and assistance from the social environment (e.g., coaches; Smith & Smoll, 1997). This feedback helps students to correct their errors, to form the performance standards and to incorporate them into their own movement repertoire. At the self-control level, students should self-direct their learning by setting goals, trying to master the performance standards, and self-monitoring, paying "deliberate attention to some aspects of their behavior"

(Schunk, 1996, p. 360). Self-control techniques such as self-talk, which refers to "those automatic statements reflective of, and deliberate techniques (e.g., thought-stopping) athletes use to direct, sports-related thinking" (Hardy, Oliver, & Tod, 2009, p. 38) can be used during performance to help students to enhance their performance. At the self-regulation level students focus on performance outcomes and use these outcomes to make adjustments to their skills if necessary. They can adapt the skill and use it in changing conditions developing their own distinctive styles of performing.

Teaching styles, such as reciprocal and self-check methods, are also associated with the four-level training model, because they can be used during emulative and self-controlled practice (Zimmerman, 2000). In the reciprocal style, students practice a task in pairs alternating in the roles of the doer who performs the task and the observer who offers immediate and on-going feedback to the doer. In the self-check style, students practice a task independently in structured settings, self-observing and self-evaluating their performances (Mosston & Ashworth, 2002).

Previous research has examined the effectiveness of aspects of the four-level training model. Kitsantas, Zimmerman, and Cleary (2000) found that girls who experienced sequentially observational and emulative learning improve their performance and reported higher levels of self-efficacy, intrinsic interest, and satisfaction. Zimmerman and Kitsantas (1997) found that students who set a process goal first and then shifted to an outcome goal displayed the highest dart-throwing performance and reported the highest levels of self-efficacy, satisfaction, and intrinsic interest, compared to students in the other goal setting conditions. These studies provided initial support for the effectiveness of aspects of the four-level training model of self-regulated learning development.

However, many issues regarding the effectiveness of this model remain unexplored, such as the effectiveness of the sequential practice from the emulation to the self-control level. This transition is considered a critical point in the development of self-regulated learning because students proceed from the practice with social support to the self-directed practice (Zimmerman, 2000). Therefore, in our line of research we examined the effectiveness of the sequential practice at the emulation and the self-control levels. Next, we describe the core characteristics of the intervention used in our research as well as its modifications.

Description of the Intervention

Our line of research focused on the four-level training model. In particular, the purpose of the main intervention was to examine the effectiveness of the sequential practice from the emulation to the self-control level.

Students participated in this intervention individually in a single practice session during a physical education lesson. The practice session was divided into two consecutive subsections to simulate the emulation and the self-control levels. The dart-throwing skill was used. First, we provided all students with observational learning experiences (i.e., oral instructions and modeling). Then, we compared students who sequentially experienced emulative (i.e., practice with social feedback) and self-control practice (i.e., practice with process goals and self-recording) with students who missed one of these levels and control group students who simply practiced the skill.

The procedures lasted approximately 30 minutes for each student and included initial guidelines, instructions and modeling, experimental manipulations, a practice session, and post-test measures. Upon arriving in the gym, students were informed regarding the intervention, provided with instructions and observed a demonstration of the dart-throwing skill. Then, they practiced dart-throwing for 16 minutes in two consecutive practice sessions of eight minutes each, which corresponded to the emulation and the self-control level. During the emulative phase, students practiced the skill while receiving social feedback. In order for all students to receive the same quantity and quality of feedback, the experimenter used a schedule that determined the time, the type, and the content of feedback. In the self-control phase students set process goals for improving their dart-throwing performance and self-observed their performance using a self-recording card. To ensure treatment fidelity, during the procedure the experimenter was communicating with each student in a standardized manner following a specific written protocol. This protocol included in written forms the phases of each study and the guidelines that the experimenter would provide to students in each phase of the study. Immediately after the practice, students were tested in the dart-throwing skill and responded to short questions regarding their beliefs, such as their enjoyment for dart-throwing practice and their satisfaction regarding their dart-throwing skill.

Over time, this original methodological design was expanded to include other aspects of the four-level training model. For example, we implemented the four-level training model in more natural teaching conditions in physical education. In particular, we examined the effectiveness of the sequential practice from the emulation to the self-control level involving students in practice in small groups. Moreover, we used both motor (e.g., dart-throwing) and sport skills (e.g., basketball dribbling and chest pass) to increase the ecological validity of our results.

We also examined the effectiveness of the combined effects of self-talk and goal setting, proposing the incorporation of self-talk in these models. The use of self-control techniques, such as self-talk, can enhance students' performance. Furthermore, associating the four-level training model with teaching approaches, we examined the effectiveness of using two teaching styles (i.e., reciprocal and self-check styles) that are often used in sport and physical education settings to guide students' practice at the emulation and the self-control levels of self-regulated learning. In our research, both boys and girls from coeducational physical education classes participated, expanding previous research in which only adolescents girls had been used.

Next, we describe the findings of our research program that have been organized in four sections including the research on the transition from the emulative to self-controlled practice, and the effects of goal setting and self-recording, self-talk, and teaching styles.

Research Findings

In this section we present findings from our research program. We have organized these finding in four subsections. In the first subsection we describe research that examined the effectiveness of the sequential practice from the emulation to the self-control level. This line of research focused on transition from emulative to self-control phase. Next, we focused on the effects of self-regulatory processes, presenting findings regarding the effects of goal setting and self-recording on students' performance. The third subsection focuses on incorporating self-control techniques in Zimmerman's models, describing research examining the effects of self-talk on students' performance. Finally, findings regarding the incorporation of two teaching styles, the reciprocal and the self-check style, in the four-level training model are presented.

Transition from Emulative to Self-Control Phase

In this section, research findings regarding the effectiveness of the sequential practice from the emulation to the self-control level are presented. Implementing the main intervention described above, Kolovelonis, Goudas, and Dermitzaki (2010) found that students who sequentially practiced with social feedback at the emulation level and set process goals and self-recorded their performance at the self-control level displayed higher dart-throwing performance compared to control group students. Furthermore, sixth grade students who received social feedback at the emulation level and those who practiced with process goals and self-recording at the self-control level reported higher satisfaction and intrinsic motivation respectively, compared to control group students. Thus, the sequential use of the self-regulatory process of observational learning, emulative practice with social feedback, and goal setting and self-recording was effective.

Kolovelonis, Goudas, Hassandra, and Dermitzaki (2012) sought to improve the intervention implemented by Kolovelonis et al. (2010), addressing some of the limitations of the previous research (e.g., individual participation, post-test designs, lack of sport skills used). In particular, they examined the effects of setting either process or performance goals and self-recording at the self-control level after students had experienced emulative practice. They also adopted a pre- to post-test design, involved repeated demonstrations of the skill, employed teaching and testing in small groups, and used a common sport skill (i.e., basketball dribble). They found that students who received social feedback and observed repeated demonstrations at the observation and the emulation levels and then set process or performance goals and self-recorded their performance at the self-control level improved their dribbling performance from pre- to post-test. Moreover, students who did not receive social feedback at the emulation level but experienced self-control practice setting goals and self-recording improved their dribbling performance from pre- to post-test.

Kolovelonis, Goudas, Dermitzaki, and Kitsantas (in press) expanded previous interventions by introducing goals at the emulation level and examining the effects of practice at different self-regulatory levels on students' performance calibration. Calibration is the degree to which a student's perception of performance corresponds with his or her actual performance (Keren, 1991) and can have important implications regarding students' motivation (Schunk & Pajares, 2009) and self-regulation (Efklides & Misailidi, 2010). They found that students who sequentially experienced emulative practice (i.e., receiving social feedback) and self-control practice (i.e., setting either process or performance goals) improved their dribbling performance from pre- to post-test and outperformed control group students. Introducing process or performance goals at the emulation level was equally effective with setting the same goals at the self-control level. These results supported the effectiveness of the four-level training model of self-regulated learning development. Regarding the effects of practice at the emulation and the self-control levels on students' dribbling performance calibration, they found no differences among groups in performance calibration. All students overestimated their performance, with the exception of the students who set process goal for their emulative and self-control practice, who underestimated their performance. Similarly, Kolovelonis, Goudas, and Dermitzaki (2012) found that students who practiced dribbling under different self-regulatory conditions did not differ in calibration bias and accuracy, and all overestimated their performance. However, regardless of the group, sixth grade students were more accurate in estimating their dart-throwing performance compared to fifth grade students. The accuracy of the monitoring process is a factor that may have important implications regarding motivation and self-regulation and should be further explored in future research because this kind of research in sport and physical education is limited. For example, students who overestimate their performance may be reluctant to continue their learning efforts because they believe that they have already mastered the skill.

Exploring the Effectiveness of Specific Techniques: Goal Setting and Self-Recording

Kolovelonis, Goudas, and Dermitzaki (2011a) focused on the effects of different goals and self-recording on students' self-regulated learning. After experiencing observational learning, students practiced dart-throwing for 16 minutes, setting process, performance or combined process and performance goals and self-recording or not their performance using a self-recording card with a three level scale for evaluating their performances. Students were also asked to make attributions and inferences regarding their performance during practice. The results showed that self-recording had a positive effect on fifth and sixth grade students' dart-throwing performance, supporting previous findings (Cleary, Zimmerman, & Keating, 2006; Kitsantas & Zimmerman, 1998, 2006; Zimmerman & Kitsantas, 1996, 1997) and providing additional evidence regarding the effectiveness of a three-level self-recording scale. No difference was found among groups with different goals. Setting combined process and performance goals was equally effective, with setting only process or only performance goals at the self-control level. These findings did not fully support the differences among process and performance goals found in previous research (Kitsantas & Zimmerman, 1998; Zimmerman & Kitsantas, 1996, 1997). However, parallel to the approach of shifting from process to performance goals proposed by Zimmerman and Kitsantas (1997), the alternative multiple goal approach of combining process and performance goals concurrently may have positive effects—in simple tasks, at least—especially in physical education settings where the instructional time is limited. Furthermore, in line with previous research (Kitsantas & Zimmerman, 1998), this study showed that students who set goals compared to those who did not set goals attributed their lower dart-throwing performance to their technique errors and reported that they focus on improving their technique in order to improve their performance.

Use of Self-Control Techniques: Self-Talk

During performance, students should use self-control techniques to enhance their performance and to attain their goals (Zimmerman, 2000). For example, Kitsantas and Zimmerman (1998) found that the use of a strategy of analyzing the throwing process and making technical adjustments in two basic elements of dart-throwing had positive effect on students' performance. In sport settings, various techniques such as self-talk (Hardy et al., 2009) are used. Kolovelonis, Goudas, and Dermitzaki (2012) examined the combined effects of goal setting and self-talk on students' dart-throwing performance. Students were asked to use the instructional self-talk during dart-throwing practice, using the cue-word "stretch," which aimed to help them to remind themselves of the vertical forearm motion that is considered a basic element of dart-throwing. Results showed that elementary students who combined self-talk with either process or performance goals outperformed students in the goal only and control group conditions. These results supported the hypothesis of using self-talk as a self-control technique during performance for enhancing the development of self-regulated learning (Zimmerman, 2000).

Considering that two basic types of self-talk have been identified, Kolovelonis, Goudas, and Dermitzaki (2011b) compared the effects of instructional and motivational self-talk on students' performance in physical education. Instructional and motivational self-talk were equally effective regarding performance in a basketball chest pass test, but motivational self-talk was more effective compared to instructional self-talk in a modified push-ups test. That is, self-talk is an effective technique for motor task performance enhancement, but the demands of the task should be considered when physical educators select the most appropriate types of self-talk.

Teaching Styles as Self-Regulatory Facilitators

The teaching method may also affect the development of self-regulated learning. In reciprocal teaching, students practice the skill and receive feedback from their peers, whereas during self-check teaching students self-direct their practice, setting goals and self-monitoring their performance (Mosston & Ashworth, 2002). These instructional formats related directly to the basic principles of the emulation (i.e., practice with social feedback) and the self-control (i.e., practice with goals and self-recording) levels of the four-level training model. Kolovelonis, Goudas, and Gerodimos (2011) examined the effects of the reciprocal and the self-check styles on students' basketball chest pass performance and on related psychosocial variables in a single physical education session. The authors found that students who practiced within a reciprocal teaching format, the self-check style, or a combined condition outperformed control group students in chest pass accuracy and technique. However, no differences were found among the four groups in self-efficacy, satisfaction, effort, and enjoyment. Longer practice sessions may have produced positive effects on these variables. These findings provided initial evidence regarding the use of the reciprocal and the self-check styles as teaching approaches at the emulation and the self-control levels, respectively.

Students' capacity to discriminate accurately the status of their own or their peers' performance in a skill performed is an important factor for the effectiveness of the reciprocal and the self-check styles and the development of self-regulated learning as well. Kolovelonis and Goudas (in press) found that students were moderately accurate in peer- and self-recording, with a tendency to overestimate their own or their peers' performance. No difference in recording accuracy was found among students who used the reciprocal and the self-check styles. Furthermore, students who, regardless of the teaching style, received more accurate feedback outperformed in the chest pass test those who received less accurate feedback.

Reflecting on Research Findings

Our findings supported the effectiveness of the four-level training model, extending previous findings (Kitsantas et al., 2000; Zimmerman & Kitsantas, 1997) in several important ways. In particular, we expanded previous research by showing the effectiveness of the sequential practice from the emulation to the self-control level. Moreover, we increased the ecological validity of this model by (a) using both motor and sport skills, (b) employing both boys and girls from coeducational physical education classes, and (c) establishing real-life teaching conditions involving students in group practice. Furthermore, we provided evidence regarding the positive effects of using self-talk as a self-control technique during performance. Self-talk is a self-control technique that is widely used in sports and physical education contexts. Incorporating such self-control techniques in Zimmerman's models can make these models more suitable for use in sports settings. Moreover, we proposed the incorporation of the reciprocal and the self-check styles of teaching at the emulation and the self-control levels of self-regulated learning development, respectively. During emulative practice, students can receive social feedback from their peers using the reciprocal style. Moreover, the use of the self-check style can provide students with the opportunity to practice the skill independently, setting goals and self-recording their performance.

However, a consistent finding in previous research regarding the positive effects of experimental treatments on students' motivational beliefs was not fully confirmed in our research. Elementary students compared to secondary ones usually report higher levels of motivation for participating in physical education (e.g., Kolovelonis, 2007). In fact, elementary students who participated in our research scored high in the motivation measures, and thus the detection of potential treatment effects was difficult. Taking into account this innate enthusiasm of young children to participate in sport activities, physical educators and coaches should focus on teaching self-regulatory process that can help young children to enhance their competence.

PRACTICAL APPLICATIONS

Zimmerman's (2000) models and the respective research findings can be translated into practical recommendations for physical educators and coaches. Next, we offer such recommendations regarding the self-regulatory processes we examined in our research, and then we present an instructional approach for teaching motor and sport skills that combines all these processes. We also illustrate the use of these self-regulatory processes in a hypothetical scenario.

Modeling

Modeling serves as a primary vehicle through which social agents (e.g., teachers) socially convey self-regulatory skills to children (Zimmerman, 2000). In the initial learning phases, students watch a model performs and listen to his or her verbal descriptions to cognitively acquire the key elements needed for performing a new skill. Modeling includes not only motor and sport skills but also the use of self-regulatory skills. For example, a physical educator can demonstrate the use of a self-control technique, such as self-talk, during practice. Moreover, physical educators can demonstrate to their students how to adopt a process goal to guide practice during the self-control level and how to use a self-monitoring technique, such as self-recording, to monitor their performance.

From an instructional view, modeling should include a teacher's or an expert student's demonstrations of the skill, as well as the use of videos or pictures if they are available. Verbal instructions can be combined with behavioral modeling to help students focus on the critical elements of the skill (Bandura, 1997). Skills should be demonstrated before students start practicing. However, physical educators may repeatedly demonstrate a skill to a student who strives to acquire performance standards or to a whole class when the skill is complex and difficult to master. Physical educators and coaches should secure that all students stand in a position from which they have a clear view to observe the demonstration of the skill (Bandura, 1986). Furthermore, physical educators should demonstrate motor and sport skills using both sides of the body and not only the dominant one.

Social Feedback

Social feedback should include affirmative performance feedback, reminders about the proper performance, positive reinforcements, and attributional feedback. An effective approach of providing these types of feedback is the "positive sandwich" approach (Smith & Smoll, 1997), in which students receive affirmative feedback between reminders about the proper performance and positive reinforcements. Social feedback can be provided not only by physical educators, but also by peers through the use of the reciprocal style of teaching. A key point for developing self-regulated learning is the way of providing social feedback. In particular, as students progress in mastering the skill, the social feedback should be gradually withdrawn (Schmidt & Wrisberg, 2008). Thus, students become less dependent on social assistance and start to generate internal feedback information through self-monitoring processes. In our research, for reasons of equal experimental treatment, we used a predefined feedback schedule to provide students with the same quantity and quality of social feedback, which was reduced towards the end of the practice. However, in applied settings students do not always need the same amount of social feedback. Some students may need less feedback and some others more. Thus, physical educators should be more flexible and should observe each student's progress to provide the right amount of social feedback at the appropriate time. The use of a checklist with students' progress in mastering the performance standards could help physical educators to decide when to reduce the amount of feedback and when to introduce students to self-monitoring processes. In such a checklist physical educators can mark students' progress in mastering the performance standards. When the successful performances of a student increase (are more than the unsuccessful), then the physical educator can gradually reduce the provision of the social feedback until he or she totally withdraws the feedback when the student is successful in the majority of his or her executions.

Goal Setting

Self-regulated learning is a goal-directed process and thus, physical educators should incorporate goal setting in their approaches of teaching motor and sport skills. In sport and physical education settings, performance goals are often emphasized because they can be easily set and evaluated through numerical criteria (Kingston & Wilson, 2009). However, in the first phases of learning new skills, students should also set process goals for acquiring the performance standards of the skill. Process goals should be used as flexible and controllable stepping stones to realize intermediate performance-based goals (Kingston & Wilson, 2009). The multiple goals approach is an avenue to combine performance with process goals. During initial learning efforts, students should focus on process goals, and after mastering the skill, they should focus on performance goals to maximize their performance (Zimmerman & Kitsantas, 1997). In simple tasks, these types of goals can be combined from the beginning of the practice with possible positive results (Kolovelonis et al., 2011a).

Goals should be specific, proximal, challenging, and personal. Moreover, the number of goals that students pursue during a practice session should be kept small (i.e., one or two goals). However, young students may confront difficulties in setting appropriate goals by themselves. They may set general, very easy or very difficult, and long term goals (Zimmerman, 2008). Thus, physical educators should help and instruct students to set specific, proximal, and challenging goals and persuade them to adopt and pursue these goals. A practical way that we used in our interventions was to ask students to repeat their goals prior to the practice and to provide them with reminders regarding their goals during practice. Another important issue is students' commitment to attain their goals. This commitment can be increased if students write their goals on a card (e.g., on the self-recording card) and sign that they would try to pursue these goals. Students should also monitor their progress in attaining their goals during, as well as after, the end of the practice.

Another practical issue is when to introduce goals during practice. Based on our findings and the social cognitive models, goals should be set from the very beginning of the practice. In particular, during the practice with social feedback students should pursue specific and explicit process goals that should represent the performance standards of the skill performed. These goals should further be pursued when students practice the skill independently self-monitoring their performance, and should be combined with specific performance goals.

Self-Recording

To become self-regulated learners, students should monitor their performance to generate internal feedback. Self-recording is a simple technique that students can use to monitor their performance in motor and sport skills. In our research students used simple recording cards to observe and to record their performance (Appendix 12.1). This three-level self-recording scale was effective in enhancing students' performance because it is wide enough to provide students with the necessary feedback information without confusing them with detailed descriptions of their performance.

Physical educators and coaches should be aware that the self-recording process may interfere with the skill and be time consuming. For example, many argue that it is difficult or disturbing for students to carry pencils and paper throughout the gym. To avoid such problematic circumstances, physical educators could create stable recording stations where all the necessary materials are available to students (i.e., recording cards, pencils). Thus, students would not have to carry all these materials throughout the gym during practice. In the case that students must move around the gym and must have the self-recording card with them, another idea is to use simple small cards printed in hard paper with small pencils that students hold in their pockets. Moreover, students should be asked to record their performance not in every single trial but after a block of trials or during breaks to minimize the interference of self-recording technique with the practice and the learning process. Moreover, consistent with the notion that the number of goals should be kept short, self-monitoring should focus on one or two elements each time.

Students should first be taught to monitor large and gross body movements because it is easier to discriminate performance on such movements and then the finer ones. Furthermore, emphasis should be given not only in the mechanistic process of recording, but also in the process of discriminating the correct performance in order for students to become accurate in their recordings. That is, students should not simply record their performance, but they should reflect on this performance, comparing it with the performance standards to decide if this is consistent or not with these standards.

Self-Talk

During practice students should also use self-control techniques such as self-talk to enhance performance and to attain their goals. Physical educators could teach students how to use self-talk during practice right from the first efforts of learning a new skill. Both instructional and motivational self-talk are effective. However, the demands of the task should be considered. Thus, the process of selecting cue words is very important. Physical educators should discern the basic features of each task and select the appropriate cue-words for each task. According to Landin (1994) cue words should be: (a) brief and phonetically simple, (b) logically associated with the referent element of the skill, and (c) compatible with the sequential timing and the rhythm of the task. When students are beginners in using self-talk, the physical educator should select the appropriate cue words. As students progress and become experienced in use of self-talk, the physical educator should prepare a list of alternative cue words, and each student should select the cue word that best suits him or her.

Another issue is whether the cue words should be said overtly or covertly. The use of overt self-talk in the first phases of the practice has the advantage that physical educators can observe if the cue words are being used appropriately, and thus they can instruct and provide appropriate feedback. Later on in practice, students may use self-talk covertly. However, in all cases, students' preferences should be considered (Hardy et al., 2009).

Apart from teaching students to use specific cue words to enhance performance, physical educators and coaches should train students to be aware of their thoughts and self-talk during practice or competition. Zinsser, Bunker, and Williams (2006) have proposed interesting methods for enhancing awareness and fostering an in-depth understanding of students' or athlete's use of self-talk. These include retrospection via the viewing of video footage, the use of imagery, self-talk logbooks, and a paper clip activity. This activity involves the transferring of clips from one pocket to another when a targeted statement has been identified. For example, when students identify a negative thought during practice, they stop, transfer a clip from one pocket to another, transform the negative thought to a positive one, and continue their practice. With this activity, students practice to become aware of their negative thoughts during practice (e.g., "I am foolish; I missed this easy shot") and to convert them into positive ones (e.g., "I will try to improve myself").

The Use of the Reciprocal and Self-Check Styles

The reciprocal and the self-check styles can enhance students' learning and performance in physical education, transferring learning responsibilities to students and helping them to become more independent and self-regulated learners. Thus, physical educators should incorporate these styles in their teaching repertoires. However, as students are usually unfamiliar with student-centered teaching approaches, physical educators should teach them how to practice with these teaching styles. These instructions may contain tips for communicating errors, providing praise, and assessing task completion (Metzler, 2000).

In the reciprocal style, pairs should be randomly formed and should be mixed regarding students' gender or ability, unless physical educators want to take advantage of some students' previous experience or higher competence and use these students as tutors of the less experienced students. Furthermore, physical educators may offer students the chance to select their partners, because it has been found that students feel more comfortable and provide more specific feedback when they practice with friends (Byra & Marks, 1993).

The self-check style requires students to practice independently, and this may challenge students, as it is a shift away from what they are accustomed to. Training students to practice pursuing learning goals and to use simple forms to observe and record the attainment of these goals is important for the effectiveness of the self-check style. Students should be taught to self-reflect on their performance and compare this performance with the performance standards.

The criteria cards are critical factors for the effectiveness of these two teaching styles. Thus, they should be carefully designed and usually include instructions for the practice, the description of the task, focusing on performance standards, pictures to illustrate these standards, and a space to check their accomplishment (Mosston & Ashworth, 2002). Criteria cards should not contain large texts, and performance standards should be illustrated by a picture and highlighted by short and specific key words.

Next we first describe the four-phase instructional approach, followed by a hypothetical case scenario

INSTRUCTIONAL APPROACH OF TEACHING MOTOR AND SPORTS SKILLS

Physical educators and coaches either systematically or spontaneously may use some of the self-regulatory process presented above. For example, coaches and physical educators when teaching motor and sport skills usually focus on modeling and providing feedback (Coté, Salmela, Trudel, Baria, & Russell, 1995; Williams & Hodges, 2005). However, the development of self-regulated learning requires physical educators and coaches to establish structured learning environments that help students to self-direct their practice setting goals and self-monitoring their performance. The four-level training model (Zimmerman, 2000) is an integrated approach that can incorporate and combine sequentially all the self-regulatory process discussed in this chapter (see Figure 13.1). Learning new skills involves in a sequence the observational phase (i.e., oral instructions, demonstration of the skill), the emulative practice (i.e., practice with social feedback), the self-controlled practice (i.e., practice with goals and self-monitoring), and the self-regulated practice (i.e., practice in changing conditions). Next we present these phases in detail.

Observational phase. Learning of motor and sport skills begins with the provision of oral instructions followed by the demonstration of the skills. Instructions should be short and focus on the key elements of the skill represented by appropriately selected cue words. The demonstration can be performed by the teacher, by an experienced student, or pictures and videos can be used. At this observational level (Zimmerman, 2000), students cognitively acquire the performance standards that are necessary for the subsequent practice in the skill. Repeated demonstrations of the skill may be needed if students confront difficulties with a complex task, even if they make progress in the next phases. Furthermore, watching demonstrations from different models may help students to observe different variations of the skill executions (Williams & Hodges, 2005), and this may facilitate the development of their personal movement repertoire. In this phase, connections with previous knowledge may facilitate the transfer of knowledge (Schmidt & Lee, 2005).

Emulation phase. During this phase students practice the skill in a supportive learning environment, receiving social feedback from their physical

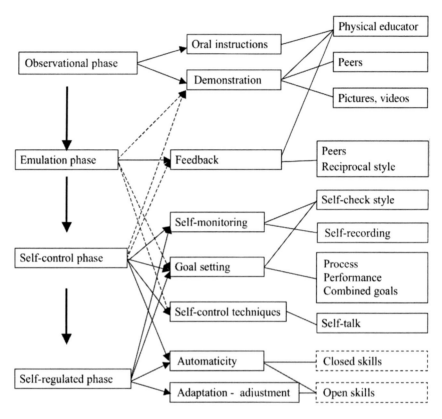

Figure 13.1 Instructional approach of teaching motor and sport skills. Arrows with solid lines connect practice phases with their respective processes. Arrows with dotted lines connect practice phases with processes that belong to a previous or to a next practice phase.

educator or coach in order to acquire the performance standards and to incorporate them into their personal movement repertoire (Zimmerman, 2000). These performance standards represent students' goals for their practice. Moreover, peers can be used as providers of feedback adopting the reciprocal teaching style. Social feedback should include affirmative responses, positive reinforcements, performance reminders, attributional, and progress feedback (Schunk, 1999). Social feedback should be reduced towards the end of the practice when students progress in mastering the skill. Thus, students should start producing their own intrinsic feedback (Williams & Hodges, 2005), reducing the necessity of remaining dependent on social feedback. This is a critical point in the process of self-regulated learning development and helps students to proceed from the practice with social support to the autonomous and self-directed practice.

Self-control phase. During this phase students self-direct their practice in structured settings, setting goals and self-monitoring their performance (Zimmerman, 2000). The role of the physical educator in this phase is to prepare and to structure the appropriate learning environment that facilitates students' learning efforts. Physical educators should be available to support students if necessary (e.g., feedback, demonstration). Physical educators should also help students to set appropriate (i.e., proximal, specific, challenging) goals for their practice and to train them to use self-monitoring techniques. The self-check style can be used in this phase because it involves students in goal-directed practice and in the process of self-monitoring. Furthermore, in this phase students should use self-control techniques, such as self-talk, to facilitate the attainment of their goals and to enhance their performance. The effectiveness of these self-control techniques should also be monitored, and the performance results should be related to the use of these techniques.

Self-regulated phase. Students who reach the self-regulation level practice the skill and make the necessary adjustments based on observation of performance outcomes (Zimmerman, 2000). The type of the skill plays a role in the nature of this phase. In closed skills, where the environment is stable, the automaticity of the skill should be pursued. Repetitive trials and observations of performance outcomes are common in this case. In open skills, however, students should practice the skill in changing conditions, developing their competence in adjusting their skills and adapting them in the changing environmental conditions. Thus, the practice in different aspects of the skill (e.g., different shooting positions in basketball), in changing conditions (e.g., practice with different opponents), in game simulations (e.g., combination of different skills), and in extra demanding conditions (e.g., 2 vs. 3 in basketball) can help students to develop their skills.

Adjusting the Instructional Approach

The instructional approach presented above can be used to facilitate learning of motor and sport skills. However, considering that self-regulatory skills are context dependent (Zimmerman, 2000), this instructional approach would be more effective if it can be adjusted in the different learning conditions and students' learning styles (Coker, 1996). Next, we provide such recommendations for adjusting this approach.

Motor and sport skill learning is optimal when students proceed sequentially through the four phases (Zimmerman, 2000). However, it is possible and in some cases necessary for students to use processes from previous phases even if they have proceeded to the next phase. In fact, self-regulatory skill is context dependent, and students may encounter performance problems that require additional social learning experiences (Zimmerman, 2000). For example, a student who practices with social feedback may ask his physical educator for an additional demonstration of the skill or a part of the skill that has not been mastered yet. Moreover, a student who self-directs his practice with goals and self-monitoring and has doubts about his performance may ask his physical educator to observe his execution and to provide him with affirmative feedback.

The length of each phase depends on various factors including the type and the complexity of the skill, students' previous experience, as well as their progress with the task. For example, students may need more practice with social feedback to master a complex skill. Moreover, students may practice for a longer period of time to automatize a closed skill, whereas in the case of an open skill students may need more practice in changing conditions and in various aspects of the skill. Furthermore, experienced students may pass the phase of the supportive practice faster, as they acquire the performance standards sooner, and then practice more in self-directed conditions and in variations of the skill. It is also possible for students to return to an earlier phase if they encounter difficulties mastering a skill. For example, a student who self-directs his practice may ask his physical educator to provide him with some kind of help or feedback or even a demonstration of the skill.

This instructional approach can be used for individualizing the teaching process in physical education, considering differences among students in previous learning experiences or in their athletic competence. In fact, students in a physical education class may practice at different self-regulatory levels and may spend different practice times in each phase. For example, some students who display higher competence or have previous experience in a skill may self-direct their practice setting goals and self-monitoring their performance or practicing the skill in changing conditions, whereas some other students who strive to acquire the performance standards may practice the skill receiving social feedback from the physical educator or from a peer who has already mastered the skill. Moreover, physical educators can take advantage of some students' previous experience by using them either as models or as tutors. At the same time, these students can benefit from this peer learning process, as students can learn a skill not only through practicing and receiving feedback, but also through the process of teaching and providing feedback to their peers (Mosston & Ashworth, 2002). Physical educators should continually observe and evaluate their students' performance level in order to be aware regarding their needs and to provide each student with the right amount of practice at the appropriate level.

Teaching the Instructional Approach

Physical education students should be prepared to use this instructional approach. First, physical education students should be provided with theoretical knowledge regarding this model in order to comprehend its core characteristics and its philosophy. They should understand that the instructional approach is a sequence of teaching episodes (i.e., observational learning, practice with social feedback, self-control practice) that have different requirements and create different learning environments. Convincing evidence regarding the effectiveness of the instructional approach should be provided. Next, students should be trained to use all the processes included in the instructional approach (e.g., how to provide social feedback and help students to set appropriate goals). Moreover, they should be prepared to use teaching styles that involve students in the teaching process, offering them learning responsibilities. This is important because the implementation of the instructional approach requires students to practice autonomously in structured settings. Thus, physical educators should be prepared to structure such learning environments to offer their students opportunities for independent practice. Physical education students should implement this teaching approach during practicum. This process should include the observation of mastered teachers that teach using this instructional approach, the implementation of this approach with the supportive guidance of a mentor, and then the independent implementation of the instructional approach in natural teaching conditions (first in a group of students and then at a class level).

Next, we illustrate this instructional approach through a hypothetical case scenario. In this scenario we describe how a physical educator should implement the instructional approach, potential problems that may emerge, and suggestions regarding potential solutions to these problems. Hypothetical behaviors are also related to specific self-regulatory processes included in the instructional approach and the social cognitive perspective of self-regulated learning (Zimmerman, 2000).

PRACTICAL CASE SCENARIO

Description of the settings. George is a physical education teacher in a coeducational elementary school located in a medium sized city in central Greece. He has 12 years of teaching experience, and during his career he has always been interested in developing his knowledge, teaching skills, and professional status. This school year he teaches 12 physical education classes (i.e., two classes each, from first to sixth grade). Classes have an average of 20 students each. The teacher has access to open facilities (e.g., a basketball court) and one small, closed multi-use recreation room. The Greek national curriculum for elementary physical education involves team sports (basketball, soccer, volleyball, and handball), individual sports (athletics and gymnastics) and folk dance. Elementary students receive two compulsory 45-minute physical education sessions per week.

George's regular teaching approach included the provision of oral instructions, the demonstration of the skill, and the provision of feedback during practice. Next, he asked students to apply the learned skills in modified or regular games. Although this method seemed to have positive effects on students learning, he feels that it is inadequate to help students achieve high levels of performance and to become autonomous learners. In fact, social cognitive views emphasize the role of both social and self sources on the development of self-regulated learning (Zimmerman, 2000). Recently, he attended a seminar regarding an instructional approach for teaching motor and sport skills in physical education, and he decided to incorporate this approach into his teaching repertoire. That is, George decided to use the four-level model and specifically to provide students with modeling, practice with social support, and self-controlled and self-regulated practice. For the next month he has planned to teach basic basketball skills (i.e., dribbling, passing, and shooting) to fifth grade students. These students were beginners in basketball, and none of them participated in basketball clubs out of school.

Implementation of the instructional approach. Upon arriving at the gym, students were informed that the lessons of the basketball unit would start, and the aim of the first lesson was to learn basketball dribbling. Next, George offered students observational learning experiences that can facilitate the process of learning motor and sports skills. Observational learning is the first phase in the four-level training model of self-regulated learning development (Zimmerman, 2000). In particular, he provided students with short oral instructions regarding the basic elements of dribbling that he summarized for them in two specific cues (i.e., fingers-wrist and low bounce) that represented the performance standards that students would have to acquire during practice. Next, he demonstrated the dribbling, giving emphasis on these two performance standards and reminded students to focus on them during practice.

Next, students formed pairs, took one ball per pair, and practiced the dribble receiving social support. One student practiced, and the other took a rest. Three drills were used: (a) standing dribbling with both hands, (b) dribbling for a distance of 15 meters and return with the opposite hand, and (c) dribbling between five cones back and forth using both hands. Before introducing each drill, George demonstrated it and reminded students about the two performance standards. During practice, George was observing students and was providing them individually affirmative responses to correct performance and provide positive reinforcements. Periodically, he reminded all students to focus on the two basic elements of the dribble that represented the goals of their practice. This social feedback helped students to correct their errors, to improve their performance, and to acquire and incorporate the performance standards into their personal repertoires. In this emulative phase of self-regulated learning development, the source of learning of self-regulatory skills is primarily social (Zimmerman, 2000).

Moreover, George told students that they could ask him for help at anytime during practice. In such a case, Helen, a girl with little previous experience in sports, encountered a problem with controlling the ball during stable dribbling, and she asked her teacher for help. After observing her executions, George realized that Helen put her right foot in the wrong place and the ball hit her foot and bounced away. He demonstrated the right position of the leg and asked Helen to repeat the execution, offering her affirmative feedback and positive reinforcement (e.g., "Good work Helen, you put your leg back and dribbled with your fingers, bouncing the ball low"). Thus, Helen had the opportunity to gain from the teacher's support and improved her performance, saving time and effort. In the case of an absence of social support, Helen may have used a trial and error approach, spending time and resources with questionable results.

During the drill of dribbling among cones, George observed that many students did not dribble with a low bounce changing hands before they passed along the cones. Thus, he decided to stop the practice and to remind students the correct movement. Moreover, he demonstrated the proper execution highlighting the specific performance standard (i.e., low bounce). Repeated demonstrations of the skill help students improve performance, especially in the case of complex and difficult tasks (Zimmerman & Cleary, 2009). The practice restarted, and students were asked to focus on bouncing the ball low. George observed students and provided them individually with affirmative feedback regarding the performance standard of low bouncing.

After students had practiced the dribble for 10 minutes, George observed that the majority of students performed the two performance standards at a satisfactory level. Thus, he decided to proceed to the next phase of the four-level model involving students in self-control practice. The transition from the practice with social feedback to the self-control practice is critical for the development of self-regulated learning (Zimmerman, 2000). Goal setting and self-recording are key components in this self-control level of self-regulated learning. The role of teacher in this phase is to structure the appropriate learning environment. For this purpose, George decided to use the self-check style of teaching and prepared criteria cards for dribbling. Each student took a criteria card. Because it was the first time that this teaching approach would be used, George first explained to students how they would use the criteria cards. He also offered students a demonstration of using the criteria card. Then he asked students to practice dribbling among the cones and to use the criteria card in order to compare their performance with the criteria included in the card. He also asked them to record their performance after a block of three trials. Students practiced dribbling using the self-check style for 10 minutes. During this period, George was walking around the gym, observing students' practice and was available to provide them with support (i.e., feedback, demonstrations). Furthermore, he reminded students regarding their goals in the case that they did not remember them. Although in this phase students self-direct their practice, they may need social support. Thus, the physical educator should be available to provide this support if necessary.

During the practice with the self-check style, George observed that some students, including John, self-recorded their performance in a mechanistic way (e.g., he recorded immediately after executions without looking at the performance standards included in the recording card to compare his performance with these standards). George observed John's performance and compared his evaluations with John's recordings. This comparison revealed that John was inaccurate in his performance evaluations. George asked John to self-reflect on his performance, to compare his performance with the performance standards, and then to self-record. He asked him to perform the skill, to evaluate his performance, and to reflect on these evaluations. Then, he provided John with feedback regarding his performance and the accuracy of his evaluation and asked him to focus on the two performance standards during the practice. That is, self-regulatory processes should be purposefully taught through modeling and practice with feedback.

Some other students did not use the self-check criteria card but simply practiced the skill. George approached these students and asked them to use the criteria card in order to improve their dribbling performance. Moreover, he offered to these students a short demonstration of the practice using the self-check criteria card. During the self-control phase students practice the skill in structured settings outside the presence of their teacher in order to master the skill (Zimmerman, 2000). This is a challenge for both students and teachers, and thus physical educators should support students' efforts to be self-regulated and independent learners. In the rest of the lesson students played games that were based on dribbling (i.e., chasing with dribbling).

In the next lesson, George briefly reminded students the basic elements of dribbling and demonstrated the skill. Then, students practiced dribbling using the self-check style for five to ten minutes. Then he involved students in self-regulated practice, asking them to dribble in changing conditions. For example, he used a drill in which students had to dribble against an opponent who would try to steal the ball, thus simulating game-like conditions. Using and adapting the skill in changing personal and contextual conditions means that students have reached the self-regulated level of performing the skill (Zimmerman, 2000). For the next part of this lesson, George introduced students to the next basketball skills (i.e., chest pass) using the same instructional approach. As students acquired the performance standards of the basic skills of dribbling, passing, and shooting, George introduced drills that combined all these skills to help students to master all these skills and to use them in game-like conditions. The approach of introducing these combined skills was similar to the simple skills and followed the order of the phases proposed by the instructional approach (i.e., observational learning, practice with feedback, self-directed practice).

George also has to teach the same skills at a more advanced level to sixth grade students. These students had some experience in dribbling from the previous school year, and this could have implications regarding the implementation of the instructional approach. Thus, considering students' previous experience, George decided to use the reciprocal style of teaching. During emulative practice, in addition to teachers, peers can also be used for providing social support during practice (Mosston & Ashworth, 2002). Students received brief oral instructions and a demonstration of dribbling skill and instruction regarding the practice with the reciprocal style, because it was the first time that they would use this style. Then students formed pairs randomly and practiced dribbling for 10 minutes using the same drills used for fifth grade students, following the instructions on the criteria cards. During practice, George walked around the gym, observed students practicing, and was available to provide them with support. Moreover, he evaluated students' progress in mastering the dribbling performance standards using a checklist. After some minutes of practice, he observed that some students had already mastered the performance standards, and thus he decided to offer these students the opportunity to self-direct their practice. Thus, he reorganized the class, and the students who had acquired the performance standards continued their practice using the self-check style, whereas students who had not acquired the performance standards continued their practice receiving social feedback (from their peers or from the teacher). Moreover, George decided to introduce self-control techniques (i.e., self-talk) during practice to help students to enhance their performance (Zimmerman, 2000). Thus, he instructed students to use the cue words "fingers-wrist" and "low bounce" to help them focus on these two performance standards of dribbling.

In this hypothetical case scenario, we described how a physical educator can implement the four-level training model as an instructional approach to teach motor and sport skills in physical education and sports contexts. We presented potential problems that a physical educator may encounter during the implementation of this instructional approach and how these problems could be fixed. These hypothetical behaviors were related with self-regulatory processes included in a social cognitive perspective of self-regulated learning (Zimmerman, 2000). Considering that each instructional environment and each class of students has unique characteristics, physical educators should carefully observe students' progress and their needs in order to adapt this approach if necessary. What is important is to support students' practice and to offer them with opportunities for autonomous practice in order to develop their self-regulatory competence.

This instructional approach can help students to develop their self-regulatory competence. However, further research is needed to examine the effectiveness of this approach. Next, we present some issues that may be examined in future research.

FUTURE RESEARCH

Although previous research has provided evidence regarding the effectiveness of the four-level training model (Zimmerman, 2000), many aspects of this model remain relatively unexplored and thus need further examination. Next we present four lines for future research including the effectiveness of the four-level training model in real life teaching conditions, the incorporation of self-control techniques in this model, the role of self-efficacy, and the transferability of self-regulatory skills.

Four-level training model. Future research should examine the effectiveness of the four-level training model in natural teaching conditions in physical education and sport contexts. These interventions should be implemented at class level, in coeducational physical education settings, using a variety of motor and sport skills with different characteristics (e.g., open or closed skills, simple or complex skills) to increase the ecological validity of the results. Skills with different characteristics may require a different teaching approach or an adjustment in the instructional approach. Moreover, the effectiveness of individualizing teaching at class level using the four-level training model should be examined focusing on potential age or gender differences in students' capacity to self-regulate their learning. Large scale interventions are also necessary to examine the effectiveness of the four-level training model in a sequence of lessons because previous research has been conducted at a micro-level. Furthermore, the effectiveness of subprocesses included in the four-level training model should be examined. For example, regarding emulative practice the effectiveness of other kinds of feedback (e.g., attributional feedback) and the use of other means of providing social feedback (e.g., classmates) should be explored.

Self-control techniques. Future research should examine the effectiveness of incorporating self-control techniques (e.g., self-talk) into the multilevel training model of self-regulated learning development and the most effective level of this model during which to introduce these techniques. For example, research should examine if self-talk is more effective when it is introduced at the emulation or at the self-control level. Furthermore, future research should examine the effectiveness of incorporating other self-control techniques used in sports such as imagery, relaxation and attentional focus techniques.

Self-efficacy. The sources of students' self-efficacy and their affective responses to various tasks during the implementation of the four-level training model should be investigated. The effects of practice under different self-regulatory conditions on students' self-efficacy have been widely examined. Future research should focus on how self-efficacy can affect students' use of self-regulatory processes (e.g., modeling, goal setting, self-monitoring), the selection of activities, and the implementation of the four-level training model. Moreover, the role of students' affective responses in developing self-regulated learning should be examined (Efklides, 2011).

The transfer of self-regulatory skills. Finally, a fruitful area for future research concerns the transfer of self-regulatory skills in other domains to become life skills. Previous research has shown that the self-regulatory processes can enhance learning and performance. However, the issue of using these self-regulatory skills in other domains remains largely unexplored. Goudas (2010) has proposed a graded approach for examining the stability and the transfer of life skills. First, the temporal stability, that is, whether students continue to apply the skills they learned, in the setting they learned them should be examined. Then, it would be examined whether students use the skills in the same context (e.g., physical education) but in different circumstances. The next step would be to examine whether the skills are employed without instruction in a similar setting (e.g., classroom) in a different subject (e.g., math), and the final step would be whether the skills are employed at home while studying and so on. Furthermore, an interesting idea would be to use the four-level training model to teach the self-regulatory process, such as goal setting, self-recording and self-talk so as to become self-regulatory life skills. Following the sequential nature of this model, students should first observe the use of a self-regulatory process (e.g., self-talk), then they should use this process in a supportive environment (e.g., receiving feedback regarding the appropriate use of self-talk), and next they should use this process autonomously, self-monitoring its effectiveness. Finally, students should try to use this process in changing conditions and to transfer its use in different environments (e.g., in different tasks or using different types of self-talk).

CONCLUSIONS

Zimmerman's social cognitive models of self-regulated learning have influenced researchers in different domains including sports and physical education. These models guided our research regarding the examination of self-regulated learning in elementary physical education. The results of these studies showed that elementary students can effectively use self-regulatory processes included in these models. From an applied perspective, the social cognitive model of self-regulated learning development can be used as an instructional approach for teaching motor and sport skills in sports and physical education and developing students' self-regulated learning.

APPENDIX

Card for self-controlled practice		
Name: Nick Grade: 5th Lesson: Basketball dribbling		
My goals are: to dribble with my fingers absorbing the bounce of the ball with my wrist and to bounce the ball low Self-record your performance in the squares aside using the following symbols: ✓ when your performance is consistent with the criterion + when you need improvement – when your performance is not consistent with the criterion	Fingers–wrist	Low bounce

REFERENCES

Bandura, A. (1986). *Social foundations of thought and action*. Englewood Cliffs, NJ: Prentice-Hall.

Bandura, A. (1997). *Self-efficacy: The exercise of control*. New York, NY: W.H. Freeman and Company.

Boekaerts, M. (1996). Self-regulated learning at the junction of cognition and motivation. *European Psychologist, 1,* 100–112.

Byra, M. & Marks, M. (1993). The effect of two pairing techniques on specific feedback and comfort levels of learners in the reciprocal style of teaching. *Journal of Teaching in Physical Education, 12,* 286–300.

Cleary, T. & Zimmerman, B. J. (2001). Self-regulation differences during athletic practice by experts, non-experts, and novices. *Journal of Applied Sport Psychology, 13,* 185–206. doi:10.1080/104132001753149883

Cleary, T. J., Zimmerman, B. J., & Keating, T. (2006). Training physical education students to self-regulate during basketball free throw practice. *Research Quarterly for Exercise and Sport, 77,* 251–262.

Coker, C. A. (1996). Accommodating students' learning styles in physical education. *Journal of Physical Education, Recreation and Dance, 67*(9), 66–68.

Coté, J., Salmela, J., Trudel, P., Baria, A., & Russell, S. (1995). The coaching model: A grounded assessment of expert gymnastic coaches' knowledge. *Journal of Sport and Exercise Psychology, 17,* 1–17.

Crews, D. J., Lochbaum, M. R., & Karoly, P. (2001). Self-regulation. In R. Singer, H. A. Hausenblas, & C. M. Janelle (Eds.), *Handbook of sport psychology* (2nd ed., pp. 497–528). New York, NY: John Wiley & Sons.

Dermitzaki, I. (2005). Preliminary investigation of relations between young students' self-regulatory strategies and their metacognitive experiences. *Psychological Reports, 97,* 759–768.

Dermitzaki, I., Leondari, A., & Goudas, M. (2009). Relations between young students' strategic behaviours, domain-specific self-concept, and performance in a problem-solving situation. *Learning and Instruction, 19,* 144–157. doi:10.1016/j.learninstruc.2008.03.002

Efklides, A. (2005). Motivation and affect in the self-regulation of behavior. *European Psychologist, 10,* 173–174. doi:10.1027/1016-9040.10.3.173

Efklides, A. (2011). Interactions of metacognition with motivation and affect in self-regulated learning: The MASRL model. *Educational Psychologist, 46,* 6–25. doi:10.1080/00461520.2011.538645

Efklides, A. & Misailidi, P. (2010). Introduction: The present and the future in metacognition. In A. Efklides & P. Misailidi (Eds.), *Trends and prospects in metacognition research* (pp. 1–18). New York, NY: Springer.

Goudas, M. (2010). Prologue: A review of life skills teaching in sport and physical education. *Hellenic Journal of Psychology, 7,* 241–258.

Gould, D. & Chung, Y. (2004). Self-regulation skills in young, middles, and older adulthood. In M. R. Weiss (Ed), *Developmental sport and exercise psychology: A lifespan perspective* (pp. 383–402). Morgantown, WV: Fitness Information Technology.

Hardy, J., Oliver, E., & Tod, D. (2009). A framework for the study and application of self-talk within sport. In S. Mellalieu & S. Hanton (Eds.), *Advances in applied sport psychology. A review* (pp. 37–74). New York, NY: Routledge.

Keren, G. (1991). Calibration and probability judgments: Conceptual and methodological issues. *Acta Psychologia, 77,* 217–273.

Kingston, K. M. & Wilson, K. M. (2009). The application of goal setting in sport. In S. Mellalieu & S. Hanton (Eds.), *Advances in applied sport psychology. A review* (pp. 75–123). New York, NY: Routledge.

Kitsantas, A. & Zimmerman, B. J. (1998). Self-regulation of motor learning: A strategic cycle view. *Journal of Applied Sport Psychology, 10,* 220–239. doi:10.1080/10413209808406390

Kitsantas, A. & Zimmerman, B. J. (2006). Enhancing self-regulation of practice: The influence of graphing and self-evaluative standards. *Metacognition and Learning, 1,* 201–212. doi:10.1007/s11409-006-9000-7

Kitsantas, A., Zimmerman, B. J., & Cleary, T. (2000). The role of observation and emulation in the development of athletic self-regulation. *Journal of Educational Psychology, 92,* 811–817. doi:10.1037/0022-0663.92.4.811

Kolovelonis, A. (2007). Grade and gender differences in students' self-determination for participating in physical education. *Education Sciences and Psychology, 11(2),* 23–30.

Kolovelonis, A. & Goudas, M. (in press). Students' recording accuracy in the reciprocal and the self-check styles in physical education. *Educational Research and Evaluation: An International Journal on Theory and Practice,* doi:10.1080/13803 611.2012.724938

Kolovelonis, A., Goudas, M., & Dermitzaki, I. (2010). Self-regulated learning of a motor skill through emulation and self-control levels in a physical education setting. *Journal of Applied Sport Psychology, 22,* 198–212. doi:10.1080/10413201003664681

Kolovelonis, A., Goudas, M., & Dermitzaki, I. (2011a). The effect of different goals and self-recording on self-regulation of learning a motor skill in a physical education setting. *Learning and Instruction, 21,* 355–364. doi:10.1016/j.learninstruc.2010.04.001

Kolovelonis, A., Goudas, M., & Dermitzaki, I. (2011b). The effects of instructional and motivational self-talk on students' motor task performance in physical education. *Psychology of Sport and Exercise, 12,* 153–158. doi:10.1016/j.psychsport.2010.09.002

Kolovelonis, A., Goudas, M., & Dermitzaki, I. (2012). Students' performance calibration in a basketball dibbling task in elementary physical education. *International Electronic Journal of Elementary Education, 4,* 507–517.

Kolovelonis, A., Goudas, M., & Dermitzaki, I. (in press). The effects of self-talk and goal setting on self-regulation of learning a new motor skill in physical education. *International Journal of Sport and Exercise Psychology, 10,* 221–235. doi: 10.1080/1612197X.2012.671592

Kolovelonis, A., Goudas, M., Dermitzaki, I., & Kitsantas, A. (in press). Self-regulated learning and performance calibration among elementary physical education students. *European Journal of Psychology of Education.* doi:10.1007/s10212-012-0135-4

Kolovelonis, A., Goudas, M., & Gerodimos, V. (2011). The effects of the reciprocal and the self-check styles on pupils' performance in primary physical education. *European Physical Education Review, 17*, 35–50. doi:10.1177/1356336X11402265

Kolovelonis, A., Goudas M., Hassandra, M., & Dermitzaki, I. (2012). Self-regulated learning in physical education: Examining the effects of emulative and self-control practice. *Psychology of Sport and Exercise, 13*, 383–389. doi:10.1016/j.psychsport.2012.01.005

Landin, D. (1994). The role of verbal cues in skill learning. *Quest, 46*, 299–313.

Metzler, M. (2000). *Instructional models for physical education.* Needhan Heights, MA: Allyn & Bacon.

Mosston, M. & Ashworth, S. (2002). *Teaching physical education* (5th ed.). San Francisco, CA: Benjamin Cummings.

Petlichkoff, L. M. (2004). Self-regulation skills for children and adolescents. In M. R. Weiss (Ed.), *Developmental sport and exercise psychology: A lifespan perspective* (pp. 269–288). Morgantown, WV: Fitness Information Technology.

Schmidt, R. A. & Lee, T. D. (2005). *Motor control and learning. A behavioral emphasis* (4th ed.). Champaign, IL: Human Kinetics.

Schmidt, R. A. & Wrisberg, C. A. (2008). *Motor learning and performance. A situation-based learning approach* (4th ed.). Champaign IL: Human Kinetics.

Schunk, D. H. (1996). Goal and self-evaluative influences during children's cognitive skill learning. *American Educational Research Journal, 33*, 359–382.

Schunk, D. H. (1999). Social-self interaction and achievement behaviour. *Educational Psychologist, 34*, 219–227.

Schunk, D. H. & Pajares, F. (2009). Self-efficacy theory. In K. R. Wentzel & A. Wigfield (Eds.), *Handbook of motivation at school* (pp. 35–53). New York, NY: Routledge.

Smith, R. E. & Smoll, F. L. (1997). Coach-mediated team building in youth sports. *Journal of Applied Sport Psychology, 9*, 114–132. doi:10.1080/10413209708415387

Williams, A. M. & Hodges, N. J. (2005). Practice, instruction and skill acquisition in soccer: Challenging tradition. *Journal of Sports Sciences, 23*, 637–650. doi:10.1080/02640410400021328

Zimmerman, B. J. (2000). Attaining self-regulation: A social-cognitive perspective. In M. Boekaerts, P. Pintrich, & M. Zeidner (Eds.), *Handbook of self-regulation* (pp. 13–39). San Diego, CA: Academic Press.

Zimmerman, B. J. (2008). Goal setting: A key proactive source of academic self-regulation. In D. H. Schunk & B. J. Zimmerman (Eds.), *Motivation and self-regulated learning: Theory, research, and applications* (pp. 267–295). New York, NY: Lawrence Erlbaum Associates.

Zimmerman, B. J., & Cleary, T. (2009). Motives to self-regulate learning. A social cognitive account. In K. R.Wentzel & A. Wigfield (Eds.) *Handbook of motivation at school* (pp. 247–264). New York, NY: Routledge.

Zimmerman, B. J. & Kitsantas, A. (1996). Self-regulated learning of a motoric skill: The role of goal setting and self-recording. *Journal of Applied Sport Psychology, 8*, 60–75. doi:10.1080/10413209608406308

Zimmerman, B. J. & Kitsantas, A. (1997). Developmental phases in self-regulation: Shifting from process goals to outcome goals. *Journal of Educational Psychology, 89*, 29–36. doi:10.1037/0022-0663.89.1.29

Zimmerman, B. J. & Kitsantas, A. (2005). The hidden dimension of the personal competence. Self-regulated learning and practice. In A. J. Elliot & C. S. Dweck (Eds.), *Handbook of competence and motivation* (pp. 509–526). New York, NY: The Guilford Press.

Zimmerman, B. J. & Schunk, D. H. (2001). *Self-regulated learning and academic achievement: Theoretical perspectives* (2nd ed.). Mahwah, NJ: Lawrence Erlbaum.

Zinsser, N., Bunker, L., & Williams, J. M. (2006). Cognitive techniques for building confidence and enhancing performance. In J. M. Williams (Ed.), *Applied sport psychology: Personal growth to peak performance* (5th ed., pp. 349–381). New York, NY: McGraw Hill.

CHAPTER 14

THE USE OF SELF-REGULATION INTERVENTIONS IN MANAGING CHRONIC DISEASE

Noreen M. Clark

Almost one half of the U.S. population lives with a chronic condition. Heart disease, respiratory disease, diabetes, epilepsy, digestive conditions, and many other ailments require day-to-day management. Management by the patient is taken in the recognition that while the disease can't be cured, it can be controlled. Control means keeping the illness from getting worse, from leading to acute complications that require immediate attention, and from disrupting personal and family life, school and work, social connectedness and so on. For chronic conditions, management often entails using medicines correctly, maintaining a given lifestyle (usually related to diet, physical activity, stress), employing particular medical devices, communicating with health care professionals, or using health services, not to mention a range of other behaviors unique to an illness (Steptoe, 2010).

Complicating disease management is the fact that it is a very dynamic process. The context in which people function and the content that com-

Applications of Self-Regulated Learning across Diverse Disciplines, pages 417–444
Copyright © 2013 by Information Age Publishing
All rights of reproduction in any form reserved. **417**

prises effective therapeutic approaches to management continually change. New medicines are discovered. New approaches to clinical treatment are developed. Personal and family demands vary. As individuals age they will often experience physical, psychological, and emotional changes related to the chronic condition. With change comes the need to learn new ways to manage, and self-regulation is the means by which this learning occurs.

The demands on a person successfully managing a chronic disease suggest that those who are self-regulating will be more able to continuously learn what is needed to keep the condition under control. This chapter will describe how self-regulation has contributed to understanding management, provide a model for managing chronic disease and give details regarding the utility of the model, describe interventions using the self-regulation model that have aimed to help people manage more effectively, and suggest areas of needed research regarding self-regulation in health. It also highlights the links between Zimmerman's work and the development of the disease management model.

SOCIAL COGNITIVE THEORY, SELF-REGULATION, AND HEALTH

Over many years, a body of work previously referred to as social learning theory and now called social cognitive theory has generated concepts and evidence for the role of self-regulation in learning. Many theoreticians contributed to the evolution of this perspective on how individuals use their cognitive abilities to adopt new behaviors, often simultaneously changing the social and physical environments that shape their behavior. The work of Bandura (1986) has been fundamental to explicating, refining and elaborating the principles comprising social cognitive theory. He has illustrated conceptually and through compilation of empirical data the cyclical nature of behavioral learning wherein the personal attributes, current behavior, and existing environmental characteristics of individuals and their situations reciprocally determine behavior. Change occurs when any or all of the characteristics are modified. More recently, Bandura has compiled ideas developed since the 1970s into a comprehensive elucidation of the central role of self-efficacy in learning, the belief that one is capable of engaging in a behavior that produces change (Bandura 1977, 1997).

Self-regulation, as part of social cognitive theory, attracted significant attention before and, especially, following Bandura's articulation of the concept. Self-regulation in general has been discussed (Vohs & Baumeister, 2011) and self-regulation related to specific areas such as health have also been examined generally, related to the idea of monitoring a situation or condition (Baumeister, Gailliot, DeWall, & Oaten, 2006; DeWall, Baumeister, & Vohs, 2006; Leventhal, Safer, & Panagis, 1983; Ryan, 2009; Ryan & Sawin, 2009).

Drawing from theoretical assumptions of social cognitive theory, Zimmerman began, over 20 years ago, to extract elements from the theory that explain how youngsters engage in self-regulation to acquire basic skills (Zimmerman 1989, 1990a, 1990b). A major contribution of this work was to move from general ideas regarding self-regulation to identify phases and subprocesses that comprise it in academic learning—that is, progressing from overall depictions to description of specific cognitive, behavioral and social processes occurring in particular contexts (Zimmerman & Campillo, 2003). In his formulation, Zimmerman described three self-regulatory phases (forethought, performance, and self-reflection) that interact and are reciprocally influential in the acquisition of reading, mathematical and related academic skills (Zimmerman, 2000).

In Zimmerman's formulation, the *forethought phase* is a task analysis process and entails goal setting, strategic planning, and developing self-motivating beliefs including self efficacy, outcome expectation, value of and interest in the task, and goal orientation. The *performance phase* is characterized by self-control, a set of subprocesses including self-instruction, imagery, focusing attention, and strategies for accomplishing tasks. It also involves self-observation where metacognitive monitoring occurs and self-recording is often employed. The *self-reflection phase* includes different types of self-judgments, such as self-evaluation and causal attribution, as well as self-reactions including perceptions of satisfaction and adaptive inferences. Each phase *reciprocally informs the others, and together they produce new capacities and application of skills.*

Although Bandura and colleagues examined a number of principles of social cognitive theory and especially self efficacy in relation to individual or collective health (Baumeister et al., 2006; DeWall et al., 2008; Leventhal et al., 1983; Ryan, 2009; Ryan & Sawin, 2009), Zimmerman also examined the nature of the relationship between his phase subprocesses of self-regulation and health behavior change regarding management of respiratory disease (Zimmerman, Bonner, Evans, & Mellins, 1999). With colleagues in the health field, he explored how the use of self-regulation principles might enhance the management of asthma by individuals living with the condition (Clark & Zimmerman, 1990). He also developed a measure for evaluating a person's capacity to self-regulate related to his or her disease. The measure aims to enable targeting of interventions to individuals' capacities. It has also been used to assess changes subsequent to intervention (Zimmerman, Bonner, & Kovach, 1996). These efforts led to application of his principles in several important studies of pediatric asthma (Zimmerman et al., 1999; Bonner et al., 2002), which demonstrated that Zimmerman's model and the subprocesses of self-regulation could be applied beyond academic learning.

THE MODEL FOR MANAGING CHRONIC DISEASE

As a result of collaborative work with Zimmerman (Clark, Evans, Zimmerman, Levison, & Mellins, 1994; Clark & Zimmerman, 1990) and drawing on his recognition of the importance of describing the subprocesses and phases of self-regulation, the model for managing chronic disease (MMCD) was developed (Clark, Gong & Kaciroti, 2001). The model was formed from exploration of the specific capacities that adults, whether directed at themselves or when acting on behalf of their children, need to possess in order to manage conditions that have no cure but can be controlled with day-to-day actions. It evolved from the understanding that most individuals confronting a long-term illness will respond in one of several ways. For example, there might be great variations in what people do in their daily lives to reduce the effects of the condition, in part because they may perceive the recommendations of clinicians as ranging from mundane to ineffective or excessively difficult. Some individuals with chronic disease may exhibit greater efforts to apply recommended therapeutics but will either continue or discontinue those efforts depending on their experience, for example becoming bored with the routine, lacking self-regulation skills, or encountering competing priorities. On the other hand, individuals who might be considered competent self-regulators may or may not decide to successfully apply clinically provided regimens and explore additional, optimal ways to control the condition. This range of responses indicates that people with chronic illness may possess varying levels of self-regulatory skill, have different degrees of interest and ability regarding motivation and development of skills needed to change their behavior, and live in differing social and environmental conditions that shape it.

Figure 14.1 presents the MMCD and illustrates the reciprocal and continuous nature of self-regulation processes in chronic disease prevention and management (Clark et al., 2001). It draws on Bandura's (1991) explication of processes of self-regulation and on Zimmerman's (Schunk & Zimmerman, 1994) model, particularly related to the inclusion of personal goals as motivational factors. In this model, the ability of the person to be self-regulating is viewed as central to achieving desired end points (Clark & Starr, 1994). Three aspects of self-regulation are central to this model: observation, judgment, and reactions. The observation and judgment processes are consistent with Zimmerman's performance phrase, with the reaction process aligned with his concept of the self-reflection phase. The content and skills of disease management are derived and refined through the process of being self-regulating. A person is motivated to be self-regulating by a desired goal or end point analogous to

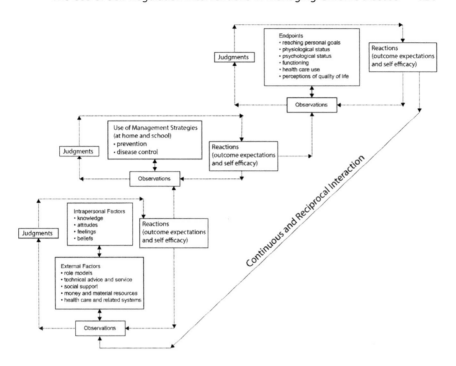

Figure 14.1 The continuous and reciprocal nature of self-regulation processes in disease prevention and management. Adapted from "A model of self-regulation for control of chronic disease," by N. M. Clark, M. Gong, & N. Kaciroti, 2001, *Health Education and Behavior, 28*(6), p. 771. Copyright 2001 by Sage Publications. Reprinted with permission.

Zimmerman's forethought phase. The more salient the goal, the more self-regulating the person will try to be. The power of the goal is associated with its value and personal meaningfulness to the individual. Being self-regulating in this model means being observant about one's own behavior and the social and physical environments that comprise the context for behavior, and making judgments based on observation (versus habit, fear, or tradition). It entails reacting appropriately to trying and achieving steps toward one's personal goal when attempting change. The model is also predicated on the idea that the processes comprising self-regulation are continuous and reciprocal. Information, behavior, understanding, feelings, and conclusions generated from any one element of self-regulation as defined in the model (i.e., observing, judging, reacting) continually influence other elements.

The MMCD suggests that intrapersonal and external factors give rise to and are modified by the observations, judgments, and reactions of the individual, leading him or her to undertake disease management strategies (including modification of the physical and social environments) so as to achieve the desired end point or goal. One reaction is to determine whether the action taken produced the expected outcome (outcome expectancy is the belief that the behavior will produce the goal). Another reaction is whether one feels the confidence to continue the action (self-efficacy; Bandura, 1986). Over time, continuous observation, judgment, and reaction lead to modification of management strategies and sometimes modification of the goal itself. Each of these elements is discussed in greater detail below.

Self-observation is the attempt to view one's behavior or physical or social factors associated with it in a detached, objective way so as to identify key influences and potential areas for change. Self-observation efforts may be, for example, a person with asthma using a peak flow meter to assess air flow through the airways when exposed to changes in the environment or a person with heart disease using a pedometer to measure the achievable level of physical activity without symptoms. It may involve tracking symptoms in a log or diary to determine what might trigger them. Or it may simply be recognition of a situation where signs of a serious episode of breathlessness or chest tightness appear. Noting influences on behavior generates information to guide the learner to options for trying modifications to or introducing new practices.

Judgment in the model refers to using the data derived from observation to develop and try out change strategies, that is, disease management strategies that may improve the situation (e.g., control pain, reduce symptoms, function more fully). Developing strategies may involve the same processes of observation, judgment and reaction and may involve such things as acquiring new medicine, increasing activity level, removing environmental triggers, using stress reduction techniques, and so on. Judging what to try and how to implement the trial entails analysis of the information generated through observation and selection of potential solutions based on personal determinations such as potential for success, manageability, affordability, personal relevance, and other salient criteria. Trial behavior can target small changes such as alteration of the time scheduled for taking medicine or larger ones—for example, enrolling in nutritional counseling to make significant changes in one's diet and so on. Through the process an individual makes judgments regarding what to do and how to do it.

Reaction in the MMCD relates to two important concepts from social cognitive theory. One is assessment that the change introduced produces the desired outcome—for example, a change in the schedule for medicine taking will reduce side effects. This is the concept of outcome expectancy. Another is self-efficacy—the belief that one is able to engage successfully in the behavior again. A positive reaction to both processes is needed for the behavior change to "take" or environmental modifications to be sustained. As posited in social cognitive theory, observation, judgment, and reaction are reciprocally determined, each shaping and informing the others in a process leading to change of significant consequence for the learner, in this case, the disease manager.

The MMCD subprocesses are similar to those identified by Zimmerman regarding academic learning (Zimmerman & Campillo, 2003), lending further credence to the idea that distinct but highly reciprocal behaviors combine to enable self-regulation. Further, although reciprocal, an underlying sequence is implicit in this view. Observation leads to judgments that lead to action and, subsequently, reactions following trial of a change strategy. In the MMCD, additional elements of self-regulation are considered central to achieving desired change. These elements in one sense comprise the "content" of change and have been labeled *internal and external factors* and *management strategies*, which to some extent also reflect Zimmerman's concepts of phases of self-regulation (Zimmerman & Campillo, 2003). *Endpoints* are equivalent to the acquisition of Zimmerman's academic skills such as reading or writing.

Internal and External Factors

The MMCD posits that when taking a disease management action, an individual is influenced by intrapersonal factors—that is, information and beliefs he or she has concerning the specific health problem. For example, when attempting to manage asthma, people will use (or not use) inhaled corticosteroids (anti-inflammatory drugs) based, in part, on what they know about the role and importance of inflammation in asthma control and about using a metered dose inhaler (Clark & Partridge, 2002). The action is also influenced by aspects of outcome expectancy, or what the person believes to be the benefits of using the medicine to reach his or her personal goal and his or her belief that the benefits outweigh the costs (e.g., safety of the medicine, side effects, financial burden, etc.; Becker, 1985). The extent to which the person holds the requisite knowledge and beliefs to support an action also depends, in part, on a range of external factors. These may include role models that can be observed making efforts in asthma situations. They include interpersonal relationships through which emotional and instrumental social support is given and received. Almost certainly involved is technical advice from a clinician who provides therapeutic recommendations. Availability of money and other material resources (e.g., the price of medicine and a way to get to the pharmacy) also will influence the person's behavior.

Management Strategies

Management strategies comprise the individual's means to keep the disease and its effects under control (Clark et al., 1998; Karoly & Kanfer, 1982). These strategies may be effective or ineffective and may be consistent with clinicians' recommendations or not. In addition, whereas some people will independently derive ways to achieve disease control that physicians or health educators would applaud (e.g., a susceptible asthma patient removing environmental precipitants to symptoms from the living quarters), others do not exhibit this strategic skill (e.g., the person overusing bronchodilators in an effort to reduce symptoms). The point here is that a management strategy evolves from the person's observations, judgments, and reactions given the aforementioned internal and external factors. Others (role models, technical experts, and family and friends) can influence the strategy chosen, but in the end, the individual's personal goals, combined internal and external resources and the degree of self-regulation, will dictate which management strategy will be derived and further employed. In addition, the combination of these factors is very specific to particular problems and may not be generalizable from one behavior (e.g., using medicines) to another (e.g., removing environmental precipitants). Self-regulation (including self-efficacy as part of the self-regulatory process) is not considered a personality trait or characteristic such as being Type A or having low or high self-esteem. Rather, it comprises skills that are applied to a specific goal and problem within a given context. It may be that one's ability to be self-regulating in a specific circumstance helps one to be more self-regulating in another circumstance. However, this result is not necessarily so.

Endpoints

The predominant motivating factor in taking a disease management action is a personal goal. Goals are highly idiosyncratic. When an educator or clinician (or any other person attempting to assist with disease management) has a different goal than the individual, the opportunity for successful goal attainment is attenuated. Usually, the clinician has a goal (say a better peak expiratory flow rate in a patient with asthma) that, although considered a gold standard in medical practice, is not likely to be perceived by the patient as important as his or her personal goal (say spending time with a loved one whose cat precipitates asthma symptoms). When the clinician or educator focuses on achieving the patient's personal goal, the chances are greater that the therapeutic regimen will appeal to the interests of the patient and be implemented by him or her. Evidence that clinical and personal goals are not always compatible is found, for example, in the work of Juniper et al. (1996), whose data showed little relationship between clinical measures such as clinical scores on pulmonary function tests and patients' own ratings of the asthma-related quality of their lives, or being able to do what they wished to do.

A TEST OF THE MODEL FOR MANAGING CHRONIC DISEASE (MMCD)

The particular challenges in managing a chronic disease and the considerable level of self-regulation entailed requires a conceptual framework that explicates influences on self-regulation and how the regulatory subprocess interfaces with these influences. Of course, the best evidence for an explanatory model is that it produces the desired outcomes. The MMCD as noted was developed to specifically describe self-regulation as it functions in management by the patient with an illness that can be controlled although not cured.

In considering the utility of such a model, two questions immediately arise. The first question is: do the elements of the model remain stable over time? In other words, if at different time points one assessed the presence of and relationships among the elements describing self-regulation of chronic disease as explicated in the MMCD, would the elements be present and exhibit similar patterns of relationship? A second question is: do these elements predict outcomes that are of interest in disease control? In academic learning, for example, the acquisition of reading or writing skills is one potential end point of self-regulation. In managing a chronic condition, different end points to consider could include a patient reaching his or her personal goals, stabilizing or improving one's physical condition, securing needed health care that is appropriate to the level of the illness, and attaining an acceptable level of quality of life.

To generate answers to the utility questions regarding the MMCD, we undertook two studies. A large research project on asthma management provided the opportunity. The randomized clinical trial has been discussed in detail in the literature, and a large longitudinal sample generated data for examination of self-regulation (Janevic et al., 2003). The data set comprised responses from 637 parents of children with asthma living in the Detroit, Michigan and New York City environs. The children were between one and 12 years of age, and their parents were interviewed by telephone by trained data collectors at baseline and at six months and one and two years subsequently regarding the parents' self-regulatory processes. Cumulative logistic regression analysis assessed stability of the model elements at the three points in time.

Figure 14.2 presents the results of cross section correlations between the model's elements of self-regulation (observation, judgment, reaction, the last of these labeled "confidence" and combining self efficacy and outcome expectation) at three points in time. These constructs were measured by questionnaire items that tapped the extent to which parents engaged in actions to observe the child in various asthma-related situations, used information for management decision making, assessed whether actions were perceived to produce the desired endpoint, and ascertained the parents' confidence to take the action. It illustrates a consistent and relatively stable pattern of relationships over a two-year period. The subprocess of judgment regarding asthma management correlates with efforts to observe the child in asthma relevant situations ($r = .36$, $p < .001$; $r = .62$, $p < .001$). Observation consistently correlated with using more asthma management strategies ($r = .36$, $p = .000$; $r = .46$, $p = .000$). Significant associations were also evident between *judgment* and *use of management strategies* ($r = .18$, p $= .001$; $r = .18$, $p = .001$) and *judgment* and *confidence* ($r = .02$, $p = .03$; $r = .30$, $p = .004$). A correlation was also seen between *external factors* and *confidence* ($r = .02$, $p = .04$; $r = .16$, $p = .0001$). No consistently significant associations were evi-

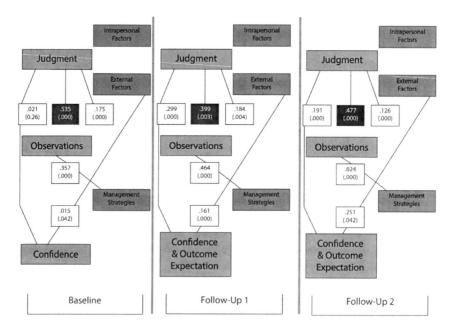

Figure 14.2 Stage elements of self-regulation: correlations at three points in time. Adapted from "A model of self-regulation for control of chronic disease," by N. M. Clark, M. Gong, & N. Kaciroti, 2001, *Health Education and Behavior, 28*(6), 777. Copyright 2001 by Sage Publications. Reprinted with permission.

dent between the intrapersonal factors component of the model at each of the three time points. Although correlations regarding two elements (judgment and confidence; external factors and confidence) are negligible, the presence and direction of association of all model elements indicate a stable pattern across two years. Findings suggest the particular importance of self-regulation as individuals manage a disease over time (Clark et al., 2001).

A second study using the same data set examined the model elements as predictors of health outcomes. Figure 14.3 presents findings of the longitudinal analysis and Table 14.1 provides the correlations among and between model elements. For purposes of this discussion, the associations between the model's subprocesses of self-regulation and asthma outcomes are the most interesting. Two of these subprocesses were significantly associated with subsequent outcomes. The higher a parent's baseline score for *observation* of the child in asthma-related situations, the higher the quality of life score two years later ($r = .54$, $p = .04$). The greater the parent's baseline level of *confidence* (self efficacy and outcome expectancy) to manage asthma, the lower the subsequent use of emergency services for asthma ($r = -.52$, $p = .003$) and the less frequently the family needed follow up visits to the

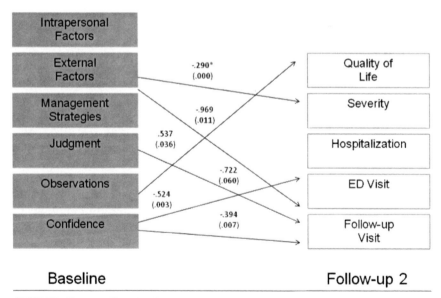

NOTE: ED = Emergency Department
*Beta and p values.

Figure 14.3 Elements of self-regulation as predictors of outcomes at end point in time. Adapted from "A model of self-regulation for control of chronic disease," by N. M. Clark, M. Gong, & N. Kaciroti, 2001, *Health Education and Behavior, 28*(6), 778. Copyright 2001 by Sage Publications. Reprinted with permission.

TABLE 14.1 Longitudinal Relationship Between Self-Regulation Elements and Outcomes Controlling for Program Participation and Baseline Score Reporting Estimates (beta) and *p* Values of the Predictors in the Model

Predictors at Baseline	Quality of Life	Severity Parent Reported	Hospital Admissions	Emergency Department Visits	Follow-up Office Visits
		Outcomes at End Point (follow-up 2)			
Intrapersonal factor	−.149	.011	.401	.269	.365*
	(.101)	(.765)	(.265)	(.140)	(.055)*
External factors	−.076	−.290*	−.429	−.969*	−.102
	(.593)	(.000)*	(.500)	(.011)*	(.731)
Management strategies	−.107	−.212	−.154	.914	.342
	(.466)	(.070)	(.896)	(.148)	(.491)
Observations	.537*	.145	1.250	−.799	.428
	(.036)*	(.387)	(.464)	(.439)	(.608)
Judgment	−.203	.007	.196	−.144	−.722*
	(.075)	(.923)	(.700)	(.677)	(.060)*
Confidence	.105	.105	−.385	−.524*	−.394*
	(.117)	(.117)	(.184)	(.003)*	(.007)*

Note: Adapted from "A model of self-regulation for control of chronic disease," by N. M. Clark, M. Gong, & N. Kaciroti, 2001, *Health Education and Behavior, 28*(6), 779. Copyright 2001 by Sage Publications. Reprinted with permission.
* $p < .06$.

physician following the child's asthma episode ($r = -.39$, $p = .007$). *Judgment* was marginally predictive of follow-up physician visits ($r = -.72$, $p = .06$). External factors as explicated in the model were significant to reducing disease severity and emergency health care visits. Management strategies and intrapersonal factors were not significant (Clark et al., 2001).

The results of these studies illustrate that the subprocesses of self-regulation, at least in the case of parents self-regulating regarding a child's illness, explicated in the MMCD are stable and evident at different points in time. This suggests that they are not arbitrary capacities. Further, findings illustrate that they are related to ultimate outcomes that are of importance to people with chronic disease. That is, subprocesses lead to achievement of goals that enhance well-being, a motivating factor for change. Again, the model subprocess of observation and judgment are analogous to Zimmerman's performance phase in his investigation of self-recording to outcomes (Kitsantas & Zimmerman, 1998).

Of course, a model is only useful in so far as it depicts reality and, in the case of a model related to chronic disease, is associated with finding ways to bring about productive change regarding health and well-being. Efforts to assess the utility of the model in this regard, in particular the subprocesses of observation, judgment and reaction, have been included in clinical trials of disease management. These studies have illustrated that interventions incorporating self-regulatory processes as defined in the model can produce significant differences in outcome (Clark et al., 1995; Clark et al., 2001; Clark et al., 2007; Clark et al., 2008).

APPLICATIONS OF THE MMCD

The model for managing chronic disease has been utilized in a number of intervention studies in asthma (Clark et al., 2007), epilepsy (Clark et al., 2010b; Dilorio et al., 2010) and in efforts to enhance the ability of clinicians to care for and communicate with their patients (Cabana et al., 2006, Clark et al., 2008). In each of these, the model has been useful in designing the intervention itself, and outcomes from the interventions have been associated with better health status and use of health services. To illustrate the application of the model here, one condition, heart disease, will be the focus. The goals of this section are to (a) describe the application of MMCD to managing heart disease, (b) examine group difference in response to MMCD, (c) present a formatting variation of MMCD, (d) and provide an overview of actual implementation procedures of MMCD.

Heart Disease and Self-Regulation

Several trials of interventions including self-regulation subprocesses of the MMCD have been conducted. Each focused on a different population and slightly different iteration of the processes. The rubric "take PRIDE" has been used to label these interventions, as all follow a self-regulatory problem-solving approach that encapsulates self-regulation: P = problem selecting; R = researching the daily routine; I = identifying a heart management goal; D = developing a plan to reach the goal; E = establishing expectations and rewards. Group meetings, coaching phone calls, and individual self-directed work characterize the interventions.

There are two goals of the "take PRIDE" interventions. The first is to make participants more conscious of the processes of self-regulation and to enable them to engage more effectively in self-observation, judgment, and reaction regarding their heart disease. The second is to assist participants in developing strategies that modify or direct their own actions and the social and physical environments in which they manage the condition.

Managing heart disease is a highly individualistic activity. What one patient finds difficult another finds easy to do. In iterations of "take PRIDE," both during group and individual activities, participants address their specific personal management priorities. They select from among recommendations made by their clinicians the one they wish to carry out and determine through the observation process what is hindering their ability to do so. Participants establish a change goal and decide based on their observations what behavioral strategies will be most productive in achieving change. They develop outcome expectancy (what will indicate that their strategy produce the desired result) and self-efficacy (whether they feel capable of undertaking and continuing the new behavior). Participants are supported through the process by health educators and coaches. The evaluation of the interventions proceeds from the point of view that although participants will have differing goals, strategies, and priorities, enhanced management will increase the chances of positive outcomes related to more symptom control, higher levels of physical and/or social functioning, and less health care use. These desired outcomes are shared by participants (and health care providers as well) and are considered appropriate measures of the success of the interventions. In other words, for purposes of evaluation, the intervention inputs to self-regulation "content" are varied and the outputs are similar.

Evaluation of the Heart Disease Management Interventions

Older men and women with cardiovascular disease. The first iteration of take PRIDE involved both men and women with cardiovascular disease and sought to introduce skills in observation, judgment and reaction specific to management of a heart condition (Clark et al., 1997). A focus was the participants' priority for change within the set of recommendations provided by his or her clinician. A randomized controlled trial was conducted involving 636 older individuals who worked with a facilitator in groups of eight to 10 individuals. Through video, mini lectures and a manual based on the self-regulation subprocesses, participants worked together and individually at home to understand the dimensions of the change they were interested in achieving and to try out self-regulatory subprocess and new management strategies. Data were collected by phone interview and through review of medical records at the baseline, at 12 months, and at 18 months from individuals randomly assigned to the program or a control group. Items included health status, health care use, and daily functioning. By the 12 month follow up, compared to controls, program participants experienced less impact of their illness on psychosocial functioning ($p < 0.05$) measured by the sickness impact profile (SIP; Bergner, Bobbit, Pollard, Martin, & Gilson, 1976; Gilson et al., 1975), especially in emotional behavior ($p < 0.05$) and alertness ($p < 0.01$). Males experienced improvements in their physical functioning, specifically their ability to ambulate ($p < 0.05$) and the frequency and severity of their symptoms. By 18 months some effects began to decay, suggesting the need for strategic follow up activities to sustain results. Lack of physical activity outcomes for women indicated a need for reformulating the intervention to assist them on this aspect of heart disease management.

Women with heart disease. Recognizing that the intervention for men and women produced differing outcomes related to ambulation and physical activity levels (both of key importance in managing heart disease), a second iteration of the intervention called "Women take PRIDE" was developed. In this version, when presenting the self-regulation subprocesses, physical activity was used as the case example, and while still able to select the management problem of their choice, participants were encouraged to consider whether adequate exercise was important in their particular situation. Information about the particular challenges women face in controlling a heart condition comprised part of the activities of the program, and female peer leaders were deployed as coaches in learning self-regulation processes.

A total of 570 women 60 years or older entered a clinical trial of the intervention (Clark, Janz, Dodge, Fingerlin, & Schork, 2000). They were randomly assigned to the program or a control group. Evaluative data were collected through telephone interviews, physical assessments, and medical records at baseline, four, and 12 months. One year subsequent to the intervention, compared to controls, women in the program had fewer heart related symptoms ($p < 0.05$), had a higher level of physical functioning as measured by the SIP ($p < 0.05$), had improved ambulation as measured by the six-minute walk ($p < 0.01$), and had lost more body weight ($p < 0.001$). No differences in psychosocial factors as measured by the SIP were noted. The last of these findings differed from the results of the first iteration of the program involving both men and women. It may have resulted from the intentional shift in the revised program to emphasize physical activity, or it may reflect a measurement factor. The standardized tests used to assess outcome may not have been sufficiently sensitive to the changes in women's levels of confidence or their views of themselves as managers of their condition. Both were evident in the formative evaluation of the program, where women expressed high levels of satisfaction with these cognitive constructs and attributed change to the intervention. However, the shift in focus for learning self-regulation appeared to produce the desired outcomes related to physical activity for women. An important finding of this study was that program women needed less health care than those in the control group, experienced 46% fewer in-patient hospital days ($p < 0.05$) and had 49% lower in-patient costs ($p < 0.10$). Hospital cost savings exceeded program costs by a ratio of five-to-one (Wheeler, 2003).

Group and individual approaches to control of heart disease. An important question for designing self-regulation based interventions is format. Which learning formats are more or less suitable for enhancing observation, judgment and reaction? Self-regulation is an internal, cognitive-behavioral activity. Are there advantages or disadvantages in teaching it to groups of learners or to individuals by themselves? To address this question, two iterations of "Women take PRIDE" were developed. One took face-to-face groups of eight to 10 participants through the processes where it was assumed that social support from other members would enhance the learning process, and activities were guided by a group facilitator. The other version assisted individuals in working at home at their own pace through telephone guidance from a coach. In the latter version it was assumed that self-directed learning would appeal to time and scheduling priorities of participants.

A randomized controlled trial of the two formats was conducted (Clark et al., 2009). Older women ($n = 575$) were randomly assigned to one or the other formats or a control group. Data regarding symptoms, functional health status, and weight were collected at baseline, four, 12 and 18 months. Findings illustrated that both formats were suitable for learning self-regulation processes, but they produced different results. The self-directed format was better than the control condition in reducing the number ($p < 0.02$), frequency ($p < 0.03$), and bothersomeness ($p < 0.02$) of cardiac symptoms. It was better than the group format in reducing symptom frequency of all types ($p < 0.04$). The group format produced improved ambulation ($p < 0.04$) and weight loss ($p < 0.03$), and group participants were more likely to complete the program ($p < 0.05$). It appeared that the self-directed format was more effective for learning symptom control and practices that are highly individualistic and require person-specific remedies. The group format appeared more effective in changing behavior where social support has shown to be important (e.g., weight loss, increased physical activity). Findings confirmed that enhancing self-regulation is amenable to different formats and that format will influence outcome.

The Content and Process of the Take PRIDE Interventions

As a case for study, the original iteration of the take PRIDE program will be used to illustrate how the program processes evolve. It comprises four meetings held in a convenient location (e.g., a clinic or a community organization site) and facilitated by a health educator. Table 14.2 outlines these activities of the program organized by self-regulation subprocesses.

The first meeting. Initially the program focuses on the desired disease management behaviors and what level of performance will be acceptable to

TABLE 14.2   Activities of the "take PRIDE" Programs Designed to Address the Subprocess of Self-Regulation

Subprocess of Self-Regulation	Program Activity Addressing the Subprocess
Observation	Viewing a video model carrying out the steps of self-regulation in meetings one and two.
	Receiving instruction in the steps from the health educator in meetings one and two.
	Selecting a problem area as the target for self-observation in meeting one.
	The required week between meeting one and two of at home "research" or self-observation of one's own behavior in relation to the target problem area using the "take PRIDE" workbook.
	Continuing use of the workbook over the four-week period and notation of actions taken and their effectiveness.
Judgment	Discussion in meeting one of heart management behavior as recommended by the physician and desired by the participant.
	Comparison with the ideal of one's own pattern of behavior as discerned through self-observation (1) using the workbook at home and (2) in group discussion in meeting two.
	Consideration of one's own behavior as discerned through self-observation in light of common reasons for noncompliance (1) using the workbook at home and (2) in group discussion in meeting two.
	Identifying a behavioral goal in meeting two that will help to resolve the target management problem.
	Developing a plan in meeting two based on self-observation information that will modify personal, social, and environmental factors so the behavioral goal might be reached.
	Continuing use of the workbook that requires judgments about the effectiveness of the plan that is producing results.
Reaction: Outcome Expectation and Self-Efficacy	Seeing the video model successfully carry out the self-regulatory process in meetings one and two.
	Identifying a behavioral goal in meeting two that is manageable and achievable.
	Establishing a reward in meeting two as explicit acknowledgment of making progress. That is, being self-efficacious.
	Writing a contract in meeting two that is a public statement of one's confidence to reach the behavioral goal.
	Noting progress in meetings three and four, being persuaded by the health educator that one is able to achieve the goal, and receiving encouragement from others in the group.
	Seeing the video model in meeting four recognize successes and abilities.

Note: Adapted from "Self-regulation of health behavior: The 'take PRIDE' program," by N. M. Clark, N. K. Janz, J. A. Dodge, & P. A. Sharpe, 1992, *Health Education and Behavior,* *19*(3), 345. Copyright 2001 by Sage Publications. Reprinted with permission.

individuals. There are three program elements constituting the initial segment. First, the physician's recommendations provided to the patient on the health regimen form, the set of behaviors that the doctor believes are necessary for the individual to "do well" clinically, are reviewed. The second is the social role model "Margaret," provided in a video. Margaret is an individual like the group participants, who becomes an active and successful self-manager. Margaret is not idealized. Her level of disease management appears reachable, and her behavior becomes a standard against which individuals can measure their own self-management skills. Third, the individual's own vision of what ideal disease management entails is addressed. Social cognitive theory posits that one reason individuals engage in behavior is the belief that the behavior will result in the desired outcome (outcome expectation). In the video case, for example, Margaret believes that taking medicines as prescribed will make her feel and function better. The physician's medical opinion and the health educator's reassurances are important ingredients in helping group members see how to improve their management skills and believe that by doing so, they will realize important benefits.

The "take PRIDE" videotape instructs participants on how to self-observe or research their routines to discover the factors contributing to the problem they have targeted. Self-observation enables individuals to determine how close to the desired goal they are. Margaret, who has chosen as her target problem "forgetting her medicines," goes through a week of observing and recording the events in the physical and social environment that influence her medicine-taking behavior. She keeps a record in her "take PRIDE" notebook and uses worksheets in the book to identify the potential causes of her problem and to discover patterns in her behavior. Subsequent to the group viewing of the videotape, the health educator reviews with group members the procedure for researching their own routines during the week prior to the next meeting.

The "take PRIDE" process provides a systematic way to review daily activities, note the times when the target problem occurs (e.g., the occasions when medicines were forgotten), and describe the events and circumstances surrounding the event. Participants are asked to keep records at home for seven days. At the end of the period of observation, before returning for the second meeting, they are encouraged to review their notes and look for themes or patterns of behavior (e.g., in video the model participants have viewed, Margaret habitually misses her noontime medication). Included in the "take PRIDE" notebook is a worksheet listing categories of factors compiled from the research literature that contribute to compliance problems. Group members are asked to use the list and to decide if their own experience fits any of the categories explaining non-compliance. They are also asked to think about how their behavior compares to ideal behavior that would resolve the target problem.

Attending to a specific behavior enables participants to become aware of aspects that have become habitual. It serves as a self-diagnostic device (Bandura, 1986) for gaining a better sense of what conditions lead to certain behaviors and lays open the possibility of varying things in daily life to effect change. During the week of observing their behavior, participants also begin to make self-judgments. They compare the information generated through self-observation against their own standard for self-management. They decide what level of competence is needed to resolve the target problem informed by what the physician has recommended, the verbal persuasion of the health educator, and the model in the videotape. Is one's behavior at the level one wishes, given the standards?

The second meeting. The objectives of meeting two are to enable participants to identify a behavioral goal to work towards as a result of researching their target problems during the observation week, to develop a step-by-step plan to meet the behavioral goal, and to establish a reward for making progress or accomplishing the goal. This group meeting attempts to increase the potential for self-judgment and to encourage the third subprocess in the MMCD self-regulation model: self-reaction. In this session, the group members view another segment of the videotape. In role model Margaret's case, the behavioral goal identified is taking medications at the prescribed time every day. She evolves a plan that includes acquiring an organizing pill box, scheduling a time in the morning to review the box, and posting reminders on the phone, near the dining table, and other key places to trigger her memory about the need for medication—especially the noontime pill. She decides that her reward will be to treat herself and a friend to a night at the movies when she goes a full week without missing any of her doses.

In this meeting, the health educator asks one group member to share his or her results of the week of self-observation. The health educator and group members help the individual to identify a specific behavioral goal from these observations and to work out a step-by-step scheme for reaching it. Group members also discuss the concept of rewarding themselves and brainstorm a variety of rewards that they might find reinforcing. Using this experience as a guide, each individual works with a partner to identify his or her behavioral goal and develop a manageable and realistic plan, one where progress might be measurable in a few weeks. The reward may be external or an internal one, for example, for some individuals, self-congratulation may be sufficient reward. Throughout the session, the health educator verbally encourages and praises group participants as they develop their plans, provides needed information, and works with individuals to ensure the plans made are feasible.

The final activity is writing a contract. The concept of contracting is discussed, specifically, the idea that making participants' intentions public often increases motivation to achieve a goal and is a statement of the level of confidence. Participants challenge themselves in written form to meet their goals (or some aspect of them) by a certain date and ask the health educator or another group member to sign the contract as a witness to the self-challenge. Members are encouraged by the health educator to try out their plans during the week prior to the third meeting.

Meeting two emphasizes self-judgment, coming to conclusions about the effectiveness of participants' actions as a result of self-observation. It entails assessing a situation or problem, responses to it, and the physical and social context in which it occurs. Participants use their personal standards to judge their performance related to the target problem. They form their standards in light of the recommendations provided by the physician, the ideas of other participants in the "take PRIDE" program, and the information presented by the health educator.

Meeting two also introduces the concept of self-reaction. Self-reactions (Seligman, 1975) are responses to observations and judgments about personal behavior and the impact of the behavior on the desired outcome, in terms of expected results on self-confidence. Reactions can also include self-reward for successful behavior (Clark & Zimmerman, 1990), which is reinforcing and can lead to repetition of the behavior. A sense of efficacy or mastery over the behavior is a stronger reinforcer and is frequently more compelling than external rewards (Bandura, 1986).

Meeting two is also based on the assumption that self-observation alone does not ensure behavior that will move towards goal attainment. The results of self-observation sometimes increase the behavior being noted (Bandura, 1986), sometimes decrease it, and sometimes have no effect. Setting goals helps people to direct their efforts and energy. The kind of behavioral goals people set and their commitment to them are determined by individuals' perceptions of their capabilities (Bandura & Cervone, 1983). Using strategies to reach the goal is basic to problem solving (Anderson 1980; Brim, Glass, Lavin, & Goodman, 1962; Spivack, Platt, & Shure, 1976). For participants in the "take PRIDE" program, reaching the behavioral goal (e.g., always taking medicines as prescribed) is expected to produce the desired outcome, for example, feeling better. The stronger the outcome desired and the stronger the feeling of self-efficacy, the greater the effort expanded to enact the plan to reach the goal.

The "take PRIDE" activities guide participants step-by-step though the cognitive processes of self-regulation. Parallel to that process, the program provides verbal persuasion, exercises, and written materials. All underscore the benefit to be derived from better management of the condition, suggest strategies for reaching goals, and provide assurance that the achievement of the goal is within the grasp of the individual.

The third meeting. The objectives of meeting three are to enable participants to determine if they are making progress towards their goals, to assess difficulties and successes in carrying out their plans, and to obtain feedback and support. This session also emphasizes self-judgment and reaction. Individuals share information about their progress or lack thereof. Difficulties in implementing their plan are discussed. Plans are fine-tuned. The health educator also introduces specific information regarding medications, diet, exercise, and stress reduction for older heart patients as the information is pertinent to the participants' behavioral goals and action plans.

Helping group members to identify indicators of progress is an important element of the program. Being able to discern that one is achieving mastery over a complicated behavior is essential to continued efforts. If one who habitually forgets to take her heart medicine develops a reminder system and sees that she is missing doses less often, she is more likely to feel efficacious and make further efforts to take heart medicine.

The fourth meeting. The objectives of the fourth meeting are to review further progress in reaching the behavioral goal, and to determine if the "take PRIDE" process has led to new or different goals and desired outcomes. The final meeting of the group intends to foster feelings of self-efficacy. The last video segment is shown, in which Margaret reflects that once having mastered medicine taking, she has made further progress in managing her heart condition. She makes the point that she has set new behavioral goals for herself (e.g., getting out more with her friends). She feels greater mastery over her situation. The videotape is used as a trigger for discussion by group members. The emphasis in discussion is the level of efficacy each feels in meeting the stated behavioral goal. The health educator provides praise and encouragement and asks members to identify other management problems they may wish to target using the PRIDE process. The meeting ends with a review of the contract each member initially wrote in light of the progress that has been made. The intention is to recognize some level of achievement and improved competence on the part of every participant. It is hoped that, based on their experience of self-observation and judgment as guided by the educational program, group members are able to put their behavior and hear management goals into perspective. The program asks that participants not set goals that are too broad, unrealistic, or complicated. They are encouraged to recognize all indicators of change. Noticing even small amounts of progress leads to stronger belief that the desired behavior can be ultimately achieved. This heightened self-efficacy in turn is thought to lead to more effort to achieve an objective.

OBSERVATIONS ON APPLICATIONS OF MMCD SELF-REGULATION PRINCIPLES

Applications of elements of the MMCD suggest that incorporating observation, judgment, and reaction as specific skills to be built into interventions for managing chronic disease can help individuals and families to achieve endpoints that are of importance to them and to the health system more generally. Understanding how to move health care professionals from conceiving of skill acquisition by patients as an exercise solely of information-giving is a critical shift in the quality of chronic disease care provided. In order to effectively give assistance to people managing their own conditions, focus on a more behavioral approach, such as the subprocesses of self-regulation are necessary.

In studies of disease management using the MMCD (Clark et al., 2007; Clark et al., 2010a), two things are evident. First, self-regulation skills improve as a result of an intervention, but capacity across all three elements (observation, judgment, reaction) does not necessarily increase to the same degree. Observation may improve more than judgment and so on. This is, in part, due to the baseline level of skill of the participant. Some will already be more observant, or able to make evaluative judgments or feel greater self-efficacy or be likely to choose efficacious actions. An intervention's effect, therefore, is likely to be differential regarding these processes. Second is that the number of management strategies needed to keep disease in control is closely associated with the severity or level of control of a condition. More symptoms require more management strategies. Interventions based on the model's self-regulation elements aim to ensure that the right strategies are selected and not necessarily that fewer strategies are the right outcome.

As they relate to chronic disease management, the shift to enhancing self-regulation skills appears to enrich interventions. Focusing on the three self-regulatory processes of the MMCD seems a clear benefit as opposed to solely providing content about disease, its pathophysiology, and so on—that is, the conventional mode in health education based on providing information and increasing knowledge levels. This is not to say that information is not needed by the person managing a chronic condition. Rather, the information required is sought as relevant in the process of observing, judging, and reacting to a disease management situation. The information becomes much more relevant, timely, and salient in the learning process. Program processes can enable individuals to build their observation skills, for example, through various means of self-monitoring. A program can build the ability to make judgments, for example, by establishing criteria for making assessments (Cleary & Sandars, 2011). It can increase the capacity to react appropriately, for example, by encouraging realistic evaluations of self-efficacy and analysis of means-ends relationships.

Programs may also be designed in such a way that learners have the opportunity to try out a range of management alternatives. Attempts to manage may aid learners to hit upon or adapt an existing strategy that is more promising for controlling a disease. Trying out alternatives likely improves the basic skills of self-regulation. External resources as an element in the MMCD are an important feature. Diligent attention to helping learners to acquire the external resources they need to be effective in disease management is likely a necessary component of most, if not all, disease management interventions and most certainly those of low income patients. Details regarding the mechanisms of self-regulatory elements of change, however, are still scant and deserve further investigation.

NEEDED RESEARCH IN SELF-REGULATION

Thanks to the important foundational studies of Zimmerman (Zimmerman et al., 1999; Zimmerman et al., 1996; Zimmerman & Campillo, 2003) over the past two decades, great strides have been made in understanding self-regulatory subprocesses. Adaptations of his principles have moved research beyond academic learning to create new models relevant to health and related fields of endeavor. This work has, as would be expected, opened the door to possibilities for deeper examination of the concepts and new directions for research.

There may be theoretical limits to self-regulation and a number of obstacles to acquiring self-regulating skills. Even if people are equally capable of self-regulation, they may differ in their motivation to self-regulate. Full use of self-regulatory processes requires the conscious decision to change, as well as additional preparation, vigilance, and effort. Individuals who lack the motivation to self-regulate are not sufficiently accounted for in theories related to health behavior to date, which treat the concept as an autonomous, internal process. Zimmerman's model has been critical in exploring self-motivation in academic learning and can guide advancements in other arenas of work. In the MMCD there is no sharp dichotomy between internal and external processes, and thus, external factors such as modeling, social reinforcement, and verbal instruction can be used to initiate regulation of health behavior and, subsequently, ensure that control moves to the domain of the learner. However, the way in which a chronic disease intervention might be shaped to appeal to the motives of learners remains less well understood. The MMCD posits that the most powerful motivating factor for individuals is their personal goal for improving disease management. However, the most valued personal goal, as discussed in social cognitive theory, is often, if not always, covert, that is, rarely made public or shared with others. What are means by which personal goals can be understood and addressed in self-regulatory processes initiated by external programs? Describing the means to enhance motivation is a primary target for further research.

To date there is evidence in academic learning research that there are sizeable individual differences in an individual's development of learning strategies that have been linked to achievement (Zimmerman, 2008). Measures to asses self-regulating as a dynamic process have been developed by several investigators related to management of chronic disease; however, little is known about how to uncover, measure, and account for these individual differences in the learning process. Modal versus novel means to develop strategies deserve attention (Cleary, 2011; Zimmerman, 2008).

It is reasonable to ask, regarding self-regulation and chronic disease, if all types of chronic conditions are appropriate for self-regulatory control. Illnesses vary in a number of dimensions that might affect the processes described in the MMCD. These differences include the speed and severity with which symptoms respond to self-regulated actions or strategies. In an illness such as diabetes, failure to self-regulate might lead to rapid and serious physical consequences, whereas the effect on asthma of self-regulatory actions might be variable and take longer to emerge. Improving self-regulation in the latter case may be more challenging because observation and appropriate strategy attributions may be more difficult to achieve. Comparative research regarding the appropriateness of self-regulatory models for various diseases and for various situations within a given condition and across conditions is needed.

Another ripe area for investigation is how health care providers whose interactions with individuals with chronic conditions are intermittent and infrequent can foster self-regulatory skills in their clients and patients. At least one study (Cabana et al., 2006) has shown that using self-regulatory processes to enhance clinicians' capacity to improve communication with and provision of education to their patients produces important outcomes. However, the key emphases, priorities, and actions that must be developed in health care providers to carry out this new role within the constrained environments in which health services are delivered are not clear. The shift required is enormous to go from a health care system in which professionals dominate and management of disease by the patient is undervalued to one in which patients become the managers and clinicians their coaches in the self-regulatory process. What are the basic skills needed by health care providers directly working with patients to make this transformation possible?

CONCLUSIONS

Zimmerman's most important contribution to the Model for Management of Chronic Disease was his elaboration of principles of social cognitive theory as described by Bandura, and his recognition of the need to clarify subprocesses of self-regulation. Much of health care practice today relies on providing individuals with relevant facts and information, verbally persuading them to behave differently, and assisting with a few aspects of problem solving. Although these approaches to change can be effective, they do not directly tap into the primary and most powerful way by which most individuals learn to control their health conditions, including chronic disease. Self-regulation appears to be a potent concept around which to organize interventions. By providing opportunity for individuals to become aware of and assess the subprocesses of their learning and by enabling them to devise strategies based on these processes, we may evolve more effective means for changing health and illness management behavior. The contributions of Zimmerman to the recognition of the role in subprocesses of self-regulation cannot be overstated.

REFERENCES

Anderson, J. R. (1980). *Cognitive psychology and its implication.* San Francisco, CA. Freeman.

Bandura, A. (1977). *Social learning theory.* Englewood Cliffs, NJ: Prentice Hall.

Bandura, A. (1986). *Social foundations of thought and action: A social cognitive theory.* Englewood Cliffs, NJ: Prentice-Hall.

Bandura, A. (1991). Social cognitive theory of self-regulation. *Organizational Behavior and Human Decision Processes, 50,* 248–287. doi:10.1016/0749-5978(91)90022-L

Bandura, A. (1997). *Self-efficacy: The exercise of control.* New York, NY: Freeman.

Bandura, A., & Cervone, D. (1983). Self-evaluative and self-efficacy mechanisms governing the motivational effects of goal systems. *Journal of Personality and Social Psychology, 45,* 1017–1028. doi:10.1037/0022-3514.45.5.1017

Baumeister, R. F., Gailliot, M., DeWall, C. N., & Oaten, M. (2006). Self-regulation and personality: How interventions increase regulatory success, and how depletion moderates the effects of traits on behavior. *Journal of Personality, 74*(6), 1773–1801. doi: 10.1111/j.1467-6494.2006.00428.x

Becker, M. H. (1985). Patient adherence to prescribed therapies. *Med Care, 23*(5), 539–555. doi:10.1097/00005650-198505000-00014

Bergner, M., Bobbit, R. A., Pollard, W. E., Martin, D. P., & Gilson, B. S. (1976). The sickness impact profile: validation of a health status measure. *Medical Care, 14*(1), 57–67. doi:10.1097/00005650-197601000-00006

Bonner, S., Zimmerman, B. J., Evans, D., Irigoyen, M., Resnick, D., & Mellins, R. B. (2002). An individualized intervention to improve asthma management among urban Latino and African-American families. *Journal of Asthma, 39*(2), 167–179. doi:10.1081/JAS-120002198

Brimm, O. G., Jr., Glass, D. C., Lavin, D. E., & Goodman, N. (1962). *Personality and decision processes.* Stanford, CA. Stanford University Press.

Cabana, M. D., Slish, K. K., Evans, D., Mellins, R. B., Brown, R. W., Lin, X., . . . Clark, N. M. (2006). Impact of physician asthma care education on patient outcomes. *Pediatrics, 117*(6), 2149–2157. doi:10.1542/peds.2005-1055

Clark, N. M., Cabana, M. D., Nan, B., Gong Z. M., Slish, K. K., Birk, N. A., & Kaciroti, N. (2008). The clinician-patient partnership paradigm: Outcomes associated with physician communication behavior. *Clinical Pediatrics, 47*(1), 49–57. doi:10.1177/0009922807305650

Clark, N. M., Evans, D., Zimmerman, B. J., Levison, M. J., & Mellins, R. B. (1994). Patient and family management of asthma: Theory based techniques for the clinician. *Journal of Asthma, 31*(6), 427–435. doi:10.3109/02770909409089484

Clark, N. M., Gong, M., & Kaciroti, N. (2001). A model of self-regulation for control of chronic disease. *Health Education and Behavior, 28*(6), 769–782. doi:10.1177/109019810102800608

Clark, N. M., Gong, M., Schork, M. A., Evans, D., Roloff, D., Hurwitz, M., . . . Mellins, R. B. (1998). Impact of education for physicians on patient outcomes. *Pediatrics, 101*(5), 831–836. doi:10.1542/peds.101.5.831

Clark, N. M., Gong, M., Wang, S. J., Lin, X., Bria, W. F., & Johnson, T. R. (2007). A randomized trial of a self-regulation intervention for women with asthma. *Chest, 132*(1), 88–97. doi:10.1378/chest.06-2539

Clark, N. M., Janz, N. K., Dodge, J. A., Fingerlin, T., & Schork, M. A. (2000). Changes in functional health status of older women with heart disease: Evaluation of a program based on self-regulation. *Journal of Gerontology Series B: Psychological Sciences and Social Sciences, 55*(2), S117–126. doi:10.1093/geronb/55.2.S117

Clark, N. M., Janz, N. K, Dodge, J. A., Lin, X., Trabert, B. L., Kaciroti, N., . . . Keteyian, S. R. (2009). Heart disease management by women: Does intervention format matter? *Health Education and Behavior, 36*(2), 394–409. doi:10.1177/1090198107309458

Clark, N. M., Janz, N. K., Dodge, J. A., Schork, M. A., Wheeler, J. R., Keteylan, S. J., & Santinga J. T. (1997). Self-management of heart disease by older adults: Assessment of an intervention based on social cognitive theory. *Research on Aging 19*(3), 362–382. doi:10.1177/0164027597193005

Clark, N. M., Janz, N. K., Dodge, J. A., & Sharpe, P. A. (1992). Self-regulation of health behavior: The "take PRIDE" program. *Health Education and Behavior, 19(3),* 341–354. doi:10.1177/109019819201900306

Clark, N. M., Nothwehr, F., Gong, M., Evans, D., Maiman, L. A., Hurwitz, M. E., . . . Mellins, R. B. (1995). Physician-patient partnership in managing chronic illness. *Academic Medicine, 70*(11),957–959. doi:10.1097/00001888-199511000-00008

Clark, N. M., & Partridge, M. R. (2002). Strengthening asthma education to enhance disease control. *Chest, 121*(5), 1661–1669. doi:10.1378/chest.121.5.1661

Clark, N. M., & Starr, N. (1994). Management of asthma by patients and families. *American Journal of Respiratory and Critical Care Med, 149,* S54–66. doi:10.1164/ajrccm/149.2_Pt_2.S54

Clark, N. M., Stoll, S. C., Youatt, E. J., Sweetman, M., Derry, R., & Gorelick, A. (2010a). Fostering epilepsy self-management: The perspectives of professionals. *Epilepsy & Behavior, 19,* 255–263. doi:10.1016/j.yebeh.2010.08.033

Clark, N. M., Stoll, S. C., Youatt, E. J., Sweetman, M., Derry, R., & Gorelick, A. (2010b). Fostering epilepsy self management: The perspectives of professionals. *Epilepsy &_Behavior, 19,* 255–263. doi:10.1016/j.yebeh.2010.08.033

Clark, N. M., & Zimmerman, B. J. (1990). A social cognitive view of self-regulated learning about health. *Health Education Research, 5*(3), 371–379. doi:10.1093/her/5.3.371

Cleary, T. J. (2011). Emergence of self-regulated learning microanalysis: Historical overview, essential features, and implications for research and practice. In B. J. Zimmerman & D. Schunk (Eds.), *Handbook of self-regulation of learning and performance* (pp. 329–345). New York, NY: Taylor & Francis

Cleary, T. J., & Sandars, J. (2011). Assessing self–regulatory during clinical skills performance: A pilot study. *Medical Teacher, 33*(7), e368–e374. doi:10.3109/0142159X.2011.577464

DeWall, C. N., Baumeister, R. F., & Vohs, K. D. (2008). Satiated with belongingness? Effects of acceptance, rejection, and task framing on self-regulatory performance. *Journal of Personality and Social Psychology, 95*(6), 1367–1382. doi:10.1037/a0012632

Dilorio, C. K., Bamps, Y. A., Edwards, A. L., Escoffery, C., Thompson, N. J., Begley, C. E.,...Price, P. (2010). The prevention research centers' managing epilepsy well network. *Epilepsy & Behavior, 19,* 218–224. doi:10.1016/j.yebeh.2010.07.027

Gilson, B. S., Gilson, J. S., Bergner, M., Bobbit, R. A., Kressel, S., Pollard, W. E., & Vesselago, M. (1975). The sickness impact profile. Development of an outcome measure of health care. *American Journal of Public Health, 65*(12), 1304–1310. doi:10.2105/AJPH.65.12.1304

Janevic, M. R., Janz, N. K., Dodge, J. A., Lin, X., Pan, W., Sinco, B. R., & Clark, N. M. (2003). The role of choice in health education intervention trials: A review and case study. *Social Science and Medicine, 56,* 1581–1594. doi:10.1016/S0277-9536(02)00158-2

Juniper, E. F., Guyatt, G. H., Feeny, D. H., Ferrie, P. J., Griffith, L. E., & Townsend, M. (1996). Measuring quality of life in children with asthma. *Quality of Life Research, 5*(1), 35–46. doi:10.1007/BF00435967

Karoly, P., & Kanfer, F. H. (1982). *Self management and behavior change.* New York, NY: Pergamon.

Kitsantas, A., & Zimmerman, B. J. (1998). Self-regulation of motoric learning: A strategic cycle view. *Journal of Applied Sport Psychology, 10*(2), 220–239. doi:10.1080/10413209808406390

Leventhal, H., Safer, M. A., & Panagis, D. M. (1983). The impact of communications on the self-regulation of health beliefs, decisions, and behavior. *Health Education and Behavior, 10*(1), 3–29. doi:10.1177/109019818301000101

Ryan, P. (2009). Integrated theory of health behavior change: Background and intervention development. *Clinical Nurse Specialist, 23*(3), 161–170. doi:10.1097/NUR.0b013e3181a42373

Ryan, P., & Sawin, K. J. (2009). The individual and family self-management theory: Background and perspectives on context, process, and outcomes. *Nursing Outlook, 57*(4), 217–225. doi:10.1016/j.outlook.2008.10.004

Schunk, D. H., & Zimmerman, B. J. (1994). *Self-regulation of learning and performance: Issues and educational applications.* Hillsdale, NJ: Erlbaum.

Seligman, M. E. P. (1975). *Helplessness: On depression development and death.* San Francisco, CA, Freeman.

Spivack, G., Platt J. J., & Shure M. B. (1976). *The problem-solving approach to adjustment.* San Francisco, CA. Jossey-Bass.

Steptoe, A. (Ed.). (2010). *Handbook of behavioral medicine: Methods and application.* New York, NY: Springer.

Vohs, K. D., & Baumeister, R. F. (Eds.). (2011). *Handbook of self-regulation: Research, theory, and applications* (2nd ed.). New York, NY: Guilford.

Wheeler, J. R. (2003). Can a disease self-management program reduce health care costs? The case of older women with heart disease. *Medical Care, 41*(6), 706–715. doi:10.1097/01.MLR.0000065128.72148.D7

Zimmerman, B. J. (1989). A social cognitive view of self-regulated academic learning. *Journal of Educational Psychology, 81*(3), 329–339. doi:10.1037//0022-0663.81.3.329

Zimmerman, B. J. (1990a). Self-regulated academic learning and achievement: The emergence of a social cognitive perspective. *Educational Psychology Review, 2*(2), 173–201. doi:10.1007/BF01322178

Zimmerman, B. J. (1990b). Self-regulated learning and academic achievement: An overview. *Educational Psychology, 25,* 3–17. doi:10.1207/s15326985ep2501_2

Zimmerman, B. J., (2000). Becoming a self-regulated learner: An overview. *Theory Into Practice, 41*(2), 64–70. doi 10.1207/s15430421tip4102_2

Zimmerman, B. J., (2008). Investigating self-regulation and motivation: Historical background, methodological developments, and future prospects. *American Educational Research Journal, 45*(1), 166–183. doi 10.3102/0002831207312909

Zimmerman, B. J., Bonner, S., Evans, D., & Mellins, R. B. (1999). Self-regulating childhood asthma: A developmental model of family change. *Heath Education and Behavior, 26*(1), 55–71. doi:10.1177/109019819902600106

Zimmerman, B. J., Bonner, S., & Kovach, R. J. (1996). *Developing self-regulated learners: Beyond achievement to self-efficacy.* Washington, D.C.: American Psychological Association. doi:10.1037/10213-000

Zimmerman, B. J., & Campillo, M. (2003). Motivating self-regulated problem solvers. In J. E. Davidson & R. J. Sternberg (Eds.), *The Psychology of Problem Solving* (pp. 233–262). New York, NY: Cambridge University Press. doi:10.1017/CBO9780511615771

CHAPTER 15

APPLYING THE MODEL OF DEVELOPMENT OF SELF-REGULATORY COMPETENCE TO MENTORING

Maria K. DiBenedetto and Marie C. White[1]

In recent years, mentoring has been increasingly studied as an important component for the learning and development of academically successful students (Lankau & Scandura, 2002). *Mentoring* is a process whereby a mentor engages the learner in activities that encourage successful completion of a task through a series of interactions on both a professional and personal level. Both mentor and mentee agree to form a mutually beneficial relationship, which often determines the success or failure of the mentee's career goals (Healy & Welchert, 1990). Critical to the design of the relationship is the degree to which the mentor's actions facilitate the growth and development of the mentee as a self-directed, independent learner during the process. The concept of mentoring can be dated back to Homer's *Odyssey* and has since then been discussed and portrayed in many literary works (Rose, 2003). Mentor is defined as someone of advanced rank or experience who guides, teaches, and develops a novice (Zerzan, Hess, Schur,

Applications of Self-Regulated Learning across Diverse Disciplines, pages 445–472
Copyright © 2013 by Information Age Publishing
All rights of reproduction in any form reserved.

445

Phillips, & Rigotti, 2009). This instrumental perspective of mentoring suggests that the driving force is the mentor's ability to engage the mentee in challenging, goal-directed activities. The mentoring relationship fosters the development of skills, exploration of opportunities, and goal attainment.

Definitions of mentoring describe the functions of the mentor's role as that of a sponsor, coach, role model, and counselor and have been done so primarily within the business context, and to a limited degree within the academic context. In either setting, the mentor fosters a reciprocal learning relationship, which is characterized by trust, respect, and commitment. The mentor supports the professional and personal development of another by sharing his or her life experiences, influence, and expertise (Zellers, Howard, & Barcic, 2008). While numerous attempts have been made to define the mentoring relationship (Haggard, Dougherty, Turban, & Wilbanks, 2011), the literature has only begun to give attention to specific mentoring processes that lead to learning and development in the academic setting. It is important to evaluate mentoring practices by paying closer attention to which actions on the part of the mentor can be credited with the learner's development and an increase in independent learning. Mentoring relationships should promote accomplishments in both academic and professional fields; researchers should consider further investigation of empirically based methods in these areas. Mentoring should also promote self-regulated learning and performance. Barry J. Zimmerman has developed a self-regulated learning model that could serve to understand the mentoring process. *Self-regulation of learning* refers to the process through which learners engage in actions, behavior, feelings, and thoughts in order to pursue important academic goals and to acquire academic skills (Zimmerman, 2000a).

Through extensive research and practice, Zimmerman has provided the educational community with a model of the development of self-regulatory competence that could be applied to the mentoring context, in particular, to the doctoral mentor and student relationship. This model enables the mentee to develop self-regulatory competencies as he or she progresses through four levels of development (Zimmerman, 2000a). Zimmerman is unique in that he, himself, uses his model as he strategically mentors doctoral candidates to develop into independent self-directed learners. He does this through each of the levels of self-regulatory skill attainment: *observation, emulation, self-control,* and *self-regulation.* Zimmerman presents a different perspective in that his model begins by engaging the doctoral student through the modeling of research practices, followed by encouraging the student to emulate the general pattern of his actions. He remains supportive as the doctoral candidate acquires skills through deliberate practice. The outcome of the process enables the student to adapt behavior across changing conditions, independent of the mentor (Zimmerman, 2000a).

Doctoral candidates mentored by Zimmerman have reported their ability to detect the shift from dependence to independence with minimum apprehension (DiBenedetto, 2011; White, 2011a). Increased self-efficacy sustains motivation and competence as Zimmerman withdraws his authority from the project and gives autonomy to the learner. It is at this final level of development of self-regulatory competence that the learner becomes what the mentor intended from the beginning: an integral part of the field of educational psychology (see Bembenutty, 2008).

In general, the purpose of this chapter is to present three models, two of which directly define the mentoring relationship, and a third, which prior to this chapter, has not been examined in this way. This third approach involves a developmental model of SRL competency. This approach describes specifically how Zimmerman's model of development of self-regulatory competence explains the many processes engaged in by a mentor and mentee within a growth framework. This chapter differs from the other chapters in this edited book in that it discusses how Zimmerman's developmental model of self-regulatory competence can be used to understand the psychological processes through which mentees become competent, specifically at the doctoral level. In order to accomplish this objective, we first provide a brief review of the literature focusing on mentoring practices with examples of two effective mentoring models. The second purpose of this chapter is to present Zimmerman's model as an exemplary process applicable to doctoral education. Zimmerman's model clearly attributes learner growth and independence to the strategic planning of the mentor by highlighting how students are provided with opportunities to develop self-efficacy through mastery experiences. Third and foremost, illustrations are provided that show the link between mentoring, using characteristics aligned with the levels of self-regulation skill development, and Zimmerman's own mentoring style. Statements from former doctoral students that demonstrate Zimmerman's direct application of his self-regulatory competency model during mentoring are presented as examples of how Zimmerman uses his own theory in his work with students. Lastly, we discuss educational implications by providing educators with a self-regulatory method of mentoring that can be applied to other educational settings and suggest recommendations for further research.

OVERVIEW OF MENTORING

The study of mentoring and mentoring relationships has evolved during the past 25 to 30 years (Ragins & Kram, 2007). Researchers, practitioners, policy makers, educators, the business community, and the general population have been interested in mentoring (Allen & Eby, 2007). In a meta-analytic review, Allen, Eby, Poteet, Lentz, and Lima (2004) reported indicators of stronger career success for mentored versus non-mentored individuals. Results also showed that mentoring is associated with a range of favorable behavioral, attitudinal, health-related, relational, motivational, and career outcomes (Eby, Allen, Evans, Ng, & Dubois, 2008). Mullen (2011) suggests that successful mentoring relationships foster self-efficacy and self-actualization. Overall, these findings indicate that an understanding of the mentoring processes is important for professionals and educators who want their organizations and legacies to succeed.

Three major areas of mentoring have emerged as distinct streams of mentoring scholarship: youth, academic, and workplace. Researchers have provided insights into the mentoring process within these specific domains focusing on mentoring relationships (Haggard et al., 2011; Jacobi, 1991; Kram, 1983). One review of the mentoring literature (Ragins & Kram, 2007) indicated that the field has moved forward from the study of a single mentoring relationship to the study of a range of relationships that offer developmental assistance at various points in individuals' lives and careers. In addition, mentoring usually occurs over a period of several years where mentors agree to invest significant amounts of their time to support and guide a mentee, and the mentee agrees to invest considerable amounts of time to learning, developing self-efficacy, and working towards achievement of professional, academic, or personal goals (Mullen, 2011). While there is research suggesting that mentoring is an important component of organizational behavior, little has been done exploring the role of mentoring in doctoral education, where the success of the doctoral student is often contingent on the quality of the doctoral mentor and student relationship (Mullen, 2009).

In doctoral education, the relationship formed between doctoral students and their mentors plays a critical role in facilitating the completion of the degrees in addition to impacting students' professional, cognitive, and emotional development (Bell-Ellison & Dedrick, 2008). Doctoral candidates' needs and motives change significantly as they progress through the program. Mentors fill multiple roles providing sponsorship, protection, challenge, exposure, visibility, counseling, acceptance, confirmation, and/or coaching to their graduate students (Rose, 2005). Ideally, the mentoring relationship is collaborative and reciprocal. It focuses on the mentee's personal and professional development as the learner strives for independence (Zerzan et al., 2009).

The following section presents two mentoring models from different disciplines, which focus on fostering the development of the mentee, from a novice to an accomplished independent professional or academic, under the direction of a nurturing mentor. The third model used uses Zimmerman's model to explain the processes that take place in the doctoral mentor–student relationship as the candidate progresses to the ultimate goal of self-directedness. These three approaches were selected because they each present information about the processes involved in mentoring relationships; and while each presents valuable contributions to the understanding of mentoring, they each have different end objectives in mind.

ORGANIZATIONAL MODEL

Kram's research on mentoring relationships has dominated the mentoring field within the organizational context for the past 30 years, and it continues to provide insight on the mentoring relationship and focuses on the *professional development* of an individual (Chandler, 2011). Kram describes mentoring functions, which are summarized using two broad categories: career and psychosocial functions. The *career functions* involve helping the protégé develop in his or her professional role by providing sponsorship, exposure and visibility, coaching, protection, and challenging assignments. These functions are possible if the mentor is someone who is widely respected and influential with traits desirable to the protégé. The mentor helps the protégé learn about the expectations associated with the career, knowledge related to the professional role, and organizational protocol. In addition, the mentor works to develop and foster the career growth of an individual within the mentor's professional area. The *psychosocial functions* involve role-modeling, acceptance and confirmation through support, encouragement, feedback, counseling, and friendship and are geared towards helping the protégé develop a sense of competence and effectiveness in his or her career. The quality of the psychosocial functions depends on the level of the interpersonal relationship between the mentor and protégé.

Kram's (1983, 1985) theory predicts that as young adults enter the workforce, they move through four phases as they learn to become successful managers. These phases occur as a result of the interactions between the mentor and protégé and can last from two years to an indefinite period of time. They are labeled initiation, cultivation, separation, and redefinition.

The *initiation phase* is when the mentorship relationship is formed and increases in strength as the mentor models and provides support and encouragement. The mentor sees this as an opportunity to pass on knowledge and experience to someone more junior. As seen in Table 15.1, the protégé is seeking someone who will provide support, guidance, counseling, and confirmation, which will foster intellectual, professional, and psychological growth. The *cultivation phase* enables the mentor and the protégé to increase work tasks and to form a mutually beneficial strong bond. This is a key phase because it is during this time that the beliefs each hold of the other are tested and confirmed. The mentor provides coaching, role-modeling, protection, challenging activities, exposure-visibility, and sponsorship while the protégé begins to develop a sense of self-worth, competence

TABLE 15.1 Three Theoretical Frameworks Relevant to Mentoring

Theoretical Framework	Characteristics of Mentor	Characteristics of Protégé/Student	Distinguishing Characteristics
Kram's Organizational Mentoring Relationship Theory	Expertise in the field Models to protégé with focus on psychosocial and career functions Through functions and phases provides: • Sponsorship • Exposure and visibility • Coaching • Protection • Challenging assignments • Support and encouragement • Feedback • Counseling • Friendship	Seeks role model to provide: • Guidance • Opportunities to promote competence and increased self-worth • Organizational knowledge • Challenging tasks • Opportunities for professional growth • Emotional support • Friendship	Career and psychosocial functions' objectives are targeted at promoting and supporting *professional growth* in protégé's career
Zipp and Olson's Layered Learning Mentorship Model of Education	Mentor focuses learning on: • Gagne's hierarchy of sequential learning • Bloom's taxonomy of cognitive domain • The process of learning is emphasized over content • Overarching goal is to promote higher level thinking, abstract reasoning, and analytical problem solving skills	Student moves within three layered levels: First level: • Learns basic content and acquires knowledge and comprehension Second level: • Behavior changes where student is applying and analyzing research, interpreting new information, making inferences, and adaptations Third level where student is: • Capable of synthesizing information to form new patterns of thinking and reasoning • Capable of developing presenting, evaluating new information	Learning objective is to advance the student through a hierarchy of distinct layers until capable of higher order *academic scholarship and expertise* in doctoral candidate's field

TABLE 15.1   Three Theoretical Frameworks Relevant to Mentoring (continued)

Theoretical Framework	Characteristics of Mentor	Characteristics of Protégé/Student	Distinguishing Characteristics
Zimmerman's model of development of self-regulatory competence supplements existing approaches as follows:			
Heavy emphasis on: • Social modeling • Environmental settings and social influences • Goal setting • Building self-efficacy • Repetition leading to automaticity • Strategic planning • Self-monitoring • Metacognition • Self-evaluation • Self-reflection • Self-standards of success • Dynamic responses and flexibility	Mentor also an expert in the field Mentor: • Guides and paces student according to student's developmental level • Models cognition and behavior • Provides opportunities throughout four levels for the development of self-efficacy and the acquisition of mastery performance experiences • Ultimate goal for student is independence Specifically provides: • Role modeling and coaching • Support as a scaffold • Challenging assignments • Constructive feedback • Regulation of cognition behavior	Student moves through four levels of development of self-regulation competence. Student seeks mentor to provide: • Instruction, advisement, guidance, and evidence of higher order thinking and reasoning • Opportunities to build self-efficacy and problem solving abilities • Support, encouragement, monitoring and feedback of performance • Challenging experiences requiring adaptations and regulation of behavior	Mentoring objective is *self-regulation*: the ability to regulate one's beliefs, thoughts, and actions towards goal attainment; involves feeling self-efficacious in one's ability to adapt and adjust, and it extends beyond the academic and professional environment to *all aspects of life*

and mastery. This phase represents a shift from a unilateral relationship to a more collegial one where a friendship begins to take shape.

During the *separation phase*, the protégé becomes less dependent and looks for opportunities to work autonomously; and as a result, both participants in the process experience anxiety, loss, and turmoil, as well as excitement and great satisfaction. The mentor loses direct influence over the protégé as the protégé struggles with a loss of security and protection. The mentor experiences pride in seeing the protégé move to other positions, and the protégé feels a sense of personal accomplishment in his or her ability to move on and handle new challenges. Finally, during the *redefinition phase*, a peer status may be established or the relationship may cease to exist. If the relationship continues, the mentor may provide support and guidance from a distance while the protégé feels indebted as he or she enters roles that are now equal to that of the mentor. While this theory has had a significant amount of research in support of it, the application has been restricted to relationships within managerial contexts, the timeframe extends indefinitely, and it provides little on the specific strategic processes used by the mentor as he or she paces the growth of the protégé within each phase.

LAYERED LEARNING MENTORSHIP MODEL (LLMM) OF EDUCATION

Zipp and Olson (2008) introduced a mentorship model at the doctoral level, which focuses on empowering students to develop and refine their intellectual processes through cognitive processing and reasoning. The layered learning mentorship model (LLMM) of education emphasizes *how to* learn, in contrast to *what to* learn. This requires faculty to invest a considerable amount of time and effort working individually with students throughout the doctoral process, implementing strategies, and promoting critical thinking. As with most doctoral programs, the core of the LLMM is focused on a research agenda, which includes a teaching component and outcomes of scholarly presentations and publications (Zipp, Cahill, & Clark, 2009). Specifically, it is designed to enable students to discuss ideas, methods, and findings with program faculty. These educational experiences are organized to meet the overall program's goals within three sequential layers of learning experiences during which the student progresses from observer to presenter.

At all three sequential layers, the doctoral candidate is closely monitored by the mentor and expected to move beyond the acquisition of facts through the six levels of the cognitive domain identified in Bloom's taxonomy (Zipp & Olson, 2008). As seen in Table 15.1, the first layer includes participating in core and research courses during which the doctoral candidate acquires *knowledge* about the field and produces literature reviews, annotated bibliographies, assessment tools, and integrated papers. The mentor looks for evidence of the candidate's ability to recall and *comprehend* information by restating material accurately when responding to questions. The second layer encompasses the *application* of content specific to the doctoral candidate's area of research. At this point, the doctoral student prepares oral presentations, uses assessment tools, and participates in projects that require research *analysis* and self-reflection. The mentor determines evidence of growth in the candidate's use of higher order reasoning skills through problem solving and exploration of new ideas. The third layer includes activities associated with the dissertation process, including practicum, research, and independent study. The mentor observes as the candidate displays the ability to *synthesize* and *evaluate* information, making independent decisions during the dissertation process.

At each layer described above, mentors are given the task to communicate and incorporate strategies to assist the mentee in developing higher level thinking and reasoning skills, and in refining intellectual processing. The entire process is based on Gagné's (1962) cognitive hierarchy of learning theory. The model embraces both pedagogy and andragogy. *Pedagogy* is the art and science of teaching children, conveying timeless unchanging knowledge to a passive student, while *andragogy* is the art and science of teaching adults to develop into independent engaged thinkers (Zipp & Olson, 2008). Survey results on both faculty and student perceptions on the LLMM consistently show the model to positively foster the mentee's skills in knowledge development, information comprehension, application of skills, analysis of information, and the synthesis and evaluation of information (Zipp et al., 2009). The objective of the LLMM is to provide opportunities for the doctoral student to proceed through a hierarchy of learning where with each advancement, the student becomes more capable of higher order cognition, reasoning, and analysis. While this model is applicable to the doctoral mentor-student relationship, it does not extend beyond the scope of doctoral learning nor does it explain many of the psychological processes involved in the interaction between a mentor and student. Further, while this model offers an approach to explain the doctoral mentor-student context, its application is limited to the academic context, and it does not explain how individuals may use what has been learned in other situations. In other words, exactly how do doctoral graduates take what has been learned from the doctoral mentorship relationship and use this knowledge and understanding beyond the scope of obtaining the doctorate within an academic setting?

SELF-REGULATION AND THE DOCTORAL
MENTORING RELATIONSHIP

The mentoring relationship models described above derive from components of theories of development and social modeling but do not address the various processes such as self-efficacy, goal setting, self-monitoring, self-reflection, and self-evaluation, which are key components of self-regulated learning. In both cases, the mentee is not a passive observer but rather an active participant whose prior learning experiences, other significant relationships, expectations, and values influence what is learned and not learned as well as how the mentee grows over time. Furthermore, most learning and mentee behavioral changes can be expected to occur from the mentor's example, not through tedious discourse (Thomas, Murrell, & Chickering, 1982). Armstrong (2008) illustrated how Bandura's social cognitive learning theory can be applied to student learning when mentors use role modeling as teaching and learning strategies in a clinical setting. Students not only identify and observe how specific skills are performed, they also observe how the mentor interacts with others, prioritizes, time-manages activities, and deals with various problems within different academic contexts. Students who are fortunate to have a role model (or in the case of doctoral programs, a mentor) who is well-liked because of strong interpersonal skills and the ability to communicate effectively, is knowledgeable, and is well-respected are more likely to adopt the model's behavior (Bandura, 1977, 1997). Conversely, students who are exposed to poor mentoring behavior will not challenge the behavior, but often adopt the bad behavior (Bandura, 1986).

Present research describes graduate mentoring as a process of regulated learning because doctoral students are successful when they systematically direct their thoughts, feelings, and actions toward the attainment of their goals (Mullen, 2011). This determinant makes the connections among self-regulated learning, social cognitive theory, and the mentoring processes. Specific to the graduate level, mentors are known to regulate cognition and emotion and assist the candidate in organizing learning experiences through goal-directed activities (Mullen, 2011). While researchers have obtained support for Kram's theory of mentoring, there is growing support for an approach to mentoring that stems from Bandura's social cognitive theory while reflecting many of the career and psychosocial functions described by Kram (Mullen, 2011), as well as the higher level learning seen in the LLMM. The Zimmerman model of self-regulatory competence presents a framework that includes the theoretical foundation considered to be lacking in most mentoring models, and it encompasses a developmental view in which the ultimate goal is self-directed independence. In addition to filling the gaps of the Kram and LLMM models, this framework can be applied beyond the mentoring of doctoral candidates into an array of educational arenas. Whether the relationship exists over a period of years or decades, the model provides both the mentor and mentee a systematic format for learning from one another.

THEORETICAL FOUNDATION: SELF-EFFICACY AND ACADEMIC SELF-REGULATION

Most educators would agree that a major purpose of education is to instill lifelong learning (Chickering, 1994). Social cognitive theory suggests that modeling is a key environmental component that influences personal and behavioral outcomes (Bandura, 1986). This perspective suggests that models provide a source for conveying and building self-efficacy, and for how to use self-regulatory processes (Schunk & Zimmerman, 1997). *Self-efficacy* refers to one's belief about the capability to perform an activity; it affects one's choice of behavior, effort, and persistence (Bandura, 1986). An observer's self-efficacy can increase when there is a perceived similarity between the model and observer and if the model is viewed as competent (Bandura, 1997; Schunk & Zimmerman, 1997). Modeling is particularly important in the development of a doctoral student. A doctoral candidate, for example, who observes the mentor confidently respond to criticism about his or her scholarship may envision responding in a similar way in the future.

Academic self-regulation has its theoretical roots in social cognitive theory and stresses the reciprocity among one's environment, personal variables (such as affect and cognition), and behavior (Bandura, 1986). *Self-regulated learners* self-generate feelings, thoughts, and behaviors while pursuing important academic goals (Zimmerman, 2000b). There is evidence that a self-regulated student will engage in processes such as strategic planning, metacognitive monitoring, and self-reflection, which have been linked to student success (DiBenedetto & Zimmerman, 2010). Academic self-regulation and self-efficacy beliefs can be applied to learners in the earlier grades as well as to students enrolled in doctoral programs (Zimmerman 2000a; Mullen, 2011). Social cognitive theory postulates that modeling, which occurs in the environment of the observer, is a precursor to self-regulation (Schunk & Zimmerman, 1997). Self-regulation is dynamic because the learner is continually evaluating and adapting as he or she compares performance against a standard or a model.

The discussion above on self-efficacy and self-regulation serves as a catalyst for an understanding of how Zimmerman's model explains the changes that take place in a doctoral student as he or she is transformed into an independent, self-regulated learner. Zimmerman's model on how one develops self-regulation incorporates the concept of self-efficacy. Schunk and

Zimmerman (1997) suggest that students' sources of self-efficacy initially begin externally, by means of modeling, and ultimately become internalized when self-regulation is reached. For example, a doctoral student may look to the mentor for reinforcements of behavior, such as praise for conducting a good analysis of a journal article, and then eventually shift the origins of the reinforcement as deriving from his or her own beliefs that he or she has done a good job. This change in the origins of self-efficacy sources in the doctoral mentoring relationship marks a significant growth in the doctoral student as the student progresses through Zimmerman's four levels of development of self-regulated competence.

LEVELS OF DEVELOPMENT OF SELF-REGULATORY COMPETENCE

According to Zimmerman, Bonner, and Kovach (1996), educators need to effectively help students learn to be self-regulated. A unique characteristic of Zimmerman's model is that it offers an approach to helping students become self-regulated learners in control of their own academic destiny. The model consists of four levels: *observation, emulation, self-control,* and *self-regulation,* which students pass through sequentially (Zimmerman, 2000b). It is important to note that this is not a stage theory in that its "emphasis is on a sequence of social learning interactions rather than an invariant sequence of age-related personal traits or cognitive stages" (Schunk & Zimmerman, 1997, pp. 199–200). The following description outlines the four levels of development of self-regulated competence within the context of the doctoral mentoring relationship and is summarized in Table 15.2.

Level 1: Observation. Observation is where learning takes place vicariously, and the mentor views this as an opportunity to begin shaping and building a self-regulated individual. The doctoral student learns as he or she *discriminates* and *differentiates* among different academic functions associated with earning the doctorate such as producing scholarly work, teaching, coaching others, reviewing manuscripts, defending one's work, and having self-efficacy. The doctoral student observes the mentor receive reinforcement in various forms such as having work published or cited, receiving recognition in the field and among colleagues, or in conducting successful experiments.

Bandura and others emphasize that when one observes a model, one learns thought patterns or behavior not present before, and that these new patterns would have had zero probability of occurring without the presence of the model (Bandura, 1986; Schunk 1981; Schunk, 2012). A skilled doctoral mentor spends a significant amount of time *talking* with students. The mentor models his or her own self-efficacy and provides verbal persuasion

TABLE 15.2 Relationship Distinctions in the Four Levels of Development of Self-Regulatory Competence

Level	Student's behavior	Student's cognitions and beliefs	Mentor promotes use of self-regulatory processes	Mentor's behavior	Relationship Control	Independence Level
Observation	Student discriminates, and differentiates; observes, absorbs, considers	Student initially begins to internalize observations of mentor	Mentor models self-efficacy and self-regulatory processes	Mentor uses cognitive modeling (thinking aloud) and demonstrates behavior	Mentor paces according to student; determines when student is ready to move to next level based on conversations	Student entirely dependent on mentor
Emulation	Student duplicates style of mentor observed in the first level; experiences motoric behavior as student is physically replicating mentor	Student experiences sensory and cognitive feedback from within him or herself as the student begins to internalize beliefs of self-efficacy	Mentor communicates performance standards, and demonstrates evaluation of strategy use effectiveness	Mentor scaffolds, guides, provides constructive feedback and encouragement; provides opportunities for practice; gives direct social reinforcement and additional persuasive self-efficacy information	Mentor continues pacing according to student; upon duplication of mentor's behavior and expressed cognitions, mentor moves student to next level	Student dependent on mentor, though transitioning towards independence

(continued)

TABLE 15.2 Relationship Distinctions in the Four Levels of Development of Self-Regulatory Competence (cont.)

Level	Student's behavior	Student's cognitions and beliefs	Mentor promotes use of self-regulatory processes	Mentor's behavior	Relationship Control	Independence Level
Self-control	Student employs patterns learned in first two levels with automaticity; not yet capable of adapting or deviating from mentor's form; student uses representational standards; focuses on processes; experiences mastery	Student self-reinforces depending on ability to match work against model's; beginning to internalize standards and becoming more self-efficacious	Mentor provides opportunities for student to model observed behavior and experience mastery in mentor's absence	Mentor provides feedback and advice and encourages some level of independence; does not jump in when student experiences difficulty, but rather observes student's ability to respond to and handle unexpected situations	Mentor decides if more practice is necessary, has allowed student to work independently though closely monitoring; mentor paces development of self-regulation to the student	Student is less dependent on mentor; practices in mentor's absence
Self-regulation	Student adapts performance to personal and environmental changes; student self-monitors, evaluates, uses transfer of knowledge and now focuses on outcomes	Student has internalized what has been learned from the mentor; is self-efficacious, and can adjust behavior as needed	Mentor's role has changed to a more collegial one; assists doctoral candidate when asked by student	Mentor advises and guides the student based on the student's request	Student is now in the position of managing relationship; will call on the mentor only when, and as needed	Self-regulatory competency is reached; student has reached independence

to students about their capability to accomplish a task, thus working to build self-efficacy. The mentor also models self-regulatory behavior by *doing*. The mentor demonstrates self-regulatory processes such as setting short and long-term goals, planning strategically, monitoring one's progress, communicating effectively through verbal and written forms, and developing and fostering professional interpersonal relationships. The doctoral student observes, considers, absorbs, and begins to internalize the self-regulatory processes modeled by the mentor, including self-efficacy. The mentor controls the relationship and *paces* his or her guidance according to the doctoral student and through numerous conversations, and the mentor recognizes when the doctoral student is ready to move to the next level. The doctoral student has grown to respect and trust the mentor, and acknowledging that he or she is ready, accepts the decision to transition. The decision may take many forms but is marked by encouragement to move ahead in a more independent manner.

Level 2: Emulation. This level differs from the observation level in that it requires motoric behavior of the doctoral student as he or she replicates the self-regulatory patterns of thought and behavior observed. The doctoral student learns as the student tries to *duplicate* the skills modeled by the mentor, such as thinking through the steps involved in writing a sample manuscript, designing a research study, working as a research assistant, presenting before classmates, and working collaboratively with fellow doctoral students. The doctoral mentor scaffolds, guides, and provides constructive feedback and encouragement. The mentor gives direct, social reinforcement and additional persuasive self-efficacy as the student attempts to replicate the style observed in the first level. Through these closely monitored learning experiences, the learner begins to experience mastery, and a sense of self-efficacy is developing. A doctoral student, for example, may be second author on a manuscript, present the findings at a conference with the mentor in the audience, or teach a class using the mentor's syllabus and teaching style. As seen in Table 15.2, the doctoral student must demonstrate evidence of learning in a capacity that closely duplicates the mentor's expertise, behavior, and expressed cognitions. Once this is evident to the mentor, the mentor will give additional support, guidance, and encouragement to the student to transition to a more independent level. The doctoral student accepts this decision with the understanding that the mentor will be close at-hand as needed.

Level 3: Self-control. This level is marked by a change in the origins of self-regulatory behavior and self-efficacy from external sources (mentor) to internal sources (self), which leads to a degree of independence of the doctoral student. The student employs the self-regulatory behavior patterns learned in the first two levels with automaticity, but no longer in the direct presence of the mentor. The doctoral student is not yet capable of adapting or deviating from the mentor's original form. The mentor provides opportunities for the student to engage in self-regulatory behavior under structured conditions. The development of the doctoral student at this level occurs as the student performs the activities more closely aligned with a doctorate than a student.

Keeping the mentor's *representational standards* in mind, the doctoral student practices self-regulated learning activities—the focus is on the *processes* used (i.e., goal setting, strategy use), rather than outcomes. For example, with a large amount of oversight, the mentor provides opportunities for the student to have mastery experiences that build self-efficacy. A doctoral student may design a pilot study as a test for the dissertation. The student is motivated because the mentor has increased the doctoral student's level of self-efficacy by indicating that the student is *ready* to begin this important step in the doctoral program. The student prepares the proposal and defends it, carries out the investigation, and writes up the findings, independently, but yet under the tight supervision of the mentor. The mentor provides feedback and advice, and the student's *self-reinforcement* depends on the ability to match his or her work against the covert standard of the model as the student acquires more evidence in the ability to build mastery independently (Zimmerman, 2000b).

At this level the expert mentor does not jump in when the doctoral candidate experiences difficulties, but rather observes the student's ability to respond to and handle unexpected situations (e.g., challenges during the proposal defense, or analysis of poor data results). The strategic mentor decides whether the doctoral student is ready to move to the next level or if more practice is necessary, again pacing the development of self-regulation to the individual doctoral candidate, who accepts the decision of the mentor based on trust in the mentor's expertise.

Level 4: Self-regulation. A key characteristic of a self-regulated individual is the ability to *adapt* one's performance to personal and environmental changes (Zimmerman, 2000b). In the mentoring relationship, this becomes evident when the doctoral student is able to vary the use of strategies depending on the situation, independent of the doctoral mentor. The doctoral student engages in strategies and skills with little process monitoring, as the focus is now on goals and *performance outcomes.* This is possible because the doctoral student has *internalized* what has been learned from the mentor, is *self-efficacious,* and can *adjust* his or her self-regulatory behavior with little support from the mentor. The student monitors his or her own performance and evaluates the outcomes in a dynamic way. Now, independent of the mentor, the student transfers what was learned from previous situations under the mentor's guidance, and begins to develop his or her own distinct style of performing (Zimmerman, 2000a). The mentor's role has changed to a more collegial one where the mentor discusses issues and guides the doctoral student based on the doctoral student's request. This shift is important because the doctoral student is now in the position of managing the relationship, whereas in the prior levels the mentor maintained control. The mentor continues to be a source of social support and provides specific and constructive feedback.

Self-regulation is most evident in the doctoral dissertation processes, where the student must employ self-regulatory strategies such as forethought planning, performance monitoring, and intense self-reflection (Zimmerman, 2000a). The doctoral defense requires high levels of self-efficacy, as candidates must argue and defend their knowledge about the theories, their contribution to research, and the methods they employed. At the defense, the mentor remains a presence, a quiet source of expertise and strength in his or her power as the chair of the committee. Upon successfully defending, the mentor relationship changes further as the doctoral student advances in educational status matching that of the mentor's.

During Level 4, the mentor and doctoral candidate may learn from each other as the new doctorate continues to provide advances in the field and in some cases, work collaboratively with the mentor. In other instances, the mentor may serve as a distant but available source of advice and feedback on projects, manuscripts, and career decisions. This level is marked by independence as the doctorate has exhibited self-regulatory competence and may even result in a true separation between mentor and new doctorate as he or she continues on the path through life.

RESEARCH ON THE DEVELOPMENT
OF SELF-REGULATION COMPETENCE

While there is no evidence in the sequential development of the levels of self-regulation competence in the doctoral mentoring relationship, there is a body of research supporting the hierarchical levels within specific athletic and academic contexts among younger students. In a recent study, Ramdass (2011) found that fifth graders who observed modeling of mathematics strategies performed better during the emulative level (while practicing) than those who did not. An earlier study found similar results when researchers tested the sequential nature of the first two levels on a dart throwing task with high school girls (Kitsantas, Zimmerman, & Cleary, 2000). Further, Zimmerman and Kitsantas (2002) conducted a study on writing revision tasks among college students and found that students who observed models and then received feedback while practicing (emulation level) surpassed others.

Zimmerman and Kitsantas (1997) tested the transition from third to fourth levels by using the same athletic task (dart throwing) and found that high school girls who shifted their focus from process goals (after receiving feedback during practice) to outcome goals performed better than those who did not. In a second study also testing the shift from third to fourth level, of high school girls on a writing revision task, it was found to also be consistent with the hierarchical model (Zimmerman & Kitsantas, 1999). In each of the studies described above, in addition to improvement of skills, students' self-efficacy increased. While the evidence offers promise for support of the transition through the levels of development, more is needed, particularly as the development of self-regulation competence is currently being applied to different educational contexts and doctoral mentoring relationships.

THE DEVELOPMENT OF SELF-REGULATION
AND TRADITIONAL MENTORING MODELS

Zimmerman's model of the development of self-regulatory competence supplements Kram's mentoring relationship theory, in particular regarding the quality of the mentoring relationship and the characteristics of the mentor and protégé within the career and psychosocial functions. With regard to the career function, both the senior level manager and the doctoral mentor see their roles with the learner as an opportunity to share expertise, wisdom, experience, and knowledge as well as to develop a new generation of leaders through feedback and support. As a doctoral mentor, Zimmerman used the career functioning skills characterized by Kram such as providing guidance, exposure, and coaching as he worked with his students in various settings. For example, former doctoral student Adam Moylan ascribes to Zimmerman's multiple roles during his time as a doctoral candidate:

> I interacted with Dr. Zimmerman in various mentoring roles such as advisor, teacher, researcher, and dissertation chair. I associated with him in the classroom, office, "laboratory," and at professional meetings. Despite his eminent status in the field, he was always approachable and receptive. In each one of these settings his support and feedback were consistently available with the intent of modeling and developing independence and self-regulatory competence in his student.

Because the nature of the mentoring relationship involves a desire on the part of the organizational manager to see the protégé succeed, the mentor also interacts with the protégé using skills within the psychosocial function. This is done by providing emotional support in the forms of counseling, promoting self-competence, and acceptance and confirmation. In Zimmerman's model, the doctoral mentor discerns the needs of the doctoral student and also provides emotional support through advising, building self-efficacy, and acceptance and confirmation. An example of this type of support is evident in this commentary by former doctoral student, Darshanand Ramdass, about doctoral mentor, Zimmerman:

> When I received my first set of revisions for an article I submitted for publication, it was quite long and detailed. I emailed Dr. Zimmerman stating that the challenge of completing the revisions was overwhelming. His support and reference to previous work I had accomplished enhanced my belief that I was capable of revising the article. After two sets of revisions, the article was accepted for publication in a peer reviewed journal.

Both the LLMM model and Zimmerman's model require a strong relationship between a mentor and a mentee where the mentor has committed a significant amount of time to guide the doctoral candidate through the demands of the process. Both models are sequential: the candidate must successfully complete one level or layer before moving ahead. The mentor in both models closely monitors the doctoral candidate's progress and frequently provides honest, constructive, and supportive feedback.

In addition, all three models discussed in this chapter identify how the protégé/student grows over time and how the balance of the relationship between mentor and protégé/student changes as a result of the growth. What initially begins as an unequal relationship becomes one in which two people become equal. However, Zimmerman's model adds and describes additional processes to an understanding of successful mentoring relationships than those described by Kram and the LLMM.

Kram's mentoring relationship theory focuses on the growth of an individual with the primary objective being career or professional advancement. Zipp and Olson's model is focused on the cognitive and behavioral growth of the doctoral student within his or her field of academic scholarship. Zimmerman's model emphasizes an approach in which a developmental change takes place within the learner. This change empowers the learner to be able to apply what has been learned to various contexts, situations, and environments, whether it be in a professional, academic, or personal context. This is possible through the model by developing self-efficacy in one's capability to regulate oneself as described below.

Zimmerman emphasizes a developmental approach in which the sources of reinforcement move from external to internal (Schunk & Zimmerman, 1997). This is significant because the reinforcements serve as sources of motivation. Once the doctoral candidate has internalized the feelings of self-efficacy and mastery, he or she will be motivated from within. Bandura (1997) has emphasized how self-efficacy influences the choices people make, the efforts they will put in, and the degree of persistence. The development of self-regulatory competence involves the development of self-efficacy, which grows as the learner is moving from a dependence on the mentor to independence, thereby explaining the application of the term *self* in self-regulation.

Zimmerman's model also involves an understanding of what it actually means to regulate. Social cognitive theory postulates that regulation refers to the ability to exercise control; the *self* suggests that the control is within the individual, whereby the learner is self-directed, meaning he or she has acquired the capability of *regulating* his or her own thoughts, actions, and behaviors towards accomplishing goals (Bandura, 1986; Schunk & Zimmerman, 1997). This implies that the learner may make changes or adjustments to the goals that are set, the strategies used to reach these goals, and the thought patterns and beliefs around the process of goal attainment. Thus, the growth of the learner into someone who is competent in his or ability to self-regulate is a unique characteristic of Zimmerman's model. This is evident in the way Zimmerman mentors his own doctoral students where independence, his primary goal, remains a thread throughout each of the levels. The ways in which Zimmerman directly applies his model can be seen in how he personifies each of the four levels of development of self-regulatory competence.

PERSONIFYING THE THEORY: ZIMMERMAN, THE DOCTORAL MENTOR

As a doctoral mentor, Zimmerman modeled self-regulatory behavior in and outside the classroom. While mentoring doctoral students, Zimmerman described the process and modeled how he designed studies, analyzed data, and write manuscript. Through cognitive modeling, students become *observers* of his thoughts and reasons for performing certain actions (Meichenbaum, 1977). For example, Zimmerman reflects out loud when communicating with his students, thus modeling the thought processes of a scholar. He does this with the goal that what he has modeled will eventually become internalized. In addition, Zimmerman provides opportunities for students to observe his research skills. Anastasia Kitsantas describes this experience with her doctoral mentor:

> The highlight of my doctoral personal experience was when Dr. Zimmerman actually arrived at the data collection site where I had the opportunity to observe a researcher articulate what he was doing as he collected the data. It was an uplifting and a very motivating shared experience, which served as a source of self-efficacy for me to conduct research in the future.

At the *emulation* level, Zimmerman is aware that a student is still internalizing what has been observed, and he keeps this in mind in each interaction he has with his doctoral student. Cognizant of the developmental growth goal he has set for his doctoral students, he creates learning opportunities by which he continually introduces more difficult tasks as the student works towards mastery—with his goal of eventually reducing his social support (Zimmerman, 2000b). Zimmerman models, discusses the performance standards he expects, and has students practice through written assignments. Through weekly discussions, he asks students to articulate understandings of theories and research. This forces students to review research in the ways he modeled and to verbalize what they are thinking; thus, he is shaping students in the strategies they use to examine, review, and articulate. An example of how Zimmerman worked with a doctoral student on her writing and of how he controlled the pacing of the developmental levels may be drawn from Linda Sturges:

> As I neared the completion of my dissertation, I was having difficulty writing the final chapter. Dr. Zimmerman opened the conversation by stating he had a similar problem when he began to publish. Dr. Zimmerman modeled how to rewrite the first paragraph. I was then encouraged to emulate his style of sentence structure. As I received feedback on subsequent drafts, I gained self-control of my writing skills.

At the *self-control* level, Zimmerman initially works with his students to co-construct goals and to structure tasks so that the assignments can be completed independently and with a certain degree of automatization. As a doctoral mentor, Zimmerman establishes a learning environment in which doctoral students obtain rewards from their own work that help them to feel more self-efficacious and self-reinforced. As suggested by Schunk and Zimmerman (in press), at this level, the growth to self-regulation competence does not mean that students become entirely independent, but rather they increase their ability to internalize what they have learned and to be self-directed. Thus the self-control level marks a transition towards a greater self-reliance as the behavior is practiced outside of the presence of the doctoral mentor (Zimmerman, 2000b). Peggy Chen, a former doctoral student of Zimmerman's, describes how he worked with her in preparation for her first job interview, which required a candidate to perform outside the presence of her mentor:

> While completing my dissertation, I sought a teaching position and received invitation job talks. Dr. Zimmerman offered to meet with me for a dry-run of my research presentation, and on a Friday afternoon, he came to the university just to do so. His invaluable insights, encouragement, and support helped me land a position successfully.

Zimmerman's interactions with students are centered on teaching educational psychology, modeling how to conduct research, providing opportunities to emulate his behavior and to practice independently. The dissertation level represents the ultimate stage of development into *self-regulatory competence*, even though students or graduates who are self-regulated may continue to seek help as needed from Zimmerman (White, 2011b). One component of Zimmerman's legacy is his ability to use his theoretical models to help doctoral students develop into self-regulated educators and scholars. His high standards communicate expectations that students will succeed, and his mentorship provides students with the support, encouragement, and self-efficacy that they are capable of doing so. Former doctoral student Rajkumari Wesley describes the nature of her relationship with her mentor, which highlights the skillful pacing towards independence:

> Our meetings were focused and quite challenging. Dr. Zimmerman was as enthusiastic as I was about getting to the next step. He set the highest standards, and I was challenged to give my very best—he read every word I wrote, fixed it, then we revised it again and again; and when Dr. Zimmerman finally said, "OK"—we set up a defense date.

EDUCATIONAL IMPLICATIONS

Within the doctoral mentoring context, the focus of the mentoring relationship should be on the development of a specific skill that will enable the student to move forward with a project. Zimmerman's mentoring of doctoral candidates, for example, often emphasized the importance of proficiency in specific areas such as writing, statistical analysis, research methods, and other areas critical to the successful completion of a dissertation. This requires the mentor to be aware of the degree of skill knowledge the student has and to, through instruction, devote more time to students who require a more intensive approach, thus pacing the development according to the student's needs. What is required of the mentor, teacher, instructor, or educator is an initial strategic intervention through modeling and guided practice, which results in increased self-control and self-regulation on the part of the student. Mentoring requires the presence of a highly competent, self-efficacious expert, who is able to call attention to critical features of his or her performance and can transform cognitive representations into actions (Carroll & Bandura, 1987). Zimmerman incorporates the use of visual representations, such as writing samples or modeling how research is conducted, along with verbal explanations, which facilitate retention. Monitored performance encourages mentees to move towards independence not constrained by time and provides them with the opportunity to build self-efficacy through effective practice until the skill can be performed independent of the model.

The development of self-regulatory competence may be used in different educational contexts with the teachers serving as mentors as they guide and pace students' learning. Although for the most part educators accept the important role that self-regulatory behavior plays in student's activities, they often have not been trained in how students develop self-regulatory competence. Teacher education programs are content based, focusing on pedagogy and methods, not in learning, development, and motivation. When many teachers enter the classroom, they become so overwhelmed with the material that must be covered to pass state standardized evaluations that they forego teaching self-regulation (Schunk & Zimmerman, 1998). Students and parents do not realize that self-regulation can be taught as a skill when working within the four levels of development. To be effective, self-regulatory skills must be applied persistently in the face of difficulties, stressors, and competing attractions (Zimmerman, Bandura, & Martinez-Pons, 1992). This approach can help students to develop the intellectual tools, self-efficacy beliefs, and self-regulatory capabilities needed while gaining proficiency one step at a time. A classroom teacher, for example, may *model* how to perform algebraic math problems over a period of a few weeks, have the students *emulate* by practicing very similar problems in their seats while she circulates and provides feedback, require homework that involves practice without the presence of the teacher (*self-control*), then administer an exam whereby students can demonstrate the ability to solve similar, and perhaps more challenging math problems on their own (*self-regulatory competence*). Thus the potential and excitement surrounding Zimmerman's model is that the application can extend beyond the arena of doctoral education to include early learners.

RECOMMENDATIONS FOR FURTHER RESEARCH

While research has begun to provide empirical evidence of the development into self-regulatory competence, more is needed (Zimmerman, 2000b). The studies cited earlier suggest that observations and emulations of an exemplary teacher can provide students with information on the processes involved in learning, which helps them advance in levels of self-regulation (Kitsantas et al., 2000). In addition, the shift from the social sources to the internal sources occurs when learners proceed through the hierarchy and learners receive feedback (Ramdass, 2011; Schunk & Zimmerman, 1997; Zimmerman, 2000b; Zimmerman & Kitsantas, 1999). This feedback may be initially in the form of social reinforcements provided by an exemplary educator and then ultimately in the form self-reinforcements as one self-monitors and grows in self-regulation competence. Much is needed to understand the processes taking place within each of the levels and how the pacing and transitions to the subsequent levels actually occur. Research is needed across various grade levels, beginning with the earlier grades and up through doctoral programs, and across various academic contexts.

There is no research to date on the application of Zimmerman's model of development of self-regulatory competence to the doctoral mentoring relationship. The research could provide insight to the specific characteristics of the relationship between mentors and students at the different levels to understand exactly how Zimmerman has been so successful in his use of his own model with the students he has worked with. The theory may be tested to provide further information on how doctoral mentors effectively promote learning and development as students progress towards independent professionals, and hopefully how the doctoral candidates then become competent in their ability to regulate their own learning.

In addition, it would be important to examine whether Zimmerman's model applies or changes if the doctoral mentor and doctoral graduate reconnect. For example, once the doctoral student has graduated and is self-regulated, if he or she were to work collaboratively with the doctoral mentor, what would the nature of the relationship be? Would Zimmerman's levels no longer apply now that the doctoral graduate is self-regulated, and would the relationship take a more collegial form; or would the mentor, still senior in expertise to the doctoral graduate, continue to apply the levels of development of competence but within a different relationship context such as that of a senior and junior faculty member? There is no research to date exploring the changes that inevitably take place in mentoring once the student has reached self-regulated competence, and this could provide additional theoretical information about the nature of mentoring relationships.

CONCLUSION

Mentoring relationships are important because they can significantly impact the lives of the mentees. Findings suggest that mentoring can improve work effectiveness, academic achievement, doctoral dissertation completion and defense, and the ability to self-regulate in all aspects of life (Bandura, 1986; Kram, 1985; Mullen, 2011; Scandura, 1992). The present chapter discusses two models of mentoring that have been applied to organizational and doctoral program contexts. Kram's theory of the career and psychosocial functions and phases of the mentoring relationship have been widely studied and offer suggestions about how mentoring may be applied and evolve within professional settings. Zipp and Olson's (2008) LLMM theory suggests that doctoral mentors frame student learning according to a hierarchy whereby the end result is higher order cognitive processing and reasoning. While both models offer insight on the mentoring process, the current authors propose that Zimmerman's model of development of self-regulatory competence offers an approach to mentoring that fits well within various educational contexts, particularly in doctoral education, because it describes how the mentor is directly responsive to the learner and is strategically pacing his mentorship according to the student's developmental level. It provides a model for which the ultimate goal is for the learner to become independent, self-directed, and capable of controlling his or her own trajectory. Although additional research is needed, this multilevel approach offers promise to educators who are seeking ways in which instruction can be used to assist students develop self-efficacy beliefs and academic self-regulatory skills that can eventually be sustained, adapted, and adjusted in other academic situations and contexts outside of the learning environment.

Zimmerman's own approach to mentoring doctoral students fits within his model of development of self-regulatory competence. In carefully shaping his doctoral students, he is cognizant of the developmental process and of each student's standing within each of the levels. He regulates his own mentorship according to this knowledge and understanding, and according to the goals of where he would like the student to be. Through this process, Zimmerman empowers students by helping them develop a sense of personal agency. He derives great satisfaction from the success of his students, and Zimmerman's legacy is his ability to help doctoral students develop into self-regulated educators, scholars, and mentors as they internalize what they have learned and demonstrate that they will be capable of self-regulating their behavior in life's many challenges that lie ahead.

NOTE

1. Both authors were equal contributors to the chapter; names are written in alphabetical order.

REFERENCES

Allen, T. D. & Eby, L. T. (Eds.). (2007). *The Blackwell handbook of mentoring; A multiple perspectives approach.* Malden, MA: Blackwell Publishing._doi:10.1111/b.9781405133739.2007.00001.x

Allen, T. D., Eby, L. T., Poteet, M. L., Lentz, E., & Lima, L. (2004). Career benefits associated with mentoring for protégés: A meta-analysis. *Journal of Applied Psychology, 89,* 127–136. doi:10.1037/0021-9010.89.1.127

Armstrong, N. (2008). Role modeling in the clinical workplace. *British Journal of Midwifery, 16,* 596–603. Retrieved from http://www.intermid.co.uk/cgi-bin/go.pl/library/contents.html?uid=2251;journal_uid=12

Bandura, A. (1977). *Social learning theory.* Englewood Cliffs, NJ: Prentice Hall.

Bandura, A. (1986). *Social foundations of thought and action: A social cognitive theory.* Englewood Cliffs, NJ: Prentice-Hall.

Bandura, A. (1997). *Self-efficacy: The exercise of control.* New York, NY: Freeman.

Bell-Ellison, B. A. & Dedrick, R. F. (2008). What do doctoral students value in their ideal mentor? *Research in Higher Education, 49,* 555–567. doi:10.10007/s11162-008-9085-8

Bembenutty, H. (2008). The last word: An interview with Professor Barry Zimmerman: Achieving self-fulfilling cycles of academic self-regulation. *Journal of Advanced Academics, 20*(1), 174–193. doi:10.4219/jaa-2008-885

Carroll, W. R. & Bandura, A. (1987). Translating cognition into action: The role of visual guidance in observational learning. *Journal of Motor Behavior, 19,* 385–398. Retrieved from http://www.des.emory.edu/mfp/Bandura1987Translating.pdf

Chandler, D. E. (2011). The maven of mentoring speaks: Kathy E. Kram reflects on her career and the field. *Journal of Management Inquiry, 20*(1), 24–33. doi:10.1177/1056492610369937

Chickering, A. (1994). Exploring lifelong self-development. *NACADA Journal, 14*(2), 50–53. Retrieved from https://www.mcgill.ca/files/oasis/Empowering_Lifelong_Self-Development.pdf

DiBenedetto, M. K. (2011, April). *Barry J. Zimmerman: An educator with passion for developing self-regulation of learning through social learning.* Paper presented at the Annual Meeting of the American Educational Research Association, New Orleans. Retrieved from http://www.eric.ed.gov/ERICWebPortal/detail?accno=ED518491

DiBenedetto, M. K. & Zimmerman, B. J. (2010). Differences in self-regulatory processes among students studying science: A microanalytic investigation. *The International Journal of Educational and Psychological Assessment. 5*(1), 2–24. Retrieved from http://tijepa.books.officelive.com/Documents/V5_TIJEPA.pdf#page=5

Eby, L. T., Allen, T. D., Evans, S. C., Ng, T., & DuBois, D. (2008). Does mentoring matter? A multidisciplinary meta-analysis comparing mentored and non-mentored individuals. *Journal of Vocational Behavior, 72*(2), 254–267. doi:10.1016/j.jvb.2007.04.005

Gagné, R. M. (1962). The acquisition of knowledge. *Psychological Review, 69,* 355–365. doi:10.1037/h0042650

Haggard, D. L., Dougherty, T. W., Turban, D. B., & Wilbanks, J. E. (2011).Who is a mentor? A review of evolving definitions and implications for research. *Journal of Management, 37*(1), 280–304. doi:10.1177/0149206310386227

Healy, C. C. & Welchert, A. J. (1990). Mentoring relations: A definition to advance research and practice. *Educational Researcher, 19*(9), 17–21. doi:10.3102/0013189X019009017

Jacobi, M. (1991). Mentoring and undergraduate academic success: A literature review. *Review of Educational Research, 61,* 505–532. doi:10.3102/00346543061004505

Kitsantas, A., Zimmerman, B. J., & Cleary, T. (2000). The role of observation and emulation in the development of athletic self-regulation. *Journal of Educational Psychology, 91*, 811–817. doi:10.1037//0022-0663.92.4.811

Kram, K. E. (1983). Phases of the mentor relationship. *The Academy of Management Journal, 26*(4), 608–625. doi:10.2307/255910

Kram, K. E. (1985). *Mentoring at work: Developmental relationships in organizational life.* Chicago, IL: Scott, Foresman and Company.

Lankau, M. J. & Scandura, T. A. (2002). An investigation of personal learning, learning in mentoring relationships: Contents, antecedents, and consequences. *Academy of Management Journal, 45*, 779–790. doi:10.2307/3069311

Meichenbaum, D. (1977). *Cognitive behavior modification: An integrative approach.* New York, NY: Plenum Press.

Mullen, C. A. (2009). Re-imagining the human dimension of mentoring: A framework for research administration and the academy. *Journal of Research Administration, 40*(1), 10–31. Retrieved from http://www.srainternational.org/sra03/uploadedfiles/journal/09/JRA_Vol_40_1.pdf#page=12

Mullen, C. A. (2011). Facilitating self-regulated learning using mentoring approaches with doctoral students. In B. J. Zimmerman & D. H. Schunk (Eds.), *Handbook of self-regulation of learning and performance* (pp. 137–152). New York, NY: Routledge.

Ragins, B. R. & Kram, K. E. (Eds). (2007). *Handbook on mentoring at work: Theory, research & practice.* Los Angeles, CA: SAGE.

Ramdass, D. (2011). Enhancing mathematics skill and self-regulatory competency through observation and emulation. *The International Journal of Research and Review, 7*(1), 24–43. Retrieved from http://journalofresearchandreview.books.officelive.com/Documents/A2_V7_1_TIJRR.pdf

Rose, G. L. (2003). Enhancement of the mentor selection using the ideal mentor scale. *Research in Higher Education 44*(4), 473–494. doi:10.1023/A:1024289000849

Rose, G. L. (2005). Group differences in graduate students' concepts of the ideal mentor. *Research in Higher Education, 46*(1), 53–79. doi:10.1007/s 11162-004-6289-4

Scandura, T. A. (1992). Mentorship and career mobility: An empirical investigation. *Journal of Organizational Behavior, 13*, 169–174. doi:10.1002/job.4030130206

Schunk, D. H. (1981). Modeling and attributional effects on children's achievement: A self-efficacy analysis. *Journal of Educational Psychology, 73*, 93–105. doi:10.1037//0022-0663.73.1.93

Schunk, D. H. (2012). *Learning theories: An educational perspective.* Boston, MA: Pearson Education, Inc.

Schunk, D. H. & Zimmerman, B. J. (1997). Social origins of self-regulatory competence. *Educational Psychologist, 32*, 195–208. doi:10.1207/s15326985ep3204_1

Schunk, D. H. & Zimmerman, B. J. (1998). *Self-regulated learning: From teaching to self-reflective practice.* New York, NY: Guilford Press.

Schunk, D. H. & Zimmerman, B. J. (in press). Self-regulation and learning. In W. M. Reynolds & G. E. Miller (Eds.), *Handbook of psychology. Vol. 7: Educational psychology* (2nd ed.). Hoboken, NJ: Wiley.

Thomas, R., Murrell., P. H., & Chickering, A. W. (1982). Theoretical bases and feasibility issues for mentoring and developmental transcripts. In R. Brown &

D. DeCoster (Eds.) *New directions for student services; mentoring-transcript systems for promoting student growth* (pp. 49–65). San Francisco, CA: Jossey-Bass. doi:10.1002/ss.37119821906

White, M. C. (2011a). Predicting success in teacher certification testing: The role of academic help-seeking. *The International Journal of Educational and Psychological Assessment, 7*(1). Retrieved from http://tijepa.books.officelive.com/Documents/A3_V7_1_TIJEPA.pdf

White, M. C. (2011b, April). *Barry J. Zimmerman: An expert mentor through cyclical phases of self-regulatory feedback.* Paper presented at the Annual Meeting of the American Educational Research Association, New Orleans, LA.

Zellers, D. F., Howard, V. M., & Barcic, M. A. (2008). Faculty mentoring programs: Reenvisioning rather than reinventing the wheel. *Review of Educational Research, 78*, 552–588. doi:10.3102/0034654308320966

Zerzan, J. T., Hess, R., Schur, E., Phillips, R. S., & Rigotti, N. (2009). Making the most of mentors: A guide for mentees. *Academic Medicine, 84*(1), 140–144. doi:10.1097/ACM.0b013e3181906e8f

Zimmerman, B. J. (2000a). Attaining self-regulation: A social cognitive perspective. In M. Boekaerts, P. R. Pintrich, & M. Zeidner (Eds.), *Handbook of self-regulation* (pp. 13–39). San Diego, CA: Academic Press. doi:10.1016/B978-012109890-2/50030-5

Zimmerman, B. J. (2000b). Achieving self-regulation: The trial and triumph of adolescence. In F. Pajares & T. Urdan (Eds.), *Academic Motivation of Adolescents* (pp. 1–27). Greenwich, CT: Information Age Publishing.

Zimmerman, B. J., Bandura, A., & Martinez-Pons, M. (1992). Self-motivation for academic attainment: The role of self-efficacy beliefs and personal goal setting. *American Educational Research Journal, 29*, 663–676. Retrieved from http://www.jstor.org/stable/1163261?origin=JSTOR-pdf

Zimmerman, B. J., Bonner, S., & Kovach, R. (1996). *Developing self-regulated learners: Beyond achievement to self-efficacy.* Washington, DC: American Psychological Association. doi:10.1037/10213-000

Zimmerman B. J. & Kitsantas, A. (1997). Developmental phases in self-regulation: Shifting from process goals to outcome goals. *Journal of Educational Psychology, 89*, 29–36. doi:10.1037//0022-0663.89.1.29

Zimmerman, B. J. & Kitantas, A. (1999). Acquiring writing revision skill: Shifting from process to outcome self-regulatory goals. *Journal of Educational Psychology, 91*, 1–10. doi:10.1037//0022-0663.91.2.241

Zimmerman, B. J. & Kitsantas, A. (2002). Acquiring writing revision and self-regulatory skill through observation and emulation. *Journal of Educational Psychology, 94*, 660–668. doi:10.1037//0022-0663.94.4.660

Zipp, G. P., Cahill, T., & Clark, M. (2009). The role of collaborative scholarship in the mentorship of doctoral students. *Journal of College Teaching and Learning, 6*(8), 29–36. Retrieved from http://journals.cluteonline.com/index.php/TLC/article/view/1111/1095

Zipp, G. P. & Olson, V. (2008). Infusing the mentorship model of education for the promotion of critical thinking in doctoral education. *Journal of College Teaching and Learning, 5*(9), 9–11. Retrieved from http://journals.cluteonline.com/index.php/TLC/article/view/1229/1213

BARRY J. ZIMMERMAN

Brief Bio

Barry J. Zimmerman is an emeritus and distinguished professor of Educational Psychology at the Graduate School and University Center of the City University of New York. He is the Thorndike Award winner (2012) of the American Psychological Association, Division 15 (Educational Psychology). He served as president of Division 15 of the American Psychological Association (1996–1997). Professor Zimmerman has received other countless honors and awards, including Senior Scientist Award of American Psychological Association, Division 16 (School Psychology) and the Sylvia Scribner Award of the American Educational Research Association for exemplary research in learning and instruction. He has received grants from the U.S. Department of Education and the Institute for Educational Science to develop applied interventions in academic contexts to enhance the self-regulation, motivation, and academic success of highly at-risk students. He has also conducted research on families' self-regulation of children's asthma funded by grants from the U.S. Institutes of Health. He received the New York City Department of Health Award for preventive care of childhood asthma and was elected chair of the Behavioral Science Assembly of the American Thoracic Society and council member of the American Lung Association. Professor Zimmerman is a prolific scholar and author. He has published over 200 journal articles and book chapters and is a member of numerous editorial boards. Of particular note were his collaborations with Ted Rosenthal in publishing *Social Learning and Cognition* (Academic Press,

Applications of Self-Regulated Learning across Diverse Disciplines, pages 473–474
Copyright © 2013 by Information Age Publishing
All rights of reproduction in any form reserved.

1978) and with Grover Whitehurst in producing the edited volume *Functions of Language and Cognition* (Academic Press, 1979). He is author with Bonner and Kovach of *Developing Self-Regulated Learners, Beyond Achievement to Self-Efficacy* (American Psychology Association, 1996) and has edited five highly influential books with Dale H. Schunk on self-regulated learning, with the most recent volume, *Handbook of Self-regulation of Learning and Performance* (Routledge), published in 2011.

CPSIA information can be obtained at www.ICGtesting.com
Printed in the USA
BVOW020230200213

313735BV00003B/20/P

9 781623 961329